IFIP Advances in Information and Communication Technology 565

IFIP – The International Federation for Information Processing

IFIP was founded in 1960 under the auspices of UNESCO, following the first World Computer Congress held in Paris the previous year. A federation for societies working in information processing, IFIP's aim is two-fold: to support information processing in the countries of its members and to encourage technology transfer to developing nations. As its mission statement clearly states:

> *IFIP is the global non-profit federation of societies of ICT professionals that aims at achieving a worldwide professional and socially responsible development and application of information and communication technologies.*

IFIP is a non-profit-making organization, run almost solely by 2500 volunteers. It operates through a number of technical committees and working groups, which organize events and publications. IFIP's events range from large international open conferences to working conferences and local seminars.

The flagship event is the IFIP World Computer Congress, at which both invited and contributed papers are presented. Contributed papers are rigorously refereed and the rejection rate is high.

As with the Congress, participation in the open conferences is open to all and papers may be invited or submitted. Again, submitted papers are stringently refereed.

The working conferences are structured differently. They are usually run by a working group and attendance is generally smaller and occasionally by invitation only. Their purpose is to create an atmosphere conducive to innovation and development. Refereeing is also rigorous and papers are subjected to extensive group discussion.

Publications arising from IFIP events vary. The papers presented at the IFIP World Computer Congress and at open conferences are published as conference proceedings, while the results of the working conferences are often published as collections of selected and edited papers.

IFIP distinguishes three types of institutional membership: Country Representative Members, Members at Large, and Associate Members. The type of organization that can apply for membership is a wide variety and includes national or international societies of individual computer scientists/ICT professionals, associations or federations of such societies, government institutions/government related organizations, national or international research institutes or consortia, universities, academies of sciences, companies, national or international associations or federations of companies.

More information about this series at http://www.springer.com/series/6102

Clement Fortin · Louis Rivest ·
Alain Bernard · Abdelaziz Bouras (Eds.)

Product Lifecycle Management in the Digital Twin Era

16th IFIP WG 5.1 International Conference, PLM 2019
Moscow, Russia, July 8–12, 2019
Revised Selected Papers

Springer

Editors
Clement Fortin
Skolkovo Institute of Science
and Technology
Moscow, Russia

Alain Bernard
École Centrale de Nantes
Nantes, France

Louis Rivest
École de Technologie Supérieure
Montréal, QC, Canada

Abdelaziz Bouras
Qatar University
Doha, Qatar

ISSN 1868-4238 ISSN 1868-422X (electronic)
IFIP Advances in Information and Communication Technology
ISBN 978-3-030-42249-3 ISBN 978-3-030-42250-9 (eBook)
https://doi.org/10.1007/978-3-030-42250-9

This Springer imprint is published by the registered company Springer Nature Switzerland AG
The registered company address is: Gewerbestrasse 11, 6330 Cham, Switzerland

Preface

Since 2003, the IFIP WG 5.1 PLM International Conference has brought together researchers, developers, and users of Product Lifecycle Management (PLM), an ICT and integrated business approach to the collaborative creation, management, and dissemination of engineering data throughout extended enterprises that create, manufacture, and operate engineered products and systems.

The PLM conference is the official conference for the IFIP WG 5.1. The conference aims at involving all stakeholders in the broad concept of PLM, hoping to shape the future of this field and advance the science and practice of the extended enterprise.

Issues of design methodologies across the whole product lifecycle, their supporting digital tools including the implementation of digital-twins, and integration challenges in the context of cyber-physical systems were key topics covered at the conference. The organizer of the PLM 2019 conference was the Skolkovo Institute of Science and Technology (Skoltech). The conference, which was held during July 10–12, 2019, included keynote lectures, scientific paper presentations, and industry-oriented sessions, with an extensive social program. The conference was preceded by a Doctoral workshop which took place during July 8–9, 2019.

Skoltech hosted the conference in Moscow, Russia, which offers many touristic attractions and a very rich cultural program all year round. Moscow also supports an important part of Russian industry, playing a key role in aerospace, software development, and manufacturing. Moreover, Moscow is a very important Russian center of research in many scientific areas and leads the educational transformation for the whole country in a number of strategic areas.

All submitted papers were reviewed by at least two reviewers following the single blind review process with at least 2 reviewers for each paper; 63 submissions were received in total, 22 were evaluated with minor corrections and 16 with major revisions that were reviewed before final publication. The Proceedings include 38 reviewed papers that will be indexed in Scopus and are grouped into 8 topical sections representing the current research state of the art in the field. They are namely:

1. 3D Modeling and Data Structures
2. PLM Maturity and Industry 4.0
3. Ontologies and Semantics
4. PLM and Conceptual Design
5. Knowledge and Change Management
6. IoT and PLM
7. Integrating Manufacturing Realities
8. Integration of In-service and Operation

The technical conference started with a high-level keynote talk by Dr. Thierry Chevalier from Airbus, France; his talk titled "Are PLM software soon to be dinosaurs?" challenged all participants about the evolution of the PLM technologies in this

Digital Twin era. His talk was followed by a keynote panel moderated by Prof. Lionel Roucoules from ParisTech, France, on the topic: "PLM ontologies, knowledge management and artificial intelligence." This high-level panel session was followed by parallel technical sessions for the rest of the day.

The second day of the conference was reserved for industrial talks on PLM implementations from various viewpoints by top experts from the Russian Industry. Three keynotes and an industrial panel were presented, followed by a presentation by the Skolkovo Innovation Center and a pitch session for technological start-ups supported by the Skolkovo Innovation Centre. The program of the day was concluded by a tour of the Skolkovo Technopark facilities and a gala dinner cruise on the Moscow River.

The PLM 2019 conference was concluded by a third day of technical sessions, which were presented in the morning, and a private tour of the Starcity, the astronauts training center in the suburb of Moscow, which was very much appreciated by all participants.

These proceedings are the result of many important contributions at all levels as presented in the organization description below. We sincerely thank all those listed below and also those who are not included but were instrumental in making this PLM 2019 conference a great success.

December 2019

Clement Fortin
Louis Rivest
Alain Bernard
Abdelaziz Bouras

Organization

Honorary Chair

Alexander Kuleshov	Skoltech, Russia

Program Committee Chairs

Clement Fortin	Skoltech, Russia
Louis Rivest	École de Technologie Supérieure (ETS), Canada
Binu Gurumoorthy	India Institute of Science (IISC), India

Steering Committee

Alain Bernard	École Centrale de Nantes, France
Abdellaziz Bouras	Qatar University, Qatar
Paolo Chiabert	Politecnico di Torino, Italy
Erastos Filos	European Commission, EU
Lionel Roucoules	ParisTech, France
Alexander Smirnov	SPIIRAS, Russian Academy of Science, Russia

Program Committee

Cordula Dorothea Auth	TU Darmstadt, Germany
M.-Lounes Bentaha	Université de Lyon, France
Giulia Bruno	Politecnico de Torino, Italy
Kay Burow	Bremer Institut für Produktion und Logistik, Germany
Christophe Danjou	Polytechnique Montréal, Canada
Benoit Eynard	Université de technologie de Compiègne (UTC), France
Sebti Foufou	New York University Abu Dhabi, UAE
Mikhail Gusev	Skoltech, Russia
Mikhael Gardoni	École de technologie supérieure (ETS), Canada
Lars Hagge	DESY, Germany
Hiroyuki Hiraoka	Chuo University, Japan
Hannu Tapio Karkkainen	Tempere University, Finland
Stefan Kehl	Volkswagen Group, Germany
Michael Abbot Maginnis	University of Kentucky, USA
Nicolas Maranzana	Arts et Métiers ParisTech, France
Fernando Mas	Airbus, Spain
Mahmoud Masmoudi	SUPMECA, France
Grant McSorley	University of Prince Edward Island, Canada
Sergei Nikolaev	Skoltech, Russia

Semih Otles	Ege University, Turkey
Yacine Ouzrout	Université de Lyon, France
Romain Pinquié	Grenoble INP, France
Jose Rios	Universidad Politécnica de Madrid, Spain
Monica Rossi	Politecnico de Torino, Italy
Nikolay Shilov	SPIIRAS, Russian Academy of Science, Russia
Anderson Luis Szejka	Pontifical Catholic University of Parana, Brazil
Nikolay Teslya	SIIRAS, Russian Academy of Sciences, Russia
Klaus-Dieter Thoben	Bremer Institut für Produktion und Logistik, Germany
Ighor Uzhinsky	Skoltech, Russia
Carlos Vila	Universitat Politècnica de València, Italy
Eduardo Zancul	University of São Paulo, Brazil

Organizing Committee

Clement Fortin	Skoltech, Russia
Ighor Uzhinsky	Skoltech, Russia
Monica Rossi	Politecnico de Torino, Italy
Yacine Ouzrout	Université de Lyon, France
Sergei Nikolaev	Skoltech, Russia
Valeria Verlina	Skoltech, Russia
Ivan Popov	Skoltech, Russia
Nicola Garzaniti	Skoltech, Russia
Sophia Salas	Skoltech, Russia

Sponsors

Siemens

DATADVANCE

Dassault Systemes

Industrial Guests and Speakers

Airbus
Roscosmos
Joint Airconstruction Corporation
KAMAZ Innovation Center (engineering manufacture)
Chelyabinsk Pipe Plant
Moscow Helicopter Plant
Central Scientific Research Automobile and Automotive Engines Institute NAMI
New Lipetsk Steel Plant NLMK

Contents

Ontologies and Semantics

PLM and Conceptual Design

Knowledge and Change Management

IoT and PLM

Integrating Manufacturing Realities

Integration of In-service and Operation

3D Modeling and Data Structures

Augmented Reality for Operator Training on Industrial Workplaces – Comparing the Microsoft HoloLens vs. Small and Big Screen Tactile Devices

Andreas Pusch and Frédéric Noël(✉)

Univ. Grenoble Alpes, CNRS, Grenoble INP, G-SCOP, 38000 Grenoble, France
frederic.noel@grenoble-inp.fr

Abstract. The digital revolution towards the industry standard 4.0 offers many ways to improve established methods and processes. In this paper, we report on the lessons learned about the pros and cons of Augmented-Reality-based operator training using the Microsoft HoloLens as compared to small and big screen tactile devices. Together with our industrial partner, we have chosen an encapsulation assembly task as use case. We have enriched the original training material with digital twins of the workplace, animations, videos, and contemporary forms of interaction, all of which made available in an optimised fashion on three different support technologies. Feedback from our testers, and those in charge of designing training courses, is suggesting that notably the HoloLens version of our prototype has the potential not only to replace current training methods, but to go beyond them up to the point where even novices can pass the training autonomously. It thus seems promising to integrate Augmented Reality into training programmes and so to complete the digital chain within the industry life management.

Keywords: Industry 4.0 · Digital twins · Augmented Reality · MS HoloLens · Tactile displays · Operator training · Assembly tasks · Ergonomics · Usability

1 Introduction

In the course of the industrial revolution towards the *Industry 4.0* standard (or *Smart Factories*, or *Cyber-Physical Systems*), systems and processes become entirely interoperable, information fully transparent up to *digital twins*, and automated assistance available at both decision making and operational levels. Communication and cooperation between all involved entities takes place in real-time, internally as well as across organisations, allowing for highly efficient value chains and product life cycles.

This paper addresses issues related to the automated assistance during operator training in the automotive supplier industry, notably for the assembly of encapsulations. We consider this an important first step towards other through-life services, such as maintenance or everyday operation support. Having the factory and all its workplaces represented as virtual models helps transform traditional *work instructions*

Published by Springer Nature Switzerland AG 2019
C. Fortin et al. (Eds.): PLM 2019, IFIP AICT 565, pp. 3–13, 2019.
https://doi.org/10.1007/978-3-030-42250-9_1

(WI), often available only on paper, card board, or as static charts, into multi-platform, interactive training modules that benefit from all the recent advances also in fields of *Human-Computer-Interaction (HCI)* and *Augmented Reality (AR)* (see [1] for a survey).

Our overall objectives consisted of **(1)** integrating the digital workplace and product twins with the standard WI used at our industrial partner's factory (=> *Cooper Standard Vitré*, France), **(2)** providing interactive, automated training modules optimised for three platforms (=> *Microsoft HoloLens, NVIDIA SHIELD tablet, iiyama ProLite touch-screen monitor*), while **(3)** designing each version iteratively and compliant with their specific ergonomic principles (=> mainly adopted from the HCI domain), in order to **(4)** compare their utility experimentally by also looking at potentials and limitations.

However, novel AR applications and processes will have to prove their added value before they can become an integral part of the everyday manufacturing business. With this comparative work, we intent to take the current state of the art one step forward towards identifying the potentials and limitations of recent devices and methods.

2 Related Work

Production line workers usually are specialised on specific tasks or task sequences, such as the part assembly we have studied at Cooper Standard Vitré. But since products like car models, for instance, change rapidly, they also need to adapt to new workplaces within short periods of time. In addition, there is a relatively high fluctuation among workers, as workforce requirements get continuously adjusted to the factory's actual production needs. As a consequence, factories often employ interim staff, which makes efficient training a crucial element for an efficient operational functioning. We will here review "traditional" training methods as well as the current streams in HCI exploring modern AR technologies and interaction techniques for the use in industrial training contexts. We further discuss the ergonomic foundations for interactive AR applications.

2.1 "Traditional" Operator Training

In many cases, training is being done "on the job". An experienced worker takes the role of a trainer, unless there is dedicated training staff available, and the trainee discovers step-by-step what is to be done and how. Tasks are either being explained or demonstrated, and then have to be repeated in a training environment, or, sometimes, directly be applied productively.

A means to standardise the training process are static WI charts. "Static" means that they are printed on paper, card board, or any other type of support. The trainer uses these instructions, which typically include brief textual descriptions, pictures, and critical checks to be performed, for recalling and communicating all key elements, whereas the trainee uses them as basic learning tool. Advancement and success are being evaluated and approved by the trainer.

2.2 Operator Training in Augmented Reality

Overview of AR Technologies and Interaction Techniques. While training in *Virtual Reality (VR)* has been studied and applied for decades in various professional domains [2], AR had (and still has) to overcome major technological issues before reaching the maturity required for practical use. When talking about AR, we can differentiate three main approaches to display augmented information on top of the real world – or images of it – each having its own advantages and disadvantages: (1) *Video see-through AR* [3], (2) *optical see-through AR* [4], and (3) *spatial AR* [5]. For the sake of conciseness, we will here only focus on optical see-through AR, which uses prisms, semi-transparent micro displays, or retinal laser scanners in front of one or both eyes to let images "float" on top of the real environment. Tracking techniques are sensor- or camera-based. However, due to the optical complexity and other technological challenges, it was only recently, with the advent of devices such as Microsoft's HoloLens [6] (=> for further details, see Sect. 4.1), that we see optical see-through AR passing a fundamental frontier.

Operator Training in AR. AR has been studied for many years in the context of education and training (see e.g. [1] and [7] for extensive surveys). Hence, various applications, methods, and advanced strategies for information presentation exist, meant to facilitate assembly tasks in a number of domains, incl. the restricted medical sector [8], covering hierarchical structures [9], but also to assist in maintenance and repair [10]. However, it has been found that AR still does not meet the rigorous requirements of operational use in the industry [11], in part due to device constraints, but also due to the way how and when interactive augmented contents are being displayed. Radkowski et al. [12] reported that it is crucial to present appropriate visual features during assembly, corresponding to the difficulty of the task, whereas [13] introduced a rule-based expert system optimising information presentation depending on the trainee's progress. In [14], an (automated) process for the actual creation of augmented contents based on assembly instructions and 3D product models is being proposed.

Ergonomics Principles for Interactive AR. For AR to be successfully employed in industrial environments, it is vital that methods and applications be robust and error-prone. Beside best practices and domain experience acquired in the field over time, another central source for the design of reliable and easy to use systems are national and international norms and standards. Although AR is still rarely being mentioned explicitly (=> a number of related standards are currently under development), we have been able to identify recommendations for system and interaction design, as well as for human factors in a broader sense. As a basis for our research, we have used the comprehensive EN ISO 9241 (*The ergonomics of human system interaction*) [15], with Travis' guide as an initial orientation aid [16], knowing that there are other important standards to be taken into account in the future. These principles have been among the main elements used for the initial design of our below training prototypes, before we have iteratively refined them together with our industrial partner.

3 Assembly Use Case

Workplaces in our partner's factory are arranged along different production lines. The workplace chosen for further study is called the *Finishing table*, a final assembly workplace (see Fig. 1). As it is usually being operated standing, its height can be adjusted by a wired controller, while the lifting mechanism can be interrupted by an emergency stop. The tabletop can also be inclined. The encapsulation to be assembled is made up of 5 separate pieces. During assembly, various checks and other actions have to be carried out, as indicated in the WI (=> not shown here for reasons of confidentiality).

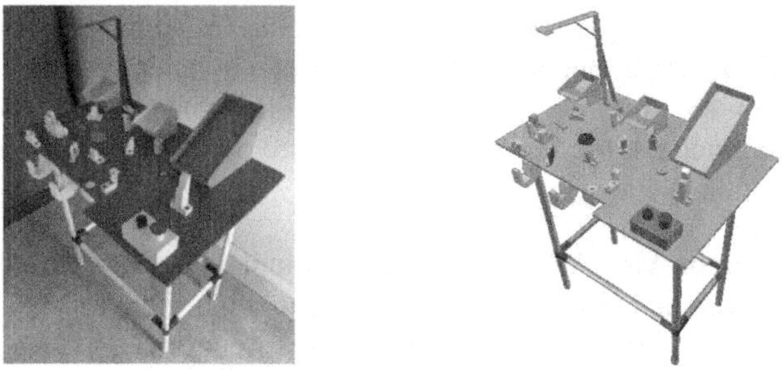

(a) (b)

Fig. 1. The *Finishing table*: (a) the physical prototype and (b) its digital mock-up.

4 Prototypes

4.1 AR Prototype Using the Microsoft HoloLens

The MS HoloLens. The MS HoloLens is a powerful, hands-free, completely self-contained optical see-through head-mounted display (HMD) which allows to see virtual contents overlaid on the real environment. It comes with 6 degrees-of-freedom (DoF) tracking, environment understanding, spatial sound, as well as with basic gesture interaction and voice recognition. The resolution per eye is 1268 × 720 pixels, the field-of-projection (FoP) approx. 30° horizontally × 17.5° vertically. It is further equipped with a 2 megapixels forward-pointing camera. Various possibilities exist to fix the device to the user's head. There also is a small physical button device, called the *clicker*, which can be strapped to the middle finger, and then be held between the index and the thumb.

AR Training Application. In compliance with the protocols at Cooper Standard Vitré, we had to organise our training applications in phases and subphases. We further had to make sure that all key contents have been visited by the trainee, before allowing her or him to proceed. The application starts each training phase with an overview of all steps to be completes (see Fig. 2a). At first, the trainee would see only the main labels, later also the detailed instructions, pictures, and animations etc. (see Fig. 2b). To avoid or limit occlusions of the real environment, added contents can always be switch off. Videos for each step are available at any time in the video pane, which also accommodates alternative navigation controls as well as the access to the overview. Trainees can navigate forth and back through the steps, pause videos and animations, replay audio instructions, and reposition the video pane, if needed.

(a) (b)

Fig. 2. Screenshots of the training application in AR mode: (a) Overview of the assembly task, (b) WI details of a specific step, plus added contents. (Color figure online)

Interactive user interface (UI) items and buttons can be selected using a 3D cursor and then performing either the *Air tap* gesture, saying "select", or using the clicker.

Limitations. Among the most important limitations of the current version of the HoloLens is its limited FoP. The AR training application has been designed to both show where the actual FoP ends (=> a blue border frame, not shown above) and guide the trainee's gaze, if relevant objects are being shown outside the current AR view. So, whenever any such object appears, its location with respect to the main camera's viewing frustum (=> the user's view) will be determined, and guidance cues (=> red arrows for step transitions, yellow arrows for additional contents of a given step) will be shown at the extremities of the projection space. These cues disappear as soon as the target object has been "found", so, when it has been seen or gazed at by the trainee.

Further limitations are the weight of the device, but also the modes of interaction. The Air tap gesture turned out to be difficult to perform, and the default speech recognition is restricted to US English. Rapid head movements may decompose the RGB images into their primary components, leading to chromatic aberrations. Head fixations, although rich and flexible, are complicated to adjust. As for the tracking, fluctuations of a few cms will have to be accepted. The device is generally rather fragile, making it risky to be used, notably in industrial settings.

Implementations Details. The training application has been developed on a standard workstation installed with *Unity 2017.3.0f3, Visual Studio Community* (needed for deployment), *Windows 10 SDK*, and all respective, freely available *HoloLens toolkits*. All 3D models have been generated with SolidWorks, and further been exported to the OBJ file format. Once running on the device, an external keyboard is needed to control certain aspects of the application, notably the manual calibration for aligning the virtual to the real workplace. A stopwatch module registers various times for further analyses.

4.2 Tablet Prototype

NVIDIA SHIELD Tablet. This (gaming) tablet comes with an 8″ multi-touch display (=>1920 × 1200 pixels). We have installed it with Android 7.0. It is equipped with two 5 megapixels cameras (=> forward- and backward-pointing), a microphone, as well as with position, orientation, and location tracking sensors. The tablet also allows for stylus input, direct stereo sound output, and for connecting up to Bluetooth 4.0 devices.

Tablet Training Application. As in the HoloLens prototype, we had to reflect the existing multi-phase training protocol. While multimodal contents are exactly the same, they are arranged differently to fit the tablet's small display (see Fig. 3a).

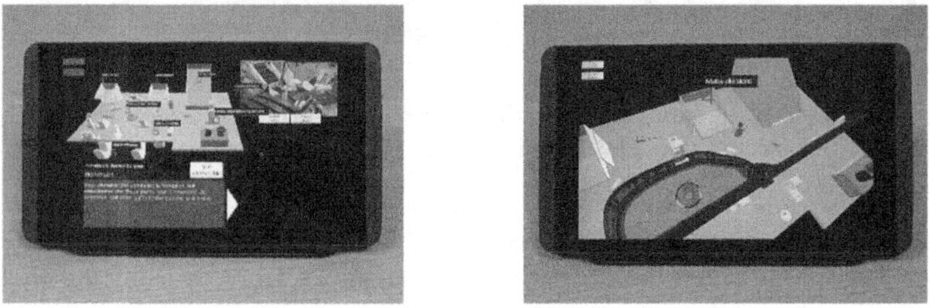

(a) (b)

Fig. 3. Tablet prototype: (a) Initial training screen. Note the decomposition of the UI in dedicated zones for animations, videos, textual instructions, and additional images, (b) full-screen 3D view, which can be manipulated freely.

The dedicated zones allow to focus on the essential elements, without having to search for them. All non-textual contents can be zoomed by tapping on them. With one exception: The full-screen 3D view (see Fig. 3b). Once entered, the trainee can move the 3D scene around, turn it, and zoom further into it. Animations can be paused at any time.

Limitations. Despite its autonomy, maturity, and robustness, it will be difficult to use a tablet in a hands-free fashion with it being constantly in front of the eyes. In other words, even if a video see-through AR approach could theoretically be applied, practically, the tablet has to be mounted somewhere on or nearby the workplace. The trainee will thus have to force her- or himself to look at it, which means that information can be missed. Finally, the screen is small, limiting visibility and readability of the training material. For audio instructions, wireless headphones are highly recommended.

Implementation Details. The main differences as compared to the HoloLens prototype are that the *Android SDK* will be required instead of the Windows 10 SDK, and Visual Studio is purely optional. The deployment chain is otherwise completely integrated into Unity (=> for direct deployment, the tablet has to be switch into "developer mode"). All media should be transcoded for the Android target platform.

4.3 Big Screen Prototype

iiyama ProLite Touchscreen Monitor. The iiyama PL2735M has a 24″ full HD (=> 1920 × 1080 pixels) multi-touch display. It can be driven through a variety of graphics ports. Its USB 3.0 host connexion allows for an immediate integration with Windows 10 systems. So, touch events are being handled just as mouse clicks, or as touch events on a tablet. Microphone, camera, and stereo speakers are integrated as well.

Big Screen Training Application. The big screen version of the training application looks and behaves exactly the same as the tablet version. The major difference is in the display size. However, while visually more comfortable and easier to interact with due to its size, not to interfere with the physical workplace, but keeping the monitor accessible at the same time, can be challenge. A separate stand may be a good choice.

Limitations. The biggest advantage of a big display, its size, can quickly turn into its biggest disadvantage, if space matters. Also, manipulating bulkier pieces can be difficult, if a bigger screen is in the way somewhere. In addition, unless a complete system with a computer integrated into the display is being used, it will further be necessary to accommodate space for the central unit, cables etc.

The risk of missing important information is imminent here as well, although visual notifications are more likely to be detected (in the periphery), since they are bigger. For audio instructions, wireless headphones should be provided.

Implementation Details. Made with Unity, too, the development environment corresponds largely to that of the tablet training app (without the Android SDK). In fact, by changing the target platform during the build process, Unity allows to generate platform-specific executables from the same sources. It is also at that time, when all media will (usually automatically) be transcoded for the selected target platform.

5 Pilot Evaluation

5.1 Testing Conditions

Our current training prototypes have been preliminarily evaluated by 2 usability experts (=> heuristic evaluation and walkthroughs), 7 of our project partners from the industry, including 5 training specialists of different responsibility levels from Cooper Standard Vitré (=> free exploration), as well as 10+ invited researchers, engineers, and students (=> informal usability tests). The usability experts and 3 colleagues from Cooper Standard Vitré have also been involved in the iterative design process. Given the nature of the tests conducted so far, it should be noted that the results presented in Sect. 5.2 are mainly based on qualitative data and observations.

5.2 Results

The tables below (see Tables 1, 2 and 3) provide a condensed summary of the feedback obtained. Where appropriate, we explain our observations in more detail.

Table 1. Comparison of the device ergonomics.

	MS HoloLens	NVIDIA SHIELD	iiyama ProLite
Wearing comfort	Poor	Moderate	Good
Viewing comfort	Moderate	Moderate	Good
Field-of-view	Moderate	Poor	Moderate
Visual quality	Good	Poor	Moderate
Acoustic quality	Good	Moderate	Moderate
Hands-free use	Yes	Yes	Yes
Interaction	Multimodal	Tactile	Tactile
Device autonomy	Moderate	Good	n/a
Device robustness	Poor	Good	Moderate

Table 2. Comparison of the training applications as a function of the support technology.

	MS HoloLens	NVIDIA SHIELD	iiyama ProLite
Content visibility	Good	Poor	Moderate
Inform. awareness	Good	Very poor	Poor
Co-located AR	Yes	No	No
Real-time 2D/3D	Both	Both	Both
Comprehension	Good	Moderate	Moderate
Ease-of-use	Good	Poor	Moderate
Acceptance	Good	Moderate	Moderate

Table 3. Overall comparison from the manager's perspective.

	MS HoloLens	NVIDIA SHIELD	iiyama ProLite
Training time	Good	Poor	Moderate
Success rate	Good	Poor	Moderate
Autonom. training	Probably yes	No	Probably not
Auton. validation	At most partially	No	No
Eff. WI alternative	Yes	Probably not	Maybe
Work support tool	No	Yes	Maybe

Managers and training experts further asked about the cost of creating training modules. The good news is that, between systems, there is no big difference. And once created for one platform, having it on another will be considerably less expensive due to shared contents and codes, especially in the case of the two tactile versions which currently do not differ at all. However, it is clear that an authoring tool on top of Unity (or any similar engine) will be required in order to render the production process cost-effective and profitable.

6 Discussion

The benefits of the *MS HoloLens* make it a very interesting device for future industrial applications, incl. AR-based training or maintenance, where the operator immediately sees synthetic contents right on top of the real environment. It is self-contained, wireless, and fully equipped with all necessary tracking, multi-modal feedback, and interaction features. Development using Unity and Visual Studio is fairly straight-forward.

But despite its obvious advantages, it also (still) suffers from important limitations. Beside the poor wearing comfort and the relatively small FoP, its fragility makes it hard to imagine to see it being employed "in the industrial wild" any time soon. In controlled environments, however, it may already substitute traditional training methods.

The *NVIDIA SHIELD tablet*, on the other hand, is a well-proven and robust device. Its computational power is sufficient even for displaying more sophisticated real-time 3D graphics. Interacting with it via touch can nowadays be considered "natural". But its display size and the fact that the trainee has to actively look at it, make it a rather poor candidate for autonomous training programmes. In addition, it requires some space to be fixed to the workplace, so as to assure a hands-free use. It may prove useful, though, as a complement to the traditional training, or as an everyday support tool.

The iiyama ProLite touchscreen monitor is in most cases doing better than the tablet, of which it basically is a (much) bigger version. Its generous display size can become a handicap, if the workplace does not offer enough space to accommodate it. Moreover, manipulating bulky pieces can be a risky endeavour with such a big screen nearby.

To summarise, on most of the dimensions we have investigated, the MS HoloLens performs best, followed by the iiyama ProLite and the NVIDIA SHIELD tablet, resp. But the existing ergonomic constraints suggest to view even the "winner" with some caution! The tablet version of our training application may be a promising tool for recalling certain aspects of the work to be conducted, useful in job rotation contexts.

7 Conclusion and Future Work

We have demonstrated that it is timely and beneficial to integrate the development of novel training methods based on recent advances in HCI and AR into the transition process towards a Factory 4.0. Iterative design and first pilot tests helped us identify both positive and negative points of our three prototypes. The AR version based on the MS HoloLens, with co-located contents being projected right on top of the real workplace, appears to be the most efficient for actual training, despite its ergonomic constraints (=> wearing and viewing comfort). The tactile tablet version, however, may prove useful as an everyday assistance or recall tool. Somewhere in the middle in terms of utility and acceptance landed the big screen version of our training application. For practical reasons (=> need for more space, risk of being "in the way" while manipulating more bulky pieces), we do not yet see it being employed operationally.

Among our next steps is to conduct formal experiments under lab and field conditions, i.e. with real operators at Cooper Standard Vitré, in order to confirm – or disprove – the various expert expectations. We also plan to study ways to render the validation phase more autonomous. In this context, we will exploit the MS HoloLens's hand tracking combined with the detection of operator actions and workplace state changes.

Finally, we plan to refine our development process, so that it can be applied to other use cases, incl. maintenance and control tasks. To this end, we will generalise code and content production, but also link with the evolving business knowledge. To support this process, and benefit all stakeholders, we intent to deepen and enlarge our partnerships.

Acknowledgements. We would like to thank Vincent Guizouarn, Pascal Lenormand, and Anthony Compassi from Cooper Standard Vitré for their highly valuable comments and suggestions. We are further grateful for the time our testers have spent evaluating the current prototypes.

This work has been funded by a BPI-France partnership project. The G-SCOP laboratory is member of the Persyval Laboratory of Excellence (French LabEx) and contributes to the Authoring Augmented Reality (AAR) research action.

References

1. van Krevelen, D.W.F., Poelman, R.: A survey of augmented reality technologies, applications, and limitations. Int. J. Virtual Real. **9**(2), 1–20 (2010)
2. Wang, P., Wu, P., Wang, J., Chi, H., Wang, X.: A critical review of the use of virtual reality in construction engineering, education, and training. Int. J. Environ. Res. Public Health **15**(6), 1204 (2018)
3. Edwards, E.K., Rolland, J.P., Keller, K.P.: Video see-through design for merging of real and virtual environments. In: Proceedings of VRAIS (1993)
4. Kiyokawa, K., Kurata, Y., Ohno, H.: An optical see-through display for mutual occlusion of real and virtual environments. In: Proceedings of IEEE & ACM ISAR (2000)
5. Bimber, O., Raskar, R.: Spatial Augmented Reality: Merging Real and Virtual Worlds. A K Peters/CRC Press, Boca Raton (2005)
6. Microsoft HoloLens (2008). https://www.microsoft.com/en-gb/hololens
7. Lee, K.: Augmented reality in education and training. TechTrends **56**(2), 13–21 (2012)
8. Nilsson, S., Johansson, B.: Fun and usable: augmented reality instructions in a hospital setting. In: Proceedings of 19th Australasian Conference on Computer-Human Interaction, pp. 123–130 (2007)
9. Zauner, J., Haller, M., Brandl, A., Hartman, W.: Authoring of a mixed reality assembly instructor for hierarchical structures. In: Proceedings of ISMAR, pp. 237–246 (2003)
10. Henderson, S., Feiner, S.: Exploring the benefits of augmented reality documentation for maintenance and repair. IEEE TVCG **17**(10), 1355–1368 (2011)
11. Tiefenbacher, P., Lehment, N.H., Rigoll, G.: Augmented reality evaluation: a concept utilizing virtual reality. In: Shumaker, R., Lackey, S. (eds.) VAMR 2014. LNCS, vol. 8525, pp. 226–236. Springer, Cham (2014). https://doi.org/10.1007/978-3-319-07458-0_22

12. Radkowski, R., Herremaa, J., Olivera, J.: Augmented reality-based manual assembly support with visual features for different degrees of difficulty. Int. J. Hum. Comput. Interact. **31**, 337–349 (2015)
13. Syberfeldt, A., Danielsson, O., Holm, M., Wang, L.: Dynamic operator instructions based on augmented reality and expert systems. In: Proceedings CIRP Conference on Manufacturing Systems.(CMS) (2015)
14. Sääski, J., Salonen, T., Hakkarainen, M., Siltanen, S., Woodward, C., Lempiäinen, J.: Integration of design and assembly using augmented reality. In: Ratchev, S., Koelemeijer, S. (eds.) IPAS 2008. IIFIP, vol. 260, pp. 395–404. Springer, Boston (2008). https://doi.org/10.1007/978-0-387-77405-3_39
15. EN ISO 9241 - The ergonomics of human-system interaction (2018). https://www.iso.org/
16. Travis, D.: Bluffers' Guide to ISO 9241, 9th edn. Userfocus Ltd., London (2014)

Octree Based Voxel Model for Representation of Spatial Conflicts Across Multiple Design Domains

Arun Kumar Singh[1,2(✉)], B. Gurumoorthy[2], and Latha Christie[1]

[1] Microwave Tube Research and Development Centre (DRDO), Bangalore 560013, India
arunsingh_aks@yahoo.com, drchristie07@gmail.com
[2] Centre for Product Design and Manufacturing, Indian Institute of Science, Bangalore 560012, India
bgm@iisc.ac.in

Abstract. This paper discusses use of octree based voxel model for representation of spatial conflicts across multiple design domains. A framework has been developed to create octree based voxel model linked with intended empty spaces in product, which are associated with design requirements, product lifecycle states and connected design domains. Knowledge in System Modelling Language (SysML), is used to select criteria for building octree voxel model. A case study of Coupled cavity travelling wave tube (CCTWT) Slow Wave structure (SWS) design has been taken to showcase the code capabilities. Octree voxels inside CAD platform show and represent spatial conflicts, detected by associativity modelling of Empty space blocks inside CAD along with the Product knowledge in SysML model.

Keywords: Octrees · Voxelization · Spatial conflicts

1 Introduction

Product designs are carried out with objectives to satisfy multifunctional domain requirements. In every product design, some spaces are intentionally left empty to satisfy specific requirements of different domains. For example, space may have been provided for electrical insulation, thermal isolation, clearance for moving part, port accessibility, Electron beam transmission or Radio frequency signal travel, expansion of material, tool access, sensors, bolts accessibility, welding tools, or for removal/replacement of parts. There may be cases, where the same space is used for different purposes but in different product states. The space, which has been provided for moving parts clearance in operation state also serves the purpose for accessibility in maintenance state. That is the same space, which is used for two different purposes but in different states. Knowledge regarding these space usages for moving part clearance under operation state, may not have been documented or is not available to designer, who is searching for empty space to locate new module into the product. This may create spatial conflict with workspace of other designer in the same domain or with other domain designers. This also incurs time

Published by Springer Nature Switzerland AG 2019
C. Fortin et al. (Eds.): PLM 2019, IFIP AICT 565, pp. 14–23, 2019.
https://doi.org/10.1007/978-3-030-42250-9_2

wastage; if these spatial conflicts are detected and resolved through conventional methods of multi-domain design stakeholder reviews. Electro-Mechanical systems exhibit more examples of these types of conflict. Designers from different domains have spatial conflicts, who claim over same empty space in coupled design iterations at different timelines.

CAD tools only hold the geometry information of the product, while beyond geometry information is not captured in CAD models. Product design information like requirements, product states, and actors involved at different product states, functional model and behavior model, is not available in CAD model. Use of tools like System Modelling Language (SysML) by incorporation of system engineering domain, provides a way to capture and to represent product's non-geometry design knowledge.

In our earlier work for modelling Intended empty spaces for detecting multi-domain spatial conflict, a top down approach was discussed and implemented [1]. A bulk of empty space was detected inside CAD assembly model by Boolean operations and then it was decomposed into smaller empty space (ES) blocks. In subsequent work, the concept of modelling intended empty spaces by parametric primitive blocks was introduced [2]. Subsequent step is modelling inter-dependencies and building associativity among these empty spaces, product structure and other product knowledge in SysML. Further to this, graph based and matrix based approaches were adopted to model these interdependencies and relationships. Design Structure Matrix (DSM)/Domain Mapping Matrix (DMM)/Multi-Domain Matrix (MDM) were used to detect the spatial conflicts among multiple design domains in different product lifecycles states. Upon identifying these conflicts, knowledge based spatial suggestions can be made for efficient assembly and layout planning in product design. In this paper, focus is on to build an octree based voxel model for representation and computation purpose, which uses CAD model and ES Blocks with spatial conflicts.

2 Octree Based Voxel Model to Represent CAD Model

Voxel based method is an extension of the concept of pixels into 3D. Space is considered as a regular array of cells (usually cubes). Each cell is called voxel. Voxelization provides an alternative to geometric representation for volume modelling outside CAD. It provides a uniform, simple and robust description to synthetic and measured objects and gives the basis of volume graphics [3]. Voxelization of 3D model is done to represent the volumetric space of geometric objects using the primitives of array of voxels in the 3D discreet space. Voxel model approximates the shape of the model as closely as possible. The concept of voxelization was first introduced for volume graphics in 1993 [3]. Voxelization has application in different fields as volume modelling [4], virtual medicine [5], heptic rendering [6], visualization of geometric model [7], CSG Modelling [8], Collision detection [9–11] and spatial analysis [12]. Voxel models are used for geospatial applications as computational methods for voxelating spatial datasets of 3D city models containing 3D surfaces, curve and point cloud data models [13]. OctoMap is also an Octree based Voxel model, used as 3D mapping framework for various robotic applications [14].

Goal of voxelization here is to device a method to discretize the whole product assembly and empty spaces into smaller pieces and computationally model the empty spaces available free of spatial conflicts, to make valuable knowledge based spatial suggestions. Voxelization of 3D Solid models in CAD is one way to model volume and have empty space representation. Voxel information can be represented in form of 3D array data structure in cases where the CAD model space is small. Voxel enumeration at different voxel sizes is shown in Fig. 1. A moderate 3-dimensional array $1000 \times 1000 \times 1000$ will result in 1 billion voxels. Handling associated computations and rendering of such big number of voxel information is difficult task for any CAD software. Once the 3D model is voxelized, Boolean operations such as union and subtraction are computationally efficient.

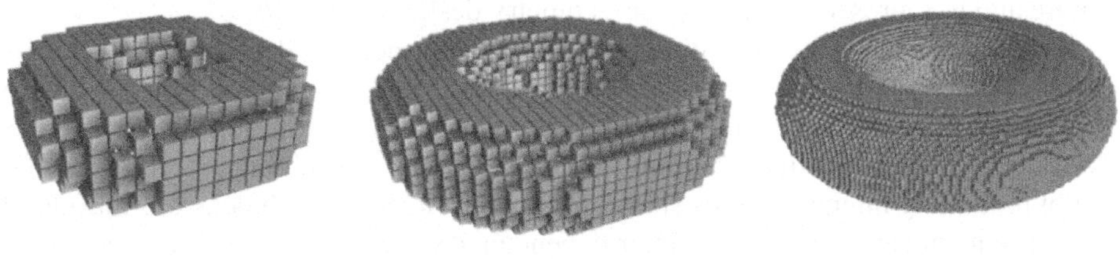

18 x 6 x 18 35 x 10 x 35 111 x 31 x 111

Fig. 1. Voxel enumeration at different voxel sizes

Voxelization of 3D model needs efficient conversion of geometry in CAD to Voxels. Octree as data structure, enable efficient storage of 3D voxel data. Octree is a 3D generalization of a Quadtree (for 2D). Each node in an Octree has eight children as shown in Fig. 2.

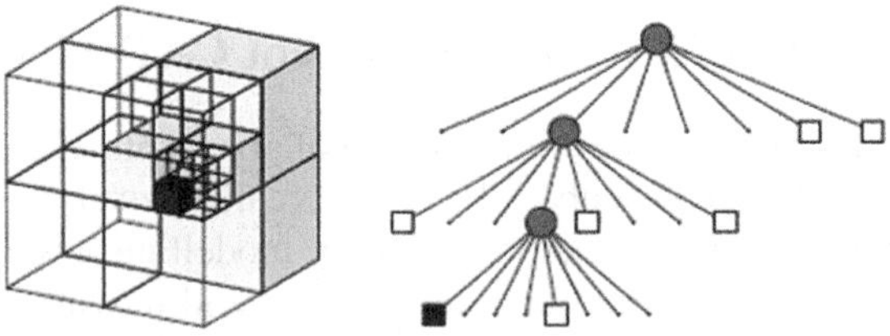

Fig. 2. Octree containing empty and occupied nodes

Modelling of intended Empty space blocks as geometry items in CAD model has been carried out in continued work earlier. Further division of these blocks in voxels provide a way to efficiently represent and compute independent of CAD Software for meaningful space suggestions to users. Figure 3 shows a UML class diagram of octree based voxel model implemented. UML class diagram has been used for easy representation of the code structure. Any Octree object contains a root Octree node, which can be further divided into eight octree nodes. Node can contain an Octree leaf object, which are used as a condition to divide, the octree upto a user given voxel resolution. CAD model is ray intersected using a standard ray intersection method with CAD APIs. This results into a point cloud of CAD geometry surfaces. Individual point is added as Octree Leaf to Octree node and based on the location of Octree leaf in root octree object, the octree nodes are further sub-divided.

Every octree node is having variables for Inner node, Empty Node and associated solid body in CAD model. Every Octree Node is having an object for octree bounds to define its boundaries modelled as class in Fig. 3. It has been implemented using C# language and the code interacts with CAD model using CAD APIs. Octree Voxel model visualization is done using OpenGL libraries outside CAD environment.

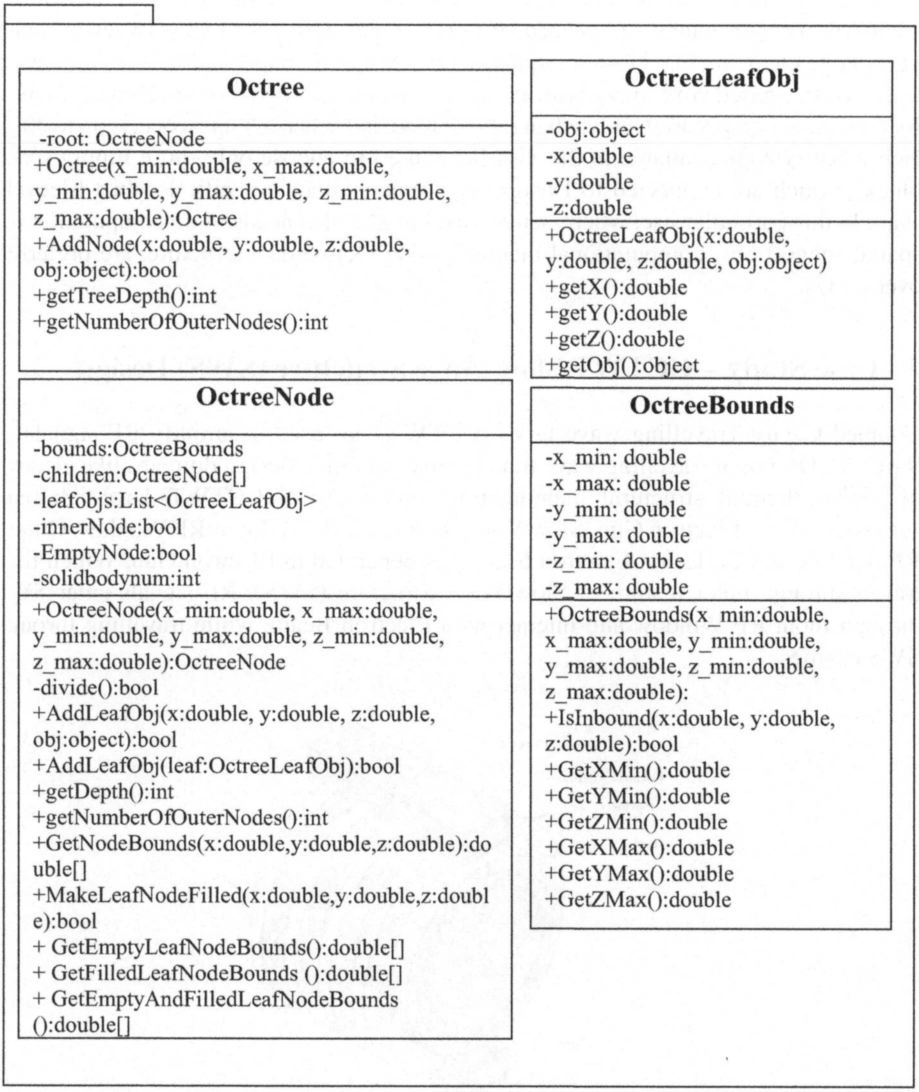

Fig. 3. UML class diagram for Octree based voxel model representation of CAD model and empty spaces

Purpose of this representation and modeling, is to embed the knowledge available in System Modelling language (SysML) with the CAD model. SysML is the extension of UML, which is developed to provide standard system modelling tools [15]. SysML supports capturing requirements of system and capturing structural & behavioral models. Block Definition Diagrams (BDD) and Internal Block Diagrams (IBD) are used to define classes and instances. Use of SysML tools, provides the way to capture, represent and associate the product's non-geometry information. This knowledge is stored in SysML compatible XML file for further processing along with the CAD model. Octree based voxel model is created on the fly instead of saving it in XML or other formats, whenever a representation is needed of CAD model with ES blocks associated with knowledge elements like Design requirements, Design domains and Product Lifecycle states. Octree based voxel models are compact and have an edge over array data structure for representation purpose, only when ratio of modeled space to total space, is up to 30%. Hence Knowledge available in the SysML, is used to choose only those Empty space blocks, which are connected to Design requirements under specific Product lifecycle state. In this particular use, where octree voxel model also needs to do computation for spatial suggestions, computational methods using Octree data structure, are preferred over arrays.

3 Case Study – CCTWT Slow Wave Structure (SWS) Design

Coupled Cavity Travelling wave tubes (CCTWT) are used to amplify RF signals in RADAR. Design of travelling wave tube involves multiple design domains like electromagnetics, thermal, structural, manufacturing and electrical. CCTWTs have five main sub-assemblies - Electron Gun, Slow Wave Structure (SWS), Input RF Window, Output RF window and Collector. Electron beam gets generated in Electron Gun, Which then travels through inner feature of Slow Wave Structure (SWS). RF signals enter SWS through Input RF Window and interact with Electron Beam, while travelling through SWS cavities.

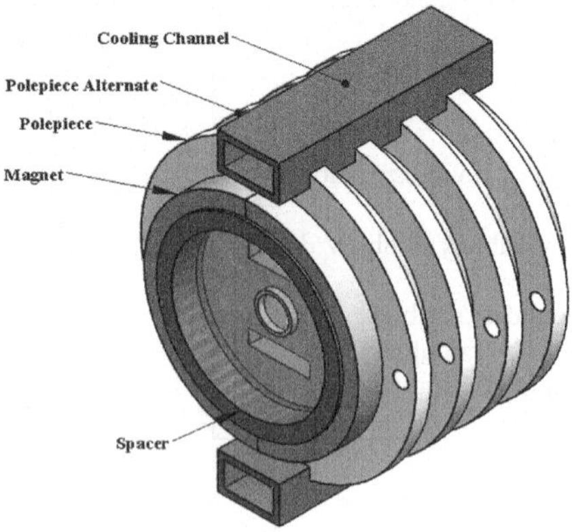

Fig. 4. Slow wave structure (SWS) solid model

SWS is an important sub-assembly of TWT and is a perfect example, where multiple design domain teams need collaboration to resolve spatial conflicts to have an efficient product design. SWS consists of alternate pattern of pole-pieces and spacers. Solid model of typical SWS is shown in Fig. 4. SWS CAD model has been represented in Octree Voxel model in Fig. 5. Complete process of getting point cloud of representing surfaces to full voxel model not differentiating filled and empty nodes to separate Empty space leaf nodes and SWS model filled leaf nodes have been shown in Fig. 5.

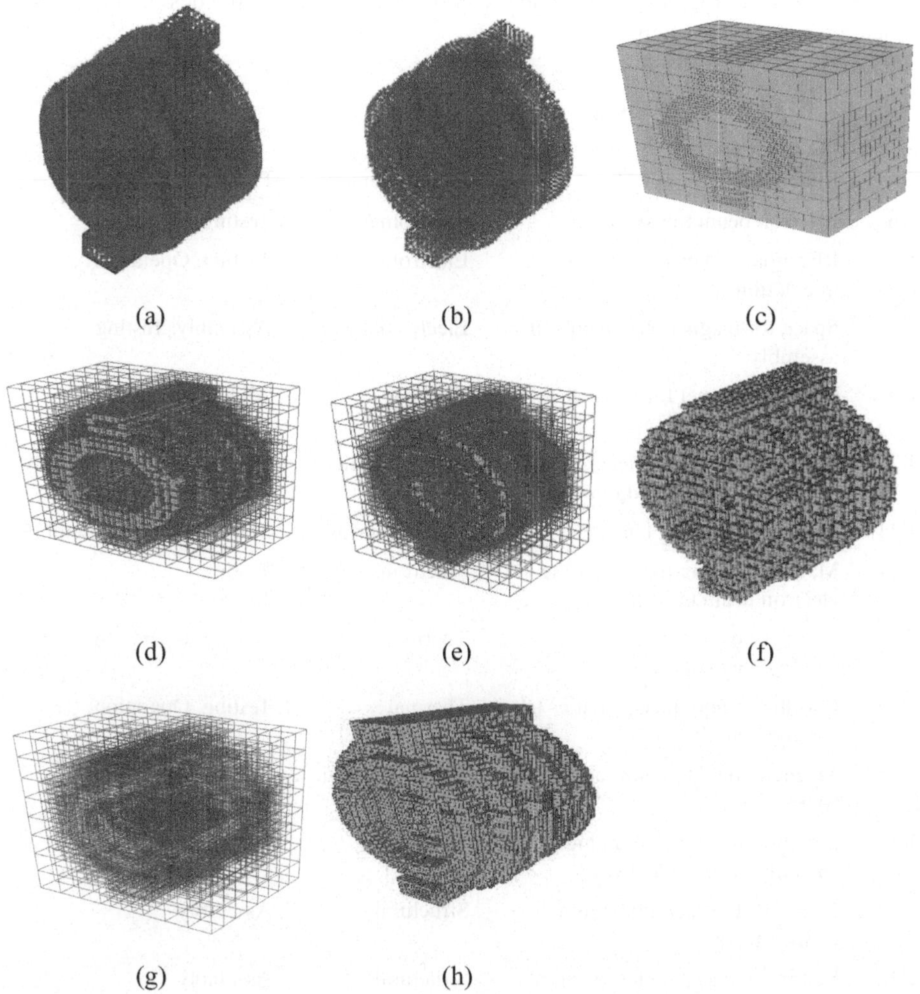

Fig. 5. Octree Based voxel model generated using ray intersection on CAD model. (a) Ray intersecting CAD model from x, y and Z direction with equal resolution. (b) Point cloud generated by standard ray intersection method with CAD APIs. (c) Voxel model showing complete SWS with its bounding box (CAD model with empty spaces). (d) Empty Spaces shown with wireframe and filled octree nodes with their faces modelled. (Empty nodes visible between filled SWS). (e) Filled nodes between surface nodes to model it as a volume (f) Surface octree node SWS model. (g) Octree voxel model of empty space (h) Octree voxel model of only SWS geometry

Design requirements for SWS with connected design domain and meant to be for particular product lifecycle states, are listed in Table 1. Design mapping matrix (DMM) of ES blocks and requirements in different product lifecycle state is shown in Fig. 6. It also shows the spatial conflicts in red color, depicting multiple usage of single ES Block in multiple design domains. This information is used to select the ES blocks shown in DMM rows, for creating the octree voxel model. Design requirements listed in Table 1, are allocated to different ES blocks. SWS modelled with intended empty space blocks has been shown in Fig. 7. Empty spaces can be associated with the design requirement, which are satisfied by them.

Table 1. Design requirements table

ID	Requirement	Design domain	Product lifecycle states
R6	Electron beam transmission	Electromagnetic	Testing, Operation
R7	RF signal and electron beam interaction	Electromagnetic	Testing, Operation
R8	Space for magnet placements in assembly	Electromagnetic	Assembly, Testing
R9	Cooling channel for thermal management	Thermal	All States
R10	Holes to align pole-pieces of SWS stack in assembly and brazing	Manufacturing	Manufacturing, Assembly
R11	Brazing of cooling channels	Manufacturing	Manufacturing, Assembly
R12	Magnetic tuning for increasing electron beam transmission	Electromagnetic	Testing
R13	Coolant flow inside pole-piece cooling channels	Thermal	Testing, Operation
R14	Cooling of pole-piece cavities to avoid de-gassing	Thermal	Testing, Operation
R15	Magnetic field to compress electron beam	Electromagnetic	Testing, Operation
R16	Structure to sustain ultra high vacuum level inside TWT	Structural	All States
R17	Materials to sustain brazing temperatures	Structural	Assembly
R18	Materials to sustain temperatures under processing	Structural	Assembly
R19	RF power gain requirement	Electromagnetic	Testing, Operation
R20	RF frequency bandwidth requirement	Electromagnetic	Testing, Operation

Manufacturing	R10
ESBlock5	0
ESBlock8	0
ESBlock9	0
ESBlock11	0
ESBlock14	0
ESBlock17	0
ESBlock18	0
ESBlock19	0
ESBlock20	0
ESBlock21	0
ESBlock22	0
ESBlock23	0
ESBlock24	0
ESBlock25	0
ESBlock26	0
ESBlock27	0
ESBlock28	0
ESBlock29	0
ESBlock30	0
ESBlock31	0
ESBlock32	0
ESBlock33	0
ESBlock34	0
ESBlock35	0
ESBlock36	0
ESBlock37	0
ESBlock38	0
ESBlock39	0
ESBlock40	0
ESBlock41	0
ESBlock42	0
ESBlock43	0
ESBlock44	0
ESBlock45	0
ESBlock46	1
ESBlock47	0
ESBlock48	1
ESBlock49	1
ESBlock50	1
ESBlock51	1
ESBlock52	1
ESBlock53	1
ESBlock54	1

Assembly	R8	R10
ESBlock5	0	0
ESBlock8	0	0
ESBlock9	0	0
ESBlock11	0	0
ESBlock14	0	0
ESBlock17	0	0
ESBlock18	0	0
ESBlock19	0	0
ESBlock20	0	0
ESBlock21	0	0
ESBlock22	0	0
ESBlock23	0	0
ESBlock24	0	0
ESBlock25	0	0
ESBlock26	0	0
ESBlock27	0	0
ESBlock28	0	0
ESBlock29	0	0
ESBlock30	0	0
ESBlock31	0	0
ESBlock32	0	0
ESBlock33	0	0
ESBlock34	0	0
ESBlock35	0	0
ESBlock36	0	0
ESBlock37	0	0
ESBlock38	1	0
ESBlock39	1	0
ESBlock40	1	0
ESBlock41	1	0
ESBlock42	0	0
ESBlock43	0	0
ESBlock44	0	0
ESBlock45	0	0
ESBlock46	0	1
ESBlock47	1	0
ESBlock48	0	1
ESBlock49	0	1
ESBlock50	0	1
ESBlock51	0	1
ESBlock52	0	1
ESBlock53	0	1
ESBlock54	0	1

Testing	R6	R7	R8	R12	R14
ESBlock5	0	1	0	0	0
ESBlock8	0	1	0	0	0
ESBlock9	0	0	0	0	0
ESBlock11	0	1	0	0	0
ESBlock14	0	1	0	0	0
ESBlock17	1	0	0	0	0
ESBlock18	0	1	0	0	0
ESBlock19	1	0	0	0	0
ESBlock20	1	1	0	0	1
ESBlock21	1	1	0	0	1
ESBlock22	0	1	0	0	0
ESBlock23	1	0	0	0	0
ESBlock24	1	0	0	0	0
ESBlock25	1	0	0	0	0
ESBlock26	0	1	0	0	0
ESBlock27	1	0	0	0	0
ESBlock28	1	1	0	0	1
ESBlock29	1	1	0	0	1
ESBlock30	1	0	0	0	0
ESBlock31	1	1	0	0	1
ESBlock32	1	0	0	0	0
ESBlock33	0	1	0	0	0
ESBlock34	1	0	0	0	0
ESBlock35	1	0	0	0	0
ESBlock36	1	0	0	0	0
ESBlock37	1	0	0	0	0
ESBlock38	0	0	1	1	0
ESBlock39	0	0	1	1	0
ESBlock40	0	0	1	1	0
ESBlock41	0	0	1	1	0
ESBlock42	0	0	0	1	0
ESBlock43	0	0	0	1	0
ESBlock44	0	0	0	1	0
ESBlock45	0	0	0	1	0
ESBlock46	0	0	0	0	0
ESBlock47	0	0	1	1	0
ESBlock48	0	0	0	0	0
ESBlock49	0	0	0	0	0
ESBlock50	0	0	0	0	0
ESBlock51	0	0	0	0	0
ESBlock52	0	0	0	0	0
ESBlock53	0	0	0	0	0
ESBlock54	0	0	0	0	0

Operation	R6	R7	R14
ESBlock5	0	1	0
ESBlock8	0	1	0
ESBlock9	0	0	0
ESBlock11	0	1	0
ESBlock14	0	1	0
ESBlock17	1	0	0
ESBlock18	0	1	0
ESBlock19	1	0	0
ESBlock20	1	1	1
ESBlock21	1	1	1
ESBlock22	0	1	0
ESBlock23	1	0	0
ESBlock24	1	0	0
ESBlock25	1	0	0
ESBlock26	0	1	0
ESBlock27	1	0	0
ESBlock28	1	1	1
ESBlock29	1	1	1
ESBlock30	1	0	0
ESBlock31	1	1	1
ESBlock32	1	0	0
ESBlock33	0	1	0
ESBlock34	1	0	0
ESBlock35	1	0	0
ESBlock36	1	0	0
ESBlock37	1	0	0
ESBlock38	0	0	0
ESBlock39	0	0	0
ESBlock40	0	0	0
ESBlock41	0	0	0
ESBlock42	0	0	0
ESBlock43	0	0	0
ESBlock44	0	0	0
ESBlock45	0	0	0
ESBlock46	0	0	0
ESBlock47	0	0	0
ESBlock48	0	0	0
ESBlock49	0	0	0
ESBlock50	0	0	0
ESBlock51	0	0	0
ESBlock52	0	0	0
ESBlock53	0	0	0
ESBlock54	0	0	0

Design Domain: Electromagnetic
Design Domain: Manufacturing
Design Domain: Thermal

Single Design Domain spatial allocation to multiple requirements
Multiple Design Domain Spatial Conflict

Fig. 6. DMM of ES blocks and design requirements for slow wave structure for each product lifecycle state showing multiple usage of single ES block within Single domain and in multiple design domains depicting spatial conflict (Color figure online)

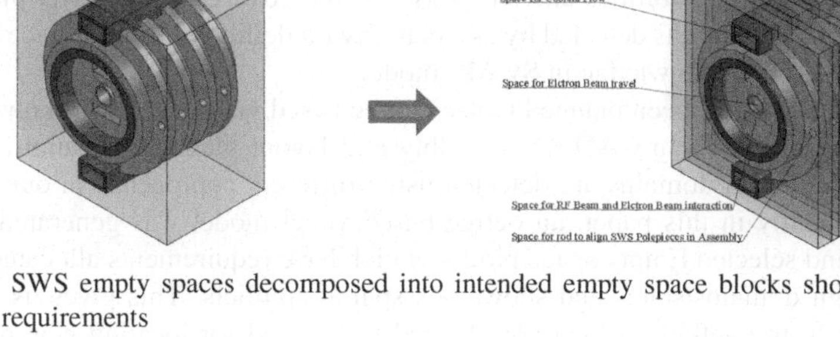

Fig. 7. SWS empty spaces decomposed into intended empty space blocks showing allocated design requirements

3D solid model of SWS empty space blocks and Cut-sectional model views of intended empty spaces of SWS for different requirements, have been shown in Fig. 8(a) and (b). This method enables us to correctly differentiate and demarcate spaces inside SWS like for RF Signal and Electron beam. ES Blocks depicting multi-domain spatial conflicts in CAD model are shown in Fig. 8c. ES block list is computed from DMM shown in Fig. 6 for different product lifecycle states. This list in addition with Product structure, is the criteria, used to model octree Voxel model shown in Fig. 8(d).

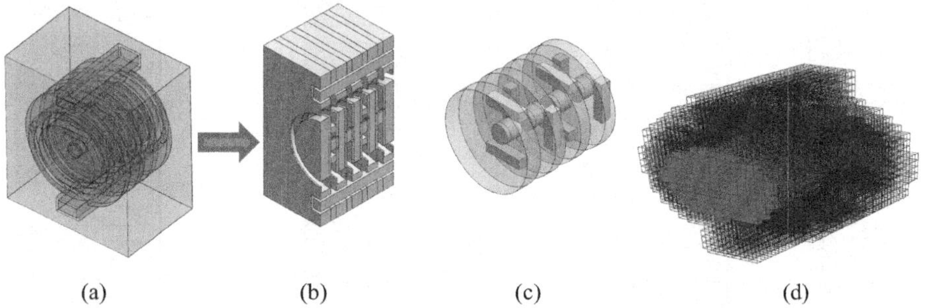

Fig. 8. (a) 3D solid model of SWS empty spaces (b) Cut sectional model of SWS's bulk empty space decomposed into intended empty space blocks to be allocated to different design requirements. (c) ES blocks depicting multi-domain spatial conflicts in CAD model (d) Multi-domain spatial conflict representation using Octree voxel model by rendering conflicting ES blocks in red with wireframe SWS octree voxel model outside CAD environment using OpenGL. (Color figure online)

4 Conclusion

This paper discusses use of octree based voxel model for representation of spatial conflicts across multiple design domains. A framework has been developed to create octree based voxel model linked with intended empty spaces in product, which are associated with design requirements, product lifecycle states and are also connected with functional design domains. Knowledge in SysML, which was elaborated in our earlier work [1], is used to select criteria for building octree voxel model. A case study of Coupled cavity travelling wave tube (CCTWT) Slow Wave structure (SWS) design has been taken to showcase the code capabilities and showcase Octree voxels outside CAD platform representing spatial conflicts detected by associativity modelling of Empty space blocks along with the Product knowledge in SysML model.

In future work, it has been planned to use Octree based voxel model for knowledge based spatial suggestions in CAD for assembly and layout planning. Spatial conflict across multiple design domains are detected using different approaches in our earlier work. Subsequently in this paper, an octree based voxel model was generated using CAD model and selected Empty space blocks, which have requirements allocated from multiple design domains/states and showcases spatial conflicts. This gives us spaces available free from conflicts, which are planned to be used for locating new parts in assembly and carry out layout planning.

Acknowledgement. The First author is thankful to Director, Microwave Tube Research & Development Centre (MTRDC) for providing the opportunity and encouragement in carrying out the work presented in the paper.

References

1. Singh, A.K., Gurumoorthy, B., Christie, L.: Empty space modelling for detecting spatial conflicts across multiple design domains. In: Ríos, J., Bernard, A., Bouras, A., Foufou, S. (eds.) PLM 2017. IAICT, vol. 517, pp. 223–230. Springer, Cham (2017). https://doi.org/10.1007/978-3-319-72905-3_20
2. Singh, A.K., Gurumoorthy, B., Christie, L.: Empty space modelling using primitive shapes and associated constraints for detecting spatial conflicts across multiple design domains. In: Proceedings of the International Conference on Product Lifecycle Modelling, Synthesis & Simulations (PLMSS) (2017)
3. Kaufman, A., Cohen, D., Yagel, R.: Volume graphics. Computer **26**(7), 51–64 (1993)
4. Wang, S.W., Kaufman, A.E.: Volume-sampled 3D modeling. IEEE Comput. Graph. Appl. **14**, 26–32 (1994)
5. Kreeger, K., Kaufman, A.: Mixing translucent polygons with volumes. In: Proceedings of the Conference on Visualization 1999: Celebrating Ten Years, CA, USA (1999)
6. McNeely, W.A., Puterbaugh, K.D., Troy, J.J.: Six degree-of-freedom haptic rendering using voxel sampling. In: Proceedings of the 26th Annual Conference on Computer Graphics and Interactive Techniques - SIGGRAPH 1999 (1999)
7. Westermann, R., Sommer, O., Ertl, T.: Decoupling polygon rendering from geometry using rasterization hardware. In: Lischinski, D., Larson, G.W. (eds.) Rendering Techniques 1999. Eurographics, pp. 45–56. Springer, Vienna (1999). https://doi.org/10.1007/978-3-7091-6809-7_5
8. Liao, D., Fang, S.: Fast CSG voxelization by frame buffer pixel mapping. In: 2000 IEEE Symposium on Volume Visualization (VV 2000) (2000)
9. He, T., Kaufman, A.: Collision detection for volumetric objects. In: Proceedings of the 8th Conference on Visualization 1997, Los Alamitos, CA, USA (1997)
10. Boyles, M., Fang, S.: Slicing-based volumetric collision detection. J. Graph. Tools **4**, 23–32 (1999)
11. Gagvani, N., Silver, D.: Shape-based volumetric collision detection. In: Proceedings of the 2000 IEEE Symposium on Volume Visualization - VVS 2000 (2000)
12. Beckhaus, S., Wind, J., Imk. Ve, F., Strothotte, T.: Hardware-based voxelization for 3D spatial analysis (2002)
13. Nourian, P., Gonçalves, R., Zlatanova, S., Ohori, K.A., Vo, A.V.: Voxelization algorithms for geospatial applications. MethodX **3**, 69–86 (2016)
14. Hornung, A., Wurm, K.M., Bennewitz, M., Stachniss, C., Burgard, W.: OctoMap: an efficient probabilistic 3D mapping framework based on octrees. Auton. Robot. **34**, 189–206 (2013)
15. OMG systems modelling language specifications (2015). www.omg.org/spec/SysML/1.4/

A Review, Focused on Data Transfer Standards, of the Uncertainty Representation in the Digital Twin Context

José Ríos[1(✉)], Georg Staudter[2], Moritz Weber[2], and Reiner Anderl[2]

[1] Universidad Politécnica de Madrid, José Gutierrez Abascal 2, 28006 Madrid, Spain
jose.rios@upm.es

[2] TU Darmstadt, Otto-Berndt-Straße 2, 64287 Darmstadt, Germany
{staudter,m.weber,anderl}@dik.tu-darmstadt.de

Abstract. In the context of the digital twin, the relevance and challenges of the uncertainty quantification are recognized. Data acquired in the physical domain are incorporated into a cyber-space to assist in predictive and decision-making processes. The acquisition of data in the physical domain involves the measurement of physical magnitudes. The digital as-built or as-manufactured model derives from measured or scanned data of a physical product. Thus, it is relevant to know how much the data are true. The uncertainty of a measured magnitude is a significant indicator of the data truthfulness. This work shows how the uncertainty is being modeled in standards related to product data representation and in an engineering data fusion context. The ongoing uncertainty modeling work in the Collaborative Research Center (SFB 805) at TU Darmstadt is presented as an example of a data fusion context.

Keywords: Uncertainty representation · Digital twin · Data fusion · Standards

1 Introduction

The digital twin concept involves integrating data from development, functional and industrial design with data from the physical domain along the whole lifecycle. This basic idea applies both to products and to production systems. It is grounded on the creation of a digital as-built model of a physical product [1] and in the integration of computation with physical processes, named as cyber-physical systems (CPS) [2]. A digital twin can be seen as the digital representation of a specific physical artifact, identified by its serial number, at a specific point in time.

In the context of production, designers and engineers define what must be achieved in the physical domain and how to accomplish it. They used different software applications along the development and design process, to define how the product must be, and how, where, for how long and in what quantity, it must be manufactured. The result is an extremely big amount of data related to the product itself, the processes to execute and the resources to use. Using a concept coined in the 1990s, we could frame such data into

Published by Springer Nature Switzerland AG 2019
C. Fortin et al. (Eds.): PLM 2019, IFIP AICT 565, pp. 24–33, 2019.
https://doi.org/10.1007/978-3-030-42250-9_3

a kind of industrial digital mock-up [3]. Then data and working instructions, which are defined as mandatory, are transferred into the physical domain to manufacture physical products. The physical product exists, and therefore, it is the true one, but the digital one is the mandatory one. The physical product is assessed by performing a comparison against the mandatory one, i.e. the digital one. A clear extension of the digital mock-up concept is the current concept of the digital twin.

In the widest sense, a digital twin requires to implement an unbroken closed-loop data flow [4], where data, acquired from test specimens, physical scale models, physical products and production systems, are incorporated into a cyber-space to assist in predictive and decision-making processes [5, 6]. Data obtained from test specimens and physical scale models are used to perform engineering calculations, e.g. material property data [7] and performance data [8]. Data obtained from the physical product are used to validate and certify the product against engineering requirements [9]. In the cyber-physical production systems (CPPS), configuration and run-time data are used to implement production and maintenance adaptive strategies that rely on system simulations [5]. In parallel, to the digital twin concept, the digital thread concept was defined. The digital thread comprises linking data and information generated along the product lifecycle through a data-driven architecture of shared resources, this way, data from the physical domain can be fed back and linked to design data (cyber domain) [6]. The assumption, behind the unbroken closed-loop data flow, is that incorporating "true data", from the physical domain into the cyber domain, allows reducing uncertainty, improving predictions and designing adaptive products and systems.

From an engineering perspective, the implementation of the digital twin concept is an ongoing process that faces challenges: data acquisition, gathering and processing of large data sets, data fusion, data standardization, uncertainty quantification, trustworthiness of data, data security, models interoperability, high-fidelity computational models for simulation and virtual testing at multiple scales, modeling of physical part variations, synchronization between the physical and the digital world to establish closed loops, complexity and cost of state-of-the-art IT-infrastructure [5, 9–12].

The acquisition of data in the physical domain involves the measurement of physical magnitudes or quantitative properties. In many occasions, the measurement result is expressed by a twofold structure: the nominal value of the magnitude and the measurement unit. The nominal value is considered as numerically exact and it is propagated throughout successive processes [13]. However, the result of measurement should be a threefold structure, where the uncertainty of the measurement is the third component. The uncertainty is a way to indicate how good a nominal value is [14]. The benefits derived from the digital twin implementation, depend on incorporating "true data" from the physical domain into the digital domain. Therefore, it is relevant to know how much the data are true. In the process of data transfer from the physical to the cyber domain, the trustworthiness of data depends on several factors, mainly: integrity, reliability, security, and quality [15]. The most widely used data quality dimensions are: accuracy, completeness, currency, and consistency. Within the accuracy dimension, the uncertainty of a measured magnitude is a significant contributor to the indicator of the data truthfulness.

This work provides a review of how the uncertainty is being considered in the context of the digital twin. The literature points out the relevance, the challenges and the lack of uncertainty quantification in the context of the digital twin [12, 13, 16, 17]. Section 2 provides a review of the uncertainty definition. Section 3 points out some of the main challenges of its quantification. Section 4 deals with the uncertainty representation, how it is modeled in standards related to product data representation, how it is considered in a data fusion context, and in particular, in an engineering data fusion context represented by the case of the Collaborative Research Center (SFB 805) at TU Darmstadt. The communication ends with conclusions and future works.

2 Uncertainty

In general, uncertainty involves imperfect, imprecise or unknown data, information or knowledge. There are two facts to keep in mind. The first one is that uncertainty refers to something: a property, a measurement, a model, an assumption, a specific data. The second one is that the existence of uncertainty imposes that truth exists [18]. In engineering, the truth exists in the physical domain: products and production systems.

Based on its nature, uncertainty is usually classified under two main types: epistemic and aleatoric [19]. Epistemic uncertainty relates to the lack of knowledge. Aleatoric uncertainty relates to the variability of physical processes. Epistemic uncertainty can be introduced by means of poor assumptions, poor models and missing data. Aleatoric uncertainty is inherent to the non-deterministic nature of the manufacturing and measurement processes [16]. Different approaches are proposed to evaluate the epistemic uncertainty, e.g. evidence theory, possibility theory and interval analysis [19]. The evidence theory uses basic probabilistic assignments to indicate the degree to which a piece of evidence supports a hypothesis. Aleatoric uncertainty is quantified by means of statistical methods using a probability distribution [19, 20]. Considering the design and development of complex multidisciplinary engineering systems, Thunnissen [21] proposed two additional uncertainty types: ambiguity and interaction. Ambiguity uncertainty relates to the use of imprecise terms and expressions by individuals when communicating a specification. Interaction uncertainty relates to situations where several disciplines, individuals and factors are involved but their interaction was not properly foreseen, or a disagreement arises.

3 Quantification of Uncertainty

The quantification of uncertainty is widely acknowledged and affects both the collected data and the models created for a process of interest. It can be seen as a process of determining uncertainties associated with model-based predictions. A sensitivity analysis is also required to quantify the impact that each input data have on the results provided by the model. It involves identifying and characterizing all the key sources of uncertainty and propagating input uncertainties through the model [19, 20].

One of the main challenges of uncertainty quantification in the digital twin context is that different types of uncertainty are present when transferring data from the physical domain into the digital or cyber domain. Material mechanical properties derived from test specimens, with values considered as exact, are used as input in models to estimate and simulate the result from manufacturing processes. However, the physical part may exhibit a microstructure that is not uniform and so are its mechanical properties [7, 22]. Data derived from functional tests of scale models are merged with simulation data, numerical uncertainties are derived from approximations to geometry and boundary conditions, and from physical models and parameters [8]. Different sensing and measuring devices are used to monitor and measure parameters, both in products and in production systems. This situation leads to fuse data from different sources. Quantifying the quality of the data, or uncertainty, provided by the different sensors and devices is critical, overall, when data from different sources are conflicting [23]. The quantification of the uncertainty of the true data gathered in the physical domain is an impediment to achieve an appropriate fusion of physical and virtual systems, and a limitation for the digital twin concept implementation [5, 11–13].

When analyzing current practices at the physical level, literature also shows examples of how the uncertainty quantification is an issue. The complexity in calculating the measurement uncertainty derives from the significant number of factors that affect it, e.g. human-caused, environmental, logical, mechanical, methodological and numerical [24]. As an example, Abollado et al. [25] concluded that at the shop-floor level, the quantification of uncertainty in the industry requires support with the identification of uncertainty key drivers and the definition of best practices.

4 Representation of Uncertainty

The formal representation of concepts, in a computer-processable way, is addressed by creating data models, information models or ontologies. This section shows how the concept of uncertainty is being represented in the context of CPS and the digital twin. A formal representation depends on how the concept of uncertainty is defined.

In a Cyber-Physical Systems (CPS) context, heterogeneous physical elements communicate via networking equipment and interact with applications and humans. Zhang et al. [17] consider uncertainty, as a lack of confidence, due to the interactions between hardware, software and humans, and the need for them to be context aware. Uncertainty represents a state where an agent does not have full confidence in a belief that it holds, and it can be represented by a measurement. Uncertainty is specialized into: content, environment, geographical location, occurrence, and time; and it can follow a pattern or be random. A measurement can be represented by vagueness, probability, and ambiguity.

In the context of virtual product development, Anderl et al. [13] and Heimrich et al. [26] consider uncertainty in properties related to products and processes. Uncertainty is modeled in the form of single values, intervals, fuzziness, and stochastic measures. They proposed an approach based on three layers: representation, presentation, and visualization. The representation layer comprises an ontology-based information model that supports an Uncertainty Mode and Effect Analysis (UMEA) process. The model extends concepts provided by the standard ISO 10303 for the exchange of product model data (STEP), e.g.: *UncertaintyType*, *UncertaintyDriverProduction*, and *UncertaintyDriverUsage*.

4.1 Uncertainty in the Standard ISO 10303 (STEP)

The standard ISO 10303 is an enabler of the digital thread and defines the basic concepts related to uncertainty in: ISO 10303-41 [27] and ISO 10303-45 [28]; which are part of the STEP Module and Resource Library (SMRL). The concepts are based on the definitions provided by the guide to the expression of uncertainty in measurement [20], which considers that a measurement is only complete when accompanied by a quantitative value of its uncertainty. The Part 41 defines the *product_property_definition_schema*, which specifies concepts to define product properties; the *measure_schema*, which specifies the concepts to describe physical quantities, e.g.: *measure_value, unit, si_unit, named_unit, measure_with_unit* [27]. In the Part 45, the *material_property_definition_schema*, specifies concepts to define material properties; the *qualified_measure_schema*, specifies concepts to qualify quantities by their uncertainty, e.g.: *value_qualifier, uncertainty_qualifier, standard_uncertainty, qualitative_uncertainty, measure_qualification, measure_representation_item* [28]. Additionally, basic concepts, dealing with geometric shape variation tolerances, are defined in the ISO 10303-47. The ISO 10303-50 defines basic concepts dealing with the definition of mathematical structures and data related to the properties of a product.

In addition to the basic definitions, application protocols are developed to specify information requirements to specific engineering application contexts. The ISO 10303-235 is the application protocol (AP) related to engineering properties for product design and verification [29]. It defines the processes for the testing, measurement, and approval of engineering properties, both of product samples and the manufactured product itself. The normative model, designed as Application Interpreted Model (AIM), comprises all the uncertainty related concepts defined in the STEP (SMRL). This AP is of interest when aiming to feedback data related to material properties derived from test specimens, and data derived from functional tests of scale models.

The ISO 10303-242 is for managed model-based 3D engineering, its scope is limited to product data related to design and manufacturing planning of mechanical parts and assemblies [30]. It substitutes the former applications protocols AP 203 and AP 214. In addition to schemas from the ISO 10303-41 and the ISO 10303-45 previously mentioned, it adopts schemas defined in the ISO 10303-59, related to the quality of product shape data. Among many other concepts, within the mechanical design, it comprises the definition of properties of parts and tools, data defining surface conditions, dimensional and geometrical tolerance data, quality criteria and inspection results of 3D product shape data. Successful implementation tests of the AP 242, to exchange 3D models with the specification of tolerances are reported in the literature [31]. The AP242 comprises schemas such as: *product_data_quality_criteria, product_data_quality_definition, product_data_quality_inspection_result*. Some of the main uncertainty related concepts are: *QualitativeUncertainty, StandardUncertainty, ValuewithTolerances, ValueWithUnit, MeasuredQualification, MeasuredCharacteristic, PropertyValue*. *PropertyValue* represents the value of a property and is an abstract supertype of: *StringValue, ValueList, ValueSet* and *ValueWithUnit*. It has an optional attribute named qualifications where the uncertainty or the precision of the value could be specified. A *ValueWithUnit* is an abstract supertype of: *NumericalValue, ValueRange*, and

ValueWithTolerances. These concepts allow expressing the value of part properties for its propagation throughout different processes.

Another relevant AP is the AP 219 for dimensional inspection information exchange [32]. This AP could be considered as an antecedent to the aimed closed-loop data flow from manufacturing (physical domain) to design (digital/cyber domain). Where data and results from the part inspection could be feedback to design. It comprises all the basic concepts defined in the STEP integrated generic resources that were commented previously, however, its industrial implementation has not been reported. In that sense, it can be stated that to achieve the digital thread concept only with STEP related technology is not feasible yet. As an alternative, the Quality Information Framework (QIF) was defined to support manufacturing quality information.

4.2 Uncertainty in the Standard QIF

QIF is an ANSI standard that defines a set of information models to enable the closed-loop exchange of metrology data from product design to inspection planning to inspection execution to data analysis and results reporting. It defines several areas of quality information: measurement plans, measurement results, measurement rules, measurement resources and results analysis [33]. It is a feed forward and feedback data quality flow that supports the digital thread concept [34].

QIF is structured into six application area information models: Model-Based Design (MBD), Plans, Resources, Rules, Results, and Statistics; and it is specified in a set of XML schemas. It allows the definition of rules by means of the called QIF Rules model. Rules can be defined by each organization to define working practices, e.g. how a product should be measured based on measurement requirements [33]. It adopts the uncertainty definitions provided by the guide to the expression of uncertainty in measurement [20]. However, it considers it as an optional attribute. In instance files, QIF allows quantities to appear without explicit unit and uncertainty for each value. Units can be specified in a QIF instance file by using the *FileUnits* element defined in the *Units* schema. This schema defines also the concepts: *SpecifiedDecimalType* and *MeasuredDecimalType*. The former allows specifying a decimal type value with two optional attributes: *decimalPlaces* and *significantFigures*. The latter defines a *SpecifiedDecimalType* with two additional optional attributes: *combinedUncertainty* and *meanError*. While this approach may provide flexibility, it also means that different implementations of QIF are possible, which at the end may turn into interoperability problems among different organizations.

4.3 Uncertainty Representation and Engineering Data Fusion

Data fusion deals with integrating multiple data streams into one single consistent information stream. The Intl. Soc. of Information Fusion has created an ontology named URREF (Uncertainty Representation and Reasoning Evaluation Framework) to facilitate the communication and data processing in the context of complex, distributed, and operational information fusion systems [35]. It distinguishes between low-level information fusion, e.g. physical-based parameters, and high-level information fusion, e.g.

the World Wide Web. The ontology comprises the classes: *UncertaintyNature, UncertaintyType, UncertaintyDerivation*, and *UncertaintyModel*. The uncertainty nature distinguishes between epistemic and aleatory. The uncertainty type refers to what makes information uncertain: ambiguity, incompleteness, vagueness, randomness, and inconsistency. The uncertainty derivation refers to how the uncertainty can be assessed, subjectively or objectively. The uncertainty model class refers to mathematical theories for representing and reasoning with the uncertainty types.

As previously mentioned, different devices are used to monitor and measure physical magnitudes. Both complex products and CPPS can be seen as large-scale measurement platforms were multiple data streams need to be integrated [23].

In this context, we may consider two possible data inducted conflict scenarios. One scenario, where different devices provide different values for the same magnitude. And a second one, where different data sources use different semantics for the same magnitude. The first scenario could be addressed by introducing two parameters. The reliability degree of the source, which expresses its level of trust for delivering true data over time. And the credibility degree of the data, which depends on its confirmation by other sources and its conflict with other data [36]. The second scenario refers to industrial interoperability and it can be addressed mainly in two ways. By harmonizing and implementing standards to transfer data, both from the cyber domain to the physical domain and from the physical domain to the cyber domain. And by automating the mapping and integration of different semantic definitions, e.g. ontologies.

An example of the need to harmonize standards can be illustrated by the previously commented ways to represent uncertainty. When considering the data transfer from the physical domain to the cyber domain, additional standards, to the ones commented in the two prior subsections, have to be considered. The standard IEC 62541, known as OPC UA, is a service-oriented framework that supports a client-server architecture to model and transport data that will be exchanged between industrial applications [37]. It provides the basis to define companion information models that specify the data content to exchange. MTConnect, although developed separately, has been harmonized with OPC UA and it can be considered as an example of such companion information models [38]. In itself, MTConnect is a standard to transfer data from the manufacturing equipment to the cyber domain and it is used as part of the digital thread implementation [34]. By means of an MTConnect Agent, a piece of manufacturing equipment can report data, e.g. an axis position. Data to be reported is modeled by means of the *DataItem* element, which has mandatory attributes: *id, type* and *category*; and optional attributes: *name, subtype, statistic, units, nativeUnits, nativeScale, coordinateSystem, compositionId, sampleRate, representation*, and *significantDigits*. The optional *statistic* attribute allows describing any type of statistical calculation that has been performed to provide the reported data value [39]. However, how to represent the uncertainty of the reported data is still unclear.

The automated integration of different semantic definitions obtained from different sources may lead to issues of incomplete and contradictory concepts. The resolution of these issues could be addressed by combining deductive and inductive reasoning mechanisms. In deductive reasoning, the truth of the conclusion is based on the truth of the data. In inductive reasoning, the truth of the conclusion cannot be asserted because of the uncertainty of the data. In this case, a certainty or truthfulness level of the conclusion could be provided. This approach is currently under research in the SFB 805 for Control of Uncertainty in Load-bearing Syst. of Mech. Eng. [40].

4.4 Uncertainty Representation in the Context of the SFB 805

Within the SFB 805, one of the main objectives is to manage uncertainty along the product lifecycle, from development to usage. The quantification of uncertainty is considered from three perspectives: data, model, and structural [41].

Data uncertainty relates to the values of parameters and measured magnitudes. Stochastic or aleatoric uncertainty is quantified by means of statistical methods using a probability distribution. When a probability distribution is unknown and only a nominal value is provided, then it is the case of unobserved uncertainty.

Model uncertainty derives from the input data and from the way it was created. Models can be deductive, empirical and hybrid. Empirical models can be derived from observed or measured data and or based on the experience of an expert. In any case, an evidence should be available to support the creation of the model. In empirical models it is necessary to identify the relationship between the different parameters, which may lead to three different situations: (1) the relationship is suspected, verified and validated, (2) the relationship is only suspected, (3) the relationship is unknown or ignored. It is a typical situation where epistemic and aleatoric uncertainties need to be quantified and integrated.

Structural uncertainty is originated during the product development phase. It derives from the typical multiplicity of functional decompositions and design solutions. The generation of design solutions from requirements involves executing tasks related to requirements formalization, functional decomposition, selection of physical principles, and structural decomposition. In general, the process is iterative and results in a combinatorial explosion of the solution space that cannot be fully identified. The part of the solution space that remains unknown constitutes ignorance. The structural uncertainty comprises epistemic, ambiguity and interaction uncertainties.

5 Conclusions

A bidirectional semantic harmonization of the uncertainty representation in the standards used to transfer data, both from the cyber domain to the physical domain and vice versa, could facilitate the attainment of the digital twin or the CPPS. It demands to consider also the data to accomplish the measurement traceability. This approach requires a deeper analysis of the modeling capabilities and the existing data transfer mechanisms provided by: STEP, QIF, MTConnect, and UPC-UA.

In addition to the already ongoing work on automated integration of different semantic definitions by combining deductive and inductive reasoning, the SFB 805 data fusion context provides a platform, where part of the standard harmonization approach could be tested.

Acknowledgment. The authors would like to thank the Deutsche Forschungsgemeinschaft (DFG, German Research Foundation) for funding this research – Project number 57157498 – SFB 805.

References

1. Tuegel, E.J., Ingraffea, A.R., Eason, T.G., Spottswood, S.M.: Reengineering aircraft structural life prediction using a digital twin. Int. J. Aerosp. Eng. **2011**, 1–14 (2011)
2. Lee, E.A.: Cyber-physical systems-are computing foundations adequate. In: Position Paper for NSF Workshop on Cyber-Physical Systems: Research Motivation, Techniques and Roadmap, vol. 2, pp. 1–9 (2006)
3. Ríos, J., Morate, F.M., Oliva, M., Hernández, J.C.: Framework to support the aircraft digital counterpart concept with an industrial design view. Int. J. Agile Syst. Manag. **9**(3), 212–231 (2016)
4. Kiritsis, D.: Closed-loop PLM for intelligent products in the era of the Internet of things. Comput. Aided Des. **43**(5), 479–501 (2011)
5. Monostori, L., et al.: Cyber-physical systems in manufacturing. CIRP Ann. **65**(2), 621–641 (2016)
6. Singh, V., Willcox, K.E.: Engineering design with digital thread. AIAA J. **56**(11), 4515–4528 (2018)
7. Tekkaya, A.E., et al.: Metal forming beyond shaping: predicting and setting product properties. CIRP Ann. **64**(2), 629–653 (2015)
8. Slotnick, J., et al.: CFD vision 2030 study: a path to revolutionary computational aerosciences. NASA/CR–2014-218178 (2014)
9. Lindau, B., Rosenqvist, M., Lindkvist, L., Söderberg, R.: Challenges moving from physical into virtual verification of sheet metal assemblies. In: ASME 2015 International Mechanical Engineering Congress and Exposition, Volume 2B: Advanced Manufacturing ASME (2015)
10. Uhlemann, T.H.J., Lehmann, C., Steinhilper, R.: The digital twin: realizing the cyber-physical production system for industry 4.0. Procedia CIRP **61**, 335–340 (2017)
11. Tao, F., Zhang, M.: Digital twin shop-floor: a new shop-floor paradigm towards smart manufacturing. IEEE Access **5**, 20418–20427 (2017)
12. Schleich, B., Anwer, N., Mathieu, L., Wartzack, S.: Shaping the digital twin for design and production engineering. CIRP Ann. **66**(1), 141–144 (2017)
13. Anderl, R., Maurer, M., Rollmann, T., Sprenger, A.: Representation, presentation and visualization of uncertainty. In: Chakrabarti, A. (ed.) CIRP Design 2012, pp. 257–266. Springer, London (2013). https://doi.org/10.1007/978-1-4471-4507-3_25
14. Coleman, H.W., Steele, W.G.: Experimentation, Validation, and Uncertainty Analysis for Engineers. Wiley, New Jersey (2018)
15. Bertino, E.: Data trustworthiness—approaches and research challenges. In: Garcia-Alfaro, J., et al. (eds.) DPM/QASA/SETOP 2014. LNCS, vol. 8872, pp. 17–25. Springer, Cham (2015). https://doi.org/10.1007/978-3-319-17016-9_2
16. Morse, E., et al.: Tolerancing: managing uncertainty from conceptual design to final product. CIRP Ann. **67**(2), 695–717 (2018)
17. Zhang, M., Selic, B., Ali, S., Yue, T., Okariz, O., Norgren, R.: Understanding uncertainty in cyber-physical systems: a conceptual model. In: Wąsowski, A., Lönn, H. (eds.) ECMFA 2016. LNCS, vol. 9764, pp. 247–264. Springer, Cham (2016). https://doi.org/10.1007/978-3-319-42061-5_16
18. Briggs, W.: Uncertainty: The Soul of Modeling, Probability & Statistics. Springer, Heidelberg (2016). https://doi.org/10.1007/978-3-319-39756-6
19. Roy, C.J., Oberkampf, W.L.: A comprehensive framework for verification, validation, and uncertainty quantification in scientific computing. Comput. Methods Appl. Mech. Eng. **200**(25–28), 2131–2144 (2011)
20. BIPM, IEC, IFCC, ILAC, IUPAC, IUPAP, ISO, OIML: Evaluation of measurement data-guide for the expression of uncertainty in measurement. JCGM 100: 2008

21. Thunnissen, D.P.: Uncertainty classification for the design and development of complex systems. In: Proceedings of the 3rd Annual Predictive Methods Conference, pp.1–16. Newport Beach, CA (2003)
22. Hu, Z., Mahadevan, S.: Uncertainty quantification in prediction of material properties during additive manufacturing. Scr. Mater. **135**, 135–140 (2017)
23. Rattadilok, P., McCall, J., Burbridge, T., Soppera, A., Eardley, P.: A data fusion framework for large-scale measurement platforms. In: Proceedings of the IEEE International Conference on Big Data, pp. 2150–2158 (2015)
24. Michaloski, J., Hedberg, T., Huang, H., Kramer, T., Michaloski, J.: End-to-end quality information framework (QIF) technology survey. US Department of Commerce, NIST (2016)
25. Abollado, J.R., Shehab, E., Rose, M., Schröter, T.: Uncertainty assessment for measurement processes in the aerospace manufacturing industry. Procedia CIRP **60**, 326–331 (2017)
26. Heimrich, F., Anderl, R.: Approach for the visualization of geometric uncertainty of assemblies in CAD-systems. J. Comput. **11**(3), 247–257 (2016)
27. ISO 10303-41:2018: Industrial automation systems and integration - Product data representation and exchange - Part 41: IGR: Fundamentals of product description and support
28. ISO 10303-45:2018: Industrial automation systems and integration - Product data representation and exchange - Part 45: IGR: Material and other engineering properties
29. ISO 10303-235:2009: Industrial automation systems and integration - Product data representation and exchange - Part 235: AP: Eng. properties for product design and verification
30. ISO 10303:242:2014: Industrial automation systems and integration - Product data representation and exchange - Part 242: AP: Managed model-based 3D engineering
31. Trainer, A., Hedberg, T., Feeney, A.B., Fischer, K., Rosche, P.: Gaps analysis of integrating product design, manufacturing, and quality data in the supply chain using model-based definition. In: Proceedings of the 11th International Manufacturing Science and Engineering Conference, ASME (2016)
32. ISO 10303:219:2007: Industrial automation systems and integration - Product data representation and exchange - Part 219: AP: Dimensional inspection information exchange
33. QIF Ver. 3.0, ANSI/DMSC QIF 3.0 2018. Digital Metrology Standards Consortium, Inc.
34. Bernstein, W.Z., Hedberg Jr., T.D., Helu, M., Feeney, A.B.: Contextualising manufacturing data for lifecycle decision-making. Int. J. Prod. Lifecycle Mgmt. **10**(4), 326–347 (2018)
35. Costa, P.C., Laskey, K.B., Blasch, E., Jousselme, A.L.: Towards unbiased evaluation of uncertainty reasoning: the URREF ontology. In: Proceedings of the IEEE 15th International Conference on Information Fusion (FUSION), pp. 2301–2308 (2012)
36. Cholvy, L.: Plausibility of information reported by successive sources. In: Deshpande, A., Hunter, A. (eds.) SUM 2010. LNCS (LNAI), vol. 6379, pp. 126–136. Springer, Heidelberg (2010). https://doi.org/10.1007/978-3-642-15951-0_16
37. IEC TR 62541-1:2016: OPC unified architecture - Part 1: Overview and concepts
38. MTConnect Institute: MTConnect OPC UA Companion Specification, Rel. 2.0.5 (2018)
39. MTConnect Institute: MTConnect Part 2 Devices Information Model, V 1.4 (2018)
40. Weber, M., Staudter, G., Anderl, R.: Comparison of inductive inference mechanisms and their suitability for an information model for the visualization of uncertainty. Appl. Mech. Mater. **885**, 147–155 (2018)
41. Engelhardt, R.A., et al.: A model to categorise uncertainty in load-carrying systems. In: Proceedings of the 1st International Conference on Modelling and Management Engineering Processes, vol. 19, pp. 53–64 (2010)

Review of CAD Visualization Standards in PLM

Stephane Nzetchou[1](✉), Alexandre Durupt[1], Sebastien Remy[2], and Benoit Eynard[1]

[1] Université de Technologie de Compiègne, Laboratoire Roberval FRE CNRS 2012, Rue du Dr Schweitzer, 60203 Compiègne Cedex, France
{stephane.nzetchou,alexandre.durupt,benoit.eynard}@utc.fr

[2] Université de Technologie de Troyes, Institut Charles Delaunay LASMIS FRE CNRS 2848, 12 rue Marie Curie, 10010 Troyes Cedex, France
sebastien.remy@utt.fr

Abstract. The rise of new technologies has led to a growth in the number of 3D data types. Also 3D data are more voluminous and include a greater number of interrelationships between the data. These data can come from various sources, hence their heterogeneity and complexity. The level of data access is often a function of the user's expertise since the 3D data are complex and registered to different file formats. A 3D data file format is used for storing information about 3D models. Each sector adopts his own 3D file format for different reasons. In this article, we are going to learn about 3D file formats and survey the functionality differences between some popular file formats, able to ease the integration of data, by analyzing on 3D viewing technology, some models made by two different CAD systems.

Keywords: PLM · 3D modelling · File formats · Data exchange · Application interoperability

1 Introduction

The way companies communicate has changed. Companies send most of their information digitally instead than on paper and it is considered as a great step forward in reduced time and money. One of the ways to save money is the business mindset of Product Lifecycle Management (PLM).

Inside the PLM system, the data from which the information is extracted, are heterogeneous by their type (photo, video, text file, CAD file, etc.); the CAD data can be heterogeneous by their formats: legacy formats (CATIA, CREO, NX, etc.), neutral formats (STEP, JT, IGES, STL, etc.), but also from the expertise that created the data or which it is intended for. Thus, the links and the dependences, which appear between heterogeneous CAD data, are becoming more complex during the daily activities of users. When products are developed in 3D for the engineering domain, the data are initially stored in the legacy file format of the used CAD software. If this 3D CAD data is to be made available to people who do not have this software, neutral 3D formats are needed. Some file formats are: 3D PDF from Adobe, X3D, U3d from Web3D consortium, JT and STEP [1]. The proprietary nature of CAD vendor specific data limits the possibility

Published by Springer Nature Switzerland AG 2019
C. Fortin et al. (Eds.): PLM 2019, IFIP AICT 565, pp. 34–43, 2019.
https://doi.org/10.1007/978-3-030-42250-9_4

of open-ended analysis of the 3D data and creates restricted universality of such tools since they work only for the format or API of the particular application [2]. The access to the information becomes a laborious task due to the unstructured data and the lack of information sharing capability. "How can we overcome dependence on legacy formats in order to access geometric and topological information? How can we allow any user to query and retrieve geometric and topological information to a desired granularity?" This raises the need to analyze 3D neutral formats to see their distinctive features view and PMI (product & manufacturing information).

2 Product Lifecycle Management

PLM is made to be composed of digital product definition and delivery. The tasks are based on computer models processed with computer assistance. According to Terzi [3], most of the product data are generated at the beginning of life (BOL). The software owned by a company, particularly 3D CAD systems, have to be able to communicate with each other. This type of tool is developed to help product designers and to provide a traceability support of the evolution of an artefact from the requirements to the product use and even recycling. The digital product definition forms the origin and core of PLM. Product definition has evolved from engineering drawings to computer-aided X (CAx) as mentioned in [4]. Most CAD systems enable exchange of the shape models with CAx (CAE, CAPP, CAM etc.) systems. Tools are being developed to optimize the design subject to conflicting requirements in one pass. This enables designers to transfer physical testing and simulation to digital simulation and prototyping for much of the design.

For PLM to be successful, data formats of digital products must be able to convey design intent, be machine interpretable, and lose as little information as possible in the translation process. From McHenry [5], some problems arise when companies have different file formats and due to format conversions and companies outsourcing have missing, collapsed, inverted faces, models that do not form closed solids such as those with surfaces and edges that do not connect. The major problem at hand is the interoperability between 3D CAD systems. Companies can have an issue even in-house if multiple 3D CAD systems are used.

3 Research Background of Some Interoperable 3D File Format

3.1 Studies of Interoperable Files

The Research Triangle Institute at the National Institute of Standards and Technology has performed a research to determine the differences between STEP and lightweight file formats in 1999. This study analyzed the transfer of models from one CAD package to another through STEP and an outdated standard, IGES [6]. It was very simple and maybe effective for 1999, but the technology, the standard and other variables have improved and changed since then. More recent studies performed on lightweight file formats like lightweight Formats for Product Model Data Exchange and Preservation [7]. However, this study only covers the basics of model fidelity, metadata support, security, features, file size, software support, and it is important since it compares basic differences between many lightweight formats. Academia has performed studies to try and to evaluate the differences between STEP, JT, 3DXML, and U3d. This study was performed to demonstrate all the differences regarding the functionality of part registered inside these formats [8]. ProSTEP iViP Association is an international association that helps drive the development of vendor-neutral file standards and validates the quality of software solutions for interoperability. ProSTEP performs research on the benchmarking of STEP and JT formats. ProSTEP published a comparison in 2010 between 3D Formats in the field of Engineering, in which JT, STEP, and 3D PDF were analyzed using multiple CAD systems and several attributes. The CAD systems used were CATIA V5, CREO, and Siemens NX [9].

It is clear that an in-depth multi-level comparison should be done with the STEP standard and other new coming file formats such as JT, because the design in context is one of the most important processes which could be based on JT and structured information (STEP AP242XML [10] - Fig. 2) coming from various 3D CAD systems. The latter two file formats include the annotations and attributes associated with the edges and faces of the CAD model in order to detail the product geometry and specifications from a manufacturing perspective. Also, non-geometric data such as surface texture specifications, finishing requirements, process notes, material specifications and welding symbols are include [11] (Fig. 1).

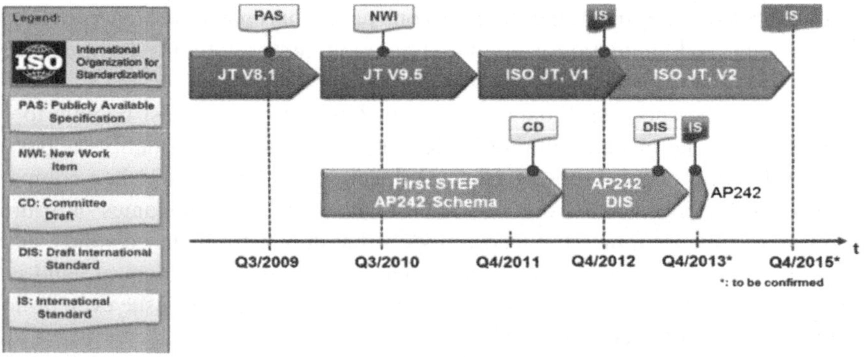

Fig. 1. ISO roadmap for JT and STEP AP242 [1].

3.2 Features of 3D File Formats

Different CAD systems have different ways of representing a CAD model, which is determined by the system's modelling kernel. Some CAD systems use the same modelling kernel as other systems. For example, ACIS by Spatial Technology Corporation and Parasolid by Siemens. Other companies use completely proprietary modelling kernels that are not shared. The modelling kernel determines how the CAD model is mathematically represented, semantically represented, and its internal accuracy of the geometric definitions [12].

The issue of legacy information has brought forward interoperable and neutral (lightweight) file formats into existence. The problems between those formats are mainly perceived when we look at the features (the shape, the appearance and the scene) of the models in each neutral file format and also the PMI.

- The shape of a model is often stored as a set of 3D points or vertices. The surfaces are stored as a series of polygons or faces that are constructed by indexing these vertices. This kind of format is known as the tessellated format. If truly smooth surfaces are required, at any scale, then a convenient option is the use of Non-Uniform Rational B-Spline patches (or NURBS). These parametric surfaces are made up of a relatively small number of weighted control points and a set of parameters known as knots. B-Rep provides explicit representations for the geometrical elements such as vertexes, edges, faces, etc. Designing a shape can be done along the lines of constructive solid geometry (CSG) that uses Boolean operations on simple shape primitives such as cubes, cylinders, spheres, etc.
- The appearance, in its most common form associated with materials, entails applying an image or texture to the surface of the model. A model that does this must store these texture coordinates within the 3D data file. Most 3D file format support texture mapping. There would be three dimensions for three-color components corresponding to color spaces, such as RGB. Many file formats are supported to store material properties. However, an application that loads material properties usually ignores many of these properties when a user is manipulating the object.
- The scene describes the layout of the 3D model in terms of cameras, light sources, and other nearby 3D models. The camera is defined by some parameters as magnification and principal point, location, the direction the camera is facing and an arrow indicating which direction is up.

4 Case Study

Due to the ephemeral nature of CAD file formats and the applications that work with them, the migration of CAD information into lightweight formats could be a solution for preserving, exchanging and recovering information in the future. So, the need to correctly visualize the model, access the geometric and topological information with the geometric definitions and tolerances, entails the analysis and choice of some standard formats; but it also needs to answers the following question: Which format are we going to choose? Which free viewers are available? Have the formats been recognized by some standard organization? What about the data exchange and the visualization?

Based on the formats supported by the community, those used by most of the companies and the CAD packages and third party software available to our use, we selected STEP, JT, 3D PDF, and STL in order to evaluate their discrepancies with respect to some chosen criteria.

The chosen criteria are:

- *File size:* Since we are dealing with the so-called lightweight file format, the data size is an important criteria. This criterion could affect the opening of the model. A smaller file could take less time to manipulate in a PLM system.

- *PMI*: It includes the geometric dimensioning and tolerancing (GD&T), which is used to communicate permissible deviations of the product to manufacturing. It is provided by the CAD system to describe linear and diametral dimensional tolerances, and geometric tolerances of flatness, perpendicularity, position, surface profile, and run-out [13].
- *Documentation*: Is there a structured document able to contain the 3D model and access the PMI?
- *Data exchange*: In a PLM environment, Companies want to share and exchange information. The standardized methods aim to improve the performance of data exchange. The standardized formats can also be used to convert CAD format to layers for 3D printing.
- *Visualization*: The translation from one file format to another can cause some issues. It is important to understand if the tree view's representation is missing, if the parts' names are the same and if the formats support geometric dimensioning and tolerancing.

4.1 Software and Hardware

CATIA from Dassault Systèmes and CREO from PTC were used to perform the test. CrossManager (dkt) software from DATAKIT was used to convert legacy CAD file format to STEP, STL, JT and 3D PDF. CAD Assistant from Open Cascade was used to analyze the completeness of the interoperable file formats and the integrity of all the CAD models. It could not read file formats as STL, 3DPDF at the time of testing. So, the tested file formats were STEP and JT. For visualizing 3D PDF component, we used adobe reader and for visualizing STL component, we used the "window 3D viewer".

4.2 Survey Data Analysis

Figure 2 shows the set of models used. The approach is, by taking one 3D model designed in CATIA and CREO with the same characteristics, same features and converted to STEP, STL, 3D PDF and JT formats through the means of CrossManager, what could be the difference in terms of the chosen criteria? Are the file formats influenced by the translation process or by the legacy CAD systems?

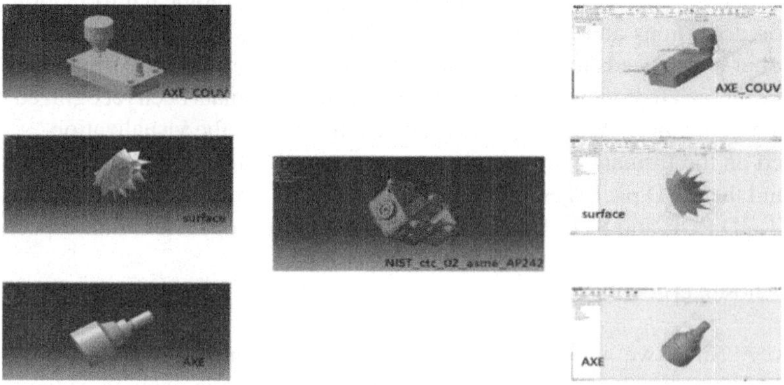

Fig. 2. Set of models used.

NIST_ctc_02_asme1_ap242 is used for observing the discrepancies with respect to the same model translated to other formats.

Figure 3 shows the synopsis of the translation process. AXE_COUV represents an assembly model. Surface is a surface part. The same 3D models are represented in CATIA and CREO in order to be analyzed and to observe the differences.

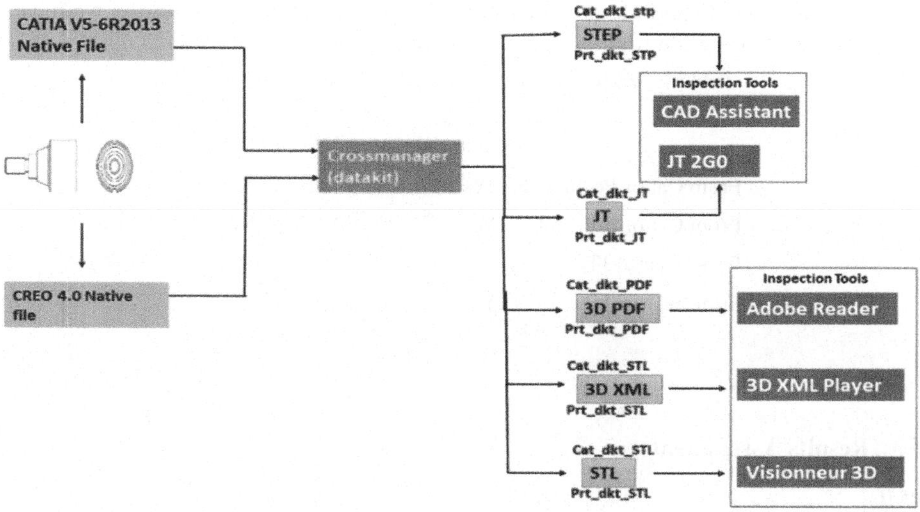

Fig. 3. Direct translation from legacy files format to another through Crossmanager

Cat_dkt_stp and Prt_dkt_stp are the STEP file format got, using directly the translation of the legacy file format through Crossmanager.

Cat_dkt_JT and Prt_dkt_JT are the JT file formats got, using directly the translation of the legacy file format through Crossmanager.

NIST_ctc_02asme1_ ap242_JT is the original file format from NIST translated in JT.

Cat_dkt_PDF and Prt_dkt_PDF are the PDF file formats got, using directly the translation of the legacy file format through Crossmanager.

Cat_dkt_STL and Prt_dkt_STL are the STL file formats got, using directly the translation of the legacy file format through Crossmanager.

The file formats are analyzed and compared. The data analysis is based on the preservation of information. The results are compared to each other in various ways to help determine possible trends. If changes occurred within 3D models after translation processes, then those changes are determined using percent change where applicable. Percent change is determined by the relative change between the attribute of the newly translated 3D model and the original attribute of the 3D model in the legacy CAD.

Regarding the area and the volume, the comparison is just performed using STEP and JT thanks to the information obtained in CAD assistant. Therefore, we compared the area of legacy file format with respect to JT and STEP by doing:

$$\text{Delta\_Area} = (\text{Area of the translated file format} / \text{Area of the legacy file format}) * 100 \quad (1)$$

$$\text{Delta\_Volume} = (\text{volume of the translated file format} / \text{volume of the legacy file format}) * 100 \quad (2)$$

During our analysis, we have observed an increase of the 3D model's areas from CREO during the translation process to other formats, while those from CATIA decrease their areas in comparison to the original ones. The volumes of the STEP files are almost equal to the legacy formats while those from JT are a little bit different. The difference regarding the volume and the area is around 4% on average. Consequently, we have a slight difference between regions and volume of objects in the two files.

Table 1. Translation path material property preservation

	Material name	Colour	Density
From Cat or Prt to STP	Yes	Yes	No
From Cat or Prt to JT	Yes	Yes	No
From STP to JT	Yes	Yes	No
From JT to STP	Yes	Yes	No

4.3 Results Assessment

PMI

STEP AP242 and JT integrate Table 1 and cover many computable representations for several types of 3D model data, including geometric definition and tolerances. The STEP and JT characteristics allow 3D PMI module to represent product information that is machine-readable. The module uses XML and EXPRESS schema languages to define product data model. CAD assistant shows the material converted in STEP and JT. In addition, the color of the part is visible. STL is dedicated to printing format, which has been used to transfer information from CAD software to printing hardware. The STEP and JT files keep the characteristics of precise geometry, tessellated geometry and tolerances as we can see in Fig. 4-a and b.

Additional features of lightweight formats not part of STEP specification and 3D PDF, as advanced material lighting properties, level of detail mechanism, some level of compression or many STEP features not available in the lightweight formats as from features, construction history drafting capabilities. Some possibly features, not available by default need to be extended manually in the GT2Go. Consequently, JT and STEP are suited for this task.

SIZE

Regarding the file size of the different 3D models, the test results were found using the file size of the legacy CAD. STEP and STL are the ones much sized and JT file sizes are the lowest in most cases. By doing some calculations with respect to our samples, JT files are almost 60% lighter than STEP files and, it is the best one in terms of size. The size of the data is determined by the data content instead of the format itself. The fact that JT is less size that another format could make JT file format, the ideal candidate suited in a PDM system because its opening could be faster than the others.

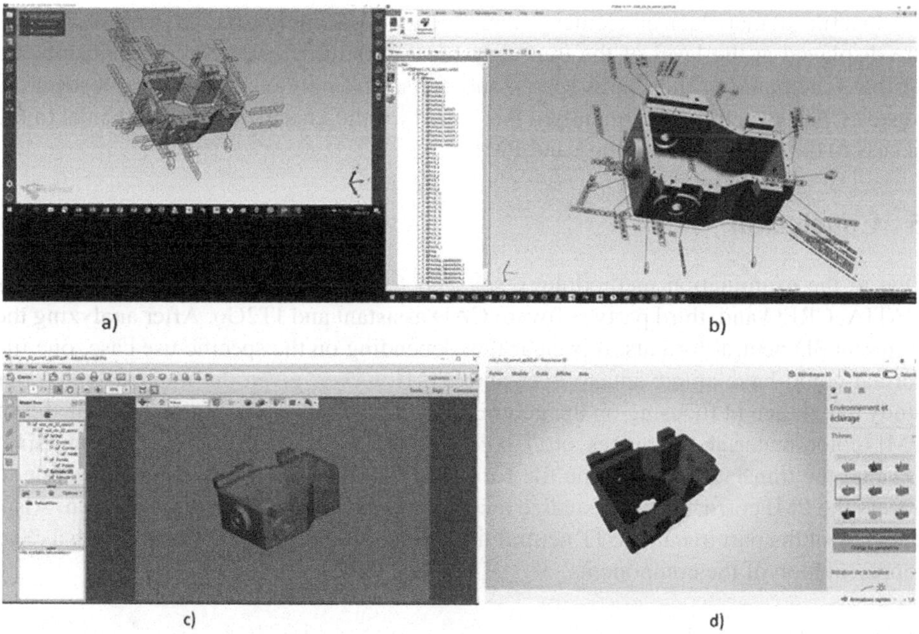

Fig. 4. NIST model in (a) STP; (b) JT; (c) 3D PDF; (d) STL

DOCUMENTATION

Because of its document-oriented structures, 3D PDF is an excellent solution for this purpose and any device that allows adobe reader can read it. STEP and JT can also be suited for this since they have been standardized ISO, so they provide a very good container for 3D models.

With respect to PLM context, 3D PDF is the most suited because it allows 3D information to be represented together with other information. All the data are contained in a single document or file.

DATA EXCHANGE

Because of the numerous applications, STEP seems best suited for that since it matured long time ago. JT is also suited to exchange information, but compared to STEP, it needs to mature. Regarding 3D PDF or STL, because of the lack of exact representation and the lack of some information, they are not suitable.

VISUALIZATION

With the translation of files through Crossmanager, we can obtain either a faceted or a tessellated representation. In addition, the capacities of the available viewers make JT (Fig. 4-b) and 3D PDF (Fig. 4-c) ideal for visualization. In fact, with JT and 3D PDF, we can notice in the tree view, the parts forming the assembly of the legacy file translated, while with STEP, it is not possible.

In terms of metadata, all elements constituent the assembly structure in these formats are displayed at the level of the tree view regardless the viewer. So, the metadata are visible. The name of the shares (parts, sub-parts, assembly etc.) is as described in the legacy CAD system. Consequently, JT is suited for the visualization case thanks to the access to the geometry, topology and PMI.

5 Conclusion

Due to the examination methodology selected for this study, we used CAD systems CATIA, CREO and, third party software CAD assistant and JT2Go. After analyzing the different 3D neutral formats, it is clear that depending on the specific use case, one file format could have an advantage over another. However, given the interest which our study has shown in focusing on the geometric and topologic information and transfer of PMI (color, material, tolerances, etc.), it could be said that the JT file is very promising. Despite the translations from one file format to JT file format, it is always possible to access the PMI correctly and visualize the geometric and topological information. Also, the view of the part tree in the JT neutral file format is done unambiguously, with a clear representation of the components.

References

1. Katzenbach, A., Handschuh, S., Vettermann, S.: JT Format (ISO 14306) and AP 242 (ISO 10303): the step to the next generation collaborative product creation. In: Kovács, G.L., Kochan, D. (eds.) NEW PROLAMAT 2013. IAICT, vol. 411, pp. 41–52. Springer, Heidelberg (2013). https://doi.org/10.1007/978-3-642-41329-2_6
2. Solihin, W., Eastman, C., Lee, Y.: Multiple representation approach to achieve high-performance spatial queries of 3D BIM data using a relational database. Autom. Constr. **81**, 369–388 (2017)
3. Terzi, S., Bouras, A., Dutta, D., Garetti, M., Kiritsis, D.: Product lifecycle management: from its history to its new role. Int. J. Prod. Lifecycle Manage. **4**(4), 360 (2010)
4. Zhu, W., Bricogne, M., Durupt, A., Remy, S., Li, B., Eynard, B.: Implementations of model based definition and product lifecycle management technologies: a case study in chinese aeronautical industry. IFAC-PapersOnLine **49**(12), 485–490 (2016)
5. McHenry, K., Bajcsy, P.: An overview of 3D data content, file formats and viewers. Technical report: National Center for Supercomputing Applications (2008)
6. Tassey, G., Martin, S.A.: Interoperability Cost Analysis of the U.S. Automotive Supply Chain. Final report: Research Triangle Institute Final Report. RTI Project (1999)
7. Ball, A., Ding, L., Patel, M.: Lightweight formats for product model data exchange and preservation. In: PV 2007 Conference Oberpfaffenhofen, Ger. 9–11 October, no. 1, pp. 1–7 (2007)
8. Hartman, N.W., Ed, D., Lim, A.: A comparison of functionality between STEP AP 203 E2, 3DXML, JT, and U3D technologies. In: 3D Collaboration and Interoperability (2008)
9. PROSTEP AG: 3D formats in the field of engineering - a comparison. www.prostep.com
10. Boy, J., Rosché, P., Hirel, G., Haenisch, J.: Recommended practices for AP242 business object model XML assembly structure. CAx-IF Recomm. Pract, pp. 1–184 (2015)
11. Xiao, J., Eynard, B., Anwer, N., Le-Duigou, J., Durupt, A.: Information exchange standards for design, tolerancing and Additive Manufacturing: a research review. Int. J. Interact. Des. Manuf. **12**(2), 495–504 (2018). https://doi.org/10.1007/s12008-017-0401-4

12. Gerbino, S.: Tools for the interoperability among CAD systems. In: Proceedings of ADM-INGEGRAF International Conference on Tools and Methods Evolution in Engineering Design (2003)
13. Lipman, R., Lubell, J.: Conformance checking of PMI representation in CAD model STEP data exchange files. Comput. Aided Des. **66**, 14–23 (2015). https://doi.org/10.1016/j.cad.2015.04.0022012

PLM Maturity and Industry 4.0

PLM Implementation Success Rate in SME. An Empirical Study of Implementation Projects, Preliminary Findings

Bas Koomen[1,2](✉), Marko Hoogeboom[2], and Vera Schellens[3]

[1] University of Twente, Enschede, The Netherlands
s.p.koomen@utwente.com
[2] Cadmes B.V., 's-Hertogenbosch, The Netherlands
bas@cadmes.com
[3] Avans University of Applied Science, Tilburg, The Netherlands

Abstract. Research on the implementation of Product Lifecycle Management (PLM) has been published since the beginning of the 21st century. Some researchers claim that the success rate of PLM implementation projects is below 50%, but the authors have found no evidence of that figure. In this paper's research, a number of PLM implementation cases have been analyzed for their project goals, implementation challenges, and project results. The research data are retrieved from project files and interviews with project managers. The investigated implementation cases are in Small to Medium-sized Enterprises (SME). The results have been structured and compared with findings from the authors' earlier literature research on SME specific implementation challenges and recommended implementation methods. From this comparison, a conclusion is drawn regarding the implementation success rate and a hypothesis for causes of observed failure.

Keywords: PLM · PDM · Implementation · Case studies · SME

1 Introduction

Product Lifecycle Management (PLM) is a business activity or strategy to manage products and product information across the lifecycle, from idea to disposal or recycling [1–5]. It helps to manage the increasing complexity of product structures, organizations, and processes. PLM is supported by PLM software. This software can be authoring software (for example Computer Aided Design; Computed Aided Manufacturing; Finite Element Analysis) or information system software (for example Product Data Management; Project Management).

When PLM emerged at the end of the 20th century, mainly large companies deployed PLM initiatives. Nowadays, Small and Medium-sized Enterprises (SMEs) also have an increasing need for PLM. An SME is a company with less than 250 employees and an annual turnover of less than 50 Million Euros, according to the definition of the European Union. A large part of the industry consists of SME companies. For example in 2014,

Published by Springer Nature Switzerland AG 2019
C. Fortin et al. (Eds.): PLM 2019, IFIP AICT 565, pp. 47–57, 2019.
https://doi.org/10.1007/978-3-030-42250-9_5

98% of companies in the machinery and equipment sector of the European Union were SME, responsible for 41% of the annual turnover [6].

A general problem with PLM implementation is that many projects fail to achieve the project goal. Some authors claims a failure rate of 50%, but no further sources are mentioned [3, 7, 8]. Moreover, industry surveys show that companies struggle to implement PLM successfully [9]. While this is a problem for large companies, it is a considerable risk for SMEs. The relative cost of a PLM implementation is higher for SMEs because the fixed part of the investment is divided over fewer people. Failure has a high relative impact on the financial health of the company [10].

To overcome implementation problems, researchers have proposed ways to model companies in a formal structure of more efficient organization and processes. For example, Bitzer [11] has reviewed and compared a number of implementation guidelines suitable for large companies. These guidelines work with organizations who already have a formal structure where current state assessment can be done successfully. Conversely, SMEs do not have formal processes, but organizations rely heavily on personal interaction. Factors such as trust, fairness, intuition, and empathy play an essential role in SMEs' business processes [12]. This makes an SME a more dynamic and agile enterprise in comparison to larger enterprises. On the other hand, knowledge management is not formalized, and most SME organizations are not able to describe their current or future state without external help, because they lack internal resources with process analysis and design skills.

From earlier research [13] we learned that case studies on the implementation of PLM at SME companies were described from a customer's perspective in most cases. We did not find papers that described cases from the perspective of a software vendor or implementation service provider.

The research question for this paper is: "Does a relation exist between the outcome of a project and the circumstances of the implementation project?" We investigated implementation cases in smaller SME companies, from the implementation service provider's perspective.

2 Theoretical Background

Three elements are used to structure the empirical research for this paper:

1. PLM Challenges for SME.
2. PLM implementation guidelines.
3. PLM goals and benefits.

The first two elements are taken from our previous paper, [13].

2.1 PLM Challenges

Companies face many challenges when they transform their business processes into a more PLM oriented way of working. The PLM challenges for SME, identified in our paper [13], are shown in Fig. 1, Sect. 4.

2.2 PLM Implementation Guidelines

Researchers have proposed various methods to implement PLM in companies. We have investigated a number of these methods during the earlier literature research [13]. We derived a general PLM implementation guideline, visible in Fig. 2, Sect. 4.

2.3 PLM Goals and Benefits

Goals for PLM are diverse. Authors have used various structures to categorize goals for PLM in their books. In Table 1, we have summarized the goal definitions found in PLM literature. We selected academic books that are frequently cited by other papers. These books contain more in-depth elaborations of goals and benefits.

In the survey results, we observed cases where the implementation of the software itself or replacement a current software was the goal of the project. This type of goals does not fit into the categories in Table 3.

Table 1. PLM goal examples

Author	Goal categorization	Examples
Feldhusen and Gebhardt [14]	Product	Make a product configurable, standardize a product family, manage variants
	Process	Shorten time-to-market, establish unambiguous milestones, reduce the number of process steps
	Organization	Shorten communication lines, make organization more flexible, define clear responsibilities
Arnold et al. [10] Stark [3]	Strategic	Higher customer satisfaction, increase market share, improve competitiveness
	Economic/operational	Information transparency, reduce rework, improve quality
Grieves [5]	External drivers	Scale, complexity, cycle times, globalization, and regulation
	Internal drivers	Productivity, innovation, collaboration, and quality
	Boardroom drivers	Income, revenue, and costs
Saaksvuaori and Immonen [15]	Time	Less rework, less search time, and automation
	Quality	Change control, documentation, standardization, and security

(*continued*)

Table 1. (*continued*)

Author	Goal categorization	Examples
	Reduce capital tie-up	Reduce the number of different and special items, reduce component stock, and manage production load with product structure information
Eigner and Stelzer [4]	Time	Reduce effort on development, search, and data exchange
	Quality	Reduce errors and therefore warranty costs
	Reuse	Improve search capability
	Synergy effect	Make product and process information available and hence improve better decision making

In our research we looked for a relation between goals, impact on the company and success rate. Therefore, we organize the project goals into three categories:

1. Strategic goals, related to the future of the company and include aspects as growth, market share, competitiveness, or survival.
2. Operational goals, related to the performance of business processes. Typical aspects are cost, efficiency, quality, time-to-market, and resource capacity.
3. Functional goals, related to technical requirements. Examples are the replacement of software, consolidation of data, and protection of intellectual property. Fundamentally, there might be an underlying goal for these functional requirements, but they are not made explicit. Therefore, this category is added.

3 Methodology

For this research, we surveyed project managers who were involved in PLM-software implementation projects with SME companies on behalf of an implementation service provider. The surveys were conducted in live interviews. During the interviews, we also had access to project management records. In total, we collected information about 9 projects, executed between 2012 and 2019.

3.1 Case Selection

We selected cases based on the following criteria:

- The project must be finished and executed in an SME company.
- The project must contain a strategic element, related to company processes, for example Product Data Management (PDM) or Design Automation.

- The project must impact multiple processes, not just engineering.
- The project manager and documentation must be available.

3.2 Interview Questions

The surveys are structured to use them for comparative analysis. We used multiple-choice (M/C) questions if possible. The questions are listed in Table 2.

Table 2. Interview questions

Topic	Questions	Q. type
1. Company details	1a. Nr. of employees	M/C
	1b. Type of industry	M/C
	1c. Number users involved in implementation	Open
2. Goals	2a. Were goals defined before the project?	Y/N
	2b. What were the goals?	Open
	2c. Who defined the goals?	M/C
	2d. Were new goals defined during the project?	Y/N
	2e. What were the additional goals?	Open
	2f. Who defined the additional goals?	M/C
	2g. Were the goals achieved?	Y/N
3. Challenges	3a. Which PLM challenges were relevant? (list)	M/C
	3b. Additional challenges identified?	Open
	3c. Impact of the challenges on the project?	Open
4. Guidelines	4a. Which guideline steps were relevant in the project?	M/C
5. Change impact	5a. Impact areas (IT/Process/Organization)	M/C
	5b. Was this impact foreseen before the project?	Y/N
6. Project performance	6a. Planned software investment (Euro)	Open
	6b. Realized software investment (Euro)	Open
	6c. Planned hours of service (Hours)	Open
	6c. Realized hours of service (Hours)	Open
	6e. Planned delivery time (Months)	Open
	6f. Realized delivery time (Months)	Open
	6g. Was the project a success?	Y/N

3.3 Definition of Project Success

We can define project success in more ways. On the one hand, we can look at a project quantitatively and measure how the project performed on time, budget and project goal achievement. From a project manager's standpoint, a project may have failed if there is a substantial budget overrun. On the other hand, we can look at the project outcome holistically: did the project leave a better world behind? A PDM project may have failed on its goals, but the company has learned more than it would have otherwise.

In our research, we primarily asked whether the project goals are achieved. We also asked for "planned delivery time and budget" versus "realized delivery time and budget" for comparison. At the end of the survey, we asked the project manager if he regarded the project to be a success as a holistic evaluation.

4 Results

We have investigated 9 cases with 5 different project managers. In Table 3, we have listed the case characteristics. In this section, we summarize the main results.

Table 3. Characteristics of the investigated project cases.

ID	PrjMngr	Industry	Size	Users	Delivered	All goals achieved
P1	M1	Machinery	100–249	25	2014	Yes
P2	M2	Installed equipment	25–49	4	2018	Yes
P3	M1	Machinery	100–249	52	2018	No
P4	M3	High-Tech	100–249	50	2017	Yes
P5	M3	Engineering services	100–249	25	2015	No
P6	M4	Machinery	100–249	65	2015	No
P7	M5	Machinery	50–99	50	2018	No
P8	M5	Machinery	50–99	14	2019	Yes
P9	M5	Machinery	50–99	20	2019	Yes

4.1 Goals

The project managers have named goals for the projects. We have categorized them into the goal types, identified in Sect. 2.3. Functional and operational goals were found in all cases. Only 3 cases contained strategic goals. In 5 cases, the primary goal was to replace an existing PDM system for functional reasons.

In 8 cases, the implementation service provider defined the goals, after an analysis of the customer's situation. In 3 cases, the customer (also) defined goals for the project. Furthermore, only two cases contained goals that are measurable quantitatively. In none of the cases did the customer use a third party for advice.

4.2 PLM Challenges

We asked the project managers for each PLM challenge in Fig. 1 to indicate if it played a role in the implementation project. The number of cases, relevant to each PLM challenge, is shown in Fig. 1. With the color we also indicate the number of related project that failed to achieve all goals.

What stands out in this diagram is that "high cost of implement" is mentioned in only 3 cases, despite being mentioned in literature most frequently. Conversely, the project managers mention "lack of strategic business planning" in 7 cases, with only one reference from literature.

The interviewed project managers added "Lack of leadership commitment" as an additional challenge. Some projects fail to achieve goals or suffer delays, due to the low priority of the implementation project from high management.

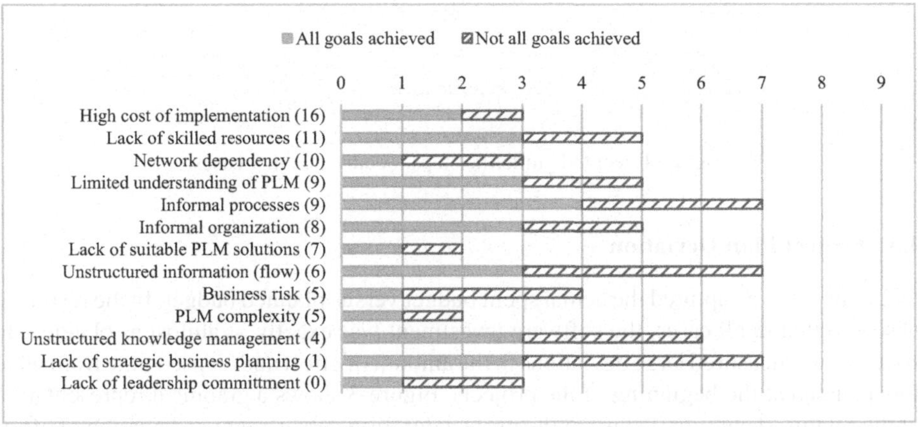

Fig. 1. Relevant SME specific PLM challenges, occurrence in 9 cases. The number between parentheses indicates the number of papers that identified the challenge [13].

4.3 Implementation Guidelines

We also asked the project managers, which of the steps in the general implementation guidelines were taken. The result is shown in Fig. 2. We noticed that towards the end of the implementation process, most steps were deemed as relevant in the projects. Most steps in the design and implement phases have a high relevance score. Conversely, we observe the absence of preparation and part of the analysis phase for the majority of projects. A maturity level assessment is absent in all cases, and a PLM strategy is created in only one case.

4.4 Project Success Rate

We assessed the project outcome in two questions. Firstly, if all goals were achieved. Secondly, if the project manager subjectively qualified the project as successful. In 5 cases, all goals were achieved. In 7 cases, the project manager qualified the project as successful.

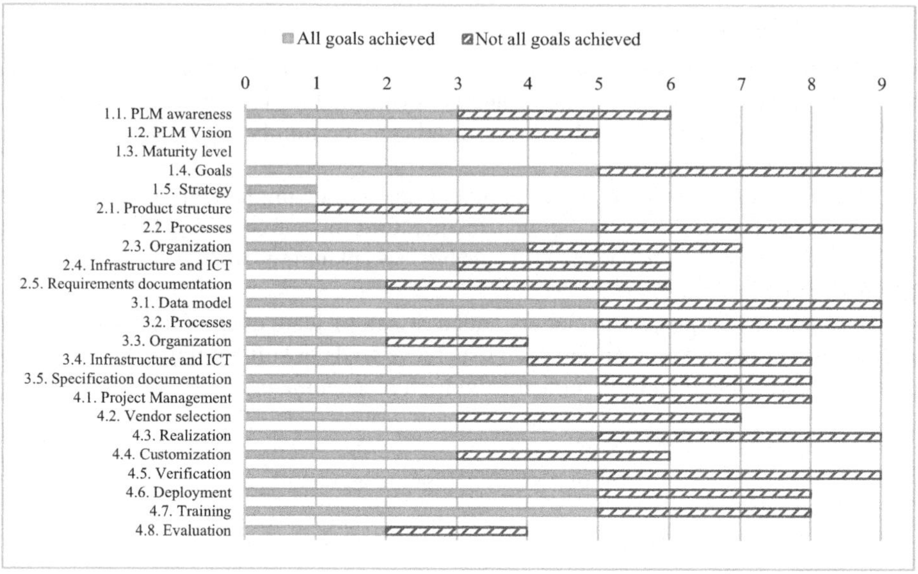

Fig. 2. Executed guideline steps, occurrence in 9 cases.

4.5 Project Plan Deviation

In the survey, we captured the actual spent budget versus planned budget. In the result we observed that in all cases, the software investment was exactly or almost as planned. In contrast, we measured large deviations in the amount of effort and elapsed time from what was planned at the beginning of the projects. Figure 3 shows a graphical representation of the relative deviation (delay) of the project duration versus relative deviation of effort (hours of external implementation services). The size of the circles indicate the amount of planned hours for the projects, ranging from 112 h (P2) to 800 h (P3). The projects that did not achieve all goals are marked with dashed red circles, the project with all goals achieved are marked in solid green circles.

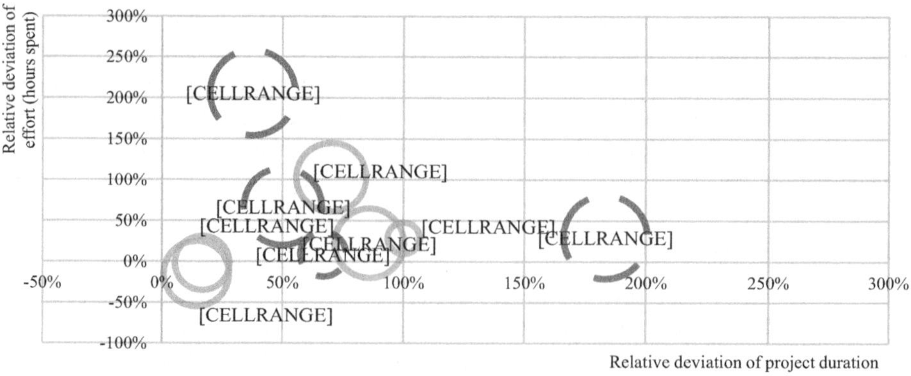

Fig. 3. Relative deviation of project effort and duration. (Color figure online)

4.6 Limitations in this Research

With the interpretation of the results, we considered the limitations of our research method. We have in-depth access to a specific implementation service provider and all project managers it employs. Within the scope of the research it is not feasible to have the same data access with a competitive provider. This, by default, causes a bias for the specific method of implementation. We try to compensate this by interviewing as many different project managers as possible, and use cases over a longer period of time.

The answers of the project managers are subjective. Moreover, the information about the companies' goals is indirect, because it is the interpretation of the project managers. To overcome this limitation, we used cases of which project records were available. We compared the answers with the project records, together with the project managers, and clarified answers where needed. Furthermore, we used dichotomous answers (Yes or No) to avoid introduction of unjustified detail.

5 Conclusions

5.1 Measurement of Goals

The operational goals, as defined in the project plans of the surveyed cases, are not measurable in most cases. They contain qualifications like "more efficient", "fewer errors", and "higher quality". The surveyed project managers are aware of this weakness, but claim that the SME companies do not have enough metrics to measure improvement.

5.2 Project Failure

Did we find evidence for the claim that 50% of the projects do not achieve their goal?

Based on the sample size and the limitations, we do not claim to have statistical proof. Nevertheless, the preliminary results are not contradicting the claim either.

More important is that our research shows the importance of goal setting. If project failure is measured as the achievement of all goals, then the definition of goals is just as important as the project outcome. More attention should be paid to help customers to define better goals, related to business strategy, and measurable.

The alternative measure for project success, where we asked the project managers for their personal opinion, shows success with 7 out of 9 cases. A conclusion could be that we need to look for another definition of project success, for example to look at the deviation from project plan and budget.

5.3 Requirements, Goals and Specifications

An important conclusion is that the companies in the cases focus on specifications. Apparently, there is a need in the company that leads to a decision to invest in PDM. Only in 3 out of 9 cases, the customer has stated the goals for the project themselves, but in 8 cases, the implementation service provider has helped to define goals.

Moreover, the majority of goals is functional. The companies expressed their desire to improve IT-related functionality. In 5 cases, an important goal was to replace another PDM system. Additionally, we observe that companies initially desire to automate their current process with little changes.

We suspect the lacking activity during the preparation phase to be the reason for this desire. This relates to the absence of maturity level assessment, which makes companies unaware of their position relative to what could be achieved, and a lacking strategy for most cases. Furthermore, the awareness and vision steps are mostly limited to explaining how PDM benefits the organization and processes of the company, according to the explanation of the surveyed project managers. The result of this lacking preparation is that the primary goal for most projects in this survey is to deliver a particular functionality, regardless of the business value of this functionality.

5.4 Causality

With 9 cases surveyed, we are not able to perform a quantitative statistical analysis for causality or correlation. At first glance, the distribution of relevant PLM challenges and implementation show little apparent relation in a qualitative sense. An exception is customization of off-the-shelf functionality. Customizations cause more substantial budget overruns. 6 of 9 cases contain customization. In these cases, the number of service hours was 69% over budget. The cases without customization were only 12% over budget. The two common reasons for customization are integration to ERP and migration of legacy data.

5.5 Future Research

We also looked for individual reasons for project failure and budget deviations. Most projects used more time and resources than planned, although the project managers have built in buffers in their project plans. The project managers believed that the initial plan was realistic before the start, so unforeseen events and circumstances must play a role in the deviations. Based on the preliminary findings of this empirical research, we plan to two direction to improve PLM implementation projects for SME.

Improve the decision making process for technical and functional solutions during the implementation: From the survey results, we conclude that project often contain loopbacks. Technical and functional problems occur in the later stages of the project, causing unplanned rework. Ward and Sobek describe this phenomenon as "wishful thinking" [16]. In their proposed method, alternative solutions for subsystems are evaluated in parallel until enough knowledge is gathered to make a confident decision. This method could also apply to PLM implementations.

Improve the goals definition for implementation projects: The project goals are important for the project. Goals are strongly related to benefits. A better understanding, and definition of benefits could improve the overall project performance.

References

1. CIMdata.: About PLM (2017). https://www.cimdata.com/en/resources/about-plm. Accessed 26 Jan 2019
2. Gartner: IT Glossary - Product Lifecycle Management (2018). https://www.gartner.com/it-glossary/product-lifecycle-management-plm. Accessed 26 Jan 2019
3. Stark, J.: Product Lifecycle Management, pp. 1–29. Springer, Cham (2015). https://doi.org/10.1007/978-3-319-17440-2_1
4. Eigner, M., Stelzer, R.: Product Lifecycle Management; Ein Leitfaden für Product Development und Life Cycle Management (Product Lifecycle Management; A Guideline for Product Development and Lifecycle Management). Springer, Heidelberg (2009). https://doi.org/10.1007/b93672
5. Grieves, M.: Product Lifecycle Management: Driving the Next Generation of Lean Thinking. McGraw-Hilll Education, New York (2005)
6. European_Commission: Key Figures on European Business — with a Special Feature on SMEs. Publications Office of the European Union, Luxembourg (2011)
7. Wognum, P.M., Kerssens-van Drongelen, I.C.: Process and impact of product data management implementation. Int. J. Prod. Dev. **2**(1), 5–23 (2005)
8. Siddiqui, Q.A., Burns, N.D., Backhouse, C.J.: Implementing product data management the first time. Int. J. Comput. Integr. Manuf. **17**(6), 520–533 (2004)
9. Woo, T.: Data Management in PLM: Optimize your Business Performance. AberdeenGroup, Boston (2016)
10. Arnold, V., et al.: Product Lifecycle Management Beherrschen: Ein Anwenderhandbuch für den Mittelstand (Mastering Product Lifecycle Management: A User Manual for Medium Enterprises). Springer, Heidelberg (2011). https://doi.org/10.1007/978-3-642-21813-2
11. Bitzer, M.A.: Entwicklung einer Methode zur prozessorientierten Planung und Optimierung von Product-lifecycle-Management-Lösungen: am Beispiel der Automobilindustrie (Development of a Method for Process Oriented Planning and Optimization of PLM Solutions : by Example of the Automotive Industry). TU Kaiserslautern, Kaiserslautern, p. 165 (2008)
12. Dhillon, G., Stahl, B.C., Baskerville, R.: Creativity and intelligence in small and medium sized enterprises: the role of information systems. In: Dhillon, G., Stahl, B.C., Baskerville, R. (eds.) IS&O 2009. IAICT, vol. 301, pp. 1–9. Springer, Heidelberg (2009). https://doi.org/10.1007/978-3-642-02388-0_1
13. Koomen, B.: PLM in SME, what are we missing? An alternative view on PLM implementation for SME. In: Chiabert, P., Bouras, A., Noël, F., Ríos, J. (eds.) PLM 2018. IAICT, vol. 540, pp. 681–691. Springer, Cham (2018). https://doi.org/10.1007/978-3-030-01614-2_62
14. Feldhusen, J., Gebhardt, B.: Product Lifecycle Management für die Praxis: Ein Leitfaden zur Modularen Einführung Umsetzung und Anwendung (Product Lifecycle Management for Practitioners: A Guideline for Modular Implementation and Application.). Springer, Heidelberg (2008). https://doi.org/10.1007/978-3-540-34009-6
15. Saaksvuori, A., Immonen, A.: Product Lifecycle Management. Springer, Heidelberg (2008). https://doi.org/10.1007/978-3-540-78172-1
16. Ward, A.C., Sobek II, D.K.: Lean Product and Process Development, 2nd edn. The Lean Enterprise Institute, Cambridge (2014)

Towards a Novel Comparison Framework of Digital Maturity Assessment Models

B. Cognet[1(✉)], J.-P. Pernot[1,2], L. Rivest[1], C. Danjou[3], T. Wuest[4], H. Kärkkäinen[5], and M. Lafleur[6]

[1] Département de Génie des Systèmes, École de Technologie Supérieure, Montréal, Canada
bruno.cognet.1@ens.etsmtl.ca, louis.rivest@etsmtl.ca
[2] Arts et Métiers, LISPEN EA 7515, HeSam, Aix-en-Provence, France
jean-philippe.pernot@ensam.eu
[3] Département de Mathématiques et Génie Industriel, École Polytechnique, Montréal, Canada
christophe.danjou@polymtl.ca
[4] Departement of Industrial and Management Systems Engineering, West Virginia University, Morgantown, USA
thwuest@mail.wvu.edu
[5] Laboratory of Industrial and Information Management, Tampere University of Technology, Tampere, Finland
hannu.karkkainen@tuni.fi
[6] AéroMontréal, Montréal, Canada
martin.lafleur@aeromontreal.ca

Abstract. The fourth industrial revolution is forcing companies to rethink their status quo – creating a need to assess their digital maturity as a basis for improvements. As a result, there is a variety of maturity models available in the literature. This paper introduces a novel comparison framework designed to compare different digital maturity assessment models. Our framework has several steps: reverse engineering of criteria from existing models, criteria matching analysis, as well as computation of the coverage and spread ratios. These two metrics characterize respectively the similarity of two maturity models, and the spread between them. We tested the proposed approach with two well-known maturity self-assessment approaches, namely the IMPULS and PwC methods. From our analysis, we were able to derive several insights that will help to develop a new maturity model specifically dedicated to support SMEs in the aerospace industry and manufacturing sector.

Keywords: Industry 4.0 · Smart manufacturing · Digitalization · Maturity models · Comparison framework · Coverage and spread ratios · Assessment

1 Introduction

Manufacturing companies feel increasing pressure to adopt the Industry 4.0 paradigm to evolve and remain competitive on the market worldwide [1]. To support Small and Medium-sized Enterprises (SMEs) with their digital transformation, seen as a pillar of

Published by Springer Nature Switzerland AG 2019
C. Fortin et al. (Eds.): PLM 2019, IFIP AICT 565, pp. 58–71, 2019.
https://doi.org/10.1007/978-3-030-42250-9_6

the Industry 4.0, several maturity models have been developed that allow evaluating the level of digital maturity of individual companies [2, 3]. The results of these evaluations are then used to design and setup a digital transformation plan. However, there are many different approaches to evaluate the digital maturity of a company available today and it can be difficult to identify the most appropriate option as they do not always focus on the same set of criteria.

The current literature shows that each maturity model has its specific benefits and challenges. Therefore, a suitable solution may lie in the partial exploitation of some of their core advantages. It has to be noted that most digital maturity models do indeed share some common characteristics and goals. For example, most of them are using a set of questions to evaluate certain criteria which are grouped in dimensions, and possibly sub-dimensions. However, when they have been formalized, criteria are not always evaluated in the same way. This is in some cases performed by asking the user to self-assess the levels or by using some black box mechanisms to compute a mark from multiple user-specified answers. Regarding the questionnaires, some approaches are referring to self-assessment whereas some others are focused on guided-assessment.

This paper is a first attempt towards understanding and identifying the possible key criteria to be used when developing a digital maturity model. Actually, when evaluating the digital maturity of a company, the so-called criteria can be considered as Key Performance Indicators (KPIs) used to monitor the status of the company; this is the terminology that is used in this document. To reach this objective, a novel digital maturity assessment models comparison framework is introduced. At its core the framework works at the level of the KPIs, rather than at the level of the questions/answers or dimensions/subdimensions. We consider that focusing on the KPIs is a good tradeoff as it reduces the subjectivity and increases the objectivity when comparing different models. In most cases, questions are directly linked to certain KPIs, making them explicit for the target end-users, i.e., the ones who will answer the questionnaire. The alternative, i.e. working at the level of the dimensions is considered too high-level, which in turn would make the comparison significantly more difficult.

The framework counts several steps: reverse engineering of KPIs from existing models, KPIs matching analysis, as well as computation of the so-called coverage and spread ratios. These two metrics characterize respectively the similarity between two maturity models overlap and the spread between them. The proposed approach has been tested with two well-known maturity self-assessment approaches, namely the IMPULS [4] and PwC ones [5]. The contribution is threefold: (i) a three-step comparison framework, (ii) new quantitative metrics to characterize the coverage and spread of two maturity models, and (iii) a summary of the key findings obtained when analyzing two maturity self-assessment approaches.

This paper is organized as follows. The proposed comparison framework is introduced in Sect. 2 together with the newly defined coverage and spread ratios. Section 3 discusses the results obtained following the proposed framework to compare two maturity self-assessment approaches (IMPULS, PwC). The last section concludes this paper and discusses the next steps.

2 Overall Comparison Framework

2.1 Background Literature

In general, the term "maturity" refers to a "state of being complete, perfect, or ready" [6]. Maturity models provide a structured approach to initiate and accompany short-term operational projects, as well as medium- term tactical changes and long-term strategic change [7]. Currently, there is a variety of available digital maturity models to support companies in their digitalization activities. Their common goal is to assess the digital maturity level of an organization, providing an indication of required activities to increase the maturity level. Existing studies have reviewed most common maturity models, in general [8], as well as digital maturity models in particular [9]. According to the above and other related studies, common features for maturity models include their incorporation of maturity dimensions (usually 3–7 dimensions descriptive of the maturity to be assessed by means of maturity models, which are often divided into more detailed maturity criteria, descriptive of the related maturity dimensions), maturity levels and related maturity descriptions. Maturity dimensions, in general, can be divided into three broader categories: maturity of people/culture (e.g. skills, capabilities), processes/structures, and objects/technology (such as ICT tools). A recent literature review-based conceptual paper related to the broad concept of digital maturity [9] demonstrates that in current digital maturity studies, digital maturity has included aspects of digital maturity that can be divided into eight capability dimensions (i.e. broad digitalization related maturity categories): strategy, leadership, business and operating model, people, culture, governance, and technology. Prior research [10], in addition, presumes that the development of a specific set of the above types of digital capabilities leads to higher digital maturity, and moreover, the higher degree of digital maturity can lead to superior corporate performance. However, such maturity models can be very different in terms of their structure, scope and industry focus [11]. Furthermore, currently, in current research, there has been conceptual unclarity and fragmented views about the concept and the measurement frameworks for digital maturity [9], while Rossman's recent study has been among the first to bring a more unified conceptualizations for the topic. It is also our attempt to clarify the topic and the concept of digital maturity, through our framework designed to compare different digital maturity assessment models.

2.2 Comparison Framework

To ease the description of the proposed comparison framework of digital maturity models, and to start generalizing the approach, a proper formalization is introduced. A maturity model $\mathcal{M}^{\kappa}$ (with $\kappa \in$ {IMPULS, PwC, ADN, ...}) contains N_c^{κ} criteria denoted $\mathcal{C}_i^{\kappa}$ (with $i \in [1..\mathrm{N}_c^{\kappa}]$) and grouped in N_d^{κ} dimensions denoted $\mathcal{D}_j^{\kappa}$ (with $j \in [1 \ldots \mathrm{N}_d^{\kappa}]$). The jth dimension $\mathcal{D}_j^{\kappa}$ contains $\mathrm{N}_{c,j}^{\kappa}$ criteria, which start at index s_j^{κ} and end at index e_j^{κ}. The criteria can be gathered together in the list $\mathcal{L}_j^{\kappa} = \left\{\mathcal{C}_i^{\kappa}, i \in \left[\mathrm{s}_j^{\kappa} \ldots \mathrm{e}_j^{\kappa}\right]\right\}$. The following rules apply:

$$\mathrm{N}_c^{\kappa} = \sum_{j=1}^{\mathrm{N}_d^{\kappa}} \mathrm{N}_{c,j}^{\kappa} \tag{1}$$

$$s_1^{\kappa} = 1, \text{ and } \forall j \in [2 \ldots N_d^{\kappa}], s_j^{\kappa} = s_{j-1}^{\kappa} + N_{c,j-1}^{\kappa} \tag{2}$$

$$\forall j \in [1 \ldots N_d^{\kappa}], e_j^{\kappa} = \sum_{k=1}^{j} N_{c,k}^{\kappa} \tag{3}$$

In the rest of the document, the so-called criterion C_i^{κ} (with $i \in [1 \ldots N_c^{\kappa}]$) of a maturity model $\mathcal{M}^{\kappa}$ will be considered as a KPI. The overall comparison framework of two maturity models $\mathcal{M}^{\kappa_1}$ and $\mathcal{M}^{\kappa_2}$ is composed of three main steps which are further detailed in the next subsections (Fig. 1):

- Reverse Engineering (RE in Fig. 1): when the maturity models to be compared do not explicitly formulate the adopted KPIs, they are reverse engineered before starting the matching phase;
- Matching of the KPIs: the KPIs of the two compared maturity models are cross-checked and systematically compared in pairs so as to evaluate the levels of matching, which are captured in the so-called matching matrix;
- Coverage and spread ratios computation: quantitative metrics are computed from the matching matrix to further analyze the coverage and spread ratios of the KPIs against the models and their dimensions.

Fig. 1. Overall comparison framework of two maturity models $\mathcal{M}^{\kappa_1}$ and $\mathcal{M}^{\kappa_2}$

2.3 Reverse Engineering of KPIs

This step is only required for maturity models that do not provide enough information on the KPIs used to assess the maturity levels. More specifically, this happens in cases when the considered maturity models are not sufficiently detailed and internal assessment mechanisms resemble black boxes.

This step aims at extracting and formalizing the list of KPIs that best characterize the criteria adopted by a given method to assess the maturity levels by using all available resources describing the considered maturity model (e.g., online self-assessment tools, questionnaires, benchmarking reports, articles). The output list of KPIs results from consensual exchanges meetings involving a pool of experts in the domain. During the evaluation, experts are requested to focus on the explicitly available information rather than on more implicit data whose interpretation could be questionable. Following this process, the risk of bias due to reinterpretations is reduced, but cannot be fully disregarded.

2.4 Matching of KPIs

The comparison of the maturity models is performed at the level of the KPIs. To characterize the 'KPIs match', three levels are introduced: *Strong match*, *Partial match*, and *No match*. Two KPIs are considered a Strong match if the experts involved in this process identify sufficient similarity between the two. Conversely, if the two KPIs do not share any similar features, a No match is considered. In between, when the KPIs share some similar features, but also have dissimilarities, a Partial match is assigned. Such a three-level matching analysis presents a good tradeoff between an under-segmentation, which would lead to a coarse analysis, and an over-segmentation that would complexify the comparison making it cumbersome and not practical.

Therefore, the matching function CCmat, evaluating the matching level of two KPIs $\mathcal{C}_{i_1}^{\kappa 1}$ and $\mathcal{C}_{i_2}^{\kappa 2}$ of two maturity models $\mathcal{M}^{\kappa_1}$ and $\mathcal{M}^{\kappa_2}$, is defined as follows:

$$\text{CCmat}\left(\mathcal{C}_{i_1}^{\kappa 1}, \mathcal{C}_{i_2}^{\kappa 2}\right) = \begin{cases} \text{Strong if } \mathcal{C}_{i_1}^{\kappa 1} \text{ and } \mathcal{C}_{i_2}^{\kappa 2} \text{ strongly match} \\ \text{Partial if } \mathcal{C}_{i_1}^{\kappa 1} \text{ and } \mathcal{C}_{i_2}^{\kappa 2} \text{ partially match} \\ \text{No otherwise} \end{cases} \quad (4)$$

This matching function is then called to fill in the matching matrix MMmat containing the $(\text{N}_{\mathcal{C}}^{\kappa 1} \times \text{N}_{\mathcal{C}}^{\kappa 2})$ values returned by the function when composed with the KPIs of $\mathcal{M}^{\kappa_1}$ and $\mathcal{M}^{\kappa_2}$. Clearly, due to the adopted procedure, one can notice that the matching function CCmat is symmetric, i.e., it returns the same matching level no matter the order of the arguments.

Here again, the assessment of the matching levels results from consensual exchanges meetings involving a pool of experts. In a first individual phase, experts are asked to suggest a matching level for each KPIs couple. Then, during a consensus phase, experts exchange on their classifications and further discuss the matching levels for which there are discrepancies. When the discussion fails to reach an adequate consensus, a simple majority rule can be used, while weighting differently the choice of the most experimented experts. Ultimately, an additional expert is to be considered to solve the residual conflicts. Thus, the matching process final results strongly rely on the exchanges between the involved experts, and consequently on their knowledge and experience in the domain. Clearly, similar results could hardly be obtained using simple text-based similarity analysis tools. This is further discussed in the conclusion.

2.5 Coverage and Spread Ratios Computation

The computation of the coverage and spread ratios is directly based on the counting of the number of KPIs assigned to the three previously introduced matching levels, as well as on the overall number of KPIs and dimensions of the compared maturity models. Thus, two counting functions are first introduced to track the number of matched KPIs of a certain level within the overall matching matrix. The first function, CMLcount, counts the number of times a KPI of the first maturity model is matched to the KPIs of the second maturity model with a given matching level. The second function, CDLcount, performs a similar search but on a particular dimension of the second maturity model.

They are expressed as:

$$\mathrm{CMLcount}\left(\mathcal{C}_{i_1}^{\kappa 1}, \mathcal{M}^{\kappa 2}, \mathrm{level}\right) = \sum\nolimits_{i_2=1}^{\mathrm{N}_c^{\kappa 2}} \left[\mathrm{CCmat}\left(\mathcal{C}_{i_1}^{\kappa 1}, \mathcal{C}_{i_2}^{\kappa 2}\right) == \mathrm{level}\right] \tag{5}$$

$$\mathrm{CDLcount}\left(\mathcal{C}_{i_1}^{\kappa 1}, \mathcal{D}_{j_2}^{\kappa 2}, \mathrm{level}\right) = \sum\nolimits_{i_2=\mathrm{s}_{j_2}^{\kappa 2}}^{\mathrm{e}_{j_2}^{\kappa 2}} \left[\mathrm{CCmat}\left(\mathcal{C}_{i_1}^{\kappa 1}, \mathcal{C}_{i_2}^{\kappa 2}\right) == \mathrm{level}\right] \tag{6}$$

where "level" corresponds to one of the previously introduced levels, i.e. Strong match, Partial match or No match. The equality test (==) returns 1 in case the two compared levels are the same, and 0 otherwise. Capital letters used in the name of the functions help understanding the type of processed data, i.e. C for criteria, M for model, L for level, D for dimension, S for strong, P for partial and N for no. This naming strategy is adopted for each newly introduced function.

Based on those definitions, the two following functions can be defined so as to consider both Partial and Strong matching levels at the same time:

$$\begin{aligned}\mathrm{CMcount}\left(\mathcal{C}_{i_1}^{\kappa 1}, \mathcal{M}^{\kappa 2}\right) = &\ \mathrm{CMLcount}\left(\mathcal{C}_{i_1}^{\kappa 1}, \mathcal{M}^{\kappa 2}, \mathrm{Strong}\right)\\ &+ \mathrm{CMLcount}\left(\mathcal{C}_{i_1}^{\kappa 1}, \mathcal{M}^{\kappa 2}, \mathrm{Partial}\right)\end{aligned} \tag{7}$$

$$\begin{aligned}\mathrm{CDcount}\left(\mathcal{C}_{i_1}^{\kappa 1}, \mathcal{D}_{j_2}^{\kappa 2}\right) = &\ \mathrm{CDLcount}\left(\mathcal{C}_{i_1}^{\kappa 1}, \mathcal{D}_{j_2}^{\kappa 2}, \mathrm{Strong}\right)\\ &+ \mathrm{CDLcount}\left(\mathcal{C}_{i_1}^{\kappa 1}, \mathcal{D}_{j_2}^{\kappa 2}, \mathrm{Partial}\right)\end{aligned} \tag{8}$$

Coverage Ratios. These percentages characterize how much two maturity models overlap. The four ratios are computed while evaluating the number of strongly, partially, strongly-and-partially, and not matched KPIs of a maturity model $\mathcal{M}^{\kappa 1}$ when compared to the KPIs of another maturity model $\mathcal{M}^{\kappa 2}$. Thus, the four following functions make use of the previously introduced counting functions:

$$\mathrm{SMMcover}\left(\mathcal{M}^{\kappa 1}, \mathcal{M}^{\kappa 2}\right) = \frac{1}{\mathrm{N}_c^{\kappa 1}} \times \sum\nolimits_{i_1=1}^{\mathrm{N}_c^{\kappa 1}} \left[\mathrm{CMLcount}\left(\mathcal{C}_{i_1}^{\kappa 1}, \mathcal{M}^{\kappa 2}, \mathrm{Strong}\right) \geq 1\right] \tag{9}$$

$$\begin{aligned}\mathrm{PMMcover}\left(\mathcal{M}^{\kappa 1}, \mathcal{M}^{\kappa 2}\right) = \frac{1}{\mathrm{N}_c^{\kappa 1}} \times \sum\nolimits_{i_1=1}^{\mathrm{N}_c^{\kappa 1}} \Big[&\left(\mathrm{CMLcount}\left(\mathcal{C}_{i_1}^{\kappa 1}, \mathcal{M}^{\kappa 2}, \mathrm{Partial}\right) \geq 1\right)\\ &\mathrm{AND}\ \left(\mathrm{CMLcount}\left(\mathcal{C}_{i_1}^{\kappa 1}, \mathcal{M}^{\kappa 2}, \mathrm{Strong}\right) == 0\right)\Big]\end{aligned} \tag{10}$$

$$\mathrm{SPMMcover}\left(\mathcal{M}^{\kappa 1}, \mathcal{M}^{\kappa 2}\right) = \mathrm{SMMcover}\left(\mathcal{M}^{\kappa 1}, \mathcal{M}^{\kappa 2}\right) + \mathrm{PMMcover}\left(\mathcal{M}^{\kappa 1}, \mathcal{M}^{\kappa 2}\right) \tag{11}$$

$$\mathrm{NMMcover}\left(\mathcal{M}^{\kappa 1}, \mathcal{M}^{\kappa 2}\right) = 1 - \mathrm{SPMMcover}\left(\mathcal{M}^{\kappa 1}, \mathcal{M}^{\kappa 2}\right) \tag{12}$$

where the inequality (≥) and AND tests return 1 if true and 0 otherwise. From Eq. (10), one can see that a KPI of $\mathcal{M}^{\kappa 1}$ is considered as partially covering the KPIs of $\mathcal{M}^{\kappa 2}$, if it matches to at least one KPI of $\mathcal{M}^{\kappa 2}$ at a Partial level, and if there is however no Strong match. Indeed, a Strong match absorbs a Partial match. Of course, the above functions are no more symmetric and are to be evaluated in both directions, i.e. coverage of $\mathcal{M}^{\kappa 1}$ when compared to $\mathcal{M}^{\kappa 2}$, and from $\mathcal{M}^{\kappa 2}$ to $\mathcal{M}^{\kappa 1}$.

Spread Ratios. These percentages characterize how much a KPI of a maturity model spreads over another maturity model, i.e. how much a KPI is interlaced inside a given maturity model. Thus, the spread ratios are KPI-dependent and are to be evaluated for each KPI of each maturity model. Two spread ratios can be distinguished. The first radio (SPCMspread) evaluates the number of matched KPIs between a given KPI and all the KPIs of a maturity model, when compared to the overall number of KPIs of that maturity model. The second ratio (SPCDspread) evaluates the number of dimensions of a maturity model to which a KPI is matched, when compared to the overall number of dimensions of that maturity model. Here, Strong and Partial matching levels are considered all together using both CMcount and CDcount counting functions:

$$\text{SPCMspread}\left(\mathcal{C}_{i1}^{\mathcal{K}1}, \mathcal{M}^{\mathcal{K}2}\right) = \frac{1}{\text{N}_c^{\mathcal{K}2}} \times \text{CMcount}\left(\mathcal{C}_{i1}^{\mathcal{K}1}, \mathcal{M}^{\mathcal{K}2}\right) \tag{13}$$

$$\text{SPCDspread}\left(\mathcal{C}_{i1}^{\mathcal{K}1}, \mathcal{M}^{\mathcal{K}2}\right) = \frac{1}{\text{N}_d^{\mathcal{K}2}} \times \sum_{j2=1}^{\text{N}_d^{\mathcal{K}2}} \left[\text{CDcount}\left(\mathcal{C}_{i1}^{\mathcal{K}1}, \mathcal{D}_{j2}^{\mathcal{K}2}\right) \geq 1\right] \tag{14}$$

where it is assumed that the test of inequality returns 1 if true and 0 otherwise. The names of the functions follow the previously introduced naming strategy which makes use of capital letters to specify the type of data manipulated. For instance, SPCMspread refers to the computation of the spread ratio of a criterion (C) over the KPIs of a maturity model (M), when considering both strong and partial (SP) matching.

3 Results and Discussion

Even though there is a wide variety of different maturity and assessment models available in literature, the proposed comparison framework has been tested and validated with two first maturity models: IMPULS and PwC. Those two maturity models have been selected because they both are digital maturity self-assessment tools easily available online, and the number of questions and the number of dimensions are quite similar and reasonably low for a first testing phase of our novel comparison framework. Of course, the proposed approach is to be tested and validated with other available maturity models and this is further discussed in the conclusion.

3.1 IMPULS and PwC Maturity Models

Considering the formalization introduced in Sect. 2, the two maturity models can be quantitatively characterized by the values gathered together in Table 1.

From this table, one can clearly see that the two maturity models have the same number of dimensions, whose description has been reported in Table 2. Clearly, this is a particular case as there is no obvious reason to have $\text{N}_d^{\text{IMPULS}} = \text{N}_d^{\text{PwC}}$. It is also clear from this initial analysis that each dimension is not evaluated with the same number of KPIs. For instance, the first dimension of IMPULS includes four KPIs whereas its fourth dimension has only two KPIs. This might be a good indicator to stress implicitly how important the dimensions are in the overall maturity assessment, independently of additional weights that could also be more explicitly used.

Table 1. Numerical characteristics of the compared maturity models

κ	κ_1 = IMPULS	κ_2 = PwC
N_d^κ	6	6
N_c^κ	19	33
$\{N_{c,j}^\kappa, j \in [1 \ldots N_d^\kappa]\}$	{4, 4, 4, 2, 3, 2}	{6, 6, 5, 6, 6, 4}

Table 2. Dimensions of the compared maturity models

j_1	Dimension $\mathcal{D}_{j_1}^{\text{IMPULS}}$	j_2	Dimension $\mathcal{D}_{j_2}^{\text{PwC}}$
1	Strategy & organization	1	Business models, product & service portfolio
2	Smart factory	2	Market & customer access
3	Smart operations	3	Value chains & processes
4	Smart products	4	IT architecture
5	Data-driven services	5	Compliance, legal, risk, security & tax
6	Employees	6	Organization & culture

Table 3. KPIs from IMPULS maturity model

i_1	KPI $\mathcal{C}_{i_1}^{\text{IMPULS}}$		
1	Implementation status of I4.0 strategy	11	IT security
2	Operationalization and review of I4.0 strategy through a system of indicators	12	Autonomous processes
3	Investment activity relating to I4.0	13	Add-on functionalities
4	Use of technology and innovation management	14	Data collection and use
5	Digital modeling through the collection, storage and processing of data	15	Availability of data-driven services
6	Functionalities of the equipment infrastructure	16	Share of revenues derived from data-driven services
7	Data usage	17	Share of data used
8	IT system	18	Skill levels
9	Information sharing	19	Effort of the company to acquire new skills
10	Cloud usage		

Table 4. KPIs reverse engineered from PwC maturity model

i_2	Reverse engineered KPI $C_{i_2}^{\mathrm{PwC}}$		
1	Contribution of digital features, products and services to the overall value creation of the organization's portfolio	18	Degree of consideration of the digitalization and I4.0 requirements in IT architecture
2	Degree of digitalization of the organization's products and/or services	19	Level of use of a Manufacturing Execution System (MES) or similar to control the manufacturing process
3	Products customization possibilities by the customers	20	Level of maturity of the IT and data architecture to gather, aggregate and interpret real-time manufacturing, product and client data
4	Degree of digitalization of the products life cycle phases	21	Importance of new technologies (social media, mobility, analytics and cloud computing) to enable business operations
5	Importance of data usage and analysis for the organization's business model	22	Ability of the IT organization to fulfill business requirements in the requested time, quality and cost
6	Intensity of the collaboration with external partners and clients for the development of products and services	23	Level of IT integration with customers and partners
7	Level of integrated sales channels used to sell the organization's products	24	Degree of sophistication of the digital compliance policy
8	Level of integration of communication channels for customer interactions	25	Levels of the organization's IP protection and of the external IP consideration
9	Degree of digital enablement of the organization's sales forces	26	Level of consideration of the digital product portfolio and production factory in the risk management
10	Degree of dynamic customization of the prices based on customer's willingness to pay	27	Level of management of the digital components of the organization's value chain with respect to tax related topics
11	Degree of customer data analysis to increase customer insight	28	Level of consideration of the production in the organization's IT security concept
12	Level of collaboration with partners regarding customers access approach	29	Level of consideration the service partners or customers into the organization's compliance and risk management
13	Degree of vertical value chain digitalization from product development to production	30	Capability to create value from data so as to optimize operations and foster new business models
14	Capability to monitor production and to dynamically respond to changes in demand	31	Level of the organization's capabilities and resources related to I4.0
15	Degree of integration of the end-to-end IT enabled planning and steering process over the entire value chain	32	Level of involvement, support and expertise of the organization's managers with regards to I4.0

(continued)

Table 4. (*continued*)

i_2	Reverse engineered KPI $C_{i_2}^{\mathrm{PwC}}$		
16	Degree of digitalization of the production equipment up to a virtual representation of the factory	33	Level of collaboration of the organization with external partners (e.g. academia, industry, suppliers, customers) on I4.0 topics
17	Degree of horizontal value chain digitalization from customer order to service		

The first part of the proposed framework aims at reverse engineering the KPIs of the maturity models to be compared. Actually, for IMPULS, it has been decided to keep the available and already formalized criteria, even though they are sometimes quite generic without considering the underlying dimensions and corresponding questions (Table 3). Thus, only the KPIs of PwC have been reverse engineered through a consensus workshop involving four experts (Table 4). Starting from the available online self-assessment tool of PwC, each question and possible answers have been carefully analyzed and discussed to come out with a consensual formalization of the KPIs. This step is not straightforward and required several in-depth discussions to achieve a consensus. The main difficulty was to avoid over-interpretation of the online questionnaire and to remain as objective and factual as possible.

3.2 Matching Matrix MMmat

Following the proposed comparison framework, the matching matrix MMmat then had to be filled out while evaluating the matching levels between the KPIs of the two maturity models. This step involved six experts who took part in a two-step evaluation process as discussed in Sect. 2. Here again, during the consensus phase, particular attention has to be paid in order to avoid over-interpretation of what the KPIs are supposed to assess. The individual assessment phase revealed several conflicts due to multiple possible interpretations of the IMPULS's KPIs. Clearly, those original KPIs (Table 3) are not sufficiently detailed and are very much linked to the underlying dimensions and questions. As a consequence, to proceed with those issues, the experts decided to come back to the dimensions and questions in order to better integrate the context in which the KPIs are supposed to be assessed. This has clearly shown the requirement for developing self-understandable KPIs which would directly embed the context within their formulation.

The matching matrix resulting from the consensual phase is shown in Table 5. Green colors correspond to Strong matches between two KPIs, and yellow colors to Partial matches, whereas no color indicates No match. For instance, one can observe that five KPIs from each maturity model had a strong match. We can also observe, for instance, that KPI 4 from IMPULS partly matches with four KPIs from PwC.

Table 5. Matching matrix MMmat of the considered maturity models (IMPULS, PwC) wherein Green cells correspond to Strong matches, and yellow cells to Partial matches.

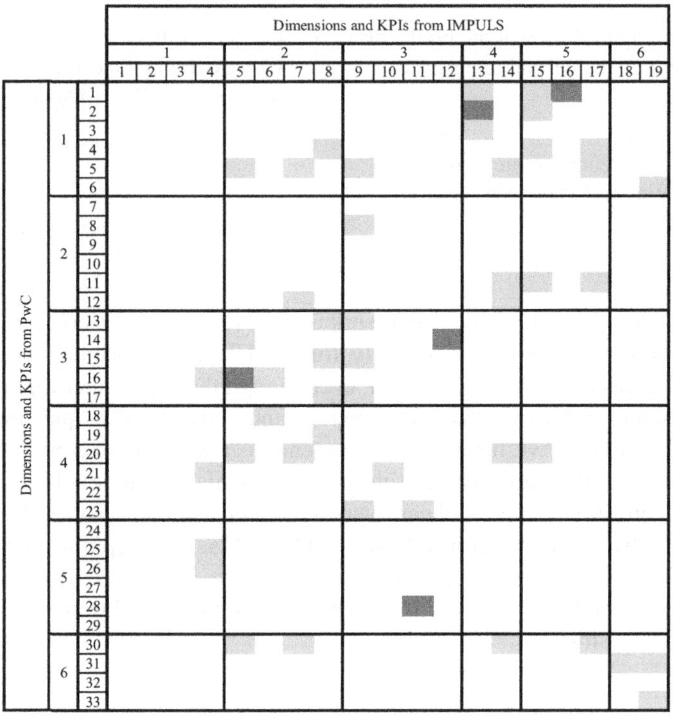

3.3 Coverage and Spread Ratios

The coverage ratios can be computed using the formula introduced in Sect. 2. They are expressed as percentages. They evaluate in both directions and through their KPIs how much $\mathcal{M}^{\text{IMPULS}}$ covers $\mathcal{M}^{\text{PwC}}$, and reversely how much $\mathcal{M}^{\text{PwC}}$ covers $\mathcal{M}^{\text{IMPULS}}$. Table 6 gathers together the results obtained using Eqs. (9) to (12), which consider four levels: No, Partial, Strong and Strong-and-Partial overall coverages.

Table 6. Coverage ratios computed from MMmat in both directions

Direction	No	Partial	Strong	Overall
Coverage from $\mathcal{M}^{\text{IMPULS}}$ to $\mathcal{M}^{\text{PwC}}$ (%)	16	58	26	84
Coverage from $\mathcal{M}^{\text{PwC}}$ to $\mathcal{M}^{\text{IMPULS}}$ (%)	24	61	15	76

Overall, when considering the strongly and partially matching KPIs, the coverage is quite high in both directions (84% and 76%). Here, it is important to stress that a very high coverage ratio could be reached even though the coverage matrix has very few colors and a lot of white cells. For instance, the matching matrix of IMPULS compared to itself would be a square matrix with only green cells on its diagonal and having 100% of KPIs strongly matched.

Furthermore, strongly matching KPIs can be clearly distinguished from the others (five KPIs for IMPULS and five for PwC). Indeed, they match so strongly that a common formulation could be thought and the shortlist of newly formulated KPIs could be considered as a common kernel of the two maturity assessment models. This is an important finding for the development of our own maturity model in the next stage. Similarly, the KPIs which do not match at all can be considered specific to a particular maturity model and no common formulation is suggested.

Furthermore, the spread ratios of each KPI can then be evaluated using the Eqs. (13) and (14). The results of those evaluations are gathered together in Tables 7 and 8, depending on whether the spread ratios are considered from IMPULS to PwC, or reversely from PwC to IMPULS.

Table 7. Spread ratios of IMPULS's KPIs when compared to the overall list of KPIs and dimensions of PwC. Results are sorted according to the overall spread ratios.

Rank	**1**	**2**	**3**	**4**	**5**	**6**	**7**	**8**	**9**	**10**	**11**	**12**	**13**	**14**	**15**	**16**	**17**	**18**	**19**
KPI	1	2	3	10	12	16	18	6	11	13	19	7	4	17	8	15	5	14	9
Overall (%)	0	0	0	3	3	3	3	6	6	9	9	12	12	12	15	15	15	15	18
Dimension (%)	0	0	0	17	17	17	17	33	33	17	33	67	50	50	38	50	67	67	67

Table 8. Spread ratios of PwC's KPIs when compared to the overall list of KPIs and dimensions of IMPULS. Results are sorted according to the overall spread ratios.

Rank	**1**	**2**	**3**	**4**	**5**	**6**	**7**	**8**	**9**	**10**	**11**	**12**	**13**	**14**	**15**	**16**	**17**
KPI	7	9	10	22	24	27	29	32	3	6	8	18	19	25	26	28	33
Overall (%)	0	0	0	0	0	0	0	0	5	5	5	5	5	5	5	5	5
Dimension (%)	0	0	0	0	0	0	0	0	17	17	17	17	17	17	17	17	17

Rank	**18**	**19**	**20**	**21**	**22**	**23**	**24**	**25**	**26**	**27**	**28**	**29**	**30**	**31**	**32**	**33**
KPI	23	31	2	12	13	14	15	17	21	1	4	11	16	20	30	5
Overall (%)	11	11	11	11	11	11	11	11	11	16	16	16	16	21	21	26
Dimension (%)	17	17	33	33	33	33	33	33	33	33	33	33	33	50	50	67

Both lists are sorted according to the overall spread ratios. Vertical lines split the tables to group the KPIs which have the same overall spread ratios, and consequently the same number of matched KPIs. For instance, Table 7 shows that KPI 9 of IMPULS has the greatest overall spread ratio (rank $=$ 19) since it spreads on six out of 33 KPIs of PwC (6/33 $\approx$ 18%). It also has the greatest spread ratio over the dimensions since it spreads on 4 out of 6 dimensions of PwC (4/6 $\approx$ 67%). One can also see that several KPIs do not spread at all (values of 0% in Tables 7 and 8), which reveals the specific KPIs of each maturity model. Spreading over too many KPIs or dimension can be confusing. As already highlighted, this can be due to the fact that some KPIs of IMPULS are certainly too generic and can therefore be matched to several of the PwC model's KPIs. From those values, one can see that some strongly matched KPIs spread on a single KPI and on a single dimension (e.g. KPIs 12 and 16 of IMPULS over the KPIs and dimensions of PwC). Again, this configuration is suitable to circumvent the action level of the considered KPIs. Furthermore, the analysis reveals that the two maturity models are not organized in the same way for some reasons not yet been fully identified.

As introduced in Sect. 2, the spread ratios somehow characterize how much a given KPI is interlaced with the KPIs and dimensions of another maturity model. Such an understanding can be very beneficial to split existing KPIs in lower-level KPIs that would evaluate more circumscribed criteria. Furthermore, this can also be interesting to define new KPIs and assign new dimensions so as to limit the spread over several KPIs and dimensions. Those improvements can certainly help to better rationalize the evaluation, and consequently limit the duplications and misunderstandings when performing a digital maturity self-assessment.

4 Conclusion and Future Works

Digital maturity models help identifying the maturity level of SMEs with respect to specific KPIs and dimensions, and consequently they provide important inputs to better design and setup the digital transformation plans. Today, many countries and consulting firms have been engaged in the development of their own model, and it is therefore required to understand the positioning of each model with respect to the others. This paper has introduced a framework to compare two digital maturity models within the Industry 4.0 paradigm. The new comparison framework consists of three successive steps: (1) reverse engineering of the KPIs when not explicitly available; (2) matching of the KPIs to identify the Strong matches, Partial matches, and No matches; and (3) computation of the coverage and spread ratios to further characterize the overlap and interlace of the two maturity models assessed. The proposed framework has been tested and validated with two maturity models, namely from IMPULS and PwC.

Our results show that the proposed approach is capable to successfully capture the similarities and differences between the KPIs of two maturity models. The reverse engineering and matching steps could have hardly been performed with some automatic text-based or corpus-based similarity evaluation tools. Thus, the pool of experts has played a key role. Of course, the work now needs to be extended and tested with additional maturity models. For instance, this will certainly help defining a strong, common kernel of KPIs, i.e., those identified as strongly matching across the board. This will be very helpful to specify a new maturity model, together with its KPIs and dimensions.

Through the analysis, some limitations clearly appeared. First, mitigation measures had to be set-up to avoid over-interpreting the KPIs. In this sense, experts were asked to focus on explicit and tangible information rather than on implicit ones whose interpretation can be discussed endlessly. Second, KPIs should be as much self-explanatory as possible in order to avoid going back to the dimensions or questions to clearly understand the context of use. Finally, to avoid working on too much interlaced KPIs, criteria should be decomposed in low-level KPIs.

References

1. Taisch, M.; et al.: World manufacturing forum 2018 report. World Manufacturing Forum (2018)
2. Scremin, L., Armellini, F., Brun, A., Solar-Pelletier, L., Beaudry, C.: Towards a framework to assess the maturity for Industry 4.0 adoption in manufacturing companies. In: Brunet-Thornton, R., Martínez, F. (eds.) Analyzing the Impacts of Industry 4.0 in Modern Business Environments, Chapter 12, pp. 224–254. IGI-Global (2018)
3. Mittal, S., Khan, M., Romero, D., Wuest, T.: A critical review of smart manufacturing & industry 4.0 maturity models: implications for small and medium-sized enterprises (SMEs). J. Manuf. Syst. **49**, 194–214 (2018)
4. Lichtblau, K., et al.: IMPULS - Industrie 4.0-readiness. VDMA (2015)
5. Geissbauer, R., Vedso, J., Schrauf, S.: Industry 4.0: building the digital enterprise. 2016 global industry 4.0 survey (2016)
6. Simpson, J.A., Weiner, E.S.C.: The Oxford English Dictionary. Oxford University Press, Oxford (1989)
7. Felch, V., Asdecker, B., Sucky, E.: Maturity models in the age of industry 4.0 – do the available models correspond to the needs of business practice? In: Proceedings of the 52nd Hawaii International Conference on System Sciences (2019)
8. Wendler, R.: The maturity of maturity model research: a systematic mapping study. Inf. Softw. Technol. **54**(12), 1317–1339 (2012)
9. Rossman, A.: Digital maturity: conceptualization and measurement model. In: Proceedings of Thirty Ninth International Conference on Information Systems (2018)
10. Westerman, G., Bonnet, D., McAfee, A.: Leading Digital: Turning Technology into Business Transformation. Harvard Business Review Press, Brighton (2014)
11. Schwer, K., Hitz, C., Wyss, R., Wirz, D., Minonne, C.: Digital maturity variables and their impact on the enterprise architecture layers. Prob. Perspect. Manage. **16**(4), 141–154 (2018)

Evaluating the Smart Readiness and Maturity of Manufacturing Companies Along the Product Development Process

Claudio Sassanelli(✉), Monica Rossi, and Sergio Terzi

Department of Management, Economics and Industrial Engineering, Politecnico di Milano, Via R. Lambruschini 4/b, 20156 Milan, Italy
{claudio.sassanelli,monica.rossi,sergio.terzi}@polimi.it

Abstract. Nowadays, manufacturing industries are compelled to go down the river of Industry 4.0 to either become or remain competitive on the market: in this context digital technologies represent the most important means for manufacturers to drive their transformation. However, investing in this kind of technologies could be not enough to go through this transformation in an effective way: manufacturers need to realize which is their actual digital status and at the same time to evaluate how they support their product development process. In addition, it has not to be neglected the importance of how the process of product development is organized and managed throughout the several functions involved. So far, different methods and maturity models have been proposed in literature to help practitioners to evaluate the readiness and maturity of either their smart level or their design and engineering process. Nevertheless, a suitable combination of these tools still needs to be implemented to fully and systematically measure and gauge a company under a PLM and digital perspective: to do this, a case study has been conducted.

Keywords: Industry 4.0 · Assessment method · Readiness model · Maturity model · Process waste · PLM · Case study · DREAMY · CLIMB · MyWaste

1 Introduction

The advent of digital technologies is strongly affecting manufacturers' behaviour, always more pushed to enhance their manufacturing systems. Gathered under the umbrella of Industry 4.0 [1], they can contribute to address a threefold scope: (i) Digitization and integration of vertical and horizontal value chains, (ii) Digitization of product and service offerings, (iii) Digital business models and customer access.

In particular, these technologies have been grouped in 11 different types (among which IoT platforms, 3D printing, smart sensors, augmented reality), leading to a huge amount of practical applications for manufacturers. However, investing in this kind of technologies could often not be enough to improve competitiveness on the market and to move effectively towards the Industry 4.0 transformation. Manufacturers need to realize first of all which is their actual digital level: a model, DREAMY (Digital REadiness

Published by Springer Nature Switzerland AG 2019
C. Fortin et al. (Eds.): PLM 2019, IFIP AICT 565, pp. 72–81, 2019.
https://doi.org/10.1007/978-3-030-42250-9_7

Assessment MaturitY model) [2–4], already exists. It is able to assess a manufacturing company's readiness level to trigger its digital transitioning process and also to identify a manufacturing company's strengths, weaknesses and opportunities, creating a roadmap for investments in digitization and transitioning to smart manufacturing.

Moreover, manufacturers need to understand and to evaluate how these new digital technologies are used to support their product development process along the entire company. Indeed, in order to deliver successful solutions in the market, companies can choose among various best practices to apply in their development process. CLIMB (Chaos-Low-Intermediate-Mature-Best practice) model [5] measures maturity in product development activities: it aims at concretely supporting the identification and selection of the most suitable best practices to be implemented in the product development process. Indeed, the final aim to obtain a faster and more effective process could be achieved applying lean techniques in product development. In this context, MyWaste and MyTime [6, 7] are formalized and structured methods to identify wastes and to lead designers to improve and streamline the process.

Therefore, as shown above, so far different methods and maturity models have been proposed in literature to help practitioners to evaluate the readiness and maturity of either their smart manufacturing level or their design and engineering process and to analyse the existing wastes along the development process. Nevertheless, a suitable and systematic combination of these tools still needs to be implemented to fully measure and gauge a company in a complete way: to do this, a case study has been conducted. Indeed, this paper aims at analyzing the AS IS situation of the order development process of a selected company, Company A, with particular attention to the digitization level of the areas involved. The main result of this study is represented by a systematized integration of the models and methods so far proposed in literature and presented in Sect. 2: DREAMY and CLIMB models and MyWaste and MyTime methods. Section 3 reports a detailed description of the adopted methodology used to combine these different approaches: formerly the used criteria in the case study approach are reported, then an introduction of the assessed company is also given. Section 4 explains the results of the study, also presenting the analysis of the specific company, and Sect. 5 is dedicated to their discussion. Finally, Sect. 6 concludes the paper, triangulating results with theory and providing further researches and limitations.

2 Research Context

With the aim of being able to perform a complete evaluation and assessment of the actual status of a company, before introducing the models and methods adopted in the case study, it is necessary to clarify the research context they refer. Models as DREAMY and CLIMB were selected since capable to perform an assessment based on a comparison with consolidated best practices codified according an advancement/maturity degree. While, analysis methods as MyWaste and MyTime, have been chosen to gather data regarding the AS-IS company situation according to a referring format. In order to detect the touching points among them, it is necessary to provide a definition of heterogeneous concepts, on one side readiness and maturity and on the other value and waste related to Lean Thinking and continuous improvement:

1. 'smart manufacturing readiness' is the capability of a manufacturing company to deploy smart manufacturing concepts;
2. 'smart manufacturing maturity' concerns how well a manufacturing company has employed smart manufacturing concepts or its smart manufacturing capability;
3. Lean Thinking is based on the idea to give the customer what he wants, when he wants it and at the right amount he desires. It means companies must create value, intended as everything the customer is willing to pay for, and banish waste, which literature classifies in 8 macro-classes (Overproduction, Inventory, Waiting, Motion, Transportation, Defects, Processing, Unused employees creativity) [8–10]. The entire process is based on and guided by the continuous improvement concept [11].

In the following sub-sections, the single approaches, based on these concepts and used in this study, are shown.

2.1 DREAMY

DREAMY is an assessment model based on the idea that, to be able to invest in digital technologies, companies should know their *status quo*. The model evaluates a manufacturing company's digital readiness and maturity along four dimensions: Process, Monitoring and Control, Technology, and Organization [2]. These dimensions can mutually involve five areas (A1. Design & Engineering; A2. Production Management; A3. Quality Management; A4. Maintenance Management; A5. Logistics Management), composing together the digital backbone of the company and affecting the value generation along the key processes (Fig. 1). The main output of this model consist in the categorization of the company analyzed: this is presented in both a 5-levels maturity scale and a radar chart composed at its angles by the four dimensions considered.

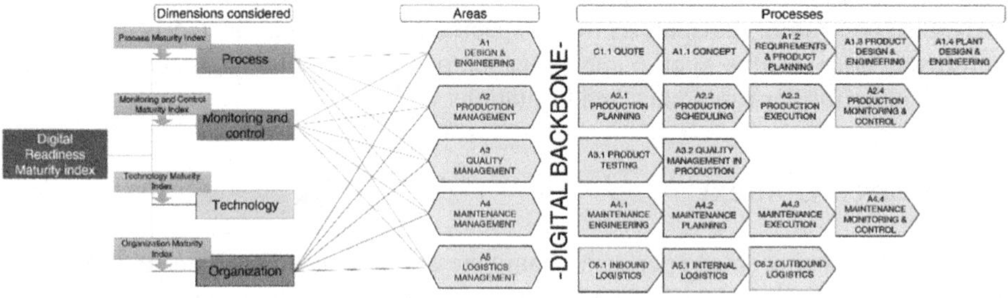

Fig. 1. DREAMY (adapted from [2])

2.2 CLIMB

CLIMB is a maturity assessment model based on a selection of the prevalent product development best practices from literature. Its aim is twofold:

(1) to create awareness and understanding in academia and industry, on the existing best practices in product development – thanks to the product development best practice framework;
(2) to retrieve an AS-IS picture of the practices usage in the industrial context, providing practitioners with the possibility of self-assessing their processes: this represents a support for their improvement initiatives and to benchmark with what is believed best in literature and eventually with other industrial cases.

The model is structured into a questionnaire, an evaluation scale made of five maturity levels and a radar chart. The questionnaire is semi-structured, based on the proposed product development best practice framework, and each of the questions investigates one of the best practices. The framework categorizes 107 product development best practices, across eight areas: 1 activities and flow, 2 decision making, 3 training, 4 roles and collaboration, 5 knowledge management (KM) process, 6 km techniques, 7 methods, 8 computerization and software. These areas are grouped into four categories (Table 1):

1. Process (how the flow of the development process is managed, the activities performed, the decision-making methods, the orientation to the client and the value, and the methods used),
2. People (how the development process is structured, which are the actors involved, the respective roles and competences),
3. KM (methods and tools used in the company to support knowledge management, accumulation, maintenance and reuse of the same)
4. tools (tools used to support the product development process and to improve the data integration level along it).

In this categorization, the process, tools and people vision are considered independent from KM, crucial in product development.

Table 1. CLIMB: Categories and Constructs

Category	Construct
1. Process	1. Activities and flow
	2. Decision making
2. People	3. Training
	4. Roles and collaboration
3. Knowledge Management (KM)	5. KM process
	6. KM tech
4. Tools	7. Methods
	8. Computerization and software

2.3 MyWaste

MyWaste is a simple methodology that companies can use in order to improve their New Product Development (NPD) processes in a continuous fashion: it allows to evaluate and rank a given library of product development wastes. The methodology is composed of 5 steps which can be recursively applied in order to continuously improve: companies are led through NPD process waste and criticalities analysis and removal, resulting in better performances of the whole development process. The method improves an existing process under lean perspective, reflecting lean principle of pursue perfection through progressive improvement actions. Figure 2 shows the framework of the methodology. The 5 steps can be grouped into 3 macro-activities: MyWaste Analysis, Map-it Process and Change Implementation.

Fig. 2. MyWaste method

2.4 MYTIME

MyTime is a method aimed at measuring through a questionnaire how time along the NPD process is spent. It analyzes how time of the actors involved in this process is divided among main activities (design and test), knowledge recovery (through traditional sources or informatics ones), specification and documentation development, data input in informative tools, coordination with other colleagues or partners and other activities. In the meanwhile, it also detects and ranks the main problems faced by actors working along this process, unveiling how time allocation is perceived by each of them.

3 The Case Study: The Methodology and the Company

In order to practically investigate the maturity level of manufacturing industries to integrate digital technologies along their value-adding processes, with a special focus on NPD, an explanatory case study has been conducted. The study conducted followed the embedded single-case design approach and included semi-structured interviews to gather data [12]. Based on the primary aim of the research, the first step has been the definition of the unit of analysis. The choice fell on Company A and in particular on its two main embedded macro-areas: on one side, production and ICT were considered to assess the digital readiness and maturity of the company, on the other technical department and R&D were chosen to evaluate the design and engineering process, appraising its readiness and analyzing its main criticalities. More than 15 interviews and 3 workshops were conducted in the company, with a total duration of about 53 h. Interviews were distinguished in two categories, based on the embedded unit of analysis of the company considered. Actors from production, supply chain, operations and ICT were involved to go through the DREAMY model. Instead, CLIMB required technical director, managers of product platform department, system engineering, R&D, service, electrical/SW BU and mechanical BU. Instead, MyWaste and MyTime were submitted to all of them. In addition, the workshops were useful to raise the awareness of both CEOs and top management regarding the topics coped along this study and to calibrate and align the objective of the study to the needs of the company.

More specifically, Company A is an Italian engineering to order company, specializing in packaging systems flowpack allowing a small wrapper to wrap a single product or group of products with a plastic film. Among the various sectors in which these types of packaging are used, there is first of all the food sector (industrial baking monotype and assorted biscuits, chocolate, products for breakfast, sweet and savory snacks, bread substitutes, coffee pods for automatic and semi-automatic coffee maker, cheese, frozen products), but also non-food, cosmetic and pharmaceutical industries. The packaging arena, fueled by more demanding customers requiring creative and innovative solutions, has contributed to the ever growing complexity of projects, and has driven the increase of system performance specifications and guarantees. To operate in this new arena and to offer to their customers the best service, simultaneously optimizing development steps and workflow management, Company A wants to analyze its order development processes and to identify critical factors with a particular attention to the digitalization level of the areas involved. Finally, the company would like to find the correct solutions to intervene on them.

Therefore, the research approach adopted (Fig. 3), composed by the integration of DREAMY and CLIMB models with MyWaste and MyTime methods, defined in Sect. 2, was used to conduct the case study, providing the following results.

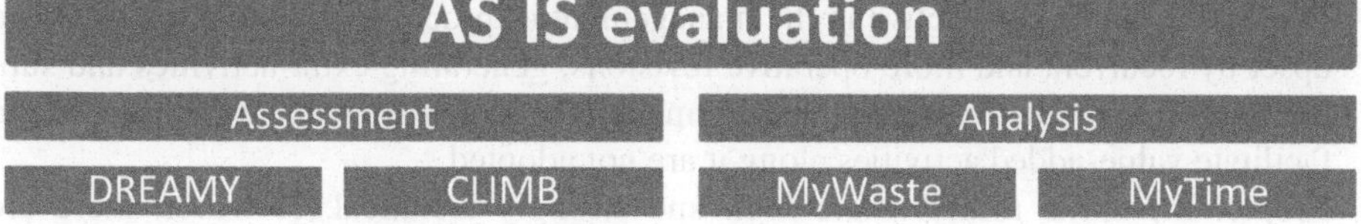

Fig. 3. AS IS evaluation research approach

4 Results

The first main result of this research is the positive outcome obtained with the application of the approach reported in Fig. 3 through the case study selected. The joint use of the models and methods selected, adequately put together and shown in Fig. 4, resulted able to grasp the data needed to evaluate the maturity level of manufacturing industries to integrate digital technologies along their value-adding processes, providing a special focus on NPD.

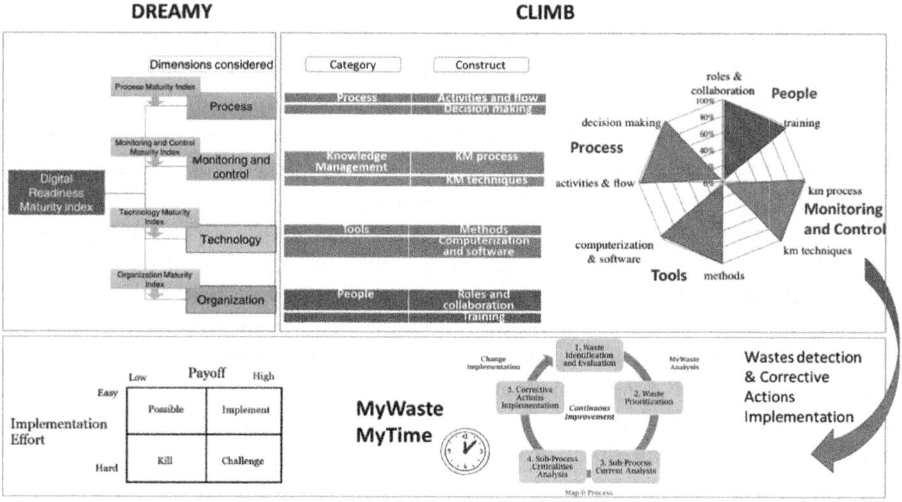

Fig. 4. The lifecycle approach evaluation

First of all, the models DREAMY and CLIMB, seemed to be compatible since structured on the same four pillars: process, monitoring and control (supported by KM practices), technology (consisting in tools, methods and computerization level) and organization (concerning roles, collaboration and training of people). This allowed authors to cross the results coming from the two models. Thanks to this integration, a more complete perspective of each of these four dimensions were obtained and the related main issues were detected, briefly reported in the following:

- Process: a macro-perspective in the management of processes' is often opposed and upset by recurrent and more operative revisions, generating extra-activities and subtracting value to the overall process. Formal methods able to manage the process and facilitate value-added activities along it are not adopted.
- People: the skills available are high and strongly technical. However, there are inefficiencies in roles allocation along the process.
- Tools: basic tools of virtual prototyping are used and there is also a basic support of PDM. However, the functionalities of these tools are not strictly concentrated in the technical office and are not shared efficiently with all the functions.

– Monitoring and Control & KM: there is a widespread tendency to an over-control of operative activities, linked to the issues raised above in the people dimension. On the other side, there is a significant problem in the formalization of knowledge and its sharing: apart from the basic IT tools, no other methods for storing, accumulating and sharing knowledge are used.

Moreover, MyWaste and MyTime methods contributed to confirm and enrich these results. The main wastes along the NPD process (grouped in the 8 macro-categories according to the lean theory) were detected. The two most relevant wastes are related to the conduction of an inappropriate process, i.e. waits along the process (for decisions, people, resources, data, etc.) and excessive or not necessary activities during its phases. They are followed by:

- wastes belonging to knowledge dimension, as for example incapacity to reuse already existing knowledge (with an impact on the product) and development of already designed components and products,
- organizational oversights (too many meetings with customers),
- over-engineering (development of components, materials or functionalities not required) and
- time lost in reworks and revisions.

The wastes detected were also linked, per each of the 8 macro-categories, to specific causes and effects. In general, the majority of them were triggered by organizational factors (29,1%), followed by process (25,6%), knowledge (21,9%), resources, tool (17,5%) and others (5,9%) causes. It was also found that wastes mostly lead to an increase of development costs and time and of product costs, to the generation of delays and inefficiencies, to a reduction of productivity and customer satisfaction and to repetition of errors.

5 Discussion

Based on the analysis conducted, in the company there is a good perception of what a waste entails (effects) and where it plausibly comes from (causes), for each of the eight waste areas. The vast majority of interviewees had clear impact of wastes on costs and time. Additionally, MyTime method revealed that the main issues in the NPD process are linked to the excessive time spent in codification, management, sharing and retrieval of knowledge (46%), not neglecting the time dedicated to coordination and organization (23%). Indeed, the majority of daily time (70%) resulted to be quite squeezable through the implementation of a major level of automation and digitization and a more efficient operability.

As a direct consequence of this general process inefficiency, also confirmed by DREAMY results, it emerged that Company A grounds its daily activities, both operative and adding-value, on the personal experience of its employees. Knowledge, not codified through structured mechanisms, remains tacit in people. Despite some digitalization attempts, the scarce interoperability level among the available systems cause several not adding-value activities along the process, as for example transcoding.

Again, also results from CLIMB model highlighted that, while the company should be organized according to a product-centric holistic approach, its knowledge appears scattered in separate silos, lacking hence of a paramount process perspective.

Finally, dedicated resources to be allocated on knowledge management and the continuous improvement of both the process and the organization could represent the first step to start reducing the detected wastes and issues. Together, digital tools and codified methods could further support the enhancement of both process efficiency and effectiveness, fostering an integrated, cooperative and collaborative management of the product knowledge along the order process and its lifecycle.

6 Conclusions and Further Researches

This paper has been aimed at practically investigating the maturity level of manufacturing industries to integrate digital technologies along their value-adding processes, with a special focus on NPD process. To achieve this result an explanatory case study has been conducted in an engineering to order Italian company, Company A, following an embedded single-case design approach. The research method adopted was designed with the intention of consistently combining four already existing models and methods aimed at evaluating and assessing different aspects in the company, unveiled as complementary for the achievement of the final objective of the research.

Assessment models (DREAMY and CLIMB) and analysis methods (MyWaste and MyTime) have been chosen and put together: they are based on concepts of readiness and maturity concerning digitization and design practices but also of waste and continuous improvement related to the Lean theory. The first main result of the study has been the positive systematic combination of these approaches in a more complete integrated one. Together, they resulted to be able not only to provide a complete assessment of the company adding-value processes but also to detect and raise the main issues and wastes occurring along them. These wastes currently hamper the company transition towards an industrial digitization and compromise its order development process effectiveness and efficiency. However, if adequately managed, they represent the key for the company to switch toward a more proficient product centric knowledge management and continuous improvement approach: this unveil the capacity of the joint method adopted and presented to outline a plan of possible interventions through which the existing situation could be improved.

On the contrary, the research method adopted has also limitations: it is all based on interviews, requiring several hours both from companies and researchers side. Moreover, compared to the single approaches, the joint method proposed in this research requires from the company side the involvement of different and heterogeneous profiles and from researchers side a big effort to analyse and put together the results obtained (that needed to be fully integrated and triangulated among them). Moreover, it has to be specified that the scope of each single method used is limited by definition. Each of them deals with specific facets (digital readiness and maturity, NPD maturity, NPD continuous improvement) of the more complex object of the research presented in this article, i.e. the smart readiness and maturity of manufacturing companies along the product development process. This justifies the need to put together and combine different approaches, obtaining as a result a more valid and complete approach.

A further improvement of this research could be to focus even more on issues with digital tools implementation in the company, since these tools actually should drive the digitization of the companies: right understanding its opportunities and prerequisites would be vital during digitization.

References

1. PwC and GMIS: Industry 4.0: Building the Digital Industrial Enterprise (2016)
2. De Carolis, A., Macchi, M., Negri, E., Terzi, S.: Guiding manufacturing companies towards digitalization. In: 23rd ICE/IEEE International Technology Management Conference, pp. 503–512 (2017)
3. De Carolis, A., Macchi, M., Negri, E., Terzi, S.: A maturity model for assessing the digital readiness of manufacturing companies. In: Advances in Production Management Systems. The Path to Intelligent, Collaborative and Sustainable Manufacturing, APMS 2017. IFIP Advances in Information and Communication Technology, vol. 513, pp. 13–20 (2017)
4. De Carolis, A., et al.: Maturity models and tools for enabling smart manufacturing systems characterization. In: Chiabert, P., Bouras, A., Frédéric Noël, J.R. (eds.) 14th IFIP International Conference on Product Lifecycle Management, Seville, Spain, pp. 23–35. Springer (2017)
5. Rossi, M., Terzi, S.: CLIMB: maturity assessment model for design and engineering processes. Int. J. Prod. Lifecycle Manag. **10**(1), 20 (2017)
6. Rossi, M., Taisch, M., Terzi, S.: Lean product development: a five-steps methodology for continuous improvement. In: 18th International ICE Conference on Engineering, Technology and Innovation (ICE) (2012)
7. Rossi, M., Kerga, E.T., Taisch, M., Terzi, S.: Proposal of a method to systematically identify wastes in new product development process. In: ICE, pp. 1–9 (2011)
8. Liker, J.K., Morgan, J.M.: The Toyota way in services: the case of lean product development. Acad. Manag. Perspect. **20**(2), 5–20 (2006)
9. Ohno, T.: Toyota Production System: Beyond Large-Scale Production. CRC Press (1988)
10. Womack, J.P., Jones, D.T.: Lean thinking—banish waste and create wealth in your corporation. J. Oper. Res. Soc. **48**(11), 1148 (1997)
11. Womack, J.P., Jones, D.T., Daniel, R.: The Machine That Changed the World: The Story of Lean Production–Toyota's Secret Weapon in the Global Car Wars That is Now Revolutionizing World Industry. Simon and Schuster, New York (2007)
12. Yin, R.K.: Case Study Research Design and Methods. Applied Social Research Methods Series, 4th edn. SAGE, Los Angeles and London (2009)

Empirical Study of Multi-party Workshop Facilitation in Strategy Planning Phase for Product Lifecycle Management System

Satoshi Goto[1,2(✉)], Osamu Yoshie[2], and Shigeru Fujimura[2]

[1] Business Transformation Management, PTC Japan Co. Ltd., Tokyo, Japan
sgoto@ptc.com
[2] Graduate School of Information, Production and Systems, Waseda University, Fukuoka, Japan
{yoshie,fujimura}@waseda.jp

Abstract. This paper proposes a framework of short term and intensive workshop facilitation for multi-party stakeholders in PLM strategy planning phase. We have been empirically pursuing what a valuable facilitation for the workshop is; how multi-party PLM stakeholders can build proactively a mutual consensus in as short a time as possible. PLM project promotion members always encounter a difficulty of consensus building. This is because various stockholders have different opinions and responsibilities through sales, engineering, manufacturing, and service departments. Firstly, we mention key challenges of multi-party consensus building in PLM strategy planning phase. Secondly, we propose a programmatic framework on intensive workshop-facilitation which is configured twelve steps. The key outcome of the workshop is to craft a PLM Success Value Roadmap (PSVR) which is contained various hypothesis defined by the workshop participants helping by facilitators (KPIs). For example, there are PLM vision, strategy, initiative, process, and key performance indicator. Thirdly, we mention an empirical case study conducted our proposed workshop-facilitation method for an industrial company. Seventeen stakeholders were joined as the workshop participants who were invited from three different business units. It was held as a two-day intensive PLM trial workshop. Finally, we found that the proposed workshop-facilitation as a consensus building method contributed to the satisfaction of more than 60% of the participants. 85% of the participants commented that they would encourage colleagues to participate in the workshop that we have developed. We conclude that the multi-party intensive workshop was a valuable experience that it allows stakeholders to produce a PLM strategy in a relatively short time.

Keywords: PLM strategy planning · Multi-party consensus building · Workshop facilitation · Product lifecycle management system

1 Introduction

According to the Digital Transformation 2025 government report in Japan published by Ministry of Economy, Trade and Industry, many Japanese companies will become

C. Fortin et al. (Eds.): PLM 2019, IFIP AICT 565, pp. 82–93, 2019.
https://doi.org/10.1007/978-3-030-42250-9_8

concerned that their current legacy information and communication technology (ICT) systems cannot cope with operational changes in the era of digital transformation [1]. This means that there will be an increasing need in Japan to either replace or rebuild aging product lifecycle management (PLM) systems as well as other corporate legacy business systems. Consequently, such companies must plan new PLM strategies. Regarding the current technological capabilities of commercial PLM software packages, an increasing number of out of the box (OOTB) PLM functionalities are available based on enterprise product information and process management. For example, we note that in Japan, PLM packages provide many of the standard functions required by PLM end users while requiring minimal customization [2]. Given all of the above, now would be a good time for PLM project promotion members to start planning new PLM strategies. The time is right to replace existing legacy PLM systems with up-to-date PLM solutions that have as many OOTB functionalities as possible. However, it will be difficult for members to devise new PLM strategies rapidly. In particular, PLM project promotion members must overcome the following outstanding issues regarding a negative mindset:

- difficulty of justifying why end users need PLM itself;
- no PLM alignment between corporate strategies and business operations;
- no specific key performance indicators that all stakeholders can understand;
- differing views among departments regarding new PLM initiatives;
- no idea of up-to-date PLM application package functionalities;
- no alignment between business unit and IT department members;
- trauma associated with the failure of a previous PLM project; and
- uncertainty about how to define PLM vision and strategy.

Ultimately, PLM project promotion members are uncertain about the manner in which to align with PLM strategy and corporate business goals getting common consensus among multi-party stakeholders. A key initiative for a PLM strategy is to "build with good people" [3]. This suggests to us that strategy planning must involve a variety of people with different skills across the product lifecycle (Fig. 1). During the last five years, we sought empirical answers to the questions of (i) what constitutes valuable facilitation for a workshop and (ii) how multi-party stakeholders throughout whole product lifecycle can build mutual consensus proactively in the short-term [4]. Herein, reflecting our past outcomes of empirical research and studies, we propose a framework of short-term intensive workshop facilitation for multi-party consensus building at PLM strategy planning phase.

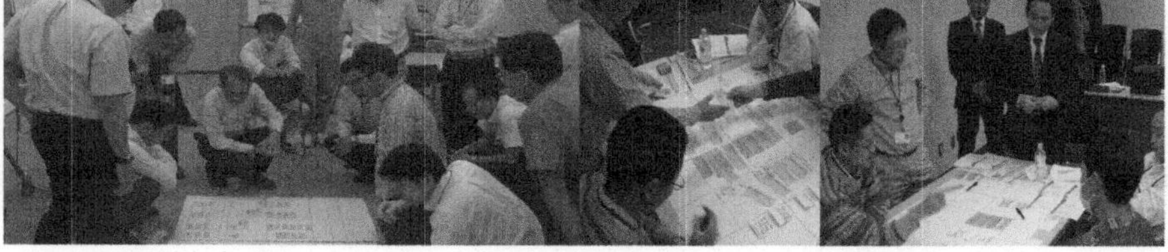

Fig. 1. Example of workshop atmosphere on multi-party consensus building

2 PLM Success Value Roadmap (PSVR)

To overcome the challenges facing PLM project promotion team members as described in Sect. 1, several PLM strategy case studies of larger Japanese firms have been reported [5]. It also suggests that small and medium sized enterprises should have to prepare and define a PLM vision and strategy as well as larger enterprises [6]. Following that, we have also conducted preliminary research involving requirement-gathering sessions with some of specific Japanese manufacturers who were planning to implement PLM systems. We asked them about the contexts of PLM strategy planning, including business strategy, key challenges, target business processes, and key critical capabilities. Finally, from the interview outcomes, we developed a simple A3-size one-page summary format (Fig. 2) that we refer to as the PLM Success Value Roadmap (PSVR). The PSVR is a deliverable of the PLM strategy-planning phase that we are proposing herein, and it must cover the understanding of every stakeholder working in any variety of organizations. As stated in Fig. 2, the PSVR as a one-page summary can be simply overviewed by the stakeholders. There are 12 different views regarding PLM strategy, including PLM vision, business strategy, difficulties experienced by existing end users, ICT best practices, focused processes, and key performance indicators. The PSVR allows PLM promotion members and related stakeholders to understand globally the comprehensive PLM strategy as planned. The contents of the PSVR are defined in the proposed workshop-facilitation steps explained in Sect. 3.

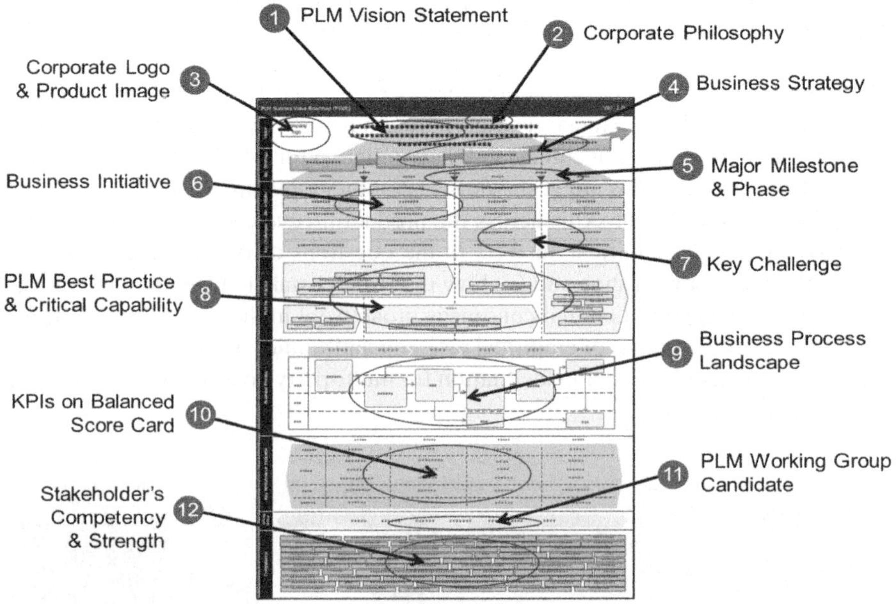

Fig. 2. Illustrative example of PLM Success Value Roadmap (PSVR) – as A3 size one-page summary

3 Design of Workshop Facilitation for PLM Strategy Planning

We designed a strategic workshop-facilitation framework for PLM stakeholders who are selected from various departments including sales/marketing, product planning, product engineering, quality assurance, production/procurement, and service/maintenance. We assume that these stakeholders are selected by level-C executives and that the former become corporate PLM promotion members. However, the workshop members are not always available to work full-time on the assigned mission. Consequently, the workshop must be held over a relatively short time (e.g., several days) to allow the members to establish rapidly a single common PLM vision and strategy that contributes to the executives' strategic business goals. This paper aims to provide a pragmatic step-by-step approach that facilitates various elements of PLM strategy planning in such business situations.

3.1 Proposed Workshop Facilitation Framework

The following explains the three primary sessions in terms of the proposed workshop-facilitation framework for multi-party participants invited from the various departments of the enterprise.

Session A: Defining the vision and strategy
The aim of Session A (the first session) is to establish a common and single PLM vision statement. The PLM vision should conform to the corporate strategy based on the consensus of all participants. Session A also identifies the key challenges that must be overcome across the departments.
Session B: Understanding the technology and processes
Session B (the next session) concerns technology experience. The aim is to get the workshop participants to identify and experience state-of-the-art commercial PLM software packages based on proven business processes. This is an important experience to smoothly imagine the ideal business process innovation with critical PLM capabilities.
Session C: Configuring the metrics and roadmap
The aim of Session C (the final session) is to achieve a single consensus among the participants. The KPIs are defined based on the balanced scorecard (BSC) methodology. Encompassing all the items discussed by the participants, a PSVR is created as a one-page summary.

3.2 Workshop Facilitation Steps

In Sessions A–C, the facilitator leads the workshop through the following 12 steps (Table 1). These steps encourage the participants to explore the various critical topics that are necessary to define a PSVR as mentioned in Sect. 2. The aim of these steps is to support the workshop participants in preparing the fundamental contents of their PLM strategy both smoothly and efficiently.

Table 1. Proposed workshop facilitation framework.

Session		Step	Key facilitation
A	Vision & Strategy	1	**Identify** the corporate strategy and operational issues
		2	**Realize** the participants' negative challenges and positive motivations
		3	**Recognize** operational PLM initiatives and map them to business processes
		4	**Define** the PLM vision statement to build common consensus
B	Technology & Process	5	**Understand** commercial PLM systems regarding business scenarios
		6	**Discuss** case studies of PLM best practices
		7	**Discover** new PLM initiatives regarding commercial PLM functionality
		8	**Experience** the OOTB functions of a PLM system with own product data
		9	**Select** favorite PLM functionalities from PLM hands-on experience
		10	**Devise** intended business processes based on new PLM initiatives
C	Metrics & Roadmap	11	**Configure** a strategy map to define the KPIs
		12	**Complete** an original PSVR for the stakeholders

Step 1: Identify the corporate strategy and operational issues
By reviewing the results of the pre-questionnaire that the workshop participants completed beforehand, the participants agree on (i) the direction of the corporate management strategy, (ii) the key challenges, and (iii) the business process. These are compared with the participants' corporate direction and the PLM-related best practices of other companies.

Step 2: Realize the participants' negative challenges and positive motivations
To determine the participants' mindsets regarding PLM strategy, the workshop facilitator asks the participants to write down existing negative operational problems and positive motivations using sticky notes. These are then gathered together, and the KJ method [7] is used to categorize all the various phrases and sentences into clusters. This encourages the participants, in the opening session of the workshop (i.e., as early as possible), to obtain a mutual understanding of their key competences.

Step 3: Recognize operational PLM initiatives and map them to business processes
Having obtained a mutual understanding of the negative and positive topics in step 2, the facilitator then asks the participants to consider what the ideal PLM initiatives are.

Several initiatives and action items are gathered together on sticky notes, whereupon these topics are mapped to some of the 26 business processes that we have defined as PLM best practices.

Step 4: Define the PLM vision statement to build common consensus

One single PLM vision statement is defined as a common contribution by all the workshop participants. This represents an important final direction for implementing future PLM solutions. Having defined the PLM vision statement, the PLM stakeholders can always refer to it during the PLM promotion project. This is a fundamental starting point when making a PLM strategic plan.

Step 5: Understand commercial PLM systems regarding business scenarios

Nowadays, major commercial PLM software packages have many usable OOTB functionalities, thereby allowing the participants to imagine how their own PLM strategy could be realized during the PLM system implementation phase. This step provides the participants with a standard demonstration session so that they understand which OOTB functionalities are suitable for their business situations. Once the participants understand the PLM OOTB functionalities, the workshop facilitator encourages them to discuss which PLM capabilities are suitable for them and how those capabilities can be adapted to their new business process.

Step 6: Discuss case studies of PLM best practices

The facilitator presents global case studies of PLM best practices in other companies. This is an important opportunity for the participants to learn about previously unknown PLM initiatives beyond the realm of their own company. The facilitator introduces as wide a variety of case studies as possible, not merely cases from the same industries with which the participants are familiar.

Step 7: Discover new PLM initiatives regarding commercial PLM functionality

The participants are now starting to imagine using the commercial OOTB PLM functionalities while incorporating their own intended business processes. In step 7, they establish a high-level definition of their ideal business-process landscape. This is in the form of a swim-lane diagram [8], which is a mapping diagram containing business phases and related organizations. This diagram helps the participants to prioritize new PLM initiatives.

Step 8: Experience the OOTB functions of a PLM system with own product data

To allow the participants, as future end users of PLM system, to experience the reality of OOTB PLM functionalities, this step provides a hands-on session with a PLM application system. The participants use their own original real product data as created on a 3D CAD system. A benefit of this hands-on experience is that it minimizes the number of subsequent unnecessary customization requirements.

Step 9: Select favorite PLM functionalities from PLM hands-on experience

Having experienced the hands-on session in step 8, the participants know which functionalities should be used in their own business processes. In this step, the facilitator encourages the participants to select as many of these preferred functionalities as desired and then map them onto the previously defined swim-lane diagram.

Step 10: Devise intended business processes based on new PLM initiatives

Referring to the template provided by the swim-lane diagram, which represents all the business processes and the relationships with all the PLM organizations, the participants devise their ideal intended business processes with one single common consensus. They then map the new PLM initiatives that they defined in step 7 on the intended processes.

Step 11: Configure a strategy map to define the KPIs
The participants tentatively define metrics for the PLM initiatives. This activity again uses the Balanced Score Card (BSC) method [9]. For a PLM strategy, the BSC is configured with four different views, namely (i) corporate management, (ii) business process, (iii) adoption, and (iv) information technology. The facilitator asks the participants to define KPIs through the BSC activity by working in groups.
Step 12: Complete an original PSVR for the stakeholders
Finally, having worked through steps 1–11, the participants complete a PSVR as a comprehensive one-page summary of their PLM strategic planning.

4 Case Study

4.1 Background and Opportunity

Company X (as a pseudonym) is a medium-sized manufacturer of high-tech electronics and comprises three different business units. It deals in high-tech products and components for electronic equipment, electrical machinery, and automotive industries. The operating officer Mr. A (as a pseudonym) of the corporate business planning department of the company has decided to implement an enterprise PLM system to manage all product data and processes throughout the three different business units. A key challenge is that the PLM user candidates of the three business units have never experienced business collaboration each other at all, and there are no job-rotation opportunities for them among the business units. We had the opportunity to use our developed multi-party PLM strategy-planning workshop method to organize consensus building for the stakeholders of the business units. To support mutual communication, a dedicated professional facilitator was also assigned from a PLM solution company.

4.2 Characteristic of Participants

The executive officer nominated 17 employees as the workshop members (see Table 2). Reviewing the preliminary questionnaire answered in step 1, it was clear that the participants all had different expectations regarding the PLM system itself. By following the 12 workshop facilitation steps, they attempted to craft an original one-page PSVR facilitated by the professional PLM consultant. This was a two-day event held at the company's employee training center.

4.3 Discussion

After the workshop event at Company X, we asked the participants the following eight questions. The aim of this survey was to assess whether our developed workshop-facilitation steps helped to plan a PLM strategy in such a multi-party environment. We received 14 responses to this survey.

Table 2. Attendees list of the workshop at company-X

Business unit	Participant	Affiliation department	Expectation of PLM system
BU-1	1	Sales	Product information sharing among departments
	2	Procurement	Supplier collaboration with open and close
	3	Manufacturing	Reformation of working process and data
	4	Production Engineering	Project management with product data
	5	Design Engineering	Improvement of product quality and reliability
BU-2	6	Sales	Standardization for product and related parts
	7	Sales	Delivery date management
	8	Procurement	Standardization and trade-off
	9	Manufacturing	Clear role and responsibility
	10	Design Engineering	Standardization and motivation management
	11	Business Development	Launch process management
BU-3	12	Sales	Eliminate duplicated activities
	13	Sales	Clear responsibility and eliminate non-valued tasks
	14	Procurement	Process reengineering
	15	Manufacturing	Resource management and process management
	16	Manufacturing	Replace existing systems reducing maintenance cost
	17	Design Engineering	Information sharing with up-to-date contents

Q1: How satisfied were you with the workshop?

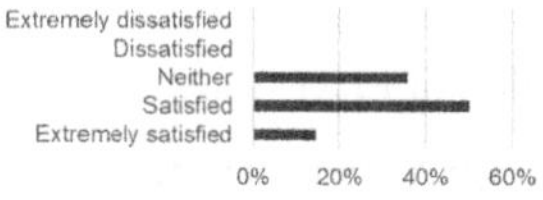

Fig. 3. Result of Q1

More than 60% of the participants were either satisfied or strongly satisfied with the workshop. This means that the workshop method that we have developed was evaluated positively and accepted comprehensively (Fig. 3).

Q2: Did you find the multi-party discussion during the workshop effective?

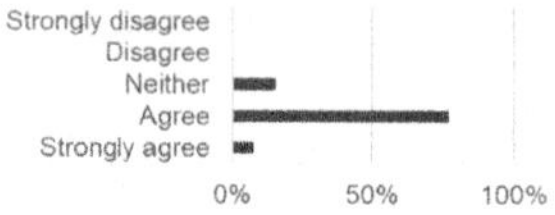

Fig. 4. Result of Q2

Most of the respondents (more than 80%) found that multi-party discussion such as group work across different departments was effective. In fact, we received positive feedback on multi-party discussion in the free description in question 7 (Fig. 4).

Q3: How was the utilization and actual progress of the external facilitator?

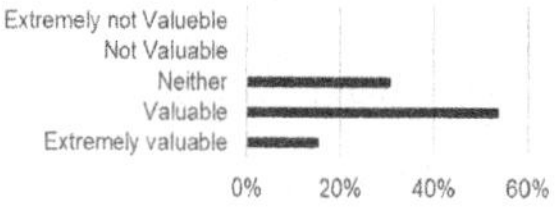

Fig. 5. Result of Q3

The replies to this question indicate that using an external facilitator made an important contribution to the trial workshop. However, more research is needed to determine whether this feedback was dependent on the skills of the professional facilitator (Fig. 5).

Q4: Did the problem hypothesis presented during the workshop correlate with problems in the actual workplace?

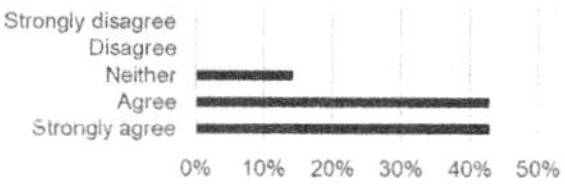

Fig. 6. Result of Q4

Most of the respondents agreed that they were able to extract a hypothesis that was appropriate to real issues in the workplace. This was one of our aims and a significant indicator for our study (Fig. 6).

Q5: In the discussion during the workshop, did you identify the root cause of the business problems?

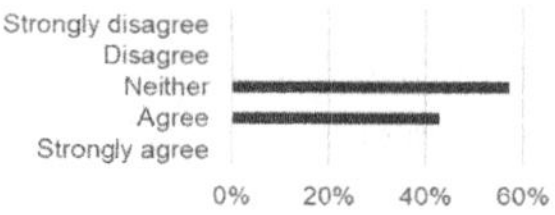

Fig. 7. Result of Q5

40% of the respondents agreed that they were able to identify the root cause. However, the majority neither agreed nor disagreed (Fig. 7), pointing out in question 7 that it was necessary to have more discussion time.

Q6: What are your opinions about the PLM success value roadmap that you crafted through the workshop group discussion? (free comment)

- *I felt that "high-level discussion" was very important regarding the vision that I created.*
- *I realized what my department's strong and weak points are; I found a direction to solve.*
- *I think that it describes exactly the issues regarding my division.*
- *I feel that its content is very effective, so I definitely want to realize it.*

- *I realized that we all had the same common understanding even if different departments.*
- *I am concerned that it might be lacking in detail.*

Q7: Regarding the workshop that you experienced, please list what you felt were the pros and cons (free comment)

- *Pro: I was able to exchange opinions across departments.*
- *Pro: I had a common recognition in related divisions.*
- *Pro: I could share my PLM vision with my members.*
- *Pro: It was a very valuable opportunity for discussions with other department members.*
- *Pro: By sharing problems, the task has been clarified.*
- *Pro: I was able to proceed with the tempo well in a short time.*
- *Pro: I was glad that I could think of it with different thought circuits.*
- *Pro: Because I got away from daily work, I was able to concentrate quietly take a lecture.*
- *Pro: It was refreshing for me to extract problems in a short time.*

- *Con: In discussions with members of the same division, it was difficult to come up with new ideas.*
- *Con: I think that participants were biased by department.*
- *Con: Time was limited, and some discussion was inadequate.*
- *Con: I thought that there was not enough time for group discussions.*
- *Con: I wanted to hear about the problems of other departments in advance.*
- *Con: I would like to have received a little more advice from the facilitator.*
- *Con: Our discussions took place in an intentionally made atmosphere, which I felt was far from practical.*
- *Con: Even if we concluded in this workshop, we would be not able to solve it at work by ourselves.*
- *Con: I wanted to talk a bit more about the current ICT system problems.*

Q8: Would you recommend this workshop method to your coworkers and colleagues?

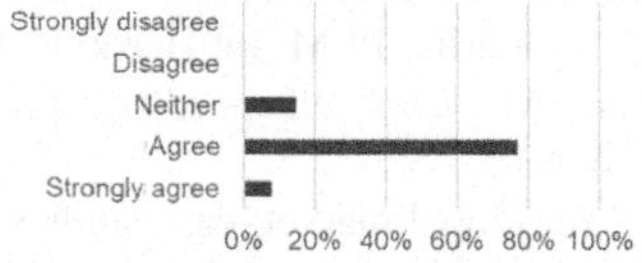

Fig. 8. Result of Q8

85% of the participants commented that they would encourage colleagues to participate in the workshop that we have developed. This means that the multi-party intensive workshop would be a valuable experience for many of the stakeholders for PLM strategy planning (Fig. 8).

5 Conclusions and Future Work

We proposed a workshop-facilitation framework for the PLM strategic planning phase, the aim being to encourage multi-party participants to discuss proactively in a positive discussion atmosphere. We defined 12 steps as the facilitation workstream, and we had an opportunity to work through these steps with an industrial company. Having conducted this empirical trial study with the company, we found that the proposed consensus-building method contributed to the satisfaction of more than 60% of the participants. 85% of the participants commented that they would encourage colleagues to participate in the workshop that we have developed. We conclude that the multi-party intensive workshop was a valuable experience that helped that stakeholders to produce a PLM strategy in a relatively short time. However, because in their feedback some of the participants requested more leadership from the facilitator, we must consider the role of the facilitator in the requirement-gathering phase (e.g., cons in Q7 discussed in the above Sect. 4.3). We must also identify whether the outcome was due to our proposed method or the skills of the professional facilitator. For example, during the workshop time, the facilitator noticed that even silent participant had the similar opinions as other participants had. Facilitators should be aware of such equal dialogue without prejudice. Therefore, as a future work, we intend to apply probabilistic latent semantic analysis, such as *topic modeling* [10], to the raw data arising from participants' dialogs. This aims to incorporate a scientific objective metric into the workshop outcome. Additionally, because it was obtained from an experiment with just one company, our trial data set was relatively small. We require more data so that we can be confident in our developed facilitation method.

References

1. The Ministry of Economy, Trade and Industry (METI): DX Report: Overcoming of '2025 Digital Cliff' Involving IT Systems and Full-fledged Development of Efforts for DX (2018)
2. Stark, J.: Product Lifecycle Management. PLM Case Studies, vol. 4. Springer, Heidelberg (2019)
3. Stark, J.: Product Lifecycle Management. The Executive Summary, vol. 3. Springer, Heidelberg (2019)
4. Goto, S., Trolio, E., Yoshie, O., Tamaki, K.: Multi-party interactive visioneering workshop for smart connected products in global manufacturing industry considering PLM. In: Harik, R., Rivest, L., Bernard, A., Eynard, B., Bouras, A. (eds.) PLM 2016. IAICT, vol. 492, pp. 501–511. Springer, Cham (2016). https://doi.org/10.1007/978-3-319-54660-5_45
5. Park, Y.W., Abe, T., Goto, S.: Product lifecycle management for global market: case studies of Japanese firms. In: 9th International Conference on Product Lifecycle Management (2009)
6. Koomen, B.: PLM in SME, what are we missing? An alternative view on PLM implementation for SME. In: Chiabert, P., Bouras, A., Noël, F., Ríos, J. (eds.) PLM 2018. IAICT, vol. 540, pp. 681–691. Springer, Cham (2018). https://doi.org/10.1007/978-3-030-01614-2_62
7. Susumu, K.: A Japanese problem solving approach: the KJ-Ho method. In: Proceedings of Kicss, Kanazawa (2013)
8. Geary, R., Brache, A.: Improving Performance: How to Manage the White Space on the Organization Chart. Wiley, Hoboken (2012)

9. Robert, K., Norton, D.: Using the Balanced Scorecard As a Strategic Management System. Harvard Business Review, Brighton (1996)
10. Chemudugunta, C.: Text Mining with Probabilistic Topic Models: Applications in Information Retrieval and Concept Modeling. Lambert Academic Publishing, Saarbrücken (2010)

Practical Implementation of Industry 4.0 Based on Open Access Tools and Technologies

Ahmed Awouda(✉), Khurshid Aliev, Paolo Chiabert, and Dario Antonelli

Politecnico di Torino, Corso Duca degli Abruzzi 24, 10129 Turin, Italy
{ahmed.awouda,khurshid.aliev,paolo.chiabert,
dario.antonelli}@polito.it

Abstract. Industry 4.0 provides a major breakthrough for innovating processes in contemporary manufacturing companies, it arises from the simultaneous presence of an opportunity and a necessity. The opportunity is the availability of powerful ICT technologies, that everyone uses every day with smart phones thanks to the well-established and expensive infrastructure provided by tech giants. The necessity is the achievement of Lean transformation in western enterprises through a deep knowledge on manufacturing processes and an incessant training of workforce.

Industry 4.0 will provide us with an integrated holistic view of the manufacturing processes and the possibility to control them according to appropriate forecasts and evaluation of performances and results. Industry 4.0 was born in 2011 and it is in its early stage, there are many research gaps which must be studied and large applications that must be fully integrated in the Industry 4.0 framework.

In this paper a simple application of Industry 4.0 is presented with the aim of demonstrating that, using commercially available open source components, it is possible to integrate different technologies belonging to industry (robotics) and commercial components into one eco-system. Moreover, it integrates different I4.0 enabling technologies namely: Robotics, IoT and fog/edge computing. Finally, the proposed framework can serve as an educational and practical tool for demonstration of Industry 4.0.

Keywords: Industry 4.0 · Internet of things · Collaborative robots · Open source · Data acquisition systems

1 Introduction

The Fourth industrial revolution promotes the "smart factory" idea, this idea is not only limited to the factory but is extended to the whole supply chain. Industry 4.0 integrates up-to-date technologies, which are equipped with sensors and intelligent control units able to simultaneously communicate and to autonomously exchange information about machines, plants or products. The underlying concepts of Industry 4.0 is the pervasive connection of devices, applications, operators belonging to the different levels of the automation stack illustrated by ISA 95 standards.

Published by Springer Nature Switzerland AG 2019
C. Fortin et al. (Eds.): PLM 2019, IFIP AICT 565, pp. 94–103, 2019.
https://doi.org/10.1007/978-3-030-42250-9_9

The Cyber-Physical Systems (CPS) promoted by Industry 4.0, can be easily assimilated to the human nervous system: a set of sensors (nerve endings) monitor physical processes and transfer signals to fog computing devices (peripheral nervous system) that control actuators (automated reaction to the stimulus) or transfer the information to the higher decision levels (the human brain) for a more elaborated and proactive answer.

In such Industry 4.0 scenario there are many research gaps which must be studied and there is no standard road map for developing solutions both from academic and industrial point of view.

The paper deals with a small part of the Industry 4.0 scenario: It's concerned with the usage of IoT solutions to monitor different systems belonging to: The Industrial realm and the commercial realm. Section 2 introduces the Industry 4.0 enabling technologies and highlight their use in the proposed solutions. It explores the connectivity of devices and illustrates the specific protocols chosen in this solution. Section 3 describes the implementation methodology: hardware components and supported functionalities are illustrated in more details. Section 4 summarizes the results of the study and highlights the possibilities for future developments.

The adoption of the open-source paradigm promotes reduced implementation costs, widespread portability of solutions and complete owning of process data.

2 Background

2.1 Enabling Tools and Technologies

To develop the fourth revolution of industry the following enabling technologies or techniques are studied [1]. These Enabling technologies (Both hardware and software based) represent the building blocks of Industry 4.0 as shown in Fig. 1, this section starts by introducing the technologies used and implemented in the proposed application and gives a brief description of the other possible technologies that can be added to the system in the future.

Cobots (collaborative robots) are the main hardware tool that has a big demand for implementation in Industry 4.0 applications. Cobots are designed to actively collaborate with human co-worker in the same workplace to complete the assigned tasks but they can work also as autonomous robots. Another advantage of cobots is their ease of programing, deployment and re-deployment to different applications. Therefore, as an example of cobots the UR3 (Universal Robot) has been utilized in the proposed system. The acquired data from UR3 allows to monitor the performance of the cobot and can serve the increase of production productivity.

Internet of things (IoT) means to utilize intelligently connected devices and systems to acquire data from embedded sensors and actuators in machines and other physical objects. Industrial Internet of Things (IIoT) is the subcategory of IoT and IIoT will serve to enhance manufacturing and industrial processes. IIoT allows field devices to communicate and interact both with one another and with more centralized controllers [2]. In the proposed system, IoT is deployed to connect different Industrial devices and sensors. Furthermore, the collected data can be used to perform decentralized analytics and to enable real-time responses.

Cloud computing models will serve to store and analyze increased datasets of Industry 4.0 applications and enable data sharing across sites and company boundaries by dividing the physical resources with virtualization tools. Cloud computing performances will improve respond times (milliseconds) between machines by deploying data to the cloud and enabling data driven services for production systems [3]. Cloud services have been partially implemented into the proposed system by enabling storage data of machines, sharing data across sites and integration visualization tools.

The enabling tools of industry 4.0 are not limited to the abovementioned technologies but also include: *Big data, Augmented reality, Additive manufacturing, Simulation, Horizontal integration, Vertical integration* and *Cyber security* [4–7]. These technologies and tools are not addressed in this work but can be added to this work as a future improvement to the proposed system.

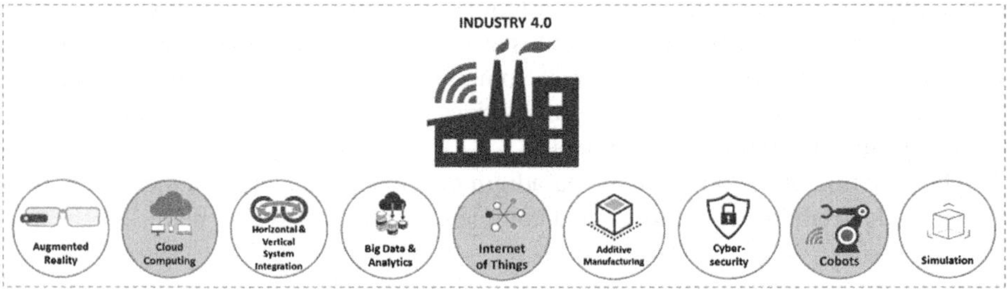

Fig. 1. Implementation of Industry 4.0 technologies are colored with green and future tools are indicated with a white color. (Color figure online)

2.2 Connectivity

Connectivity is the backbone of IoT [14], in the vision of I4.0 advanced connectivity of anything such as devices, systems and the granted access to the users at any time in any place to these systems is a must [15]. Communication protocols provide the set of rules for such devices to communicate and coordinate decisions.

There is a big variety of protocols used in today's industrial scene and the choice among these different protocols is totally application dependent and device specific. These industrial communication protocols fall into two main categories; Fieldbus protocols (such as Modbus RTU, Profibus DP and many other non-ethernet based protocols), and Industrial ethernet protocols (such as Modbus TCP and Profinet).

Industrial ethernet is practically the use of standard ethernet in industrial environments with protocols that satisfy the deterministic and real-time control requirements of factory floor and other industrial environments [8]. The growing popularity of Internet technology and IT usage stimulated a new wave of ethernet based industrial networks that borrowed basic technology from the IT world and tailored it towards usage in an industrial setting. According to a study conducted by [9] in 2018, industrial ethernet networks now hold a greater market share (52%) than traditional fieldbus technologies (48%) in factory automation with an annual growth rate of 22%. This transition to industrial Ethernet is driven by the need for high performance integration between factory installations and IT, interoperability requirements of industrial automation and control devices, as well as the growing adoption of Industrial IoT-systems.

Standardization of IoT connectivity is far from fruition and there is no clear de facto standard for IoT communication systems, however discussions within industry alliance are active such as the IIC (Industrial Internet Consortium) [17] and IEC (International Electrotechnical Commission) [18]. Nevertheless, the MQTT protocol is becoming a de facto standard in IoT applications especially for applications of remote device connectivity. Another protocol that stands out in the realm of industrial communications and is widely adopted in legacy factory floor systems is the Modbus protocol which has been the de facto standard in factory floor settings for many years. For this reason, MQTT and Modbus have been chosen as suitable Protocols for our study since this will allow our framework to combine legacy systems of the factory floor with the emerging technology paradigm of IoT. This allows the creation of a true cyber-physical systems which are the primary enabler of Industry 4.0 [19].

Modbus TCP (Also Modbus TCP/IP) is a variant of the modbus protocol where the modbus message frame is incapsulated in a TCP/IP wrapper [10]. TCP/IP refers to the Transmission Control Protocol and Internet Protocol, which provides the transmission medium for Modbus TCP messaging. The primary function of TCP is to ensure that all packets of data are received correctly, while IP makes sure that messages are correctly addressed and routed.

As seen in Fig. 2, Modbus TCP uses a Client server model where the Client sends a request to the server to initiate a transaction, this transaction can be a data read or write. The server receives the request as an indication, performs the necessary action required from the transaction and then replies with a response. Finally, the client receives the response in the form of a confirmation.

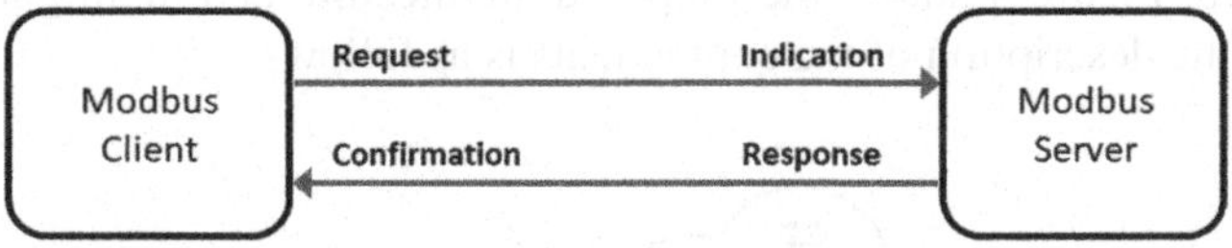

Fig. 2. Use case of Modbus TCP: Client-Server model where the Client sending a request to the server to initiate a transaction

MQTT provides connectivity between applications and users at one end, network and communications at the other end. MQTT is designed to minimize network bandwidth and device resource requirements whilst also attempting to ensure reliability and some degree of assurance of delivery, also MQTT protocol is a good choice for wireless networks that experience varying levels of latency due to occasional bandwidth constraints or unreliable connections [11].

As shown in Fig. 3, MQTT uses the Publish/Subscribe Model which consists of three main components: publishers, subscribers, and a broker. Publishers are the lightweight sensors and devices that connect to the broker to send their data and go back to sleep whenever possible. Subscribers are applications or devices that are interested in a certain topic, or sensory data, so they connect to brokers to be informed whenever new data is received. The brokers classify sensory data in topics and send them to subscribers interested in those topics only. A device can behave as a publisher and a subscriber at the same time by publishing to specific topics and subscribing to others, the term MQTT client is used to distinguish publishers/subscribers from brokers [12].

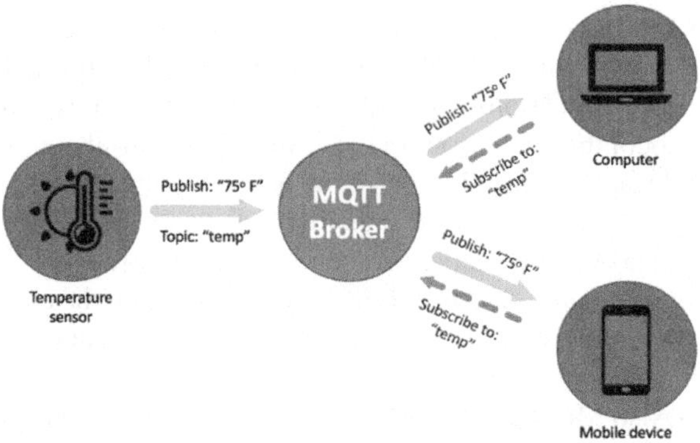

Fig. 3. MQTT Publish/Subscribe model between sensor & devices [13]

3 Implementation Methodology of Proposed Architecture

3.1 Hardware and Software Components

The internet of things allows devices to communicate and coordinate with each other in order to be able to make consensus decisions that benefit many applications. The proposed framework is a system able to collect data from different devices and allow this data to be accessible from anywhere in the world (via the internet) in the form of a dashboard. Figure 4 shows the proposed architecture and highlights its different components; the description of the components is as follows:

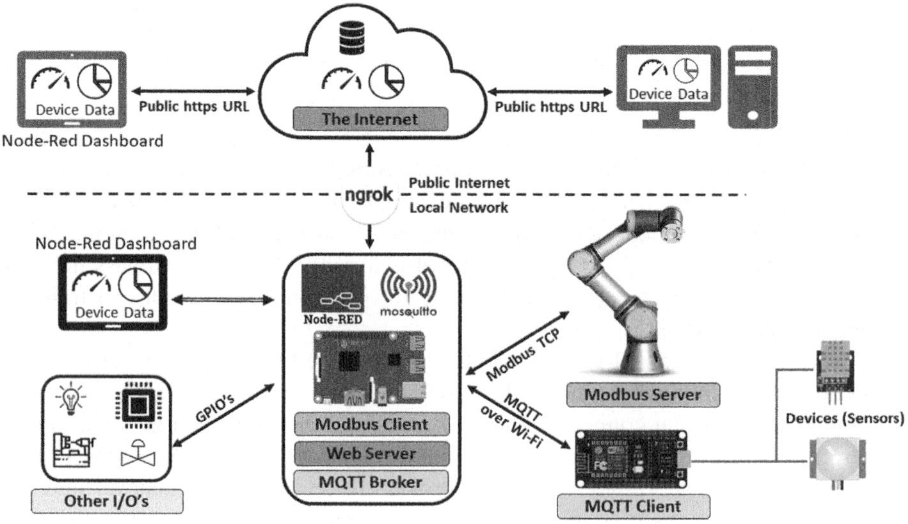

Fig. 4. Proposed architecture

Raspberry Pi is a single board computer that runs on open source software, it contains a Broadcom system on chip (SoC) with an ARM compatible CPU. In the proposed system the raspberry pi plays many roles: Modbus Client for the UR3 (Modbus Server);

Hosts the MQTT Broker (Mosquitto); Web Server for the Dashboard UI; Communication Gateway for GPIO connected Devices.

Node-Red is a flow based open source programming tool built upon Node.js that is used to connect hardware devices, API's and other online services belonging to the realm of IOT. Node-Red provides a browser-based flow editor which can be used to create JavaScript functions in the form of interconnected blocks that together construct a flow. One of the biggest advantages of Node-Red is its ability to run at the edge of the network on low-cost hardware such as the Raspberry Pi, in the cloud and locally on a standard PC. In the proposed framework Node-Red is ran on the Raspberry Pi and the editor is accessible via any web browser on the local network.

As seen in Fig. 5 which shows the developed node-red flow, Node-Red has been used to create the interactions between devices, sensors, robot ("things") and then to present the live data acquired from the devices on an interactive dashboard.

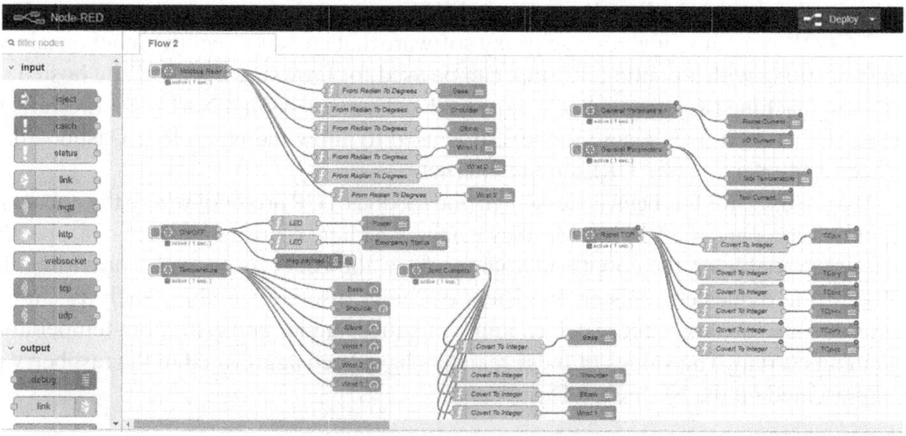

Fig. 5. Node-red flow image

The Node-Red dashboard is an add on module of Node-Red that is used to create and present a live data graphical user interface on a web browser. Figure 6 shows the developed dashboard, it can be seen from the figure that the dashboard package allows the addition of many UI components such as buttons, sliders, leds and gauges.

Mosquitto is an open Source message broker that implements the MQTT protocol, it can run on many devices from single board computers to powerful servers. It has been used to control the MQTT message flow between the ESP8266 and the Raspberry Pi but its limitations are much further as it can also be used manage MQTT communication between a magnitude of devices.

The ESP8266 (also known Node_MCU) is a low power Wi-Fi module with a full TCP/IP Stack and microcontroller capability. As seen in Fig. 4, it has been operated

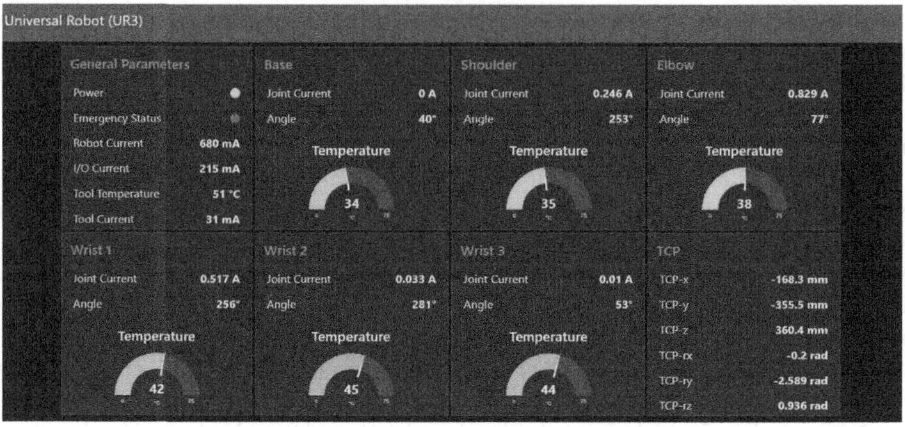

Fig. 6. Node-red dashboard

as an MQTT client that acquires sensor data from the sensors connected to it and then transmits the data to the Raspberry Pi via MQTT protocol.

NGROK is a tunneling, reverse proxy software that creates a secure tunnel on a local machine along with a public URL that can be used for browsing the local site hosted on the local machine (Raspberry Pi), it exposes local servers behind NATs and firewalls to the public internet over secure tunnels. It is used to allow the Node-Red Dashboard to be accessible via a public URL on the internet.

Data in the UR3 has been accessed via the modbus TCP protocol where the cobot is a Modbus Server and the RPi is a Modbus Client, the client sends requests to read specific registers available on the cobots internal memory, the cobot responds by providing the value of the requested register. Registers can hold discrete variables such as On/Off status and also analog values such as joint velocities, angles and also robot temperature and input current. The values of these registers have been aggregated in the raspberry pi and presented on the Node-Red Dashboard.

3.2 Functions Supported by the Demonstrator

The proposed framework is a generic, open source data acquisition system able to collect data from multiple devices and provide easy accessibility for this data via the internet. As seen previously in Fig. 4, this system is based on a Raspberry Pi that acts as a data collection buffer by holding the device data temporarily and as a gateway to the internet by presenting all the data on a web page GUI. By exploiting the multiple interfaces available on the raspberry pi one is able to have higher flexibility when it comes to data sources.

The presented system will allow (i) the collection of real-time data from various devices using different technologies and protocols of data transmission which in turn grants higher flexibility and lowers the limitations faced when acquiring device data (ii) remote monitoring of processes and sensor data from anywhere in the world via the internet (iii) usage of low cost devices and sensors to present a practical implementation of IoT based on open access tools that can be used for educational purposes and other applications.

By exploiting the flexibility of the open source Node-Red packages, several nodes can be used to serve different applications, In the presented work the system acquires data via Modbus TCP, MQTT and hardwired GPIO's.

As seen in Fig. 7; a different set of nodes is used for each method of data acquisition. For the Universal robot a modbus tcp node is used, by defining the IP address of the Modbus TCP server (the robot), the function code and the data length, node-red can access the internal registers of the universal robot. From the robot point of view, a set of registers containing various parameters are present, by knowing the parameters held in each register (also known as the modbus map) one can read or write to those registers. An example of these parameters are joint angles, velocities, joint motor currents, temperatures, robot state and many other parameters measured by the robots internal sensory. In addition to the existing registers, the UR3 contains a set of general-purpose registers that can be customized to store other parameters or variables.

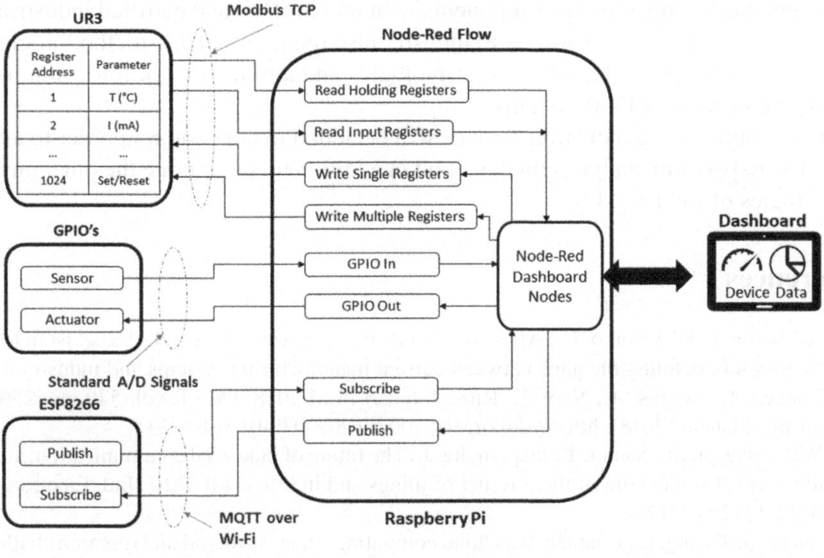

Fig. 7. Functional diagram of the proposed system.

For the ESP8266, the MQTT protocol over Wi-Fi is employed, the ESP8266 publishes messages to specific topics that the raspberry Pi is subscribed to, the Pi can also publish messages to topics that the ESP is subscribed to, messages can contain the sensor readings or commands to the ESP. By using this "Publish/Subscribe" model of MQTT a sort of 2-way communication can exist between the Raspberry Pi and the ESP8266.

The GPIO's onboard the Raspberry Pi are also used to acquire data. By connecting sensors and actuators used in standard small-scale electronics directly to the Raspberry Pi, Node-Red can read/write from/to these devices using an existing RPi library that provides access to all the hardware interfaces on the Raspberry Pi such as USB ports, sense HAT modules and GPIO's.

Data from all the sources presented previously is then passed onto the Node-Red Dashboard Nodes which presents the data in a graphical user interface accessible through a web browser in a real-time manner. Node-red dashboard allows the data to be presented in various forms such as charts, text fields and gauges, Commands are also triggered from the GUI using sliders, switches, text fields and buttons.

4 Conclusions and Future Works

This paper proposed a framework and a practical implementation of an Industry 4.0 application by integrating recent developed tools and technologies. The Proposed technologies are based on open access systems and protocols which gives more flexibility and allows one to reap the benefits of the open source paradigm.

The proposed framework can be an appropriate tool for academics to explain Industry 4.0 in education systems but integration of the system into Industry requires some improvements by substituting components with more robust and certified industrial like tools. Furthermore, the transition into industry also requires suitable methodologies and standards to manage such tools and technologies and a trained work force that has the knowledge to work in I 4.0 systems.

In the future, more industrial devices will be added to the system in order to acquire more data to perform analytics on the cloud in addition to incorporate the other enabling technologies of Industry 4.0.

References

1. Kambarov, I., D'Antonio, G., Aliev, K., Chiabert, P., Inoyatkhodjaev, J.: Uzbekistan towards industry 4.0. defining the gaps between current manufacturing systems and industry 4.0. In: Chiabert, P., Bouras, A., Noël, F., Ríos, J. (eds.) PLM 2018. IAICT, vol. 540, pp. 250–260. Springer, Cham (2018). https://doi.org/10.1007/978-3-030-01614-2_23
2. Wollschlaeger, M., Sauter, T., Jasperneite, J.: The future of industrial communication: automation networks in the era of the internet of things and industry 4.0. IEEE Ind. Electron. Mag. **11**(1), 17–27 (2017)
3. Zhang, Q., Cheng, L., Boutaba, R.: Cloud computing: state-of-the-art and research challenges. J. Internet Serv. Appl. **1**(1), 7–18 (2010)
4. Lee, J., Kao, H.A., Yang, S.: Service innovation and smart analytics for industry 4.0 and big data environment. Proc. Cirp **16**, 3–8 (2014)
5. Gattullo, M., Scurati, G.W., Fiorentino, M., Uva, A.E., Ferrise, F., Bordegoni, M.: Towards augmented reality manuals for industry 4.0: a methodology. Robot. Comput.-Integr. Manuf. **56**, 276–286 (2019)
6. Dilberoglu, U.M., Gharehpapagh, B., Yaman, U., Dolen, M.: The role of additive manufacturing in the era of industry 4.0. Proc. Manuf. **11**, 545–554 (2017)
7. Thames, L., Schaefer, D.: Cybersecurity for Industry 40. Springer, Heidelberg (2017). https://doi.org/10.1007/978-3-319-50660-9
8. Jasperneite, J., Schumacher, M., Weber, K.: Limits of increasing the performance of industrial ethernet protocols. In: IEEE Conference on Emerging Technologies and Factory Automation, ETFA 2007, pp. 17–24. IEEE, September 2007

9. The website of HMS networks. https://www.hms-networks.com/press/2018/02/27/industrial-ethernet-is-now-bigger-than-fieldbuses. Access 20 Feb 2019
10. Modicon, I.: Modicon Modbus Protocol Reference Guide, pp. 28–29. North Andover, Massachusetts (1996)
11. OASIS Standard: MQTT version 3.1. 1 (2014). http://docs.oasis-open.org/mqtt/mqtt/v3, 1
12. Salman, T., Jain, R.: A survey of protocols and standards for internet of things. Adv. Comput. Commun. **1**(1), 1–20 (2017)
13. https://www.appcelerator.com/blog/2018/03/api-builder-and-mqtt-for-iot-part-1/. Accessed 1 Feb 2019
14. Samuel, S.S.I.: A review of connectivity challenges in IoT-smart home. In: 2016 3rd MEC International Conference on Big Data and Smart City (ICBDSC), pp. 1–4. IEEE, March 2016
15. Cho, J.Y., Lee, H.S., Lee, B.G.: Connectivity issues on IoT business-the Korean case of smart home network. In: The Second International Conference on Electrical Electronics Computer Engineering and their Applications (EECEA2015) (2015)
16. https://developer.ibm.com/articles/iot-lp101-connectivity-network-protocols/
17. Industrial Internet Consortium website. http://www.iiconsortium.org/
18. International Electrotechnical Commission website. https://www.iec.ch/
19. O'Donovan, P., Gallagher, C., Leahy, K., O'Sullivan, D.T.: A comparison of fog and cloud computing cyber-physical interfaces for Industry 4.0 real-time embedded machine learning engineering applications. Comput. Ind. **110**, 12–35 (2019)

Ontologies and Semantics

Building a Multi-aspect Ontology for Semantic Interoperability in PLM

Alexander Smirnov[1], Nikolay Shilov[1(✉)], and Vladimir Parfenov[2]

[1] SPIIRAS, St. Petersburg, Russia
{smir,nick}@iias.spb.su
[2] ITMO University, St. Petersburg, Russia
parfenov@mail.ifmo.ru

Abstract. Interoperability support is a key task to enable seamless integration between various information systems. Today, in the era of Internet of Things and cyber-physical systems more and more systems have to collaborate. Product lifecycle management is not an exception. It covers multiple processes related to all stages of the product lifecycle and usually aimed at solving various tasks using different apparatus. As a result, a dilemma arises: on the one hand, there is a need of common information models enabling seamless information exchange, and on the other hand, the existing information models need to be preserved in order not to lose the already achieved efficiency in solving various tasks. In the present research, the problem of developing a single ontology for PLM support is investigated taking into account differences between terminologies (multi-aspect ontology) used at various stages of the PLM cycle. In this paper, the process of the multi-aspect PLM ontology building is presented based on the case study of PLM support at the automation equipment producer, Festo AG & Co KG.

Keywords: Information management · Interoperability · Multi-aspect ontology

1 Introduction

Current trend towards digitalization and the fourth industrial revolution (or Industry 4.0) assumes an intensive usage of information and telecommunication technologies at all stages of the product lifecycle value chain process – from design and engineering to manufacturing, distribution and discontinuation.

As a result, a successful implementation of this concept requires a tight integration along all the processes what leads to the implementation of cyber-physical system platforms that provide possibilities of integration between the physical equipment and IT services & applications [1].

However, such an integration is usually a challenge since different PLM processes have different goals, solve different tasks, and apply different methods that assume application of information models, which fit well to the corresponding tasks, but usually are not interoperable with each other.

Published by Springer Nature Switzerland AG 2019
C. Fortin et al. (Eds.): PLM 2019, IFIP AICT 565, pp. 107–115, 2019.
https://doi.org/10.1007/978-3-030-42250-9_10

This would not be a problem if each PLM process had to deal with its own piece of information, however in reality these information pieces overlap and changes made during one process have to be taken into account at the others. As a result, an efficient information exchange between different PLM processes requires solving the problem of interoperability support.

Since knowledge sharing can be viewed as an enabler for almost any kind of collaborative action, one of the main problems is the problem of interoperability between independent heterogeneous information resources [2]. In Europe, this issue today is receiving a great attention.

In the concept of a new European interoperability framework (New EIF [3, 4]), interoperability is defined as the "ability of organizations to interact towards mutually beneficial goals, involving the sharing of information and knowledge between these organizations, through the business processes they support, using the exchange of data between their ICT systems".

In Europe, the need for standardization and interoperable systems was recognized almost thirty years ago with the launch of the European Commission's CADDIA program in 1985, the IDABC program in 1995, the ISA program in 2009 (decision 2009/922/EC) and the creation of current compatibility solutions for European e-government services (ISA^2) in 2016 [5]. However, support for interoperability and integration of information resources into common ecosystems is still an unsolved interdisciplinary problem.

There are four levels of interoperability [4]: technical, semantic, organizational and legislative. Semantic interoperability is understood as semantic interpretation of data presented using meta-models such as the Unified Modeling Language (UML [6]) class diagrams and the Ontology Web Language (OWL [7]).

The semantic web (Semantic Web) is one of the ways to solve the problem of semantic interoperability, but today it does not allow working with information as seamlessly as necessary.

Ontologies are formal conceptualizations of domains of interests sharable by heterogeneous applications [8]. They provide means for machine-readable representation of domain knowledge and enable to share, exchange, and process information & knowledge based on its semantics, not just the syntax. Usually, ontologies include concepts existing in a domain, relationships between these concepts, and axioms. Ontologies have proved themselves as one of the most efficient ways to solve the problem of semantic interoperability support. Still there is a need for common ontologies of problem areas with supporting multiple modifications in a quick and simple way, as well as semantic queries in a given context; but applying ontologies to digital ecosystems is still a problem due to different terminologies and formalisms that the members of the ecosystems use.

It is generally accepted that models of specific problem areas (for example, configuration models of complex systems) can be obtained by inheriting or extending a common ontology. However, in systems with a dynamic structure, such as PLM systems, this solution does not allow to achieve the required level of flexibility, since the expansion of the general ontology with the appearance of new information objects requires ontology matching. It should be noted that the automatic ontology matching methods are still not sufficiently reliable (except in narrow domains), and manual ontology matching significantly reduces the efficiency.

The presented work is aimed to solve this problem at the level of semantic interoperability. In the previously reported work [9], different approaches have been analyzed and the apparatus of describing the PLM-related knowledge via a multi-aspect ontology was selected. The contribution of this paper is the application of the multi-aspect ontology to PLM interoperability support and sharing experience of the design process of such an ontology. The paper is structured as follows. Section 2 presents the motivation of the carried-out research. Section 3 describes the most relevant works in the area of PLM and multi-aspect ontology design. Section 4 describes the process of multi-aspect ontology building. The main results are summarized in the conclusion.

2 Motivation

The need to solve the semantic interoperability problem between different PLM stages has appeared due to a long-term collaboration with the company Festo AG & Co KG.

Festo AG & Co KG is an equipment producer providing for industrial automation technologies with a wide range of products (more than 40 000 products of approximately 700 types, with various configuration possibilities) ranging from simple products (e.g., an electric motor) to complex systems (e.g., a complete production line).

During several years of collaboration, an eco-system of software tools aimed at supporting the various PLM processes within the company has been developed as shown in Fig. 1. This eco-system covers several processes from product engineering (NOC and CONCode systems) through definition of possible configurations (CONSys) and product range segmentation (SePa) to customer-driven product configuration sales (encoway). The detailed description of these tools and supported processes can be found in [9].

Though most of these systems were developed as a result of the same collaboration, each of these was aimed at a particular task and used the most appropriate information model with some information duplicated. The further extension of the eco-system required a complete re-thinking of the used information model that has led to the present research.

The common ontology would provide for semantic interoperability between the systems. However, in its classical form the information models appropriate for each particular task would have been lost, since they would have to be converted into the common model. The multi-aspect ontology would make it possible not only to provide for semantic interoperability between information models of each PLM process but also would preserve the existing models.

3 Some Existing PLM Ontologies

In order to build the multi-aspect PLM ontology, existing PLM ontologies have been studied. The most interesting ones are described below. There exist a number of ontologies for PLM and similar domains, however, most of them are either high-level or oriented to a narrow domain.

The authors of [1] propose an ontology for Industry 4.0, which has a slightly different perspective considering the PLM from the Industry 4.0 point of view. As a result, they introduced into the ontology such concepts as Cyber-Physical System, Internet of Things,

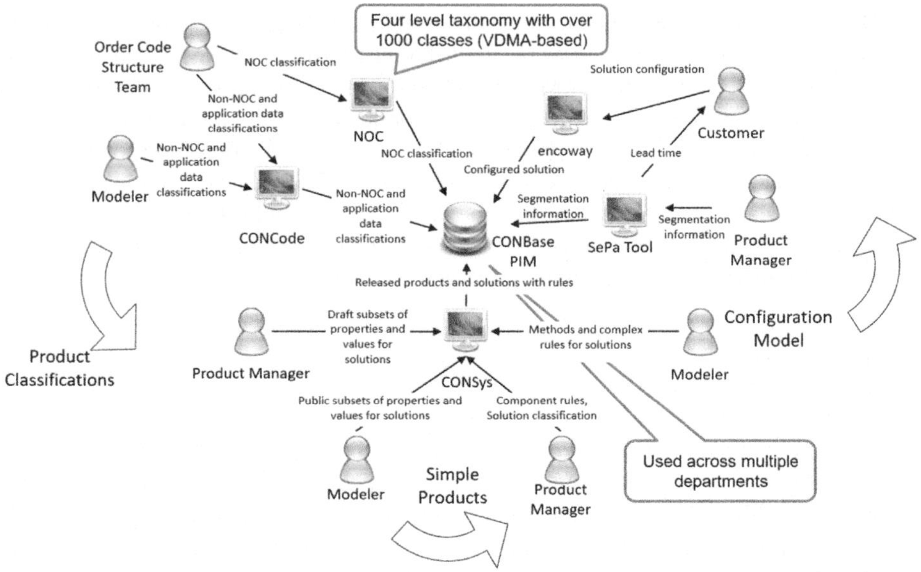

Fig. 1. Developed eco-system of information and knowledge management systems.

Smart Factory, Smart Product and others. The proposed ontology supports both vertical and horizontal integrations in a distributed production system.

In [10], a very high-level PLM ontology is presented that can be instantiated for each particular application (the authors present an example for an assembly process). This approach, however, will not help in solving the interoperability problem, since newly created instances have to be transferred between all the related application ontologies.

The ontology proposed in [11] is a generic but complete solution for a high-level PLM ontology aimed at knowledge reuse in SMEs. On the one hand, it tries to cover all the main aspects of SME functions so that new applications could be developed without significant ontology modifications, and on the other hand, the limited complexity of SMEs makes it possible for the ontology to stay at a reasonable size.

The PLM ontology survey [12] considers mostly high level generic ontologies (SUMO, Cyc, Generalized Upper Model, Enterprise, TOVE, and OntoWeb). The authors point out SUMO, Enterprise and TOVE ontologies as those that had the highest potential. They also conclude that it is practically impossible to have just one ontology for PLM thus confirming the main problem addressed in this paper.

In [13], a survey of ontologies for modelling the manufacturing process as a part of the PLM cycle is presented. The authors consider the integration of three notions: Product, Process and Resource. Though the considered ontologies usually cover a wider topic than just Product or Process, they are still mainly aimed at one task. The authors notice that there still exists a lack of semantics integration between the heterogeneous systems. Among the ontologies oriented towards narrow domains, there are two that should be considered in detail.

In [14], a PLM ontology is proposed, which covers only high level classes and supports instances and reasoning for only some particular tasks such as a product (vehicle) configuration. Usage of the ontology for other tasks is possible only when corresponding instances are added and only those based on OWL-DL logic.

In [15], the proposed PLM ontology covers a wide range of domains, mainly product-centered, namely: quality, environment, after development issues, marketing, product engineering, process engineering, strategic planning and production, supply chain, costs (found in [16]) as well as two additional domains: high level abstraction (for defining generic terms) and standards and best practices. Their entire ontology is quite detailed with 624 classes; however, it still can be used only as a vocabulary for interoperability support. It cannot support the solution of specific tasks that would require specific information representation formalisms.

4 Multi-aspect PLM Ontology Building

The difficulty of supporting conciliated ontologies that capture different views of the same problem, as well as developing an ontology model for representation and processing of information used for solving problems of different nature, lies in the necessity to operate not only with different terminologies but also with different formalisms used to describe different domains. The terminologies and formalisms, in turn, depend on the tools used for efficient solving of the domains' problems. In the previous publication [9] several paradigms of building multi-aspect ontologies have been analyzed and the granular multi-aspect ontology proposed by [17] has been selected.

The next step was to choose the notation. The most important progress in this direction was achieved by M. Hemam who in co-authorship with Z. Boufaïda proposed in 2011 a language for description of multi-viewpoint ontologies - MVP-OWL [18], which was extended in 2018 to support probabilistic reasoning [19].

In accordance with this notation, the OWL-DL language was extended in the following way (only some of the extensions are listed here; for the complete reference, please, see [18]). First, the viewpoints were introduced (in the current research they correspond to ontology aspects). Classes and properties were split into global (observed from two or several viewpoints) and local (observed only from one viewpoint). Individuals could only be local, however, taking into account the possibility of multi-instantiation, they could be described in several viewpoints and at the global level simultaneously. Also, four types of bridge rules were introduced that enable links or "communication channels" between viewpoints (only the bidirectional inclusion bridge rule stating that two concepts under different viewpoints are equal is used in the example below, indicated with the symbol $\overset{\equiv}{\leftrightarrow}$).

The ontology presented below is based on integration of several existing ontologies. The top-level ontology proposed in [15] was used as the basis. The described simplified but illustrative example Fig. 2 considers three aspects: "*Product Engineering*", "*Sales*", "*Strategic Planning and Production*" corresponding to different PLM stages. The three aspects are aimed at different tasks (only one per aspect is considered in the example) and, as a result, they use different formalisms (below, these are described in detail with references considering each of the aspects). However, some of the concepts (e.g., "*Product*") are used across the viewpoints.

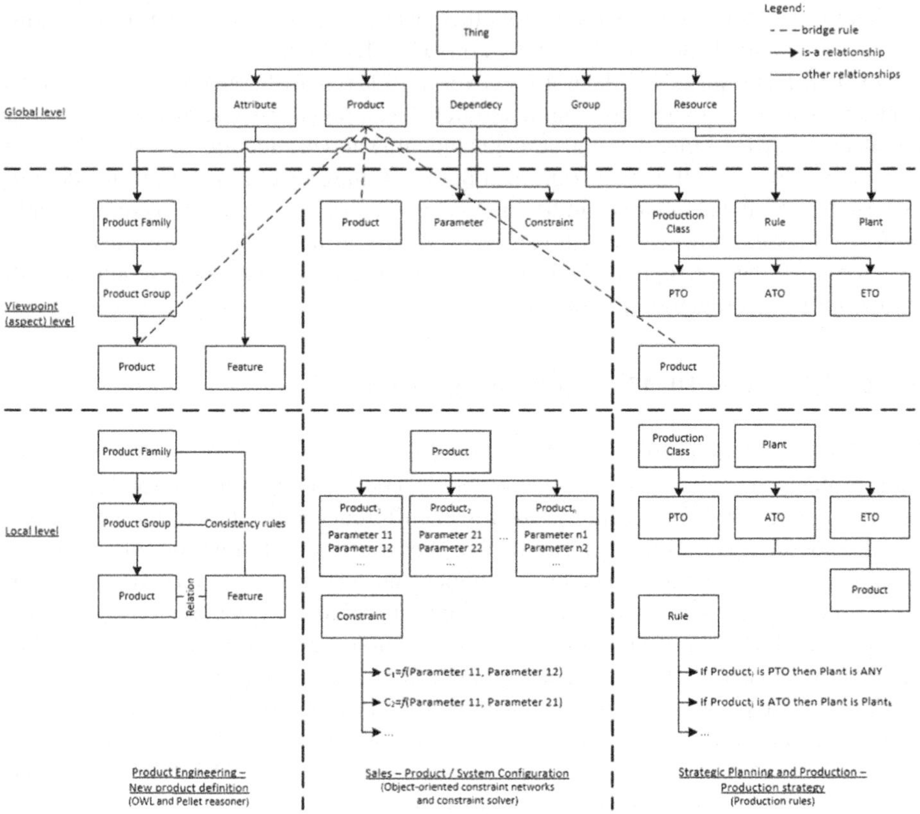

Fig. 2. Multi-aspect ontology for three viewpoints.

The task considered in the *Product Engineering* aspect, is the definition of a new product and its possible features [20]. The formalism used in this domain is OWL, and the example classes are "*Product Family*", "*Product Group*" (subclass of *Product Family*), "*Product*" (subclass of *Product Group*), and "*Feature*" (associated with the class *Product*). The product engineer needs to be able to define new classes of products and new products with their possible features and feature attributes (e.g., *Cylinder XXX* is a subclass of *Pneumatic Cylinder* and has such features as "*diameter*", "*stroke*", "*lock in end position*", and others, that, in turn, have certain attributes). However, there still has to be a possibility to ensure the consistency of product classes that is achieved via OWL and reasoning (the Pellet reasoner is currently used).

In the *Sales* aspect, the task is definition of functional dependencies between parameters of products and their processing when a product or an assembly of products are being configured by/for a customer [21]. There are three main classes in this aspect: "*Product*", "*Parameter*" (product parameter such as "*mass*", "*power*", etc.), and "*Constraints*". The formalism of object-oriented constraint networks makes it possible to define functional dependencies (represented by constraints) between product parameters and then process these via a constraint solver when a particular product or a system is being configured.

The "*Parameter*" in this aspect is not the same as "*Feature*" in the previous aspect. In certain cases, they can coincide, however, generally this is not the case.

The third aspect taken as an example, is *Strategic Planning and Production* where a production strategy is defined based on corresponding rules. The products are divided into three production classes: "PTO" (pick to order), "ATO" (assemble to order), and "ETO" (engineered to order) [22]. Based on this class, the lead time for each product is defined together with the plant, where it is to be produced. As a result, the following classes are considered in this aspect: "Production Class", "Product", "Plant". In this view, production rules ("if … then …") are used.

In accordance with [18] the following ontology elements have been defined:

Viewpoints (aspects): *Product Engineering*, *Sales*, *Strategic Planning and Production*

Global classes: *Thing, Product, Attribute, Dependency, Group, Resource.*
Local Classes:

Product Engineering: Product Family, Product Group, Product, Feature
Sales: Product, Parameter, Constraint
Strategic Planning and Production: Product, Production Class, Plant, Rule

Bridge Rules:

$Product \overset{\equiv}{\leftrightarrow} Product_{Sales}$

$Product \overset{\equiv}{\leftrightarrow} Product_{ProductEngineering}$

$Product \overset{\equiv}{\leftrightarrow} Product_{StrategicPlanningAndProduction}$

i.e., the products from different viewpoints (aspects) are the same products.

When the viewpoints and bridge rules are defined, one can use any required formalism inside each of the viewpoints. Besides, the existing models can be integrated into such a multi-view ontology without significant modification.

5 Conclusion and Future Work

The paper considers the problem of interoperability support across PLM processes via application of an ontology. The problem of heterogeneity of the processes and their respective information models is addressed through having multiple aspects within the common ontology. On the one hand, the multi-aspect ontology provides for the common vocabulary enabling the interoperability between different PLM processes and IT systems supporting these, and, on the other hand, it makes it possible to preserve internal notations and formalisms suitable for efficient solving particular tasks (e.g., configuration, planning, consistency checking, and others).

The contribution of this paper is the application of the multi-aspect ontology to PLM interoperability support and sharing experience of the design process of such an ontology. The proposed ontology is built using the OWL-MVP language aimed at support of different views (aspects) within the same ontology. It is illustrated though an example from IT projects implemented during collaboration with the automation equipment producer Festo AG&Co KG including three aspects "*Product Engineering*", "*Sales*", "*Strategic Planning and Production*"), each of them has one task.

Integration of knowledge across PLM stages is an important task and its automation is always plausible. The proposed approach has shown its efficiency for the selected case. Unfortunately, no qualitative analysis can be done to support this. Comparison of the amount of time spent for programming or the amount of code would not produce any rational results. Hence, the final decision on application of the presented approach or another, mostly depends on the goals pursued, e.g.: MBSE relies on modeling to manage systems through their entire lifecycle but does not address the semantic interoperability [23, 24], and the presented approach concentrates on the latter.

In the future, it is planned to extend the built ontology for other aspects and use it more intensively in real applications.

Acknowledgements. The paper is due to collaboration between SPIIRAS and Festo AG & Co KG, projects funded by grants ## 18-07-01201, 18-07-01272, 18-07-01203 of the Russian Foundation for Basic Research. The work has been partially financially supported by Government of Russian Federation, Grant 08-08.

References

1. Bruno, G., Antonelli, D.: Ontology-based platform for sharing knowledge on industry 4.0. In: Chiabert, P., Bouras, A., Noël, F., Ríos, J. (eds.) PLM 2018. IAICT, vol. 540, pp. 377–385. Springer, Cham (2018). https://doi.org/10.1007/978-3-030-01614-2_35
2. Ordiyasa, I.W., Nugroho, L.E., Santosa, P.I., Kumorotomo, W.: Enhancing quality of service for egovernment interoperability based on adaptive ontology. In: 2016 2nd International Conference on Science and Technology-Computer (ICST), pp 102–107. IEEE (2016)
3. European Commission Communication from the Commission to the European Parliament, the Council, the European Economic and Social Committee and the Committee of the Regions, European Interoperability Framework – Implementation Strategy (2017). https://eur-lex.europa.eu/legal-content/EN/TXT/HTML/?uri=CELEX:52017DC0134&from=EN
4. European Commission New European Interoperability Framework: Promoting seamless services and data flows for European public administrations (2017). https://ec.europa.eu/isa2/sites/isa/files/eif_brochure_final.pdf
5. European Commission ISA^2 Interoperability solutions for public administrations, businesses and citizens (2017). https://ec.europa.eu/isa2/home_en
6. Object Management Group (OMG) About the Unified Modeling Language Specification. Version 2.5 (2015). https://www.omg.org/spec/UML/2.5.1/
7. McGuinness, D.L., van Harmelen, F.: OWL web ontology language overview. W3C Recommendation (2004). https://www.w3.org/TR/owl-features/
8. Gruber, T.R.: A translation approach to portable ontology specifications. Knowl. Acquis. **5**, 199–220 (1993). https://doi.org/10.1006/knac.1993.1008
9. Smirnov, A., Shilov, N.: Multi-aspect ontology for semantic interoperability in PLM: analysis of possible notations. In: Chiabert, P., Bouras, A., Noël, F., Ríos, J. (eds.) PLM 2018. IAICT, vol. 540, pp. 314–323. Springer, Cham (2018). https://doi.org/10.1007/978-3-030-01614-2_29
10. Bruno, G., Villa, A.: The exploitation of an ontology-based model of PLM from a SME point of view. IFAC Proc. **46**, 1447–1452 (2013). https://doi.org/10.3182/20130619-3-RU-3018.00141
11. Bruno, G., Antonelli, D., Villa, A.: A reference ontology to support product lifecycle management. Procedia CIRP **33**, 41–46 (2015). https://doi.org/10.1016/j.procir.2015.06.009

12. Mostefai, S., Bouras, A.: What ontologies for PLM: a critical analysis. In: 2006 IEEE International Technology Management Conference (ICE), pp 1–8. IEEE (2006)
13. Cao, Q., Zanni-Merk, C., Reich, C.: Ontologies for manufacturing process modeling: a survey. In: Dao, D., Howlett, Robert J., Setchi, R., Vlacic, L. (eds.) KES-SDM 2018. SIST, vol. 130, pp. 61–70. Springer, Cham (2019). https://doi.org/10.1007/978-3-030-04290-5_7
14. Matsokis, A., Kiritsis, D.: An ontology-based approach for product lifecycle management. Comput. Ind. **61**, 787–797 (2010). https://doi.org/10.1016/j.compind.2010.05.007
15. Borsato, M., Estorilio, C.C.A., Cziulik, C., et al.: An ontology building approach for knowledge sharing in product lifecycle management. Int. J. Bus. Syst. Res. **4**, 278 (2010). https://doi.org/10.1504/IJBSR.2010.032951
16. Rozenfeld, H., Forcellini, F., Amaral, D.C., et al.: Product development management – a reference for process improvement (in Portuguese). Saraiva, Sao Paulo (2006)
17. Tarassov, V., Fedotova, A., Stark, R., Karabekov, B.: Granular meta-ontology and extended allen's logic: some theoretical background and application to intelligent product lifecycle management systems valery. In: Schwab, I., van Moergestel, L., Gonçalves, G. (eds.) INTELLI 2015 : The Fourth International Conference on Intelligent Systems and Applications, St. Julians, Malta, pp 86–93 (2015)
18. Hemam, M., Boufaïda, Z.: MVP-OWL: a multi-viewpoints ontology language for the Semantic Web. Int. J. Reason. Intell. Syst. **3**, 147 (2011). https://doi.org/10.1504/IJRIS.2011.043539
19. Hemam, M.: An extension of the ontology web language with multi-viewpoints and probabilistic reasoning. Int. J. Adv. Intell. Paradig. **10**, 1 (2018). https://doi.org/10.1504/IJAIP.2018.10003857
20. Oroszi, A., Jung, T., Smirnov, A., et al.: Ontology-driven codification for discrete and modular products. Int. J. Prod. Dev. **8**, 162–177 (2009). https://doi.org/10.1504/IJPD.2009.024186
21. Smirnov, A., Kashevnik, A., Teslya, N., et al.: Knowledge management for complex product development framework and implementation. IFIP Adv. Inf. Commun. Technol. **409**, 110–119 (2013)
22. Smirnov, A.V., Shilov, N., Oroszi, A., et al.: Changing information management for product-service system engineering: customer-oriented strategies and lessons learned. Int. J. Prod. Lifecycle. Manag. **11**, 1–18 (2018). https://doi.org/10.1504/IJPLM.2018.091647
23. Mordecai, Y., Orhof, O., Dori, D.: Model-based interoperability engineering in systems-of-systems and civil aviation. IEEE Trans. Syst. Man. Cybern. Syst. **48**, 637–648 (2018). https://doi.org/10.1109/TSMC.2016.2602543
24. Shani, U., Jacobs, S., Wengrowicz, N., Dori, D.: Engaging ontologies to break MBSE tools boundaries through semantic mediation. In: Conference on Systems Engineering Research (2016)

A Preliminary Method to Support the Semantic Interoperability in Models of Manufacturing (MfM) Based on an Ontological Approach

Anderson Luis Szejka[1](✉), Osiris Canciglieri Jr.[1], and Fernando Mas[2,3]

[1] Industrial and Systems Engineering Graduate Program (PPGPES), Pontifical Catholic University of Parana (PUCPR), Curitiba, Brazil
{anderson.szejka,osiris.canciglieri}@pucpr.br
[2] Airbus, Seville, Spain
fernando.mas@airbus.com
[3] Universidad de Seville, Seville, Spain

Abstract. The product design and manufacturing complexity have been increased in the last few years. This has challenged the manufacturing industry to rationalise different ways of bringing to the market novel products in a short lead-time with competitive prices while ensuring higher quality levels and customisation. Design and Simulation systems bring to the product developer experts an abstraction required for the design of complex products. However, for a complex product manufacturing process has required simultaneously collaborations with multiple groups, producing and exchanging information from multi-perspectives within and across institutional boundaries. Thousands of different information must be exchanged across heterogeneous systems. Semantic interoperability obstacles have been identified in view of the information heterogeneity from multiple perspectives and their relationships across different phases of product manufacturing. In this context, this paper presents a preliminary method for Models for Manufacturing (MfM) to support the semantic interoperability across the manufacturing system based on reference ontologies, application ontologies and semantic rules. The MfM has been modelled in reference ontologies and specialised to perform multiple specific applications according to the product to be manufactured. Semantic rules are used to share, convert or translate information from multiple perspectives in order to infer the relation between multiple manufacturing levels. The main research contributions are: (i) the intelligence structuring information in elementary concepts responsible for representing the MfM, modelled in the core ontologies (Reference Ontologies) and (ii) the improvement of information exchanging (translation, conversion and sharing) from heterogeneous domain across different phases of manufacturing process based on the semantic rules.

Keywords: Models for Manufacturing (MfM) · Semantic interoperability · Reference ontologies · Semantic rules

Published by Springer Nature Switzerland AG 2019
C. Fortin et al. (Eds.): PLM 2019, IFIP AICT 565, pp. 116–125, 2019.
https://doi.org/10.1007/978-3-030-42250-9_11

1 Introduction

Currently, in the aerospace industry, the 3D definition of the product using PLM, CAx tools and MBSE models are in a huge improvement in the Functional Design processes [1]. Additionally, globalization has impulse a new trend in the Product Development Process (PDP) through the creation of business collaborative and/or cooperative alliances between enterprises [2]. However, across the manufacturing system, despite the use of ERP, PLM, MES CAx tools and bespoke tools that has been improved along the last years, information and knowledge sharing across the product design and manufacturing systems are still undergoing [1].

This trend requires new methods to share information in an efficient way, without misinterpretation and mistakes. The traditional ERP, PLM, MES, CAx approaches is often hindered by the lack of clarity, multiples taxonomy and structures used by different designers, engineers and other stakeholders. Thus, thousands of heterogeneous information and knowledge must simultaneously share across different phases of the manufacturing system [3–5]. The information and knowledge sharing, therefore, presents two main problems that are known as semantic heterogeneity, (i) the same term is being applied to different concepts (semantic problem) and (ii) different terms are being applied to the same concept (syntax problem) [6].

The solution to this problem lies in addressing interoperability issues [7, 8]. Interoperability is the capacity of two or more systems to share information and to use the information that has been shared [9]. The European Commission [10] classifies interoperability, according to the typology, in three major categories: (i) technical interoperability, (ii) semantic interoperability and (iii) organizational interoperability. Technical interoperability concerns technological issues as data format and protocols, computational connections, etc. Organizational interoperability concerns the sharing of business models and processes as organization structure, business cooperation, etc. Semantic Interoperability concerns the information meaning that is proper and understandable by different systems (human, computer, machine, etc.). According to this definition, the misinterpretation and mistake issues across the product development cycle is a typical problem of semantic interoperability.

Related works [11, 12] present different approaches to support semantic interoperability through the ontology. Ontology is defined as a formal, explicit specification of a shared conceptualization [13]. In this definition, the formal model indicates that ontology isthis research, showing the essential methods and tools machine-readable, that is, the format of the ontology can be understood and processed by computers. Furthermore, ontology-based models have had an increase in their role of achieving semantic interoperability among the different stakeholders across the manufacturing systems. Nonetheless, the process of integrating and interoperating across several ontologies is still a difficult one as physical and logical differences among information sources complicate information retrieval and formalization. Even though ontology mapping and matching techniques were developed to tackle the issues of cross-ontology interoperability, they remain weak in their ability to enable relationship formalization and verification in the cross-model approach for the product design and manufacture.

In this context, this paper presents a preliminary method for Models for Manufacturing (MfM) to support the semantic interoperability across the manufacturing system based on reference ontologies, application ontologies and semantic rules. The MfM has been modelled in reference ontologies and specialized to perform multiple specific applications according to the product to be manufactured. Semantic rules are used to share, convert or translate information from multiple perspectives in order to infer the relation between multiple manufacturing levels. Moreover, the main research contributions are: (i) the intelligence structuring information in elementary concepts responsible for representing the MfM, modelled in the core ontologies (Reference Ontologies) and (ii) the improvement of information exchanging (translation, conversion and sharing) from heterogeneous domain across different phases of manufacturing process based on the semantic rules.

2 Problem Statement

Product Development Process (PDP) is used to speed up the new product launching and markets expansion while fulfilling the costumer's demand and desires. PDP has a holistic view and provides the necessary information to the different stages of product development and manufacturing. However, semantic problems can be identified across the PDP as the developers do not use the same product taxonomy, which may cause requirements misinterpretation and mistakes during the product realisation due to the information heterogeneity [2]. In this context, the research focused on the information and knowledge formalisation to support the development of a conceptual framework to provide seamless information interoperability across multiple domains in the PDP [3, 8, 12].

Semantic Interoperability issues become a significant problem as the activities of the design and manufacture cost 85% of the products final cost [12]. Therefore, the information sharing across the different stages of product development and manufacture must be done efficiently to ensure that the product developed has the desired quality with cost and time optimization.

For a complex product manufacturing process has required simultaneously collaborations with multiple groups, producing and exchanging information from multi-perspectives within and across institutional boundaries. Figure 1 illustrates the semantic interoperability obstacles which have been identified in view of the information heterogeneity from multiple perspectives and their relationships across different phases of product manufacturing. During the product design, manufacturing and production of aerospace, the information must be shared with multiples experts by different systems in across multiples phases (design, manufacturing and production).

The standardized and formalised knowledge that is captured by an ontology-driven system allows it to be retrieved, shared and reused in different stages of the product development and manufacture and, also, through the process of relating concepts made in the ontology design the information can be captured in its entirety as well as extended as the need arises. This system capability improves the collaboration in a multiple domain environment and across network based designs as it conveys several characteristics, that are often ambiguous, in a non-ambiguous manner, while the high degree of expressiveness of an ontology-driven structure enables the establishment of resolvable and meaningful

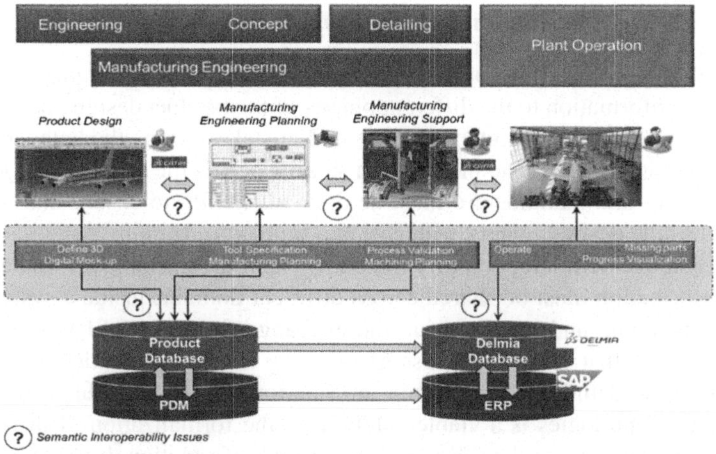

Fig. 1. Product design, manufacturing and production interdependency.

mappings across knowledge models which help support the consistency of the ontology matching while also avoiding the drawbacks of subjectivity in the mapping transaction that are a consequence of extensive human intervention.

3 Technological Background

This chapter shows the literature review responsible for the presentation of the necessary concepts to the development of this research, showing the essential methods and tools for the completion of the research. The topics approached in this review are: Semantic Interoperability and Concurrent Engineering.

3.1 Models for Manufacturing (MfM)

MfM is an approach proposed by the authors to apply Model-Based Systems Engineering (MBSE) concepts to Manufacturing [1]. Functional and data models have been published and deployed using data structures available from commercial PLM systems [14].

Some related works [15–17] are exploring the development and deployment of MBSE methodologies and tools in manufacturing systems. Some recent research topics address aspects like process planning, human resources, robotics, IoT (Internet of Things).

The MfM proposed in [18] is based on 3-Layers Model, Data Layer, Ontology Layer and Service Layer. The Ontology layer defines (i) Scope model, (ii) Data model, (iii) Behaviour model, and (iv) Semantic model, to further instance information from existing databases [18]. Scope model is required because manufacturing systems have a large and wide part of the artefact lifecycle. Data model covers different several uses across the manufacturing systems. As discussed in (Mas), software architecture to support the methodology is being developed using Free and Open Source Software (FOSS) tools. A PLM tool, ARAS Innovator [19], is the core of the system. Other tools like IDEF0 [20] and CMap [21] are used by [1] as modelling tools.

3.2 Ontology-Driven Semantic Interoperability

Even though the product development process presents a holistic approach to provide the necessary information to the different phases of the product design and manufacturing, it has been identified misinterpretations and mistakes during the latter stages of the product development [12]. The information sharing across the different stages of product development and manufacture must be done efficiently to ensure that the product developed has the desired quality with cost and time optimization.

This is a semantic interoperability issue for which the meaning associated with the captured information must be shared across different domains inside a system without any loss of meaning and intent during the exchange process [8]. The most common method to ensure that there is no loss of meaning in the information exchange process has been the definition of common information models [22]. In this context, the construction of ontologies is a viable solution on the formalization of these common information models and on the sharing of the formal information throughout the stages of the product development process, which, consequently, provides increased knowledge in the domains of application [23].

An Ontology is defined as "a lexicon of specialized terminology along with some specification of the meaning of terms on the lexicon" [24], where the lexicon is the vocabulary of a knowledge domain. The use of ontologies is restricted to the purpose of its application, that is, the knowledge structure formalized in an ontology has little reusability outside the scope of its application [8]. Despite the semantic formalism created using ontologies, a limitation appears when the need to work in multiple knowledge domains is presented, as the semantic formalism of the ontology cannot ensure the sharing of the information and its meaning through different domains. However, this problem is moderated with the development of ontology mapping methodologies, which can create relationships between terms in different ontologies of different domains [25].

The Web Ontology Language (OWL) relies only on description logic, however, both description logic and rules are required for a semantic web application because they can overcome expressiveness limitations through extensions of different knowledge domains. Nevertheless, each paradigm supports specific reasoning services and for them to work efficiently there is a need to close integration between the description logic and semantic rules [2].

3.3 Concurrent Engineering in Manufacturing Systems

The intensification of the economic competitive environment due to globalization has put more pressure on the industries to release new products to the market. This happens because an industry long time survival in this environment is made through new products, that is, in order to maintain its competitiveness, it is necessary to the industry to develop and release new products. Therefore, in the last decades, tools and methodologies to increase the efficiency and reduce the cost and time of the product development process have been developed [26]. The author uses as an example of these methods the Lean Product Development, which uses the concepts proposed by the Toyota Production System and applies them in the stages of the product development, and Concurrent

Engineering, which aims to parallelize the tasks of the product development in order to reduce costs and time.

In this context, the objective of [26] is to create a lean product development environment through the application of concurrent engineering. According to [26] and [27], concurrent engineering happens when the development team think, communicate and search solutions in a parallel way, that is, the development team communicates through the stages of the PDP searching for solutions as soon as they can identify a problem. [28] assesses the application of concurrent engineering in the Toyota enterprise and made a comparison between the parallel and sequential product development.

4 Interoperable Manufacturing System Method Concept

The Interoperable Manufacturing System method proposed in this research uses two main approaches: (i) Models for Manufacturing (MfM) approach proposed by [1]; and (ii) the Interoperable Product Design and Manufacturing System (IPDM) proposed by [29]. The MfM approach considers 3-Layers Model: (i) Data Layer, (ii) Ontology Layer, and (iii) Service Layer. The IPDMS approach is structured with 3 main perspective/view: (i) Reference View, (ii) Application Domain View and (iii) Semantic Reconciliation View. IPDMS uses semantical well-defined Core and Constraints concepts formalized in Ontology References with knowledge and information from multiple domains to simultaneously instantiate with data from the real process in the Application Domain View, according to the specific product information and technological limitations. In addition, semantic relationships can be established between instantiated information, allowing their semantic mappings of translation, sharing and conversion between different phases of product design and manufacturing. Based on two approaches, Fig. 2 presents the preliminary architecture of the Interoperable Manufacturing System Method (IMSM). ISMS is composed of 4-layers: (i) Ontology Layer; (ii) Application-Domain Layer; (iii) Semantic Reconciliation Layer; and (iv) Data Layer.

- **Ontology Layer** (Detail "A" of Fig. 2) – It defines the reference of knowledge, modelling in an elementary form, to represent different perspectives of the product and its manufacturing in a formal way. The knowledge is modelled in a common logic-based formalism using Web Ontology Language (OWL). Reference ontologies may be composed by Product Engineering, Manufacturing Engineering Reference Ontology, Machining Reference Ontology, etc. The reference ontologies formalization was explored in [30].
- **Application Domain Layer** (Detail "B" of Fig. 2) – The concepts from the Ontology Layer are specialized into a manufacturing system ontology (application ontology), according to the specific data about the product or the manufacturing process. This specialization process must respect the semantic rules to ensure the correct relationship of this information. The data constitutes the Knowledge Model with information about the Product and/or Manufacturing and comes from different phases of the lifecycle. As this information is formally defined in a common language, it is possible to compare and verify the information without losing their meaning in an interoperable manner with semantic rules. Additionally, an inference reasoner (Pellet) is in a continuous analysis to identify information inconsistencies and information traceability.

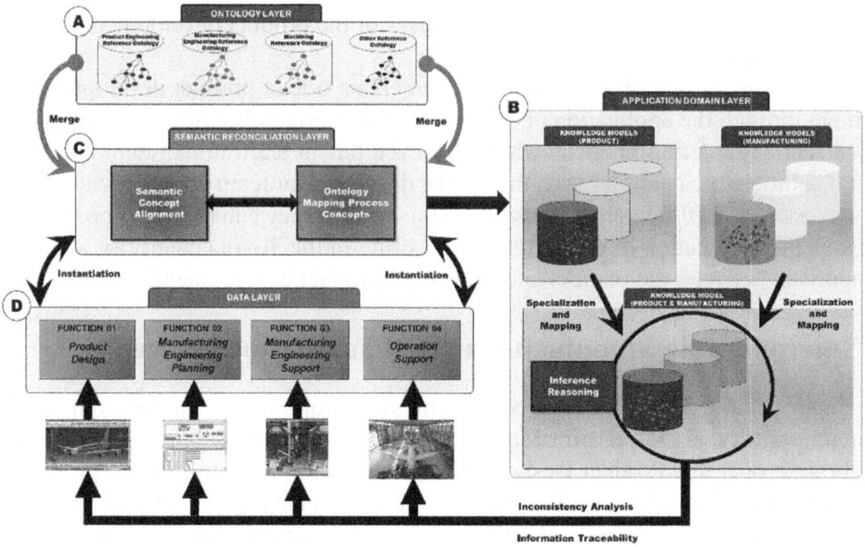

Fig. 2. Preliminary interoperable manufacturing system method architecture.

- **Semantic Reconciliation Layer** (Detail "C" of Fig. 2) – It defines the semantic rules for information relationship from Ontology Layer, Application Domain Layer and Data Layer. The Semantic Reconciliation Layer is composed of three main modules: (i) Context Alignment; (ii) Ontology Intersection; (iii) Semantic Mapping. Context Alignment is the first phase of semantic reconciliation and executes the alignment of data from data layer with the concepts in the ontology layer, i.e. the context is aligned according to the product that will be developed. Ontology Intersection is responsible for connected multiple ontologies from the ontology layer and specialized them according to specific information from the Data Layer. Finally, the semantic mapping is responsible to relate all information in the Application Domain Layer. It allows the establishment of the relationships with the information from multiple perspectives. The alignment process is enabled by the specialized semantic rules that allow inferring the semantic mapping during the Product Design, Manufacturing Engineering Planning, Manufacturing Engineering Support and Operation Support. The semantic rules are a binary relation that describes the semantic relationships from "A" to "B" ($A \Rightarrow B$), where "A" is the antecedent and "B" is consequent. "A" has multiple conditions that are from product constraints, technological restrictions, etc. All conditions in "A" must be "true" to infer the semantic mapping with "B". Table 1 presents the syntax to build the semantic rules.

Data Layer (Detail "D" of Fig. 2) – It collects all the information, databases and interfaces: legacy databases from the legacy software, databases from the commercial software applications, clouds and data lakes databases and many others. Included in the Data layer are those databases to hold the information instanced using Ontology layer.

Table 1. Syntaxes to build the conditions of semantic rules [30].

Rules	Syntax	Description
Equivalence	Equal(C_1,C_2)	Satisfied iff the first argument and the second argument are the same
Contradiction	NotEqual(C_1,C_2)	The negation of equivalence
Lesser than	LessThan(C_1,C_2)	Satisfied iff the first argument is less than the second argument
Greater than	GreaterThan(C_1,C_2)	Satisfied iff the first argument is greater than the second argument
Lesser or equal than	LessThanOrEqual(C_1,C_2)	Satisfied iff the first argument is less than or equal to the second argument
Greater or equal than	GreaterThanOrEqual(C_1,C_2)	Satisfied iff the first argument is greater than or equal to the second argument
Sum	Add(R,C_1,C_2)	Satisfied iff the first argument is equal to the arithmetic sum of the second argument through the last argument
Subtraction	Subtract(R,C_1,C_2)	Satisfied iff the first argument is equal to the arithmetic difference of the second argument minus the third argument
Multiplication	Multiply(R,C_1,C_2)	Satisfied iff the first argument is equal to the arithmetic product of the second argument through the last argument
Division	Division(R,C_1,C_2)	Satisfied iff the first argument is equal to the arithmetic quotient of the second argument divided by the third argument

5 Conclusion and Further Work

A preliminary method to support the semantic interoperability in Models of Manufacturing (MfM) based on an ontological approach is a novel way to integrate and establish the semantic relationship of multiple information from different platforms across the manufacturing system. Additionally, this method contributes to the decision support systems area and providing the right information for design and manufacturing activities. The preliminary ISMS method is based on the 4-Layer Model, that allows the development of aerospace projects in an integrated manner via formal information originated in well-defined structure data and relationships mechanisms (translation, conversion and sharing). In this way, heterogeneous data from multiple views of the Product Design and Manufacturing are instantiated in the core concepts, in a well-defined manner, through semantic rules, which enables the creation of an interoperable environment for the manufacturing system. Knowledge of the relationships between multiple views has been captured in semantic mapping mechanisms for translating, converting and sharing information across multiple views, which certifies the correct semantic information interoperability in the product design and manufacturing.

The further ISMS method tasks planned are: (i) improve the definition of semantic reconciliation layer and application domain layer; (ii) define the methods to the semantic mapping (iii) detailed the instantiation approach from the data layer. Finally, there is a requirement to evaluate the framework with an aerospace experimental case.

References

1. Mas, F., Racero, J., Oliva, M., Morales-Palma, D.: Preliminary ontology definition for aerospace assembly lines in Airbus using Models for Manufacturing methodology. Procedia Manuf. **28**, 207–213 (2019)
2. Szejka, A.L., Canciglieri Jr., O., Panetto, H., Loures, E.R., Aubry, A.: Semantic interoperability for an integrated product development process: a systematic literature review. Int. J. Prod. Res. **55**, 6691–6709 (2017)
3. Nagy, M., Vargas-Vera, M.: Multiagent ontology mapping framework for the semantic web. IEEE Trans. Syst. Man Cybern. Part A: Syst. Hum. **41**, 693–704 (2011)
4. Beau, S., Taouil, F.-T., Hassanaly, P.: Elaborate knowledge between necessity and opportunity. In: Proceedings of The Third International Conference of Information Systems and Economic Intelligence (Siie), Sousse, Tunisia, pp. 317–30 (2010)
5. Kim, K.-Y., Chin, S., Kwon, O., Ellis, R.D.: Ontology-based modeling and integration of morphological characteristics of assembly joints for network-based collaborative assembly design. AI EDAM **23**, 71–88 (2009)
6. Lin, H.-K., Harding, J.A., Shahbaz, M.: Manufacturing system engineering ontology for semantic interoperability across extended project teams. Int. J. Prod. Res. **42**, 5099–5118 (2004)
7. Belkadi, F., Dremont, N., Notin, A., Troussier, N., Messadia, M.: A meta-modelling framework for knowledge consistency in collaborative design. Ann. Rev. Control **36**, 346–358 (2012)
8. Chungoora, N., et al.: A model-driven ontology approach for manufacturing system interoperability and knowledge sharing. Comput. Ind. **64**, 392–401 (2013)
9. Institute of Electrical and Electronics Engineers, IEEE Standard Computer Dictionary: A Compilation of IEEE Standard Computer Glossaries, IEEE (1990). ISBN: 1559370793
10. European Commission, EIF 2.0 – European Interoperability Framework for European public services [white paper] (2010). http://goo.gl/4ZZLPt
11. Palmer, C., Usman, Z., Junior, O.C., Malucelli, A., Young, R.I.M.: Interoperable manufacturing knowledge systems. Int. J. Prod. Res. **56**, 2733–2752 (2018)
12. Penciuc, D., Durupt, A., Belkadi, F., Eynard, B., Rowson, H.: Towards a PLM interoperability for a collaborative design support system. Procedia CIRP **25**, 369–376 (2014)
13. Gruber, T.R.: Toward principles for the design of ontologies used for knowledge sharing. In: Formal Ontology in Conceptual Analysis and Knowledge Representation, pp. 1–22. Kluwer Academic Publishers, Padova (1993)
14. Gómez, A., Ríos, J., Mas, F., Vizán, A.: Method and software application to assist in the conceptual design of aircraft final assembly lines. J. Manuf. Syst. **40**, 37–53 (2016)
15. Ríos, J., Morate, F.M., Oliva, M., Hernández, J.C.: Framework to support the aircraft digital counterpart concept with an industrial design view. Int. J. Agile Syst. Manag. **9**, 212–231 (2016)

16. Lundgren, M., Hedlind, M., Kjellberg, T.: Model driven manufacturing process design and managing quality. Procedia CIRP **50**, 299–304 (2016)
17. Heike, G., Ramulu, M., Sorenson, E., Shanahan, P., Moinzadeh, K.: Mixed model assembly alternatives for low-volume manufacturing: the case of the aerospace industry. Int. J. Prod. Econ. **72**, 103–120 (2001)
18. Mas, F., Racero, J., Oliva, M., Morales-Palma, D.: A preliminary methodological approach to models for manufacturing (MfM). In: Chiabert, P., Bouras, A., Noël, F., Ríos, J. (eds.) PLM 2018. IAICT, vol. 540, pp. 273–283. Springer, Cham (2018). https://doi.org/10.1007/978-3-030-01614-2_25
19. Shariatzadeh, N., Gurdur, D., El-Khoury, J., Lindberg, L., Sivard, G.: Using linked data with information standards for interoperability in production engineering. Procedia CIRP **41**, 502–507 (2016)
20. NIST, "Integration Definition for Function Modeling (IDEF0)", Computer Systems Laboratory of the National Institute of Standards and Technology, December 1993. http://www.idef.com/wp-content/uploads/2016/02/idef0.pdf. Accessed Mar 2019
21. Cañas, Alberto J., et al.: Concept maps: integrating knowledge and information visualization. In: Tergan, S.-O., Keller, T. (eds.) Knowledge and Information Visualization. LNCS, vol. 3426, pp. 205–219. Springer, Heidelberg (2005). https://doi.org/10.1007/11510154_11
22. Canciglieri, O.J., Young, R.I.M.: Information mapping across injection moulding design and manufacture domains. Int. J. Prod. Res. **48**, 4437–4462 (2010)
23. Yang, S., Guo, J., Wei, R.: Semantic interoperability with heterogeneous information systems on the internet through automatic tabular document exchange. Inf. Syst. **69**, 195–217 (2017)
24. Durbha, S.S., King, R.L., Shah, V.P., Younan, N.H.: A framework for semantic reconciliation of disparate earth observation thematic data. Comput. Geosci. **35**, 761–773 (2009)
25. Yin, Y.H., Nee, A.Y.C., Ong, S.K., Zhu, J.Y., Gu, P.H., Chen, L.J.: Automating design with intelligent human–machine integration. CIRP Ann. **64**, 655–677 (2015)
26. Al-Ashaab, A., et al.: The transformation of product development process into lean environment using set-based concurrent engineering: a case study from an aerospace industry. Concurr. Eng. **21**, 268–285 (2013)
27. Sobek, D.K., Ward, A.C., Likker, J.K.: Toyota's principles of set-based concurrent engineering. Sloan Manag. Rev. **40**, 67–83 (1999)
28. Xie, Y., Ma, Y.: Design of a multi-disciplinary and feature-based collaborative environment for chemical process projects. Exp. Syst. Appl. **42**, 4149–4166 (2015)
29. Szejka, A.L.: Contribution to interoperable products design and manufacturing information: application to plastic injection products manufacturing. Thesis (PhD) – Pontifical Catholic University of Parana, Curitiba, and University of Lorraine, Nancy, p. 297 (2016)
30. Szejka, A.L., Canciglieri Junior, O.: The application of reference ontologies for semantic interoperability in an integrated product development process in smart factories. Procedia Manuf. **11**, 1375–1384 (2017)

An Approach to Semantic Interoperability for Product Development Through Automatic Requirement Extraction and Semantic Reconciliation

Matheus Beltrame Canciglieri, Athon Francisco Curi Staben de Moura Leite, Anderson Luis Szejka(✉), and Osiris Canciglieri Junior

Industrial and Systems Engineering Graduate Program, Pontifical Catholic University of Parana, Curitiba, Brazil
{matheus.canciglieri,athon.leite,anderson.szejka, osiris.canciglieri}@pucpr.br

Abstract. The strong competitiveness challenges manufacturing industry to rationalize different ways of bringing new products to the market in the shortest time with competitive prices while ensuring higher quality. Industries need to effectively share product requirements, which comes from various sources and are heterogeneous in nature, during the Product Development Process (PDP) to stay competitive. However, problems with misinterpretation of such requirements have been identified during its sharing due to semantic interoperability obstacles related to the process of automatically gathering requirements and their translation and reuse. This research proposes an approach to automatically gather product requirements, extracting its knowledge and translate it for further use and reuse along PDP. The research structure consisted of firstly studying the current issues of the topic, secondly by exploring an approach, to be validated in an experimental case. Current issues point out to gaps related to the process of semantic reconciliation and knowledge extraction perspectives, giving it a multi-dimensional panorama where semantic issues are intertwined among different perspectives. The later solution presents an approach which considers raw information being processed into product features, refining knowledge during PDP and making it reusable in different cycles. The approach brings a new view on practical methods for automatically collect product requirements, extract its knowledge and translate it into product features, based on knowledge extraction methods and by using semantic reconciliation as means for translating product's requirements. Further research will focus on expanding the approach and including more features to increasingly complex cases, to explore the full potential of the approach.

Keywords: Product Development Process · Multiple domains · Knowledge extraction · Product design and manufacturing · Semantic reconciliation · Semantic Interoperability

Published by Springer Nature Switzerland AG 2019
C. Fortin et al. (Eds.): PLM 2019, IFIP AICT 565, pp. 126–135, 2019.
https://doi.org/10.1007/978-3-030-42250-9_12

1 Introduction

The current panorama of product development is defined by sets of complex requirements, higher standards of quality, changes in value perception and products that better fulfill customer's needs. In this context, product development relates to current trends on smart factories, integrated manufacturing systems and Industry 4.0, which in the product lifecycle scenario accompanies the use of technologies and methods to improve communication and support the decision-making process.

The market needs related to quick development cycles demands parallelism of activities and knowledge from different areas, using information technologies as a basis for communication across development. An Integrated Product Development Process (IPDP), in this context, considers multiple domains and various sources of knowledge as a means of gathering requirements to new or improved products. These requirements must have a good definition and must be shared without losing their meaning, in order to avoid incoherency, misinterpretation and other negative impacts during development, such as delays and increased costs [1].

Current praxis is still not able to cope with all semantic issues within an integrated product development process, as requirements must be clear, consistent, measurable, stand-alone, testable, unambiguous, unique and verifiable [2]. These issues are mostly caused by different taxonomies, divergent views from professionals of different areas and limitations in the translation of knowledge in product development phases. Consequently, the misinterpretation of market requirements and development mistakes are a result of heterogeneous information from different domains of knowledge [2].

To address such problems, the concept of Semantic Interoperability aims to ensure the effective sharing of information in a collaborative environment with multiple domains of knowledge. Semantic Interoperability is currently being applied in the context of product design and manufacturing, to reduce mistakes and heterogeneity in information [3]. There are still, though, problems with its implementation, regarding the methods to automatic requirement extraction and translation from different sources and organize it in a standardized way [3, 4]. In this context, this research aims to develop an approach to gather, organize and translate product requirements in a standardized manner, reducing heterogeneity of interpretation during product development in multiple domain environments.

2 Conceptual Background

2.1 Product Development Process

The Product Development Process approaches different domains of knowledge, involving specialists from different areas with multiple viewpoints. The transdisciplinary nature of PDP activities represents a holistic approach, which meets the requirements and constraints (laws, specification, etc.), respecting technical limitations and enterprise's goals [1]. Authors [5–7] cite development environments as integrated, communicative, collaborative and interoperable as, according to [7], the better the product information is defined, the lesser the misinterpretation, mistakes, and semantic barriers occurrence.

Most of the more systematic approaches for PDP consider three main phases: Pre-Development, Development and Post Development. Current models normally emphasize the systematization process of the Product Development Process. Originally, PDP was defined as a linear flow, with later activities starting after the conclusion of the previous ones [1]. Later approaches review this structure by inserting parallelism along the development cycle [5–7]. This structure allows a better design of information and the understanding of how to formalize it, in order to reduce the misinterpretation. There are not, though, enough methods that ensure the seamless information interoperation along development cycles.

The representation of knowledge in PDP has a direct impact on the capability of information semantically interoperate [2]. This is due to the degree of standardization in structured information. The Product Development Process has two most significant types of model to represent its knowledge: the product model [2, 8]; and the manufacturing model [2, 9].

Current research on this field points out the need for ensuring interoperability between product and manufacturing models since there occur misinterpretation issues when the product development approaches multiple domains of knowledge [4]. The researches found on [2, 9–11] presented a tendency to use ontological approaches to gather and formalize knowledge in product and/or manufacturing models.

2.2 Ontology-Driven Semantic Interoperability

The use of ontologies has increased for the development of shared representations. Recent research, as shown in [2, 9, 11] proved that the ability for sharing semantics across these representations is supported by ontological formalisms. Currently, ontology is recognized as a key technology to deal with semantic issues related to interoperation [12]. Its computational structure has been developed to provide a machine-processable semantics of varied knowledge sources [13].

In spite of its contributions to semantic wholeness, it is worth mention that even when using ontology-based methods to assure sharing semantics, semantic heterogeneity is still unavoidable and, for this reason, methods for ontology mapping are in development to reconcile semantics between ontologies that need to interoperate [14].

In the field of application, ontologies can be categorized into three levels of abstraction, depending on the deepness in which the ontology aims to represent a knowledge [3]:

- **Foundation Ontology** - suited for general concepts and relationship, can be used in different domains;
- **Reference Ontology** - Domain-specific ontology, reusable for different activities in the same domains;
- **Application Level Ontology** - represents specific knowledge, dedicated to a task.

2.3 Semantic Reconciliation Methods

Ontology integration is the process of finding common aspects between different ontologies, creating a new ontology with its common aspects. [15] discussed the distinction among integration approaches, as follows:

- **Ontology Inclusion** - simple inclusion of an ontology in the other's structure;
- **Ontology Mapping** - processing of similarities and relations from different sources through equivalent relations and combining it at one new ontology;
- **Ontology Merging** - processing a vast number of data sources through a mediator and querying process to achieve a newly combined ontology

Even though ontology mapping/matching has been key to solve semantic heterogeneity problems, there is a present of methods that rely on lexical similarity matching, which is not optimal from a semantic interoperability viewpoint. This is because in multiple domain environments similar terms are used across different groups to refer to diverse concepts. Ergo, it is only through the semantics associated with these terms that existing differences can be identified, highlighting the need to capture semantics in the first place [3].

On the other hand, ontological formalisms lite the Web Ontology Language (OWL) support built-ins for ontology mapping, however, these built-ins have limitations when mapping the semantic content of manufacturing ontologies and their associated knowledge bases [3].

Moreover, there are requirements to aid the construction of mapping/matching techniques which can be formally interpreted and are focused at identifying potential solutions for semantic mismatches. Therefore, enabling the reconciliation process at several levels, including the instance level, of ontology-based models. These requirements aid the reconciliation process to have better accuracy, automation and reduces the time that takes to resolve cross-model correspondences [16].

3 Research Development for an Approach to Semantic Interoperability for Product Development

3.1 Problem Statement

Modern Product Development Process (PDP) has required simultaneous collaborations of multiple groups, producing and exchanging information from multi-perspectives within and across institutional boundaries. However, semantic obstacles have been identified during this process, affecting the process of product development. In this context, [] identified in their research three main issues: (i) Cross Domain issue; (ii) Cross PDP Phases Issues; and (iii) Cross Requirement Representation and Translation Issues.

In *Cross Domain issue* to standardize the structure of information in different domains, representation models were developed, such as UML (Unified Modelling Language), Model-Driven Engineering (MDE), Domain Specific Language (DSL), and others [17–19]. Despite presenting an intent to formalize and represent knowledge from various domains in a standardized manner, those models do not present in an accurate way the dynamic nature of market requirements and knowledge from different product development and manufacturing phases [19].

Recently, few models consider the consistency of requirements and performance in dynamic environments. In [20], the authors explain a design framework for cyber-physical systems, based on the design rationale, connecting different design parameters and requirements from varied sources. In [3], the authors explore the Manufacturing domain and requirement's gathering from different domains. Both researches have combined different models in order to achieve verifiable and validated information within a dynamic requirements context, but still, there is a significant presence of specialist's decisions during the process of translating requirements. This might result in semantic issues, as there are subjective factors and different methods related to each domain.

To *Cross PDP phases issue,* the communication in PDP relies heavily on the semantic interpretation of each agent [21]. Across different phases, the different set of information may cause misinterpretation due to variable meanings for a term. This occurs due to the different knowledge background of developers and their experience in different stages of product development [7, 19, 21]. Corroborating that, [19] states that the knowledge required for a stage of the development process may have different implications in later activities, being changeable due to the dynamic nature of product development requirements.

Currently, as demonstrated in [3], literature proposes a formalization through semantic annotations for semantically interoperable applications, regarding different views in PLM. There are no annotations, however, that accurately represent dynamic requirements in mentioned research. In [22], the author proposes a solution to cross-PDP issues based on a model-driven ontology, which was limited to two domains and presented no continuity for further expansion and integration for more domains.

In Cross Requirement Representation and Translation Issues, requirements represent the main inputs in an ontology-driven semantically interoperable system. This knowledge must be 'semantically whole', to avoid further interoperation issues, by using formalized structures, well-defined statements and axioms [4]. In most cases, however, the abstraction of poorly defined statements ends up generating divergent interpretation, which might result in issues related to the uniqueness, the comprehensiveness and, most important, the traceability of information [2].

Correct, consistent and traceable information can prevent further inconsistencies in product development and manufacture [23]. In [23], a framework for semantic interoperability corroborates this view. Despite that, the provided framework do not ensure the requirements' traceability and optimization of knowledge gathering and its structuring process. In [24], the author presented an interoperable model considering multiple domains to ensure traceability through validation and verification methods. This model, however, was limited only to the early phases of a system. Current research, as shown in [2], points to standardized forms of extracting knowledge and information and ensure its traceability through verification and validation, but still with no automatic requirement extraction.

3.2 Main Research Questions

Globalization, collaboration, and cooperation have contributed to the emergence of a knowledge sharing culture in open and large environments. However, communication between project teams is often hindered by the lack of clarity in the terms used. This represents that the context in which the information is exchanged affects the overall meaning and interpretation of the shared implicit and explicit knowledge. Therefore, two problems may appear: (i) *the same term is being applied to different concepts (semantic problem)* and (ii) *different terms are being applied to the same concept (syntax problem)* [25]. These problems are known as semantic heterogeneity

One approach to solve these problems is the creation of an ontology in which a specific domain's concepts and terms are defined and can be understood through the different teams across that domain. Nevertheless, this presents a different issue: *How can the knowledge be shared effectively through multiple domain systems without the problems caused by semantic heterogeneity?*

3.3 The Approach to Semantic Interoperability for Product Development Through Automatic Requirement Extraction and Semantic Reconciliation

In order to answer this problem, an approach is proposed in Fig. 1 that aims to apply semantic interoperability concepts and tools to develop an interoperable environment that can efficiently represent and translate knowledge between different stages of the product development process and analyze the consistency of the created knowledge, reducing the misunderstandings and mistakes caused by semantic heterogeneity.

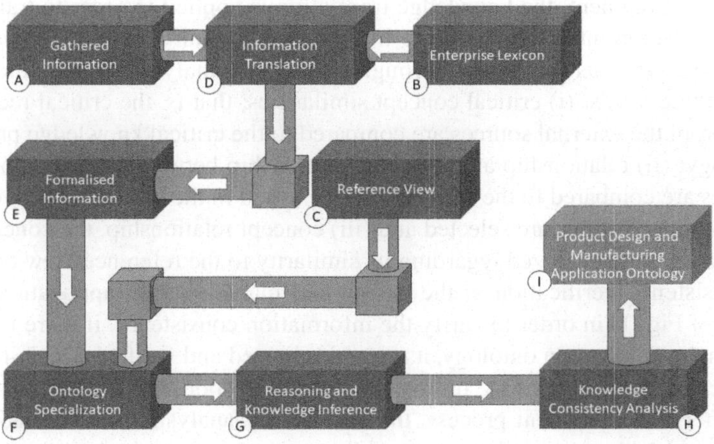

Fig. 1. Proposed semantic interoperable system for product development process and manufacturing.

The proposed approach showed in Fig. 1 is divided into 9 stages. The first one (Detail A of Fig. 1) consists in gathering knowledge from the consumer, using tools as the Quality

Function Deployment (QFD) or through an enterprise´s Customer Relationship Management software, alongside Computer Aided Design/Computer Aided Manufacturing (CAD/CAM) and production planning and control systems.

This information is gathered from different sources and, therefore, it is heterogeneous, as the information is presented differently by the different tools. Therefore, before this information can be used in the decision process, it must be translated and for this process to happen, a lexicon of the enterprise‘s terms is needed (Detail B of Fig. 1). This lexicon contains all the enterprise concepts, their associated context, and explicit meaning and is formalized in an OWL format.

Alongside the enterprise‘s lexicon, the proposed approach has a reference view (Detail C of Fig. 1), which gathers information from within the enterprise alongside the real world and represents it in a high-level abstraction of different domains through ontological models. These models are considered the knowledge core of the proposed approach.

The gathered information is translated into useful information (Detail D of Fig. 1) to the product development decision making process through an ontology alignment where the gathered information is compared to the lexicon in order to create a formalized information structure that can be used by the enterprise without mistakes. This information is structured in an OWL format to allow the proposed approach to further refine it and to share it across all stages of the product development process (Detail E of Fig. 1).

With the necessary knowledge gathered and formalized in an ontology, the proposed approach uses an ontology alignment to create the application ontology for this stage (Detail F of Fig. 1). The ontology alignment first "cuts" the useful information from the different ontologies, the gathered information ontology and the reference view ontologies, and then "merges" them into an application ontology.

After the alignment, the knowledge translation is applied in order to transform the design information into manufacturing information (Detail G of Fig. 1). This translation, as in the previous step occurs through a similarity analysis made by the inference engine in three levels; (i) critical concept similarities, that is, the critical requirements gathered from the external sources are compared to the critical knowledge presented in the ontology; (ii) relationship analysis, the relationship between concepts in the external sources are compared to the relationship presented in the reference view ontologies and any similar relations are selected and (iii) concept relationship, the concepts of the external sources are analyzed regarding its similarity to the reference view ontologies.

A consistency verification in the design and manufacturing application ontology (Detail H of Fig. 1) in order to verify the information consistency, if there is an inconsistency in the application ontology, it must be adjusted and verified which information from the external sources or the reference view was responsible for this error and corrected. After the adjustment process, the consistency analysis must be made again in order to avoid ambiguous information. If there was no inconsistency the ontology is shared with the next stage of the IPDP.

The resulting ontology from this stage shares the product design and manufacturing planning to the fabrication process, where the product will be mass produced. This planning is shared through the hierarchical structure of the design and manufacturing planning application ontology (Detail I of Fig. 1).

3.4 Experimental Case

In order to validate the proposed approach, a conceptual experimental case is proposed. For this experimental case, the product chosen Uninterrupted Power Supply (UPS) with the potency of 20 kVA as it was being reformulated, through the customer requirements gathering. by the enterprise in which this research was conducted. This product was developed without using the proposed approach. It took 20 months to be developed, using 2808 h of work and cost to the enterprise US$ 32.840,00.

From these 20 months, the project was paused through 6 months due to reviews the project had to undergo in order to comply with customer needs. This pause cost to the enterprise US$ 13.432,00.

For the experimental case, initially, the proposed approach focused on gathering the requirements from clients through an automated QFD tool. This tool gathers the information from users and automatically determines most relevant requirements, crossing with the organization's technical requirements. The product of that is an XML file, which will undergo through a semantic reconciliation process with an ontology that contains the Enterprise Lexicon, to correctly designate the organization's terminologies to customer's requirements from the QFD tool. This process consisted of adapting the generated XML from the QFD into a formal taxonomy (new ontology) by a computational algorithm, which identifies similar terms in the Enterprise Lexicon ontology and the customer's requirements.

The formalized knowledge gathered is presented as an ontology and it is further refined by comparing them to the design reference ontology and manufacturing reference ontology. This comparison is made through an ontology alignment process and will work as a guide to the product design and the manufacturing planning process. In the experiment, the technical requirements and manufacturing restrictions are translated into design requirements which reduced the problems in the production line and more aligned with the consumer needs.

After the Alignment the design information is translated into manufacturing planning information to assist the production planning and control. In the experiment, the design information gathered from the CAD systems (Altium for the circuit boards and SolidWorks for the mechanical parts) is translated into manufacturing information, such as tool path, process order, etc. Alongside, a consistency analysis is made through the inference engine in order to establish if the manufacturing information is coherent with the enterprise's production facilities.

With the consistency analysis performed and with no inconsistency found the resulting ontology is used to control the production and usage of the product, with the aim of creating a prioritization for further improvements on the product.

The reformulation of the UPS using the proposed approach reduced the development time from 20 months to 12 months and the cost of the project was 30% as there was no need to pause the development to adjust the product to the customer needs.

4 Conclusion

As this application was of a conceptual nature, this research could not completely explore the full potential of the proposed approach. However, even with this limitation, the approach presented significant benefits in the integration of the product development process and manufacturing, as it reduced the time and cost of the development of a product and improved the overall quality as there was no need to redesign the product afterward. Further research will focus on expanding the approach and including more features to increasingly complex cases, to explore the full potential of the approach.

Acknowledgments. The authors would like to thank Pontifical Catholic University of Parana (PUCPR) and NHS Sistemas Elétricos for the financial support to the development of this research.

References

1. Rozenfeld, H., et al.: Product development management: a reference for process improvement. Saraiva, Sao Paulo (2006)
2. Szejka, A.L., Júnior, O.C., Loures, E.R., Panetto, H., Aubry, A.: Proposal of a model-driven ontology for product development process interoperability and information sharing. In: Harik, R., Rivest, L., Bernard, A., Eynard, B., Bouras, A. (eds.) PLM 2016. IAICT, vol. 492, pp. 158–168. Springer, Cham (2016). https://doi.org/10.1007/978-3-319-54660-5_15
3. Chungoora, N., et al.: A model-driven ontology approach for manufacturing system interoperability and knowledge sharing. Comput. Ind. **64**(4), 392–401 (2013)
4. Szejka, A.L., Aubry, A., Panetto, H., Júnior, O.C., Loures, E.R.: Towards a conceptual framework for requirements interoperability in complex systems engineering. In: Meersman, R., et al. (eds.) OTM 2014. LNCS, vol. 8842, pp. 229–240. Springer, Heidelberg (2014). https://doi.org/10.1007/978-3-662-45550-0_24
5. Andreasen, M.M., Hein, L.: Integrated Product Development. IFS Publications Ltd, Bedford (1987)
6. Sosa, M.E., Eppinger, S.D., Rowles, C.M.: The misalignment of product architecture and organizational structure in complex product development. Manag. Sci. **50**(12), 1674–1689 (2004)
7. Pereira, J.A., Canciglieri, O.J.: Product development model oriented for the R&D projects of the Brazilian electricity sector. Appl. Mech. Mater. **518**, 366–373 (2014)
8. Canciglieri, O.J., Young, R.I.M.: Information mapping across injection moulding design and manufacture domains. Int. J. Prod. Res. **48**(15), 4437–4462 (2010)
9. Chungoora, N., Canciglieri, O., Young, R.I.M.: Towards expressive ontology-based approaches to manufacturing knowledge representation and sharing. Int. J. Comput. Integr. Manuf. **23**(12), 1059–1070 (2010)
10. Panetto, H., Dassisti, M., Tursi, A.: ONTO-PDM: product-driven ontology for product data management interoperability within manufacturing process environment. Adv. Eng. Inform. **26**(2), 334–348 (2012)
11. Imran, M., Young, B.: The application of common logic based formal ontologies to assembly knowledge sharing. J. Intell. Manuf. **26**(1), 139–158 (2013)
12. Palmer, C., et al.: Reference ontologies to support the development of global production network systems. Comput. Ind. **77**, 48–60 (2016)

13. Fensel, D.: Triple-space computing: semantic web services based on persistent publication of information. In: Aagesen, F.A., Anutariya, C., Wuwongse, V. (eds.) INTELLCOMM 2004. LNCS, vol. 3283, pp. 43–53. Springer, Heidelberg (2004). https://doi.org/10.1007/978-3-540-30179-0_4
14. Fahad, M., Moalla, N., Bouras, A., Qadir, M.A., Farukh, M.: Disjoint-knowledge analysis and preservation in ontology merging process. In: Software Engineering Advances (ICSEA), pp. 422–428 (2010)
15. Malucelli, A.: Ontology-based services for agents interoperability. Thesis (Ph.D.) - University of Porto, Porto, p. 266 (2006)
16. Kumar, S., Harding, J.: Ontology mapping using description logic and bridging axioms. Comput. Ind. **64**(1), 19–28 (2013)
17. Canciglieri, O.J., Young, R.I.M.: Information sharing in multiviewpoint injection moulding design and manufacturing. Int. J. Prod. Res. **41**(7), 1565–1586 (2003)
18. Haveman, S.P., Bonnema, G.M.: Requirements for high level models supporting design space exploration in model-based systems engineering. Procedia Comput. Sci. **16**, 293–302 (2013)
19. Nattermann, R., Anderl, R.: Approach for a data-managment-system and a proceeding-model for the development of adaptronic systems. In: ASME 2010 International Mechanical Engineering Congress and Exposition, pp. 379–387 (2010)
20. Moneva, H., Hamberg, R., Punter, T.A.: Design framework for model-based development of complex systems. In: 32nd IEEE Real-Time Systems Symposium 2nd Analytical Virtual Integration of Cyber-Physical Systems Workshop, Vienna (2011)
21. Stechert, C., Franke, H.J.: Managing requirements as the core of multi-disciplinary product development. CIRP J. Manuf. Sci. Technol. **1**(3), 153–158 (2009)
22. Liao, Y., Lezoche, M., Panetto, H., Boudjlida, N., Loures, E.R.: Semantic annotation for knowledge explicitation in a product lifecycle management context: a survey. Comput. Ind. **71**, 24–34 (2015)
23. Pohl, K.: The three dimensions of requirements engineering: a framework and its applications. Inf. Syst. **19**(3), 243–258 (1994)
24. Cleland-Huang, J., Chang, C.K., Sethi, G., Javvaji, K., Hu, H., Xia, J.: Automating speculative queries through event-based requirements traceability. Requirements Eng. **2002**, 289–296 (2002)
25. Lin, H.-K., Harding, J., Shahbaz, M.: Manufacturing system engineering ontology for semantic interoperability across extended project teams. Int. J. Prod. Res. **42**(24), 5099–5118 (2004)

Communication Protocol Application for Enhanced Connectivity of Sensors, Machines and Systems in Additive Manufacturing and Production Networks

Cordula Czwick(✉), Stefan Kugler, Jennifer Greven, and Reiner Anderl

Department of Computer Integrated Design, TU Darmstadt, Otto-Berndt-Str. 2, 64287 Darmstadt, Germany
czwick@dik.tu-darmstadt.de

Abstract. The connection between sensors, systems and machines in the production environment enables new concepts to increase quality or flexibility. Integrated sensors can measure machine performance parameters. The measurements serve for monitoring of process stability and quality or for affecting production planning through a new agile routing. To realize the new concepts, data needs to be transmitted from the sensors to a data management system, where the collected data can be analyzed and stored. The communication between sensors, machines and systems is a central aspect and, therefore, a big challenge. There exist different protocols to enable communication, but choosing the proper protocol for a special use case is difficult. There does not exist a method that supports the choice of the protocol depending on the initial situation and the user's preferences. Therefore, the aim of this paper is the development and implementation of a method that supports the selection of a communication protocol in an Industrie 4.0 surrounding for enhanced connectivity between sensors, systems and machines in the production depending on the individual initial situation and the personal preferences. After a short motivation and state of the art, two use cases are described and the development of the concept is explained. The following implementation shows the realization of the concept and enables the use of the concept on the two use cases. The paper ends with a conclusion and outlook.

Keywords: Industrie 4.0 · Digitalization · Communication · OPC UA · MQTT · Production network · Project ArePron

1 Introduction

Developments in the field of digitalization enable new business models and help to enhance products in the whole lifecycle. One technical requirement for Industrie 4.0 is the clear identification of all instances. A well-defined description helps to identify all components, machines and systems. Another technical requirement is the localization, which describes the precise and actual location of a certain component. For the communication between machines and components, the third technical requirement is very

Published by Springer Nature Switzerland AG 2019
C. Fortin et al. (Eds.): PLM 2019, IFIP AICT 565, pp. 136–145, 2019.
https://doi.org/10.1007/978-3-030-42250-9_13

important. This is the addressing, which helps to control devices through the mapping of an individual address for connection and communication. [1]

Communication between components, machines and systems enables the vision of a flexible and autonomous production especially for individualized products or small lot sizes [2, 3]. In this paper, the requirements to enable an adequate communication are investigated and described. The aim of this paper is the development of a method, which helps to choose a proper communication protocol for the connection of sensors, machines and systems in the production environment. Until now, a user-friendly method for the selection of a communication protocol in Industrie 4.0 does not exist.

For the communication in an Industrie 4.0 surrounding, several protocols exist as an option. The mostly known options are OPC UA, MQTT and DDS. The protocols enable the data flow between sensors, machines and systems and therefore the connection between all devices in the production environment. This paper compares the three protocols OPC UA, MQTT and DDS and analyses the advantages and disadvantages of each possibility. OPC UA stands for "Open Platform Communications Unified Architecture" and is a standardized communication protocol for machine-to-machine communication. The strengths of the protocol are the high security standard through an additional message encryption and authentication and the semantic transmission of data or even complex data [4–6]. The protocol MQTT (MQ Telemetry Transport) is even suitable for devices with limited resources and works well with instable connections and nets [7, 8]. DDS or "Data Distribution Service" is a communication protocol developed by the Object Management Group in 2004 and features a decentral structure with an opportunity of data filtering [9, 10]. Section 3 deals with a detailed evaluation of the three protocols. Based on the analysis of the three protocols, the resulting information gives an advice, which protocol shall be selected for communication. Therefore, a concept is created and presented in the next parts of the paper.

2 Uses Cases for Additive Manufacturing and Production Networks

This section deals with the use cases and their usage. There exist two use cases, which, on the one hand, support the motivation for the concept development, and, on the other hand, serve for implementation and validation of the theoretical concept. The use cases are real existing systems with different characteristics and requirements, which are described in the following.

Use Case "Additive Manufacturing Lifecycle"

The Additive Manufacturing (AM) lifecycle for fused deposition modeling (FDM) comprises the different lifecycle phases starting with the material production. A material extruder represents the material production phase. Granulate material is transformed into filament. The next phase is the product development phase. After designing the part, the machine preparation takes place. A small FDM printer represents the preparation and printing process. After the product development phase, the product distribution and product use phase follow. The last phase is the product end of life. A shredder represents the product recycling phase and produces new granulate material of old components [11]. To control the production process and the quality of the printed part, several sensors are integrated into the machines. The measurements of the sensors and the information of the machine control are collected in a database [12]. To transfer data, a proper communication protocol is needed. Requirements on the protocol are in this use case: fast and reliable transmission of data, simple implementation, good expandability of new machines or sensors and reliable function with instable nets.

Use Case "Production Network in ArePron Project"

The name ArePron stands for agile resource efficient production network. The project is approved by the Hessian Ministry of Economics, Energy, Transport and Regional Development (HMWEVL) and financed by the European Regional Development Fund (ERDF) and the Hessian Ministry [13]. It started in January 2018 and ends in December 2020. The aim is an increase of the resource efficiency of the production with the help of an agile, cross-location linking of production systems. Rules and performance indicators are created, that can lead to an increase of the resource efficiency. The collected data help to calculate the performance indicators and rules. Therefore, the resource efficiency of a manufactured part can be determined and, in the end, optimized. The improvement of the resource efficiency enables a cost reduction while the ecological footprint of the company reduces. In the work package of the Department of Computer Integrated Design, the information and communication infrastructure is developed and implemented, which enables the acquisition und usage of data. Therefore, a communication protocol for machine and systems communication is needed. This protocol has to fulfill standards of a real industrial production concerning the security and the function of the protocol. Sensors of the machines and information of the programmable logic controller need to be transferred to a database, where the defined rules and key performance indicators determine the best production route in the production network.

3 Development of a Concept for Selection of a Communication Protocol

The aim of this paper is the development of a concept that helps to choose a proper protocol to enable an Industrie 4.0 communication within machines, systems and components in a production environment. Therefore, the first step is the selection of criteria that can characterize communication and that can help to decide which protocol is suitable. The next step is the characterization of the three protocols OPC UA, MQTT and DDS. Each protocol is evaluated concerning the decision criteria. An overview summarizes all advantages and disadvantages of every protocol. The information serves as general input for the method. The next step is the concept development. The overall method and the single steps of the concept are introduced and presented. After this, the implementation and validation take place in the following section.

The concept and the method have two significant layers. The first layer proofs the technical abilities. The three protocols are analyzed concerning the strengths and weaknesses. In this layer of the method, a first request on the user takes place. The user has to insert his requirements depending on categories. The three protocols are evaluated for every category. The result of this first layer are all protocols that can satisfy the technical requirements. For this first layer, rating criteria need to be chosen and evaluated for the three protocols. The second layer of the method comprises the preferences of the user. With the help of a utility analysis, the user can bring his individual preferences into the method. For the utility analysis, the user decides the weighting of meaningful criteria. Depending on this, the method ranks the protocols and gives an advice, which protocol is suitable for the defined use case. Figure 1 presents an overview of the method.

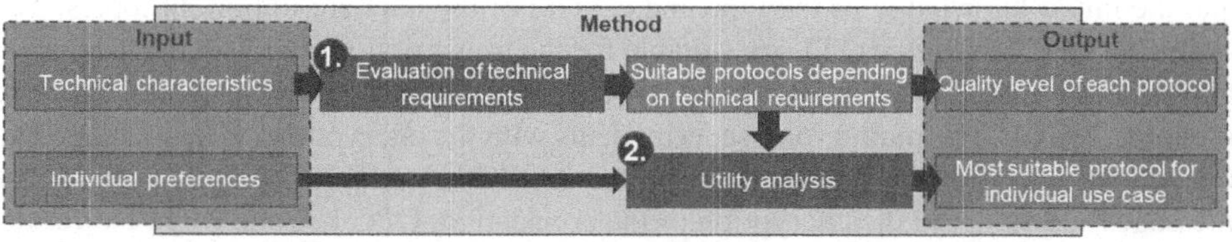

Fig. 1. Two layers of the method in an overview

To fulfill the technical requirements, rating criteria are necessary. The selection of criteria is an important first step for a meaningful method. The analysis of requirements of Industrie 4.0 helps to identify important criteria. The most important requirement of Industrie 4.0 is the vertical and horizontal integration. Vertical integration means that data is available for every authorized person or machine of every step of the process chain. Horizontal integration describes the exchange of data between individual enterprises. In terms of scalability, the connection of hundreds of devices has to be enabled. The three requirements generally count for all Industrie 4.0 activities. For the method, special requirements on the communication and especially the protocol are important. The transmission rate describes the time between an event on one device and the arrival of data on another device. Industrie 4.0 adequate transmission rates have times of few milliseconds. The real-time capability describes the awareness of the latest possible arrival time of a message at a certain device. Therefore, the real-time capability can reduce security risks. Through the independence of the protocol from the manufacturer or certain systems, the communication is possible with every system or device. Standard interfaces support an easy change of clients. An easy implementation of the protocol and a high flexibility in the structure of the protocol simplify the protocol itself and its use. A communication with the help of the internet enables a communication of devices separated by open ground. The stability ensures the function of the protocol even under poor connections or high data traffics. For the data, additional requirements exist. The requirements are a permanent availability of the data with several access facilities, a guaranty for the transmission of the data and the consistent access and output of data independent of the data type. For the devices or clients, the localization, identification and addressing are important requirements as explained in the introduction. Besides, a high flexibility enables an easy change of clients. To maintain a certain security level, only authenticated users have access to the system and the messages. A high safety level ensures a safe use without accidents even with incorrect operation [2].

The important requirements on the protocol, the clients and the data can be divided into four main groups: transmission, structure, function and security. The four groups are used as cluster for the decision criteria. The protocols OPC UA, MQTT and DDS have different strengths. The decision criteria help to point out the strengths and weaknesses. The first three questions represent the main group transmission. The transmission group deals with the latency, the real-time and the possibility to transfer complex data. A transmission faster than milliseconds works only with the protocol DDS. The protocols MQTT and DDS predict the maximum time when the message arrives the recipient at the latest. Complex data can only be sent with the protocol OPC UA. For the main group structure, the general structure with or without a broker (centralized or decentralized) and the initial knowledge of the type and content of the data are important topics. The protocols OPC UA and MQTT are suitable for the transmission even if it the data is not known and filtered initially. Only the protocol DDS supports a decentralized structure without a broker. The main group security deals with the encryption of the message and the authentication of the devices. The protocol OPC UA enables an encryption of the messages additional to the encryption of the connection. OPC UA and MQTT offer the possibility to authenticate devices. The forth group is the function that includes encoding and the quality of the connection in the network. The protocols DDS and OPC UA enable the encoding that enables a faster transmission. With a changing connection, MQTT can be used. Figure 2 shows the decision criteria separated into the four groups and the evaluation of the three protocols OPC UA, MQTT and DDS in an overview.

Categories	User questions for the decision criteria	Evaluation			
		if	OPC UA	MQTT	DDS
Transmission	Must it be possible to predict the maximum time when the message will reach the recipient at the latest?	yes	X	✔	✔
	Does the transmission have to be faster than in ms-range?	yes	X	X	✔
	Does the protocol also have to be able to transfer complex data such as control data?	yes	✔	X	X
Structure	Is it not known at the time the protocol is set up which data must be transmitted and / or should the content of the data be filtered?	yes	✔	✔	X
	Should the data be transferred via a decentralized structure (no central broker)?	yes	X	X	✔
Security	Should the message be encrypted in addition to the connection encryption?	yes	✔	X	X
	Should it be possible to authenticate devices?	yes	✔	✔	X
Function	Do the data have to be encoded for example for a faster transmission of large data packages?	yes	✔	X	✔
	Is there not always a constant connection in the network?	yes	X	✔	X

Fig. 2. Decision criteria with an evaluation of the three protocols

Depending on the necessary technical requirements, a ranking of the protocols takes place. If the protocol fulfills all requirements, the protocol reaches the first quality level with nine points. For the second quality level, the protocol achieves seven or eight points.

Protocols of the first or second quality level satisfy the technical requirements. In the next layer of the method, only the protocols of this quality levels are considered.

The second layer deals with the utility analysis. With the help of the utility analysis, the user can place his individual preferences. Through the analysis of the user stories, four important categories result. The first category is the simple implementation. The time of becoming acquainted with the protocol shall not exceed the time of the implementation. Especially in traditional enterprises, a simple and adequate implementation motivates a project for digitalization. The next category is the fast transmission of the data. On the one hand, a fast transmission saves time and in the end money. Fast transmission enables an optimization of routing or machine scheduling. Therefore, a fast transmission bears new business cases in an enterprise. On the other hand, a fast transmission supports a long-term use of the protocol. With the increasing digitalization, transmission speeds and the use of data increase as well. Choosing a protocol with a fast transmission now helps to keep the actuality of the technical state for a longer time. The following category is the semantical data description. This can be important for the user, because it enables a simple and compact read-out of the data. The last category addresses the connection of devices. If the connection shall only take place between sensors, the user can put his focus on this. After the request of the preferences, the method presents the most suitable protocol to the user. In case of several options, the method asks for the country of the use case. The place of implementation is an interesting factor because the use of the protocols differs strongly between the countries. If the protocol is often used in a country or region, there exists a better infrastructure for costumer support. After considering all aspects of the technical requirements and the individual preferences, the best protocol for the user's case is presented in the end.

4 Implementation and Application on the Use Cases

The implementation of the method tend to an easy and efficient use. Therefore, requirements are a self-explanatory handling and a clear view. The use of the implemented method shall be possible directly without a long training. Besides, the implemented method shall be operated without an additional software with the common operating systems. Based on the requirements, the software Delphi is chosen for the implementation. Delphi works with the programming language Pascal and enables the preparation of clear user interfaces.

In a first step, the user interface is developed through drag and drop. The choice of objects is limited on a fixed number, but still suitable for a productive implementation. Just as the concept of the method, the implementation is separated into two parts. The first part serves for the evaluation of the technical feasibility. For every decision criterion, the necessity is determined. The user can answer with a "yes" or a "no" for every decision criterion. If a decision criterion is important, the user can mark the "mandatory" button. This decision criterion cannot be neglected in the choice. The protocol has to fulfill this decision criterion otherwise the protocol is suspended. After the evaluation, the user presses the "calculate" button. A direct evaluation gives feedback and shows the ranking of the three protocols OPC UA, MQTT and DDS depending on the user's input. Besides the quality level and the achieved quality points, the evaluation tells the missing properties for every protocol. This gives a first information to the user how many protocols can be considered in the second part of the method. If all protocols show a negative rating, the user can either reconsider his input or interrupt the method directly. The user pushes the "next" button to reach the utility analysis. The user inserts his preferences with the help of percentages. If the sum of the four inputs does not result in 100%, the method adapts the weighting factors for intern calculation. After pushing the "calculate" button, the method shows the results of the utility analysis for the three protocols. If the difference between the values of the protocols is small (<10 points) a new input mask appears. The user chooses the county where the project takes place. After pushing the "final decision" button, the method gives an advice which protocol is the most suitable option for the descripted use case. Besides the recommendation of a protocol, all properties that are not fulfilled are mentioned. The advised protocols match the technical requirements, if not, they are not included in the second part of the method.

For an application of the method, the use cases are used. Section 2 describes the two use cases "Additive Manufacturing Lifecycle" and "Production Network in ArePron Project". Use case one "Additive Manufacturing Lifecycle" has technical requirements on the transmission and the security. Figure 3 shows an extract of the method.

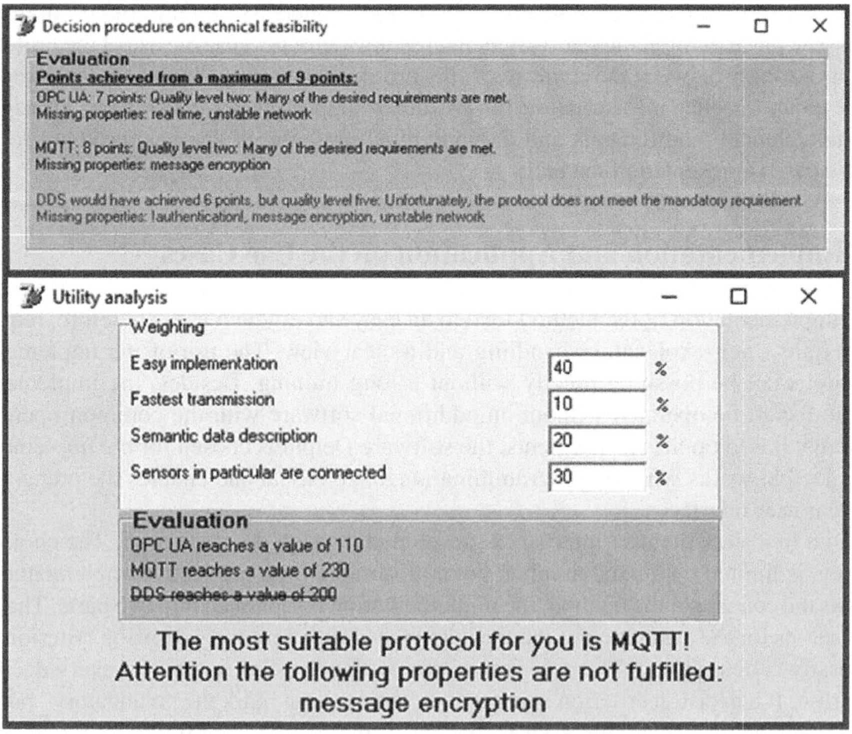

Fig. 3. User interface of the method used for the additive manufacturing lifecycle

In this case, the maximum time when the message will reach the recipient needs to be predictable. Besides, the message has to be encrypted additionally to the connection encryption. The authentication of the devices is mandatory. Based on the mentioned technical requirements, the method recommends OPC UA and MQTT with the quality level two. OPC UA does not offer real time. MQTT misses the message encryption. In the next step, the utility analysis takes place for the final decision. For the "Additive Manufacturing Lifecycle" an easy implementation is most important and assessed with 40%. Most of the devices are sensors. Therefore, this criterion is weighted with 30%. The semantic data description is rated with 20%, the fast transmission is assessed with the last 10%. Based on this rating, the method recommends the use of the protocol MQTT with the hint of the missing functionality of message encryption.

Use case two "Production Network in ArePron Project" has technical requirements on the categories transmission, structure and security. To plan and determine the agile routing in the production, the maximum time of the transmission has to be predictable. Besides, the protocol has to be able to transfer complex data like the control data for the machines. In the actual state of the project, doubts exist concerning the collected data and a potential sorting of the raw data. The data is used for determining the ecological efficiency of a product and adapt the agile routing. There do not exist a key performance indicator that considers the influences of the digitalization in the economic efficiency of products. Therefore, this indicator is developed in the project and this is why the final data is not indicated yet. The ArePron project is a funded Hessian transfer project. Therefore, all results have to be transferable to small and medium-sized enterprises. For enterprises, security of the data is the most important point to keep the business secrets and therefore the competitiveness. Hence, the authentication of the devices and the additional encryption of the messages are mandatory. With the mentioned technical requirements, the method advices OPC UA for the project. MQTT and DDS do not meet the mandatory requirements concerning the security. Therefore, MQTT and DDS are eliminated as alternatives. Figure 4 presents the user interfaces for the evaluation for the second use case.

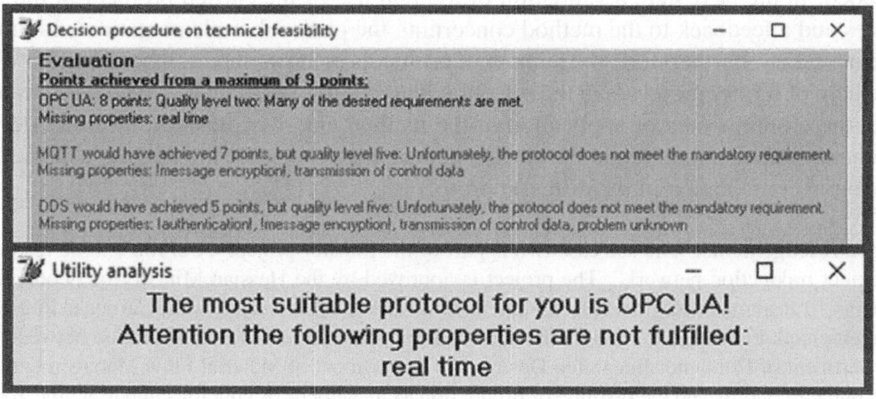

Fig. 4. User interface of the method for the production network in ArePron

In this case, the utility analysis is overleaped and the method is presenting the most suitable protocol directly. For the second use case, the suitable protocol is OPC UA.

The use cases evaluate the function of the developed method. The advised protocols match with the strengths and weaknesses that are described in the beginning of the paper. Therefore, the method serves as assistance in the selection process of a protocol for communication in Industrie 4.0 environments.

5 Outlook and Conclusion

The paper presents the development of a method for the selection of a communication protocol depending on technical and individual requirements. Therefore, in a first step, requirements of Industrie 4.0 and the protocols OPC UA, MQTT and DDS for communication are described in an overview. The next section deals with the two use cases. In the use case "Additive Manufacturing Lifecycle", mostly sensors need to be connected to a data management system. For this research project, an easy implementation and a reliable function in case of inconstant connection is important. The use case "Production Network in ArePron Project" deals with the acquisition of production data to determine a new agile resource efficient routing. Especially the requirements on the security are mandatory, because the project pictures a real production environment of a small or medium-sized enterprise. The following section describes the development of the method. The method consists of two layers. The first layer is the evaluation of the technical requirements. The user answers questions of the four categories transmission, structure, security and function. With the answers, the technical suitability of the three protocols is evaluated. The second layer consist of a utility analysis. The user can weight four factors. Based on the user's preferences the most suitable protocol is displayed. For implementation, the software Delphi with programming language Pascal is chosen. The two use cases enable the application and validation of the method. For the first use case, the protocol MQTT is recommended, for the second use case the method advises the protocol OPC UA. This shows that for different applications different protocols are needed. In the next step, a validation of the real use of the chosen protocol in the use cases and a feedback to the method concerning the protocol implementation and usage are necessary. Furthermore, the number of protocols in the method can be enlarged. With the help of further protocols in the selection, the requirements can be covered accurately and therefore the area of application of the method enlarges. Besides, a further development of the communication protocols is necessary to enable the flexible use and the potential combination of the different protocols.

Acknowledgements. The use case two is part of the transfer project "ArePron – agile resource efficient production network". The project is approved by the Hessian Ministry of Economics, Energy, Transport and Regional Development (HMWEVL) and financed by the European Regional Development Fund (ERDF) and the Hessian Ministry. The project is a collaboration between the Department of Computer Integrated Design, the Department of Material Flow Management and Resource Economy and the Institute of Production Management, Technology and Machine Tools. The project started in January 2018 and ends in December 2020.

References

1. Anderl, R., Anokhin, O., Arndt, A.: Effiziente Fabrik 4.0 Darmstadt – Industrie 4.0 Implementierung für die mittelständige Industrie. In: Sendler, U. (ed.) Industrie 4.0 grenzenlos. X, pp. 121–136. Springer, Heidelberg (2016). https://doi.org/10.1007/978-3-662-48278-0_8
2. Plattform Industrie 4.0: Umsetzungsstrategie Industrie 4.0 – Ergebnisbericht der Plattform Industrie 4.0 (2015). https://www.bitkom.org/noindex/Publikationen/2015/Leitfaden/Umsetzungsstrategie-Industrie-40/150410-Umsetzungsstrategie-0.pdf
3. Kellner, F., Lienland, B., Lukesch, M.: Produktionswirtschaft. Springer, Heidelberg (2018). https://doi.org/10.1007/978-3-662-54341-2
4. OPC Foundation: What is OPC? https://opcfoundation.org/about/what-is-opc/
5. Mahnke, W., Leitner, S.-H., Damm, M.: OPC Unified Architecture, 1st edn. Springer, Heidelberg (2009). https://doi.org/10.1007/978-3-540-68899-0
6. OPC Foundation: OPC Unified Architecture: Interoperabilität für Industrie 4.0 und das Internet der Dinge. https://opcfoundation.org/wp-content/uploads/2016/05/OPC-UA-Interoperability-For-Industrie4-and-IoT-DE-v5.pdf
7. Raymor, B., Coppen, R.: OASIS Message Queuing Telemetry Transport (MQTT) TC. https://www.oasis-open.org/committees/tc_home.php?wg_abbrev=mqtt
8. Obermaier, D.: So funktioniert MQTT: Schlankes IoT-Protokoll. http://www.elektroniknet.de/elektronik/kommunikation/so-funktioniert-mqtt-148672.html
9. Object Management Group: DDS – The Proven Data Connectivity Standard for the IoT. https://www.omgwiki.org/dds/
10. Happacher, M.: DDS versus OPC UA. https://www.computer-automation.de/unternehmensebene/produktionssoftware/artikel/121784/
11. Auth, C., Arndt, A., Anderl, R.: Development of a concept for a holistic knowledge-based additive manufacturing over the entire lifecycle. In: Chiabert, P., Bouras, A., Noël, F., Ríos, J. (eds.) PLM 2018. IAICT, vol. 540, pp. 726–735. Springer, Cham (2018). https://doi.org/10.1007/978-3-030-01614-2_66
12. Auth, C., Anderl, R.: Additive manufacturing lifecycle – data collection and analysis for process and component optimization. In: 23rd International Seminar on High Technology - Smart Product Development: Challenges and Requirements, Piracicaba, Sao Paulo, Brazil, 04 October 2018 (2018). http://scpm.eng.br/en/palestrantes/m-sc-cordula-auth/additive-manufacturing-lifecycle-data-collection-and-analysis-for-process-and-component-optimization/
13. Agiles ressourceneffizientes Produktionsnetzwerk: Entwicklung einer transparenten und vergleichbaren Bewertungsgrundlage als Entscheidungsbasis für den optimierten Ressourceneinsatz innerhalb eines Wertschöpfungsnetzwerks. http://www.arepron.com/

Tracking the Capture of Tacit Knowledge in Product Lifecycle Management Implementation

Daniela Oliveira[1(✉)], Mickael Gardoni[1], and Kimiz Dalkir[2]

[1] École de Technologie Supérieure, Montreal, QC H3C 1K3, Canada
daniela.innovation.oliveira@gmail.com

[2] School of Information Studies, McGill University, Montreal, QC H3A 1X1, Canada

Abstract. This study outlines the importance of tacit knowledge for engineering organizations, specially engineer-to-order organizations, and its impact in Product Lifecycle Management (PLM) implementations. The use of maturity models as roadmaps and its functions in PLM and knowledge management (KM) are explored. Difficulties of managing knowledge to prepare an organization for PLM implementation, and how PLM maturity models lack the granularity to support KM for PLM implementations are also explored. To support KM for PLM implementations, a tacit knowledge codification scale is developed from KM and PLM maturity models. The scale intends to help knowledge managers better prepare the organization for a PLM implementation and better support the implementation effort.

Keywords: Tacit knowledge codification · Explicit knowledge · Product Lifecycle Management · Knowledge management · Maturity models · Content analysis

1 Introduction

A lot of knowledge in an organization resides in people's heads and nowhere else. How does this knowledge relate to Product Lifecycle Management (PLM) initiatives and how to measure its integration in those initiatives?

When knowledge is codified, written, explained, be it in policies, procedures, detailed estimates, patents or any other kind of document, it can be said to be "explicit". Explicit knowledge is visible, can be regrouped and analyzed without interaction with the people who hold that knowledge. There is however a great amount of knowledge that has never gone through the codification process. It is, for instance, the knowledge of which policies apply in a specific case, which procedures interact in a process, what is the consequence of including an information in a detailed estimate and so on. This kind of knowledge is recognized by the term "tacit knowledge", which covers all knowledge that is not codified. Tacit knowledge may have never been articulated, discussed or exposed to management. It is, however, the kind of knowledge that helps organizations

Published by Springer Nature Switzerland AG 2019
C. Fortin et al. (Eds.): PLM 2019, IFIP AICT 565, pp. 146–155, 2019.
https://doi.org/10.1007/978-3-030-42250-9_14

build success in new projects and deal with uncertainty. Tacit knowledge is built through diversified experience, interaction with other knowers, observation, on-the-job training, mentorship, and other activities with high level of interaction between participants. Tacit knowledge is the power behind situations where engineers make recommendations that would apparently go against standards but that effectively solve a problem with no further repercussions. Another example is where an activity is theoretically dependent on a piece of equipment, but engineers know that the task can be completed without it just fine. It is the knowledge that empowers the worker to do the right thing even when conditions are not optimal. This kind of knowledge is less visible because it resides in people's minds and, as such, cannot be exposed without interaction with the people who hold it. Tacit knowledge may be less visible but is still the doorway for the application of the organizational knowledge to the operational environment [17].

The success of an organization in creating, producing, commercializing and supporting the sales of a given product at any point in time depends on how it employs the knowledge it holds. If there are no policies or procedures, all the knowledge involved is tacit. Codified tacit knowledge, or explicit knowledge, enables department integration, data production and software implementation and, therefore, allows for PLM implementation. Explicit knowledge also reduces the risk of knowledge loss. Many initiatives in knowledge management focus on codifying tacit knowledge, or, in other words, creating documents or systems out of tacit knowledge, in order to attain these advantages. However, the process is rather costly.

Tacit knowledge, on the other hand, enables flexibility, out-of-the-box thinking and innovation. These elements are especially important for engineer-to-order organizations. Engineer-to-order organizations are defined by Schönsleben [15] as industries where "at least some design or engineering work occurs during delivery lead time, according to customer specifications" (p. V). In engineer-to-order organizations, knowledge workers must adapt their interventions to the order requirements. Implementing PLM in engineer-to-order organizations is particularly difficult [9] because of the importance of tacit knowledge in those organizations.

The need to understand the impact of tacit knowledge in PLM implementations is twofold: Firstly, to maximize the use of resources by prioritizing codification initiatives where it would have the most impact. Secondly, to codify tacit knowledge to the optimal extent – the point where an acceptable compromise is reached between standardization and flexibility. In this study, maturity models in knowledge management (KM) and in PLM were analyzed to identify stages of tacit knowledge codification. A scale of tacit knowledge codification is then proposed.

2 Overview of Literature

Organizations place high expectations on PLM implementation [20]. One of the objectives of PLM is to centralize the product knowledge residing in individuals of the organization [14]. However, the management of knowledge, especially its tacit dimension, has been noticeably left out of PLM [8]. To verify this statement, we performed a bibliometric analysis of the field in Scopus, a major bibliographic database indexing journal articles, books and conference proceedings, among other kinds of documents. 2163 documents were retrieved with the query "product lifecycle management" applied in title, abstracts and keywords fields or in any of them [5]. Of this body of published literature, little more than a quarter (25.16%) also mentioned the term "knowledge". Only a little less than 7% (6.85%) of the articles mentioned "tacit knowledge", "know-how" or "experience" [3], terms that would suggest some reflection on the knowledge employed by workers in the accomplishment of their tasks. The term "tacit knowledge" itself, largely established in the knowledge management (KM) field, accounts for little more than 0% (0.32%, or seven documents) of the works on PLM [4].

Stark [18] defines Product lifecycle management (PLM) as "the business activity of managing, in the most effective way, a company's products all the way across their lifecycles; from the very first idea for a product all the way through until it is retired and disposed of" (p. 1). The need to improve the capability to manage products, according to Kale [7], comes from the traditional department-oriented paradigm, where demand is detected by marketing, the product is designed by engineering, produced by manufacturing and supported by sales. Potential benefits of applying PLM include faster and less faulty distribution of change information, the anchoring of products to its related certificates, records and test results, and easier diffusion and maintenance of standards [14] (p. 96). The common aim of adopting PLM is "to integrate people, processes, data, information and knowledge throughout the product's lifecycle, within a company and between companies" [10] (p. 97). In knowledge terms, PLM has been defined as "the ability to manage the knowledge and capabilities of an organization to respond effectively to specific customer needs, at any point in time" [7].

PLM affects a wide range of processes inside and outside the company, often involves changes to existing business processes and working practices [1], in addition to requiring new types of skills and capabilities, not to mention large-scale cultural and strategic changes [10]. A certain level of collaboration between departments within and organization and perhaps among organizations is then sought. In fact, many problems with implementation of PLM Support Systems have been considered "more of organizational nature rather than technical" [1] (p. 335) as PLM impacts working processes and activities, which includes people's roles, responsibilities and authorities [20]. PLM impacts and is impacted by the knowledge surrounding the lifecycle of a product.

To assess the readiness for PLM implementation and increase its chances of success, maturity models have been developed. The term "maturity" combines notions of evolution with levels of process formality. Maturity models provide the good and bad practices across transitional stages, intended to be used as a part of an improvement process [6]. Most maturity models are adapted from the Capability maturity model (CMM), developed by Paulk [13]. Initially defined to determine the readiness of an organization to adopt a given piece of software, maturity levels are well-defined evolutionary steps on the path to a clear goal [19].

PLM implementations depend on a certain level of codification of tacit knowledge, which might have not yet been attained by the organization. In addition, a balance has to be achieved in the codification of tacit knowledge to maintain the flexibility knowledge workers require to do well in their jobs.

In order to articulate tacit knowledge codification with PLM implementations, we performed content analysis on a KM and PLM maturity models to obtain a gradient of tacit knowledge codification and better inform knowledge management initiatives in PLM implementations.

3 Methodology

In order to analyze tacit knowledge codification states, a KM and a PLM maturity model were selected.

Dalkir [2] accounts for the existence of about twelve knowledge management maturity models. To allow for mapping to the PLM maturity model, the knowledge management maturity model should present descriptions of initiatives and/or outcomes in each level that are rich enough to associate them with the corresponding PLM maturity model initiatives and/or outcomes. Among the twelve knowledge management maturity models presented by Dalkir [2], the Kochikar [12] model was selected because of the richness of details presented for each level.

The Kochikar [12] maturity model has five incrementally complex phases. In phase one, Default, the organization is completely dependent on individual skills and abilities; in phase two, Reactive, the organization is capable of performing the basic business tasks repeatedly; in phase three, Aware, the organization is somewhat capable of supporting decision-making with data; in phase four, Convinced, there is quantitative decision making for strategic and operational; in phase five, Sharing, the organization is able to manage organizational competence.

The Kochikar model intends to reflect an organization's intention and ability to manage knowledge. Intentional codification of tacit knowledge is a part of knowledge management. Phase one, Default, suggests no intentional codification of tacit knowledge is attempted, resulting in the organizational dependence on individuals' skills and abilities. Tacit knowledge is produced individually only. In this phase, basic business activities are at risk when an individual leaves the organization. To reduce this risk, two complementary knowledge management solutions can be applied: (1) sharing tacit knowledge through job shadowing, on-the-job training and mentoring, for example, and (2) codifying tacit knowledge, through the creation of documents enumerating position and department responsibilities, procedures and policies. This reduction of knowledge loss, joined by the organizational ability to repeat basic business tasks through personnel movement, h is represented by phase two of the maturity model, Reactive. The third phase, Aware, denotes a greater degree of tacit knowledge codification, as the coverage of data produced is enough to support decision-making. Indeed, tracking a task implies the acknowledgement that the task exists. The appreciation of the value of that task implies knowledge of the process the task belongs to. The two subsequent levels imply greater levels of conjoined work between departments in an organization. At these levels, departments are not only aware of the work in other departments, but they are able to collaborate and adapt to new business realities or new product requirements demanding collaboration between departments. Tacit knowledge is produced jointly.

On the PLM side, Kärkkäinen and Silventoinen [9] identified nine maturity models specifically conceived for PLM. As organizations have different PLM needs, the authors analyzed the focus of these maturity models along three dimensions: (1) from Functional, Organizational to Inter-organizational; (2) from Data/Information to Knowledge/People and (3) from Process automation to Ad-hoc process integration. Engineer-to-order organizations need more flexibility in adapting tasks to the product requirements at hand, meaning they need a strong Ad-hoc process integration. Of the nine PLM maturity models analyzed by Kärkkäinen and Silventoinen [9], the Sharma [16] model had the strongest ad-hoc process integration. In addition to that, it allowed for a balanced description of needs in the Data/Information to Knowledge/People spectrum. Still according to Kärkkäinen and Silventoinen [9], the Sharma [16] model also focuses on process automation.

The Sharma model was conceived to facilitate collaboration among organizations, product development and innovation and has six phases: The first phase, Manual/Ad hoc, is paper-based; in the second phase, Standardization, there is some integration; in the third phase, Visibility, there is a cross-platform visibility; in the fourth phase, Business Activity Reinvention, there is intra-organization integration; in the fifth phase, Real time track and trace, there is flexible inter-organization application integration; in phase six, Collective optimization, there is need-based inter- and intra-organization event and business process integration [16].

In terms of knowledge, at the base of the Sharma model, there is ad hoc integration due to kinships and other cultural reasons, with no intentional knowledge management. In the second level, integration between departments assumes formalization of procedures or, in other words, some tacit knowledge codification. The third level evokes the possibility of a department understanding the work involved in the inputs it receives and in the outputs it produces, denoting an understanding of roles, responsibilities and tasks of each department. The fourth level represents the possibility of a department to influence the course of production depending on specific and/or business requirements. Here, a certain degree of collaboration is implied, indicating the creation of tacit knowledge involves more than one department. Subsequent levels indicate an increasing number of departments, inside and outside of the organization, sharing the fourth level state. In other words, more and more departments share the same understanding – the same knowledge - about departments' tasks and impact in the product lifecycle. As departments work more closely together, the tacit knowledge produced becomes more collectively produced and used by more and more departments.

Table 1 summarizes both maturity models levels regarding tacit knowledge.

Table 1. Tacit knowledge codification and production in KM and PLM maturity models

Level	KM maturity model (Kochikar)	PLM maturity model (Sharma)
1	No tacit knowledge codification supported by organization	No tacit knowledge codification supported by organization
2	Some tacit knowledge codification; Tacit knowledge sharing	Some tacit knowledge codification
3	Tacit knowledge codification at the process level	Tacit knowledge codification at the process level; Tacit knowledge sharing
4	Conjoined production of tacit knowledge	Collective production of tacit knowledge
5	Greater, conjoined production of tacit knowledge	Greater, collective production of tacit knowledge
6	–	Greater, collective production of tacit knowledge by greater number of departments

4 Results

In both KM and PLM maturity models, tacit knowledge codification precedes the sharing and collective production of tacit knowledge. This finding suggests that efforts for codification of tacit knowledge are necessary to foster the collective production of tacit knowledge. Tacit knowledge is first produced individually, then codified, and therefore shared, by department, then an understanding of the positioning of the department in the product lifecycle takes place, before the production of tacit knowledge can be undertaken by two or more departments together. The aim of PLM is to level all departments touching a product lifecycle to a stage where they can produce tacit knowledge together. Joint production of tacit knowledge, however, demands a shared context and some closeness between teams.

Evaluation of levels of tacit knowledge codification, sharing or collective production seems possible at the department level and presents a good indicator of the readiness of two or more departments to implement a PLM initiative.

The collective production of tacit knowledge implies the shared understanding of two or more departments regarding their positioning in the product lifecycle and how one department's work influences the other. However, departments might not have the same level of understanding. Departments might develop their understanding of the impact of another department over their work before understanding their own impact on another department.

Table 2. Tacit knowledge codification scale

Level	Definition	Codified tacit knowledge
Uncharted	Tacit knowledge resides only in individuals	Workers' *Curricula vitae* and personal notes
Interrelated	Tacit knowledge relations between departments have been identified and codified	Workflows; Fishbone diagrams [11] representing the product lifecycle; Data maps and dictionaries
Aware	Departments are aware of factors influencing work before their intervention and afterwards; Department production of tacit knowledge considers other departments	Requests for task changes in other departments; Communication of special circumstances concerning sub products to other departments; Comments regarding other departments in interdepartmental meeting minutes
Joined	Departments work together to find some solutions; tacit knowledge is produced jointly	Sub products produced by two or more departments
Appropriated	Departments have a history of working together to find solutions; tacit knowledge is produced collectively	Complex sub products produced by two or more departments

This beginning of understanding seems to be a necessary stage before the implementation of PLM, in order to avoid the organizational issues mentioned by Batenburg [1].

Based on these findings, we suggest a scale of tacit knowledge codification in Table 2.

5 Application

To illustrate the application of the Tacit Knowledge Codification Scale, we present a case involving a regional branch of an organization charged with the maintenance of road infrastructure.

The case concerns the Maintenance Planning department charged with planning major maintenance projects. The department needed information about the state of existing products in order to predict maintenance measures. The information would be submitted to an asset management system able to predict the degradation of road quality, allowing for accurate planning of maintenance measures. This information was obtained by on-site analysis, which is quite costly. A list of roughly ninety terms, each one representing one road composition formula, was used by the asset management system to create degradation scenarios. This list had been used in previous attempts to gather information from other departments, without success. With the mediation of an information professional, it came to light that this list assumed a great deal of knowledge of road composition, knowledge that seemed to be present only in the Maintenance Planning department. Indeed, after realizing that the list could be decomposed into combinations of materials, quantities and order of application, the information professional met with members of the Maintenance Planning team to discuss how to simplify the list using more widely known terms.

Apart from the manager, other three members took part in the Maintenance Planning team. One of the members had more than ten years of experience, another had roughly four years of experience in the department and the last one had just recently joined the team. The junior member indicated their lack of knowledge to help with the decomposition of terms. The mid-career member was able to decompose about seventy percent of the terms. The rest of the terms had to be decomposed with the help of the senior member of the team. The document with the matrix connecting the original list terms and a combination of entries of the second list – called road layers list – placed the tacit knowledge of Planning regarding road composition in the Identified level of the Tacit Knowledge Codification Scale (Table 2). The complexity of the knowledge involved in road degradation analysis was keeping other departments from collaborating with Planning. The codification effort vulgarized road composition terms into terms that other departments could understand and relate information to. The document with the matrix also served as an indicator of the tacit knowledge regarding road composition concentration in the Maintenance Planning department.

In their quest to obtain road composition information, the Maintenance Planning department mapped where the information was present. It could be found in different organizational systems. In those systems, however, data was regrouped according to a particular logic model and were available only a certain delay after construction. They did not represent a solution for the Maintenance Planning department. At this point,

Maintenance Planning turned to departments closer to the conception of the product. Because these departments intervened earlier in the product lifecycle of the product, they were also closer to the production of the needed information.

Indeed, the data was first submitted to different systems by the Project Management department. The Project Management department was however not the producer of the data. The data was produced by external contractors and were provided to comply with invoice payment requirements, which explained the particular logic used to regroup the data. Maintenance Planning had acquired the understanding of the information flow in the Project Management department, along with the challenges of obtaining this information. Maintenance Planning understood why information was managed the way it was in the Project Management department and also the correlation between that information management and their own work. Interdepartmental meeting minutes and a diagram would be evidence of the Interrelated phase of the scale.

After this first contact, Maintenance Planning sought Project Management collaboration to envision a way to obtain the information needed. Maintenance Planning used the recently gained knowledge about how Project Management operated to produce a form for data collection. The form was submitted to Project Management to request its use by external contractors. The form was an evidence that Maintenance Planning had reached the Aware stage in relation to Project Management regarding road composition data.

The logic used to regroup data in the form and the form itself, as a tool, turned out to be potentially convenient for Project Management for some of their own information needs. For this reason, Project Management sought collaboration with Maintenance Planning to include more data to be gathered in the form. The resulting form was only possible because of the collaboration of both departments and would be an evidence of the Joined level. The collaboration of the two departments was maybe still not a solid, long-term one, but already a break from the work-in-silo paradigm. This collaboration would indicate a greater readiness for a PLM initiative regarding road composition.

6 Discussion and Conclusions

As illustrated in the previous section, the application of the Tacit Knowledge Codification Scale may show evidence of shared tacit knowledge and collaboration between departments. The existence of shared tacit knowledge and collaboration between departments is a good indicator of a PLM implementation with less organizational issues. The scale does not replace maturity level assessments but may be an additional tool to assess readiness for PLM implementation. PLM implementation may prove difficult if departments do not understand the relationship between their work, knowledge, information and data to those of other departments. In those cases, it might be more interesting and cost-effective to implement knowledge management initiatives and culturally break the work-in-silo paradigm before designing a PLM support system, for example.

Some questions regarding tacit knowledge integration still persist. For instance, when assessing the tacit knowledge codification general stage of two departments, how many documents would be needed to show evidence of a specific state? The answer to this question should consider specialization and complexity of the tasks involved, as well as turnover rates and availability of similarly talented workforce that can be hired. Another issue is the identification of documents providing proof of existing tacit knowledge or the joint production of tacit knowledge, for example. In organizations where a team responsible for knowledge management exists, those professionals can be charged with assessing the evidentiary value of documents produced. How can the assessment of this evidence be explained so that smaller organizations can also appreciate their tacit knowledge codification levels? An empirical validation of the theoretical exercise in this article would shed light on these topics and on characteristics of the documents used to assess tacit knowledge codifications. An empirical validation would pave the way for automation of the identification and analysis of these documents, possibly in large scale and should be the target of future research endeavors in this area.

References

1. Batenburg, R., et al.: PLM roadmap: stepwise PLM implementation based on the concepts of maturity and alignment. Int. J. Prod. Lifecycle Manag. **1**(4), 333–351 (2006). https://doi.org/10.1504/IJPLM.2006.011053
2. Dalkir, K.: Knowledge Management in Theory and Practice. The MIT Press, Cambridge (2017)
3. Elsevier B.V.: Scopus Results Analysis Report on "((TITLE-ABS-KEY ('product lifecycle management') AND TITLE-ABS-KEY (tacit W/2 knowledge))) OR ((TITLE-ABS-KEY ('product lifecycle management') AND TITLE-ABS-KEY (experience))) OR ((TITLE-ABS-KEY ('product lifecycle management') AND TITLE-ABS-KEY (know-how)))" from 2004 to 2018
4. Elsevier B.V.: Scopus Results Analysis Report on "(TITLE-ABS-KEY ('product lifecycle management') AND TITLE-ABS-KEY (tacit W/2 knowledge))" from 2008 to 2015
5. Elsevier B.V.: Scopus Results Analysis Report on "TITLE-ABS-KEY ('product lifecycle management')" from 1996 to 2019
6. Fraser, P., et al.: The use of maturity models/grids as a tool in assessing product development capability. In: IEEE International Engineering Management Conference, vol. 1, pp. 244–249 (2002). https://doi.org/10.1109/IEMC.2002.1038431
7. Kale, V.: Enhancing Enterprise Intelligence: Leveraging ERP, CRM, SCM, PLM, BPM, and BI. CRC Press, Taylor & Francis Group, Boca Raton (2016)
8. Kärkkäinen, H., Pels, H.J., Silventoinen, A.: Defining the customer dimension of PLM maturity. In: Rivest, L., Bouras, A., Louhichi, B. (eds.) PLM 2012. IAICT, vol. 388, pp. 623–634. Springer, Heidelberg (2012). https://doi.org/10.1007/978-3-642-35758-9_56
9. Kärkkäinen, H., Silventoinen, A.: Different approaches of the PLM maturity concept and their use domains – analysis of the state of the art. In: Bouras, A., Eynard, B., Foufou, S., Thoben, K.-D. (eds.) PLM 2015. IAICT, vol. 467, pp. 89–102. Springer, Cham (2016). https://doi.org/10.1007/978-3-319-33111-9_9
10. Kärkkäinen, H., Silventoinen, A.: What is product lifecycle management (PLM) maturity? Analysis of current PLM maturity models. J. Mod. Proj. Manag. **3**, 3 (2016)
11. Kenett, R.S.: Cause-and-effect diagrams. In: Encyclopedia of Statistics in Quality and Reliability. American Cancer Society (2008). https://doi.org/10.1002/9780470061572.eqr413
12. Kochikar, V.P.: The knowledge management maturity model: a staged framework for leveraging knowledge. In: Proceedings of KM World, pp. 1–9 (2000)
13. Paulk, M.C.: The Capability Maturity Model: Guidelines for Improving the Software Process. Addison Wesley Publishing Company, Reading (1995)

14. Sääksvuori, A., Immonen, A.: Product Lifecycle Management. Springer, Berlin (2008). https://doi.org/10.1007/978-3-540-78172-1
15. Schönsleben, P.: Integral Logistics Management: Operations and Supply Chain Management Within and Across Companies. Taylor and Francis, London (2016)
16. Sharma, A.: Collaborative product innovation: integrating elements of CPI via PLM framework. Comput.-Aided Des. **37**(13), 1425–1434 (2005). https://doi.org/10.1016/j.cad.2005.02.012
17. Shoham, S., Hasgall, A.: Knowledge workers as fractals in a complex adaptive organization. Knowl. Process. Manag. **12**(3), 225–236 (2005)
18. Stark, J.: Product lifecycle management. In: Stark, J. (ed.) Product Lifecycle Management (Volume 1). DE, pp. 1–29. Springer, Cham (2015). https://doi.org/10.1007/978-3-319-17440-2_1
19. Weber, C.V., et al.: Key practices of the capability maturity model. Software Engineering Institute, Carnegie Mellon University, Pittsburgh, PA (1991)
20. Wognum, P.M., Kerssens-Van Drongelen, I.C.: Process and impact of product data management implementation. Int. J. Prod. Dev. **2**(1–2), 5–23 (2005). https://doi.org/10.1504/IJPD.2005.006666

PLM and Conceptual Design

A Novel Approach to Product Lifecycle Management and Engineering Using Behavioural Models for the Conceptual Design Phase

Stephen Peters[1], Clément Fortin[2], and Grant McSorley[1](✉)

[1] University of Prince Edward Island, Charlottetown, PE CIA 3T3, Canada
{sepeters,gmcsorley}@upei.ca
[2] Skoltech, Skolkovo Innovation Center, Moscow, Russia

Abstract. This work builds upon a previous proposal for the use of the extended SAPPhIRE model of causality as a foundation for a PLM system, and more specifically the management of design data at the conceptual design phase. During the conceptual design phase, the product definition is in a state of flux as multiple iterations and options are considered until a suitable baseline design is developed. The role of PLM systems is to manage the people, processes and products involved in developing and sustaining a product in order to increase stakeholder satisfaction and product quality while reducing lifecycle costs. At the conceptual design stage, a balance must be struck between the freedom to iterate and the need to control the design process and capture relevant data.

Currently, PLM systems are not well suited for the support of the conceptual design stage due to their reliance on the product structure, as the unavoidable, significant design changes to the physical configuration in the early design stages make it difficult to maintain a coherent product definition. This paper presents a case study of the product data created during the conceptual design phase of the SpudNik-1 CubeSat. The results demonstrate the ability of the model to represent a variety of design data representing different subsystems at several levels of maturity. This could prove to be more consistent and easier to use for conceptual design and is one part of a larger goal of redesigning PLM systems for the support of the extended product lifecycle.

Keywords: Conceptual design · Behaviour · Function · Causal · Satellite · Nanosatellite · Product lifecycle management · Behavioural model

1 Introduction

Designing, building and operating spacecraft and other complex systems involve unique challenges for engineers. To address these challenges, engineers have developed methodologies and tools that emphasize collaboration and dynamic exchanges between personnel. These methodologies form the basis of concurrent engineering and are central to the

Published by Springer Nature Switzerland AG 2019
C. Fortin et al. (Eds.): PLM 2019, IFIP AICT 565, pp. 159–169, 2019.
https://doi.org/10.1007/978-3-030-42250-9_15

systems engineering development process. Typically, the systems engineering process is represented by the V-model, and more recent work has specifically focused on the early stages of space system design [1], which can be referred to as concurrent conceptual design. Creating a proper tool for exchanging and storing design data and supporting the concurrent work and collaboration is imperative for optimizing the quality of work, schedule goals and capital expenditures.

The effective handling of data is crucial for the success of each phase of an engineering design project. Previous work focused on the design data used within the CEDESK concurrent conceptual engineering tool, which is based on parametric systems models, and was restricted to the thermal behaviour of a CubeSat [2]. CEDESK is a data exchange tool that was developed to conduct concurrent design studies in an efficient way, with previous case studies performed on satellite projects [3]. This paper will expand on the previous work in two ways. First, by examining conceptual design data in multiple formats and from multiple sources, and second by comparing the representation of multiple CubeSat subsystems.

The paper is structured as follows. After a summary of the literature review and an explanation of the Extended SAPPhIRE model, the context of the case study is established. The methodology of the data collection and analysis is explained, and the results presented. Finally, relevant insights and conclusions are made based on the case study and future work in this direction is proposed.

2 Conceptual Design Data in Product Development and PLM

During the conceptual design phase, the product definition is in a state of flux as multiple iterations and options are considered until a suitable baseline design is developed [4]. The role of PLM systems is to manage the people, processes and products involved in developing and sustaining a product in order to increase stakeholder satisfaction and product quality while reducing lifecycle costs [5].

At the conceptual design stage, a balance must be struck between the freedom to iterate and the need to control the design process and capture relevant data. To date, PLM and computer assisted engineering tools have been limited in support of conceptual design [4, 6], although some authors have proposed possible solutions, with a focus on managing and exploiting the types of information available at early versus late stages of the development process.

Rizzi and Regazzoni [7] suggest that the use of problem solving or solution generation tools such as GTI's RelEvent Diagram or TRIZ in a PLM framework could help exploit unstructured conceptual design information to improve knowledge management, identify criticalities and reduce revision times, but do not elaborate on implementation. Torres et al. [6] distinguish between geometric and non-geometric data at the conceptual design phase, and propose a knowledge-based approach combing QFD, axiomatic design and FMEA with CAD Tools in order to connect the two. However, the product structure remains the foundation for the connection, and initial geometric design parameters must be defined early on. Chandrasegaran et al. [8] explain that PLM extended the abilities of PDM systems to represent product data to the representation of product knowledge which can be "represented in terms of requirements, specifications, artifacts, forms, functions, behaviours, design rationale, constraints and relationships". However, in actual implementation, many commercial tools continue to rely primarily on the product structure as the defining element of the product. A notable exception is Sudarsan et al. [9] who propose a PLM framework centered on the Core Product Model, which includes behaviour, function and geometry, which is in line with our current work but does not include relationships of causality like SAPPhIRE.

An overall theme from the literature is that there is a distinction to be made between geometric and non-geometric data. This is consistent with the authors' experience that non-geometric data may be more important than geometric data at the conceptual design stage [2]. In this work, 'geometric' is defined as data which can be measured in physical units and directly refers to the physical dimensions or configuration of a system. The present work proposes how engineers and designers can organize these representations in a logical structure based on a behavioural model.

3 Representations of Product Behaviour for Supporting Conceptual Design

The extended SAPPhIRE (State-Action-Parts-physical Phenomenon-Inputs-oRgan-physical Effect) causality model [11] based on the work of Chakrabarti et al. [10], shown in Fig. 1, provides a visual representation of how the behaviour and function of the system are brought about through one or multiple changes of state which occur due to the physical laws acting upon the system. This model provides a richer representation, at various levels of granularity, of the relationships between the function, behaviour and structure of a system, than previous function-behaviour-structure models, such as those of [12–14]. Descriptions of each model element can be found in Table 1. Previous work

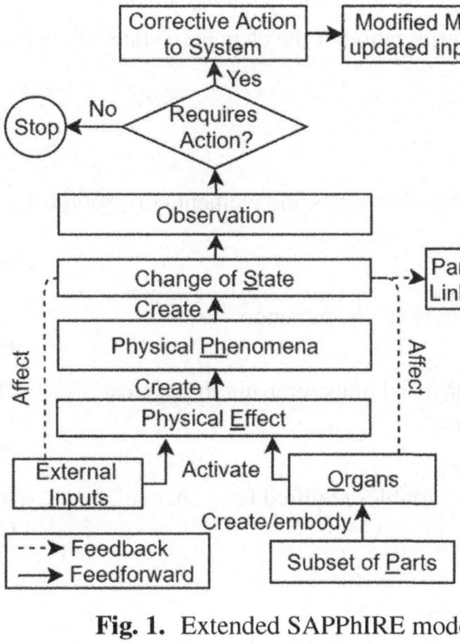

Fig. 1. Extended SAPPhIRE model

has demonstrated the use of the SAPPhIRE model for the representation of in-service [15], test [11] and conceptual design data [16], and proposed as a framework for product lifecycle management [11]. The modified Extended SAPPhIRE model was developed in order to more closely align with the product development process and to represent the evolution of the product over its lifecycle [10]. The intended benefits of this representation over traditional PLM product data structures include the ability to represent system behaviour at various level of granularity and system decomposition, as well as the focus on system functions and behaviours, which demonstrate compliance to requirements, as opposed to a primary focus on the product structure or bills of materials.

Table 1. Extended SAPPhIRE model constructs [17]

Model construct	Definition
Parts	A set of physical components and interfaces constituting the system and its environment of interaction
Change of state	The attributes and values of attributes that define the properties of a given system at a given instant of time during its operation
Organ	The structural context necessary for a physical effect to be activated
Physical effect	The law of nature governing a change
Input	The energy, information or material requirements for a physical effect to be activated; interpretation of energy/material parameters of a change of state in the context of an organ
Physical phenomenon	A set of potential changes associated with a given physical effect for a given organ and inputs
Corrective action:	Action taken (by human intervention or by system self-correction) based on interpretation of change of state
Observation	The interpretation of the change of state which may modify the current system

Table 2. Design data types and element correspondence [2]

Data type	Definition	Element
Behavioural	Corresponds to physical phenomenon	Physical effects Physical phenomenon
Geometric	Measurable via physical units referring to physical system dimensions	Organs Subset of parts Change of state
State	Important design variables required for a change	Inputs Change of state

Preliminary research has demonstrated the use of the Extended SAPPhIRE model for the structuring the design data found within parametric design models used for concurrent conceptual design of CubeSats [2]. Three categories of conceptual design data were defined and identified within parametric models managed by a concurrent conceptual design tool, CEDESK. These categories were then associated with corresponding elements of the Extended SAPPhIRE model (Table 2), providing an initial indication of the viability of the use of the model for structuring conceptual design data.

4 Case Study Context

The University of Prince Edward Island is currently in the process of designing a 2U (20 × 10 × 10 cm) CubeSat named 'SpudNik-1' in partnership with the Canadian Space Agency. This is part of the national Canadian CubeSat Project and has a target launch window of Q4 2021. The primary functional requirement for the satellite is to capture 2–10 m optical resolution of the Canadian province of Prince Edward Island (PEI) and relay it back to a ground station. This information will be used for ongoing precision agriculture research. The CubeSat standard was developed as a low cost means for universities to allow researchers and students to conduct a range of experiments [18]. These are typically launched as part of larger payloads by external partners and rely on existing infrastructure. As a result, the interfaces and safety requirements are tightly controlled by interface configuration documents and standards.

The SpudNik-1 work breakdown structure presented in Fig. 2 is based on typical breakdowns for CubeSats and complex systems engineering projects [18, 19], as well as logistical considerations.

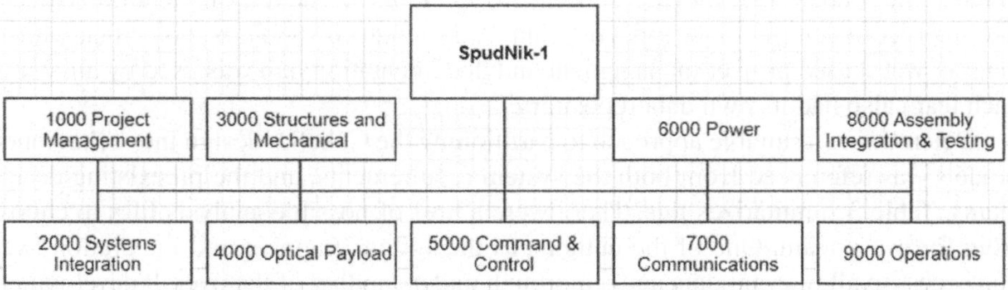

Fig. 2. Simplified work breakdown structure

The CubeSat development process (prior to launch) has been divided into four standard stages: Mission Concept Development; Preliminary Design; Detail Design; Assembly, Integration and Testing. The conceptual design activities were completed as part of the Mission Concept Development phase, and so the current work considers only the design progress up to the Mission Concept Review.

5 Methodology

The methodology for the case study consisted of five main steps:

1. Selection of a key behaviour for each subsystem
2. Representation of subsystem behaviour using the Extended SAPPhIRE model
3. Survey of design data created during the conceptual design phase (i.e. prior to the Mission Concept Review)
4. Association of conceptual design data to relevant elements of the behavioural models
5. Validation of model with designers

The subsystems selected were based on the SpudNik-1 WBS. While additional behavioural models would be needed to represent the complete CubeSat, for the scope of the present study, this was limited to one significant behaviour per subsystem. As the UPEI co-authors are involved in the project in the roles of project manager and systems engineer, they had access to all relevant design data produced by the student teams. Where possible, conceptual design data was traced to originating files or documents. These sources were related to the appropriate model elements. For example, external inputs may be derived from standards and requirements, while relevant parts may be included in a BOM or a labelled sketch.

6 Results

6.1 Model Identification and Data Collection

Based on the CubeSat system requirements and WBS, it was decided to develop six behavioural models, one for each subsystem, see Table 3. The relevant team was identified in order to determine the most relevant data sources. It should be noted that while a central, web-based project management and documentation hub was used by all teams, each team also had its own data repository.

Determining a suitable approach to partitioning the CubeSat design into behavioural models was referenced from both the system requirements, and the preexisting design teams. Table 3 summarizes this. There were a host of possible analysis files to choose from for every team. One of the authors, as the system engineer and integration lead, had access to all relevant data and a thorough understanding of the overall development process. For the purposes of narrowing the scope, each behaviour was limited to a single parametric model, selected based on its relevance to the design and its impact on the overall design definition. The selected models are presented in Table 3, along with the associated subsystem, team, and the primary driving requirements, in order to provide context.

The source and types of data used for the parametric models varies between teams. The Buckling Analysis used dimensional and mechanical property data of initial rail designs and prototypes. The Reaction Wheel Analysis was based on preliminary estimates regarding weight distribution from initial layouts and CAD assemblies provided by the Structures and Payload team. It is important to note that the analyses are iterative, due to the ongoing evolution of the CubeSat design.

Table 3. Subsystems and behavioural models

Subsystem (team)	Behavioural model	Driving requirement
Thermal (Structures and Payload)	Heat Transfer with environment	Component temperature limits
Structure (Structures and Payload)	Structural Buckling	Critical launch load case
Communications (Communications)	Data Transceiving	Link budget and power requirements
Power (Power)	Power Generation	Power budget
Optical Payload (Structures and Payload)	Optical Sensing	Image quality
Attitude (Command & Control)	Reaction Wheel Dynamics	Positioning requirements for image acquisition

6.2 Mapping of Analysis Files to the SAPPhIRE Model

The behavioural models of all six subsystems were developed, three of which are presented below in Figs. 3, 4 and 5. Due to the observed consistency across data sources (Excel spreadsheets, initial CAD models, data sheets), there is a high level of confidence that the models represent the targeted subsystem behaviours. The developed models and the information sources were also presented to the relevant designers, to garner their opinions. They expressed understanding of this representation of their system and indicated an interest in the use of functional models for organizing their files.

As reported in [2], and confirmed in this study, at the conceptual design stage, the physical phenomena are typically represented by calculations, parametric models or

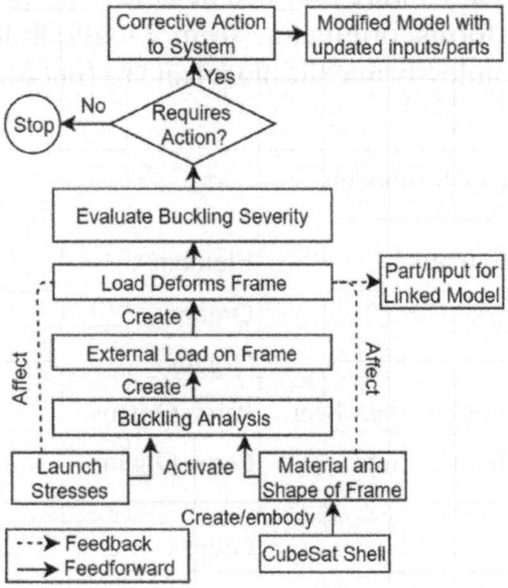

Fig. 3. Buckling Analysis

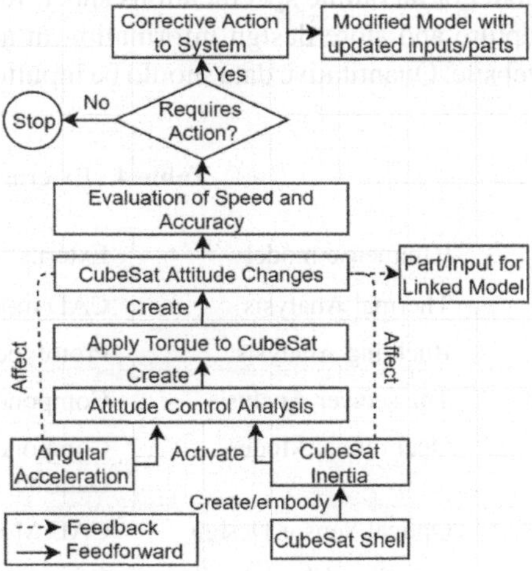

Fig. 4. Motor and Reaction Wheel Analysis

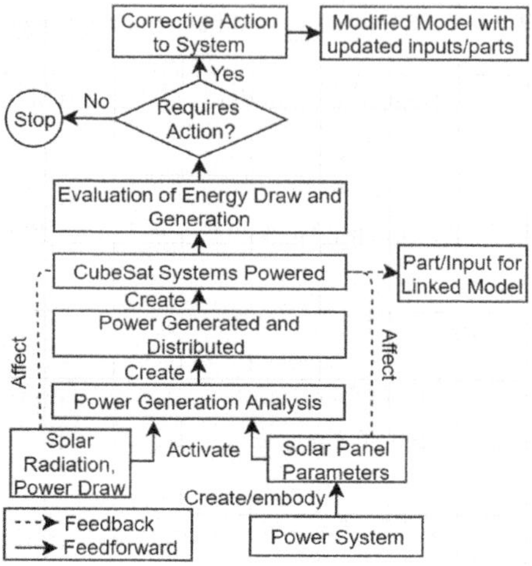

Fig. 5. Evaluation of Power Generation

simplified simulations. These representations in turn draw on external data, which can be related to the inputs, parts and organs necessary for activating the phenomena. Table 4 presents the sources for data used in each of the parametric models. We have not included project requirements and universal information (i.e. physical constants) in this summary as they are accessible project wide.

There were three models whose analyses included standard components to be outsourced, and thus used specifications from online distributors. Two models were reliant on the geometries of the CubeSat that were featured in the CAD assembly. Finally, because of the simplicity of manufacturing rails, the Buckling Analysis used geometries from the simple physical prototypes to confirm its validity.

For this case study, most of the exterior input data originated from either a CAD model or an online specifications sheet. Ideally, any future tool will be able to properly capture and store design information in all its forms, originating from a logbook to a website. Quantitative data should be inputted seamlessly into the model and its functions.

Table 4. External sources for models

Parametric model	External data source(s)	Element
Thermal Analysis	CAD model	Organs
Buckling Analysis	Prototype	Organs
Transceiver Analysis	Component, Supplier Datasheet	Parts, Organs
Operational Modes	Component, Manufacturer Datasheet	Parts, Organs
Optical Sensor Design	CAD Model	Organs
Reaction Wheel Analysis	Component Supplier Datasheet	Parts, Organs

In contrast, qualitative would be catalogued and stored as its original file type into the appropriate behavioural model element.

One difficulty encountered in representing system behaviour is capturing the different operational modes. This affects the behaviour of the power system, as other subsystems such as the optical payload, attitude control and communications have varying power requirements depending on the mode of operation of SpudNik-1. For example, the imaging mode requires more power than the hibernation mode. SAPPhIRE includes a feedback loop, so it can model these temporal variations in the data but it remains difficult to convey that here. This representation will be the focus of future work.

7 Implications of Work

Initially it was hypothesized that the buckling behaviour of the structure would be the most difficult to represent through a behavioural model due to its reliance on geometric data. However, during the mapping process it was realized that because the outer shell of the CubeSat is controlled by detailed interface requirements and pre-defined launch loads, the structure has little dependency on design changes to the other CubeSat subsystems. The Structures and Payload team can design the frame based on the load requirements, while the relative placement and design of the internal components do not have to be taken into account. This indicates that it is the unvarying nature of the geometric data rather than its total amount that is more relevant for defining the data structure (i.e. behavioural versus structural).

In contrast, the assumptions necessary for designing the reaction wheels (i.e. CubeSat inertia) are heavily dependent on geometric data that were not finalized at the conceptual design phase, for example the mass properties and distribution within the BUS. As a result, there is a high likelihood of design changes to the reaction wheels later in the development process. This indicates that the dependency between systems, in particular with respect to geometric properties, can be a critical factor.

Lastly the Power analysis is primarily concerned with non-geometric data, for example solar radiation levels in Low Earth Orbit and the power draw from the CubeSat subsystems. However, indirectly the analysis will be affected by the lack of geometric data. As the reaction wheel cannot be sourced confidently because of the lack of knowledge about the inertia, there remains uncertainty with respect to the power requirements.

An important observation that was not captured in the three models presented is the uncertainty and necessary iterations regarding the overall geometric definition and physical configuration of the CubeSat. For example, there are strict requirements regarding the allowable mass and location of center of gravity for CubeSats, and uncertainty with respect to the geometric properties of the subsystems results in an ongoing risk to meeting these requirements. Similarly, there is a strong dependency between the design of the Optical Payload and the overall CubeSat layout, due to the need to achieve as long an effective focal length as possible. The novelty of the of optical design adds to this complexity.

These observations further indicate that the high level of uncertainty regarding the physical definition of the system at the early stages of design calls into question the utility of the product structure for organizing conceptual design data, as traditionally done in PLM systems. It should be noted that there exist tools to manage the complexity described above, for example the design structure matrix and collaborative design tools aim to reduce the risk associated with coupled systems. However, these tools do not address questions of data structure for sharing and reuse, which are central to PLM systems.

8 Conclusion

This paper served to further experiment with the extended SAPPhIRE model as a potential substitute for the product data structure via a case study on a CubeSat design. To reiterate the overall objective of the work, the behavioural models shown are proposed as the framework for replacing the generic product data structure, represented by the BOMs, used in PLM systems. During the conceptual design phase, system functions, behaviour and spatial and geometric properties go through multiple iterations, which causes the product data structure to also evolve quickly. When one considers the potential scale of a PLM system and the corresponding engineering tools that rely on the product data structure the ramifications are substantial. The functional definition of the design is much more consistent, and thus a more stable foundation on which to base a data structure.

One area of future work is the study of project management data, such as schedule constraints and budget, present during conceptual design, as these can have a significant influence on design decisions. An additional goal is to eventually represent the entire CubeSat in one integrated model. Being able to show how some behaviours are more interconnected including causality relationships with regards to requirements, inputs etc. compared to others has potential for optimizing the data framework and reflecting the true reliance between design teams. Having different design teams test out a tool would be very useful for both validation and optimization. Finally, there is an option to experiment with a wider range of engineering fields i.e. aerospace and automotive industries. In general, CubeSats can be considered variant designs, comparable to sequential generations of products with common platforms seen in said industries i.e. models. Both cases involve heavily relying on previous designs as a reference for the new product, a practice that may be considered with the during the work on the tool.

References

1. Knoll, D., Fortin, C., Golkar, A.: Review of concurrent engineering design practice in the space sector: state of the art and future perspectives. In: 2018 IEEE International Systems Engineering Symposium (ISSE), Rome, Italy (2018)
2. Fortin, C., McSorley, G., Knoll, D., Golkar, A., Tsykunova, R.: Study of data structures and tools for the concurrent conceptual design of complex space systems. In: Ríos, J., Bernard, A., Bouras, A., Foufou, S. (eds.) PLM 2017. IAICT, vol. 517, pp. 601–611. Springer, Cham (2017). https://doi.org/10.1007/978-3-319-72905-3_53
3. Knoll, D., Golkar, A.: A coordination method for concurrent design and a collaboration tool for parametric system models. Concurr. Eng. **26**(1), 5–21 (2017). https://doi.org/10.1177/1063293x17732374

4. Vuletic, T., et al.: The challenges in computer supported conceptual engineering design. Comput. Ind. **95**, 22–37 (2018). https://doi.org/10.1016/j.compind.2017.11.003
5. Stark, J.: Product Lifecycle Management (Volume 1). DE. Springer, Cham (2015). https://doi.org/10.1007/978-3-319-17440-2
6. Torres, V.H., et al.: Approach to integrate product conceptual design information into a computer-aided design system. Concurr. Eng. **21**(1), 27–38 (2013). https://doi.org/10.1177/1063293X12475233
7. Regazzoni, D., Rizzi, C.: Conceptual design knowledge management in a PLM framework. In: 4th International Conference on Product Life Cycle Management (PLM 2007) (2007)
8. Chandrasegaran, S.K., et al.: The evolution, challenges, and future of knowledge representation in product design systems. Comput.-Aided Des. **45**(2), 204–228 (2013). https://doi.org/10.1016/j.cad.2012.08.006
9. Sundarsan, R., et al.: A product information modeling framework for product lifecycle management. Comput.-Aided Des. **37**(13), 1399–1411 (2005). https://doi.org/10.1016/j.cad.2005.02.01
10. Chakrabarti, A., et al.: A functional representation for aiding biomimetic and artificial inspiration of new ideas. Artif. Intell. Eng. Des. Anal. Manuf. **19**(2), 113–132 (2005). https://doi.org/10.1017/S0890060405050109
11. McSorley, G., Fortin, C., Huet, G.: Modified SAPPhIRE model as a framework for product lifecycle management. In: DS 77: Proceedings of the DESIGN 2014 13th International Design Conference, Dubrovnik, Croatia, pp. 1843–1852 (2014)
12. Hubka, V.: Principles of Engineering Design. Butterworth Scientific, London (1982)
13. Gero, J.S., Kannengiesser, U.: The situated function–behaviour–structure framework. Des. Stud. **25**(4), 373–391 (2004)
14. Umeda, Y., et al.: Supporting conceptual design based on the function-behavior-state modeler. Artif. Intell. Eng. Des. Anal. Manuf. **10**(4), 275–288 (1996). https://doi.org/10.1017/S0890060400001621
15. Jagtap, S.: Capture and structure of in-service information for engineering designers. University of Cambridge, Cambridge (2008)
16. Tsykunova, R.: Study of data structures, tools and processes to support concurrent conceptual design of space products. Skolkovo Institute of Science and Technology (2016)
17. Chakrabarti, A., Srinivasan, V.: SAPPhIRE–an approach to analysis and synthesis. In: ICED 2009: Proceedings of the 17th International Conference on Engineering Design, California, USA, pp. 417–428 (2009)
18. Munakata, R., et al.: CubeSat design specification. California Polytechnic State University, San Luis Obispo, California, 20 February 2014
19. NASA: NASA Systems Engineering Handbook. National Aeronautics and Space Administration (NASA), Washington, DC (2016)

Graph-Based Tools for ECM Search Result Analysis to Support the Ideation Step

Houcine Dammak[1], Abdellatif Dkhil[1], and Mickaël Gardoni[1,2(✉)]

[1] École de Technologie Supérieure, Montréal, Canada
{Houcine.dammak.1,Abdellatif.dkhil.1}@ens.etsmtl.ca,
Mickael.gardoni@etsmtl.ca
[2] Institut National des Sciences Appliquées, Strasbourg, France

Abstract. Enterprise Content Management tool (ECM) is defined as the technologies, tools, and methods used to capture, manage, store, preserve, and deliver content. Using ECM in the ideation step of the innovation process may enhance the creativity of users to create new knowledge. In this paper, we discuss how to access this large amount of information efficiently without overwhelming users which may decrease their creativity. The purpose of this work is to avoid this situation by replacing the classical representation of ECM results with a graphical representation using graph theory. The advantages of this approach for visualizing and analyzing the connection between contents are discussed.

Keywords: Creativity · Knowledge management · Visualization · Content management · Graph theory

1 Introduction

Organizations today have access to an enormous amount of information. This information is present everywhere in the workplace in different formats: documents, communications, databases, etc. and it represents a great asset for any organization. The reuse of information and data-driven management is considered a route to greater efficiency and decision making resulting in improved productivity, profitability and competitiveness [1].

Availability of information is one of the critical success factors for organizations to survive. While trying to overcome this critical success factor, organizations are facing different challenges like the huge volume of data and information that exist in different formats and that is not easy to use.

Since this amount of information is usually non-structured and is present in different locations in the workplace, some information management tools have appeared. From these information management tools, we consider content management tools (ECM: Enterprise Content Management) which have the main goal to manage all the organizations' content.

«ECM is defined as the technologies, tools, and methods used to capture, manage, store, preserve, and deliver content across an enterprise» [2]. It is also defined as a

Published by Springer Nature Switzerland AG 2019
C. Fortin et al. (Eds.): PLM 2019, IFIP AICT 565, pp. 170–180, 2019.
https://doi.org/10.1007/978-3-030-42250-9_16

collection of strategic resources and capabilities that provides an automated enabling framework for efficient lifecycle management of valuable organization asset, i.e. contents and processes, to carry out required business operations in a collaborative fashion, supports governance and compliance, provides integration within and outside the business boundaries to achieve business intelligence, knowledge management and decision support capabilities with focus on fulfilment of business goals and objectives for competitive advantage [3].

The main ECM steps are [4]:

- Capture: It contains all the activities related to collecting content. It is usually about identifying the content that it wants to capture and all its dimensions. This content could be captured from internal to external databases.
- Organize: It involves indexing, classifying and linking databases together. This step utilizes different techniques like OCR (Optical Character Recognition) and smart templates for indexing (to identify the metadata), workflows for classification based on business rules and ODBC connections to link content with other databases.
- Process: Analyse the content already classified in order to inform decision-makers and other existing management systems.
- Maintain: It is mainly related to the maintenance of the content. How to keep it accessible? How to link it with new content? And for how much time we should keep it?

ECM is used mainly for daily and operational tasks. Usually, the main reasons to implement ECM solutions are: reducing searching times, unifying the presentation or adhering to reporting obligations [5]. ECM has proven its efficiency not only in the industrial world but also in the research world.

In early stages of the innovation process, participants are invited to use their creativity to come up with ideas. Those ideas are usually inspired by the participants' background and own knowledge. Some researchers proposed different tools to support this important stage in the innovation process which is the ideation stage. The combination of teams existing technical knowledge and limited domain-specific knowledge provokes more original and diverse ideas, which confirms there is a creative value in the combination of KDD (knowledge discovery from databases) with teams' existing knowledge [6].

The ideation step in an innovation process is a critical step. Providing tools to participants in ideation sessions may enhance creativity. As mentioned above, ECM is a tool that will be provided to participants of ideation sessions to see its impact on the creativity of an organization. ECM users will have access to valuable information that is structured and easily accessible. This access to information may enhance the creativity of users to create new knowledge. The gap is present, and the benefits expected are really promising but unfortunately until today, in the ECM research, Creativity, Innovation and Knowledge Management have played a minor role.

With the Content Management tool, we are planning to use indexes (Metadata) related to each content to do searches. By using this metadata layer, the participant receives a list of contents as a search result. Most commercial ECM tools present the search results as a list of contents (documents) grouped by the category of the content (Example: Thesis, Article, Product catalog, Invoices…) and details with all the metadata related

(Date, field, author, location, university…). The metadata depends on the category of documents and it is configured at the implementation stage of an ECM solution. So, the participants of an ideation session, depending on the criteria that they select, they receive a list of content as a search result. This list of contents may inspire them in their ideation session to come up with innovative ideas.

2 ECM Contribution in an Ideation Session

2.1 Using ECM in an Ideation Session

As mentioned above, ECM converts non-structured content to structured content using its main functionalities. Then, by providing the ECM as a support tool to participants in an ideation session they have access to all the content indexed and classified. While doing a search in the ECM, participants have the search result in a list format (see Fig. 1). This method offers structured search results for contents to access to the most relevant ones that may support their creativity.

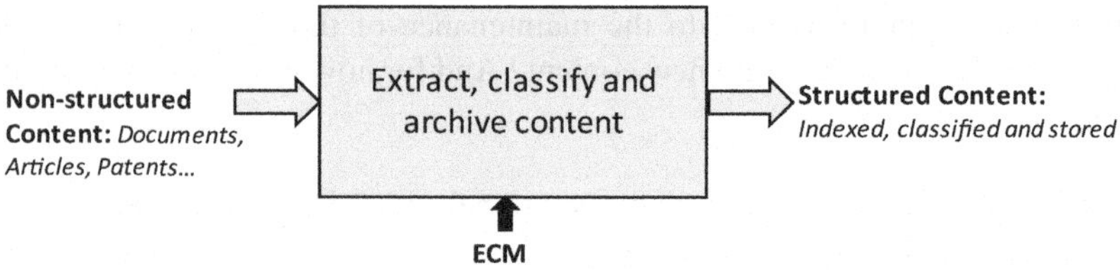

Fig. 1. Modeling the ECM system

2.2 Limitation of the Actual Method

The actual representation of search result in the ECM allows users to have access to a list of indexed contents. Usually, organizations have thousands of contents stored in an ECM which may result in a communicative limitation. By having a long list of contents, participants may lose time to demystify this list to understand the indexes and set a priority list. So, the actual method has a limitation in describing the entire structure of contents with multiple relationships. To cope with this challenge, what information should we analyze? and how to display it?

2.3 Proposed Method to Improve Using ECM in an Ideation Session

Some researchers proved that access to large databases of information can overwhelm users, in their innovation process, and tend them to return to known solutions which decrease the creativity [6]. To avoid this situation, instead of presenting the search results to participants as a list of contents with the metadata related, we are proposing a relational analysis between these contents to display them in a graph which may help them.

As mentioned previously, ECM is the platform that stores content and makes it available to users when they need it. So, we are proposing a framework that couples the ECM output and the innovation process at the ideation stage. And this by proposing a relational analysis of the list of contents displayed by the ECM and representing them in a graph (see Fig. 2). The difficulty here is about the important number of analysis properties to identify the right graphs and all the combinations between these analysis properties.

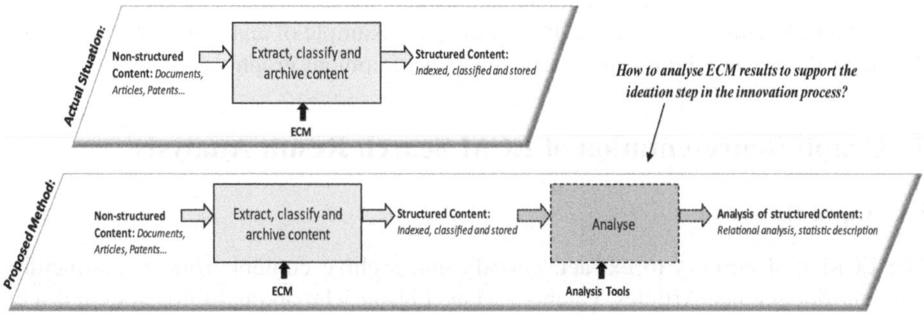

Fig. 2. Proposed method

2.3.1 Use of Graph Tools to Analyze ECM Search Results

In this study, we propose to use graphs for visualizing and analyzing the result of the ECM application. We define a content graph as a graph in with the nodes represent contents (or indexes), the lines represent the relations, and the labels on the lines represent the nature of the relations. Content Graph is a network with nodes that are connected unidirectionally by links of various relations and are intended to organize the entire relation structure between contents (or indexes). ECM result graph has several noticeable benefits compared to actual search result which is in a list format. The advantages of using graphs will be discussed in the following section.

2.3.2 Advantages of Using Graph Representation

Our methodology consists of using graph theory tools to analyze the ECM results. Using a graph representation have many different advantages. A graph is a standard tool for data visualization. This representation tool permits to minimize the reading and interpretation time. In fact, we propose to use graph representation to better understand the links between contents and to have additional analysis tools. Using a content graph presents several advantages. The content graph simplifies the representation and the relation between contents (or indexes) by using standard representation allowing a comprehensive structure of the organization's content. Graphs have long provided visual languages and have been widely used in many different disciplines as formal representation system [7, 8].

The content graph is a particularly good way of organizing the organization's content residing in the ECM especially when using the search function. Displaying a search result in a graph instead of a list brings a view of the entire content of the search result. Content graph display describes the diversity and the depth of the entire ECM search result without omitting any content residing in the bottom of a list and highlighting the relationship between them. It is essential to participants in an ideation session to understand the relationship between all their organization's content to clarify their thinking and to optimize their creativity exercise.

The other great advantage of this presentation way is the possibility to use many structural analysis tools proposed by the theory of graphs. These tools allow a quantitative analysis of connectivity and relationships between contents [8].

In the following section, we will present some example of analysis tools issued from the graph theory and their utility in the analysis of content graphs.

3 Graph Representation of ECM Search Result Analysis

3.1 Input Data

The ECM tool permits to extract, classify and archive content from Non-structured Content (documents, Articles, Patents…) (see Fig. 1). The output of this system is a list of Structured Content: Indexed, classified and stored. An example of a list of Structured Content is given in the following table.

This example considers that we have two categories of contents (the first one is Thesis) and the first category has three indexes (University, Field and Year) (Table 1). After organizing and structuring the content, ECM delivers it to users in the format of a list. We are using graph tools to change this output to a graph format that highlights the relationships between contents. The goal here is to study the links between all the contents presented in the search result and to present them in a graph format. A common way to represent a graph is the adjacency matrix which is a matrix A(n, n) where n is the order of the graph. An entry (u, v) of the matrix is either 0 if there is no edge between u and v or the weight of the edge (u, v) if it exists (this representation implies that no edge has a weight equal to 0). From the list of Structured Content, it is simple to extract two adjacency matrices which can be transformed into a graph. The first is the content/content matrix A(n, n): n corresponds to the number of content. An entry (i, j) of this matrix A(n, n) indicates the value of the link between content i and content j. The second matrix is index/index matrix. An entry (i, j) of this matrix indicates the value of the link between index i and index j.

Her, and to simplify we use only the adjacency matrix corresponding to content - content link matrix (An entry (i, j) of this matrix indicates the link between content i and content j). From this matrix, a graph called content - graph can be presented.

3.2 Introduction to Graph Theory: Basic Terminology and Notations

A graph G = (V, E) is a mathematical structure often used to define relationships between objects. It consists of a set of vertices V and pairs of vertices connecting them (edges, E). A graph can be directed or undirected. In a directed graph, given the edge e = (u, v), we say that u is the origin of e and v is the destination of e. In undirected graphs, u and v are the endpoints of the edge. An undirected graph (or graph) G = (V, E) consists of a finite set V of vertices, and a set E of unordered pairs of distinct vertices called the edges. We say that vertex v is adjacent to vertex u if there is an edge (u, v). In this paper, the used graph is an undirected graph: this graph corresponds to the content/content matrix A(n, n) [9, 10].

Table 1. Example of a list of structured content

Category				Category 1			Category 2		
				Index	Index	Index	Index	Index	Index
				University (a)	Field (b)	Year (c)	d	e	f
1	Content	c1	Thesis 1	ETS (x)	Innovation (s)	2012 (u)			
1	Content	c2	Thesis 2	McGill (y)	Innovation (s)	2012 (u)			
1	Content	c3	Thesis 3	Concordia (z)	Innovation (s)	2012 (u)			
1	Content	c4	Thesis 4	ETS (x)	Innovation (s)	2012 (u)			
1	Content	c5	Thesis 5	ETS (x)	Innovation (s)	2015 (j)			
1	Content	c6	Thesis 6	ETS (x)	Electrical (r)	2015 (j)			
1	Content	c7	Thesis 7	McGill (y)	Electrical (r)	2015 (u)			
1	Content	c8	Thesis 8	Concordia (z)	Electrical (r)	2015 (u)			
2	Content	c9					q	t	p
2	Content	c10					q	t	p
2	Content	c11					q	t	p
2	Content	c12					q	t	p
2	Content	c13					w	i	l
2	Content	c14					w	o	l
2	Content	c15					w	o	l
2	Content	c16					q	o	k

The order of graph corresponds to the number of nodes and a path in a graph is a sequence of vertices (v0, v1; . . . , vk) such that (vi − 1, vi) is an edge for i = 1, 2, . . . , k. The length of the path is the number of edges, k. A path is simple if all vertices and all the edges are distinct. A path in a graph G is a sequence of vertices such that from each of the vertices there is an edge to the successor vertex. A path is called simple if none of the vertices in the path are repeated. A cycle is a path starting and ending at the same node. A cycle is a path containing at least one edge and for which v0 = vk. A cycle is simple if its vertices (except v0 and vk) are distinct, and all its edges are distinct.

3.3 Limit of the Representation

The graph-based representation permits us to use classical graph theory tools and concepts, but some drawbacks exist. The essential limit is the loss of the details of the link. An edge represents an aggregate index between two contents. Figure 3 shows an example of the aggregation of the link between two content i and j: only one link is established. The weight of this link corresponds to the number of aggregated links.

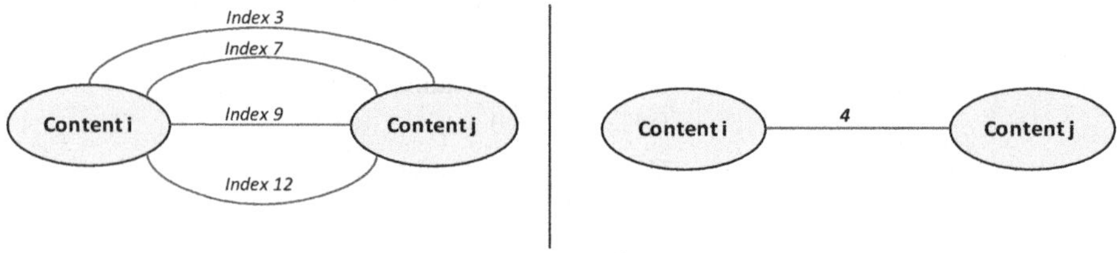

Fig. 3. Example of aggregation

4 Examples of Graph Tools and Utility for ECM Result Analysis

This section aimed to show how classical concepts of graph theory can be applied to analyze ECM search result or to give quantitative information about these results. In our specific context, we present the utility in term of analysis between contents for each concept.

4.1 Biconnected Graphs: Connected Components

Let G = (V, E) be a connected undirected graph, a graph G is connected if, for every pair of nodes v1 and v2, there is a path between nodes v1 and v2. A graph is said to be connected if it can be traveled from any one node to any others by moving along paths of edges. The graph is 2- connected if deletion of any node still keeps it connected; it is 3-connected if it still remains connected with the removal of any two nodes, and so on. It is required that a k-connected have at least k + 1 nodes [9–11].

Notice that unlike strongly connected components of an oriented graph (which form a partition of the vertex set), the biconnected components of a graph form a partition of the edge set.

A graph G = (V, E) is k-connected (k-edge-connected) if at least k vertices (edges) must be deleted to disconnect G. A graph that is 2-connected (3-connected) is also called biconnected (tri-connected).

- Utility: The identification of connected component gives an indication about the clustered nature of ECM search result: each connected component represents an independent cluster. If a graph contains only one connected component, the graph is said to be connected and corresponds to a "one block" draw while a non-connected graph can be drawn in several blocks.

4.2 Articulation Points (or Cut Vertices) and Cut Edge (or Bridge)

Let G = (V, E) be a connected undirected graph. A node in the graph G is called cut point (or articulation point) if its removal disconnects a graph, i.e. increases the number of components. Also, it makes some points unreachable from some other [9]. Articulation Point (or Cut Vertex) correspond to any vertex whose removal (together with the removal of any incident edges) results in a disconnected graph.

In graph G, a Bridge or cut edge is an edge whose removal results in a disconnected graph. An edge is a bridge if its removal results in disconnected sub-graph. A bridge is an edge such that the graph containing the edge has fewer components than the sub-graph that is obtained after the edge is removed.

Figure 4 shows an example of cut vertex and cut edge. cut the bridge disconnects the graph and forms disconnect subgraph (cluster).

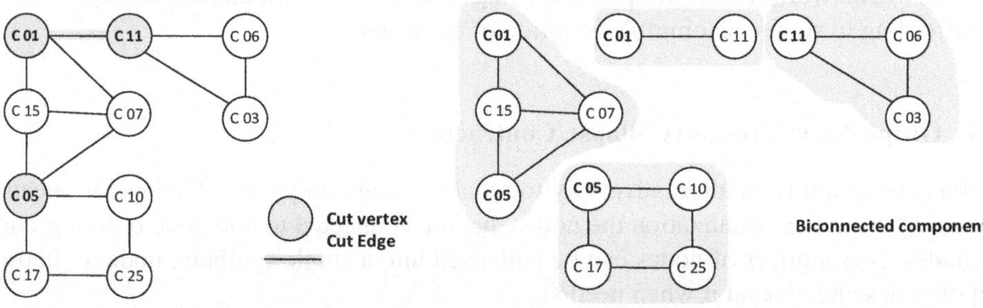

Fig. 4. Example of cut edge and cut vertex

A graph is biconnected if it contains no articulation points. (In general, a graph is k-connected, if k vertices must be removed to disconnect the graph). The concept of a cut point can be extended from a single node to a set of nodes necessary to keep graph connected. Those nodes are referred to as a cut-set. A node cut-set is a subset of the nodes of a graph, whose removal (simultaneously removing all edges adjacent to those nodes) makes the graph no longer connected. If the set is of size k, then it is called a k-node cut, denoted by k(G). That is, the K(G) of a graph is the minimum number of the nodes that must be removed to make the graph G disconnected.

- Utility: Biconnected graphs, articulation points, bridge are of great interest in the analysis of d content graph because these are the "critical" points, whose failure will result in the network becoming disconnected. Also, the biconnected components of a graph are the equivalence classes (see Sect. 4.1).

4.3 Clustering

Clustering is a process of finding such groups based on chosen semantics. According to this semantics, the current clustering approaches can be roughly classified into two categories: content-based clustering and structured based clustering. Content-based uses semantic aspects of data such a category labels, while structure-based clustering takes advantage of structural information about data. Moreover, structured-based clustering is domain-independent so that it is suitable for graph visualization.

In order to cluster a graph, a metric of a node in the graph is required to quantify its features. Based in this metric, existing approaches of partitioning graphs [10, 12] can be loosely divided into the following groups: connectivity based partitions, which use standard concepts from graph theory, distance partitions from selected subsets, Neighbourhood based partitions, and other approaches.

There are several ways how to rearrange a given matrix (correspond to the graph) determine an ordering or permutation of its rows and columns. To get some insight into its structure:

- Utility: The goal of clustering is to reduce a large, potentially incoherent network to a smaller comprehensible structure that can be interpreted more readily. A clustered graph can greatly reduce visual complexity by replacing a set of nodes in a cluster with an abstract node. Clustering, as an empirical procedure, is based on the idea that units in a network can be grouped according to the extent to which they are equivalent, according to some meaningful definition of equivalence.

4.4 Graph Node Groups (Collapse/Contraction)

Collapsing graph is an alternative way to reduce visual complexity. Collapsing means removing from the visualization the nodes that are connected to one node or to a group of nodes. Any number of nodes can be collapsed into a single synthetic node: collapse set of nodes and expand it when needed.

Such a synthetic node contains a user-provided text instead of normal disassembly listing.

- Utility: If a graph is too large to fit on the screen, groups of related nodes are (clustered) collapsed into super-nodes. The users see a "summary" of the graph, namely the super-nodes and super-edges between the super-nodes. Some clusters may be shown in more detail than others. The process collapsing involves discovering groups in the data. In the case of graph visualizing collapsing nodes Groups can be un-collapsed to display the original node content.

4.5 The Degree of a Vertex and Adjacency List

A graph consists of vertices and edges connecting these vertices. The degree of a vertex i is the number of edges incident with it, except that a loop at a vertex contributes twice to the degree of that vertex. The degree of the vertex v is denoted by deg(v) and calculate from the adjacency or the neighborhood of vertex. Two vertices u and v are called adjacent or neighbors if u and v are endpoints of an edge e of G = (V, E). The degree of a vertex represents the number of edges incident to that vertex. Figure 5 shows an example of a graph and the degree of each vertex.

- Utility: To analyze a graph it is important to look at the degree of a vertex. The degree of vertex informs the Criticality of contents. Critical contents are those that have a significant number of links to other contents. In this example, content C33 correspond to 14% of the total number of links.

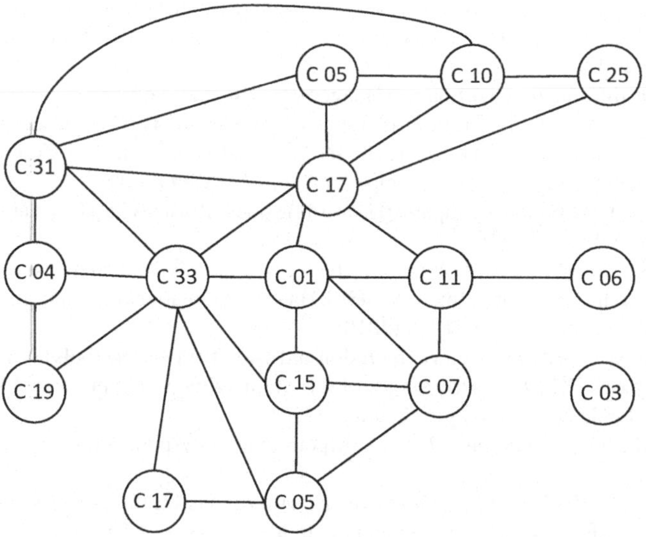

V	deg(v)
C 31	5
C 05	3
C 10	3
C 25	2
C 17	7
C 04	3
C 33	8
C 01	5
C 11	4
C 06	1
C 03	0
C 07	4
C 15	4
C 19	2
C 05	4
C 17	2

Fig. 5. The degree of a vertex

4.6 Singleton

The singleton graph is the graph consisting of a single isolated node with no edges. It is, therefore, the empty graph on one node. In Fig. 4, the vertex D03 is a singleton.

- Utility: As known, there are two types of innovation: Incremental and Disruptive (or radical). Incremental innovation is a series of small improvements or upgrades made to a company's existing products, services, processes or methods. In the other hand, disruptive innovation is an invention that changes radically an existing product, services, process or method. We believe that a singleton in our content graph may bring a disruptive idea to participants in the ideation session.

5 Conclusion

This document intersects with the improvement of the use of the ECM result in the ideation phase. We propose to use graph theory to facilitate access to the analysis results.

The advantage of using the visualization of the results in the form of a graph was presented. The tools presented in this paper permit to analyze ECM results and to give indications about the relation between the used contents.

These tools aimed to highlight some particularities which are useful in the ideation session. Future research should consider some of these suggestions to further extend this line of research. Also, it would be interesting to explore other analysis properties.

References

1. Hicks, B.J., Culley, S.J., Allen, R.D., Mullineux, G.: A framework for the requirements of capturing, storing and reusing information and knowledge in engineering design. Int. J. Inf. Manag. **22**, 263–280 (2002)
2. AIIM: Association for Information and Image Management. www.aiim.org
3. Usman, M., Muzaffar, A.W., Rauf, A.: Enterprise content management (ECM): needs, challenges and recommendations. In: 2009 2nd IEEE International Conference on Computer Science and Information Technology, 8–11 August 2009, pp. 283–289 (2009)
4. Nonaka, I.: The Knowledge-Creating Company (Harvard Business Review Classics). Harvard Business School Press, Boston (2008)
5. Brocke, J.V., Seidel, S., Simons, A.: Bridging the gap between enterprise content management and creativity: a research framework. In: 2010 43rd Hawaii International Conference on System Sciences, 5–8 January 2010, pp. 1–10 (2010)
6. Escandon-Quintanilla, M.L.: Effects of data exploration and use of data mining tools to extract knowledge from databases (KDD) in early stages of the engineering design process (EDP). Doctoral dissertation, École de Technologie supérieure (2017)
7. Bang-Jensen, J., Gutin, G.Z.: Digraphs: Theory, Algorithms and Applications. Springer, Heidelberg (2008)
8. Herman, I., Melançon, G., Marshall, M.S.: Graph visualization and navigation in information visualization: a survey. IEEE Trans. Vis. Comput. Graph. **6**(1), 24–43 (2000)
9. Eades, P., Tamassia, R.: Algorithms for drawing graphs: an annotated bibliography. Brown University (1988)
10. Harel, D., Koren, Y.: Graph drawing by high-dimensional embedding. In: Goodrich, M.T., Kobourov, S.G. (eds.) GD 2002. LNCS, vol. 2528, pp. 207–219. Springer, Heidelberg (2002). https://doi.org/10.1007/3-540-36151-0_20
11. Hossain, M.I., Rahman, M.S.: Good spanning trees in graph drawing. Theor. Comput. Sci. **607**, 149–165 (2015)
12. Everitt, B., Landau, S., Leese, M., Stahl, D.: Cluster Analysis. Wiley, Chichester (2011)

A Property Graph Data Model for a Context-Aware Design Assistant

Romain Pinquié[1(✉)], Philippe Véron[2], Frédéric Segonds[3], and Thomas Zynda[4]

[1] Univ. Grenoble Alpes, CNRS, Grenoble INP, G-SCOP, Grenoble, France
romain.pinquie@grenoble-inp.fr
[2] LISPEN, Arts et Métiers ParisTech, Aix-en-Provence, France
philippe.veron@ensam.eu
[3] LCPI, Arts et Métiers ParisTech, Paris, France
frederic.segonds@ensam.eu
[4] Capgemini, Toulouse, France
thomas.zynda@capgemini.com

Abstract. [Context] The design of a product requires to satisfy a large number of design rules so as to avoid design errors. [Problem] Although there are numerous technological alternatives for managing knowledge, design departments continue to store design rules in nearly unusable documents. Indeed, existing propositions based on basic information retrieval techniques applied to unstructured engineering documents do not provide good results. Conversely, the development and management of structured ontologies are too laborious. [Proposition] We propose a property graph data model that paves the way to a context-aware design assistant. The property graph data model is a graph-oriented data structure that enables us to formally define a design context as a consolidated set of five sub-contexts: social, semantic, engineering, operational IT, and traceability. [Future work] Connected to or embedded in a Computer Aided Design (CAD) environment, our context-aware design assistant will extend traditional CAD capabilities as it could, for instance, ease: (1) the retrieval of rules according to a particular design context, (2) the recommendation of design rules while a design activity is being performed, (3) the verification of design solutions, (4) the automation of design routines, etc.

Keywords: Design rule · Graph modelling · Knowledge management · Context-awareness · Cognitive assistant

1 Introduction

[Context] Designing a product is a knowledge-intensive activity. Thus, to prevent design errors, that is, choices that make certain designs "not allowed" or inappropriate for their intended use, design departments prescribe design rules. A design rule is a prescriptive statement – often an unstructured blend of text and graphical objects (equation, table, chart, sketch, etc.) – aiming at assisting deployed designers for the achievement of a valid design, in compliance with best practices, applicable regulations, and Design for X

Published by Springer Nature Switzerland AG 2019
C. Fortin et al. (Eds.): PLM 2019, IFIP AICT 565, pp. 181–190, 2019.
https://doi.org/10.1007/978-3-030-42250-9_17

constraints. To store the bewildering array of design rules, companies use unstructured documents – mainly in PDF format – which are over tens or hundreds of pages.

[Problem] Formerly, when companies used to store tens of design rules and share them among tens of designers in a unique design office, documents remained adequate. However, today, for various reasons, a document-based approach is not suitable anymore. First, the large number of experts and the geographically dispersed teams make the collection of design rules in documents cumbersome. That is all the more true at a time when design rules are stored in multiple repositories: documents, databases, models, expert's head, etc. Once stored in a repository, design rules must be validated "Are we defining the right design rule?", verified "Are we defining the design rule right?", and managed for decades but change management using documents is laborious. Finally, when a designer must provide a design free of errors, it has no other alternative than to go through the "Big Data" and spend a large amount of time to retrieve the subset of design rules that matches its own design context. Because of the aforementioned reasons and the recent Renaissance of the Model-Based approach encouraging a full model-based engineering, we state that unstructured documents can no longer serve as an efficient solution for storing design rules. There is a need for a context-aware design assistant that aids designers in the collection, organisation, retrieval, use, and modification of design rules.

[Proposal] The main contribution of this paper is twofold. First, we will analyse the operational view of the context-aware design assistant to identify the stakeholders and the services the assistant shall provide to them. Second, based on the identified services, we will derive the graph-property data model that will support the context-aware design assistant.

2 Literature Review

[Information retrieval] The problem of providing the right information to the right person at the right time is one of the fundamental goals that motivated academics and industrialists to work out a new strategic product-centric, lifecycle oriented and information-driven approach – Product Lifecycle Management (PLM). Numerous PLM and knowledge engineering research studies proposed state-of-the-art solutions to improve the access and reuse of information stored in engineering documents [1–5]. Although, the basic information retrieval capabilities – e.g. keyword search, faceted search, etc. – of search engines facilitate the access to textual content, the lack of a structured representation degrades the performance for many reasons (technical terms, ambiguities, etc.) [6]. This is the reason why researchers have reused semantic web techniques including modelling languages (e.g. RDF, RDFS, OWL), query languages (e.g. SQWRL), and software (e.g. Protégé) for modelling domain-specific knowledge, such as geometry and topology [7, 8], feature recognition [9], generative modelling [10], nuclear design rules [11], configuration management [12] and so on. An ontology, in its broadest sense, that is, a description providing a shared understating of a given domain, facilitate the reuse of knowledge, but it is extremely time-consuming to be developed and maintained. It is therefore interesting to use natural language processing and text mining techniques to not only automate the acquisition and processing of knowledge, but also to integrate both rule-based and machine learning-based capabilities to make the assistant "intelligent".

[Cognitive assistant] Cognitive assistants, which are also known as expert systems or knowledge-based agents, are "intelligent" computer programs that learn more or less complex problem-solving expertise from human experts so as to assist human nonexpert in solving similar problems [13]. One key feature of cognitive assistant is its ability to adapt itself to a given context that is not limited to linguistic characteristics like information retrieval systems. It can therefore provide better answers than a search engine. For instance, a cognitive assistant could process multi-factorial information including the user role, its social relationships in the company, the operational CAX environment he is using, etc. to provide personalised answers to questions asked by a designer.

[Context-aware] Many research studies on knowledge management refer to the concept of "context". For instance, Dhuieb et al. [14] propose a framework for managing manufacturing knowledge with a multiscale and context-aware approach. Although the application to manufacturing differs to design, the authors provide us with some details on the definition of the context that includes three viewpoints: operational (activities and task of the worker), organizational (team and role of the worker), and user-centric (expertise and skills). Related to our research goal, Rowson et al. [15] investigate the idea of building reusable expert knowledge using screen monitoring and contextual similarity. Context similarity is defined as the identification in real time of a resemblance between the script under elaboration and schemes in the knowledge base, but it seems to us that too many aspects of the framework are assumed, such as the form and the content of the knowledge base, the way it is fed with information, the query language and patterns, the similarity measure, etc. The concept of "context" remains therefore too fuzzy to be reused for our mission. If we extend our literature review to the theory of information retrieval in context, Ruthven [16] sums up the different way to explore context (related searches, keywords query expansion, query suggestion, etc.) based on various dimensions of the user context: task context, social context, personal context, spatio-temporal context, environmental context, etc. We may wonder, why is it so difficult to define what "context" means? The reason for this is simply that "context" is one of those suitcase-like words that we use to conceal the complexity of very large ranges of different things whose relationships we do not yet comprehend. In this paper, we propose to use a property graph data model to attempt to define the concept of context in product design.

[Property graph data model] A property graph data model is a model where data structures for the schema and/or instances are modeled as graphs for managing graph-like data and the data manipulation is expressed by graph-oriented operations using a graph query language [17]. A graph-oriented data structure facilitates the modelling of entities, relationships and properties that make up the design context. Using NoSQL graph-oriented database systems such as Neo4J is also flexible as we can create, read, update, and delete nodes and relationships without impacting the schema. This is a very important advantage since we will never come up with a complete property graph data model the first attempt.

3 A Property Graph Data Model for a Context-Aware Design Assistant

In this section, first, we detail the operational view, that is, the stakeholders, the services the context-aware design assistant shall provide to the stakeholders, and the inputs/outputs of the assistant. Second, we give the gist of the modelling process that leaded us to the property graph data model underlying the context-aware design assistant.

3.1 Operational Analysis of the Context-Aware Design Assistant

Our context-aware design assistant is a knowledge-based cognitive assistant that shall help designers to provide solutions satisfying applicable design rules.

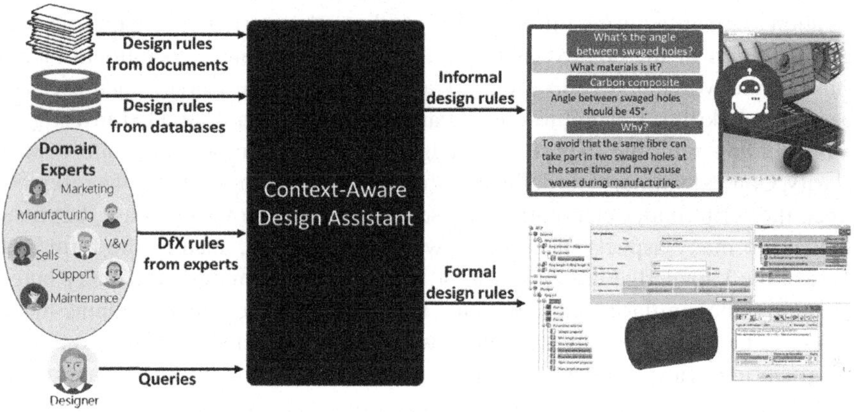

Fig. 1. Context diagram of the context-aware design assistant

Figure 1 illustrates the stakeholders interacting with the context-aware design assistant. So far, we have identified two types of intended effects (outputs). First, the context-aware design assistant shall recommend informal – i.e. not computable – design rules to the designer. We do not guess how this service will be implemented – e.g. Chatbot, recommendation engine, search engine, (un)supervised learning, etc. Second, the context-aware design assistant shall communicate computable design rules to extend CAX capabilities (e.g. automating modelling routines, enriching models with semantic annotations, verifying design solutions, etc).

To provide both services, the context-aware design assistant requires inputs. In the one hand, there are the design rules that feed the context-aware design assistant. The design rules, which are recognized and codified knowledge [18], mainly come from unstructured (e.g. PDF, Word, etc.) documents, semi-structured (e.g. Excel, XML, etc.) documents, and databases. The second main source of design rules, which are recognized tacit knowledge (e.g. commonsense) or unrecognized knowledge (e.g. expertise and skill) [18], corresponds to domain experts (e.g. marketing, manufacturing, V&V, sells, support, maintenance, etc.) who shall systematize [18] Design for X rules in the context-aware design environment throughout the product lifecycle. Finally, in addition to the inputs corresponding to design rules, designers shall provide queries to interact with the context-aware design assistant.

3.2 Modelling of the Property Graph Data Model

To derive the property graph data model that supports the mission of the context-aware design assistant, that is, "*As a designer, I want to know which design rules my design shall satisfy, so that I can provide proof design.*", we follow a systematic 4-step modelling process:

1. Find what questions the context-aware design assistant shall help designers to answer;
2. For each question, identify entities (nodes of the property graph) and relationships (edges of the property graph);
3. Express each question as a graph pattern.
4. Translate the graph pattern into a query path.

The simplest question to answer is a graph pattern corresponding to a predicate, that is, a triple (Subject – Predicate → Object) as follows:

Question	Which (design rules) [has_material] (material *X*)?
Graph Pattern	
Query Path	(:Design_rule) – [:HAS_MATERIAL] → (:Material)

Using such query, we can answer various questions, such as: Which design rule has manufacturing process *X*? Which design rule belongs to the engineering domain *X*? etc.

A graph-oriented data model brings an added-value when queries traverse richly interconnected data. We can therefore answer more sophisticated questions such as the one hereafter.

Question	Which design rules are favored by person who use the same software as me?
Graph Patterns	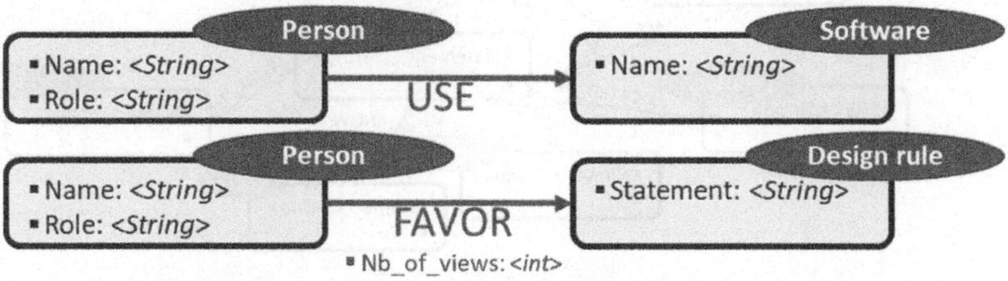
Consolidated Graph Pattern	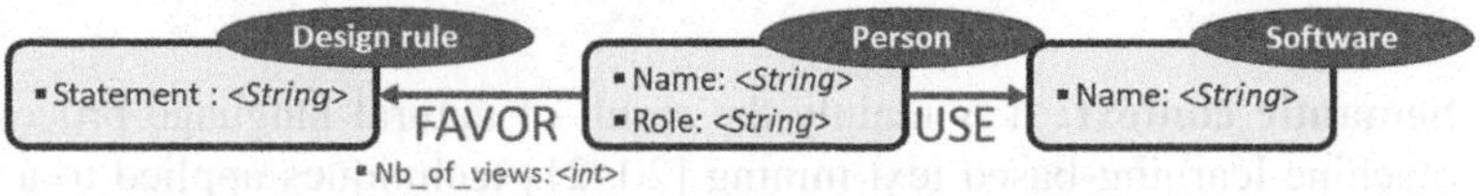
Query Path	(:Design_rule) ← [:FAVOR] – (:Person) – [:USE] → (:Software)

It is challenging to enumerate all questions that the context-aware design assistant shall answer. Another complementary reductionist approach consists in defining the parts, which are not questions but pieces of the design context, before reassembling each component to recreate the whole property graph data model (Fig. 2). In general, there is a need for zigzagging between both approaches.

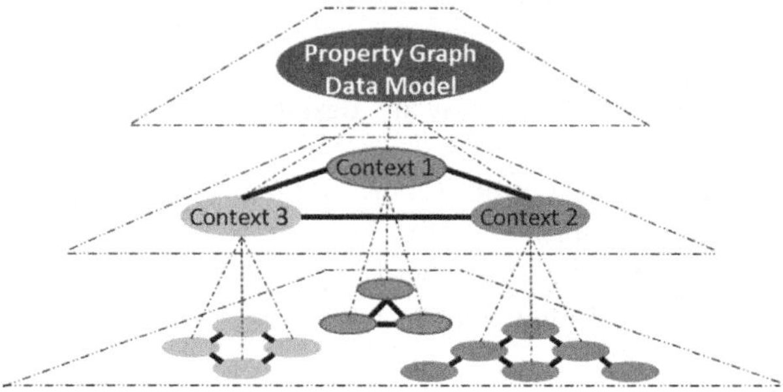

Fig. 2. Multi-level design context modelling

So far, we have identified five sub-contexts that make up the overall design context. Each sub-context is a sub-graph that we illustrate hereafter. To remain synthetic, we do not provide all properties of entities and relationships. For each context, we also give clues on how information can be acquired.

- **Social context:** It is the user profile and its relationships with colleagues. To capture the information, we ask each designer to fill a user profile form except for ":FRIEND_OF" relationships which are extracted from the social platforms deployed within the company (e.g. Slack, Skype, etc.) (Fig. 3).

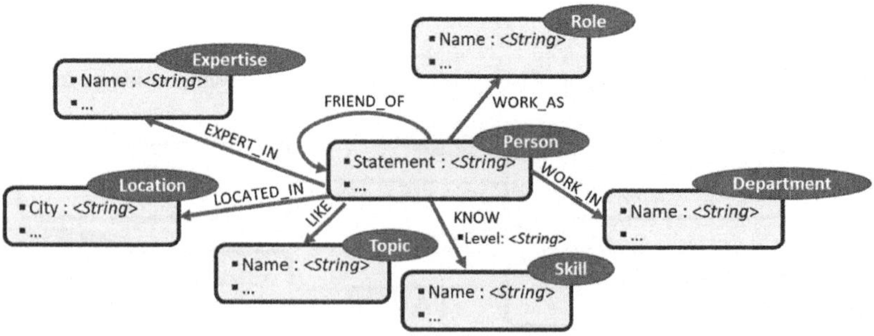

Fig. 3. Social context sub-property graph model

- **Semantic context:** It is mainly the result of natural language processing [19] and machine learning-based text mining [20, 21] techniques applied to a textual design rule. Keywords are words tagged with a part-of-speech corresponding to a noun, a verb, an adjective, or an adverb. In addition to the part-of-speech tagging, natural language processing techniques (sentence splitting, tokenization, lemmatization, and stemming) enable us to derive the stem and the lemma of each keyword. Removing the inflected forms of the keywords – lemmatization – enable us to get linguistically-related terms (synonym, holonym, meronym, hypernym, derived related terms, and the definition) from the Wordnet thesaurus. In addition to extend keywords with linguistic contextonys, we can use the open multilingual knowledge graph ConceptNet to find related concepts. For instance, using the conceptual relationship (:Airplane) – [:USED_FOR] → (:Travel) we can ease the navigation among design rules containing both entities (:Airplane) and (:Travel). The self-relationship [:SIMILAR_TO] on the (:Lemma) entity helps to retrieve similar normalised keywords (lemmas). The similarity score is computed using the Word2vec [22] and GloVe [23] language models (Fig. 4).

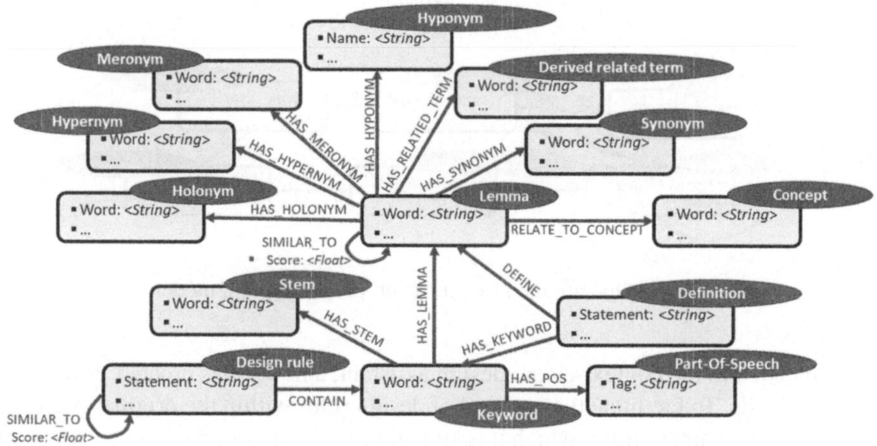

Fig. 4. Semantic context sub-property graph model

- **Engineering context:** It is a set of interrelated engineering information that is also derived by processing the text of the design rule statement. By using a rule-based classifier and taxonomies that enumerate materials, manufacturing process, and bill-of-materials we can identify keywords corresponding to specific domain knowledge. Thus, when a designer is looking for design rules related to a rib made of aluminum, he can explore such graph patterns. The (:Expertise) – e.g. electronics, mechanics, IT, etc. – entity to which the design rule belongs to can be inferred using a supervised machine-learning based classifier [20] (Fig. 5).
- **Operational IT context:** It is the current working IT situation within which the designer operates. The software (e.g. CATIA), the workbench (e.g. Part Design), and the operation (e.g. Extrusion) are software processes running on a machine and human-machine interactions that we can monitor. The data being edited (e.g. Beam.prt) and the PDM project within which the designer is working can be captured using the API of the PDM software. The self-relationship [:LINK_TO] represents link between data in the PDM software (e.g. link between a CAD model, its FEA mesh, and its 2D drawing) (Fig. 6).
- **Traceability context:** Finally, the traceability context enables designers to trace the origin of the design rules and manage their changes. When one or several documents

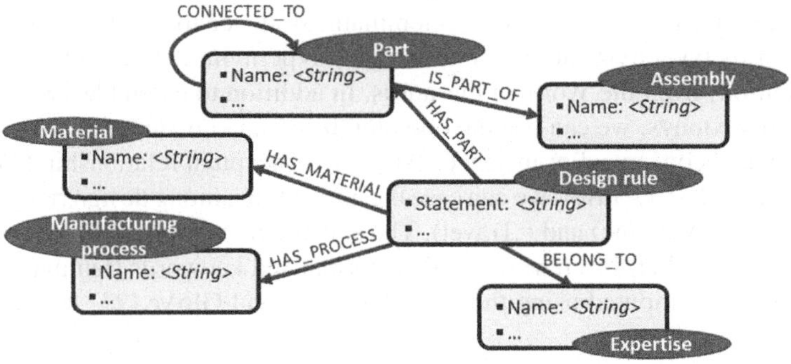

Fig. 5. Engineering context sub-property graph model

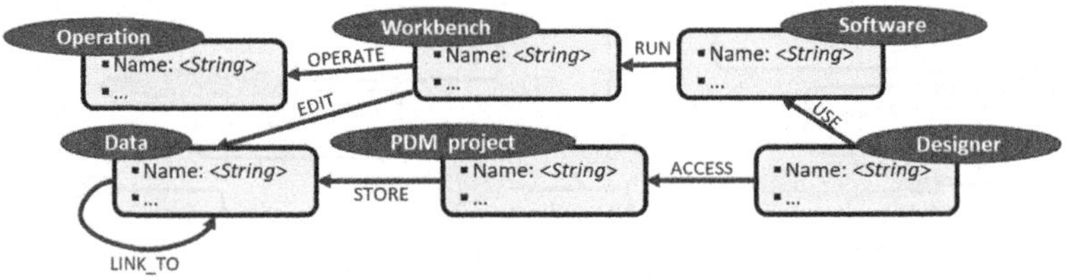

Fig. 6. Operational IT context sub-property graph model

are uploaded to the context-aware design assistant, a new job is created. Job serves to trace uploads. To facilitate the retrieval of design rules within the original documents, we trace the chapter within which it is stated. Most document parsers can retrieve the structure of documents, but there is a limit for some PDF documents encoded in a format that does not provide relevant semi-structured HTML or XML tags. The author of the design rule is either the person that directly prescribes it in the design assistant or the metadata "author" of the document source. Documents parser such as Apache Tika enables us to extract metadata. Finally, basic engineering change management concepts (maturity, revision and iteration) serve to trace the lifecycle of design rules and result from user manual inputs (Fig. 7).

3.3 Consolidation of Sub-property Graph Data Models

All sub-graphs corresponding to sub-contexts must be consolidated to end up with the property graph data model. We do not provide an overview of the whole property graph but we illustrate the concept of consolidation by merging the sub-graph of the social context and the sub-graph of the engineering context using the relationship [:HAS_TOPIC]. This consolidation enables designers to answer new questions such as "Which design rules belong to the expertise ($X = e.g.\ Mechanics$) that has topic ($Y = e.g.\ mechanical\ joints$) is liked by a designer who is a friend of mine?" (Fig. 8)

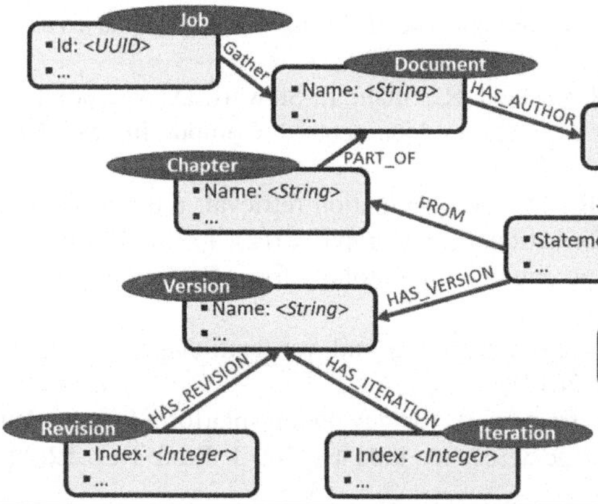

Fig. 7. Traceability context sub-property graph model

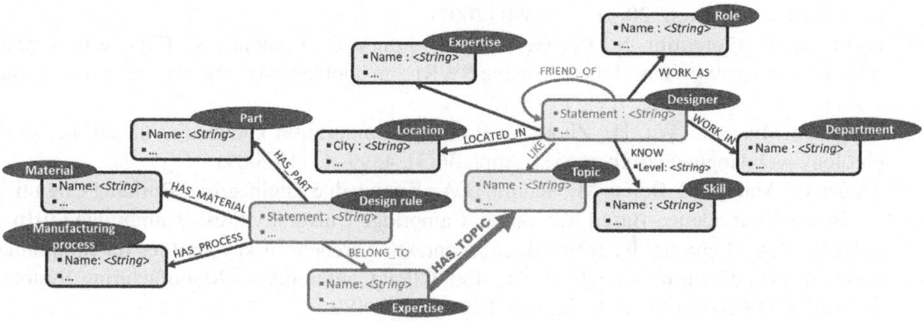

Fig. 8. Example of a consolidation of the social and engineering contexts

4 Conclusion

In this paper, we propose a property graph data model to support a context-aware design assistant. The assistant will use contextual knowledge to retrieve relevant design rules so that designers can create proof designs. The proposed property graph is the consolidation of five sub-contexts that can be queried using graph patterns.

As future work, we intend to continue to enrich our property graph data model and to develop the services that the context-aware design assistant shall provide to designers (design rules recommendation, design verification, design routines automation, etc.).

References

1. Dong, A., Agogino, A.M.: Text analysis for constructing design representations. In: Gero, J.S., Sudweeks, F. (eds.) Artificial Intelligence in Design 1996, pp. 21–38. Springer, Dordrecht (1996). https://doi.org/10.1007/978-94-009-0279-4_2
2. Marsh, J.R.: The capture and utilization of experience in engineering design. Ph.D. thesis, Cambridge University, UK (1997)

3. Song, S., Dong, A., Agogino, A.: Modeling information needs in engineering databases using tacit knowledge. J. Comput. Inf. Sci. Eng. **2**(3), 199–207 (2003)
4. McMahon, C., Lowe, A., Corderoy, M., Crossland, R., Shah, T., Stewart, D.: Waypoint: an integrated search and retrieval system for engineering documents. J. Comput. Inf. Sci. Eng. **4**(4), 329–338 (2004)
5. Yang, M.C., Wood, W.H., Cutkosky, M.R.: Design information retrieval: a thesauri-based approach for reuse of informal design information. Eng. Comput. **21**(2), 177–192 (2005)
6. Li, Z., Raskin, V., Ramani, K.: Developing engineering ontology for information retrieval. ASME J. Comput. Inf. Sci. Eng. **8**(1), 21–33 (2008)
7. Tessier, S., Wang, Y.: Ontology-based feature mapping and verification between CAD systems. Adv. Eng. Inform. **27**(1), 76–92 (2013)
8. Sanya, I.O., Shehab, E.M.: An ontology framework for developing platform-independent knowledge-based engineering systems in the aerospace industry. Int. J. Prod. Res. **52**(20), 6192–6215 (2014)
9. Wang, Q., Yu, X.: Ontology based automatic feature recognition framework. Comput. Ind. **65**(7), 1041–1052 (2014)
10. Sharka, W.: Application of MOKA methodology in generative model creation using CATIA. Eng. Appl. Artif. Intell. **20**(5), 677–690 (2007)
11. Fortineau, V., Fiorentini, X., Paviot, T., Louis-Sidney, L., Lamouri, S.: Expressing formal rules within ontology-based models using SWRL: an application to the nuclear industry. Int. J. Prod. Lifecycle Manag. **7**(1), 75–93 (2014)
12. Yang, D., Miao, R., Wu, H., Zhou, Y.: Product configuration knowledge modelling using ontology web language. Expert Syst. Appl. **36**(3), 4399–4411 (2009)
13. Tecuci, G., Marcu, D., Boicu, M., Schum, D.A.: Knowledge Engineering: Building Cognitive Assistants for Evidence-Based Reasoning. Cambridge University Press, Cambridge (2016)
14. Dhuieb, M.A., Laroche, F., Bernard, A.: Context-awareness: a key enabler for ubiquitous access to manufacturing knowledge. In: 48th CIRP Conference on Manufacturing Systems – CIRPS CMS 2015 (2016). Procedia CIRP **41**, 484–489
15. Rowson, H., Bricogne, M., Roucoules, L., Durupt, A., Eynard, B.: Knowledge capture and reuse through expert's activity monitoring in engineering design. In: Chiabert, P., Bouras, A., Noël, F., Ríos, J. (eds.) PLM 2018. IAICT, vol. 540, pp. 621–630. Springer, Cham (2018). https://doi.org/10.1007/978-3-030-01614-2_57
16. Ruthven, I.: Information retrieval in context. In: Melucci, M., Baeza-Yates, R. (eds.) Advanced Topics in Information Retrieval. INRE, vol. 33, pp. 187–207. Springer, Heidelberg (2011). https://doi.org/10.1007/978-3-642-20946-8_8
17. Angles, R.: The property graph database model. In: 12th Alberto Mondelzon International Workshop on Foundations of Data Management, Cali, Colombia, 21–25 May (2018)
18. Yoshikawa, H.: Systematization of design knowledge. CIRP Ann. – Manuf. Technol. **42**(1), 131–134 (1993)
19. Pinquié, R., Véron, P., Segonds, F., Croué, N.: Natural language processing of requirements for model-based product design with ENOVIA/CATIA V6. In: Bouras, A., Eynard, B., Foufou, S., Thoben, K.-D. (eds.) PLM 2015. IAICT, vol. 467, pp. 205–215. Springer, Cham (2016). https://doi.org/10.1007/978-3-319-33111-9_19
20. Pinquié, R., Véron, P., Segonds, F., Croué, N.: A requirement mining framework to support complex sub-systems suppliers. In: CIRP Design 2018, Nantes, France, 23–25 May (2018)
21. Pinquié, R., Véron, P., Segonds, F., Croué, N.: Requirement mining for model-based product design. Int. J. Prod. Lifecycle Manag. **9**(4), 305–332 (2016)
22. Mikolov, T., Chen, K., Corrado, G., Dean, J.: Efficient estimation of word representations in vector space (2013)
23. Pennington, J., Socher, R., Manning, C.D.: GloVe: global vectors for word representation (2014)

Toward a Hybrid Agile Product Development Process

Nicola Garzaniti(✉), Clément Fortin, and Alessandro Golkar

Skolkovo Institute of Science and Technology, Space Center, Nobel Street 3, 464 Skolkovo, Moscow 143026, Russia
nicola.garzaniti@skoltech.ru

Abstract. Both startups and traditional space industry are exploring new business opportunities and new engineering approaches in what is becoming known now as New Space.

Organizations started accelerating project schedules and challenging the V-model typically used in space product development. The need of a faster and more adaptive response to changing customer needs within an improved development productivity made Agile process a potential key enabler of New Space sector.

On the other hand, space system projects are typically executed in multi-party consortia. Each organization in a consortium adopts its own product development process and interprets "New Space" differently. For this reason, the implementation of Agile is not seamless as it requires coordination with traditional systems engineering approaches. This setup is what we refer to as "hybrid Agile product development process".

This paper provides a first definition of the architecture of hybrid product development process targeted toward systems development and lifecycle management of hardware projects developed by multi-party consortia. We consider this discussion in the context of the development of spaceflight hardware in the New Space industry. We identify the main challenges in adopting such a methodology in developing hardware systems. This work identifies opportunities of future work for defining coordination approaches in hybrid product development settings, and improved organization structures of hardware projects in hybrid development contexts.

Keywords: Collaborative product development process · Hybrid agile process · New Space · Agile PLM

1 Introduction

In the last decades we witnessed radical changes in global space activity with greater involvement from the private sector. These changes come together under the definition of "New Space" [1].

Organizations started accelerating project schedules and challenging classical product development processes such as the V-model [2] and the Stage-Gate model [3] typically used in space system developments. The need of a faster and more adaptive response

C. Fortin et al. (Eds.): PLM 2019, IFIP AICT 565, pp. 191–200, 2019.
https://doi.org/10.1007/978-3-030-42250-9_18

to changing customer needs within an improved development productivity makes Agile process [4] a potential key enabler of the New Space sector. Nevertheless, the question of whether Agile can truly fulfill its promise in complex hardware developments has not yet been thoroughly validated from a scientific perspective.

Several research projects have been dedicated to extend and tailor the Agile principles to hardware product development [5–7] but most process implementations were unsuccessful from the methodology point of view [7, 8].

The main reason behind those failures is potentially that space system projects are typically executed in multi-party consortia. Each organization in a consortium adopts its own product development process and interprets New Space differently. Therefore, the implementation of Agile is not seamless as it requires coordination with traditional systems engineering approaches.

This paper investigates this concern by providing a definition of Hybrid Product Development Process (Hybrid PDP) targeted toward systems development and lifecycle management of hardware projects developed by multi-party consortia.

We identify the main challenges in adopting such a methodology in developing hardware systems. We propose a coordination approach for hybrid Agile product developments and discuss strengths and limitations based on our initial findings. We limit the scope of the paper to the development of spaceflight hardware in the New Space industry context.

The remainder of the paper is structured as follows. Section 2 illustrates the architecture of hybrid product development. Section 3 discusses our preliminary findings on the implementation of Hybrid PDP on an industrial use case. Section 4 draws conclusions from the research and identifies avenues of future work.

2 Hybrid Product Development Architecture

The goal of our investigation is to define an approach to embed Agile in the traditional stage gate product development process. We analyze from a scientific perspective whether Agile combined with traditional stage-gate can work symbiotically, or whether the two approaches are mutually exclusive or just incompatible.

We provide a first definition of hybrid product development process from a holistic perspective targeted toward systems development and lifecycle management of hardware projects developed by multi-party consortia.

We consider this discussion in the context of the development of spaceflight hardware in the New Space industry.

2.1 Stage-Gate Model: Strengths and Weaknesses

Stage-gate approach [3], also called waterfall, phase gate, toll gate, checkpoint, or structured product development by different authors and practitioners [9] is a well-established product development process. Stage-gate has been designed to help firms to select the right projects, and once selected, to map out the key stages, best practice activities, and roles and responsibilities as part of the project, bringing discipline to "*chaotic*" new product development (NPD) activities [10].

The ideal stage-gate process proceeds in distinct stages from product planning to product release (Fig. 1). At the end of each phase is a review, or gate, to evaluate whether the previous phase was successfully completed. If the project is reviewed positively, work proceeds to the next phase. If not, then the project iterates within that phase until it can successfully pass the review or the project may be terminated.

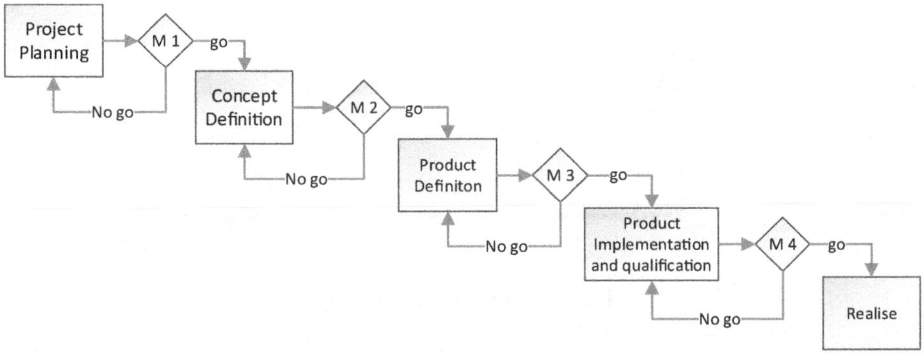

Fig. 1. Stage-Gate model

The major advantage of stage-gate processes is to provide structure to the development by reaching sharp product definitions and specifications early in product development. Technical risk is reduced because narrow iterations and reviews freeze specifications early. Rigid requirements and stable product definitions help to avoid errors by avoiding midstream corrections [9].

The main drawback of this product development process (PDP) is inflexibility. Narrow iterations cannot incorporate feedback from later phases. Failure may occur if early specifications and assumptions are proven wrong by subsequent market research or prototyping.

2.2 The Agile Way of Implementing Projects

Agile is a method that brings flexibility and speed to development projects: It includes micro-planning tools to get a working end-product quickly. This PDP is designed specifically for managing and supporting product developers in developing their system once the development project has been "approved."

Agile, particularly the Scrum version (Fig. 2) is a methodology that breaks the development process into a series of short, iterative, incremental *sprints* (i.e. development period)., each one to four weeks long. The main goal of Scrum is to deliver a *Minimum Viable Product* (MVP) at the end of each sprint (i.e. development period).

The work is decomposed into *stories* related to the development of the product. This decomposition provides structure to the development process. The collection of user stories forms the *product backlog* for the development. Each user story is characterized by a subset of the main high-level tasks (high-level product backlog) that will be divided later on, during the sprint planning, into smaller tasks that could be completed in a one-day time-frame. The goal in Sprint planning is to define a *Sprint backlog* taking tasks out

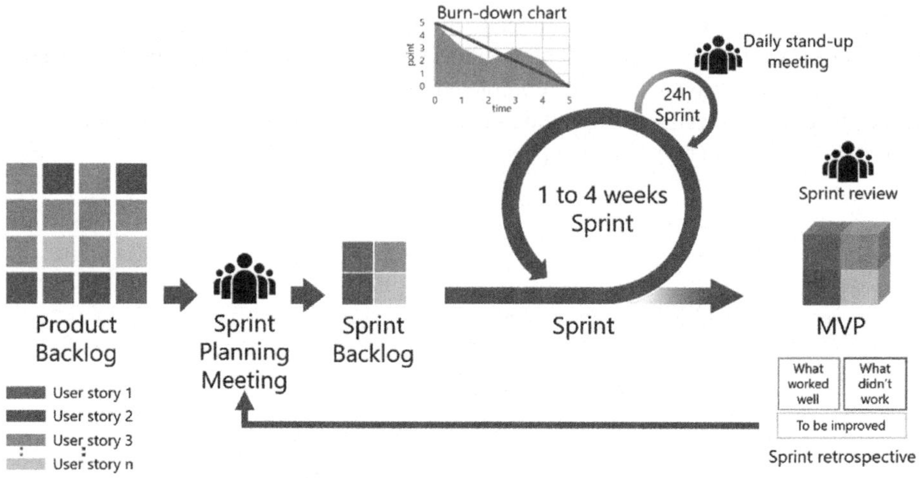

Fig. 2. Scrum process diagram

of the product backlog. Sprint planning is performed collaboratively among the members of the team using a Fibonacci sequence [11] scoring system to evaluate the complexity of the tasks and prioritize them within the one-week time box. A team member is assigned the role of "*Scrum master*," that is the facilitator in charge of coordinating inputs and running the Agile process. At the end of each Sprint, the team performs a retrospective analysis of the work in order to prepare for the next development iteration.

The tempo of the Sprint is given by daily 15-min stand up meetings and daily close-out meetings. In order to assess the correct implementation and to constantly monitor the development of the system, the team makes use of a set of tracking technologies to monitor the status of the process (e.g. Atlassian Jira [12]).

The main advantages of Agile are improved communication and coordination, quicker releases, and flexibility to allow quicker responses to changed customer requirements or technical context. However, Scrum presents some challenges for manufacturers, such as a lack of scalability, a proliferation of meetings, and very often a lack of management [13].

2.3 Hybrid Product Development Process for Physical Products

Hybrid Product Development Process embeds the Agile way of working within stage-gate driven product development. Hybrid PDP integrates traditional project management with Agile. The structure of hybrid product development can be described as a three-layer architecture (Fig. 3) composed of multiple project participants, each operating with its own product development process (Agile, stage-gate, or others).

At the top layer of the architecture we have the *consortium layer*. The consortium is the coordinating agent of the PDP; it provides overall management and coordination of the project. It is in charge of the governance of the project. The consortium defines overall mission requirements, the functional system requirements, the interfaces among

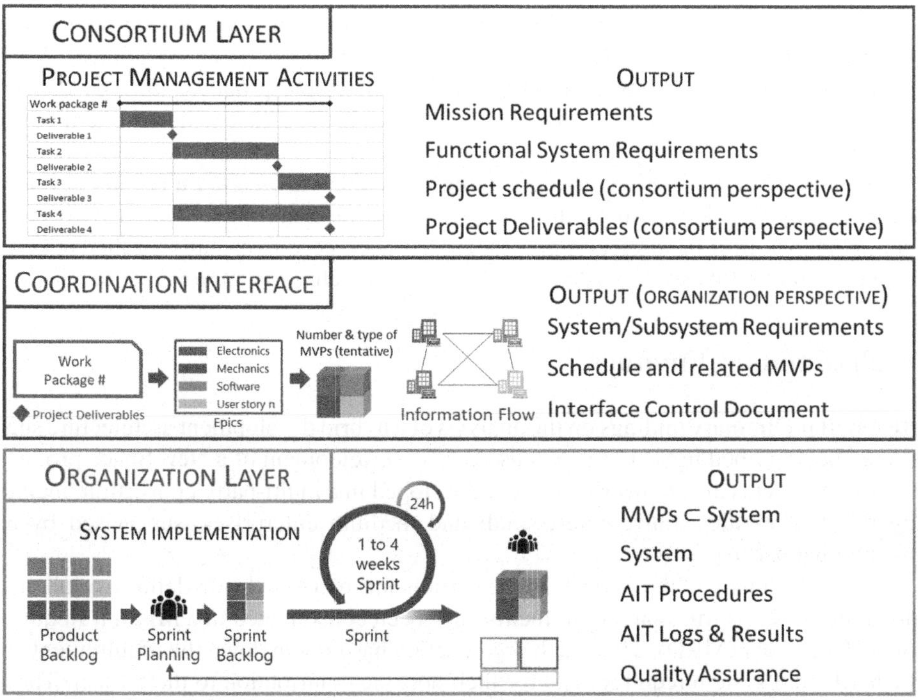

Fig. 3. Hybrid product development process architecture

all parties in the project and it coordinates project reviews and deliverables. The consortium is also in charge of making strategic decisions throughout the lifecycle of the project. Consortia can be operated using either PDP (Agile or stage-gate). In our initial investigation, we focus on consortia operating using traditional stage-gate processes.

Due to its structured nature, stage-gate provides natural means of coordination through decision gates and milestones, and it has been proven to work with very large, complex organizations. Future research, however, will investigate the possibility for having consortia operating using Agile, and investigating the conditions by which such process brings advantages (or disadvantages) compared to a more traditional stage-gate approach.

The *organization layer* sits at the bottom layer of the architecture. This layer groups together all the organizations participating the project. Each project participant operates its own product development process, and coordinates with each other through interfaces with the consortium layer.

The coordination is implemented through *coordination interface* defined at organization level. Each organization participating to the project defines the work packages or the minimum viable products (MVPs) to meet the deliverables defined in the top layer depending on the PDP they are operating. This layer can also implement information coordination through direct interfaces between the participating organizations. In the current setting we neglect the latter, and focus on the main structured means of coordination.

The key challenge in hybrid PDP architectures is reconciling coordination between Agile and stage-gate, that are designed under different operating principles. While the former aims at building incremental minimum viable products towards the target performance, the latter has the goal of achieving the target with no intermediate deliverables.

In particular organizations implementing Agile need to creating a project development backlog (for their own product) for roughing out a high-level tentative development plan that meet the project milestones. Then they need to ensure that the backlogs developed for sprints are consistent with the product definition approved at the gate.

3 Preliminary Findings

We report preliminary findings on the analysis of a hybrid development architecture such as the one described in Sect. 2.3 on a use case of development of a New Space product.

The product is an engineering system developed in a multi-party consortium including different entities: universities, small and medium enterprises, supervised by an institutional partner.

At the beginning of the project, all the participants met together to define overall mission requirements. Mission requirements have been consolidated in a Mission Requirements Document (MRD). Then each organization has broken down the requirements of the MRD into system requirements for their specific contribution to the project. Those requirements have been formalized into a System Requirements Document (SRD).

Based on those two documents (MRD and SRD), each organization has defined its own Product Development Process (PDP). The prime contractor structures the PDP at consortium level, defining in a Gantt chart the high-level activities and the main milestones. Traditional Space Flight Project Life Cycle (Fig. 5) has been adopted [14].

At the time of writing of this paper, the consortium has completed the path up to final system delivery.

In our investigation, we focus on one project participant that adopted Agile methodology to deal with fixed schedule and cost constraints. We analyze the metadata concerning the project the organization has provided. To ensure delivery of the system on a schedule of 12 months, they structured the development following an Agile approach (Scrum development process).

The organization moved directly from the *consortium layer* to the *organization layer* without implementing *coordination interfaces*. Because of this initial weakness in hybrid product development process several issues were encountered.

3.1 Work Breakdown

The organization implementing agile started decomposing the work into *user stories* related to the development of the main subsystems of the product, shaping the so called *product backlog* (Fig. 4). Within this activity the team did not set up *a priori* the Minimum Viable Products (MVPs) needed to meet the deliverable foreseen in the main schedule.

The lack of clear objective for all the MVPs and a clear view of the *big picture* yielded the rescheduling of several activities (a percentage close to the 35% $\pm$ 6% of the total

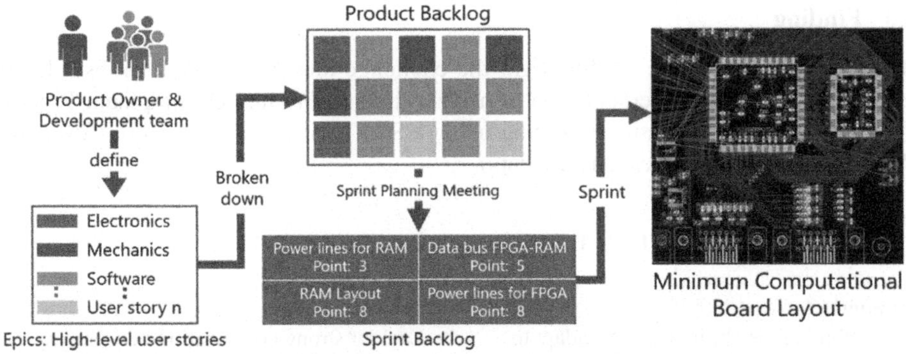

Fig. 4. Example of Agile implementation to realize one MVP

points foreseen for a given Sprint). That caused delays (in Fig. 5) and non-recurring engineering efforts (NREs). Furthermore, without a high-level tentative development plan, it was not possible to address early programmatic risks and develop a mitigation strategy.

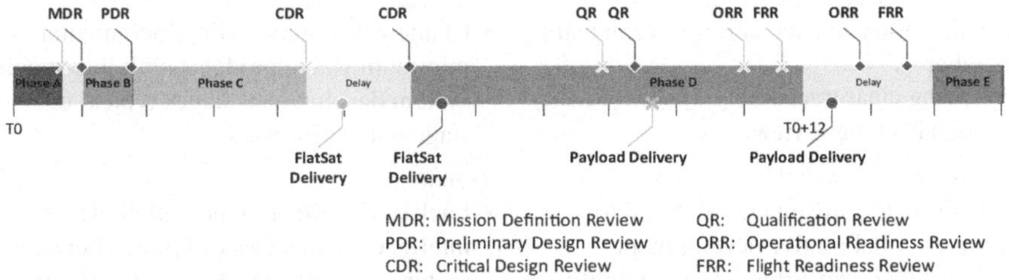

Fig. 5. Use case Project Life Cycle - we marked in yellow the foreseen milestones and in red the actual milestones (Color figure online)

3.2 Coordination with Partners

In the traditional Scrum approach all the development depends on the team. In Scrum, the development is entirely managed using Agile. Within a hybrid development architecture each organization in the consortium needs input from the other project participants and has to provide input to others.

The interfaces among all parties in the project have been defined at the consortium level. Technical interfaces have been formalized in the SRD (interface sections) and in the Interface Control Document (ICD). Due to the nature of the Agile process, most of the interfaces were not yet defined at the time of the consolidation of SRD and ICD (the system was at the concept level). Therefore, in order to deliver the document according to the schedule the development team has to make assumptions that sometimes have proven to be wrong in the later stages. This caused *requests for deviation* that impacted all the consortium.

3.3 Finding

Based on this experience we highlight the challenge they face, and use it as a lesson learned for a future implementation of a Hybrid Agile Product Development Process. We summarize the preliminary finding using a SWOT analysis framework (Strengths, Weaknesses, Opportunities, and Threats).

Table 1. SWOT analysis of Hybrid PDP

Strengths • Combining the ability to better adapt to changing requirements due to Agile, while keeping structured pace in the development through staged-gate processes • Allowing collaboration between organizations adopting heterogeneous product development processes • Accelerating project schedule by learning and adapting through rapid engineering iterations • Assigning clear responsibility and accountability of user stories to each team member • Providing clear traceability of work history through backlog review	*Weaknesses* • Lack of strong coordination between layers may lead to suboptimal results due to asynchronous pace of development • Lack of rigorous coordination methods requires tailoring of hybrid PDPs to the specific characteristics of each product development • Challenges in implementing rigorous verification and validation due to potentially diverging integration readiness of interdependent system components • Challenges in reconciling incremental minimum viable products with intermediate system development stages typical of stage-gated processes
Opportunities • Delivering the advantages of Agile to complex collaborative development projects, while ensuring interoperability with traditional PDPs • Accelerating speed of execution and product delivery to the market • Improved alignment with rapidly evolving competitive environments due to the inherent adaptability of hybrid PDPs • Potentially reducing development costs by shifting risk posture in complex hardware development projects	*Threats* • Lack of coordination potentially leading to interface mismatches or failures between system elements developed by different organizations • Lack of understanding between project participants or by the coordinating consortiums of the fundamental differences between stage-gated and Agile development processes • Lack of understanding of the motivations underlying the implementation of a hybrid PDP does not allow for efficient exploitation of benefits of Agile developments

4 Conclusion

A hybrid product development process that integrates elements of both Agile and Stage-Gate can help companies capitalize on the strengths of both.

Stages and gates remain an important part of this hybrid model. Stages provide a high-level overview of the project's main phases and a guide to required or recommended activities and expected deliverables for each stage. Gates provide vital go/kill decision points providing focus in the development pipeline.

Agile is used to structure execution within the development teams. In this way the deliverables specified for each gate are leaner, more flexible and less granular than in the classical model, and they are physical prototypes rather than reports or slide presentations.

The key element of the hybrid PDP is the *coordination interface*. It is crucial to reconcile incremental minimum viable products with intermediate system development stages typical of stage-gate processes.

The definition of high-level tentative development plan at the *coordination interface level* is needed to address early programmatic risks in the project and develop a mitigation strategy (it is not a common practice in pure Agile approach).

In this paper we described a use case of a hybrid product development architecture where the consortium did not implement a coordination layer. For this reason, coordination misalignments emerged, such as schedule and cost overrun, NREs and quality assurance issues related to the risk mitigation strategy and product verification and validation. We used the challenge faced by the project participants as a lesson learned to shape a preliminary implementation of a Hybrid Agile Product Development Process.

By combining Agile with Stage-gate, the hybrid PDP aims at accelerating project schedules and overcoming organizational limitations in New Space project development (or highly innovative projects in general). There are still challenges in reconciling the two approaches (as shown in Table 1). This work intended to contribute to this future and this vision shaping a strategy to enable the implementation of a hybrid PDP.

References

1. Paikowsky, D.: What Is new space? The changing ecosystem of global space activity. New Space **5**, 84–88 (2017). https://doi.org/10.1089/space.2016.0027
2. Lee, J.S., Miller, L.E.: INCOSE - Systems Engineering Handbook (2007). http://dl.acm.org/citation.cfm?id=552393
3. Cooper, R.G.: Stage-gate systems: a new tool for managing new products. Bus. Horiz. **33**, 44–54 (1990). https://doi.org/10.1016/0007-6813(90)90040-I
4. Beck, K., et al.: Manifesto for Agile Software Development (2001). http://agilemanifesto.org/
5. Thomke, S., Reinertsen, D.: Agile product development: managing development flexibility in uncertain environments. California Manag. Rev. **41**, 8–30 (1998). https://doi.org/10.2307/41165973
6. Huang, P.M., Darrin, A.G., Knuth, A.A.: Agile hardware and software system engineering for innovation. In: 2012 IEEE Aerospace Conference, pp. 1–10. IEEE (2012). https://doi.org/10.1109/aero.2012.6187425
7. Garzaniti, N., Briatore, S., Fortin, C., Golkar, A.: Effectiveness of the scrum methodology for agile development of space hardware. In: 2019 IEEE Aerospace Conference (2019). https://doi.org/10.1109/AERO.2019.8741892
8. Stepanova, D., Ballheimer, W., Van Ginkel, G., Joos, C., Skyrpnyk, I.: Scrum methodology in aerospace projects. In: 69rd International Astronautical Congress, Bremen, Germany (2018)
9. Unger, D.W., Eppinger, S.D.: Comparing product development processes and managing risk. Int. J. Prod. Dev. **8**, 382 (2009). https://doi.org/10.1504/IJPD.2009.025253

10. Sethi, R., Iqbal, Z.: Stage-gate controls, learning failure, and adverse effect on novel new products. J. Market. **72**, 118–134 (2008). https://doi.org/10.1509/jmkg.72.1.118
11. Falcon, S.: The k-Fibonacci difference sequences. Chaos, Solitons Fractals **87**, 153–157 (2016). https://doi.org/10.1016/j.chaos.2016.03.038
12. Jira | Issue & Project Tracking Software | Atlassian, (n.d.). https://www.atlassian.com/software/jira
13. Gregory, P., Barroca, L., Taylor, K., Salah, D., Sharp, H.: Agile challenges in practice: a thematic analysis. In: Lassenius, C., Dingsøyr, T., Paasivaara, M. (eds.) XP 2015. LNBIP, vol. 212, pp. 64–80. Springer, Cham (2015). https://doi.org/10.1007/978-3-319-18612-2_6
14. NASA, NPR 7120.8 Nasa Procedural Requirements (2008). https://nodis3.gsfc.nasa.gov/displayDir.cfm?t=NPR&c=7120&s=5E

A Data Preparation and Migration Framework for Implementing Modular Product Structures in PLM

Muni Prasad Giddaluru(✉) and James Gao(✉)

School of Engineering, University of Greenwich, Chatham Maritime ME4 4TB, UK
muniprasad3@gmail.com, J.Gao@gre.ac.uk

Abstract. This paper reports the research on the complex process of implementing modular product structures in a Product Lifecycle Management (PLM) system. There are many challenges in implementing the system. One main challenge is organising or mapping existing product data and migrating it to the new PLM system. Companies often use a PLM tool for management of CAD files, documents and drawings, but they do not take advantage of the full potential of the PLM system to support the development activities of modular products. Product data management tools are used mainly for product CAD data management and PLM systems support by automating and managing some of the operational complexity of modular product design. The aim of this research is to propose a data model that can be used for implementing modular product structures in a PLM system and a tool that can formalise the existing data so as to migrate it into the PLM system.

Keywords: Product life cycle management · Data migration · Modular product structures · Product Data Management

1 Introduction

PLM systems are now widely used in companies to manage product development and service processes from beginning to life cycle end [1]. Among the major changes in product development, the lifecycle management and time to market of new products are the big issues. Reducing the development cycle is always a challenge. There seems to have a general transformation in the industry in the last two decades from developing products in independent projects to the development of product families. Architecture based product development is one initiative in the product development area to address the changed way of developing products, which focuses on the design of product ranges instead of individual products, and by reuse of knowledge, components, processes and utilization of economies of scale in many of the activities that are necessary to provide products for customers. Product architecture development can be done through Modularization of commonality among different variants. Modularization of product structures can serve as a means to provide a variety of products that are needed for customers, and at

Published by Springer Nature Switzerland AG 2019
C. Fortin et al. (Eds.): PLM 2019, IFIP AICT 565, pp. 201–210, 2019.
https://doi.org/10.1007/978-3-030-42250-9_19

the same time re-use sub-solutions across different products to improve time-to-market [2]. To achieve this PLM tool should be implemented that will facilitate the modular structures and migrate the existing product data into the PLM system.

2 PLM System Architecture and Its Implementation Methods

By definition, PLM integrates product information, people and knowledge by controlling a company's processes [3]. The PLM concept holds the promise of seamlessly integrating all the information involved throughout all phases of a product's lifecycle to everyone in an organization at every managerial and technical level, along with key suppliers and customers. As such, PLM systems need the capability to serve up the information referred to the above, and they need to ensure the cohesion and traceability of product data. For an enterprise to be successful in today's and tomorrow's global markets, PLM is not an option, it is a competitive necessity [4].

A critical aspect of PLM systems is their product information modelling architecture. The traditional hierarchical approach to building software tools presents a dangerous potential pitfall: if PLM systems continue to access product information via Product Data Management (PDM) systems which, in turn, obtain geometric descriptions from Computer-Aided Design (CAD) systems, the information that becomes available will only be the CAD data. This is what most of the companies are using for. CAD data is a tiny portion of product information or knowledge [5]. In this research, a different approach is proposed in serving up information to PLM systems: a single PLM system support framework for product information that can access, store, serve and reuse all the product information throughout the entire product lifecycle. The full PLM system functionality can be achieved by the specific components: a Foundation Technologies (Infrastructure); Core functions; a set of business Applications; and a set of Business solutions [6].

The main elements of a typical PLM system architecture include PLM server, Web server, Mail server, Indexing server, Database server and few optional elements like Enterprise directory and administrative directory. The Java-based PLM server is the application layer of the system and provides system logic for behaviour and data element relationships. The Web server enables Web connectivity, giving Web-centric behaviour. These two elements comprise the technology core of the PLM solution. Client machines, which are the computers used by the user community, only require the latest browsers and network connectivity to access data and execute tasks. Since most PLM systems are Web-based applications, accessing information is as simple and familiar as browsing the Internet. Lightweight Directory Access Protocol (LDAP) server or Mail server to reference user, group, and organizational data. Most PLM systems also come bundled with a standalone LDAP server, the system Directory Server. You may also configure to access an existing corporate LDAP server, such as Microsoft's Active Directory. A database server, such as an Oracle server, is used as the repository for metadata. Content files may also be stored in the database, but they are often referenced and stored elsewhere in a file vault. The database server, Windchill server, Web server, and client machines, establish a three-tier architecture, which is scalable and more accessible to manage than traditional client-server environments. File vaulting is the process of storing content on an external file system, as opposed to BLOBS (Binary Large Objects) in the Windchill database. By default, contents are stored inside the database. However, file vaulting manages data on an external file system in folders and subfolders and reduces the time for uploading and downloading data. The storage location of content files is transparent to the user, so user operations do not have to be modified.

3 Data Model for Modular Product Structure Implementation

3.1 Modular Product Structure

Modular products consist of detachable modules, which can be manufactured, assembled, and serviced separately. Some of the modules may be reusable, recyclable or re-manufacturable upon product retirement. Thus, modular design can provide benefits to many aspects of the product life cycle [7]. Product modularity is primarily seen as a product structuring concept, in which the product is decomposed into smaller, more manageable chunks (modules) in order to better manage design and manufacturing complexity. The most common way this is done is by the decomposition of the product down to component level and then a grouping of the components to form modules. Modularity is a concept and process of clustering the independent components into logical units that are relatively independent of each other in functions [8]. Modular design methods that have been focused on include function-based [9, 10], manufacturing or assembly [11], and mass customization [12]. Ulrich and Tung [13] gave a summary of different types of modularity and their advantages and disadvantages.

Modularity allows the designer to control the degree to which changes in product maintenance and service processes affect the product design. By promoting interchangeability, modularity also gives designers more flexibility, with decreased cycle time, to meet these changing processes. The flexibility that modularity offers is increasingly vital as uncertainty in service requirements (due to new diagnostic and repair technology and ever-changing warranty agreements) increase. This flexibility allows some design decisions to be delayed because they have a lower impact on the total product. Controlling the effects of changes and being flexible in responding to changes are the benefits of modularity. A compliant product can more readily adapt to a late influx of service technology or a new shift in service strategy. To implement the modular product structure in PLM, a data model is proposed which is the primary task to implement the methodology. The object types and their relations are illustrated in Fig. 1.

The PLM system used in this research is Windchill which supports a number of different types of objects: Display object type 'PART' is used for all parts in the product and its Object Class is called WTPart. The product is represented as 'End Item' for display in the system and its Object Class is also called WTPart with an attribute as End Item and values Yes/No. CAD models are called as CAD Documents for display purpose and its Object Class is called EPMDocument. The objects have been carefully defined to provide the functionality of the multiple structure views, yet able to handle the interdependencies as systems split modules, modules containing elements belonging to different systems, and interfaces between different system elements.

The data model shown in Fig. 1 is proposed to implement in PLM system which facilitates to structure products with the modular methodology. The *product* is the final

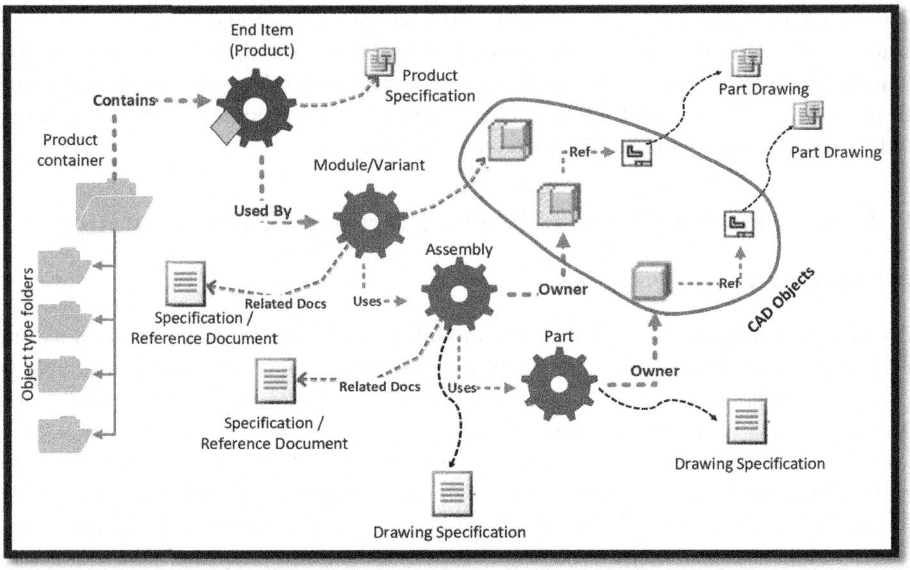

Fig. 1. Data model for modular product structure in PLM

End Item that the company will produce. This End item can be of 3 types, a Pre-Configured product, Configurable Product or Engineering to Order product. The soft type object in the system is called an End Item. As mentioned earlier this is recognized with an attribute that can be easily searchable either within the folder or in Global search. The proposed methodology is to have a single folder for each family of products. In the sponsoring company example, all products that are produced for 15 L Genset (Genset is the name of the final product). For clarity in this family, there are 2 types of configurable products and several pre-configurable products. Engineer TO Order (ETO) products are created depending on customers' requirements.

3.2 PLM Objects and Their Relations

The *End Item* or *Product* will have a Used-By relation with all the Modules called Variants in PLM terminology. Each variant may consist of one or more options depending on the requirements. All Modules will have 'Uses' relationship to all assemblies. Each option in the module shall have an assembly with Uses relationship. An assembly is the combination of physical components representing the module in three aspects, i.e., Form, Fit and Function. The assembly will have 'Owner' relation with the CAD object. There will be only one Owner for each WTPart and this is an essential object that defines the assembly. Other documents can be added as an attachment if required, but only one object will be the Owner. The *CAD assembly* is always defined by a CAD drawing and this will have Reference or Child relationship. The CAD assembly will the parent from which the CAD Drawing is created, and it is a child. The assembly will have at least one part and as more as hundred if required. The parts under an assembly are called Bill Of Material (BOM). Since the initial BOM is defined by engineering, this is known as Engineering Bill Of Materials (EBOM). As progressing this BOM is transferred to downstream functions it will be changed or converted according to their needs.

The *Part* is the single level item and it can be on its own in the product or it can be part of an assembly. This represents a manufacturable or purchased item that is used at a different level in the product. Part will have Owner relation with CAD object similar assembly explained earlier. The CAD models can have CAD drawing to define the CAD part that will have a Reference or Content relationship. Another object mentioned in the data model is Drawing Specification. This object act as a space holder for storing the CAD drawing in PDF format while that is in the process of releasing. This will only represent the CAD drawing, does not contain any reference to other specifications attached to WTPart. The WTPart can have many specifications attached likewise material specifications with which the part would be made, standards specification to which the part would comply, and Regulation specifications the part would comply to. The drawing specification does not reflect all these references.

Another document type used in the data model is *part drawing*. This is a place holder for In-Process document and final released drawing in PDF format. PLM system has got the ability to create an in-process document while the objects are in the Change Management process. Product containers will be created for each generic Product Context. The products, i.e., End Items are stored in these containers which are represented with a folder figure in the data model. Under each product container, there are multiple folders to store product information. Each folder can represent different objects types, for example, Change Management objects, CAD objects, WT Part objects, Specifications objects, End Items (Products), Project Management data and Manufacturing data. Since the objects relate to the relationships proposed earlier, they will have good traceability even though they are stored in different locations in the system. The proposed data model will bring all product information under one system with good parametric relationships between the objects created. This model would work with most PLM systems in the market. This data model is tested in the PTC Windchill PLM system. The next challenge is how to arrange the legacy, i.e., existing product data. For this, a tool has been designed and explained which is discussed below.

4 Product Data Preparation Methodology and Migration Tool Design

One of the biggest challenges in implementing any new PLM systems in the industry is to deal with existing product data or knowledge. All PLM systems provide tools for data migration, but they are mainly focused on AS-IS process, do not have many flexible methods to adopt any specific needs of companies. This is mainly because the tools from the software are developed for general-purpose, not for any specific industry or product types, which leads to having out of system solution.

4.1 Product Data Preparation Concept

Data translation and migration from one system to other system is increasingly difficult based on the volume of data, quality, and complexity. Automation of data translation and validations at each step helps to achieve a higher return on investment. Detailed planning, analysis, selection and prioritization of the data are some of the key parameters for successful data migration. It is important to try to establish the value of the data that is considered for conversion and the scope of that effort [14]. A sample data of few products are collected from the sponsoring company. The well-defined product structure of this product type is studied and incorporated into the tool.

In the industrial investigation from the sponsor company, all the configurable product structure is created in an Excel document as the part of new product development and the same is maintained manually when there are changes to the structure. This is the main document for product structure information for all products. Only the top four levels of the product structure are maintained in this document, the rest of all intended levels of product structure are maintained in Enterprise Resource Planning (ERP) system. Some levels of structures are created and maintained in CAD/CDM systems and product configurator depending on the requirements of the system. For example, the product configurator function is to configure the product that the system does not require any manufacturing or CAD product information. Each system has got its own requirements to meet its functionality and a typical system will have input information from its preceding system and generates required output for the following system. The product data is created by CAD systems stored in the Product Data Management (PDM) system and the information needed for the manufacturing process is the interfaced to ERP system. Product data required for configuration is interfaced from the ERP system. Some ERP systems have a configuration module within its system for example Oracle. Figure 2 shows the relationships of product structure with different systems and how the product data is represented in their systems.

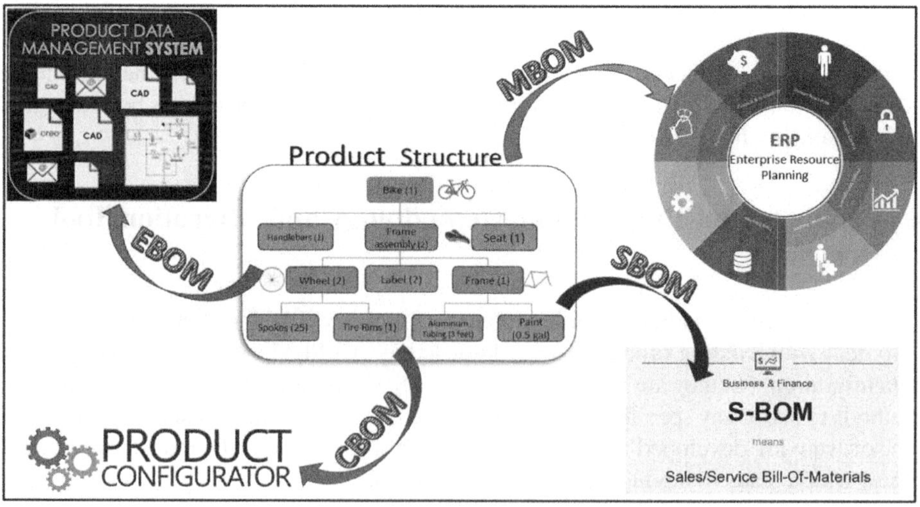

Fig. 2. Product structure connections with different systems along with BOM types

Product data stored in PDM is in the form of EBOM, it is stored in ERP system in the form of MBOM for manufacturing, in the form of CBOM in configurator and in the form of SBOM for service function. For building the module product structure and structuring the product data for migration, a tool has been proposed. For this methodology data from 3 systems are collected and by using data mining techniques [15] the product data will be migrated to PLM in the earlier proposed data model methodology.

4.2 Product Data Migration Tool Design

To demonstrate the proposed data model described above, a tool has been designed using VBA (Visual Basic) as the Front End and Excel like the back-end data collection. The tool is named as 'Integrated Product Modular Structure'. Out-Of-The-Box data migration functionality of most existing PLM systems in the market does not provide any mechanism to create a modular product structure. The proposed tool is designed to demonstrate the methodology with small sample data. The following steps will define the operation of this tool (as shown in Fig. 3).

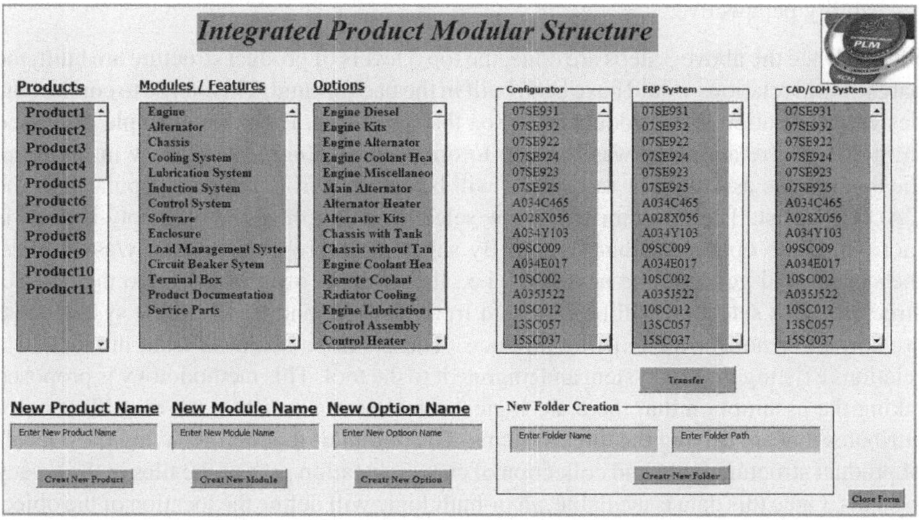

Fig. 3. The tool for creating modular product structure from legacy data [16]

Step 1. The 3 boxes on the left of Fig. 3 show the list of existing products, modules/features and options or variants as per the modular product structure. For example, *Product 1* will have *Engine* module with *Engine Kits* as an option. The tool can also create new products, features, and options if required. This can be done using the bottom-left options available in the form shown above. Once the required features and options are created, users can create a new product and select the level one module or features and level two options to create a modular structure. The main function of this tool is to create a product with modular product structure including features and options making metadata connections in the background using the Visual Basic code written.

Step 2. The existing product data is collected from three different systems, i.e., product data management, enterprise resource planning and product configurator. Since the company has been selling products for many years, ERP systems must have product BOM in some format, either in manufacturing BOM or in some other form. A configurator has overloaded BOM of the product, with rules to drive the configurable product (CBOM). From the sponsor company data, these are the two areas where the product BOM is maintained for order management and other many operations. The CAD data which is the starting point of the product development process is maintained in many locations, but mainly on the CAD data management system called Windchill PDMLink (in the sponsor company). Data from all these systems are imported into this tool. The 3 boxes on the right side of Fig. 3 show the data from 3 systems.

Step 3. Frame 'New Folder Creation' is used to create the folder structure for storing product physical data in a respective folder and make relations to corresponding parts or assemblies or options or features. Folder/containers will be created for different object types for storing product information. For example, all the CAD objects are stored in one folder, Parts are stored in another, analysis data as attachments are stored in another folder. But the relations explained in the data model will keep them connected from traceability perspective.

Step 4. Once the above 3 steps are done, the top 3 levels of product structure are built, the parent-child relations would have been built in the background. This step is to connect the design information level product data, i.e., the CAD data. From the example discussed in Step 1, the relationship was built up to option level *Engine Kits*. Now in this step, the appropriate assembly or assemblies will be selected from the data populated in the CAD/CDM list. The program will allow selecting more than one assembly if there is more than one option for that variant. By selecting appropriate assembly/assemblies, the system will generate the next level, i.e., the 4th level of information to the product structure. This selection will be validated from the ERP and Configurator systems that are correct or not for the existing products. These can be achieved from the metadata relations existing in their system and migrate it to the tool. This methodology is proposed taking the assumption that there are logical references, i.e., either the classification or attributes that are driving the three systems. The output of this step is having the 4 levels of product structure build and collection of current location path of the files in the legacy systems. Once this data is available, an in-built logic will define the location of the object in the target PLM system.

Step 5. Data from one system is retrieved into export files, then while passing through integration module it is converted into a format that is understandable by another system after removing the redundant information which is challenging [17]. In this step, the formatted data from the integrated tool VBA and Excel is exported in the XLM data format. First, a schema based on XML source data will be created. The schema defines the structure of the XML file that replicates product structure data format. Figure 4 shows the pictorial representation of this process. This must be done outside Excel and the file is saved as a schema.xml file. From the formalised Excel product data file, open the schema and export the data from excel to XML format. This will be the source file for importing the data into the PLM system. This process only covers the metadata, not the physical data which is residing in the data vault. Migrating physical data is not considered in this paper. That is considered for future study.

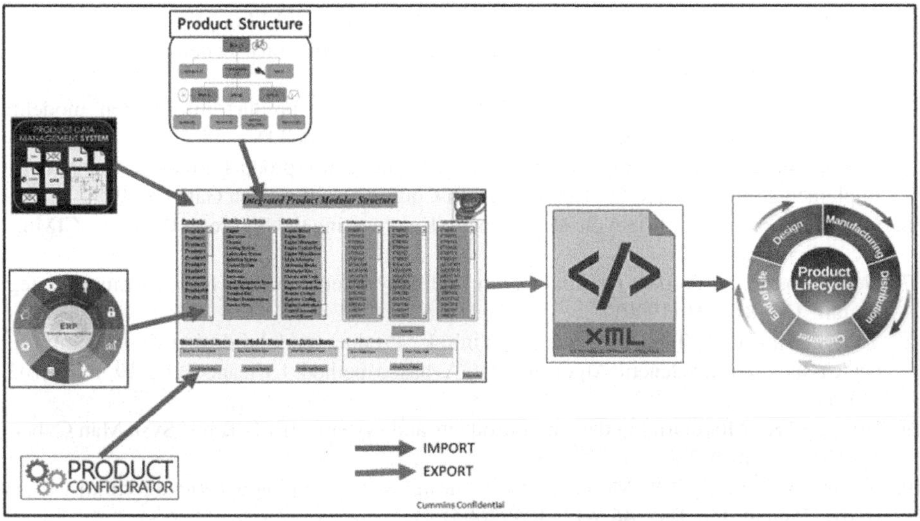

Fig. 4. Product data translation mechanism

5 Conclusions

The manufacturing industry has been evolving for so many years, and there is an immense amount of product data generated in the process of product development. Modular product structures have been developed for many years and found many benefits in implementing this methodology. Most companies adapted this methodology on the process side while very few attempted to do it in PLM systems. The proposed methodology in this research gives an opportunity to prepare the data model and prepare the product data that can be structured and transfer the data in the structure format which will enable easy manageability, integrity, consistency and traceability of the product information in the whole lifecycle. The data mining process of the product data between the engineering information systems is an achievable approach which will give seamless connection of data integrity which enables the data flow process smooth in future product changes. With the developed tool, engineers should be able to build Modular Product Structures with PLM systems and connect the product knowledge to the structure which can be traceable as and when needed for future product development. Future work from this study is to develop an application of the proposed methodology to handle a large amount of product data. The developed tool has some limitations in handling big data for demonstrations using VB and Excel.

References

1. Mourad, M., Farouk, B., Benoit, E., Abd-El-Kader, S.: System Engineering and PLM as an integrated approach for industry collaboration management. In: IFAC Symposium, pp. 135–140 (2012)
2. Bruun, H.P.L., Mortensen, N.H., Harlou, U., Worosch, M., Proschowsky, M.: PLM system support for modular product development. Comput. Ind. **67**, 97–111 (2015)

3. Bedolla, J.S., Ricci, F., Gomez, J.M., Chiabert, P.: Fostering PLM implementation in SMEs: modelling and managing verification processes. In: International Federation of Automatic Control, pp. 1762–1765 (2013)
4. Sudarsan, R., Fenves, S.J., Sriram, R.D., Wang, F.: A product information modeling framework for product lifecycle management. Comput.-Aided Des. **37**, 1399–1411 (2005)
5. Silventoinen, A., Jorma P., Hannele, L.: A roadmap for product lifecycle management implementation in SMEs. In: The XX ISPIM Conference, Research Gate (2009)
6. CIMdata Inc: Product Lifecycle Management Empowering the Future of Business. CIMdata Inc., Michigan (2002)
7. Gu, P., Sosale, S.: Product modularization for life cycle engineering. Robot. Comput. Integr. Manuf. **15**, 387–401 (1999)
8. Yua, S., Yanga, Q., Taoa, J., Tiana, X., Yinb, F.: Product modular design incorporating life cycle issues - Group Genetic Algorithm (GGA) based method. J. Cleaner Prod. **19**, 1016–1032 (2011)
9. Huang, C.K.: Modularity in design of products and systems. IEEE Trans. Syst. Man Cybern. Syst. Hum. Part A **28**(1), 66–77 (1998)
10. Krenga, V.B., Leeb, T.P.: Modular product design with grouping genetic algorithm—a case study. Comput. Ind. Eng. **46**, 443–460 (2004)
11. Bryan, A.K.: Co-evolution of product families and assembly systems. CIRP Ann.-Manuf. Technol. **56**(1), 41–44 (2007)
12. Mikkola, J.G.: Managing modularity of product architecture: toward an integrated theory. IEEE Trans. Eng. Manag. **50**(2), 204–218 (2003)
13. Ulrich, K.T.: Fundamentals of Product Modularity, vol. 3973-80. American Society of Mechanical Engineers, Design Engineering Division DE (1991)
14. Murthy, K.: Best Practices for CAD Data Migration. https://www.hcltech.com/.../Best_practices_for_CAD_Data_Migration_v01_2.pd. Accessed 2011/16/2018
15. Jiawei, H., Kamber, M., Pei, J.: DataMining: Concepts and Techniques, 3rd edn. Elsevier Inc., Waltham (2012)
16. Giddaluru, M.P., Gao, J., Bhatti, R.: Integrating product knowledge with modular product structures in PLM. In: International Conference on Innovative Design and Manufacturing. ICIDM, Milan (2017)
17. Ostroukh, A.V., Gusenitsa, D.O., Golubkova, V.B., Yurchik, P.F.: Integration of PDM and ERP systems within a unified information space of an enterprise. J. Comput. Eng. **16**, 31–33 (2014)

Knowledge and Change Management

Estimation of Prospective States of Mechanical Parts for Lifecycle Support by Part Agents

Hiroyuki Hiraoka(✉), Takeru Nagahata, Hiroki Saito, and Tsuramichi Tanigawa

Chuo University, 1-13-27 Kasuga, Bunkyo-Ku, Tokyo 112-8551, Japan
hiraoka@mech.chuo-u.ac.jp

Abstract. This paper discusses the lifecycle simulation of mechanical parts that are managed by part agents to promote their effective reuse.

It is essential to promote the reuse of mechanical parts with lifecycle management for the realization of a sustainable society. However, it is difficult to manage products in the use phase of product lifecycles owing to the unpredictable and uncontrollable behavior of consumers. This paper proposes a product lifecycle management system, called part agent system, using network agents and RFID tags attached on parts to promote reuse.

A part agent generates advice for the user regarding the maintenance of corresponding parts based on its current state and lifecycle information. The lifecycle simulation scheme performed by part agents is described herein. First, a part agent expands the part lifecycle with time. Next, it estimates by simulating the deterioration of the part and subsequently selects preferable maintenance actions. To simulate forthcoming states of the part, the possibility of events related to the part is estimated based on the causal relation of events with the acquired data on the states of the part, user operations, and detected events. Herein, a proposed method is presented to describe how the deterioration process is represented as causal relations with probabilities and how the relation is created using simulation. The simulation method is described for two example cases: fatigue of spring and deterioration of joints of a robotic manipulator.

Keywords: Part reuse · Part agent · Lifecycle simulation · Deterioration

1 Introduction

The effective reuse of mechanical parts is important for the development of a sustainable society [1]. To realize effective part reuse, it is essential to manage individual parts over their entire lifecycle because each individual part exhibits a different reuse history. However, it is difficult for manufacturers to predict such information owing to the uncontrollable and unpredictable diversity of user behavior. For users, specifically for consumers, it is difficult to access appropriate information for the maintenance of their parts. We propose a scheme whereby a part "manages" itself and supports user maintenance activities to address these issues [2].

We have proposed a scheme for a part agent to generate advice regarding the maintenance of corresponding parts [3]. We herein describe our proposed method to create

Published by Springer Nature Switzerland AG 2019
C. Fortin et al. (Eds.): PLM 2019, IFIP AICT 565, pp. 213–222, 2019.
https://doi.org/10.1007/978-3-030-42250-9_20

a causal relation of events that may occur in a lifecycle stage. This causal relation is generated based on knowledge and simulation on deterioration and is used to calculate possibilities of transition between lifecycle stages.

A framework based on a part agent that estimates the prospective states of a corresponding part is described in Sect. 2. In Sect. 3, a proposed scheme to evaluate values of lifecycle stages and lifecycle paths in the near future using causal relations on deterioration is described. Simulations of deterioration of a spring and robotic manipulator are presented for evaluation in Sect. 4. Section 5 summarizes the paper with remaining issues.

2 Estimation of Prospective States for Lifecycle Support of Parts

A part agent manages all information regarding its corresponding part throughout its lifecycle. The proposal assumes the spread of networks and high-precision RFID (Radio-frequency Identification) technology [4]. A part agent is generated at the manufacturing phase of a core part, when an RFID tag is attached to its corresponding part. The part agent identifies the ID of the RFID tag during the part's lifecycle, tracking the part through the network. The part agent communicates with various functions within the network to collect the information needed to manage its corresponding part such as product design information, predicted deterioration of parts, and market information. It also communicates with local functions on-site, such as sensory functions that detect the state of the part and storage functions for individual part data.

Based on this scheme, a part agent creates advice for the user regarding the maintenance of the corresponding part [3]. This conceptual scheme is still in planned phase and contains many development issues but we expect it can be realized in the near future considering the current emerging technologies on digitalization including IoT and cyber-physical systems.

Challenges in promoting parts reuse include selection of parts to be replaced. The decision whether a certain part should be replaced is made based on the monitored state of the part and its diagnostics. Methodologies on condition-based maintenance and predictive maintenance of a product have been developed, such as those described in [5, 6]. In addition, to detect and diagnose the current situations of parts and products using these methods, it is advisable to consider their expected state by forecasting the forthcoming stages of the lifecycle. Users require assistance on deciding whether a part should be replaced and, in the case of a replacement, when and with which part it should be replaced.

Figure 1 shows a framework for a part agent to advise its user based on the lifecycle model of a part. A lifecycle model consists of lifecycle stages and paths that represent the transfer between them. The stages are represented based on human actions related to the part, such as produce, sell, use, repair, and dispose. At each time step, the part agent predicts possible states of the part in the near future and evaluates the options of actions to provide advice to the user [7]. For the representation of life cycle model, Wuest [8] used similar representation in his case studies where the state transfer of a product captures events in MOL (middle of life) of the product.

A part agent expands the lifecycle to evaluate every option of the expanded lifecycle path for several time steps in the future. Figure 2 shows a simple example of the expanded

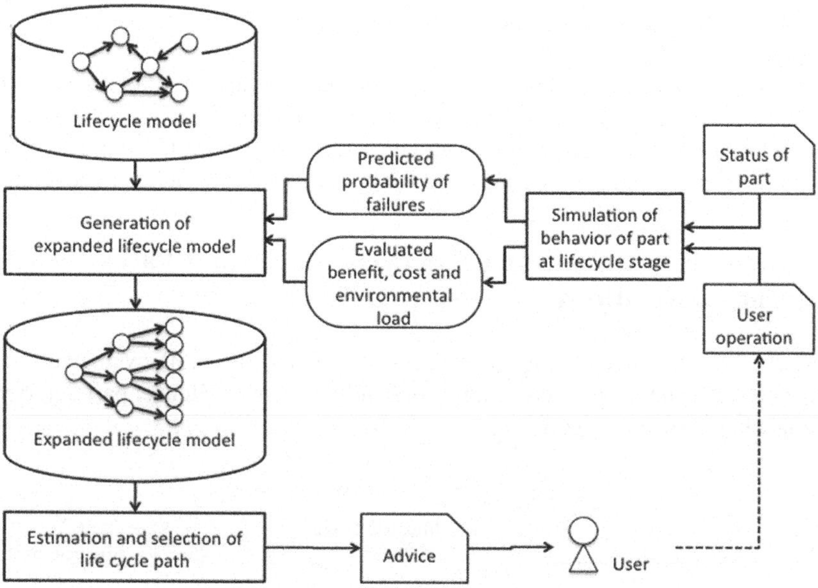

Fig. 1. Generation of advice by part agent

lifecycle of the part starting from the "use" stage. Circles represent lifecycle stages and arrows depict lifecycle paths. An expanded lifecycle of the part represents possible actions in its lifecycle over time. For every time step, a part agent evaluates every action option in next step, i.e., "use," "repair," and "dispose" stages in the case of this figure, selects the best action, and advises the user with the result.

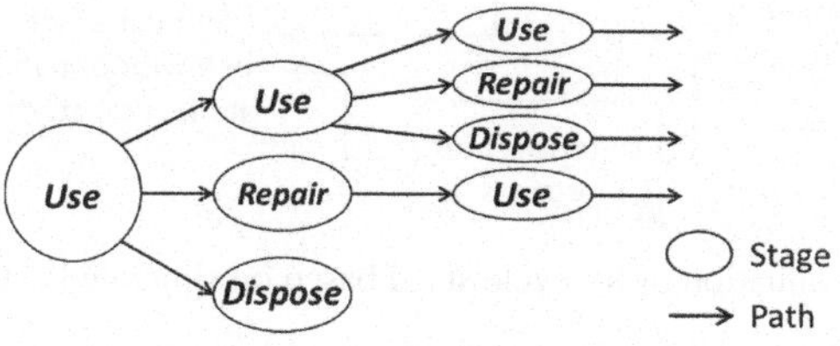

Fig. 2. Expanded lifecycle

The evaluation of actions in the lifecycle is based on the simulated state of the part, including the estimations of its environmental load, benefit, and cost. These values are estimated for every lifecycle stage in the near future. They can be estimated primarily based on the operations and usage performed in the stage, such as the load and duration of the task that the product achieves. The current status of the part, its deterioration, and the possibility of failures are considered in the estimation of the lifecycle stage. Probability is assigned to each expanded lifecycle path. It represents the probability of a part agent in taking that path and is estimated considering the probability of failures of the part.

Expected values such as environmental load, benefit, and cost for every option of the actions in the next step are calculated by accumulating the expected values of the forthcoming stages connected to the candidate stages. Each expected value is calculated as the product of the value in the stage and the possibility of the path connected to it [9].

3 Evaluation of Prospective Lifecycle Stages and Paths Based on Causal Relations

As described above, values of lifecycle stages and possibilities of lifecycle paths must be evaluated to estimate the expected values of candidate stages. Hence, part deterioration is simulated as shown in Fig. 3.

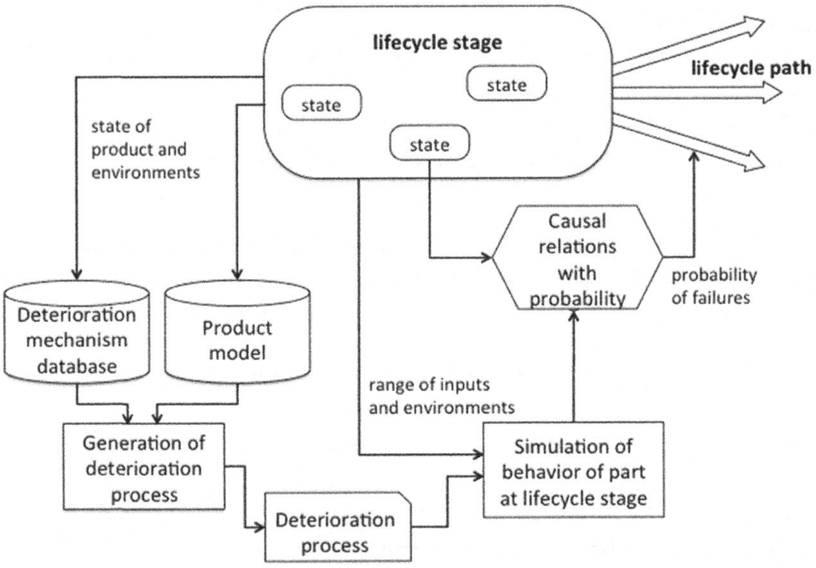

Fig. 3. Evaluation of lifecycle stage based on simulated deterioration

First, a deterioration process is constructed by combining deterioration mechanisms derived from a database or a library of deterioration mechanisms. A deterioration mechanism represents the deterioration that occurs when specific factors exist in the product and environments. A mechanism may yield other factors that cause other mechanisms. Thus, a deterioration process is generated as a tree structure comprising multiple mechanisms combined by common factors [10]. This process qualitatively depicts the progress of deterioration under specific conditions.

Next, we simulate the deterioration mechanisms to evaluate the probabilities of their occurrences. It is performed by accepting the range of user inputs and environmental values such as the temperature during the stage. We assume that the deterioration database contains, as the information of each mechanism, a function to calculate the resultant deterioration value from the input factor values. The function may be either a simple function such as a spreadsheet, or a complex function such as dedicated simulation software. A threshold for the range of each input can be assigned depending on the application to discriminate whether a certain condition holds. For example, when the parameter of an input factor is a load value, a condition "heavy load" may be defined to indicate that the load is larger than, e.g., 100 kg. Similarly, a threshold can be assigned for the resultant deterioration value to determine whether the value is acceptable. For example, when the parameter of the resultant factor is a deviation, a condition "large deviation" may be defined to indicate that the deviation is larger than 1 mm. With these factor values of range and threshold, the simulation calculates the probability of occurrence of the resultant factor against the occurrence of the input factors. In other words, the simulation generates the conditional probability of a deterioration mechanism. For example, the simulation calculates the probability that "large deviation" occurs when "heavy load" exists and the probability when "heavy load" does not exist. Furthermore, it calculates the probability of "large deviation" not occurring when "heavy load" exists and when it does not exist. Examples of deterioration simulation are described in the next section.

As the conditional probabilities are assigned to every deterioration mechanism at the stage, the deterioration process can be regarded as a causal relation model among factors. As the range of input factors is provided at the stage, the probabilities of deterioration and failures can be estimated using this model. We can infer the probabilities of the lifecycle path from the stage using these probabilities because the stages "replace" and "dispose" are closely related to deterioration and failures.

Causal relations were used in SAPPhiRE model that was originally developed for design phase and was extended for MOL (middle of life) of the products [11]. While SAPPhiRE model intends to represent MOL events and activities in a generic way using ontology technology, our study aims to simulate the deterioration of products as described in the next section.

4 Simulating Deterioration Using Product Model and Deterioration Model

We describe two examples to demonstrate how the conditional probabilities for causal relations is estimated using deterioration simulations. The deterioration phenomenon of the first example is the fatigue of a spring and that of the next example is the deterioration of manipulator joints.

4.1 Spring Deterioration

In the first example, a simple steel spring is used. It is known that metals break under repeated stress. This phenomenon called fatigue occurs according to the stress and number of repetitions. The relation between magnitude of cyclic stress and number of cycles (in logarithmic scale) to failure can be represented by an S–N curve [12]. In other words, the deterioration mechanism of fatigue is represented by an S–N curve.

The conditional probabilities for spring deterioration that are calculated based on this curve using the Monte Carlo method are as follows. See Fig. 4 for the illustration of the method.

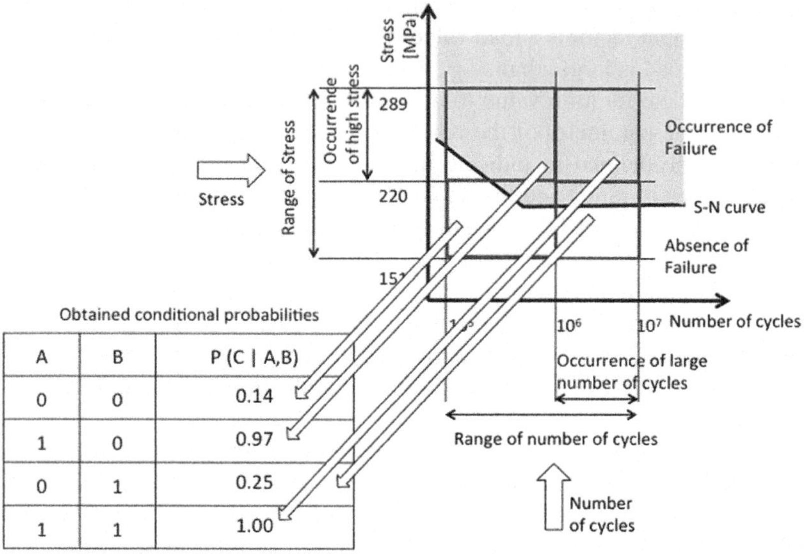

A	B	P (C | A,B)
0	0	0.14
1	0	0.97
0	1	0.25
1	1	1.00

Fig. 4. Calculation of conditional probabilities for spring failure

(a) Input values and events: The input values for this deterioration mechanism are the magnitude of cyclic stress on the spring and its number of cycles. The input events are "high stress" for the magnitude of stress and "large number of cycles" for the number of cycles. The ranges of those values and the thresholds to determine the occurrence of the input event are presented as shown in the graph of Fig. 4. Sets of input values are generated randomly within their ranges. The input values should be generated following the actual distribution if available; however, they are distributed uniformly in this example.

(b) Occurrence of spring failure: The occurrence of resultant event or spring failure is determined by comparing against the S–N curve. Failure occurs if the stress magnitude is larger than the value of the S–N curve for the number of cycles. Here, we approximate an S–N curve comprising two line segments, as shown in the figure.

(c) Conditional probabilities: For the combination of occurrence and absence of input events, i.e., whether high stress and a large number of cycles exists, probabilities of occurrence of resultant event or spring failures are calculated by adding the number of occurrences of failures against the number of input values that are generated randomly.

4.2 Deterioration of Robot Manipulator Joint

Cases exist where the resultant occurrences exhibit more complex relationships with the input values. As an example, we developed a system to calculate the position error of the end effector of a manipulator with three degrees of freedom with a deteriorated joint.

- Simulation of robotic manipulator's behavior with deterioration of its joints

Figure 5 shows the configuration of the system to simulate the kinematic behavior of a manipulator considering the deterioration of its joint. The operation of the manipulator and its environment are provided according to the situation of the lifecycle stage. The following are procedures to calculate the state of the manipulator.

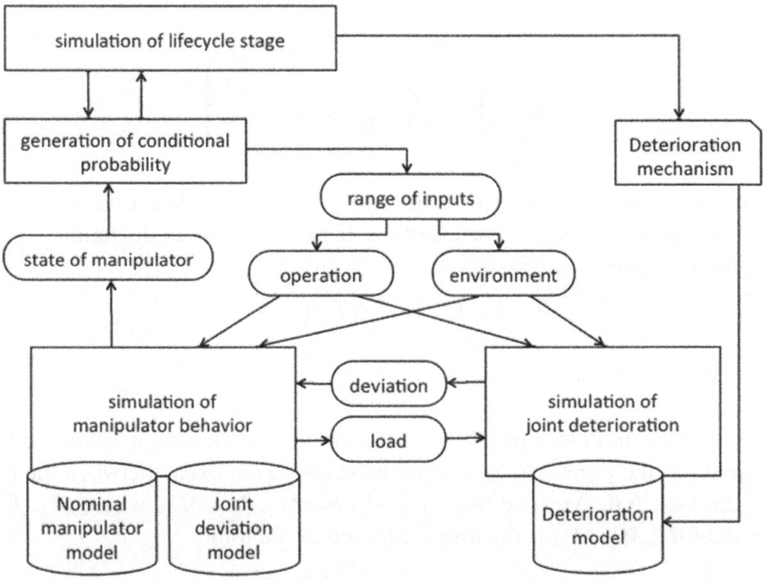

Fig. 5. Simulation of behavior of a manipulator with deterioration in its joints

1. First, simulate the behavior of the manipulator without the deterioration of joints using the nominal manipulator model and obtain loads on the joints.
2. Next, the deviations of joints are calculated based on the calculated loads using the deterioration model of the joints.
3. When the deviation of a joint is detected, the joint deviation model that provides transformation representing the deviation is associated to the nominal manipulator model.
4. Subsequently, the behavior of the manipulator is simulated again using a manipulator model with deviation in the joint to calculate the position error of the end effector.

- Kinematic model of a manipulator with deteriorated joint

The kinematic model of a manipulator is represented by a series of coordinate transformations [13]. Each transformation is a matrix of 6 × 6 elements and represents either a rigid relation between two joints in a link or a variable relation between two links in a joint. For the manipulator with three degrees of freedom, i.e., with three joints, the matrix representing the position and orientation of the end-effector is as shown in Eq. (1).

$$T_E = T_{L0}T_{j1}(\theta_1)T_{L1}T_{j2}(\theta_2)T_{L2}T_{j3}(\theta_3), \tag{1}$$

where T_{Li} denotes the transformation between two joints in a link i; $T_{ji}(\theta_\square)$ denotes the transformation between two links connected by a joint i with joint angle $\theta_\square$.

When joint k exhibits translational deviation (Δx, Δy, Δz) and rotational deviation ($\Delta\alpha$, $\Delta\beta$, $\Delta\gamma$), the transformation matrix T_{dk} representing this deviation is as follows [14]:

$$T_{dk} = \begin{pmatrix} 1 & -\Delta\gamma & \Delta\beta & \Delta x \\ -\Delta\gamma & 1 & -\Delta\alpha & \Delta y \\ -\Delta\beta & \Delta\alpha & 1 & \Delta z \\ 0 & 0 & 0 & 1 \end{pmatrix} \tag{2}$$

This transformation is inserted at the transformation of the joint to calculate the kinematics of the manipulator. For example, if joint 1 exhibits deviation T_{dl}, Eq. (1) becomes the following:

$$T_E = T_{L0}T_{d1}T_{j1}(\theta_1)T_{L1}T_{j2}(\theta_2)T_{L2}T_{j3}(\theta_3) \tag{3}$$

- Deterioration of a joint

We assume that the deterioration that causes joint deviation is caused by the force and torque applied to the joint. The following elastic relation exists between the deviation (Δx, Δy, Δz, $\Delta\alpha$, $\Delta\beta$, $\Delta\gamma$) and load (F_x, F_y, F_z, M_x, M_y, M_z), where (F_x, F_y, F_z) is the force and (M_x, M_y, M_z) is the torque applied to the joint.

$$\begin{pmatrix} \Delta x \\ \Delta y \\ \Delta z \\ \Delta\alpha \\ \Delta\beta \\ \Delta\gamma \end{pmatrix} = K^{-1} \begin{pmatrix} F_x \\ F_y \\ F_z \\ M_x \\ M_y \\ M_z \end{pmatrix}, \tag{4}$$

where K^{-1} is a compliance matrix of the joint. For simplicity, we assume that the deterioration deviation is proportional to the accumulation of this elastic deviation.

If the position error of the end effector thus calculated is greater than the predefined threshold value, the occurrence of failure is identified. In other words, the proposed system serves as a function to determine the occurrence of failures similar to the S–N curve for the spring example described in Sect. 4.1. This example illustrates how causal relations can be created with probabilities for complex systems such as robotic manipulators by simulating deterioration.

5 Conclusion

A scheme for lifecycle simulation was proposed for a part agent to predict the prospective states of the corresponding part. The scheme generated a causal relation for a lifecycle stage based on the deterioration process. The probabilities of the causal relation were calculated using simulation and described herein. A simple case of a spring and a complex case of a robotic manipulator were explained.

Issues that remain necessitate the further development of the system. A detailed implementation of the system is yet to be completed and its applicability should be verified. As the causal relation involves conditional probabilities, Bayesian estimation is applicable to calculate the current probability of failures using this model. We are currently developing this functionality. The development of an appropriate deterioration model is also an important research issue.

Acknowledgements. This study was supported by JSPS Kakenhi Grant number 15K05772. Mr. Naoki Masuda who left our team in March 2019 developed the functions of the product model for lifecycle simulation.

References

1. Hauschild, M., Jeswiet, J., Alting, L.: From life cycle assessment to sustainable production: status and perspectives. Ann. CIRP **54**(2), 535–555 (2005)
2. Nakada, T., Hiraoka, H.: Network agents for supporting consumers in the lifecycle management of individual parts. Int. J. Product Lifecycle Manag. **5**(1), 4–20 (2011)
3. Hiraoka, H., Nagasawa, A., Fukumashi, Y., Fukunaga, Y.: Replacement of parts by part agents to promote reuse of mechanical parts. In: Ríos, J., Bernard, A., Bouras, A., Foufou, S. (eds.) PLM 2017. IAICT, vol. 517, pp. 394–403. Springer, Cham (2017). https://doi.org/10.1007/978-3-319-72905-3_35
4. Borriello, G.: RFID: tagging the world. Commun. ACM **44**(9), 34–37 (2005)
5. Hashemian, H.M., Bean, W.C.: State-of-the-art predictive maintenance techniques. IEEE Trans. Instrum. Measur. **60**(10), 3480–3492 (2011)
6. Jin, C., Ompusunggu, A.P., Liu, Z., Ardakani, H.D., Petre, F., Lee, J.: A vibration-based approach for stator winding fault diagnosis of induction motors: application of envelope analysis. In: Annual Conference of the Prognostics and Health Management Society (2014)
7. Hiraoka, H., et al.: Part agent advice for promoting reuse of the part based on life cycle information. In: 20th CIRP International Conference on Life Cycle Engineering, Singapore, pp. 337–342 (2013)
8. Wuest, T., Nana, U.M.N.: State-based representation of a product's middle of life. Int. J. Product Lifecycle Manag. **9**(2), 108–138 (2016)
9. Nanjo, K., Yamamori, Y., Yokoki, Y., Sakamoto, Y., Hiraoka, H.: Maintenance decisions of part agent based on failure probability of a part using Bayesian estimation. In: The 22nd CIRP Conference on Life Cycle Engineering, Sydney (2015)
10. Takata, S., Shiono, H., Hiraoka, H., Asama, H.: Case-based evaluation of potential deterioration for facility life-cycle management. CIRP Ann. **46**(1), 385–390 (1997)
11. McSorley, G., Fortin, C., Huet, G.: Modified SAPPhIRE model as a framework for product lifecycle management. In: Proceedings of the DESIGN 2014 13th International Design Conference, pp. 1843–1852 (2014)

12. Fatigue (material), Wikipedia. https://en.wikipedia.org/wiki/Fatigue_(material). Accessed 22 Mar 2019
13. Denavit, J., Hartenberg, R.S.: A kinematic notation for lower pair mechanisms based on matrices. J. Appl. Mech. **22**, 215–221 (1955)
14. Takano, S.: Kinematics of robots in detail, Ohmsha (2004). (in Japanese)

An Approach to Assess Engineering Change Effort Retrospectively Utilizing Past Engineering Change Information

Niklas Kattner[1(✉)], Eldar Shakirov[2], and Udo Lindemann[1]

[1] Technical University of Munich, Munich, Germany
niklas.kattner@tum.de

[2] Skolkovo Institute of Science and Technology (Skoltech), Moscow, Russia

Abstract. The competitiveness of companies is nowadays highly dependent on an efficient product development. Shorter time to market, increased competition as well as accelerated market dynamics can be handled well by a continuous improvement in development efficiency. Hence, improving the development performance can have a big impact on the time to market. However, an increasing number of resources must be assigned to the management of engineering changes. The management of changes strongly influences the resources available for the actual design process. Furthermore, the increasing complexity of technical systems as well as the organization affects the engineering change situation and further induces change complexity. This paper therefore introduces an approach to retrospectively assess engineering change information to identify areas for reducing the change workload. It therefore introduces a procedure to guide users through the process of the assessment. In addition, it suggests indicators to evaluate the change situation regarding the induced workload. Finally, the approach is applied in a use case to investigate an engineering change data set.

Keywords: Engineering change management · Structural complexity management · Engineering change assessment

1 Introduction and Background

In recent years, the complexity of modern technical systems increased rapidly [1]. Hence, the organization of product development tasks becomes more complex as well and the effort to collaborate and cooperate increases within the company. As a result, the resources in form of people's minds behind the actual development and maintenance of products are increasingly valuable for the company, since the projects are more demanding due to complexity and scope. This requires a lot of man power for meetings, improvements, iterations and testing. The actual task of engineering by creating technical products and systems is pushed into the background. Hence, a lot of potential for improving the product development task – and the actual development performance – is in the optimization of tasks and cooperation influencing the product development

Published by Springer Nature Switzerland AG 2019
C. Fortin et al. (Eds.): PLM 2019, IFIP AICT 565, pp. 223–232, 2019.
https://doi.org/10.1007/978-3-030-42250-9_21

activities [2]. One major consumer for product development resources is the handling of engineering changes. These changes are usually defined as changes to parts, drawings or any other development artefact, after these artefacts have been released [c.f. 3, 4]. They are usually carried out to improve products, adapt them to new requirements and needs or to correct errors. Studies have shown that the share of the overall development capacity required to handle changes is significant. [5, 7] give a share of the change work in the total development capacity of 30–50%, partly up to 70%. [6] indicate that about 30% of the work load for reworking and implementation of additional functions is due to changes. Hence, improving the handling of engineering change management by reducing the change effort promises to be a big lever in the improvement of the overall resource usage. However, literature lack research about how to systematically investigate the efforts in engineering change management [3]. The paper therefore introduces an approach to utilize past engineering change information to retrospectively assess effort indicators for a given technical system. Hence, Sect. 2 outlines the methodology as well as the shortcomings and the goal of the paper. Section 3 introduces an initial set of effort indicators. Section 4 introduces the method and describes the systematic procedure. Section 5 briefly pictures the application of the method in a use case. In Sect. 6, the results of the application are discussed as well as the content of the paper is summarized.

2 Methodology and Shortcomings

The research is based on the Design Research Mythology [8]. Hence, a profound research clarification was conducted in the beginning of the study to refine the objective of assessing change information retrospectively. In the following step - the descriptive study 1 - a literate review revealed the current state of the art regarding retrospective change data analysis and performance measures in engineering change management. An overview of current research can be found in [c.f. 9, 10]. In this paper, the focus is on the prescriptive study, which embraces the development of a methodology to improve change handling and the overall engineering design process by assessing the technical change information retrospectively. Thus the following hypothesis defines the research of this paper: The assessment of engineering change information retrospectively helps to better understand the characteristics of high workload in engineering change management. Hence, by uncovering the root characteristics of high change effort, proactive measures can help to reduce the overall use of capacity for change management in engineering design. In Sects. 2.1, 2.2 and 2.3 we discuss shortcomings to underline the introduced hypothesis by emphasizing potential to improve engineering design. The shortcomings are derived from current state of the art in research [3, 9].

2.1 Shortcoming 1: Defining Engineering Change Effort

As discussed above, handling engineering changes has a fundamental impact on design performance, since it uses resources not available for the design task. As a result, engineering changes can be the origin of performance lacks, shortcomings in the development progress or cost drivers for companies. Since engineering changes are more a rule than the exception in companies and are often necessary to adapt to new requirements, a broader understanding of the causes of engineering change effort will allow for improving the change handling itself. Hence, a more granular approach to uncover effort indicators describing change effort to precisely understand, address and improve the use of resources for either the change handling itself or the general engineering design task is necessary.

2.2 Shortcoming 2: Methodical Approach for the Systematic Assessment of Change Effort

Many approaches in engineering change management address the actual process of engineering changes handling beginning from the first occurrence, to the evaluation of the change effects to the implementation. Furthermore, many retrospective methods focus on the support of the actual change handling [3, 9]. Therefore, a lack of methods to learn based on past change information not for the process itself, but for the knowledge gain to reduce the effort in a systematical way can help to maintain an efficient engineering change management. Hence, a methodical approach as a guidance for a continuous learning is introduced in the following.

2.3 Shortcoming 3: Utilizing Past Change Information to Investigate Drivers for Engineering Change Effort

In companies the management often ends when the change is closed, and the implementation was successful – or the change request was rejected. Nevertheless, a systematic learning and monitoring of changes regarding their capacity and resource use is crucial when it comes to an efficient development process. Hence, simplifying the process of learning from past engineering changes by decreasing the resistance to apply assessment and monitoring methods can leverage the acceptance of such approaches. Therefore, a method which adapts to the company's situation and either allows to qualitative assess past engineering change information or process change data to observe the resource use will be beneficial for industry. Since many companies must document many change relevant data, an automated assessment of change data to reveal change efforts can further lower the barrier to investigate the changes retrospectively.

2.4 Focus of the Paper

This paper therefore introduces a method for a systematic assessment of engineering change information to uncover, assess and process past engineering changes regarding the effort and its resource consumption. This helps to identify major performance lacks in engineering change management and therefore in engineering design, to proactively improve engineering design and therefore free resources for the actual development of the technical system. This can be achieved through better understanding of the origins of resource binding for the technical system.

To give an overview of the methodology, the paper furthermore emphasizes on the assessment of past engineering change data. Hence, a limited set of structural measures are introduced as an example for the calculation of the change effort indices. The actual calculation is mainly based on the approach of structural assessment [11] with engineering change data retrospectively.

3 What Induces Effort in Engineering Change Management?

The shortcomings outlined that there is a lack of research in engineering change management regarding the identification and observation of effort and feasible indicators. In addition, the actual identification and investigation of the root causes of effort drivers in engineering change management is lacking in current research. This paper thus introduces an approach to define effort in engineering change management utilizing structural assessment approaches. A broader scope to apply the investigation within the collaboration with the manufacturing department is planned for a future assessment.

To ensure a broad applicability of the indicators, the objective of deriving these indicators were to use only the most common information usually available in companies about engineering changes. The change number, the persons involved in the change handling as well as the artefacts under change are therefore used for evaluating the effort induced by engineering changes within a predefined scope of a technical system. By utilizing this structural information about the engineering change situation, interrelations and its strength, indirect dependencies and the degree of networking can be used to assess the technical system. Since the approach uses engineering change information, the assessed data is always based on actual shortcomings, technical improvement activities and cost reduction projects. Hence, the interrelations are defined by objectively generated information, i.e. the documentation of engineering changes or the retrospective reflection of experience, instead of a proactive approach with anticipation and hypothesis.

Table 1. Initial set of measures to assess engineering change effort

	Measure	Explanation	Based on
Product-based effort measures	*Frequency*	Number of Change requests per Module	[13]
	Network factor	Strength of bonding of the module (number of occurrences with other modules)	[13]
	Centrality	Centrality of the Module within the product structure	[13]
Organization-based effort measures	*Involved people*	Number of involved people	[13]
	Collaboration resistance	Collaboration Resistance per Module – average hierarchical distance between all involved people	[14]
	Network factor	Average network factor of all involved people	[13]

Reflecting the origin and driver for effort in engineering change management, there are three major categories – product, process, and organization. Either the effort can be induced and generated by the artifact under change itself – product-based change effort. Also, the effort for handling engineering changes can emerge from the organization and its entities handling the change – organization-based change effort. A third driver for change effort is the actual process management. However, since literature provide a lot of research in the reactive phase – either in the form of change processes itself or supporting methods – the third category is excluded from further investigation.

Hence, there are two groups of measures defined to assess past engineering change information regarding the effort for changes management. The groups each include three initial measures which allow for a structural assessment and are meaningful for the overall effort situation of an engineering change to an engineering artifact (see Table 1).

4 Assessing Engineering Change Information

To create a more structured approach to remedy the lack of understanding regarding the origin of resource usage for conducting engineering changes, a methodical approach is introduced guiding through the steps to create an understanding of the change situation. Thus, engineering change information from past changes – either in the form of quantitative and formalized data or in the form of informalized knowledge – is used to create a basis to retrospectively assess the technical system regarding the induced change effort. To do so, the methodical approach consists of 3 major phases depicting 5 independent steps (see Fig. 1). It is built up as a circular procedure to emphasis the recurring character of the methodology. Since the engineering change situation in companies usually is a dynamic environment, the method has to represent this character by underlining the importance of an iterative application. We assume, that by applying the method, or at least certain steps, the information is kept up to date. This ensures that the information about effort always adapts to the company's individual constraints. The methodology depicts the three major phases preparation, assessment and support.

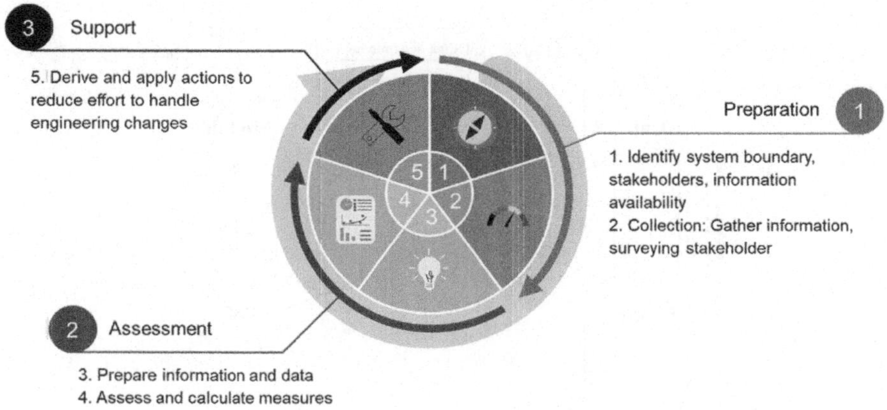

Fig. 1. Method to retrospectively assess change effort

The 3 phases of the method can be applied individually without the necessity to start with the first. However, by doing so, the certain pre-checks have to be finished to ensure that all information is available for the phase to successfully accomplish.

4.1 Preparation

In the preparation step, a change management team needs to identify and gather all information necessary to conduct the analysis. Therefore, the first step 1 of the procedure includes the identification and definition of a viable system boundary. It is important to define the scope of the assessment at the beginning – e.g. whether it is just a small assembly of a product, i.e. constraint by the engineering unit – or the investigation of a whole product or project. However, the scope of this assessment can be limited by the resources available to apply the methodology as well as the type of information available. Data driven assessment allows for a bigger scope as the analysis can be automated. The second step of the methodology includes the actual gathering of information. Dependent on the in step 1 identified situation, the information is either available in a formalized, explicit way in the form of engineering change documentation or must be collected by questionnaires to document the informalized, implicit knowledge of the people. This paper describes the situation of a situation within a company, where engineering change data is available. To prepare the assessment step, the information therefore has to be derived from a database. To do so, the respective people have to be identified and all necessary approvals for the assessment must be signed. Furthermore, a data preparation is necessary.

4.2 Assessment Phase

The assessment phase focuses on the evaluation of the previously gathered information. Depending on the information available, it either allows for an automatic calculation of the engineering change data or the manually assessment of the measures using questionnaires.

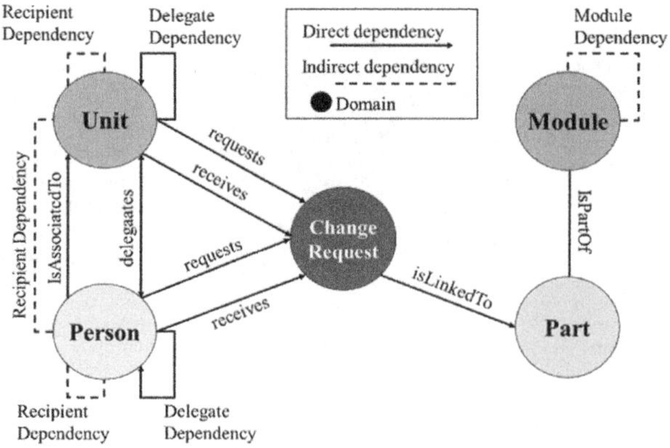

Fig. 2. Meta model of the engineering change data

Since many companies have formalized and documented information about engineering change handling, the method also considers the automatic calculation of the effort measures. Hence a meta model is introduced derived on the structure of existing literature to the main artefacts of engineering change managements and its interrelation [c.f. 3]. The metamodel was furthermore refined with the logics derived from engineering change databases from industry [12]. The overall objective of the meta model was to include as little engineering change relevant objects as possible but still allow for a usable analysis of the change effort measures.

By reducing the number of objects relevant in engineering change management, the approach is easier to apply in a variety of different companies by increasing the likelihood of the availability of all necessary information. The simplified metamodel can be seen in Fig. 2.

The meta model defines the interrelations between the information used in this method and therefore serves as the basis for the calculation of the measures. Based on this meta model, the use case in Sect. 5 introduces the analysis of the network regarding the set of structural engineering change effort measures.

4.3 Support

The support phase finally helps to address the effort indicator to improve the overall engineering change situation. Hence, either a catalog of change drivers and respective counter measures or methods to improve collaboration or reduce organizational dependencies must be considered. Due to the previously identified information, a network of stakeholder is already available. This stakeholder information is used to identify key engineers for a workshop-based processing and assessment of the information.

5 Use Case

The following use case introduces the application of the method with focus on the calculation of the indicators by using an engineering change data set from a big company in the automotive sector. The analysis was applied to data set of 711 engineering change requests – constrained by focusing on one engineering design unit. Furthermore, the data set was limited by the time period under consideration of six months to further reduce the amount of data to be calculated. A data preparation step was conducted to ensure the structural assessment can be conducted – e.g. removing incomplete information, translate data types. As a demonstrator Soley Studio was used to conduct the structural assessment. The software enables users to calculate and handle structural data and hence, allows for graph analysis. The case mainly focusses on phase two of the methodology, hence the focus will be on the actual data assessment. Therefore, the data gathering won't be discussed. In addition, the further use of the information as well as the usage is just explained initially.

In the first step, the graph network is built by importing the engineering change data into the software demonstrator. The tool then applied previously defined rules based on the meta model to generate the concerning elements (EC, persons and artefacts – in this case modules) and its interrelations to create the structural network of the data.

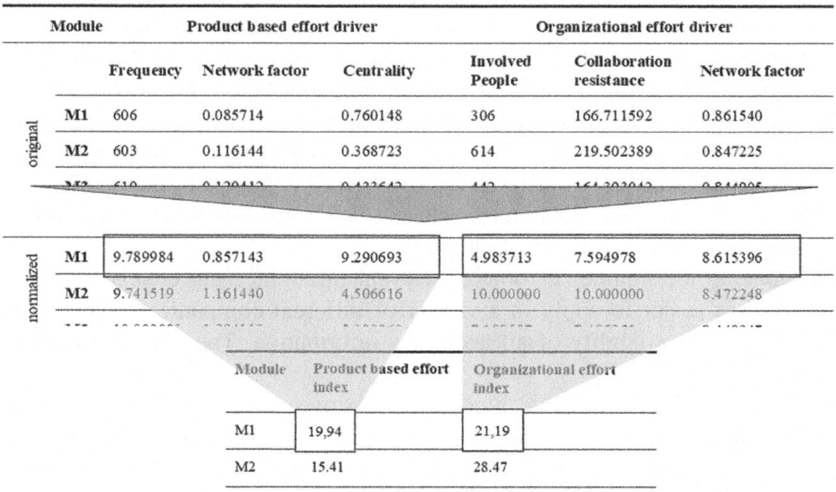

Fig. 3. Calculation of the effort index

The network allows for the calculation of the in Sect. 3 introduced measures based on the in Sect. 4.2 introduced, simplified meta model for the assessment of the change effort. Hence for each module of the technical system the measures are calculated. Since the measures are derived from network analysis, first the original calculations are conducted for each module of the system under consideration. In the case of this example, the system comprises 103 modules.

Figure 3 shows an excerpt of the analysis results. The original calculations are then normalized, and the normalized indicators then serve to calculate a cumulated value for the product-based effort and the organizational effort. Hence, these indices allow for an estimation of the product and organizational characteristics and company specific properties on the engineering change effort. Based on these two indices, a portfolio is derived which enables a simplified, visually supported assessment of the modules regarding their respective effort indices (see Fig. 4). The portfolio allows for an easy comparison of the systems modules regarding their induced effort when changed during the development. To do so, the portfolio spans the organizational effort over the system effort. Thus, the portfolio supports the assessment of the effort drivers and allows to directly reveal measure categories to improve the change situation. For organization-based effort drivers, the improvement of collaboration, the people involved as well as the unit interrelations can be a leverage to reduce effort in change handling. For product-based effort drivers, the improvement of the product structure, the reduction of changes as well as the change propagation are viable starting points to release resources for engineering design by improving the change management. In summary, the portfolio is a first approach to quantify the change effort allocated to the technical artefacts of a system. This increases the transparency of resource usage and therefore is a basis for discussing and improving the engineering change management.

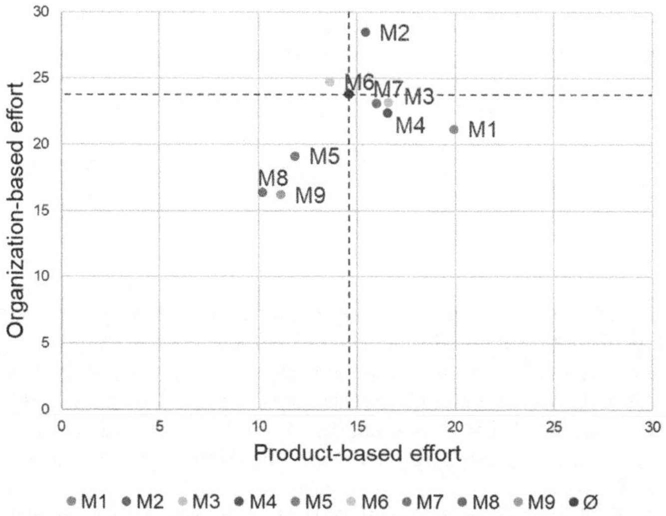

Fig. 4. Modules portfolio of engineering change effort

6 Conclusion and Summary

The paper gives an overview of a method to retrospectively assess engineering change information to investigate the effort induced by changes to the technical system and emphasizes how engineering change information can be used to improve design performance. This knowledge can then be used to either improve the resource usage by directly addressing causes of high effort or to evaluate the potential effort necessary to conduct changes to certain system artefacts. The paper showed that structural complexity measures can be applied to an engineering change dataset. Furthermore, the measures can reveal indicators for high engineering change effort retrospectively. Since the documentation of engineering changes vary in industry, the flexibility of the approach must be further investigated. In addition, the set of indicators is limited in this paper in 6 measures to reduce the effort for implementing the indicators in the software tool. However, an extension of indicators could allow for a more extensive investigation of either organizational induced effort or product induced effort. With the application of the method and the assessment of a data set, the resulting portfolio shows visually prepared information about the effort indices to characterize the system under consideration regarding the change effort. For future research, the focus is on a more in-depth application of the procedure. Hence, the measures must be applied to different types of change data. A weighting system for the individual effort values would allow for more flexible assessment of the information. Furthermore, a list of comprising actions to improve the change situation depending on the effort indicator's characteristics would allow for a focused measure to address the effort causes.

Acknowledgement. This work was supported by the German Research Foundation (Deutsche Forschungsgemeinschaft, DFG) collaborative research centre 'Sonderforschungsbereich SFB 768 "Managing cycles in innovation processes – Integrated development of product-service-systems based on technical products". Furthermore, we thank the Soley GmbH for providing the data analytics tool.

References

1. Fricke, E., Schulz, A.P.: Design for changeability (DfC): principles to enable changes in systems throughout their entire lifecycle. Syst. Eng. **8**(4), 342–359 (2005)
2. Clark, K.B., Fujimoto, T.: Product Development Performance. Strategy, Organization, and Management in the World Auto Industry. Harvard Business School Press, Boston (1991)
3. Hamraz, B., Caldwell, N.H.M., Clarkson, P.J.: A holistic categorization framework for literature on engineering change management. Syst. Eng. **16**(4), 473–505 (2013). https://doi.org/10.1002/sys.21244
4. Jarratt, T.A.W., Eckert, C.M., Caldwell, N.H.M., Clarkson, P.J.: Engineering change: an overview and perspective on the literature. Res. Eng. Des. **22**(2), 103–124 (2011). https://doi.org/10.1007/s00163-010-0097-y
5. Lindemann, U., Reichwald, R. (eds.): Integriertes Änderungsmanagement. Springer, Heidelberg (1998). https://doi.org/10.1007/978-3-642-71957-8
6. Fricke, E., Gebhard, B., Negele, H., Igenbergs, E.: Coping with changes. causes, findings, and strategies. Syst. Eng. **3**(4), 169–179 (2000)
7. Maier, A., Langer, S.: Engineering change management report 2011. Survey results on causes and effects, current practice, problems, and strategies in Denmark (no. 17), Technical University of Denmark, DTU (2011)
8. Blessing, L.T.M., Chakrabarti, A.: DRM, a Design Research Methodology. Springer, London (2009). https://doi.org/10.1007/978-1-84882-587-1
9. Tale-Yazdi, A., Kattner, N., Becerril, L., Lindemann, U.: A literature review on approaches for the retrospective utilisation of data in engineering change management. In: 2018 IEEE International Conference on Industrial Engineering and Engineering Management (IEEM), pp. 612–616. IEEE (2018)
10. Kattner, N., Wang, T., Lindemann, U.: Performance metrics in engineering change management - Key Performance Indicators and engineering change performance levels. In: 2016 International Conference on Industrial Engineering and Engineering Management, IEEM 2016, 4–7 December 2016, Bali, Indonesia, pp. 1180–1184. IEEE, Piscataway (2016)
11. Maurer, M.S., Lindemann, U.: Structural awareness in complex product design - the multiple-domain matrix. In: 9th International Design Structure Matrix Conference (2007)
12. VDA, 4965 (08/2009). ECM Recommendation Part 0 (ECM)
13. Biedermann, W.: A minimal set of network metrics for analysing mechatronic product concepts. Dissertation, Technische Universität München, München (2014)
14. Heimberger, N.: Strukturbasierte Koordinationsplanung in komplexen Entwicklungsprojekten. Ph.D. thesis. Munich, Germany: Chair of Product Development, Technical University of Munich (TUM) (2017)

Design and Manufacturing of a Device Made of Additive Manufacturing Machines for Fast and Reliable Measurement of Material Stiffness

Konstantinos Bailas(✉) and Paraskevas Papanikos(✉)

Department of Product and Systems Design Engineering, University of the Aegean, Ermoupoli, Syros, Greece
{kbail,ppap}@aegean.gr

Abstract. Additive Manufacturing (AM) technology is constantly expanding to small and large industry over the last 20 years. The vast potential of this technology has been perceived by many companies which invest in research and development for faster and more reliable machines with better capabilities and more quality products. AM expansion in industry has also been helped by a wide variety of materials, such as polymers, whose technology is developing rapidly with better mechanical properties related to stiffness and strength. In this paper we will describe a device which can be fully produced by all AM machines and enables users to measure in a fast and reliable way the stiffness of materials without the need for specialized and expensive methods, large-volume laboratory testing machines, specialized technical personnel and time. The objective is to design a small scaled three-point bending device using design intent through a parametric CAD system and manufacture it using AM technology. The device is designed to calculate the deformation and force applied to specific specimens and the Young's modulus of the material. The proposed device and its process helps users to estimate the mechanical properties of materials and apply that information on production or in a simulation system to optimize the printing quality of products by selecting the right material and adjusting the related printing parameters of the machines with the mechanical properties of the produced parts.

Keywords: Additive Manufacturing technology · 3D printing · Stiffness · Elastic modulus · Design intent · Parametric design · Product lifecycle

1 Introduction

Additive Manufacturing (AM) as a technique of 3-D printing technology has revolutionized the way which products are designed and manufactured in industry [1]. The main benefits of AM technology are the construction of complex geometries of both flexible and sustainable products and the ability of making parts with a variety of materials with no need of expensive and specialized machinery [2]. The basic principle of AM processes consists on fabricate parts by adding layers of materials which are placed one above the other [3] with most popular AM techniques being powder bed fusion, vat

Published by Springer Nature Switzerland AG 2019
C. Fortin et al. (Eds.): PLM 2019, IFIP AICT 565, pp. 233–242, 2019.
https://doi.org/10.1007/978-3-030-42250-9_22

photopolymerization, binder jetting and material extrusion [4]. There are also numerous AM desktop machines with many capabilities on building products which differ mainly in the sectors of printable size, surface quality, printing speed and the variety of materials they use during the production process, like metals, polymers, ceramics, concrete and composite materials [5, 6]. By selecting the appropriate materials and machine types, users can specify materials properties such as flexibility, hardness, stiffness, and control the quality of final products [1]. The building quality of products, other than materials selection, depends on various machine parameters that needs to be considered during the production process such as build orientation, contour width (CW), raster to raster air gap (RRAG) and others which significantly affect the printing results. Studies, using specialized laboratory machines, have showed that the values of these parameters affect the mechanical properties of the materials, such us Young's modulus and tensile and bending strength [5]. An equally important parameter that affects the mechanical properties of a product during the production process using AM technology is the viscosity of the material that is injected layer by layer mainly with the use of FDM (Fused Deposition Modelling) technology and recent studies proved that different temperatures of the dispensed material change the mechanical behaviour of a product. Another parameter that affects the strength of the produced products is fill density of the materials that determines the amount of the polymer used to print a product. It is confirmed that the tensile strength is influenced by the value of fill density during the production process [6]. Therefore, it is perceived that quality products made of AM technology requires knowledge of material mechanical properties and specific adjustments to the machine's settings such as the values of fill density, viscosity and other parameters which can be changed by the machine software during the production process [5, 6]. These parameters are related to the mechanical properties of the material before and after making products using AM technology and it is difficult for users to know the real values of the stiffness of the printed ones [1]. The objective of this paper is to design and manufacture a small scaled three-point bending device using exclusively AM machine and calculate the stiffness of selected AM materials by measuring the force and displacement of suitable selected specimens. The proposed process helps simple users and small-scale industries to know and measure the stiffness of materials and select the appropriate material from a list of available materials according to production needs by knowing and comparing their mechanical properties. The evaluation of Young's modulus was made using small deformation bending theory [7] and the results were compared with similar tests conducted on specialized testing machines.

2 Operation and Design Intent of the Device

The combination of a parametric CAD system and Fused Deposition Modelling (FDM) technology were the key factors to design and produce, a small sized three-point loading machine that consists of two different parts made of ABS material, referred to as *BTable* (Fig. 1), the steady part of the device, and *BSpike* (Fig. 2) the moving one. The operation of the device, called "BDevice", was simple. A specimen with dimensions, Length (L) = 60 mm, Width (b) = 5 mm and height (h) = 1 mm, (Fig. 3) was designed to fit the geometry of 50 mm BTable support spam. BSpike was placed at the railway of Btable with its lower end touching the upper surface of the specimen. The force was applied by hand with the index finger at the top flat cylindrical surface of BSpike. The applied force was transferred at the end surface of BSpike and therefore at the top surface of the specimen that bends and moves vertically downwards. That force was measured instantaneously using a low scale digital measuring machine which was mounted on BTable base (Fig. 4). An appropriate range of scale (0–200 g) was selected with 0.01 g accuracy, to be close to the range of applied forces that gave greater measuring accuracy. When the specimen bends 1 mm distance using finger force the steady applied force was measured each time. At that point the specimen was in equilibrium, meaning that the total effect of external forces on it equals to zero and the indication of the measuring scale shows the value of the applied force.

Fig. 1. Steady part of the device (BTable)

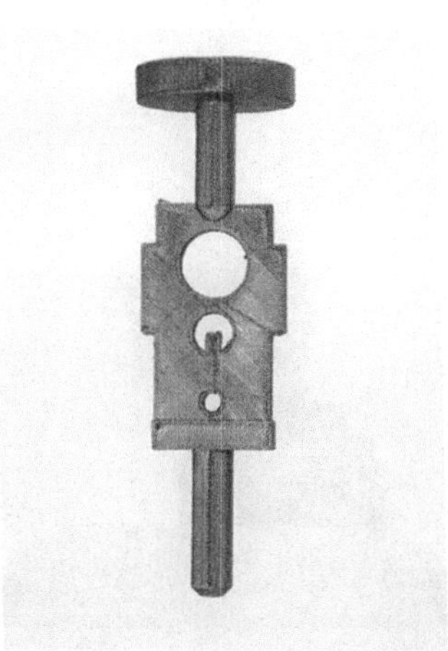

Fig. 2. Moving part of the device (BSpike)

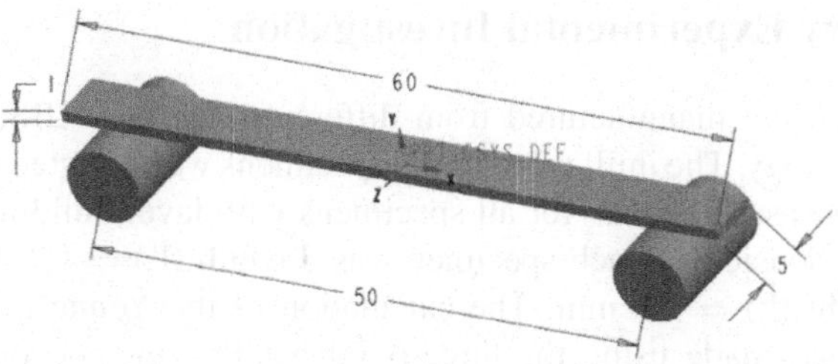

Fig. 3. Specimen dimensions

To measure as accurately as possible, the 1 mm displacement of the specimen during bending the observation of the placement of the cylindrical holes of BSpike was needed in relation to BTable. More specifically, while BSpike moves downwards to Btable and the displacement of the specimen equals to 1 mm, the geometry of the cylindrical holes of the two parts become coincident, meaning that they match perfectly (Fig. 4).

Design intent played an important role for the reliability of the device and it was the main factor that makes our device as reliable as possible to control the shifting and endurance of our device and specimens while measuring. One of the most important information that was included in the design intent of the product was the geometrical reference and topology of the cylindrical holes (C1, C2) of the two parts that consists the device and the height (d) of the specimen which had a dependent relationship between parameters such as $C1 = C2 + d$ that was included in the design intent during the design process of the device. The confirmation of the displacement is also carried out using the back pattern of BTable that has been designed with strips spaced apart by one-millimeter distance. During bending of specimen under an applied force a strip of pattern is covered, meaning that the specimen was bent exactly at a millimeter distance, d' (Fig. 5).

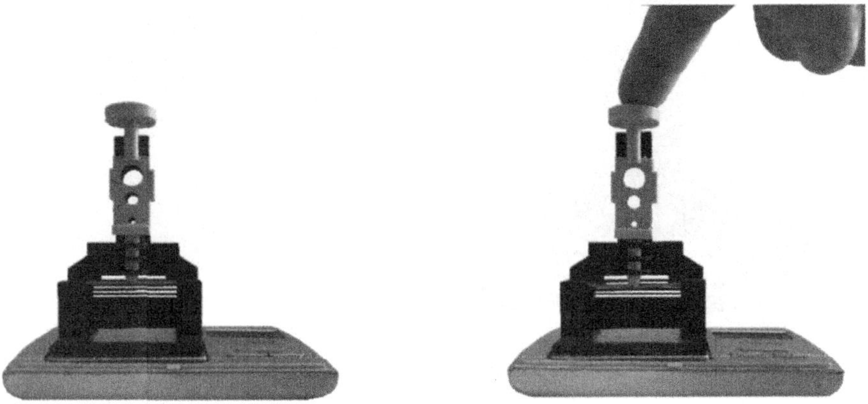

Fig. 4. Optical confirmations of the displacement of the specimen while bending using *geometry strips* and *cylindrical holes* coincidences between parts

3 Preliminary Experimental Investigation

Three specimens were manufactured from different materials ABS, PLA and PETG using FDM technology. The infill value of the specimens was adjusted through machines parameters and was set to 100% for all specimens with layer building thickness set to 0.25 mm. The dimension of each specimen was, Length (L) = 120 mm, Width (b) = 10 mm and height (h) = 1.5 mm. The calculation of the Young's modulus for each of the material was made using the three-point bending method on tensile machine SHIMADZU 100 KN at the Integrated Industrial Design Lab (INDEL) of the Department of Product and Systems Design Engineering at the University of the Aegean (Fig. 6). The displacement speed of the machine was set to 0.1 mm/s and the calculation of the Young Modulus for each of the specimens was made with the use of the force-displacement diagrams which gave as the following values: 2088 MPa for ABS, 2661 MPa for PLA and 1660 MPa for PETG.

Using the same FDM machine and settings, we manufactured three equal dimensioned specimens using the same quality of materials, ABS, PLA and PETG with the following dimensions, Length (L) = 60 mm (50 mm between support spam), Width (b) = 5 mm and height (h) = 1 mm (Fig. 7) to fit the geometry of BDevice (Fig. 4).

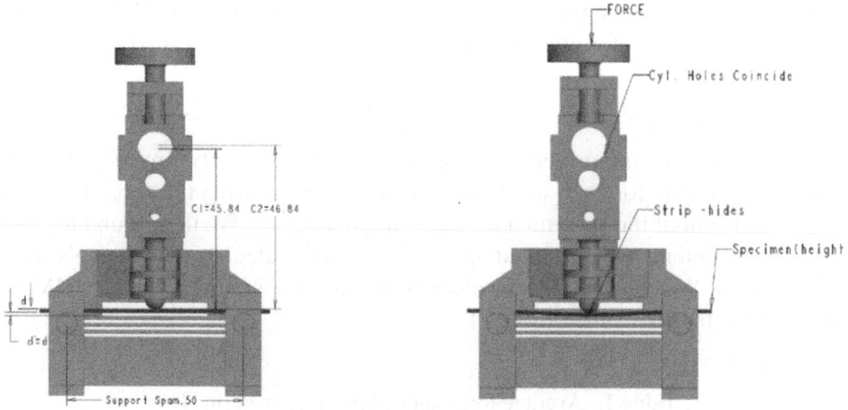

Fig. 5. Design intent of the device

Fig. 6. Three-point bend with tensile machine SHIMADZU

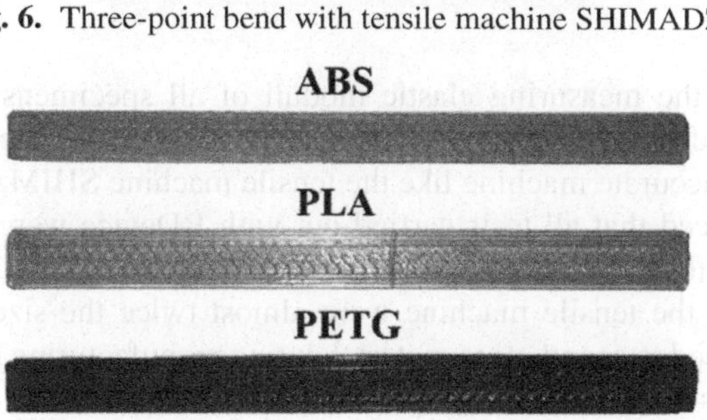

Fig. 7. Specimens made of FDM technology and ABS, PLA and PETG materials

The calculation of the Young's modulus was done using the equation

$$E = \frac{Fl^3}{4ubh^3}, \tag{1}$$

where E is the Young's modulus, F the bending force, l the distance between supports, u (=1 mm) the deflection, b the width and h the height (thickness) of the specimen.

This formula applies for elastic deformations which can be defined by

$$\sigma_{max} \leq \sigma_e \tag{2}$$

where σ_{max} is the maximum bending stress and σ_e the elasticity limit [7]. We carried out ten measurements for each of the three materials measuring the force for total displacement of 1 mm of the specimen during bending (Fig. 4). We then found the average force of all specimens (Table 1) and applied Eq. (1) to calculate the Young's modulus of each material. We compare these values with the ones we found using SHIMADZU tensile machine from INDEL (Table 2).

Table 1. Average force applied per specimen (in N).

Test Nr.	1	2	3	4	5	6	7	8	9	10	Avg.
F_{abs}	0.35	0.34	0.38	0.39	0.37	0.33	0.4	0.32	0.31	0.37	**0.359**
F_{pla}	0.41	0.47	0.42	0.47	0.46	0.47	0.42	0.43	0.47	0.44	**0.446**
F_{petg}	0.28	0.26	0.22	0.26	0.28	0.23	0.28	0.26	0.27	0.21	**0.255**

Table 2. Deviation of Young's modulus values (MPa) between two different machines.

	ABS	PLA	PETG
BDevice	2244	2788	1594
INDEL	2088	2661	1660
Deviation	8%	5%	4%

The results of the measuring elastic moduli of all specimens of the devices we used did not exceed 8% deviation, which means that BDevice reached the results of a more reliable and accurate machine like the tensile machine SHIMADZU during those tests. We also noticed that all tests carried out with BDevice were accomplished in a much shorter time than the laboratory testing machines. It is also worth noting that the specimens used in the tensile machine were almost twice the size the ones used for BDevice and we need to spend more material during manufacturing process, so they can be within the limits of the machine's specification.

4 Experimental Investigation According ASTM D790

The measurement reliability of the device was an important issue during this study and for that reason we choose to redesign BDevice and specimen's geometry according to ASTM D790 which defines strictly design standards during measurements [8]. Thus applying all the limitations and standards of that method we took new measurements of the materials Young's modulus and compare them with the ones from the previous geometry used at the preliminary experimental investigation. These standards were introduced in the form of parameters and constraints through design intent to the geometry of each part of the device and specimen. According to these standards both loading nose of BSpike and supports of Btable were designed to have cylindrical surfaces to avoid excessive indentation or failure due to stress concentration. According to the standards, for the specimens less than 3.2 mm thickness, the radius of the support should be up to 1.6 times the specimen thickness and the radius of the loading nose to be no more than 4 times the specimen thickness (Fig. 8). The specimens should have rectangular cross section and must rest on the midway between the supports during loading. The specimens we used had 1 mm thickness, which is less than 1.6 mm, and according to D790 standards for that thickness each specimen's length should be long enough on each end at least 10% of the support span but no less than 6.4 mm. Also, each specimen must be 50.8 mm long and 12.6 mm wide (Fig. 9) and the number of specimens need to be tested must be no less than five for each sample in the case of isotropic materials tested flatwise on a 25.4 mm support span.

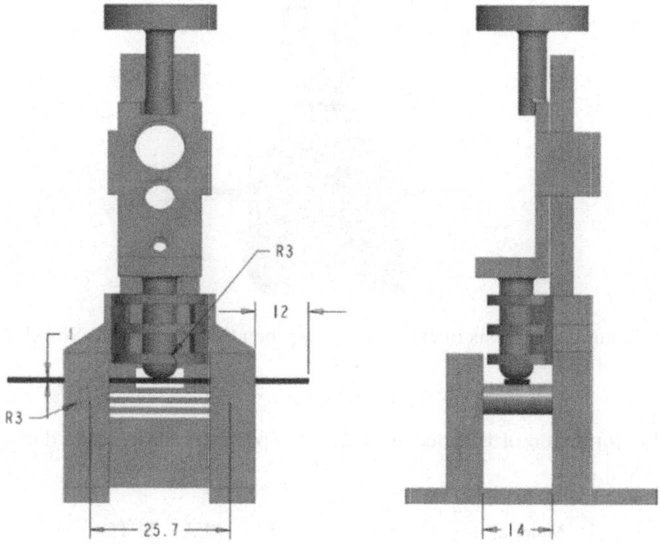

Fig. 8. BDevice geometry according to test method D790

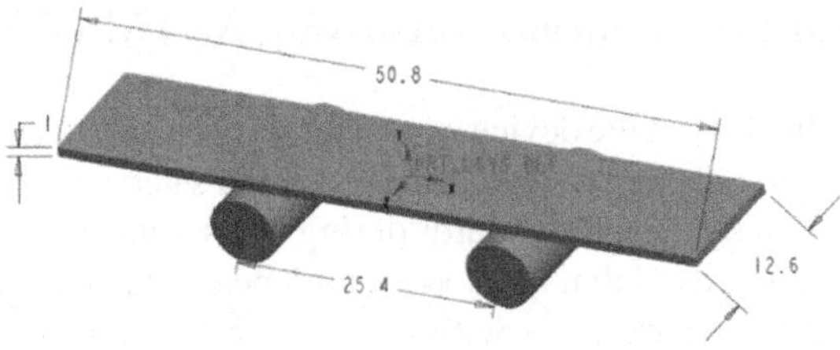

Fig. 9. Specimens geometry according to test method D790

Test method D790 also determines that the stiffness of the testing machine shall be such that the total elastic deformation of the systems does not exceed 1% of the total deflection of specimen during test. To confirm this standard, we needed to use mechanical analysis on a CAD software and to simulate BDevice loading machine as accurate as possible. To this end, apart from the exact geometry, the model included contact between the specimen and supports. We simulate three different BDevices with ABS, PLA and PETG material and we conducted the analyses using Creo Simulate platform (Fig. 10) to find and compare the results of the total elastic deformation of the testing machine with the deflection of each specimen that was, in all cases, under 1% (Table 3).

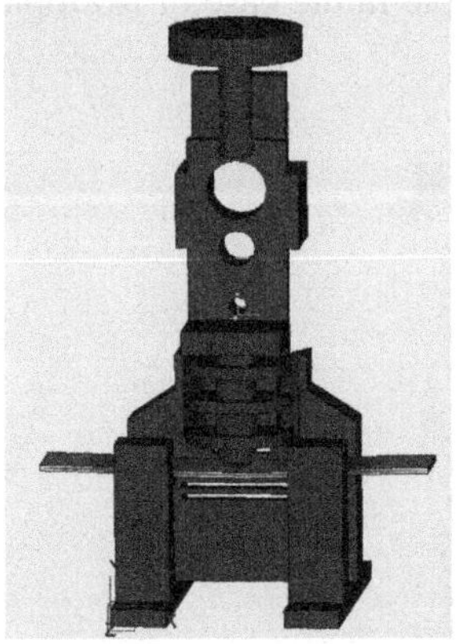

Fig. 10. Mechanical analysis of BDevice during bending using Creo Simulate software

Table 3. Total deformation of Bdevice according to specimen deformation during bending in a simulation mode.

Material	ABS	PLA	PETG
Young's modulus (MPa)	2088	2661	1660
Specimen deformation (mm)	1 mm	1 mm	1 mm
Total deformation (mm)	1.0053	1.006	1.0053
%	0.53%	0.6%	0.51%

Using FDM machine, we manufactured a new Bdevice and specimens (Fig. 11) and measured the Young's modulus of all three materials. The elasticity moduli calculated using Eq. (1) were: $E_{abs} = 2045$ MPa, $E_{pla} = 2445$ MPa and $E_{petg} = 1703$ MPa (Table 4). The new results, as it can be seen comparing with the values of Table 2 are much closer to the values obtained using the traditional testing equipment. Specifically, the deviation range from 4–8% was reduced to 2–8%.

Fig. 11. BDevice geometry using standards

Table 4. Deviation of Young's modulus values (MPa) between two different machines.

	ABS	PLA	PETG
BDevice	2244	2788	1594
New BDevice	2045	2445	1703
Deviation	9%	9%	7%

5 Conclusions

AM technology with its main capability and advantage in making complex geometries of both flexible and sustainable products helped us to manufacture a device (BDevice) with a specific geometry which includes all the necessary mechanical information such as design limits and standards that were inserted and controlled through parameters and constraints using Design Intent and a parametric CAD system. We showed that the measurements of Young's moduli of three different materials using BDevice had a small deviation considering the measurements taken from specialized and expensive laboratory testing machines that also needed to use large scaled and more expensive specimens. The reliability of the device was also proved by adjusting its geometry and specimens in an easy and fast way changing design intent under standards that method D790 requires.

Bdevice can be manufactured using any AM machine by a simple user or a small company which then can measure and compare the stiffness between the materials and thus know at any time which material is best suited for each construction. Knowing the material required for the manufacturing of a product, enable us to control and manage its lifecycle in all manufacturing phases. Using BDevice we can also estimate the real values of the Young's modulus of each polymer that differs before and after manufacturing process using AM machines. The measured modulus of each polymer can also be used after printing a model using AM machine to simulate, optimize and predict the mechanical behaviour of a single part or an assembly through FEA software. Using BDevice and the right adjustments to AM machines printing parameters we can also control the stiffness of any polymer material we use.

References

1. Gao, W., et al.: The status, challenges, and future of additive manufacturing in engineering. Comput.-Aided Des. **69**, 65–89 (2015)
2. Ngo, T.D., Kashani, A., Imbalzano, G., Nguyen, K.T., Hui, D.: A review of materials, methods, applications and challenges. Compos. Part B **143**, 172–196 (2018)
3. Wulle, F., Coupek, D., Schäffner, F., Verl, A., Oberhofer, F., Maier, T.: Workpiece and machine design in additive manufacturing for multi-axis fused deposition modeling. Procedia CIRP **60**, 229–234 (2017)
4. Turner, B.N., Strong, R., Gold, S.A.: A review of melt extrusion additive manufacturing processes: I. Process design and modeling. Rapid Prototyp. J. **20**(3), 192–204 (2012)
5. Hossain, M.S., Ramos, J., Espalin, D., Perez, M., Wicker, R.: Improving tensile mechanical properties of FDM-manufactured specimens via modifying build parameters. In: International Solid (2013)
6. Hwang, S., Reyes, E.I., Moon, K.S., Rumpf, R.C., Kim, N.S.: Thermo-mechanical characterization of metal/polymer composite filaments and printing parameter study for fused deposition modeling in the 3D printing process. J. Electron. Mater. **44**(3), 771–777 (2015)
7. Miljojković, J., Bijelić, I., Vranić, N., Radovanović, N., Živković, M.: Determining elastic modulus of the material by measuring the deflection of the beam loaded in bending. Tehnički vjesnik **24**(4), 1227–1234 (2017)
8. ASTM D 790, Standard Test Methods for Flexural Properties of Unreinforced and Reinforced Plastics and Electrical Insulating Materials (2003)

Motion-Structural Analysis of Systems Using Digital Twins

Sebastian Haag[1(✉)], Reiner Anderl[1], Klaus Schützer[2], and Eduardo Zancul[3]

[1] Department of Computer Integrated Design, Technische Universität Darmstadt, Otto-Berndt-Str. 2, 64287 Darmstadt, Germany
haag@dik.tu-darmstadt.de

[2] Laboratory for Computer Integrated Design and Manufacturing (SCPM), Methodist University of Piracicaba, Rod. Luis Ometto Km 24, Santa Barbara d'Oeste, Brazil

[3] Department of Production Engineering, Polytechnic School, University of Sao Paulo, Cidade Universitaria, Sao Paulo 05508-070, Brazil

Abstract. Digital Twins enable the analysis of systems under real world conditions using multiphysics models, sensors and bidirectional data connections between the digital and its physical twin. At the Research Lab of the Department of Computer Integrated Design (DiK) of Technische Universität Darmstadt, a Digital Twin demonstrator was developed that enables a motion-structural simulation of a bending beam test bench. The approach provides proof of many of the claimed benefits and challenges through a comprehensible Digital Twin system.

Keywords: Digital Twin · Motion-structural simulation · Test bed · Cyber-physical systems

1 Introduction

Digital Twins (DT) constitute virtual representations of physically existent systems [1]. The exchange of data between digital and physical twin takes place through bidirectional data connections [2]. The networking of technical systems, also called cyber-physical systems (CPS), is one of the key tasks of the digitization of industrial production, which in Germany is being promoted under the term *Industrie 4.0* [3]. CPS use embedded electronics, software, sensors, actuators, and network connectivity to collect, process, and communicate data about their condition or behavior over wired or wireless networks [4]. The ability to communicate allows the synchronization of physical and virtual space and thus forms the basis for the creation of Digital Twins. The transmitted data regarding state, behavior, or environment serve as input to multidimensional, physical models that make up the Digital Twin.

The use of physical data collected by sensors in real space enables Digital Twins to reproduce and analyze real conditions, to respond to changes, to optimize the operation of the system, and thus generate added value for the product usage phase [5]. The processing of the data is hereby not accomplished using classical methods of data processing, but

Published by Springer Nature Switzerland AG 2019
C. Fortin et al. (Eds.): PLM 2019, IFIP AICT 565, pp. 243–249, 2019.
https://doi.org/10.1007/978-3-030-42250-9_23

with methods of computer-aided technologies (CAx). This brings several advantages. The current state or the current behavior of the real system can be visualized using the model. This allows a much more efficient conceptualization of the situation by humans compared to a description through numbers and letters [6]. In addition, the visualization of the Digital Twin facilitates the comparison of both the current state with the desired state and all the past states stored. And lastly, visualization allows for more effective collaboration between multiple individuals, as all share the same conceptualization and are not dependent on individual interpretation [6]. These advantages are already used in product development with the help of the computer-aided design (CAD). In addition, the advantages of computer-aided engineering, in particular simulation and optimization, should also be borne by the Digital Twin to the product usage phase.

The Digital Twin allows the simulation of a system based on its real geometry, i.e. taking into account manufacturing deviations, wear and maintenance of individual components, which will increase the accuracy of the simulation in terms of behavior and in particular failure. Furthermore, through the data connection between digital and physical twin actual environmental data can be included in the simulation, which increases its accuracy in regard to the actual usage behavior of the system compared to predefined simulation scenarios [7]. The bidirectionality of the data connection also allows the control of the actuators of the physical system based on the calculated optimization results of the simulation. Ultimately, the Digital Twin forms an integral part of future autonomous systems [7]. Figure 1 summarizes the aforementioned benefits.

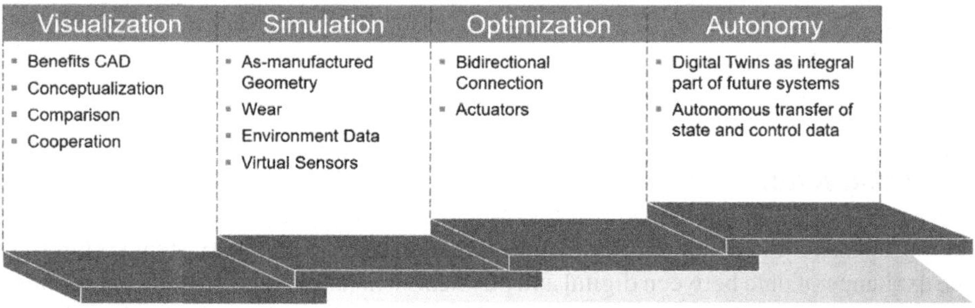

Fig. 1. Benefits of digital twins

The aim of this project is to demonstrate the application of Digital Twins using a cyber-physical bending beam test bench connected to a motion-structural model of the system, its Digital Twin. The demonstrator is located at the Research Lab of the Department of Computer Integrated Design of Technische Universität Darmstadt but can be accessed via a secure connection by any internet-capable device from anywhere in the world.

2 Test Bed Development

The test bed was developed in two phases. In the first phase the physical bending beam test bench was developed and connected to an Internet of Things (IoT) platform and a CAD system using different application programming interfaces (API). In the second phase a fully functional motion-structural simulation model of the test bench was developed and integrated into the system.

In step one of phase one, a simple bending beam test bench was developed. The bending beam was chosen because its physics are easily comprehensible thus making it ideal to demonstrate the potentials of Digital Twin technology. The test bench (see Fig. 2) represents the physical twin in this cyber-physical system. It consists of two linear actuators that can move independently from another in the vertical direction. In between the two actuators a bending beam is clamped. Two load cells are integrated into the holding fixture on one side. They measure the resulting force acting on the bending beam after displacement. The displacement is calculated as the difference between the actuator positions. The control unit is set atop the frame.

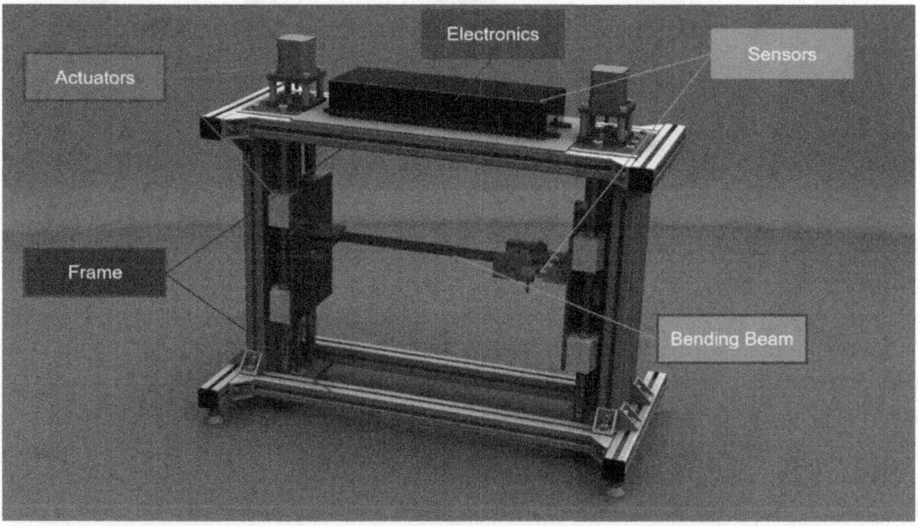

Fig. 2. Model of the developed bending beam test bench

In step two, the mechatronic test bench was transformed into a cyber-physical system by adding a microprocessor and a communication interface. Through the communication interface the test bench was connected to an IoT platform using the Message Queuing Telemetry Transport (MQTT) protocol. MQTT is an open messaging protocol based on a publish-subscribe architecture [8]. Upon connection, clients can publish messages to a broker under hierarchically defined topics. The broker saves the messages and forwards them to other clients who subscribe to this topic. The three clients in the test bed architecture are: the physical test bench, the IoT platform and the application programming interface of the CAD system.

The bending beam test bench publishes the position of each linear actuator as well as the force measured by the load cells. The IoT platform subscribes to these topics and collects the data. This sensor data is also visualized on a browser-based dashboard. Through this dashboard, the user can also control the physical demonstrator. Analogously to the sensor data, the control data is published to the broker who forwards it to the subscribing test bench. The dashboard can be accessed by any authorized device connected to the internet. Figure 3 visualizes the interaction between the single components of the test bed.

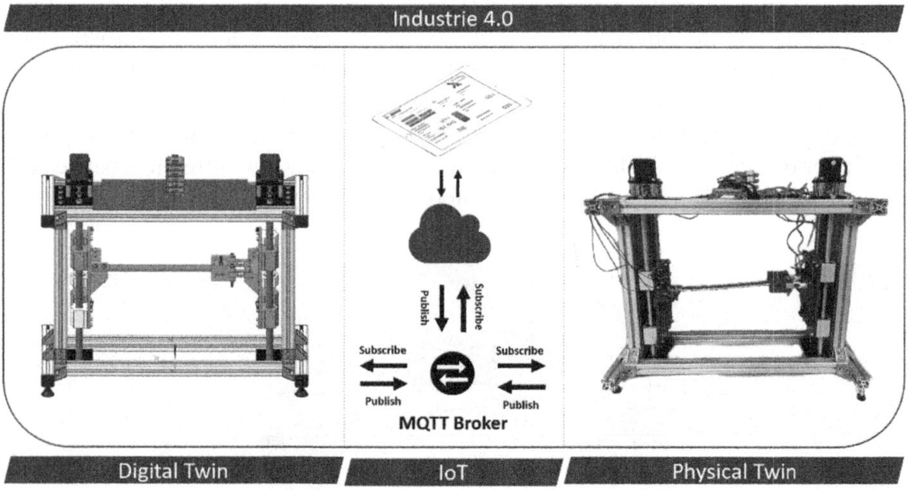

Fig. 3. Architecture of Digital Twin system

In step three, an isolated finite element analysis (FEA) model of the bending beam was modelled and also connected to the broker through the API of the CAD system. The analysis using the finite element method is done in the CAD system. The resulting geometry model forms the reference geometry on which the process chain is based. The solid model is transformed into a finite element model by generating a finite element mesh. In addition, the body is assigned material properties and loads as well as constraints. During the subsequent processing, the finite element problem is solved with the help of a solver. In post processing, the results of the calculation are prepared in graphical form for evaluation and interpretation. The FEA model represented the Digital Twin in the first phase of the project. At this point, a human user could run a bending beam test through the dashboard on both the physical system as well as the Digital Twin using any internet capable device. To start the experiment the dashboard is opened in a browser. Either the resulting force on the beam or the final displacement of the beam are put in as parameters. Pushing the Run complete test button sends the variables to the broker who distributes them to the physical twin, which then moves to the selected position until either the displacement or the force is reached and measures the other variable respectively. The variable is then sent back to the broker who forwards it to the Digital Twin and the IoT platform. The Digital Twin uses the real force or displacement values to start a fully automated FEA. The necessary inputs for the finite element calculations are predefined in this use case. However, it is possible to consider them as variables and query them from the user through the dashboard or from the physical twin through a scenario-based logic. After completion, the calculated results are pushed back to the IoT platform through the broker where they can be compared to the physical results [9].

In phase two, a motion-structural analysis model of the entire test bench was developed (see Fig. 4). Motion-structural analyses combine the process chains of multi-body simulation (MBS) and finite element analysis (FEA). MBS calculate the dynamic movement of an assembly and are used to determine motion sequences, joint positions and collision areas under the consideration of the physical constraints. Originally, in MBS elastostatics of individual components are neglected [10]. However, in motion-structural analyses, the motion simulation calculates reaction forces and loads on the individual components, which then serve as input into a structural FEA. The additional chaining provides more accurate component strength results than pure FEA under self-defined load cases and increases the understanding of the performance of components in their operating environment. The motion-structural model was similarly connected to the broker through the CAD system's API. The operator can now control the actuators individually and the Digital Twin will mirror the behavior of its physical twin as well as visualize additional data, such as actual stress and deformation characteristics during usage. Figure 4 shows the result of a motion-structural analysis of the test bench. The beam was bent by driving the right linear actuator upward through the simulation of the multi-body-system. The FEA calculates and visualizes the resulting deformation.

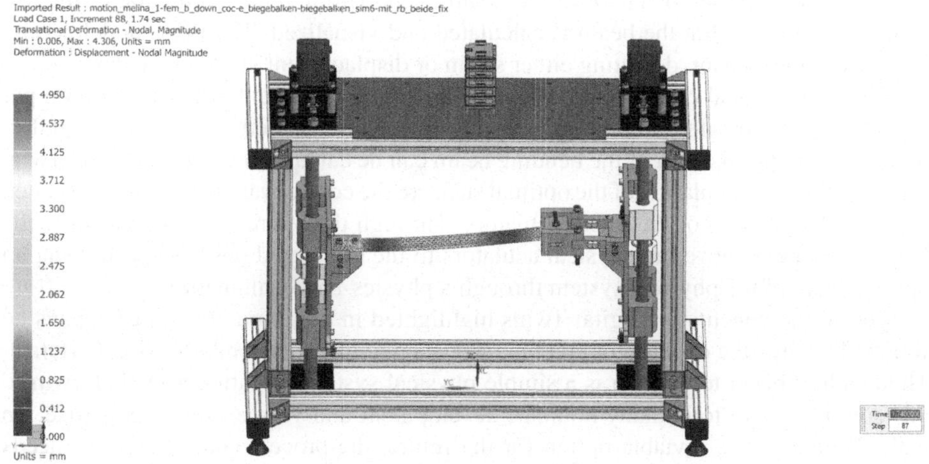

Fig. 4. Motion-structural analysis

3 Results and Discussion

As with the first phase of the project, the intention of the test bed is not to examine the deviation between real and virtual measurements. It is to demonstrate the concept of the Digital Twin. In the first phase, the virtual counterpart of the bending beam test bench only consisted of an isolated FEA model of the beam itself. In a bending beam test, this is where the focus of the analysis lies. However, representing the entire test bench in a motion-structural model opens up a wider range of benefits of the Digital Twin as described in Sect. 1.

Users can visualize the current state of the entire physical system. This is helpful whenever the system itself is not in sight. The conceptualization through a three-dimensional model is much more powerful than looking at numbers, reports and other symbolic information. This also helps the user to compare the current state to the intended state more easily. Lastly, multiple users share the same conceptualization, making it easier for them discuss it and solve potential problems together. Through technologies such as augmented and virtual reality the Digital Twin can be brought to the factory floor or any environment where a system is deployed assisting workers or maintenance personnel.

Using physics-based models throughout the product usage phase extends the concept of Model-Based Systems Engineering (MBSE) beyond the product development phase. Thus, simulation of three-dimensional physics-based models becomes available during product use. To increase the accuracy of the simulation models, as-manufactured geometries as well as wear can be taken into account. A full overview of the system can be generated by a combination of virtual and real sensors. In the demonstrated use case, a real sensor is represented by the load cells in the physical system to measure the force acting on the beam. In order to measure the strain within the beam or the displacement of the beam along its length, a variety of additional sensors would have to be installed, possibly impacting the behavior of the beam itself. Through the simulation of the test bench the strain within the beam is calculated and visualized. The FEA model hereby acts as a virtual sensor, depicting either strain or displacement graded by color.

The bidirectional connecting between the physical and the digital twin allows, per definition, data transfer from the physical to the digital as well as from the digital to physical. An optimization of the bending beam can be calculated using its Digital Twin. The result of the calculation of the optimal state are the control variables, in the presented use case the position of the linear actuators. Through the bidirectional connection, the Digital Twin can move the physical actuators to the calculated positions, achieving an optimal state of the physical system through a physics-based simulation.

For all the benefits of Digital Twins highlighted in literature, they must always be weighed against the expense of creating and maintaining this complex virtual artefact. The bending beam test bench is a simple physical system. Creating a Digital Twin to this simple system took many hours of development and very exclusive expertise. To make Digital Twins a viable option for the future, the process chain CAD-DT needs to be formally specified. Furthermore, the operation of a fully functional Digital Twin is accompanied with significant costs. These include license fees for modeling and simulation software as well as hardware costs for memory and processing power. In the presented use case a state-of-the-art workstation was used to calculate the simulations. Still, the calculation was the limiting factor of the Digital Twin operation. Quickly changing states could not be realized because the time needed for the calculation averaged at 37 s. More complex virtual representations will therefore require much more powerful computing hardware in order to gain real-time capabilities.

4 Conclusion

In summary, the concept of the Digital Twin has evolved greatly in recent years from a NASA and U.S. Air Force research project. There is a variety of benefits to be gained from implementing Digital Twins to physical systems. Most notably, Digital Twins carry the advantages of Model-Based Systems Engineering to the product usage phase. Simulation and optimization based on physical models paired with real environment data enhances insight into system operation and lays the foundation for model-based control of future autonomous systems. However, the deployment of Digital Twins is also accompanied by many challenges and costs. The development and operation of the virtual counterpart requires specialized knowledge, expensive simulation software and powerful computing performance.

The benefits and challenges of the Digital Twin concept could both be demonstrated in this project using a bending beam test bench. A motion-structural model to the physical system was developed and simulated, illustrating the added value of a three-dimensional virtual model mirroring a physical system's behavior. The performance of the applied hardware represented the limiting factor of the entire Digital Twin system. The calculation of the simulation required more than half a minute making the system far from real-time capable.

Acknowledgments. The demonstrator is part of the project "Smart Components within Smart Production Processes and Environments (SCoPE)" within the Brazilian-German Collaborative Research Initiative on Smart Connected Manufacturing (BRAGECRIM) funded by DFG. Other institutes involved in this project are the Laboratory for Computer Integrated Design and Manufacturing of the Methodist University of Piracicaba and the Department of Production Engineering of the Polytechnic School of the University of Sao Paulo.

References

1. Shafto, M., et al.: Modeling, simulation, information technology & processing roadmap. Technol. Area **11** (2010)
2. Grieves, M.: Virtually Perfect: Driving Innovative and Lean Products Through Product Lifecycle Management. Space Coast Press, Cocoa Beach (2011)
3. BITKOM, VDMA, ZVEI (eds.): Umsetzungsstrategie Industrie 4.0: Ergebnisbericht der Plattform Industrie 4.0 (2015)
4. Lee, E.A.: Cyber physical systems: design challenges (2008)
5. Anderl, R., Haag, S., Schützer, K., Zancul, E.: Digital twin technology – an approach for industrie 40 vertical and horizontal lifecycle integration. IT – Inform. Technol. **60**(3), 125–132 (2018)
6. Grieves, M.: Digital twin: manufacturing excellence through virtual factory replication (2014)
7. Boschert, S., Rosen, R.: Digital Twin - The Simulation Aspect. In: Hehenberger, P., Bradley, D. (eds.) Mechatronic Futures, pp. 59–74. Springer, Cham (2016). https://doi.org/10.1007/978-3-319-32156-1_5
8. Trojan, W.: Das MQTT-Praxisbuch, 1st edn. Elektor-Verlag GmbH, Aachen (2017)
9. Haag, S., Anderl, R.: Digital twin – Proof of concept. Manuf. Lett. **15**, 64–66 (2018)
10. Anderl, R., Binde, P.: Simulationen mit NX/Simcenter 3D. Carl Hanser Verlag GmbH & Co. KG, München (2017)

Modular Product Variety Generator Based on the Modified Genetic Algorithm: A Lego Plane

Mahmoud Masmoudi[1(✉)], Mariem Besbes[1,2], and Marc Zolghadri[1]

[1] Quartz Laboratory (EA7393), SUPMECA, 3 Rue Fernand Hainaut, 93400 Saint-Ouen, France
mahmoud.masmoudi@supmeca.fr
[2] LA2MP Laboratory, ENIS, B.P 1173, 3038 Sfax, Tunisia

Abstract. Mass customization is a business strategy that aims at satisfying individual customer needs and provides them a large product mix. To achieve this goal, it is necessary to manage the product life cycle activities especially the volume and variety of products which have to be easily customizable. Designing modular products increases the possibility of obtaining customizable products. The modular design consists of breaking down a product into more or less independent sub-elements called modules. This paper focuses on setting up a Genetic-based automatic product variants generator. The product used as the testbed is a LEGO plane composed of bricks. Different operators are used for selection, crossover and mutation of genes. Each final plane assembly is qualified based on some criteria to respect pre-defined constraints. The obtained final assemblies are discussed at the end of the paper to highlights future challenges.

Keywords: Variety · Genetic Algorithm · Modularity · Product families

1 Introduction

Today, a product exists in several variants. The Renault Megane II, for example, is produced in a few thousand variants. Mass customization is a business strategy that aims at satisfying individual customer needs by providing a large product mix. Consumer demand for ever more differentiated products, generated the notion of a variety in early 80s. During the product design, it is therefore necessary to take into account of product variety and modularity. The modular design consists of breaking down a product into more or less independent sub-elements called modules that are bundled as a unit, and which serve identifiable functions. The differentiation of the finished product is obtained by defining modules and their interfaces.

In this context, this work focuses on the design of a computer tool for the generation of variants of a product composed of LEGO bricks using MATLAB language. These bricks of LEGO represent the modules to assemble. Of course, this research work does not take account more sophisticated concepts such as architecture determination, various types of exchanges between modules and so on; it remains focused on some aspects

Published by Springer Nature Switzerland AG 2019
C. Fortin et al. (Eds.): PLM 2019, IFIP AICT 565, pp. 250–259, 2019.
https://doi.org/10.1007/978-3-030-42250-9_24

of a product definition. The following section will present the general idea about the concept of product variety as well as its advantages and disadvantages. The proposed methodology is introduced in Sect. 3 followed by presentation of the case study in Sect. 4. Section 5 focuses on the resolution technique which is the genetic algorithm, with some modifications. Finally, we discuss the obtained results before concluding by research perspectives.

2 Product Variety

Over the past decade, many research activities have been deployed to develop methods and tools to facilitate the design of product platforms and product families to provide cost-effective product variety and customization. The product platform is a relatively broad set of components, physically connected and forming a stable subset, common to different finished products [1]. Similarity in products configuration can led us to the notion of product family. A product family is a class, and variant products are instances of that family. Each instance is obtained by choosing different values of attributes [2]. According to [3] the term product family is defined as a group of interrelated products that are derivatives of a platform produced to satisfy a variety in the marketplace. The variety of products is a fundamental element of the commercial offer. However, it is subject to positive and negative pressures. Business objectives, such as the fight against competition and the arrival of new technologies, are pushing for an increase in variety to best meet customer needs. On the other hand, a variety that is too high becomes a brake on economic growth, particularly due to, for example, too much confusion that it can induce. Nevertheless, above all are the concerns of production in favor of the variety mastery. A too high variety generates too many references items to procure, store, manage, etc. Negative pressures therefore come mainly from manufacturing concerns.

Industrialists are therefore seeking to find a solution to this. In the literature [4], the modularity of products is considered among the best solutions. From a commercial point of view, a modular product presents several varieties by combining the different possible configurations of the modules. In addition, modularity reduces the complexity of the operations of the production process.

A huge number of modular methods have been proposed in the literature such as the graph and matrix partitioning method by [5], the mathematical programming method [6], the clustering methods, Genetic Algorithm [7] or Artificial Intelligence.

Generally, in previous researches, there are two main steps: (1) regroup components or identify all the modules of the product and (2) produce different product variants by testing different configurations. In addition, a technique such as UML diagrams, DSMs, IDEF0 and OPM is used to model the product architecture. But, we think that each different architecture representation is best suited for a specific purpose and not fit exactly to our need and requirements in some cases.

That's why in this paper we propose a new modular methodology for product variety generation with definition of a modular architecture representation. This study aims to contribute to this growing area of research by exploring the modularity in LEGO modelling which we consider as another way of seeing the product from a modular point of view. To our knowledge, the use and building of products in LEGO is conventionally done with the aim of designing prototypes for products and models, and this paper is the first attempt to generate alternatives or varieties of product using different design constraints. Problem resolution is done by modified GA.

3 Product Architecture and Variety: General Methodology

As said previously, we need first to define and model the Product architecture. Inspired by the definition given by [8] as "The structure (in terms of components, connections, and constraints) of a product", we propose in Fig. 1 our approach. A Product is a set of physical (components), logical (constraints) and functions connected together. In other words, Product architecture is considered as the scheme by which the functions of the product are arranged into physical chunks controlled via the existence of constraints and interacted via connections.

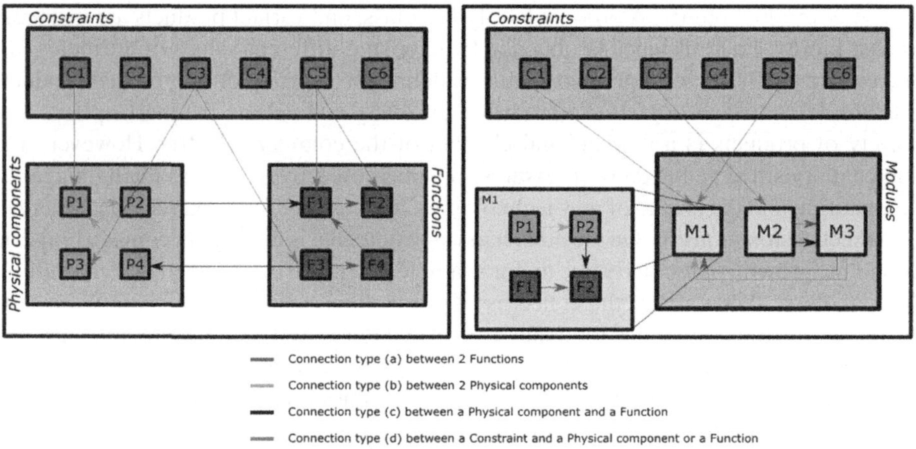

Fig. 1. Product architecture representation (Color figure online)

Four types of connections are identified here (represented in different colors in Fig. 1). One or more physical component(s) can be regrouped with single or multiple function(s) in one block called 'Module'. The Module includes also the different connections that link these functions and physical components together (type (a), (b) or (c)). And two modules are connected together if there are connections type (a), (b) or (c) between two elements (function or physical component) where each element belong to one of these modules. The steps of our methodology for variety generation are:

1. Identify the different modules, their physical and functional composition, interaction between them and connection with the constraints
2. Model modules as LEGO bricks and translate the different constraints and connections into equations
3. Simulate different combinations and find new product variants.

4 LEGO Plane

We consider that a product P that can be modelled into LEGO bricks, is the result of the assembly of a set of blocks, called "modules" M_i on a platform (a set of LEGO bricks that are fixed in specific position).

$$P = Platform + \sum_i M_i \tag{1}$$

Our case of study is a LEGO plane, modelled in Fig. 2 composed by a platform and 18 modules. We denote n_m the number of modules in one solution. The goal is to generate new plane variants respecting defined criteria.

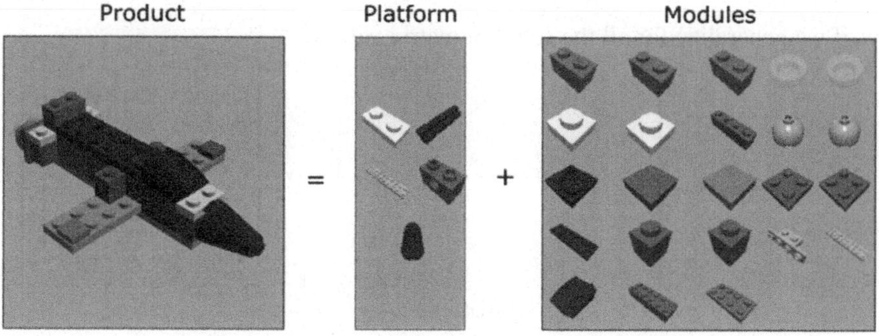

Fig. 2. 3D LEGO plane model

Each module can contain one or more LEGO bricks and it is characterized by a function and a geometric structure. For example, an "engine" module contains two bricks has a rectangular structure of defined dimensions and performs the energy transformation. We consider a discrete space of three dimensions (x, y, z); with x_{max} , y_{max} , z_{max} standing for the maximum dimensions of the space along the axis; $O(1, 1, 1)$ is the point of origin. A product can therefore be represented within the solution space $(x_{max} \times y_{max} \times z_{max})$. Each module M_i of dimension $(n_i \times m_i \times p_i)$ is represented by a matrix Mat_i of having the same dimension and containing the value i in all the cells.

$$Mat_i(x, y, z) = i \forall x \in [\![1, n_i]\!], \forall y \in [\![1, m_i]\!], \forall z \in [\![1, p_i]\!] \tag{2}$$

A module M_i is characterized by:

- Geometric dimensions: $(n_i \times m_i \times p_i)$ length, width and height.
- A position vector $P(i) = [x_i, y_i, z_i]$ that represents its position in the solution S, where x_i, y_i and z_i represent coordinates of the Module M_i in the solution space along the 3 dimensions.
- An orientation $O(i)$ signifying its orientation ('H' for horizontal or 'V' for vertical) in the solution S.

So, inserting the same module, we can get two different solutions depending on the orientation value.

Given a Module where $\begin{cases} Mat_i(x, y, z) = i \forall x \in [\![1, n_i]\!], \forall y \in [\![1, m_i]\!], \forall z \in [\![1, p_i]\!] \\ P(i) = [x_i, y_i, z_i] \end{cases}$

If $O(i) = \text{'}H\text{'}$ then

$$S(x + x_i - 1, y + y_i - 1, z + z_i - 1) = i \forall x \in [\![1, n_i]\!], \forall y \in [\![1, m_i]\!], \forall z \in [\![1, p_i]\!] \tag{3}$$

Suppose now a solution where $O(i) = \text{'}V\text{'}$, we get:

$$S(x + x_i - 1,\ y + y_i - 1,\ z + z_i - 1) = i \forall x \in [\![1, m_i]\!],\ \forall y \in [\![1, n_i]\!],\ \forall z \in [\![1, p_i]\!] \tag{4}$$

Now, if we generalize for all the solution matrix values:

$$S(a, b, c) = \begin{cases} i,\ if\ \exists i,\ where \begin{cases} Mat_i(a - x_i + 1,\ b - y_i + 1,\ c - z_i + 1) = i \forall \begin{cases} \begin{cases} a \in [\![x_i, x_i + n_i - 1]\!] \\ b \in [\![y_i, y_i + m_i - 1]\!] \\ c \in [\![z_i, z_i + p_i - 1]\!] \end{cases} \\ \cup \\ \begin{cases} a \in [\![y_i, y_i + m_i - 1]\!] \\ b \in [\![x_i, x_i + n_i - 1]\!] \\ c \in [\![z_i, z_i + p_i - 1]\!] \end{cases} \end{cases} \\ P(i) = [x_i, y_i, z_i] \end{cases} \\ 0 \text{ otherwise} \end{cases} \tag{5}$$

The platform represents the modules that are fixed (their position vector and orientation have a unique value that cannot be changed) and that exist in the chromosome. A solution is defined as a combination of placement of these matrices Mat_i in solution space fitting constraints. Design rules and assembly constraints must be defined to ensure compliance of generated products with expected functions and specifications. Mathematical modelling of different Lego pieces, constraints and rules can be done using Matrices. These constraints are classified under 3 categories:

- Constraints on the modules (type (d)): for each module, attributes are defined
  - rotational constraint (M_i can be rotated horizontally, vertically or both) $(H, V, H/V)$
  - assembly constraint above (assemble another module above M_i) (YES, NO)
  - assembly constraint below (assemble another module below M_i) (YES, NO)
  - assembly constraint on the right (assemble another module on the right side of M_i) (YES, NO)
- Constraints between the modules (type (a) or (b)), such as:
  - Plane wings must be in the front of the plane and distance between wings M_2 and the nose M_4 must be less than 50% of M_1 the platform length,
  - distance between M_1 and M_4 is null,

- each module M_i, $\forall i \neq 4$ must have at least one module M_j $j \neq i$ assembled below or above,
- the red light M_5 must be at the left side of the wing M_2 and the green one M_4 must be at right, etc...

- Constraints on the solution: The solution is a $(n_s \times m_s \times p_s)$ matrix

- $n_s \leq x_{max}$, $m_s \leq y_{max}$ and $p_s \leq z_{max}$
- All modules exist in the matrix and there is no overlap between modules
- Each module exists ones a time

All these constraints are necessary to define a plane, but not sufficient to get a good plane. The goal is to design a computer tool using MATLAB and relying on the notion of the GA to generate from these Lego pieces all possible plane variants.

5 Genetic Algorithm Principle

Genetic Algorithm (GA) is an evolutionary algorithm inspired by Darwin's theory of species evolution developed by [9]. It has proved its effectiveness in solving a wide variety of problems in various fields: robotics [10], facility layout problem, planning problem [11] and others [12–14]. For this reason, the GA is adopted in this paper.

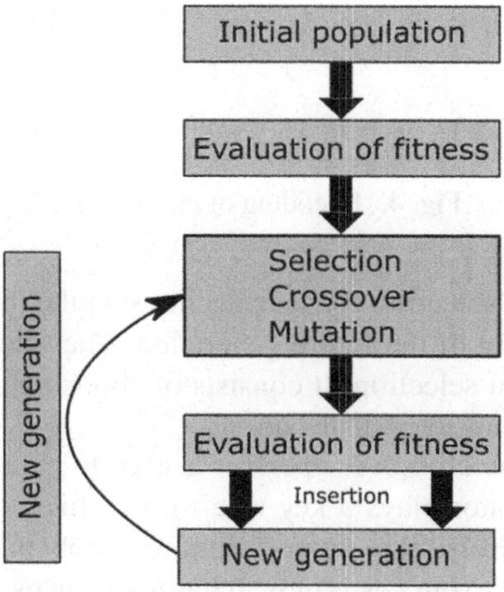

Fig. 3. Genetic Algorithm principle

The Genetic Algorithm starts with an initial population consisting of a set of individuals. Each individual is represented by a chromosome. This population evolves during a succession of iterations, called generations. At each iteration, three types of operators (selection, crossover and mutation) are applied to individuals in order to obtain new individuals. Several different operators can be used. This process of evolution is repeated until the satisfaction of a stopping criterion. The flow chart of different GA steps is shown in Fig. 3. In our case, we will focus particularly on the generation of a variety of LEGO products (an assembly of LEGO bricks).

- **Step 1: chromosome encoding:** Each individual is represented by a vector with $(n \times m \times p)$ columns as illustrated in Fig. 4. With n, m and p represent respectively the dimensions of a matrix S: number of rows, number of columns and number of layers. This matrix S represents the matrix model of the product in a $3D$ space. Each cell of the matrix S can have either the value 0 (if there are no Lego bricks in the position (i, j, k)) or the value x where x is the index of the module M_x which exists in the position (i, j, k).

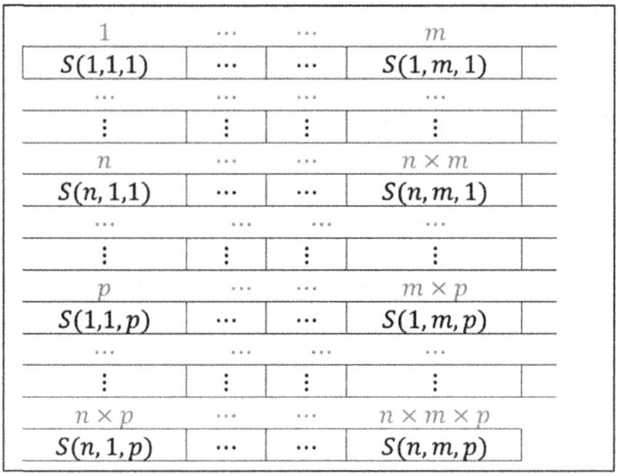

Fig. 4. Encoding of chromosome

- **Step 2: Selection:** The selection consists in choosing the individuals who will participate in the reproduction of the future generation. The selection operator adopted in this work is the random selection. It consists of choosing an individual in a random manner according to a uniform distribution.
- **Step 3: Crossover:** The crossover operator is used to combine the different parts of each parent. This operator plays a key role for the diversity of the population. It is applied with a certain probability named crossover probability. The crossing operator adopted here is specific to our case study. It has not been used before in other research works. As illustrated in Fig. 5, it is necessary to randomly choose two different cut-off points x_1 and x_2. The first child C_1 is created by keeping the first part of the first parent P_1 and the second part of P_2. The block between x_1 and x_2 consists of the random arrangement of the missing modules. The second child C_2 is made in the opposite way. NB: If a module is divided into two part: for example a part of module is before x_1 and the other is after x_1, as a result, the module belongs to the first part of the first child. As shown in Fig. 5, the cutoff point x_1 divides the module M_1 (yellow color) into two parts. So this module belongs to the first part of E_1.

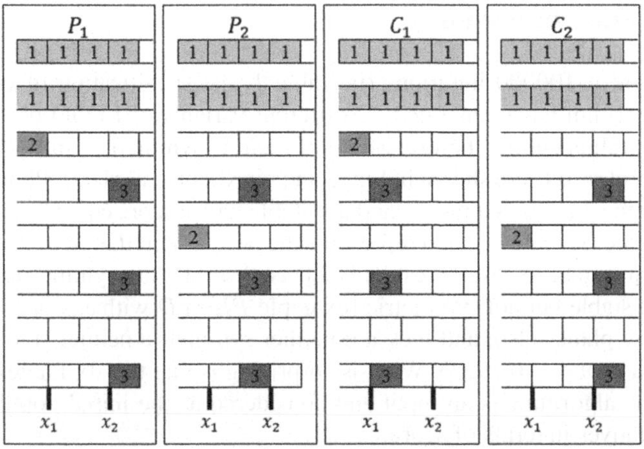

Fig. 5. Crossover operator (Color figure online)

- **Step 4: Mutation:** The mutation operator is used to apply some transformations on the chromosome structure with a low probability noted p_m. Its main objective is to keep the diversity of solutions. The mutation operator applied in this study is the "exchange operator". The principle is to choose any random module to change its position as well as all the modules that are above it in the $3D$ matrix S. The new position of these modules will be randomly chosen from one of the vacant boxes following a random order.
- **Step 5: Evaluation:** The evaluation of solutions is done by assigning an X-weighting that measures the performance of each individual by taking into account criteria. Here we chose the feasibility (A), symmetry (B) and the stability (C). The score is computed as below:

$$SCORE = A \times (1 + B) - Coefficient \times C \tag{6}$$

Where $A = \left\{ \begin{array}{c} 1 \text{ if the solution represents a plane} \\ 0 \text{ otherwise} \end{array} \right\}$

And $B = \left\{ \begin{array}{c} 2 \text{ if the plane is symmetrical} \\ 1 \text{ otherwise} \end{array} \right\}$

$C = \left\{ \begin{array}{c} 0 \text{ if the plane is stable} \\ >0 \text{ otherwise} \end{array} \right\}$ and $Coefficient = 1/1000$

A solution is considered as a plane if it responds to all constraints. Symmetry is defined here by the horizontal plane that cuts the matrix S in half and passes through the point of gravity of the plane. Stability is computed by the difference of plane weight at right and left of the vertical plane that cuts the matrix S in half and passes through the point of gravity of the plane.

- **Step 6: Stopping criterion:** The genetic algorithm evolves in several generations until the satisfaction of a stopping criterion. The criterion chosen in our case is a maximum number of iterations fixed at 100000 iterations.

6 Results and Discussion

After execution of 100000 iterations (in Table 1, the specification of our study), the developed algorithm have generated 22 different variants of LEGO plane. They obey to all the constraints defined before. Some of them is symmetric, and others are stable planes (Different results are shown in Fig. 6 and represented as stars). Plane B represents the initial design which is symmetric and not stable with a score equal to 1.9933. Plane A has the best score ($score = 2$) and represents the best variant that fit to the requirements of symmetry and stability. Some results (such as $PlaneC$) are symmetric but not stable and others are stable but not symmetric (example $PlaneD$ with a $score = 1$). The rest of solutions are planes also, and they are neither symmetric neither stable (the case of Plane E with a $score = 0.9933$). What is surprising is that the six Planes that we have provided to the algorithm as an input and considered as the initial population, are not the best alternatives in terms of score.

Table 1. Study specifications

Steps of Genetic algorithm		Specifications
Initial population		Solutions known in advance
Selection operator		Random selection
Crossover	Crossover operator	Modified crossover operator
	Crossover probability	0.6
Mutation	Mutation operator	Exchange operator
	Mutation probability	1
Stopping criterion		100000
New population		Elitist strategy

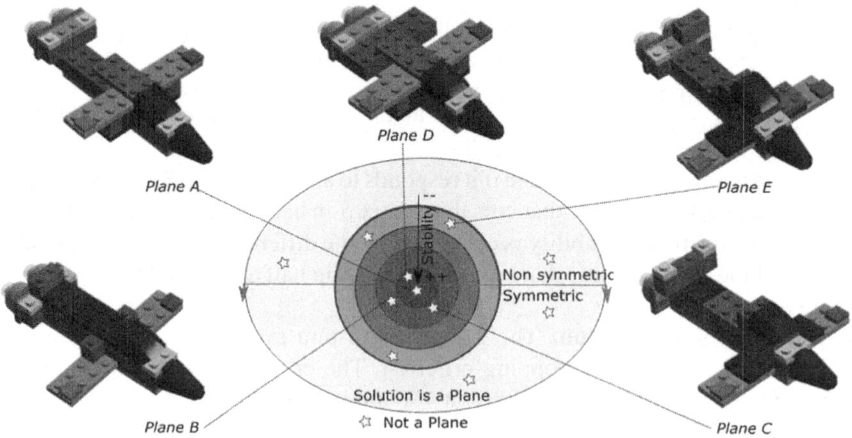

Fig. 6. Evaluation of different solutions

7 Conclusion

Product variety continues to be a major goal for companies, and architecting modular or platform-based product is becoming crucial in helping designers accomplish this. The aim of the present research was to generate new variants for a modular product. A LEGO model was used to express the modularity of the Plane. Based on a modified Genetic Algorithm (with new operators), a MATLAB program has been implemented to generate these new product variants. Results show that even if we use a small number of modules, the Genetic Algorithm is able to find in a short time (less than half an hour) product new alternatives. In this work we have chosen only three criteria to evaluate the product performances; further research might explore more criteria linked together in another combination. Some hypothesis may be considered as restrictive and need to be generalized in order to increase the degree of complexity, such as the possibility to generate solutions that contain more than 18 modules and where modules are used more than one time. In future work, the authors aim to compare different resolution techniques, such as particle swarm optimization "PSO" rather than Genetic Algorithm.

References

1. Muffatto, M.: Introducing a platform strategy in product development. Int. J. Prod. Econ. **60**, 145–153 (1999)
2. Dahmus, J., Gonzalez-Zugasti, J., Otto, K.: Modular product architecture. Des. Stud. **22**, 409–424 (2001)
3. Jiao, J., Tseng, M.: Fundamentals of product family architecture. Integr. Manuf. Syst. **11**, 469–483 (2000)
4. KöKer, R.: A genetic algorithm approach to a neural-network-based inverse kinematics solution of robotic manipulators based on error minimization. Inf. Sci. **222**, 528–543 (2013)
5. Kundakcı, N., Kulak, O.: Hybrid genetic algorithms for minimizing makespan in dynamic job shop scheduling problem. Comput. Ind. Eng. **96**, 31–51 (2016)
6. Joines, J.A., Culbreth, C.T., King, R.E.: Manufacturing cell design: an integer programming model employing genetic algorithms. IIE Trans. **28**, 69–85 (1996)
7. Huang, C.C., Kusiak, A.: Modularity in design of products and systems. IEEE Trans. Syst. Man Cybern.-Part A: Syst. Hum. **28**, 66–77 (1998)
8. Suresh Kumar, C., Chandrasekharan, M.P.: Grouping efficacy: a quantitative criterion for goodness of block diagonal forms of binary matrices in group technology. Int. J. Prod. Res. **28**, 233–243 (1990)
9. Rechtin, E., Maier, M.W.: The Art of Systems Architecting. CRC Press, Boca Raton (2010)
10. Lee, C.K.H.: A review of applications of genetic algorithms in operations management. Eng. Appl. Artif. Intell. **76**, 1–12 (2018)
11. Holland, J.H.: Adaptation in Natural and Artificial Systems: an Introductory Analysis with Applications to Biology, Control, and Artificial Intelligence. MIT Press, Cambridge (1992)
12. Hölttä-Otto, K., et al.: Modular product platform design. Helsinki University of Technology (2005)
13. Bonvoisin, J., et al.: A systematic literature review on modular product design. J. Eng. Des. **27**, 488–514 (2016)
14. Ezzat, O., et al.: Product and service modularization for variety management. Procedia Manuf. **28**, 148–153 (2019)

Computer Vision with Cognitive Learning to Improve the Decision-Making During the Sales Process in Physical Stores

Vinícius da Silva Ramalho, Anderson Luis Szejka(✉), Marcelo Rudek, and Osiris Canciglieri Junior

Industrial and Systems Engineering Graduate Program, Pontifical Catholic University of Parana, Curitiba, Brazil
{vinicius.ramalho,anderson.szejka,marcelo.rudek, osiris.canciglieri}@pucpr.br

Abstract. In a world where the information is obtained faster than ever seem, new methods to process that high volume of data are being developed frequently. This is more notorious in a virtual ambient where the data is generated in a manner that is faster and easier to analyze than in the real world. This is very evident in the retail field, where virtual stores have easy access to all the advertisement a user visited and simple to obtain user profile, on the other hand physical stores are limited to basically create a register in a database when there is a purchase. In an attempt to improve the retailers experience from physical stores to manage their business this document has the objective to develop a computational tool that will analyze the people flux going in the establishment, trying to inform the retailer the amount of people and their gender to help the sales process in physical stores. To this end, computational vision methods and algorithms were raised, which after selection, theoretical conception and tool's implementation it was tested with benchmarks to operate locally and in real time by accessing the cameras installed strategically in a real scenario. Two scenarios were tested: static ambient light and dynamic light. Two tests were conducted: YOLOv2 against background subtraction-based counter; gender classification using full body features. Even though the results were not as positive as needed for commercial use, the tool demonstrated potential and space for improvements.

Keywords: Smart retail · Retail 4.0 · Computer vision · Intelligent systems

1 Introduction

The development of a retail store is directly linked to the customers' experience, interests and exclusiveness therefore gathering more information about customers will help the retailer give the consumer a better experience and improve business growth [1]. To provide such an experience a valuable insight is needed to better understand client's shopping profile [2].

Published by Springer Nature Switzerland AG 2019
C. Fortin et al. (Eds.): PLM 2019, IFIP AICT 565, pp. 260–269, 2019.
https://doi.org/10.1007/978-3-030-42250-9_25

Consequently, physical stores are in a disadvantage when compared with virtual stores as the later can better understand their customers. Because the data is already in the digital world, virtual stores can easily access the search history, gender, age, nationality and more, which are very important to figure out client's profiles [3].

Using new tools like intelligent systems, computer vision, and internet of things (IoT), the retail 4.0 emerges as a way to lessen the difference between buying online and offline. The retail 4.0 brings more attention to digital marketing and social media, dynamic pricing of the products accordingly to demand and stock volume and, by understanding the customers profile, provide a customized experience. It is in the interest of physical stores to make a smart marketing campaign using client's data to optimize the selling process [4].

Based on this context, this paper proposes a computational tool utilizing computer vision technics to extract and provide the number of clients and their gender in real time as well as test the tool in real scenarios with benchmarks to better analyze the approach.

The tool will provide raw data, so it will need to be refined or crossed with other data. The number of clients can be cross related with weather or holidays to forecast how many clients is to be expected, so the owner can better adjust employees scheduling and stock management. Gender will give a better hint on customers taste to help, for instance, the selection of a promotional product. While this work focus on those two parameters age and emotions are also possible as demonstrated in [5].

2 Technical Background

The object detection technics can be separated in 4 classes: feature-based; template-based; movement-based; classifier-based. For its simplicity and capacity to process in real time the movement-based approach known as background subtraction was selected as well as a more robust, however computing intensive, convolutional neural network approach.

2.1 Background Subtraction

Easily found in safety and security systems to detect moving objects. A scene model is built pixel by pixel to verify, using pixel value comparison, differences in the model and the actual frame. If the difference Is very small then it is probably just noise in the image, however if it is large that means it is a moving object [6].

The background model could be a static image (when the scene is empty), a pixel wise mean/median of passed frames, a Gaussian distribution approach and many more. After the subtraction it is applied a threshold to classify whether it is background or foreground to obtain the final result. The process described can be easily expressed in the Eq. 1 [7].

$$result(x, y) = \begin{cases} 1, |I(x, y) - model(x, y)| > threshold \\ 0, |I(x, y) - model(x, y)| \leq threshold \end{cases} \tag{1}$$

Where $I(x, y)$ is the actual frame, $model(x, y)$ is the background's model and $result(x, y)$ is a bitmap that describes if a pixel belongs to the foreground (value "1") or background (value "0").

The method to model the background in this paper is based on the mean value, pixel wise, of n passed frames which is a quick technic but usually uses more memory than other methods [8]. This method is indicated for situations where the camera changes position. The background's model is obtained using the Eq. 2.

$$model(x, y, z) = \frac{1}{n} \sum_{i}^{n} history(i, x, y, z) \tag{2}$$

Where $history$ is a 4-dimension hyper volume, that for each position i there is a volume representing an image with width x, height y and z color channels (usually 3) as represented below.

$$history(i, x, y, z) = [I_0(x, y, z), I_1(x, y, z) \ldots, I_i(x, y, z) \ldots I_n(x, y, z)] \tag{3}$$

2.2 YOLOv2

The computer vision improved a lot after applications using convolutional neural networks (CNN) for object detection were developed. Using the brain as an inspiration a CNN can obtain great performance on pattern recognition tasks using extracted features learned beforehand. The difference between a CNN and a conventional artificial neural network (ANN) is that neurons are organized in three dimensions, where the height and width receive input signals and depth is an activation volume. Any neuron connects to a small region on the following layer which means that the image information will be condensed to a smaller volume [9].

There are plenty CNN architectures, but when it comes to real-time applications only some architectures can be realistically used. Using a clever approach to object detection YOLO is a very fast CNN architecture, unlike other methods like R-CNN that uses, in different steps, a feature extractor, classifier and a regressor to both detect and classify object in an image [10]. Instead, YOLO approach the whole problems as a regression problem from the image's pixel to the bounding boxes coordinates which makes it faster and easier to train [11, 12].

3 Computational Tool's Architecture

The computational tool proposed in this paper is software that will operate in a local machine processing videos from strategically placed cameras in real-time to count and classify the customers gender.

3.1 Camera's Layout

The software should be able to analyze the flux of people walking through the door with the least amount of occlusion as possible. To that end one camera should be positioned above the door and capturing the ground and people walking through. As the characteristics captured from above are not enough to classify gender another camera in front of the door, but away from the path people use, is needed to capture more features and closer.

3.2 General Working

The software is divided in two modules that work in parallel: count module, and classification module. In order to minimize the computational cost, the classification module will only engage when the count module detects someone going inside the room, when that happens a sequence of frames will be saved to be processed by the classification module. That will prevent the neural network from working on every single frame, but only on those that really matters.

The count module will have 2 options to detect people: the background subtraction and the YOLOv2-based CNN. The idea is to be able to work on modest machines as well as on more powerful computers, and as the count module must work on every single frame using the resources most the time it is the only module to receive those options. The tracking is based on the intersection of the bounding boxes along adjacent frames, the pairs with most intersected area are considered the same person throughout the frame sequence. The counting is based on a single line in the middle of the frame, if the center of the bounding box was above the line and in the next frame it appears bellow the line it is counted down. If the order is inverted the bounding box is counted up, in that case, it also saves the frames from the other camera in front of the door to be classified by the classification module.

The classification module will basically stand by until frames are saved to be processed. The module will run a different YOLOv2-based CNN trained to detect people and classify their gender using information of the whole body, instead of using face features like other methods. Face is not that easy to capture in many situations, people might look away, look at their phones, put their hands on their faces and many more, so to be able to classify in a more robust way the network was trained with the whole body. To improve the robustness, the CNN will classify a sequence of frames and if the person is classified more times as a male then the module will consider a male and vice versa.

4 Training

The first YOLOv2-based CNN was modified to detect one class (person) and the second CNN two classes (male and female), that was done by changing the number of filters in the last layer in each CNN to 30 and 35 respectively. For people detection the CNN was trained on COCO dataset plus 2800 custom images, the custom images were from cameras positioned above doors from 2 different places. It was hoped that those examples would improve detections from above the door.

For male and female detections using the full body features a dataset was created based on the WIKI and IMDB datasets. The WIKI and IMDB datasets only have the face coordinates annotated, and using the other CNN trained for people detection face coordinates were updated for the whole body. The problem is that there is always one person annotated per image in the dataset, as it is concentrated on specific personnel, causing some images to have people missing annotations. Those images were used for training ONLY. It was also added customized PASCAL VOC dataset with manually labeled gender in each image, and a chunk of those images were the only ones used to evaluate the CNN (achieved a classification F1score of 0.70).

5 Benchmarks Explanation

To measure the computational tool's performance two benchmarks were created to test each module. The benchmarks use manually annotated bounding boxes to compare with the ones the algorithm is outputting. The metrics selected were precision, recall and F1score which are vastly used to measure classification performance. A high precision means that the model is good at classifying examples of that class and recall measures how much the actual class (all data) was classified correctly. Those 2 metrics are joined to obtain F1score. The principal advantage of F1score is the ability to measure unbalanced data which means, for instance, the number of false positives doesn't need to be the same or close to false positives [13] making it easier to evaluate real scenarios, where there are more variables, balanced data is hardly acquired.

6 Real World Tests

To prove and test the proposed tool, it will be tested in 2 different scenarios. The first scenario, university laboratory, the light will be static and the second scenario, a real store, the light will be dynamic and unpredictable. The first test will compare traditional and cognitive computer vision to verify if the YOLO-based counter is better than the background subtraction approach and how much is the difference. The last will analyze the gender counting performance. 4 videos, with 1 h each, in 4 different cameras were recorded, 2 for each scenario, and manual annotations were made frame by frame in all 16 h of video.

6.1 Comparison Between Traditional and Cognitive Computer Vision

The scenario with controlled light was positioned in the middle of the frame of closed door to guarantee good visibility since before the person walking in. Calculating the selected performance metrics for each video the Table 1 is built with all results and combined, each direction has 3 metrics per video and a combined result of all the videos in the last row.

Table 1. Counting benchmark's metrics (traditional approach) in the controlled light scenario

Direction	Up			Down		
Metrics	Precision	Recall	F1score	Precision	Recall	F1score
Video 1	0.9999	0.9333	0.9655	0.8333	0.9090	0.8695
Video 2	0.3181	0.6363	0.4224	0.2258	0.5833	0.3255
Video 3	0.9999	0.7499	0.8571	0.7999	0.8888	0.8421
Video 4	0.9999	0.9999	0.9999	0.7499	0.8571	0.7999
Comb.	0.6739	0.8157	0.7380	0.5081	0.7948	0.6199

The F1score decay a lot in the second video making the combined result decrease. This bad performance issue was cause because the door was opened and closed, Fig. 1, a lot throughout the second video. This situation creates differences in the modeled background causing false positives.

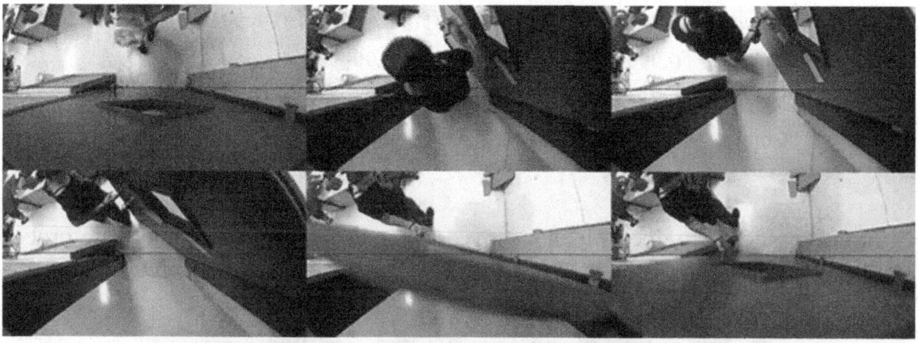

Fig. 1. Opening and closing door example causing false positives

Running the benchmarks using YOLO as detector the Table 2 was built. Even though the F1score is a little bit higher than the traditional approach the recall for people going out was low because the detector failed to detect people. In contrast the F1score increased more than 6% for people going up (inside), this improvement is visible in the second video where the door is not counted because YOLO know it is not a person resulting in better precision.

Table 2. Counting benchmark's metrics (cognitive approach) in the controlled light scenario

Direction	Up			Down		
Metrics	Precision	Recall	F1score	Precision	Recall	F1score
Video 1	0.9166	0.7333	0.8148	0.8888	0.7272	0.7999
Video 2	0.9999	0.7272	0.8421	0.8749	0.5833	0.6999
Video 3	0.8333	0.6249	0.7142	0.6666	0.2499	0.3636
Video 4	0.9999	0.7499	0.8571	0.9999	0.2857	0.4444
Comb.	0.9310	0.71	0.8059	0.8336	0.4999	0.6333

In the dynamic light scenario, the camera was installed not as close to the door causing the line to be moved to 75% the frame's height. Running the benchmark in this scenario with the traditional approach the metrics, Table 3, were obtained.

Table 3. Counting benchmark's metrics (traditional approach) in the dynamic light scenario

Direction	Up			Down		
Metrics	Precision	Recall	F1score	Precision	Recall	F1score
Video 1	0.4074	0.8461	0.5499	0.4615	0.9230	0.6153
Video 2	0.7499	0.9999	0.8571	0.6666	0.9999	0.7999
Video 3	0.9999	0.8999	0.9473	0.9999	0.6666	0.7999
Video 4	0.7142	0.7142	0.7142	0.7499	0.7499	0.7499
Comb.	0.5957	0.8484	0.6999	0.6046	0.8124	0.6933

In those videos the door was not moved as much, but during the cleaning process the squeegee, Fig. 2, was counted several times causing a decreasing precision.

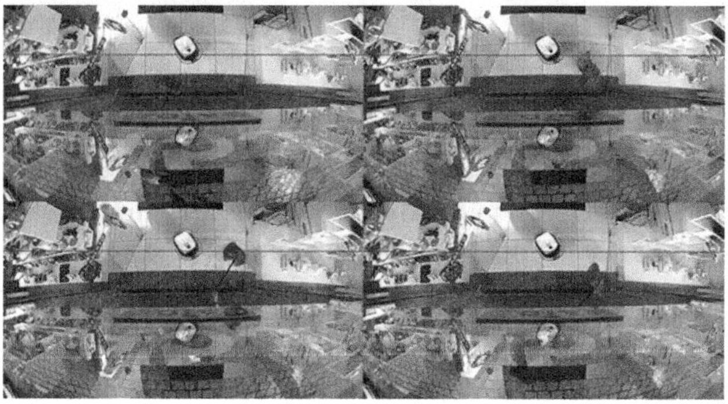

Fig. 2. Example using squeegee in the cleaning process

Table 4. Counting benchmark's metrics (cognitive approach) in the dynamic light scenario

Direction	Up			Down		
Metrics	Precision	Recall	F1score	Precision	Recall	F1score
Video 1	0.6499	0.9999	0.7878	0.6190	0.9999	0.7647
Video 2	0.7499	0.9999	0.8571	0.6666	0.9999	0.7999
Video 3	0.9999	0.8999	0.9473	0.9999	0.7777	0.8749
Video 4	0.7499	0.8571	0.7999	0.7999	0.9999	0.8888
Comb.	0.7560	0.9393	0.8378	0.7317	0.9374	0.8219

Running the same benchmark but with the cognitive approach the F1score, Table 4, improved more than 10%, improvement more visible in the first video where the cleaning squeegee was ignored by YOLO.

6.2 Men and Women Counting Performance

A camera was installed in front of the door to capture a sequence of frames (20 frames were saved for each entrance confirmation), Fig. 3.

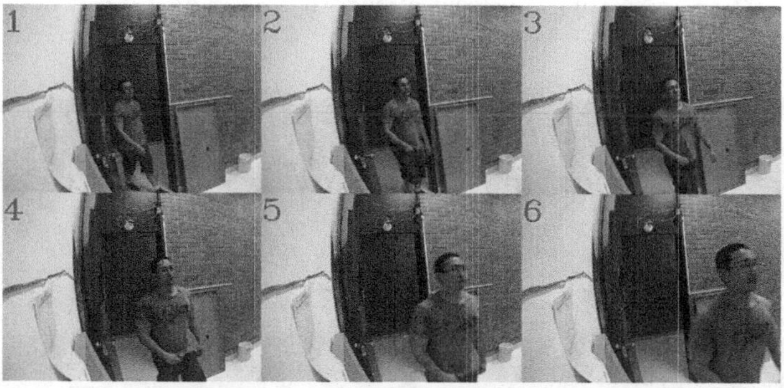

Fig. 3. Sequence of frames example of a person walking in the perfect scenario

The trigger to save the frames is the YOLO-based counter and the Table 5 contain the metrics extracted. It was observed that most the times the CNN committed a mistake the cause was occlusions and other people in the door space causing detections and tracking problems.

The benchmark done in a real store, metrics in Table 6, achieved a very low performance. As the camera was supposed to be used for other reason, it was installed far away from the door, Fig. 4, making it difficult for the CNN to detect and classify. Although YOLO detected the person as the features were poor it could not resolve to a good classification exposing a tendency to classify as a male.

Table 5. Gender classification benchmark's metrics in the perfect scenario

Direction	Up			Down		
Metrics	Precision	Recall	F1score	Precision	Recall	F1score
Video 1	0.6249	0.7692	0.6896	0.9999	0.9999	0.9999
Video 2	0.3846	0.7142	0.4999	0	0	0
Video 3	0.9999	0.7499	0.8571	0.7999	0.7999	0.7999
Video 4	0.9999	0.7499	0.8571	0.9999	0.9999	0.9999
Comb.	0.5999	0.7499	0.6666	0.7777	0.5384	0.6363

Table 6. Gender classification benchmark's metrics in the real scenario

Direction	Up			Down		
Metrics	Precision	Recall	F1score	Precision	Recall	F1score
Video 1	0.2499	0.2499	0.2499	0	0	0
Video 2	0	0	0	0	0	0
Video 3	0.7499	0.3749	0.4999	0	0	0
Video 4	0.5714	0.7999	0.6666	0	0	0
Comb.	0.4499	0.4090	0.4285	0	0	0

Fig. 4. Sequence of frames example of a person walking in the real scenario

7 Discussion

As observed in the benchmarks people walking in were counted more accurately, therefore that should be the information shown to the store's owner. Even though it demonstrated potential, the traditional-based counter achieved a F1score result of roughly 0.7 not enough for commercial use. On the other hand, YOLO-based counter achieved a F1score better than 0.8, making its information much closer to the real world.

In good and perfect conditions of light and distance to the door the gender classification module achieved a F1score of 0.66 (male) and 0.63 (female) also demonstrating potential, but not being good enough for commercial use. It is important to point that the benchmark tested the whole system and some errors were counting people module's fault.

The videos in the university laboratory were record with everybody consensus and the videos in the real store had the owner's approval, the images were used for running benchmarks only.

8 Conclusion

The disadvantages physical stores face when compared with virtual stores to obtain client's information was approached in this paper. The fact that virtual stores have better understanding of its clients, strategies will be easier and more efficiently executed on the sales process.

Even though the computational tool could not achieve the expected performance for commercial use, it demonstrated that it has potential and there is space for optimization and refinement. The counting people module using background subtraction approach needs to avoid the false positives and a possible path is to classify the detections as a person or not.

To improve the gender classification module, it could be done by improving the neural network, if it achieves a very high F1score the classification on a sequence of frames shouldn't be necessary, but only the one on the instant the person walks in. Also, as discussed on Sect. 4 the dataset used to train the current system suffers from some missing annotations and by correcting the dataset and retraining the network the performance should improve.

References

1. Hwangbo, H., Kim, Y.S., Cha, K.J.: Use of the smart store for persuasive marketing and immersive customer experiences: a case study of Korean apparel enterprise. Mobile Inf. Syst. **2017**, 1–17 (2017)
2. Quintana, M., Menéndez, J.M., Alvarez, F., Lopez, J.P.: Improving retail efficiency through sensing technologies: a survey. Pattern Recogn. Lett. **81**, 3–10 (2016)
3. Rocha, M.A.V., Hammond, H., Hawkins, D.: Age, gender and national factors in fashion consumption. J. Fash. Mark. Manag.: Int. J. **9**(4), 380–390 (2005)
4. Jayaram, A.: Smart Retail 4.0 IoT consumer retailer model for retail intelligence and strategic marketing of in-store products (2017)
5. Karim, N.T., Jain, S., Moonrinta, J., Dailey, M.N., Ekpanyapong, M.: Customer and target individual face analysis for retail analytics. In: 2018 International Workshop on Advanced Image Technology (IWAIT), pp. 1–4. IEEE, January 2018
6. Jeeva, S., Sivabalakrishnan, M.: Survey on background modeling and foreground detection for real time video surveillance. Procedia Comput. Sci. **50**, 566–571 (2015)
7. Desai, H.M.: A survey: background subtraction techniques. Int. J. Sci. Eng. Res. **5**(12), 1365–1367 (2014)
8. Takahara, K., Tori, T., Zin, T.: Making background subtraction robust to various illumination changes. Int. J. Comput. Sci. Netw. Secur. **11**(3), 241–248 (2011)
9. Zeiler, M.D., Fergus, R.: Visualizing and understanding convolutional networks. In: Fleet, D., Pajdla, T., Schiele, B., Tuytelaars, T. (eds.) ECCV 2014. LNCS, vol. 8689, pp. 818–833. Springer, Cham (2014). https://doi.org/10.1007/978-3-319-10590-1_53
10. Ren, S., He, K., Girshick, R., Sun, J.: Faster R-CNN: towards real-time object detection with region proposal networks. IEEE Trans. Pattern Anal. Mach. Intell. **39**(6), 1137–1149 (2017)
11. Redmon, J., Divvala, S., Girshick, R., Farhadi, A.: You only look once: unified, real-time object detection, pp. 779–788 (2016). https://doi.org/10.1109/cvpr.2016.91
12. Redmon, J., Farhadi, A.: YOLO9000: better, faster, stronger. In: 2017 IEEE Conference on Computer Vision and Pattern Recognition (CVPR), Honolulu, HI, pp. 6517–6525 (2017)
13. Sokolova, M., Japkowicz, N., Szpakowicz, S.: Beyond accuracy, F-Score and ROC: a family of discriminant measures for performance evaluation. In: Sattar, A., Kang, B. (eds.) AI 2006. LNCS (LNAI), vol. 4304, pp. 1015–1021. Springer, Heidelberg (2006). https://doi.org/10.1007/11941439_114

IoT and PLM

Towards a Digital Thread Between Industrial Internet of Things and Product Lifecycle Management: Experimental Work for Prototype Implementation

Piers Barrios[1,2(✉)], Benoit Eynard[2], and Christophe Danjou[3]

[1] Gfi Informatique, Meudon-la-forêt, France
piers.barrios@gfi.fr
[2] Université de Technologie de Compiègne, Compiègne, France
benoit.eynard@utc.fr
[3] Polytechnique Montréal, Montréal, Canada
christophe.danjou@polymtl.ca

Abstract. With the growing number of internet of things (IoT) and their miniaturisation, the technical possibilities associated with data collection are multiplied. In the future, it will be possible to install a sensor anywhere for a small cost. On the other hand, product lifecycle management (PLM) is a growing societal concern and products will need to be designed in such a way as to minimize their impact, while allowing businesses to have a viable business model. It will therefore be necessary to integrate data, coming from industrial internet of things (IIoT) into product lifecycle management, for companies to be able to offer product-as-a-service and pay-to-use. This paper aims to describe current advances on the integration of industrial internet of things in product lifecycle management. It also describes a prototype for a digital thread between IIoT and PLM allowing us to put forward open questions regarding the integration.

Keywords: PLM · IIoT · Digitalization · Prototype · Implementation

1 Introduction

The miniaturisation of computers allows everyone nowadays to have a handheld computer, whereas a few years ago it was a resource shared by multiple actors within a company. Everything suggests that tomorrow the miniaturisation of microelectronic systems (MEMS) will continue. These systems today have a lot of connected usage invading our day-to-day life: wireless headsets and earphones, badges of all kinds, mobile phones nec plus ultra, connected watches, speakers with voice assistants, etc. The list, of course, is not exhaustive as Internet of Things (IoT) continues to grow.

These modifications have not yet been entirely considered by companies as the difficulties and the challenges are huge: The Industrial Internet of Things (IIoT) should be dissociated from standard consumer IoT as the constraints are quite different. IIoT

Published by Springer Nature Switzerland AG 2019
C. Fortin et al. (Eds.): PLM 2019, IFIP AICT 565, pp. 273–282, 2019.
https://doi.org/10.1007/978-3-030-42250-9_26

systems need more security, better reliability, a lower response time than consumer IoT and are, most of the time, to be added to existing assets rather than IoT which starts from scratch [1]. Moreover Russell [2] phrases the difference as follows: "While IoT in general focuses on distributed sensors and control systems, the main difference in Industrial Internet of Things uses similar concepts in mission-critical/industrial facilities." This goes to further underline the duality of IoT and IIoT.

Among the difficulties related to IIoT projects, the technical limits and the diversity of applications along with the absence of a roadmap are the difficulties that are most likely to lead to a project failure. To improve the results, a global approach and methodology regarding IIoT and its integration in existing systems should be established.

On the other hand, Product Lifecycle Management (PLM) has been around for a few decades now and is defined as follows by Terzi [3]: "PLM can be broadly defined as a product centric – lifecycle-oriented business model, supported by ICT (information and communication technologies), in which product data are shared among actors, processes and organisations in the different phases of the product lifecycle for achieving desired performances and sustainability for the product and related services." Therefore, PLM talks about the full lifecycle of a product whereas PLM as implemented in most of companies' ICT systems often encompasses only certain phases of the lifecycle. Moreover, most of the time only Beginning Of Life (BOL) is taken into consideration by PLM. This dissociation appears more evidently as companies are starting to talk about Application Lifecycle Management (ALM) and Service Lifecycle Management (SLM).

Digital Thread is the ability to dispose of product information from and to any phase of the product lifecycle, hence avoiding data loss or corruption (i.e. from human copying) and enabling extended features to be developed.

It seems that only companies that are heavily liable for their products are considering the whole lifecycle (aircrafts, nuclear power plants, etc.). Only a few companies such as Michelin (for tyres) and Rolls-Royce (for aircraft motors) have, to this day, been able to switch from selling products to selling products-as-a-service. Forecasters tend to talk a lot about product-as-a-service and pay-to use. Therefore, companies are going to have to be able to manage their product from 'cradle to grave' and to do so, information coming from IIoT and IoT is going to have to interact with existing PLM information and knowledge. It is therefore crucial to think about integration of IIoT and PLM.

To address this, the current paper will describe the current state of integration between IIoT and PLM. In the third part, we shall present a prototype that is being implemented. Finally, the further improvements that need to be added and the underlying remaining questions shall be presented.

2 Current Status of IIoT and PLM Integration

To picture the current state of IIoT and PLM integration, we shall first present the current status of IIoT. Secondly, current integration of PLM and IIoT is detailed. Finally, the few papers mentioning the integration of IIoT and PLM are reviewed.

2.1 Current State of IIoT

IIoT's technology stack comprises sensors, communication protocols and gateways as well as platforms. Although the latter will interest us more than the others, it is important to have a broad view of the different aspects of the IIoT in order to grasp the diversity inherent to the domain.

Concerning sensors, the trend is toward battery-less sensors. Radio frequency identification (RFID) and Near Field Communication (NFC) allowed in the past decade to have extended item recognition as together they permitted the creation of passive tags that are remotely checked. Today, sensors are able to collect surrounding energy in order to function [4], to be activated remotely in order to get a measure [5] or even 3D-printed to send a precise signal [6]. Furthermore, improvements are made to sensors leading to a continued decrease in costs.

Protocols are legion and many lists exist. Salman [7] catalogues many of them across the multiple Open Systems Interconnection (OSI) layers and presents six IoT challenges: mobility, reliability, scalability, management, availability and interoperability. These challenges listed here were meant to be specific to communication protocols but could be generalized to any IIoT project.

Gateways are mostly hybrid components between sensors and platforms as they sometime serve as one or the other but can also be dissociated and be a communication relay or a computing on-edge device.

The main problem with "IoT platform" is the absence of a common definition. Therefore, lots of ICT based systems are identified as IoT platforms. Hoffman [8] identified 212 "IoT platforms" and proposed a long-list and a short-list of the platforms in the scope of "internet of production". However, if one wants to interact with IoT, it's most probably going to be through those kind of platforms, interoperability will therefore be key and multiple European projects are currently working on this aspect [9].

Finally, Liao [10] presents a systematic literature review on IIoT. It is interesting to notice that only 8 of the 94 articles retained talked about "practical solution" whereas the majority use "experimental solution" (72), the remainder being "review or survey" (6) and "theoretical solutions" (8). However, industry is currently looking for practical solutions therefore we shall try to work in that direction. In this sense, Anjomshoaa [11] proposed a practical solution, including analysis of feasible solutions, sensor choice and image analysis, but applied it to an adjacent field to IIoT: Smart Cities. Another sector alongside IIoT, where this work was found, is agriculture; Klein [12] proposes an IoT irrigation system allowing improved performances.

However, in these few fields, no PLM or industrial application was mentioned and no question was raised concerning integration of IoT with PLM. Similarly, no industry application was mentioned by Belapurkar [13] although a thorough analysis of smart space application was made for healthcare, public safety, environmental monitoring and commercial applications. Wang [14] presents "IoT for next-generation racket sports training" without mentioning management of the product itself via PLM for instance. However, next-generation racket sports trainings are necessarily going to need new rackets and product lifecycle management will be essential to do so.

In these numerous cases, IoT and the system as a whole would benefit from interactions with PLM. However, we found no explicit mention of this.

2.2 PLM and IIoT Integration

PLM's integration in various systems has been studied in the past. Considering IIoT as being a new ICT system, looking at previous PLM integrations, the latter could give us clues towards its integration with IoT. In [15], Bosch-Mauchand et al. proposed an integration of PLM and value-chain simulation (among others) in order to better knowledge capture. However, knowledge is low volume and high-quality data on the contrary to IoT, which consists of high volume and low quality (when considered independently).

Concerning PLM and IIoT, little was found. In [16] Menon et al. proposed a critical analysis of some IoT platform performances based on their openness from the scope of PLM. Hence, they underlined the possible use of these IoT platforms during the different phases of a product lifecycle: beginning, middle and end (BOL-MOL-EOL). However, integration between PLM's ICT and these platforms at the various stages where opportunity wasn't discussed. In [17] Hehenberger et al. talk in one paragraph (3.4) about "Product lifecycle management for CPS": IoT being part of any Cyber-Physical System (CPS), the approach stays on a high level and does not mention integration of CPS' IoT into PLM. Nevertheless, separation of PLM approaches between hardware and software mentioned could be reused as IIoT and PLM integration is discussed.

In [18], Kadiri et al. mentioned the importance of IoT in context-aware infrastructures but no system integration is studied although a focus is made on Enterprise Resource Planning (ERP) systems.

However, there is a need for PLM systems to handle the increasing amounts of data being made available by IoT [19]. As the information available on explicit PLM and IIoT integration is scarce, we investigated possibilities of semantic interoperability through ontologies.

On the PLM side, in [20] Sriti et al. proposed an ontology for product information exchange. Still from a PLM point of view, Kiritsis [21] presented various technologies, some of which are IoT ones, in order to achieve a closed-loop PLM. However, IoT is not considered as an independent system and therefore its integration with PLM was not discussed. From a more global point of view, Kadiri et al offered in [18] a broad picture on ontology-based approaches and addresses ICT as a whole without entering into PLM and IIoT specifics.

However, ontology-based integration remains in question as its adoption in industry is scarce and we want our methodology to be adopted easily by the industry. Yoo [22] describes a conceptual framework but hasn't put forward a practical use-case. Also, considering adoption by industry and the return on investment for such a project, the case study developed by Alcatel Alenia Space in [23] showed how complicated it can be to evaluate Key Performance Indicators (KPI) in large scale projects such as PLM, as both process and working methods change at the same time. It would therefore be interesting to have such data available on IIoT and PLM integration.

3 A Prototype of PLM and IIoT Integration

Along with the deductive inferences that are made above, research will also be made by inductive reasoning, via the realisation of a prototype. We shall therefore present the prototype as it is currently, from both the architectural aspect as well as from the implementation point of view. We will also introduce the next architectural target for our prototype.

3.1 Current Architecture and Implementation

The current prototype consists of a PLM platform and an IoT platform connected to a 3D virtual environment to display information from both platforms. We shall detail the infrastructure itself, why we chose these options and how it has been helpful so far.

Currently, the aim is to display information in multiple devices thanks to UMI3D [24]. This information comes from a Windchill instance (from the PTC company) as a PLM solution, where the product's information is stored and a ThingWorx instance (also from PTC) as a IIoT solution, where the information relative to the sensors located on the product is stored. These instances have been successfully tested on a local Virtual Machine (VM), a company server as well as the provider's cloud, therefore allowing more flexibility depending on the use case. The Unity server then calls this information to display it in a virtual room that is accessed by multiple devices: personal computer, virtual reality headsets, tablets, etc. All this information is summarised in Fig. 1.

Indeed, product's 3D model is the only data used at this point from PLM. However, being able to retrieve it is promising as it is the most difficult part. In future architecture, PLM metadata will be used to enhance product visualisation.

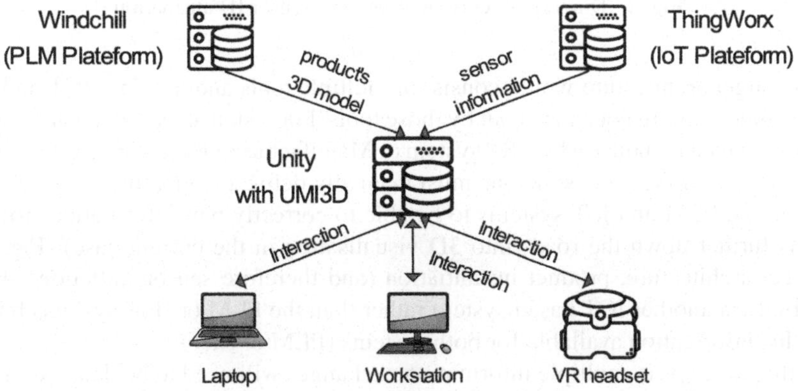

Fig. 1. Diagram of current prototype

The choice of a PLM platform was made towards Windchill as this was one of the two mastered by the team. This choice was made based on the openness of the solution, as integration of multiple solutions needs a minimum of interactivity. Concerning the choice of an IIoT platform, we are currently using ThingWorx, but are closely looking at other platforms as the multiplicity of solutions available reinforces the necessity to consider other options. Also, as underlined in [16], IoT platforms could be specific for use in for certain parts of the product lifecycle.

This prototype has been helpful in multiple ways: first, it allowed the team to understand the possibilities of interoperability on a technical level. As described previously, one could try to carry this interoperability to a higher level, even to semantic interoperability aiming to reduce adaptation cost, in case of a change of either the PLM or IoT platform. Second, we are facing questions on a practical level, which will no doubt help us to corroborate our comprehension of the theoretical ones. Finally, it moves us closer to having a complete integration of PLM and IIoT as discussed in the next section.

3.2 Target Architecture

In the long run and to investigate interactions between IIoT and PLM, we shall try to integrate closely both platforms. Therefore, we need to think a target architecture that would satisfy most needs.

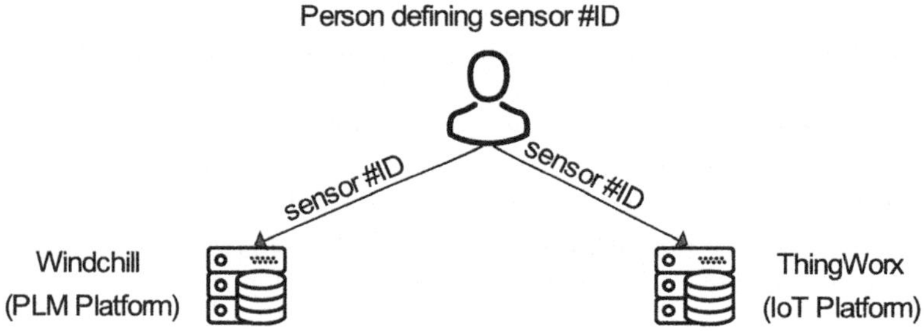

Fig. 2. Diagram of current issue with sensor ID attribution

The target architecture would consist of multiple tools and not only ICT and PLM, as some functions are not carried out by those tools. For instance, product instantiation is mostly managed in industry by ERP system or Manufacturing Execution System (MES). In the current architecture, someone must manually define the identification (ID) of the sensor in the PLM and IoT systems to be able to correctly pair information from both systems further down the road (into 3D visualisation in the current case) (Fig. 2). In the target architecture, product instantiation (and therefore sensor initiation) shall be supported via another ICT based system rather than the PLM or IIoT systems but shall make this information available for both systems (PLM & IIoT).

In the same spirit, multiple information exchanges will need to be detailed in future works as each ICT based system holds information. We represented in Fig. 3 the different interactions between inherent ICT based systems without detailing them, because much information and many orders can be given and received by those different systems. Although the current system offers the possibility to display information from multiple systems without having to do specific development for each device, in the future we would need to be able to send information back to the PLM and to the IoT solutions, based on the interactions made with the product, within the 3D environment. Also, information from both IoT and PLM systems should be available to the other systems for any actors to take any decision knowingly. The information should be delivered to the right person, in the right place and at the right time. With this in mind, we shall attempt to integrate the PLM and IIoT systems.

However, this will also depend on the use-case, as we will discuss in next section.

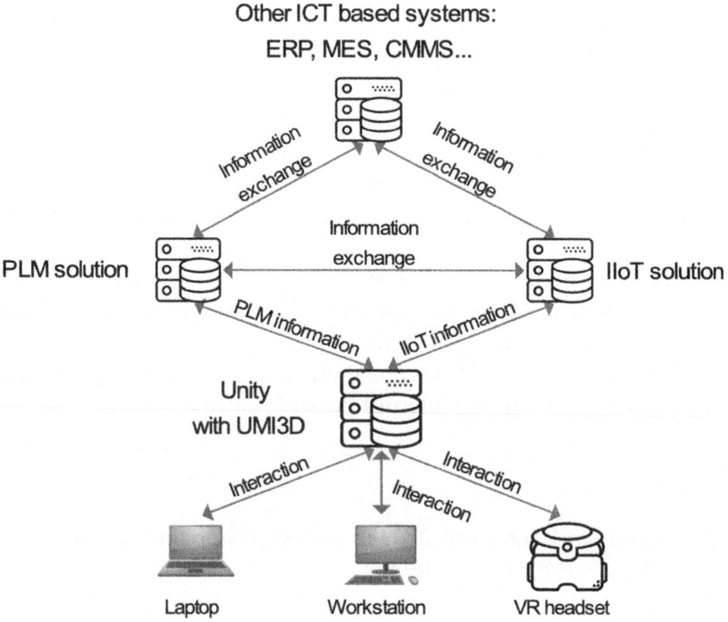

Fig. 3. Diagram of target architecture

4 Further Improvements and Related Questions

In this section, we shall present the different use-cases that our solution could match, as well as other further improvements that could be made. We will then discuss our implementation in the light of the current state of PLM and IIoT integration.

4.1 Improvements to Approach Real Use-Cases

Once the prototype is implemented, one naturally faces more practical questions coming from industrial stakeholders, such as "what is the aim of interaction between PLM and IIoT?" We shall try to present a few industrial use-cases and the necessary work in order to implement them into our prototype.

Firstly, the entry point consists of the usage feedback from the product prototype. In this case, the product is in a prototype stage and has only been produced either once or maybe a few copies. In this case, the aim is to visualise, in our 3D environment, the different measures made by the sensors to know which parts need changing and/or improving. Improvements needed to our prototype, in this use-case, would be to mark the parts in the 3D environment with a Problem Report (PR) or a Request For Change (RFC) which would be treated exclusively in the PLM environment. However, IoT information visualised at the time of issuing the PR/RFC would be needed inside the PLM to decide on the incumbent and create a Change Request (CR).

Secondly, the product is in a maintenance phase and historical data is needed on the product, both from a PLM and sensor point of view. Indeed, one needs to know the product history and what changes were made during previous maintaining phases, as well as usage data to know what happened in each phase. Moreover, any maintenance information carried out will need to be added to the PLM and then sensors could be calibrated at that point. In this case, our prototype should be able to display historical information from both PLM and IIoT systems.

Finally, products have been widely sold and this is a success; it is therefore time for a new version. Engineers are going to need agglomerated data on multiple instances of the product to visualise product information. Unfortunately, to this day, our prototype does not provide data integration in-between various phases of the product. The number of products instantiated, as well as the type and volume of information to display, would heavily impact the choice of implementation.

Here are listed only a few use-cases and these do not plan to be exhaustive, however, we went through the spectrum of numerous possible enhancements.

4.2 Discussion

As our experimental work for a full-fledged prototype implementation starts, we shall try to place it in the context of our readings.

First, the implementation of both platforms on a technical interoperability level is specific to each and every solution. Therefore, thinking of a semantic interoperability level could answer or at least diminish the integration complexity. Second, the prototype was nourished by the need to have a first-hand view on the different existing open questions. This has been very helpful to better understand the available literature.

The choice of IoT and PLM solutions were made based on the stakeholders' best knowledge. However, that turns out to give a certain bias on the solution and the questions we are facing. It would be pertinent to benchmark these choices against others. Unfortunately, no other PLM and IIoT implementation has been found by our team to this day. One of the reminding possibilities would be to carry this work. Moreover, the proposed target architecture will need further narrowing, as interaction between the different ICT based systems are studied more closely.

Last but not least, relying on industrial use-cases would allow us a more practical solution approach rather than staying on an experimental stage. However, we shall try to avoid the pitfall of a solution that is too specific and rather tend towards proposing a more global methodology.

5 Conclusion and Future Work

In the ever-changing world we live in, the products' environmental impact could be diminished by improving various product-life stages using multiple sensors thanks to the Industrial Internet of Things. This would allow for more respectable methods of consumption and allow pay-to-use & product-service systems to develop further. However, PLM and IIoT systems have not yet been successfully integrated to achieve this.

For the purpose of creating a digital thread between IIoT and PLM, we have successively presented current state of IIoT as well as IIoT and PLM integration. We then explained the state of our current experimental work toward prototype implementation.

Although not a full-fledged prototype, this allowed us to draft multiple open questions that shall be worked upon in further studies/articles, following the proposed target architecture. The possible use-cases were also drafted for such a system and finally discussed in the presented work.

Future work could consist of more thorough state-of-the-art experiments done through Systematic Literature Review (SLR). Moreover, the current prototype will be improved to lean towards the proposed architecture. During this process, integrations of both systems shall be discussed, as the information available and the process involved are quite thorough. Depicted use-cases could face some expertise from the industry to sharpen them and better answer the requests/demands. Finally, integration on a semantic level through ontologies will be investigated as an easier way to integrate PLM and IIoT systems.

Acknowledgement. Thanks to Julien Casarin, Cyriaque Dupoirieux, Christophe Theillaumas, François Loison, Dimitri Van-Wijk, Christophe Cazes & Laurent Clamens for working on the first version of the prototype.

References

1. Schneider, S.: The Industrial Internet of Things (IIoT): applications and taxonomy. In: Geng, H. (ed.) Internet of Things and Data Analytics Handbook, pp. 41–81. Wiley, Hoboken (2016)
2. Russell, L., Goubran, R., Kwamena, F., Knoefel, F.: Agile IoT for critical infrastructure resilience: cross-modal sensing as part of a situational awareness approach. IEEE Internet Things J. **5**, 4454–4465 (2018). https://doi.org/10.1109/JIOT.2018.2818113
3. Terzi, S., Bouras, A., Dutta, D., Garetti, M., Kiritsis, D.: Product lifecycle management - from its history to its new role. Int. J. Prod. Lifecycle Manage. **4**, 360 (2010). https://doi.org/10.1504/IJPLM.2010.036489
4. Ulukus, S., et al.: Energy harvesting wireless communications: a review of recent advances. IEEE J. Sel. Areas Commun. **33**, 360–381 (2015). https://doi.org/10.1109/JSAC.2015.2391531
5. Merenda, M., Felini, C., Della Corte, F.G.: Battery-less smart RFID tag with sensor capabilities. In: 2012 IEEE International Conference on RFID-Technologies and Applications (RFID-TA), pp. 160–164. IEEE, Nice (2012)
6. Iyer, V., Chan, J., Gollakota, S.: 3D printing wireless connected objects. ACM Trans. Graph. **36**, 1–13 (2017). https://doi.org/10.1145/3130800.3130822
7. Salman, T., Jain, R.: Networking protocols and standards for Internet of Things. In: Geng, H. (ed.) Internet of Things and Data Analytics Handbook, pp. 215–238. Wiley, Hoboken (2016)
8. Hoffmann, J., Heimes, P., Senel, S.: IoT platforms for the Internet of production. IEEE Internet Things J. **6**(3), 4098–4105 (2018). https://doi.org/10.1109/jiot.2018.2875594
9. Bröring, A., et al.: Advancing IoT Platforms Interoperability. River Publishers (2018). ISBN 978-87-7022-005-7
10. Liao, Y., de Freitas Rocha Loures, E., Deschamps, F.: Industrial Internet of Things: a systematic literature review and insights. IEEE Internet Things J. **5**, 4515–4525 (2018)
11. Anjomshoaa, A., Duarte, F., Rennings, D., Matarazzo, T.J., deSouza, P., Ratti, C.: City scanner: building and scheduling a mobile sensing platform for smart city services. IEEE Internet Things J. **5**, 4567–4579 (2018). https://doi.org/10.1109/JIOT.2018.2839058

12. Klein, L.J., Hamann, H.F., Hinds, N., Guha, S., Sanchez, L., Sams, B., Dokoozlian, N.: Closed loop controlled precision irrigation sensor network. IEEE Internet Things J. **5**, 4580–4588 (2018). https://doi.org/10.1109/JIOT.2018.2865527
13. Belapurkar, N., Harbour, J., Shelke, S., Aksanli, B.: Building data-aware and energy-efficient smart spaces. IEEE Internet Things J. **5**, 4526–4537 (2018). https://doi.org/10.1109/JIOT.2018.2834907
14. Wang, Y., Chen, M., Wang, X., Chan, R.H.M., Li, W.J.: IoT for next-generation racket sports training. IEEE Internet Things J. **5**, 4558–4566 (2018). https://doi.org/10.1109/jiot.2018.2837347
15. Bosch-Mauchand, M., Belkadi, F., Bricogne, M., Eynard, B.: Knowledge-based assessment of manufacturing process performance: integration of product lifecycle management and value-chain simulation approaches. Int. J. Comput. Integr. Manuf. **26**, 453–473 (2013). https://doi.org/10.1080/0951192X.2012.731611
16. Menon, K., Kärkkäinen, H., Wuest, T., Gupta, J.P.: Industrial Internet. platforms: a conceptual evaluation from a product lifecycle management perspective. Proc. Inst. Mech. Eng. Part B: J. Eng. Manuf. **233**(5), 1390–1401 (2018). https://doi.org/10.1177/0954405418760651
17. Hehenberger, P., Vogel-Heuser, B., Bradley, D., Eynard, B., Tomiyama, T., Achiche, S.: Design, modelling, simulation and integration of cyber physical systems: methods and applications. Comput. Ind. **82**, 273–289 (2016). https://doi.org/10.1016/j.compind.2016.05.006
18. El Kadiri, S., Grabot, B., Thoben, K.-D., Hribernik, K., Emmanouilidis, C., von Cieminski, G., Kiritsis, D.: Current trends on ICT technologies for enterprise information systems. Comput. Ind. **79**, 14–33 (2016). https://doi.org/10.1016/j.compind.2015.06.008
19. Holligan, C., Hargaden, V., Papakostas, N.: Product lifecycle management and digital manufacturing technologies in the era of cloud computing. In: 2017 International Conference on Engineering, Technology and Innovation (ICE/ITMC), pp. 909–918. IEEE, Funchal (2017)
20. Sriti, M.F., Assouroko, I., Ducellier, G., Boutinaud, P., Eynard, B.: Ontology-based approach for product information exchange. Int. J. Prod. Lifecycle Manag. **8**, 1 (2015). https://doi.org/10.1504/IJPLM.2015.068011
21. Kiritsis, D.: Closed-loop PLM for intelligent products in the era of the Internet of Things. Comput. Aided Des. **43**, 479–501 (2011). https://doi.org/10.1016/j.cad.2010.03.002
22. Yoo, M.-J., Grozel, C., Kiritsis, D.: Closed-loop lifecycle management of service and product in the Internet of Things: semantic framework for knowledge integration. Sensors **16**, 1053 (2016). https://doi.org/10.3390/s16071053
23. Alemanni, M., Alessia, G., Tornincasa, S., Vezzetti, E.: Key performance indicators for PLM benefits evaluation: the Alcatel Alenia Space case study. Comput. Ind. **59**, 833–841 (2008). https://doi.org/10.1016/j.compind.2008.06.003
24. Casarin, J., Bechmann, D., Keller, M.: A unified model for interaction in 3D environment. In: Proceedings of the 23rd ACM Symposium on Virtual Reality Software and Technology - VRST 2017, pp. 1–7. ACM Press, Gothenburg (2017)

Digital Twin – Integrating Cloud Services into Communication Protocols

Thomas Dasbach[1](✉), Eduardo de Senzi Zancul[2], Klaus Schützer[3], and Reiner Anderl[1]

[1] Technische Universität Darmstadt, 64283 Darmstadt, Germany
{dasbach,anderl}@dik.tu-darmstadt.de
[2] University of São Paulo, São Paulo, Brazil
ezancul@usp.br
[3] Methodist University of Piracicaba, São Paulo, Brazil
schuetzer@scpm.unimep.br

Abstract. The Digital Twin is the following development of ongoing improvements in communicational technologies, decreasing hardware costs and the need for products with decentralized decision-making abilities. In order to improve the qualities of decisions, there is the requirement for an easy, reliable way to transport data between Digital Twins, even if the network connection has a low bandwidth or is unstable. As a solution, the use of a cloud service as a broker architecture is described. A concept for communication architecture is given as well as the required design of a Digital Twin. The proposed concept has been implemented to assess the resulting advantages and limitations.

Keywords: Digital Twin · Cloud storage · Communication protocol · Product Lifecycle Management

1 Introduction

Industry and society are always subject to change. One of the major developments of nearly the last two decades has been the ongoing digitalization. Several factors, like the increased availability of wireless communication, enhanced user interfaces and arise of new technologies like cloud services led to a point where the demand of products and machines, which are to a small degree self-aware and able to decide for themselves for the most suitable usage, rises [1].

To enable reliable decisions, it is crucial to know everything or at least as much as possible related to the matter [2]. In the case of products, an approach to aggregate most of the data can be seen in Digital Twins. Over time, integrating modern information, communication, and sensor technologies developed into complex constructs, which are enhanced by simulation models and databases. They are a sufficient starting point to develop the goods of the future [3].

In order to further advance the resilience of the decisions, the amount of available data for each Digital Twin has to be increased beyond the point of just using only the sensors

Published by Springer Nature Switzerland AG 2019
C. Fortin et al. (Eds.): PLM 2019, IFIP AICT 565, pp. 283–292, 2019.
https://doi.org/10.1007/978-3-030-42250-9_27

connected to the specific product to a scenario where each Digital Twin can benefit from all sensors within the near perimeter of the product. Therefore it is necessary to exchange large sets of data between them. This can happen either with peer-to-peer connections or, as in the concept described, with the usage of cloud services as a broker. In addition to the advantage of a temporally decoupled data transfer, the actual workload for each Digital Twin is reduced: if more than one request is made, the requirement for the hardware of each Twin is lowered.

The objective of this paper is to present a concept proposal for enhancing data transfer between Digital Twins based on cloud services. The proposed concept is detailed and implemented in a test scenario to support assessment.

The remainder of this paper is structured as follows: Sect. 2 presents a literature review regarding the Digital Twins and communication protocols, followed by Sect. 3, which submits the proposed concept. Section 4 describes the pilot implementation. Finally, Sect. 5 presents the main conclusions and suggestions for further research.

2 Literature

In the following passages, the underlying key requirements of the concept will be discussed. Especially chapter 2.2 should be regarded as only a summarized segment of a large field of study with a focus on technologies which are used in the development of the proposed concept.

2.1 Digital Twin

Historically, the concept of an exact object's copy to study its real counterpart behavior can be traced back to the NASA's Apollo program, where two identical space vehicles were made. One was sent to the mission, and the other one was kept on Earth to allow mirroring the conditions faced by the mission's vehicle as accurately as possible. This monitoring was crucial to achieving a better understanding of the critical situations faced and help the astronauts more efficiently [4, 5].

This first Twin concept for monitoring a system or object, even if purely physically, was of great importance to inspire the development of software-based Digital Twins. The software-based Digital Twin has been used to monitor the real-time condition of a connected Physical Twin through modern sensing, communication, and identification technologies, such as RFID, QR-Code, Machine Vision, etc. and to validate the gathered data with the virtual model of the physical counterpart [6–9].

Over time, especially with the upcoming of *Industrie 4.0*, the focus of the concept Digital Twin shifted towards production and manufacturing of smart products [10]. The term Digital Twin has been defined in many attempts by several authors but each one with a slightly different focus. Most of them describe the Digital Twin as a comprehensive collection of information gathered throughout the entire product lifecycle [3]. A different trend is followed by Boschert and Rosen, who define the Digital Twin as only an aggregation of the currently relevant data [11].

In this paper, the Digital Twin is understood as an accumulation of all gathered data, simulation models enhanced by the real environmental influences and own decision trees to adapt the behavior of the physical counterpart regarding the perceptions from simulations and similar products in alignment to previously given definitions like the one of Haag and Anderl [3].

2.2 Communication Protocols

Concerning the communication protocol, there is a variety of available solutions at the market; most of them with advantages and disadvantages depending on the particular use case. Therefore, only a small selection is presented here. MQTT in this case can be taken as an example for several relatively new, lightweight protocols like CoAP, AMQP or STOMP.

In April 1971, the first FTP standard RFC 114 was published. After multiple subsequent RFCs, RFC 959, File Transfer Protocol (FTP) was published in October 1985. Unlike most protocols, the FTP standard does not use one TCP connection, but two. One of them is the Control/Command Connection, the other one is the Data Connection. The former connection is maintained throughout the entire FTP session and used to pass control information, such as FTP commands and replies. The latter one is used for data transfer and is opened and closed as needed [12].

The FTP standard specifies an active and a passive mode. The main difference between the two is whether the client or the server initiates the data connection [13]. Due to its design it inherits some security problems, which are hardly possible to solve, as well as complex handling to set up properly. So newer protocols like HTTP or HTTPS should be taken into account [14].

Released in 1999 by IBM, MQTT (currently Message Queuing Telemetry Transport) exchanges data using packets (or "message formats") in an organized specific manner [15]. Each of the packets contains three parts: a mandatory fixed size header, an optional header with variable length and a possible payload, again with a variable length [16].

MQTT has two kinds of participants, clients and brokers, and uses a publish-subscribe concept. Clients can be publishers or subscribers, meaning they can publish messages for the interested users, subscribe or unsubscribe in interesting subjects in order to receive messages, attach and detach from the brokers. The brokers control the distribution of information, processing requests from clients, accepting client requests, receiving published messages by clients and sending publisher messages to subscribed clients [16].

HTTP is one of the most widespread protocols within the web. Developed by Tim Berners-Lee, it is a standard since 1997. In contrast to MQTT, it uses an architecture based on clients and servers. Meaning a server will never initiate a connection and a client will never expect an incoming transmission. The server can gather data, given to them by clients, and distribute this data, once a client requests this data.

Originally designed for the web, it has some disadvantages regarding the use in IoT applications. For example, the overhead of HTTP messages is big in comparison to other protocols. HTTP has quite high hardware requirements, high latency, and a big bandwidth compared to other protocols. Despite these facts, HTTP has two advantages which are very interesting: High security standard as well as very high interoperability [16], both basic interests for IoT.

3 Concept Development

In order to create a commutation protocol for a Digital Twin, the first step is to define the design of the Digital Twin itself. No matter how complex or, more likely, how slim it needs to be, a Digital Twin will always consist of at least three functional parts – frontend, core, and backend. The following described architecture allows easy extensible design of the separate parts. Therefore, it is kept abstract with references to the recommended features. The basic layout with the extension of a cloud unit is visualized in Fig. 1.

From the perspective of an end customer, the frontend of a Digital Twin will consist of an interface unit, dedicated to general communication to other Digital Twins or customers. A various amount of communication protocols can be used to initiate data transfer. Due to the later-described method to discover other Digital Twins, the previous mentioned MQTT with its client-broker architecture is a suitable solution for the concept described in this paper.

Behind the frontend is the core of the Digital Twin. The core serves as the decision unit; it runs the decision trees, processes the sensor values of the physical counterpart and initiates communication requests to other Digital Twins or web services. Therefore, it uses the functionalities that the interface unit provides. Another key aspect of the core is to request data from other sources and pass this incoming data down to the storage unit. Besides the core, there is the possibility to include further simulation models or additional software, which will be executed by the core, if necessary. The complexity of the local simulations is limited by the hardware of the core. In practice this will result in the approach to reduce local simulations as much as possible in order to decrease costs of products. The lower boundary for the hardware decrease will be the crucial simulations for the uninterrupted running. Which simulations have to be declared as crucial depends again on the network connectivity. If the connection is very stable most simulations can be run elsewhere, otherwise more simulations need to run locally resulting in higher requirements for the hardware.

The backend is a storage unit for system variables. Furthermore, it caches all data provided by sensors and sub-ordinary Digital Twins. Data can be passed to both, the cloud, as well as to the communication interface to send it to other Digital Twins and vice versa. The storage unit can store data locally. The required size of the storage depends on the network stability of the Digital Twin. Whenever there is a disconnect data needs to be stored until it can be uploaded again. Technically the most likely implementation of such a storage unit is created by a local database or if the spare hardware resources are available by a database attached to a server.

To unburden the core unit, the storage should be able to handle the data of the sensors independently. If the values need processing, the core can request them once it is idle. In addition, the incoming data of subordinate Digital Twins can be handled at the storage unit. In case of sufficient storage capacity, there is a variety of available databases to order and process the data for later usage.

Independently of the underlying hardware, the Storage Unit may run out of free space at a point in time. Reasons for that can be an unexpected long usage of the product, peaks in the needed storage space after requesting large data sets from other sources, or extension of sensors later on.

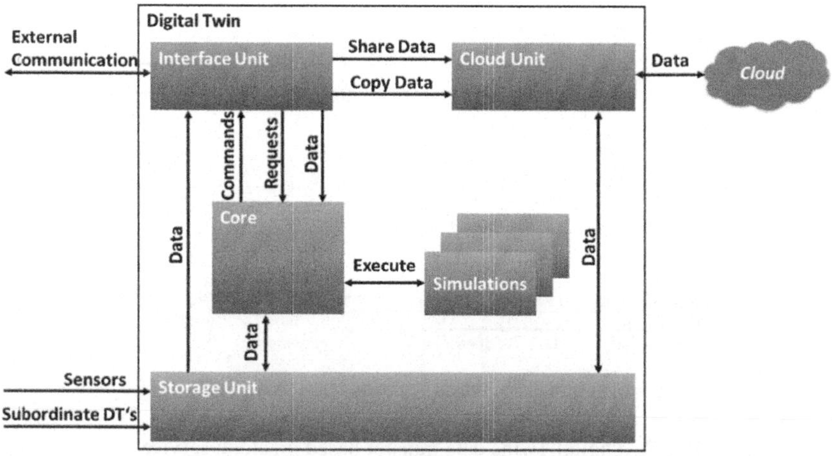

Fig. 1. Digital Twin architecture

The possible counter-strategies consist mainly of two categories: on the one hand, it is possible to decrease the stored data, and on the other hand to increase the available space. In order to decrease the stored data, it is either needed to decide which data will not be needed in future use cases and to delete those or to compress the stored data. Deleting data is in case of a Digital Twin not a longsighted strategy because the decision-making criterion cannot take future technologies and their requirements into account. Therefore, as an alternative, the storage space needs to be increased. Increasing the storage space before the deployment of the Digital Twin leads to the difficult decision of the required margin. In order to absorb every possibility, such as the extension of the product by adding additional sensors, it is necessary to aim for a very large margin, which in the end leads to an increase of production costs and needed materials.

It will be difficult to increase the storage space physically at the product, once it is needed, if the product is embedded into larger and inaccessible systems. Such a design would critically limit the usage of the Digital Twin. Thus, it needs to be accessible with a reasonable effort.

Another solution to solve the storage issue is the usage of established cloud services. Therefore, the interface unit is extended, as seen in Fig. 1, by a cloud unit. The cloud unit handles communication with a contractor's or the manufacturer's cloud. With this setup, it is possible to add further storage space without physical access to the Digital Twin.

Additional to the solved space problem, this setup enables a second way of transferring data between different Digital Twins. If the large data collection of a Digital Twin gets stored in the cloud, it is possible to transmit data within the cloud.

Figure 2 shows the steps included in the proposed data transfer. In this case, the Digital Twins store their data up to a certain degree on a local storage, but whenever possible, they update a data set located in a cloud, which includes all the data gathered over the entire life of the product.

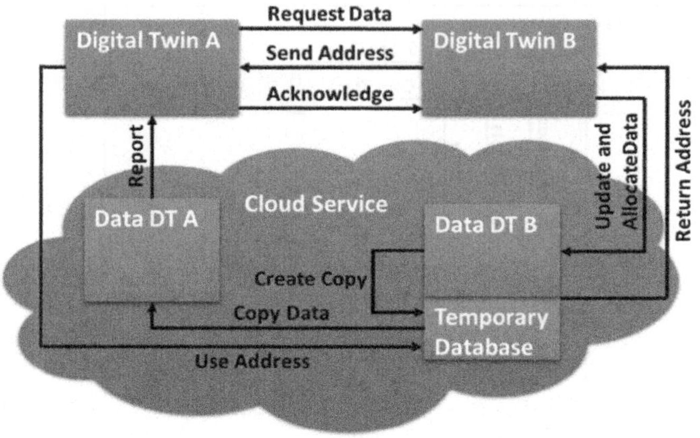

Fig. 2. Digital Twins data transfer based on cloud services

This double storage of information allows another way of transferring the data between two Digital Twins. In the described use case it is presumed that both Twins already know about each other. If Digital Twin A needs data from Digital Twin B, it will send, independently of the later used transportation method, a request to Digital Twin B. This request must already contain information about all available ways of data transfer. So, B can decide depending on varying factors, e.g. size of the requested files or stability of the connection, to use the cloud transfer. In the first steps, if necessary, B updates its data set within the cloud, then the cloud provider creates a temporary copy with the requested data and returns the address and access keys for this set to the Digital Twin. Digital Twin B passes the address and the key to Digital Twin A. With the address and the key, A can order the cloud service to copy the temporary data set into the online storage of A. Once this is finished, a report is sent to Digital Twin A and it passes an acknowledgment to Digital Twin B. Any needed information included in the transferred data can now be exchanged between the cloud service and A.

Another benefit provided by the usage of a cloud infrastructure is the possibility to use an online client as a manager for the addresses of all active Digital Twins. If all Digital Twins try to establish connections to a cloud in order to update their information, it is an easy task to keep track which Twins are active and what kind of services they could provide. Within this concept, all addresses of the participating Digital Twins were stored in a so-called phone list, in reference to a dissipating phone book.

Basically, the phone list functions as a central database for all available participants of a certain network. Digital Twins that do not store data regularly online have to regularly confirm their activeness towards the phone list, otherwise their information and addresses will be deleted to avoid degeneration of the database.

With these parts of the concept, a behavior flow chart for Digital Twins, which shows how a regular data transfer will be ordered was designed, like seen in Fig. 3. In a first step, the Digital Twin will connect to the phone list to get an address of a specific Twin or of a Twin, that can provide the services needed. After receiving the message it establishes a message via HTTP, due to its high interoperability. First step in communication between both Digital Twins has to be defining which way they will use to transmit the data. For this step, all methods available for both parties have to be considered. After a final decision, the communication switches to the selected protocol, the data is transferred and the communication channel is closed again.

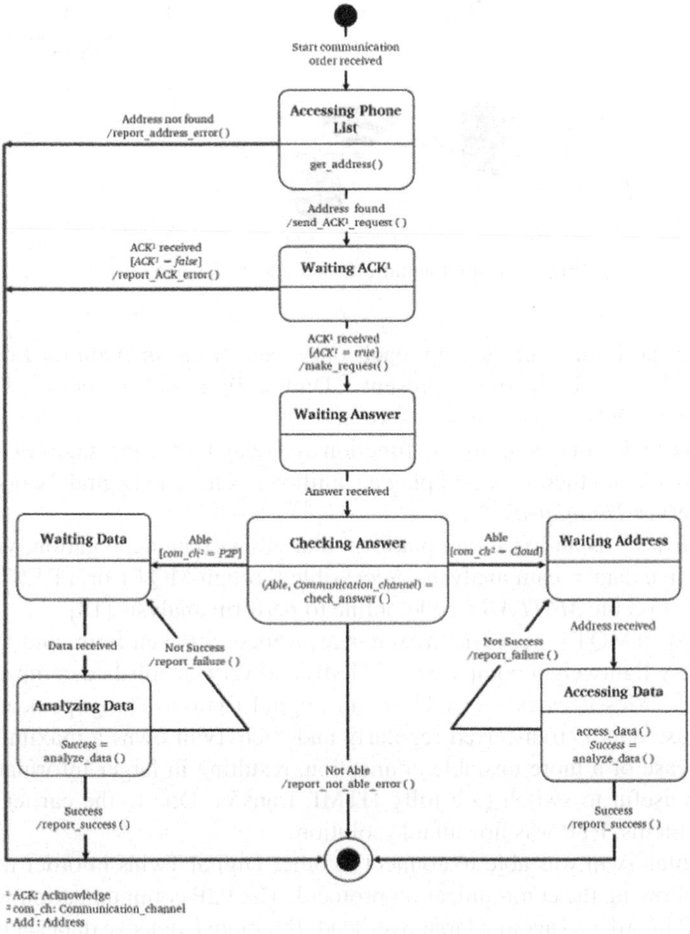

Fig. 3. Flow chart of communication selection [17]

4 Implementation

In order to test and assess the proposed concept, a pilot scenario has been implemented. For the implementation, it was crucial to use mainly low budget and low tier hardware for the Digital Twins to prove the functionality of the concept, even with limited capabilities.

The prototype was based on sensors and Arduino and RaspBerry Pi microcontrollers in order to test the algorithm with real-time data. The setup is presented in Fig. 4.

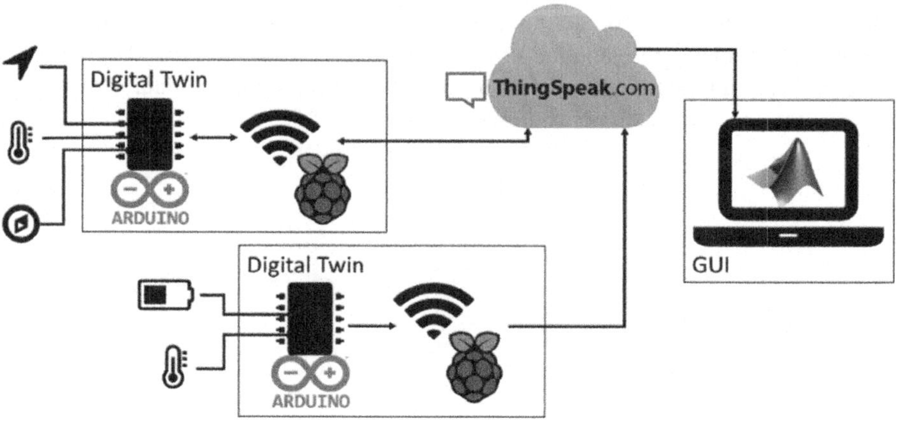

Fig. 4. Implementation for the test scenario [17]

Two Digital Twins were set up, each one made from an Arduino Leonardo and a Raspberry Pi, which together represent a Digital Twin with its physical and digital counterparts. Each Digital Twin uses several sensors to generate data. The sole purpose of the Raspberry Pis in this setup is to function as a relay for the messages of the Arduino into the network and therefor don't play a significant role. The Digital Twins connect to the Cloud server *ThingSpeak*^{TM}.

ThingSpeak^{TM} is an IoT cloud platform that allows data aggregation, visualization feature and live data stream analysis. Accessible through MQTT or a REST API it has the ability to execute *MATLAB*® code online to perform analysis [18].

The protocol MQTT is used as an exchange protocol between Twins and ThingSpeak, since it is very lightweight compared to HTML and very established compared to other protocols [19]. Messages transferred from the Digital Twins to ThingSpeak are relatively small, because data is transferred regularly and each Twin owns a maximum of three sensors. In case of a more unstable connection, resulting in larger information pieces, it would be useful to switch to a fully HTML transfer. Due to the earlier mentioned security problems, FTP was no suitable solution.

The Digital Twin was able to connect to other Digital Twins in order to receive or send data following the communication protocol. The P2P communication was handled with TCP/IP in order to avoid a large overhead. If a more extensive data set between the Digital Twins needed to be exchanged, an algorithm decided whether the data transferred directly over the TCP/IP connection or if it would be more suitable to create a new access key on *ThingSpeak*^{TM} and only send it. After the key transmission, the second Twin was able to access the stored data in the cloud and could download all shared information. Depending on what kind of permission the Twin was given, it was able to gather the data later on, if it lost connection or was busy with other tasks.

5 Conclusion

This paper presents a concept for improving Digital Twins communication. It is not the goal of the proposed concept to eliminate P2P communication entirely, but rather to propose a second, more effective way to communicate between Twins, if certain limitations are given. The benefits of the proposed communications are most relevant, if both Digital Twins have an unstable connection while the disconnection between them is not temporally connected. The described concept offers four main advantages, identified during pilot assessment. First, on a design level, the separation between the interface unit and cloud unit allows for an easy switch of the cloud service, because the cloud unit is not an essential part of the Digital Twin and can be exchanged at any time. Second, the transfer of data through the cloud decreases the time each Digital Twin needs for the data transfer, because not both of the Digital Twins need to maintain a stable internet connection at the same time. This does not imply that the data transfer in general takes shorter.

Third, given the fact the Digital Twin, which receives the request, maintained its cloud storage, the actual workload for this Digital Twin is lowered to a minimum. The whole task of reading the data and sending is done by the cloud service, with likely more sufficient hardware. Also, the storage in the cloud enables non crucial simulations being executed in the cloud. And the last benefit results from the use of the central directory for all Digital Twins, due to the easy monitoring and the slim approach for finding other Digital Twins with particular services.

The proposed concept is part of a broader research effort in order to establish the conceptual foundation, concepts, and methods to enable Digital Twin adoption in larger scale in industry. Further suggestions for research in the area include a pilot implementation using real data and extension to multiple Digital Twins communicating production environments, as well as using the accumulated data to run simulations at the cloud to unburden the Digital Twins.

Acknowledgment. The authors thank Ms. Peixoto Barbosa, Mr. Machado Lima, Mr. Carvalho Gaspar de Barros Bello, Mr. Siguematu, and Mr. Oliveira Françani for detailing the proposals technical aspects and implementing the pilot test scenario as part of a student project.

References

1. Rayes, A., Salam, S.: Internet of Things From Hype to Reality. Springer, Cham (2017). https://doi.org/10.1007/978-3-319-44860-2
2. Iselin, E.R.: The effects of information load and information diversity on decision quality in a structured decision task. Account. Organ. Soc. **13**(2), 147–164 (1988). https://doi.org/10.1016/0361-3682(88)90041-4
3. Haag, S., Anderl, R.: Digital twin – proof of concept. Manuf. Lett. **15**, 64–66 (2018)
4. Rosen, R., von Wichert, G., Lo, G., et al.: About the importance of autonomy and digital twins for the future of manufacturing. IFAC-PapersOnLine **48**(3), 567–572 (2015)
5. Schleich, B., Anwer, N., Mathieu, L., et al.: Shaping the digital twin for design and production engineering. CIRP Ann. Manuf. Technol. **66**(1), 141–144 (2017)

6. Uhlemann, T.H.-J., Lehmann, C., Steinhilper, R.: The digital twin: realizing the cyber-physical production system for industry 4.0. In: The 24th CIRP Conference on Life Cycle Engineering (2017)
7. Tao, F., Zhang, M.: Digital twin shop-floor: a new shop-floor paradigm towards smart manufacturing. IEEE Access **5**, 20418–20427 (2017)
8. Brenner, B., Hummel, V.: Digital twin as enabler for an innovative digital shopfloor management system in the ESB logistics learning factory at Reutlingen - University. Procedia Manuf. **9**, 198–205 (2017). https://doi.org/10.1016/j.promfg.2017.04.039
9. Uhlemann, T.H.-J., Schock, C., Lehmann, C., et al.: The digital twin: demonstrating the potential of real time data acquisition in production systems. Procedia Manuf. **9**, 113–120 (2017). https://doi.org/10.1016/j.promfg.2017.04.043
10. Negri, E., Fumagalli, L., Macchi, M.: A review of the roles of digital twin in CPS-based production systems. Procedia Manuf. **11**, 939–948 (2017)
11. Boschert, S., Rosen, R.: Digital twin—the simulation aspect. In: Hehenberger, P., Bradley, D. (eds.) Mechatronic Futures, pp. 59–74. Springer, Cham (2016). https://doi.org/10.1007/978-3-319-32156-1_5
12. Kozierok, C.M.: The TCP/IP Guide Version 3.0 (2005)
13. Ribak, J.: Active FTP vs Passive FTP: a Definitive Explanation (2006)
14. Bernard, F.: Sicherheitsprobleme beim FTP-Protokoll. Linux-Magazin (2002)
15. Banks, A., Gupta, R.: MQTT Version 3.1.1. OASIS Open (2014)
16. Soni, D., Makwana, A.: A Survey on MQTT: a protocol of Internet Of Things (IOT) (2017)
17. Barbosa, P., Lima, M., de Barros Bello, C.G., et al.: Design of a communication protocol for the use between digital twins, ADP, TU Darmstadt (2019)
18. Thingspeak: The MathWorks I (2019). https://thingspeak.com/pages/learn_more
19. Naik, N.: Choice of effective messaging protocols for IoT systems: MQTT, CoAP, AMQP and HTTP. In: 2017 Symposium Proceedings of 2017 IEEE International Symposium on Systems Engineering: ISSE 2017, Vienna, Austria, 11–13 October 2017, pp. 1–7. IEEE, Piscataway (2017)

Development of a Valuation Method for IoT-Platforms

Stefan Kugler, Cordula Czwick(✉), and Reiner Anderl

Department of Computer Integrated Design, TU Darmstadt, Otto-Berndt-Street 2, 64287 Darmstadt, Germany

{kugler,auth}@dik.tu-darmstadt.de

Abstract. A production facility enables the collecting of many different data with existing machinery. One reason for this are modern machines, which are usually equipped with cyber-physical-systems (CPS). CPS are the basis of Industry 4.0 and enable machines to collect and transfer data by using sensors and a communication interface. The IoT-platform can visualize and analyse the data collected. This enables production to be optimized by detecting and minimizing weak points. Due to the topicality of this topic, there is a large variety of platform providers on the market. However, the IoT-platforms of the different providers have different strengths and weaknesses. In order to be able to keep track of existing IoT-platform solutions and to be able to better point out advantages and disadvantages, this paper presents a method that supports the suitability and choice of an IoT-platform solution.

For this reason, a method will be developed which is based on a matrix in which selected IoT-platform solutions are listed. In addition, criteria for evaluation are detected and an evaluation scheme is integrated. Based on the evaluation the method determines a suitable IoT-platform by taking the customer needs into account. After a brief introduction and portraying the state of the art, the concept of the evaluation matrix is followed by an outlook and a short summary.

Keywords: Platform · Industry 4.0 · Digitalization · Project ArePron

1 Introduction

Data are often referred to as the oil of the 21st century because of their current importance. A large number of different data can be generated in a production facility with existing machinery. On the one hand, these are machine-unspecific data such as temperature or humidity inside and outside the machine hall. On the other hand, machine-specific data such as machine temperature, lubricant level, set-up time or energy consumption can also be recorded. Sensors can also be used to determine production duration or quality. One reason for the ever simpler generation of data is the implementation of cyber-physical systems (CPS) directly in the machines used in production. CPS consist of an integrated system, an actuator and a communication module. If several of these CPSs are in use for one production, this is referred to as cyber-physical production systems (CPPS).

C. Fortin et al. (Eds.): PLM 2019, IFIP AICT 565, pp. 293–301, 2019.
https://doi.org/10.1007/978-3-030-42250-9_28

CPS are the basis of industry 4.0 and enable the acquisition of physical data and the influence on physical processes by the existing actuators. Furthermore, data evaluation and storage as well as the resulting active or reactive interaction between the real and the digital world are of relevance. The prerequisite for this is a communication module that can be used for local or global communication [1].

This technology contributes to the fact that the worldwide amount of data will grow from 33 Zettabyte[1] today to 175 Zettabyte in 2025 [2]. Businesses need to prepare for this data growth and existing infrastructure should be rethought and adapted. The development of an in-house strategy should also be considered. Existing IoT-platform solutions can become very important and provide added value for companies. With the help of IoT-platforms, the data generated can be visualized and analysed. Thus, production can be optimized by uncovering and minimizing weak points. In addition, the system can independently point out errors, such as an excessively large deviation between actual data and target data. Due to the topicality of this subject, there are a large number of platform providers on the market. However, these differ with regard to various criteria, such as existing functionalities, the suitable range of applications or the provider, which is why companies must be supported in the search for and selection of a solution [3].

In order to be able to keep track of existing IoT-platform solutions and to be able to better point out advantages and disadvantages, this paper presents a method that supports the suitability and choice of an IoT-platform solution. The method is based on a matrix in which selected IoT-platform solutions are listed. In addition, criteria for evaluation are recorded and an evaluation scheme is integrated. On the basis of the evaluation and taking into account the requirements, the method determines a suitable IoT platform. This paper focuses on the core of the method, the evaluation matrix.

As part of the ArePron project (agile resource-efficient production network), two existing learning factories at TU Darmstadt will be networked to form a production network and expanded to include an IoT-platform. With the help of the IoT-platform, a component-based recording of resource use and consumption will take place. In addition, a "common currency" will be introduced to compare the whole resource consumption and therefore possibilities will be developed for converting value-added processes into a resource-optimized production process. This project is supported by the Hessian Ministry of Economics, Energy, Transport and Regional Development and the European Union [4].

2 Automation Pyramid and IoT-Platforms

The hierarchical structure of a factory and communication inside companies can be simplified using an automation pyramid [5]. Different processes are subdivided into different levels, making production boundaries visible. Automation pyramids are usually displayed with three to seven levels (see Fig. 1) [6]. In most cases, the individual levels are supported by different systems, such as PLC, SCADA, ERP or MES. Of major relevance is the data transfer within the individual levels, but also between the levels.

[1] 1 Zettabyte = 10^{21} Bytes = 1.000.000.000 Terabytes

From bottom to top, the amount of data in the individual levels increases, while the need for decreases due to low latency.

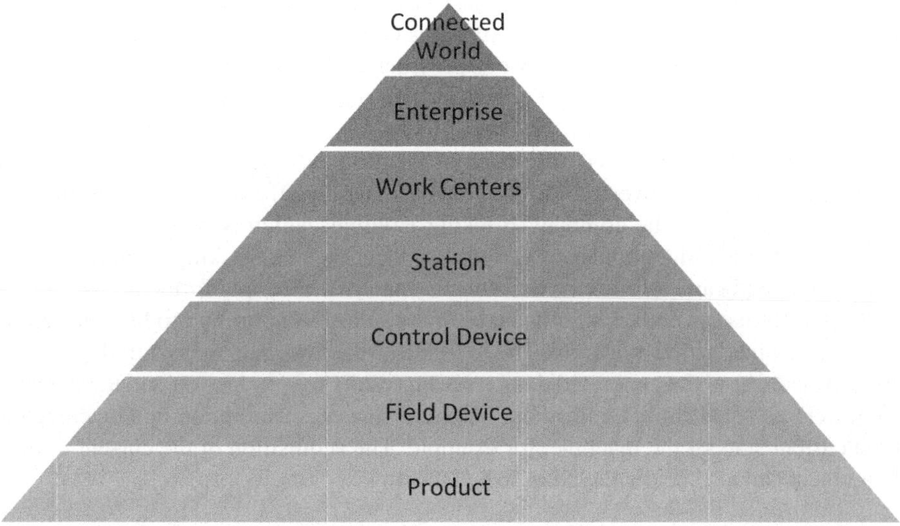

Fig. 1. Classification of IoT-platforms in an automation pyramid according to RAMI4.0 [7]

As a result of digitalization and new emerging technological possibilities, such as the use of cloud computing or the connection of a production to IoT-platforms, the pyramid is flattening more and more and the number of levels is tending to decline resulting in less hierarchical structures. The reason for this is the integration of networked, decentralized systems that make data, services and functionalities available where the need arises in production. By using CPS in production, generated data can be transferred directly to integrated systems such as IoT-platforms. Previously, data was transferred from the field level via the Control Device, Station and Work Center levels to the Enterprise level. RAMI 4.0 is followed by Connected World at the top of the pyramid, which includes the entire company group, external service providers, suppliers and customers [8]. This detour is no longer up to date due to modern and more flexible communication channels, which explains the flattening of the automation pyramid.

These developments are beneficial for the use of platforms. In case of platforms, a primary distinction must be made between transaction platforms, innovation platforms, investment platforms and integration platforms [9].

Transaction platforms such as eBay, Uber or Airbnb take on the role of intermediaries for the sale of products or services connecting buyers and sellers. Innovation platforms are platforms that provide an innovation in the form of a product or service. Building on this innovation, others can become a part of the platform through their own ideas and developments to expand it further. One example is Axoom's IoT-platform. Other companies can use the product as a basis to offer new products and services. On the one hand, these can be innovative apps with new business models for the companies. Another possibility is the sale of manufacturer-dependent machine tool data, so-called technology data, with which customers can manufacture in high quality immediately after purchase, without having to carry out samples [10]. This saves time and money and customers can immediately gain added value through the platform.

Integration platforms relate to the characteristics of transaction platforms and innovation platforms. A well-known example of this is Google's operating system Android, on which over 3.3 million apps from various providers are now available [11]. In addition, Android brings the agent and buyer together via a single platform.

Finally, there are investment platforms to be mentioned which have to be distinguished from those mentioned so far. Users of the platforms are companies that act as holding companies, investors or both, and pursue a platform portfolio strategy [9]. An example of this is the company Booking Holding, which is not a platform in the actual sense but is a shareholder of various products such as Booking.com, Kayak.com or momondo and can therefore be described as an investment platform.

IoT-platforms can deliver significant business value by capturing production data and transferring it into an IoT-platform. The IoT-platform allows data to be stored, processed and analysed. From the generated data, relevant results for production and the company can be derived. This could be information on the power consumption of a machine tool or the current state of the machine, for example. The acquisition of the current position of an object can also be displayed in IoT-platforms.

3 Concept for a Method of Valuation for IoT-Platforms

After a brief explanation of IoT-platforms in Sect. 1, now the concept of a method supporting the selection of IoT-platform will be described. This is necessary due to the large number of platform providers and the differences between different IoT-platforms. The method allows interested parties of an IoT-platform to directly access relevant requirements, add requirements as needed and evaluate the IoT-platform if necessary. The method is based on a matrix (see Table 1) in which various criteria, subcriteria and selected IoT-platforms can be found. The evaluations have to be entered into the matrix shown in Table 2.

Table 1. Structure of the evaluation matrix

Main criterion	Secondary criterion	Platform A	Platform B	Platform …
Main criterion A	Secondary criterion A1	++	−−	…
	Secondary criterion A2	+	−	…
Main criterion B	Secondary criterion B1	o	o	…
Main criterion …	Secondary criterion …	++	−−	…

Table 2. Valuation possibilities

++	Fully applicable
+	Applies largely
o	No statement possible
–	Applies in part
––	Not applicable

The valuation options are shown in Table 2.

The statement "Fully applicable" (++) means that the relevant subcriterion is fully applicable and met by the IoT-platform. In contrast, a subcriterion is not met in any way in the "not applicable" (––) rating. In case of the ratings "largely applies" (+) and "applies in part" (–), a subcriterion is met or not met with restrictions. Finally, the evaluation "no statement possible" (o) is required in order to be able to neutrally evaluate a subcriterion if information is missing. The evaluation options are decisive for the selection of an IoT-platform and are taken into account in the developed logic as part of the method.

The main criteria and their respective subcriteria are presented below. They are the core of the method and represent a collection of relevant properties for the selection of an IoT-platform. It is possible to change the criteria or add new criteria as needed. Each criteria of an IoT-platform must be evaluated as objectively as possible so that the result of the selection is not distorted.

In the following, the main criteria with associated subcriteria are presented and briefly explained:

<u>Criterion Usability</u>

The usability criterion refers to the user-friendliness of a platform. It describes the extent to which users can achieve a goal effective[2], efficient[3] and satisfactorily [4] in a defined application context.

- Platform Setup: Describes the usability of the platform setup.
- Integration of new devices: Describes the usability regarding the integration of new devices into the platform.
- Import of measurement data: Describes the usability regarding the import of measurement data into the platform.
- Intuitively usable: Describes the positive usability of the platform without prior knowledge from associated documentation or similar.
- Stability of data transmission: Describes the probability of the occurrence of unexpected effects of changes on data transmission.

2 "Accuracy and completeness with which users achieve certain goals" [12].

3 "Resources used in relation to the results achieved" [12].

4 "Extent to which the user's physical, cognitive and emotional reactions resulting from the use of a system, product or service correspond to the user's requirements and expectations" [12].

- Stability of the platform: Describes the probability of unexpected effects of changes on the platform.
- User Experience: Includes all effects, such as perception and reactions, that the use of a user interface has on a user before, during and after use [13].
- Reliability of data transmission: Describes the maintenance of a certain line level of data transmission under certain conditions over a defined period.
- Reliability of the platform: Describes the maintenance of a certain line level of the platform under certain conditions over a defined period.

Criterion Data Processing:

The criterion data processing describes the automated processing of data in electronic form within the platform. In addition, the possibilities of data processing within the platform are considered in this main criterion.

- Recording amount: Describes the upper bound for the recording amount of platform data.
- Display of a data series: Describes the possibilities, such as using different diagram types or lists, of visualization data series.
- Display of different sensor data: Describes the possibility of displaying different sensor data.
- Amount of data during transmission: Describes the size of data sent to a platform and its compression options.
- Data point display: Describes the possibilities of displaying data points.
- Exportability of the data: Describes whether data can be exported.
- Speed at which measurement data is transferred to the platform: Describes the latency between the collection of a measurement value and its appearance on the platform.
- Grouping of sensors: Possibility to classify groups of different sensors.
- Transmission frequency: Describes the support of different transmission frequencies of a platform.

Criterion Documentation

The criterion documentation describes the possibility of using manual or similar sources of information, which can explain and simplify the use of the platform. The documentation is usually integrated into the platform or made available by the provider as a document.

- Status: Describes the status of documentation with regard to the version of the platform and its available functionalities.
- Handling: Describes the transferability of documentation to real events.
- Correctness: Describes the extent to which the documentation corresponds to the real use.
- Clarity: Describes the clarity of the documentation. The structure, table of contents and intuitive finding of relevant information are taken into account.

Criterion Surface

The Surface criterion describes the structure and surface of the platform. The evaluation of design and clarity (which is not completely objective) must be taken into account. Therefore, a high weighting of these two subcriteria is not recommended.

- Design: Describes formal aesthetic functions as well as sign and symbol functions.
- Individually customizable: Describes whether a platform has the ability to customize its interface.
- Clarity: Describes the clearness of the platform.

Criterion Basic Functions

The basic functions criterion describes the existence and use of various platform functionalities. This includes, for example, the possibility of creating rules, automatic notifications when defined events occur or monitoring connected systems.

- Automatic connection: Describes the possibility of automatically connecting systems, sensors or machines to the platform on restart or reconnection.
- Own programming: Describes the possibility whether own programs or algorithms can be integrated directly into the platform.
- Creation of rules: Describes the possibility whether rules can be integrated into the platform.
- Restarting the systems: Describes whether it is possible to restart connected systems such as machines, sensors or systems from the platform.
- Monitoring active devices: Describes the possibility of recording whether the device is on or off.
- Monitoring of running production: Describes the possibility of supervisioning a running production.
- Support of different languages: Describes the support of the platform of different programming languages.
- Warning systems: Describes whether a warning system is existing within the platform.
- Condition monitoring of machine data: Describes the possibility of capturing machine data via the platform.

Criterion Administration

The criterion Administration describes the administrative possibilities within the platform.

- Platform maintenance effort: Describes the administrative effort required to maintain a platform.
- Role distribution for platform access: Describes the possibility of distributing roles so that users have different rights within the platform.
- Assignment of access rights: Describes the possibility of assigning access rights so that access to the platform can be restricted individually.

Criterion Interoperability

The interoperability criterion describes the ability of the platform to interact with different systems.

- Integration of different systems: Describes the possibility of connecting different IT systems, such as Manufacturing Execution System (MES) or Enterprise Resource Planning (ERP), to the platform.
- Communication from system to platform: Describes the possibility of sending data from different systems to the platform.
- Platform to System Sending Capability: Describes the ability to send data from the platform to different systems.
- Connection of devices: Describes the possibility of connecting different machines, which use different communication options to the platform.

After carrying out the evaluation of an IoT-platform, or using existing evaluations, a suitable IoT-platform is selected. For this purpose, the sub criteria indicate whether it is a must request, a target request or a wish request for the interested party. The more information is indicated thereby, the more suitable is the selection of the suitable solution. Specifying too many mandatory requirements can mean that no suitable IoT-platform can be found, since no IoT-platform can meet all mandatory requirements. A weighting option has therefore been added to the method, which can be used after an unsuccessful search. The most relevant mandatory requirements can be re-weighted to find an IoT-platform that comes closest to your requirements. Finally, all IoT-platforms included in the selection are listed in a table. The IoT-platforms are sorted in descending order by overlapping their own requirements and the appropriate range of functionalities of the IoT-platform. The logic used to make the selection is not described in more detail in this paper.

4 Conclusion and Outlook

Following the introduction of the IoT-platform and the associated changes to existing productions, this paper presented a method for evaluating and selecting suitable IoT-platforms. The method makes sense due to the large number of different platform providers, as there are large differences with regard to the existing IoT-platforms. The method draws on a matrix in which the functionalities and properties of an IoT-platform can be specified. The evaluation of the IoT-platforms can be carried out by the user or previous evaluations published within the ArePron project can be used. It is also possible to adapt previous evaluations. Once the relevant IoT-platforms have been integrated into the matrix and evaluated, the IoT-platform is selected. To do this, the interested party must first define mandatory, target and optional requirements. Subsequently, all IoT-platforms are presented in a table with regard to their conformity.

The ArePron project is currently conducting a market analysis of existing IoT-platforms. Selected platforms are evaluated within the framework of the project and integrated into the matrix. For this purpose, a benchmark will be carried out to ensure objectivity and comparability of the results. The results will be stored in a database that will be accessed by a program in the form of a web application. This program guides the user through the method and displays the results after using the method.

Acknowledgements. The method is part of the transfer project "ArePron – agile resource efficient production network". The project is approved by the Hessian Ministry of Economics, Energy, Transport and Regional Development (HMWEVL) and financed by the European Regional Development Fund (ERDF) and the Hessian Ministry. The project is a collaboration between the Department of Computer Integrated Design, the Department of Material Flow Management and Resource Economy and the Institute of Production Management, Technology and Machine Tools. The project started in January 2018 and ends in December 2020.

References

1. Abele, E., Anderl, R., Metternich, J., Arndt, A., Wank, A.: Effiziente Fabrik 4.0. Studie Industrie 4.0 - Potentiale, Nutzen und Good-Practice-Beispiele für die hessische Industrie, Zwischenbericht zum Projekt Effiziente Fabrik 4.0. Meisenbach GmbH Verlag, Bamberg (2015)
2. Reinsel, D., Gantz, J., Rysning, J.: Data Age 2025. The Digitization of the World. From Edge to Core (2018). https://www.seagate.com/files/www-content/our-story/trends/files/idc-seagate-dataage-whitepaper.pdf. Accessed 23 Jan 2019
3. Bayern, Z.D.: Plattformen: Ein Einstieg in Industrial IoT (2018). https://zentrum-digitalisierung.bayern/plattformen-ein-einstieg-in-industrial-iot/. Accessed 21 Jan 2019
4. Institut für Produktionsmanagement, Technologie und Werkzeugmaschinen: ArePron. Agiles ressourceneffizientes Produktionsnetzwerk. http://www.arepron.com/. Accessed 23 Jan 2019
5. Forstner, L., Dümmler, M.: Integrierte Wertschöpfungsnetzwerke – Chancen und Potenziale durch Industrie 4.0. Elektrotech. Inftech. (2014). https://doi.org/10.1007/s00502-014-0224-y
6. Meudt, T., Pohl, M., Metternich, J.: Die Automatisierungspyramide - Ein Literaturüberblick. Accessed 31 Jan 2019
7. DIN Deutsches Institut für Normung e. V.: Referenzarchitekturmodell Industrie 4.0 (RAMI4.0). Beuth Verlag GmbH 03.100.01, 25.040.01, 35.240.50(91345) (2016). Accessed 31 Jan 2019
8. VDI/VDE-Gesellschaft Mess- und Automatisierungstechnik/ZVEI: Statusreport. Referenzarchitekturmodell Industrie 4.0 (RAMI4.0) (2015). https://www.vdi.de/fileadmin/user_upload/VDI-GMA_Statusreport_Referenzarchitekturmodell-Industrie40.pdf. Accessed 31 Jan 2019
9. Evans, P.C., Gawer, A.: The rise of the platform enterprise. A Global Survey (2016). https://www.thecge.net/archived-papers/the-rise-of-the-platform-enterprise-a-global-survey/. Accessed 1 Feb 2019
10. Erner, M. (ed.): Management 4.0 - Unternehmensführung im digitalen Zeitalter. Springer, Heidelberg (2019). https://doi.org/10.1007/978-3-662-57963-3
11. Statista: Anzahl der angebotenen Apps in den Top App-Stores bis, October 2017 (2019). https://de.statista.com/statistik/daten/studie/208599/umfrage/anzahl-der-apps-in-den-top-app-stores/. Accessed 1 Feb 2019
12. DIN Deutsches Institut für Normung e. V.: Ergonomie der Mensch-System-Interaktion. Teil 11: Gebrauchstauglichkeit: Begriffe und Konzepte. Beuth Verlag GmbH, Berlin 13.180; 35.080; 35.180(9241-11) (2018). Accessed 6 Feb 2019
13. DIN Deutsches Institut für Normung e. V.: Ergonomie der Mensch-System-Interaktion. Teil 210: Prozess zur Gestaltung gebrauchstauglicher interaktiver Systeme. Beuth Verlag GmbH, Berlin 13.180; 35.180(9241-210) (2011). Accessed 6 Feb 2019

Impact of IIoT Based Technologies on Characteristic Features and Related Options of Nonownership Business Models

Karan Menon[1(✉)], Hannu Kärkkäinen[1], Sameer Mittal[2], and Thorsten Wuest[2]

[1] Tampere University, Tampere, Finland
{karan.menon,hannu.karkkainen}@tuni.fi
[2] West Virginia University, Morgantown, USA
samittal@mix.wvu.edu, thwuest@mail.wvu.edu

Abstract. Industrial internet of things (IIoT) can positively impact business from the process and the technical perspective. There is a limited understanding of the impact of IIoT on business models in general especially the novel nonownership business models (NOBMs). In this paper we analyze the literature, especially case study literature, to understand the impact of IIoT based technologies and related features on the NOBMs using a morphological box (developed by Lay et al. [4]) as a framework. We understood that IIoT- enabled technologies enables the implementation of a larger variety of NOBMs, such as, the pay-per-use, pay-per-output and pay-per-outcome business models, as well as a variety of options related to them. We also realized that there is a need to develop a morphological box for capital intensive manufacturing companies by developing new characteristic features and related options that can take IIoT enabled technologies.

Keywords: Industrial internet of things · Industry 4.0 · Business models · Nonownership business model · IIoT · IoT

1 Introduction

The academia and managers are currently having high expectations on the potential of the IIoT [1]. However, these benefits are not very apparent and easy to realize. While recognizing the uncertainties related to the realization of business benefits from IIoT, the novel types of Nonownership Business Models (NOBMs) enable collaborating companies to share both opportunities and downsides of IIoT for mutual benefit, thus creating novel networked value creation opportunities. Regarding such benefits, in general, IIoT has been demonstrated e.g. to enable decreases in transaction costs between companies in various manners [1], while increasing transparency in collaboration through increases in the quantity and quality of data and information (e.g. [2]).

Currently, there is a limited understanding in the academic literature about the value and benefits of IIoT to business and novel business models (see e.g. [3]). Therefore, the central novelty of this study is to understand the role of IIoT technologies in NOBMs

Published by Springer Nature Switzerland AG 2019
C. Fortin et al. (Eds.): PLM 2019, IFIP AICT 565, pp. 302–312, 2019.
https://doi.org/10.1007/978-3-030-42250-9_29

(especially pay-per-use, pay-per-output and pay-per outcome) in the domain of industrial (business-to-business) capital-intensive manufacturing goods. The novelty is derived, in more detail, partly also from the use of a business model structuring framework [4], previously not used, to understand the role of IIoT technologies in the NOBMs. We will review the perspective of earlier studies that have addressed this topic in the next section.

We focus on companies that not only produce products for other companies, but more specifically, on companies the products (machines or machine components) of which are used as part of the other companies' manufacturing processes, and mostly are capital-intensive in nature, i.e. B2B companies. Thus, for instance, the risk aspect, associated to all NOBMs which transfer product ownership from customers to suppliers, is emphasized, while e.g. failures in products or product components can cause even significant interruptions in the whole production process, and thus, the supplier has significantly higher responsibility of such risks.

To address the above research gaps, our aim is to answer the following main research question: "*How do IIoT- based technologies impact the characteristic features and related business model enabled options of the nonownership types of advanced business models of business-to-business manufacturing companies*?"

The structure of this study is as follows: we first introduce the major concepts, primarily IIoT and NOBM business models, and related frameworks for this study. Second, we review existing research and the research gap in more detail. Third, we introduce the methodology of this paper. Fourth, we present the results, and discuss them, leading finally into the conclusions and managerial implications.

2 Theoretical Background

2.1 Industrial Internet of Things-Based Technologies

Smart Manufacturing (SM) improves the efficiency and responsiveness of a production system by integrating data with information technology and manufacturing. IoT employs sensors to communicate between the physical world and computers and was first used in 1999 [5]. IoT can record and measure parameters like temperature, pressure, and light with the help of affordable electronic sensors and wireless processors over the internet and considered as a technology that can revolutionize the future [6]. IIoT connects the factory machines with IoT [5]. IIoT consists of devices and sensors, communication technologies, gateways and switches, analytical and optimization programs, interconnected apps, and people (that use it) [5, 7]. Based on the literature, [1] four technologies are important for IIoT, (i) *Internet and communication protocols and middleware*, (ii) *Sensors*, (iii) *Actuators*, and (iv) *IT-driven services like AI and big data analytics*.

Evolution of digital technologies has transformed B2B companies [8]. Similarly, the information interoperability possible because of IIoT, has totally changed the relationships between the customers, manufacturers and the suppliers, and thus modifying the business models of the manufacturing companies [5, 6]. For example, now the electrical engineering and information and communication technology companies are looking for novel key partner networks and automotive suppliers use IIoT to increase their cost efficiency [3]. A systematic review study [9] has also shown that the scientific work has not looked at all the aspects of the business models, and these studies mainly focus on the key resources and activities of the companies, and utterly ignored the effect of IIoT adoption from the customer perspective. Therefore, although, the literature refers to the right business models as the force behind profitable use of IIoT, it lacks a comprehensive business model that caters towards the aspect of IIoT [5].

2.2 Nonownership Business Models

Nonownership model can be defined as a*"service in which customers acquire some property rights to an asset and are offered a certain degree of freedom in using this asset for a specified period of time while the burdens of ownership remain with the owner"* [10].

The above definition describes the concept of nonownership in a clear manner from the customers point of view, as it talks about how a customer can use the asset but not own it, by keeping the ownership with the manufacturer. To take the manufacturer's point of view into consideration, the earning logic of nonownership business models must be described. This can be done by dividing the nonownership model into pay-per-use, pay-per-output and pay-per-outcome models. Pay-per-use type nonownership model implies that the customer pays for the use of the machine and every other aspect related to the machine, i.e. ownership, installation, maintenance, upgrade and recycling is taken care of by the manufacturer. Pay-per-output type nonownership model focuses on the result of the machine use, which is usually quantified in monetary terms. Pay-per-outcome type nonownership model focuses on the value derived by the customer after using the machine provided by the manufacturer.

Literature has covered the nonownership models from various different sectors; such as, software industry [11], B2C product manufacturers such as washing machine manufacturers [12], manufactured products such as the copier and printer [2]. The above-mentioned product ranges are easy to scale because the economies of scale work very well for software products, B2C products and use intensive copiers and printers. B2B manufacturers that make equipment or machines that are critical in customers process, such as the air-compressors or jet engines (critical components for an airplane manufacturer) have a very different risk profile when it comes to these nonownership models when compared to the above-mentioned products. There are some authors that discuss the risk profile for these kind of manufacturing companies [13]. Some of the authors [2, 13, 14], discuss the impact of IIoT on the business models of the manufacturing companies using the business model framework. They do not discuss the impact of IIoT on specific nonownership business models, such as the pay-per-use, pay-per-output and the pay-per-outcome models in a manner that the companies can define the value proposition for every individual model. Hence, we take the morphological box designed by [4] and understand the impact of IIoT on each and every characteristic feature as well as related options of the morphological box for manufacturing companies.

2.3 Morphological Box - Framework for Nonownership Business Models

Advanced business models that enable manufacturing companies to transition from sales-based revenue to a more continuous, service-based revenue generation are very appealing for a myriad of reasons, including closer customer relations, lock-in, more control of complex assets, and access to the system's operational data for the manufacturer. There are several tools and frameworks available that aim at supporting manufacturing companies during the early phases of this complicated transition. In this paper, we specifically focus on the strategic perspective of the business model development. One established framework is Lay et al.'s [4] morphological box that allows to describe service/based business models in a structured way. Table 1 illustrates the basic structure of Lay et al.'s morphological box. This framework is intended to allow manufacturing companies with limited experience in nonownership business models to envision their own, unique set-up.

Table 1. Morphological box framework for nonownership business concepts [4]

Characteristic Features		Options			
Ownership	During the phase of use	Equipment producer	Leasing bank	Operating joint venture	Customer
	After the phase of use	Equipment producer	Leasing bank	Operating joint venture	Customer
Personnel	Manufacturing	Equipment producer	Operating joint venture	Customer	
	Maintenance	Equipment producer	Operating joint venture	Customer	
Location of operation		Equipment producer's establishment	Establishment "fence to fence" to the customer	Customer's establishment	
Single/multiple customer operation		In parallel operation for multiple customers	Operation for a single customer		
Payment model		Pay per unit	Pay for availability	Fixed rate	Pay for equipment

Lay et al.'s morphological box depicts five different characteristic features, ownership, personnel, location of operation, single/multiple customer operation, and payment model. By "characteristic features", we mean the central features of novel manufacturing business-to-business product- related business models, which are typical, as well as centrally differentiate the different types of novel business models from each other, and thus can be used for identifying the variety of options in the case of novel business models.

The first two, ownership and personnel are split in two sub-sets of characteristic features, during/*after the phase of use*, and *manufacturing/maintenance* respectively. For each of the characteristic features, different options are provided, reflecting the different possible set-ups for nonownership business models in manufacturing companies.

2.4 Impact of IIoT Enabled Technologies on NOBMs

While there is still a relatively small amount of academic studies discussing IIoT technologies' various roles in novel business models, and furthermore, especially aiming to understand these roles from the perspective of investment- and capital intensive business-to-business products, some studies [1, 2, 14–16] have addressed the topic. This literature that focuses on software products cannot be directly applied for understanding NOBMs in manufacturing capital intensive products. This is since software products can be scaled up as well as delivered and installed to customers' machines and manufacturing lines in a very different manner than large and expensive manufactured products. Second, due to such scalability and delivery challenges, risks related to suppliers' earnings being significantly linked to manufacturing customer e.g. not using the equipment in their production, bring significant risks to NOBM use in manufacturing context, limiting the adoption of experiences received from earlier literature derived from software NOBMs or consumer product NOBMs (see e.g. [15]).

We have studied literature reviews on IoT impacts to business models, literature reviews on NOBMs (e.g. [15]), and their references through forward and backward references of these reviews. No studies were found directly addressing our research question from the selected perspectives of capital-intensive manufacturing companies and from the perspective of NOBMs and the related changes in ownership of machines. We review the literature which is most closely associated with our research aim, context and research question.

Recently, [1, 2, 14, 16] have studied the role of IoT technologies in NOBMs. However, their studies do not address the topic from the perspective of capital-intensive manufacturing products. Metallo et al. [16] studied IoT technologies in three cases (Intel, Apio and Solair), making use of BM framework of [17], the so-called business model canvas, related to BM building blocks, but of which none are about capital intensive manufacturing products. Bock & Weiner [14] aim to study IIoT technologies' roles in NOBM's, their case study is focusing on capital-intensive manufacturing products, and they make use of [18] well-known BM framework. However, their perspective is focused on how these technologies can help to manage the uncertainties and risks (upsides and downsides of IIoT technologies) associated with NOBMs. Ehret & Wirth [1] focused on the role of IIoT technologies on NOBMs' BM components (Osterwalder's (see e.g. [17] well known BM framework), making use of economic theories (transaction cost theory and entrepreneurship theory) to understand the roles in more detail. However, their study is conceptual, and not concentrating on manufacturing capital-intensive products. They do neither, however, address directly the topics and issues of changing ownership in machines, related to NOBMs.

There are also some relatively recent systematic literature reviews on links of IoT and BMs [3, 15]. However, [15] discussed IoT's impact to software business models, which, for the above reasons, cannot be applied reasonably into manufacturing companies' product-oriented business models in the case of NOBMs. Arnold et al. [3] focus on generic business model impacts of IIoT into individual business model components of Osterwalder's business model canvas framework. They do not, however, discuss directly the implications to changes in ownership of investment products or NOBMs as such, but overall benefits to BM components, or on the changes in customer relationships.

3 Research Methodology

In this research we take a literature-based approach to investigate the impact of IIoT on the morphological box for NOBMs [4]. Lay et al.'s [4] framework was published in

2002, and since then, the digital transformation within the Industry 4.0 paradigm has had a significant impact on the feasibility and design of advanced NOBMs.

After identifying the relevant papers in a literature review, in a next step we map the reported case studies to the morphological box. More specifically, we analyze first, whether a certain characteristic feature is addressed in the case studies and second, if and how IIoT had an impact on said characteristic feature. Similarly, we proceed about the different options presented in the morphological box and apply the same methodology. After identifying the impact of IIoT on the individual characteristics features and associated options, we discuss the overall impact and the validity of the morphological box given the changes in the technological landscape. Furthermore, we analyze whether there are additional aspects that are reported as relevant in the recent case studies that are not represented in the morphological box at present. These missing aspects are discussed and put into context to build the foundation for future work aiming at creating an updated framework, taking advanced digital technologies and their requirements and opportunities into consideration.

4 Results and Findings

In this section we present the findings related to the impact of IIoT based technologies on the morphological box (shown in Table 1) in two parts. Table 2 shows the impact of IIoT based technologies on the characteristic features, whereas, Table 3, shows the impact of IIoT based technologies on the options related to the characteristic features (shown in Table 2).

IIoT technologies influence the tracking of the ownership using the sensors and the actuators as well as impact the prediction of the wear and tear to estimate the recycle time of the machine after the phase of use [1]. Lay et al. [4] did not separately considered the ownership of data component (under ownership) in the morphological box. After embedding IIoT based technologies with the machines and the equipment, it is possible to collect data of processes and the condition of the machine. This collected data on further analysis can enable process optimization, wear and tear prediction and new product design with better optimization for the manufacturer. Hence, it becomes imperative to consider the ownership of data associated with the process of manufacturing and condition of the machine [2, 14]. As per Lay et al. [4], operating "personnel" characteristic feature describes the allocation of the workforce in a business concept. IIoT based technologies have a big impact on the way personnel carry out the work in a manufacturing process. IIoT technologies create a connected environment for the machines via cloud, which enables the machine operator to remotely control the machine from another location. Thus, the customer worries only about the output of the machine. For example, Kaeser Compressors while adopting the IIoT enabled nonownership model, agreed with the customer that Kaeser will be the owner of the equipment and will also manage the operation of the compressors on customers' behalf [19–21].

Kaeser made use IIoT based technologies to enable operational efficiencies resulting from big data analytics and predictive maintenance. Real-time or near real-time condition monitoring of the machine's operation makes the "location of operation" decision making simpler for the manufacturer to remotely control the process and maintenance of the

Table 2. Impact of IIoT based technologies on characteristic features of advanced business models

Characteristic Features			Impact of IIoT based technologies	References
A	Ownership	During the phase of use	Ownership of Data associated with the process of manufacturing and condition of the machine	[2, 14, 19, 20, 22]
		After the phase of use		
B	Personnel	Manufacturing	Adaptive control using predictive analytics of the machine impacts the Personnel activities. Predictive maintenance impacts overall maintenance activities.	[1, 19, 21, 24, 25]
		Maintenance		
C	Location of operation		Condition monitoring gives more freedom when it comes to selecting the location of operation	[2, 23, 24, 26]
D	Single/multiple customer operation		Real-time or near-real time monitoring allows multiple customer operations with ease.	[14, 19]
E	Payment model		IIoT based technologies enable flexible and smart contracts	[27]

machine. adaptive control allows the manufacturer to let the customer make the decision on the location of the machine [2, 22, 23]. The characteristic feature that deals with the exclusivity of use of the machinery (Lay et al. [4]) focuses on "single/multiple customer operation" aspect. IIoT technologies enable real time or near real time monitoring of the machine use. This allows the manufacturer to create a system where multiple customers in the same location can use the machine as per a dedicated timeslot.

For example, if Kaeser has five customers in the same industrial area then it can set up a compressor system in a manner that all the five customers can use the same compressor system without purchasing any compressor [14, 19]. Kaeser can monitor the usage and the wear and tear of the compressor system and control the operation using IIoT based technologies.

Finally, IIoT based technologies in combination with Blockchain technology can lean-up the payment model for the manufacturer. Manufacturers can use smart contracts [27] to create more dynamic contracts with the customers. They can customize the smart contracts in a manner that it can cater to the pay-per-use model in the beginning but as the usage intensifies the contract automatically advances to pay-per-output and then to pay-per-outcome, giving maximum benefits to the customer and increasing the profit margin for the manufacturer. Blockchain in combination with the machine's real time operational data and related analytics enables the manufacturer and customer to agree on the dynamic nature of the contract [27].

Table 3 assesses the impact of IIOT based technologies and the enabled improved process capabilities (such as condition monitoring, predictive maintenance, etc.) on the options under the characteristic features (A to E from Table 2). Table 3 enables decision making, especially for the manufacturer. IIoT based technologies allow the manufacturer

Table 3. Impact of IIoT based technologies on the options related to characteristic features of advanced business models

C.F.*	Options				Impact of IIoT based technologies
A	Equip-ment producer	Leasing bank	Operating joint venture	Customer	Condition Monitoring and Predictive Maintenance enables the equipment producer to take more risk in ownership
	Equip-ment producer	Leasing bank	Operating joint venture	Customer	
B	Equipment producer	Operating joint venture	Customer		Adaptive control allows the equipment producer to take control of the manufacturing process and maintenance
	Equipment producer	Operating joint venture	Customer		
C	Equipment producer's establishment	Establishment "fence to fence" to the customer	Customer's establishment		Optimization, prediction and geo-localization allows the equipment producer to operate the machine at any location
D	In parallel operation for multiple customers	Operation for a single customer			Usage monitoring, intensity assessment and condition monitoring allows the equipment producer to serve multiple customers with the same machine.
E	Pay per unit	Pay for availability	Fixed rate	Pay for equipment	Smart contracts based on all the IIoT based capabilities allows flexibility in payment contracts.

* C.F. – Characteristic Features as in Table 2

to select options which give them more control over the machine's operation and usage by minimizing the risks. For instance, in case of the "ownership" characteristic feature (A), the manufacturer or equipment producer can take control of the ownership related to the equipment as well as maintenance by using condition monitoring and predictive maintenance [2, 19, 20].

Similarly, adaptive control allows the manufacturer's personnel to control the operation and maintenance remotely or limiting the visits to the customers facility [2, 19]. Hence, the manufacturer can have their own "personnel" for both manufacturing and maintenance. When it comes to the "location of operation", the manufacturer can provide any of the option, equipment producer's establishment, establishment "fence to fence" to the customer, customer's establishment, because manufacturer can control the operation using optimization, prediction and geo-localization. IIoT enabled technologies allow usage monitoring, intensity assessment and condition monitoring letting the manufacturer to serve multiple customers using the same equipment system [14, 19]. Finally, when it comes to the options for payment model, smart contracts [27], give dynamic capability and freedom to the manufacturer to offer any nonownership contract, pay-per-use, pay-per-output or pay-per-outcome.

5 Discussion and Conclusions

In our paper, the objective of the morphological box (originally by [4]) was to demonstrate the larger variety of possible different types of NOBMs, making use of the characteristic features and related options (as shown in Table 1). According to the results demonstrated above, IIoT- enabled technologies and facilitated process capabilities impact the above-mentioned characteristic features and related options in a way that this enables the implementation of a larger variety of NOBMs, such as, the pay-per-use, pay-per-output and pay-per-outcome business models, as well as a variety of options related to them.

The characteristic features and related options described by [4] in Table 1 were found relevant to the NOBMs. We found it possible to implement any type of NOBM using the characteristic features and the related options in different combination as demonstrated by [4]. IIoT based technologies on the other hand, were found to impact the characteristic features and related options in a manner that manufacturers can implement the variety of NOBMs. As shown in Table 2, "ownership" changes the way NOBMs are implemented because of IIoT enabled technologies. At the business model level, IIoT based technologies were found to impact the "ownership" characteristic feature in a manner that manufacturers interested in NOBMs can take better control of the ownership. This, in turn, may impact the "personnel" provided by the manufacturer to operate and maintain the machine, impacting the "location of operation" to be at the customer's site and finally impacting the way "payment model" is designed. Bock et al. [19] discuss how Kaeser changed the way they did business by employing the NOBM (pay-per-output model). With the IIOT based technologies, Kaeser took over the "ownership" of the compressor system and provided compressed air to the customer at customer's location using Kaeser's personnel to operate the compressor system and maintain them. In return, Kaeser was able to deploy the pay-per-output model for their customers to make payments for the compressed air they received [19].

NOBMs can be implemented without IIOT technologies as well. But, IIOT technologies were found to allow the manufacturing companies to implement a large variety of NOBMs. This variety can be seen using a morphological box, which constitutes of various characteristic features and options [4]. It is the options in the morphological box, that enable the variety in the NOBMs. IIoT based technologies enable the tapping into every detailed data point in a machine, providing big data and good quality data in real time or near real time. This access to data makes all the options (as in Table 3) that can contribute the variety of NOBMs i.e. pay-per-use, pay-per-output and pay-per-outcome feasible. Manufacturer can take control of the ownership, personnel that can operate the machine and do the maintenance, location of the machine as well as whether the machine system can be used by one or multiple customers. Finally, it is using the morphological box manufacturers can recognize and design novel business model -related experiments with their customers, and thus understand better the potential of various types of NOBMs and their feasibility.

After the analyses of results making use of the morphological box by [4], originally designed for various types of novel manufacturing business models, and the related IIOT enabled technological impacts analyzed from the literature making use of the morphological box, we realize that there is a need to create a facilitated new morphological box for manufacturing companies to take better into consideration these specific types of novel business models, NOBMs (such as pay-per-use, pay-per-output and pay-per-outcome). For instance, there is a need to design new characteristic features that, for example, can take the overall changes in asset ownership into account. This means, in addition to the machine ownership, that for instance data ownership, software ownership etc. are considered in the model. These changes and additions will allow the manufacturing companies to better design the advanced NOBMs such as the pay-per-use, pay-per-output and pay-per-outcome business models.

References

1. Ehret, M., Wirtz, J.: Unlocking value from machines: business models and the industrial Internet of Things. J. Mark. Manag. **33**, 111–130 (2017)
2. Ardolino, M., Rapaccini, M., Saccani, N., Gaiardelli, P., Crespi, G., Ruggeri, C.: The role of digital technologies for the service transformation of industrial companies. Int. J. Prod. Res. **56**, 2116–2132 (2018)
3. Arnold, C., Kiel, D., Voigt, K.-I.: How the industrial Internet of Things changes business models in different manufacturing industries. Int. J. Innov. Manag. **20**, 1640015 (2016)
4. Lay, G., Schroeter, M., Biege, S.: Service-based business concepts: a typology for business-to-business markets. Eur. Manag. J. **27**, 442–455 (2009)
5. Gierej, S.: Techniques for designing value propositions applicable to the concept of outcome-economy. Eng. Manag. Prod. Serv. **9**, 56 (2017)
6. Ahuett-Garza, H., Kurfess, T.: A brief discussion on the trends of habilitating technologies for industry 4.0 and smart manufacturing. Manuf. Lett. **15**, 60–63 (2018)
7. Hossain, M.S., Muhammad, G.: Cloud-assisted Industrial Internet of Things (IIoT) – enabled framework for health monitoring. Comput. Netw. **101**, 192–202 (2016)
8. Pagani, M., Pardo, C.: The impact of digital technology on relationships in a business network. Ind. Mark. Manag. **67**, 185–192 (2017)
9. Kiel, D., Gasse, L., Arnold, C., Collisi, M., Voigt, K.-I.: The impact of the Industrial Internet of Things on established business models. In: Conference Proceedings, vo. 24 (2016)
10. Wittkowski, K., Moeller, S., Wirtz, J.: Firms' intentions to use nonownership services. J. Serv. Res. **16**, 171–185 (2013)
11. Weinhardt, C., Stößer, J., Anandasivam, A., Blau, B.: Business models in the service world (2009)
12. Manninen, K., Koskela, S., Antikainen, R., Bocken, N., Dahlbo, H., Aminoff, A.: Do circular economy business models capture intended environmental value propositions? J. Clean. Prod. **171**, 413–422 (2018)
13. Gebauer, H., Saul, C.J., Haldimann, M., Gustafsson, A.: Organizational capabilities for pay-per-use services in product-oriented companies. Int. J. Prod. Econ. **192**, 157–168 (2015)
14. Bock, M., Wiener, M.: Nonownership business models in the manufacturing industry: the role of uncertainty and the industrial Internet of Things. In: ICIS 2018 Proceedings (2018)

15. Wnuk, K., Murari, B.T.: The impact of Internet of Things on software business models. In: Maglyas, A., Lamprecht, A.-L. (eds.) Software Business. LNBIP, vol. 240, pp. 94–108. Springer, Cham (2016). https://doi.org/10.1007/978-3-319-40515-5_7
16. Metallo, C., Agrifoglio, R., Schiavone, F., Mueller, J.: Understanding business model in the Internet of Things industry. Technol. Forecast. Soc. Change **136**, 298–306 (2018)
17. Osterwalder, A., Pigneur, Y., Tucci, C.L.: Clarifying business models: origins, present, and future of the concept. Commun. Assoc. Inf. Syst. **16**, 1–25 (2005)
18. Amit, R., Zott, C.: Value creation in E-business. Strateg. Manag. J. **22**, 493–520 (2001)
19. Bock, M., Wiener, M., Gronau, R., Martin, A.: Industry 4.0 enabling smart air: digital transformation at KAESER COMPRESSORS. In: Urbach, N., Röglinger, M. (eds.) Digitalization Cases. MP, pp. 101–117. Springer, Cham (2019). https://doi.org/10.1007/978-3-319-95273-4_6
20. Gleich, R., Hypko, P., Tilebein, M.: Clarifying the concept of performance-based contracting in manufacturing industries: a research synthesis. J. Serv. Manag. **21**, 625–655 (2010)
21. Kleemann, F.C., Essig, M.: A providers' perspective on supplier relationships in performance-based contracting. J. Purchasing and Supply Management. **19**, 185–198 (2013)
22. Bigdeli, A.Z., Bustinza, O.F., Vendrell-Herrero, F., Baines, T.: Network positioning and risk perception in servitization: evidence from the UK road transport industry. Int. J. Prod. Res. **56**, 2169–2183 (2018)
23. Visnjic, I., Jovanovic, M., Neely, A., Engwall, M.: What brings the value to outcome-based contract providers? Value drivers in outcome business models. Int. J. Prod. Econo. **192**, 169–181 (2017)
24. Grubic, T., Jennions, I.: Do outcome-based contracts exist? The investigation of power-by-the-hour and similar result-oriented cases. Int. J. Prod. Econ. **206**, 209–219 (2018)
25. Bock, M., Wiener, M.: Towards a taxonomy of digital business models – conceptual dimensions and empirical illustrations. In: ICIS 2017 Proceedings (2017)
26. Liinamaa, J., Viljanen, M., Hurmerinta, A., Ivanova-Gongne, M., Luotola, H., Gustafsson, M.: Performance-based and functional contracting in value-based solution selling. Ind. Mark. Manag. **59**, 37–49 (2016)
27. Bahga, A., Madisetti, V.K.: Blockchain platform for industrial Internet of Things. J. Softw. Eng. Appl. **09**, 533–546 (2016)

Integrating Manufacturing Realities

A Concept to Integrate Manufacturing Execution and Product Data Management Systems

Christian Nigischer(✉), Martin Hennig, and Detlef Gerhard

TU Wien, Wien, Austria
{christian.nigischer,martin.hennig,detlef.gerhard}@tuwien.ac.at

Abstract. Variant rich production of individualized products and customer solutions results in new challenges for all involved industrial information systems in a producing company. To keep pace with the new requirements of a volatile future market and to exploit benefits of flexible digital production environments, it is crucial to adapt integration concepts of Industry 4.0, e.g. enhance information exchangeability by improving interconnectivity between software solutions, utilize all sources of data from a products production and use phase, and maintaining an up-to-date digital twin of the product and production assets.

This paper presents an integration concept for the interaction between Product Data Management (PDM) systems, Manufacturing Execution Systems (MES) and shop floor level client systems. It addresses the gap of information flow between the different involved key software tools in a twofold manner. On the one hand side, specific information gained from production and use phase data of products have to be looped back to the PDM system. This sets the foundation for a better understanding of production planning and execution as well as use phase issues related to the engineering phase where problems have to be addressed for continuous product improvement. On the other hand, a direct information flow from PDM to MES and shop floor clients is defined to enable forwarding of current variant product instance information. To evaluate the practical applicability and additional value of the developed integration concept, a case study with an industry partner is conducted.

Keywords: Product Lifecycle Management · Manufacturing execution · Closed loop information management · Product instance data management · Industry 4.0

1 Introduction

As presented by Khedher et al. [1], data exchange between Product Lifecycle Management (PLM) supporting industrial information systems like PDM systems, Enterprise Resource Planning (ERP) systems and MES is a crucial success factor for producing enterprises acting in today's fast-moving markets. The interconnection of smart devices among each other, but also with the mentioned established information systems, is one of the fundamental ideas of the ongoing efforts within the scope of Industry 4.0. Smart

Published by Springer Nature Switzerland AG 2019
C. Fortin et al. (Eds.): PLM 2019, IFIP AICT 565, pp. 315–324, 2019.
https://doi.org/10.1007/978-3-030-42250-9_30

interconnected products enable permanent communication which allows the collection of product data in all lifecycle stages, but especially during its use phase. With appropriate processing, this data can be used to derive useful conclusions that initiate enhancements in production processes, maintenance tasks and future engineering design processes. To benefit from these new opportunities, interaction points between involved information systems and additional data sources have to be defined to grant flawless information exchange.

While the international standard IEC 62264 [2] based on the ISA-95 specification [3] defines models and transactions for the integration of ERP and MES, a similar standard for direct communication between PDM systems and MES is missing. Furthermore, the collected data from production facilities is often used to optimize production processes but is not passed on to the product development department, which leaves a considerable product optimization potential unused. Therefore, this contribution presents a concept for closed-loop information integration within the PLM environment of producing enterprises. The following section gives a brief overview of the utilized methodology and related research activities. Section 3 presents the developed integration concept, followed by the introduction of the ongoing case studies conducted with industry partners. At the end of Sect. 4 the results that were attained so far are stated and discussed. The contribution closes with a conclusion and gives an outlook in Sect. 5.

2 Integration Challenges, Methodology and Related Work

In PLM there are three major perspectives which are considered when defining a products life cycle, i.e., engineering, production and operation [4].[1]

The engineering aspect of a products lifecycle reaches from conceptual designs to a detailed product definition maintained in many different authoring tools. That diversity in tool landscapes and development methods requires a systematic combination of approaches and tools. The complex outcome has to be managed by a PDM system [5]. The definition of a product's properties nowadays happens predominantly in virtual form and is rarely materialized during engineering using rapid prototyping techniques. The main transition from the virtual product definition to a real product is the scope of the production.

Although production aspects clearly affect a product's definition and vice versa, the two perspectives are somewhat orthogonal to each other. This becomes particularly obvious if the production system has to be developed like a product itself, with a product lifecycle of its own. Production tasks that have to be managed by or interfaced to a PDM system reach from production system conceptualization over operations planning like NC programming to resource and assembly planning tasks, like warehousing, dimensioning of production lines and production resource allocation. A MES has to be linked to an ERP solution to fulfil all tasks of order processing to meet a physical demand for a product. The materialization of a virtual product definition into many physical products can be perceived similar to instantiations of a class in object-oriented programming [6].

[1] From a more environmentally driven lifecycle management point of view, ISO 14040 also considers the acquisition of raw materials, a products distribution as well as its end of life phase. But since these are less relevant for product data this paper does not consider them.

The product instances share all properties, which they inherited from their abstract class – although within the variations that the production process imposes – but they are all independent from each other.

The operation or product use phase is a third perspective which again influences engineering and production and vice versa, but is independent from them as each product instance is operated and maintained differently in a particular environment and context. This is the case for mass produced end consumer items as well as specialized high-tech equipment for industrial applications. Information management for operations is often neglected in PDM environments. For certain products, this management task is outsourced to a dedicated maintenance, repair and overhaul (MRO) system and for a number of other products it is handled by after-sales services of ERP systems. Figure 1 shows the mentioned 3 orthogonal perspectives. The right part of the illustration points out the independence of every product instance concerning all considered perspectives.

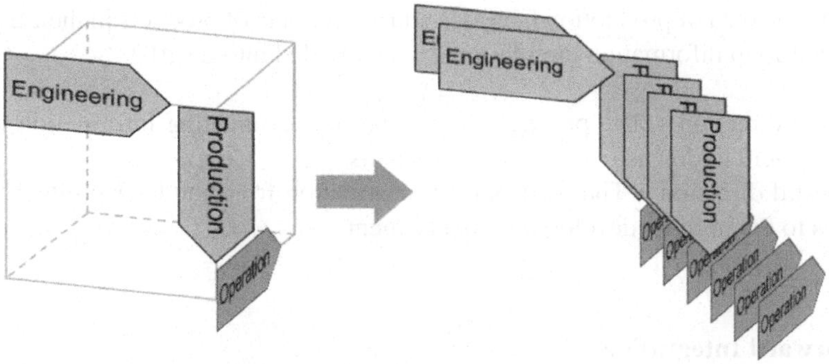

Fig. 1. Engineering, production and operation as three orthogonal perspectives on the products lifecycle. As the product is materialized, used and maintained multiple times independently there are multiple instances of each perspective. From [4]

If problems occur during the use phase of a product, the customer complaint typically traverses different departments in the organizational structure of the manufacturer before the engineering department is involved. A closer link of product instance data to the PDM system, which is the linchpin for data authored in engineering and production, would offer great opportunities to shorten problem solving intervals, provide accurate maintenance scheduling based on current operational data and to initiate continuous product engineering improvements through downstream insights.

This introduces a challenge for modern PDM systems and also points to the need for a methodology to determine which information has to be collected and fed back into a PDM system [4]. An integrated information feedback loop from production and operations back to a PDM system would be a solution but still leaves problems to be addressed, e.g. how to derive product class indicators and necessary change activities from individualized product instance information.

To date, there are not that many research activities which address a direct integration between PDM systems and manufacturing execution. Khedher et al. [1] present an integration concept using a mediation system based on ontologies and web services to interlink data of both systems. The work in this paper takes another step forward and does not only consider data linking, but also processing of manufacturing and operational data from a product's use phase to generate useful information that can be fed back to a PDM system. Gerhard [4] delivers important conceptual starting points for the integration concept introduced in this contribution. D'Antonio et al. [7] stated advantages of a PLM-MES integration and conducted a survey among Italian companies to confirm the interest in such an integration.

3 Integration Concept

To overcome the problems of outdated, locally stored product information and to be able to benefit from the available data collected during different lifecycle phases, it seems necessary to define new data exchange channels between involved information systems. The goal of the developed concept is to establish a closed-loop information flow between the involved information systems and to integrate other data sources such as production data of production facilities and sensor data of products in their use phase. The closed-loop information circulation can be divided into 2 parts:

- Forward direction – The propagation of relevant engineering information from the PDM system to downstream recipient systems
- Backward direction – The feedback of information from the later product lifecycle phases to the product development department

3.1 Forward Integration

The typical information flow in modern producing enterprises from the PDM level down to the shop floor is described in [8] and depicted in Fig. 2. At the shop floor level, product instantiation takes place and production or assembly resources also impart some information to the manufactured product instance, e.g. the firmware of a control unit. Shop floor production resources report production parameters like production times, amount of produced parts, etc. to the MES. MES forwards relevant information to ERP and creates production performance indicators that help to identify optimization potentials concerning the production process. ERP also generates performance indicators based on feedback from MES, Customer-Relations Management (CRM) tools and other systems. If there are engineering relevant incidents, ERP triggers an engineering change request workflow in PDM [9]. These basic upstream information flows are depicted as blank arrows in Fig. 2.

A widespread problem within industrial applications of these information exchange processes is often data actuality and accuracy. Delays in information propagation lead to outdated information in the downstream processes. As a result, avoidable mistakes occur and cause costly corrective actions. The forward integration idea is to avoid that problem by eliminating some data forwarding processes. Instead, necessary engineering information is directly propagated to the target systems. Up-to-date versions of CAD models, assembly instructions and soft- or firmware iterations can be retrieved from PDM using a direct information channel.

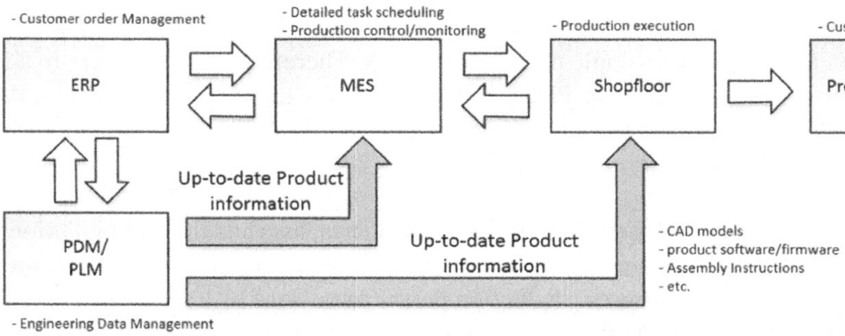

Fig. 2. Conceptual depiction of the forward integration

There are several important challenges establishing such direct channels that have to be addressed accordingly:

- All relevant product information has to be stored in PDM – no separate non-synchronized information storage in downstream information systems is allowed to avoid the usage of outdated information.
- The provided information must be easily updatable. Therefore, information has to be displayed in electronic form on a screen, no printed hard copy or locally saved document is needed.
- A feedback system has to be provided to information recipients to report errors or make improvement suggestions.

In general, a modern PDM system provides all necessary technical functionality to tackle the mentioned challenges. The first point has to be anchored in the organizational structures and the work processes of the enterprise. PDM has to be accepted as the central product information repository. All relevant and required information on product class and product instance level has to be managed in PDM. Presentation of the information can be done via thin clients running in a standard web browser on various devices, like computer terminals, handhelds, tablets, smart phones, etc. This ensures low efforts for deployment and roll-out. The possibility to give feedback can be realized via PDM workflows, triggered via the thin client.

3.2 Backward Integration

The main goal of the backward integration is to use data collected during the manufacturing processes and also the operation phase of a product to identify improvement potentials for next generation development projects and maintenance aspects. Figure 3 shows the involved information systems and a product instance.

A data analytics platform is used to generate valuable insights for product development from gathered data of production planning, production and product use (operation). The platform offers a data lake for data storage, analyzes different types of data, and calculates key indicators that are forwarded to PDM. These calculated parameters are referenced to 2 different types of information objects – product class (or product type) and product instance (or product entity). PDM data structures are usually designed to operate with product classes, not with single product instances. Therefore, it is necessary to add product instance data structures in PDM. Figure 4 depicts the mappings between the involved data structures in the data analytics platform and PDM. The different mappings are explained in the following:

A: This mapping keeps track of the link between product classes and their instantiations. It can be implemented by creating a snapshot copy of the product's class valid at the time of production. The identification of production parts can be done by a serial number and brought-in parts can be identified with their respective batch number or serial number. This mapping represents a 1:n mapping from one product class to many instantiations. As the product instance matures, the product class can mature, too. With a new production release, a product class may change. New product instances have to be mapped to the revised class and also can have new and matured properties.

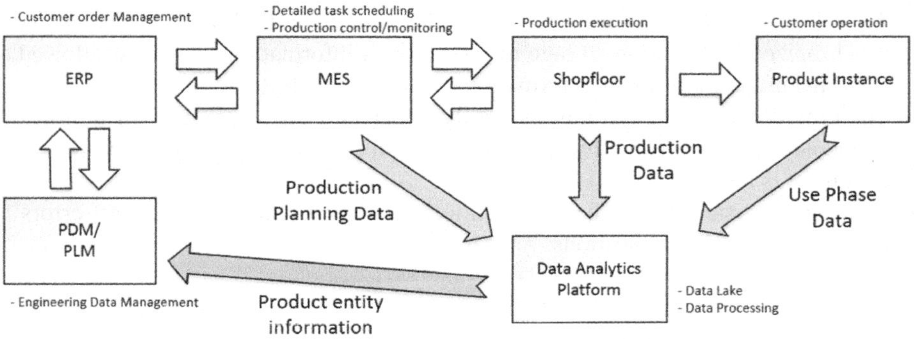

Fig. 3. Conceptual depiction of the backward integration

B: As the sensors of each product instance are connected to the data analytics platform, their data (e.g. time series) is stored as semi-structured data in a data lake and identified by a hash code. Within the platform, the stored data is mapped to individual structural data elements called assets. Assets represent a physical entity in the virtual space. The asset structure is not as deep and complete as the Bill of Materials (BOM) but it offers enough structure to link streams of sensor data to an appropriate position in a product's structure.

C: This mapping is the actual link from product instances in PDM to its structured asset data collection in the analytics platform. If there is an issue with a product instance, the manufacturer can look up the products individual as-build BOM in PDM and visualize current and historical data from the products sensors and data sources. Ideally, the data collection offers visualizations to support the identification of trends and anomalies.

D: To generalize conclusions from product instance data streams to a product class, an aggregation of data sources over all surveyed instances has to be realized. This aggregation can be as simple as showing basic statistics (e.g. mean, variance, distribution parameters) but also advanced like cluster identification, self-learned correlations of product data (e.g. operating hours and bearing temperatures) and sophisticated like pattern recognition for cause and effect analysis. The ability to offer these insights at a scalable level is one of the key arguments of using a data analytics platform.

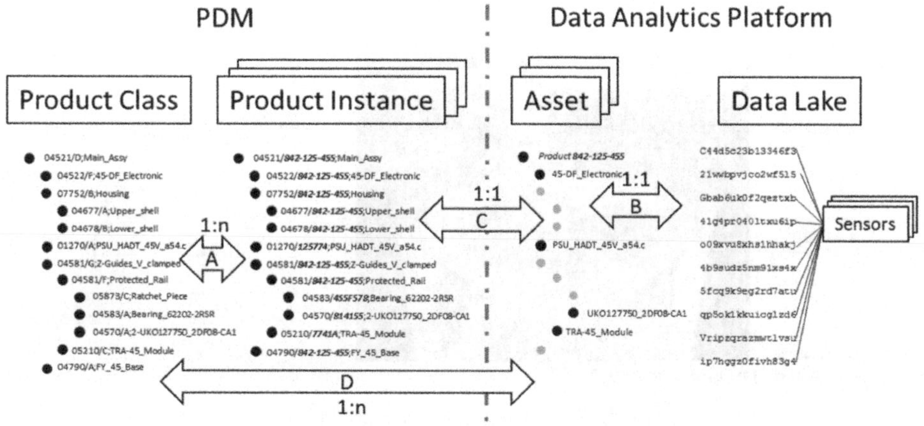

Fig. 4. Mapping of data structures in the backward integration

4 Use Cases

The following subsections give a brief overview of the use cases currently conducted in a research project of the authors together with industry partners to evaluate the feasibility of the introduced concept.

4.1 Forward Integration

A research survey of state-of-the-art solutions found that there is already a tool for the intended concept. Forwarding manufacturing and assembly information of high variance products from PDM to MES or shop floor terminals can be done by Cortona3D and Teamcenter. The software package is also known as "rapid author" and is usually used to derive detailed and visual documentations and publications from CAD data, such as customer manuals, professional maintenance instructions, training material, animated video or HTML for online publication. Being integrated into the Siemens ecosystem of PLM software Cortona3D offers an integration to Teamcenter [10]. The integration allows the import of CAD models from Teamcenter in Cortona3D and the attachment of Cortona3D-based work instructions to a Bill of Processes in Teamcenter manufacturing and production planning modules.

The goal of the use case is to document the extruder assembly process of a 3D FDM printer (shown in Fig. 5), which is produced as demonstration product at the TU Wien Pilot Factory Industry 4.0 [8]. This product can be configured with different options and dimensions, which leads to variant rich assembly processes. Cortona3D is used to build a digital documentation based on the current variant without the need to create new production drawings and assembly instruction. This documentation is visualized using the Teamcenter Active Workspace thin client. The only technical restriction for an end device to use the Active Workspace user interface is an up-to-date web browser. [11]

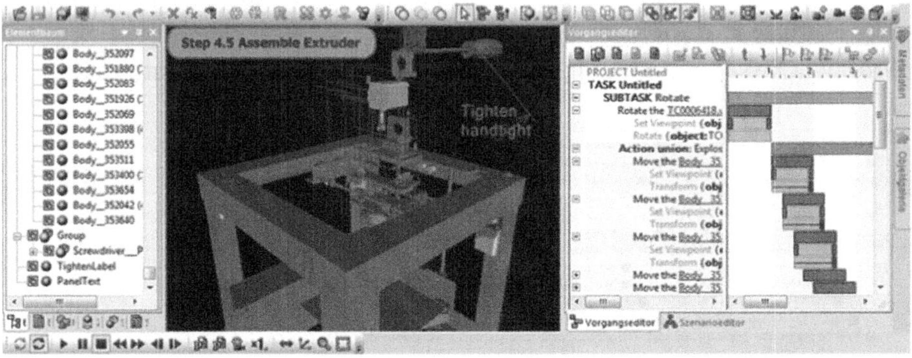

Fig. 5. Screenshot of an assembly process

4.2 Backward Integration

The use case for the backward integration concept is demonstrated by the integration of a machining center located in the TU Wien Pilot Factory. This is an excellent example as it covers aspects of the production and operation phase. The machining center delivers production data for various products, but is also a product itself and is developed and improved continuously based on insights from its utilization. Since the manufacturer of the machining center is partner of the research project, all relevant engineering data of the machining center is accessible for the use case.

Figure 6 illustrates the data and information flow between the machining center, the data analytics platform and the PDM system. The machining center is directly connected to Mindsphere – an industrial data analytics platform developed by Siemens – via Sinumerik interface, using the Manage MyMachines application to link a real-world asset to Mindsphere. Data points are stored in the data lake of the analytics platform. In the backward integration use case, there are two self-programmed applications to generate useful insights. A backend data processing application is doing the analytics, while a frontend visualization application generates graphical representations of the processed outcomes. The visualized information is then linked to the corresponding product instance or product class structures in Teamcenter using a web service developed in the project. The information retrieved from the data analytics platform can be used to trigger engineering change requests or maintenance tasks. One example of such information is the interrelation of bearing temperatures with different operational states of the main spindle. This information can be used for constructive improvements or the determination of optimal maintenance intervals.

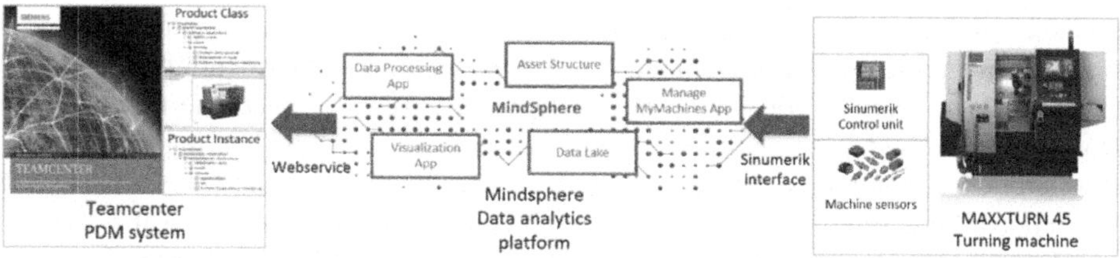

Fig. 6. Backward integration use case

Mindsphere also allows data exchange with other information systems using the MindConnect library [12]. A next step to realize the backward integration concept to its full extent would be to gather production data from the MES system as well and use it for calculations in Mindsphere, too.

4.3 Results

Both use cases are currently subject of an ongoing research project. While the concepts for both integration directions are defined, the implementation works are still in progress. Currently, the focus is put on the implementation of the backward integration in the environment of the TU Wien Pilot Factory Industry 4.0. Nonetheless, some interim results in terms of experiences made during the implementation works can already be presented here.

Mindsphere seems to be a powerful data analytics platform but has some restrictions:

- The time interval for collecting data points is limited to a few seconds in Mindsphere. For smaller intervals, an additional edge computing device has to be used.
- The limited structuring options in Mindsphere do not allow a comprehensive representation of product structures out-of-the-box. E.g. inheritance of parameters is not implemented in the Sinumerik asset type used for direct interconnectivity.
- Teamcenter is currently not able to manage product instance information out-of-the-box. Although most of the functionalities for product classes can also be applied to product instances, some crucial aspects are missing, e.g. specialized product instance elements and "derived" relations that connect product instance elements with their parent product class elements.

5 Conclusion and Outlook

The research done in the presented project shows that recent PDM systems provide only cumbersome support for managing product instance information. Recording and storing as-build structures of individualized product instances is a valuable basis for engineering changes on complex high-variant products. The sheer amount of data that comes along with product instance management in PDM has also to be addressed appropriately.

There are several challenges concerning information retrieval from raw sensor data of physical products. Different measuring intervals and accuracy complicate data analyses, but the combination of various parameters is necessary to receive meaningful information that enables engineering improvement. Another big factor is the frequency of information feedback. While some propagation is clearly event-based, e.g. machine failures, other processing-intense repetitive tasks, e.g. the comparison of spindle bearing temperatures as a function of parameters like spindle torque, speed, operating mode, etc., using data from all available product instances, have to be limited to a feasible interval.

The technical requirements to realize the forward integration approach presented above are already met by state-of-the-art PDM systems. The biggest challenge here is to create acceptance for PDM as the single central product information repository.

References

1. Khedher, A.B., Henry, S., Bouras, A.: Integration between MES and product lifecycle management. In: IEEE International Conference on Emerging Technologies and Factory Automation ETFA 2011, Toulouse, France, p. 8 (2011). https://doi.org/10.1109/etfa.2011.6058993
2. International Standard IEC 62264:2013 Enterprise-control system integration, Geneva, Switzerland (2013)
3. Brandl, D.L., Brandl, D.E.: Plant IT Integration Information Technology into Automated Manufacturing. Momentum Press, New York (2012). https://doi.org/10.5643/9781606504338
4. Gerhard, D.: Product lifecycle management challenges of CPPS. In: Biffl, S., Lüder, A., Gerhard, D. (eds.) Multi-disciplinary Engineering for Cyber-Physical Production Systems, pp. 89–110. Springer, Cham (2017). https://doi.org/10.1007/978-3-319-56345-9_4
5. National Standard: VDI 2206: Entwicklungsmethodik für mechatronische Systeme. VDI-Verlag, Düsseldorf (2004)
6. Hribernik, K.A., Rabe, L., Thoben, K.D., Schumacher, J.: The product avatar as a product-instance-centric information management concept. Int. J. Product Lifecycle Manag. **1**(4), 367–379 (2006)
7. D'Antonio, G., Macheda, L., Sauza Bedolla, J., Chiabert, P.: PLM-MES integration to support industry 4.0. In: 14th IFIP WG 5.1 International Conference (PLM 2017), Seville, Spain, pp. 129–137 (2017)
8. Hennig, M., Reisinger, G., Trautner, T., Hold, P., Gerhard, D., Mazak, A.: TU Wien pilot factory industry 4.0. In: 9th Conference on Learning Factories 2019, Braunschweig, Germany. Elsevier (2019)
9. Nadia, B., Gregory, G., Vince, T.: Engineering change request management in a new product development process. Eur. J. Innov. Manag. **9**, 5–19 (2006)
10. Cortona3D: Rapidauthor. http://www.cortona3d.com/en/rapidauthor. Accessed Feb 2019
11. Siemens Product Lifecycle Management Software Inc.: Active workspace. https://www.plm.automation.siemens.com/global/de/products/collaboration/active-workspace.html. Accessed Feb 2019
12. Siemens AG: MindConnect library. https://developer.mindsphere.io/resources/mindconnect-lib/resources-mclib-overview.html. Accessed Feb 2019

Disassembly Process Planning Under End-of-Life Product Quality

M.-Lounes Bentaha[1(✉)], Alexandre Voisin[2], and Pascale Marangé[2]

[1] Université Lyon 2, DISP Laboratory (EA 4570), Lyon, France
mohand.bentaha@univ-lyon2.fr

[2] Université de Lorraine, CRAN, UMR CNRS 7039, Nancy, France
{alexandre.voisin,pascale.marange}@univ-lorraine.fr

Abstract. Quality of post-consumer products is one of the major sources of uncertainty in disassembly systems. This paper presents a decision tool for disassembly process planning under variability of the End-of-Life product quality. The objective is to maximize the profit of the disassembly process. This latter is the difference between the revenue generated by recovered parts and the cost of the disassembly tasks. The revenue of a product (subassembly, component) depends on its quality. The proposed approach helps to take decisions about the best disassembly process and the depth of disassembly, depending on the quality of the products to be disassembled. Industrial applicability and interest are shown using an industrial case focused on the remanufacturing of mechatronic parts in the automotive industry.

Keywords: Sustainable manufacturing · Product recovery · Disassembly · Quality uncertainty management · Decision support system

1 Introduction

Reverse logistics and its processes are nowadays well accepted and understood. In addition, it is well understood that ease materials recycling, reuse and remanufacturing constitute critical factors for sustainable competitiveness [12]. Remanufacturing is a key enabler technology [8,10] not only for sustainable development but as well for economic and social developments. As such, it addresses the 3 pillars of sustainability, i.e. Economic, Social, and Environmental.

The process of re-manufacturing requires to disassemble; to clean; to inspect, diagnose and sort; to re-condition and to re-assemble [4,11]. When considering "systems", with several sub-systems as cars, computers, etc., a prior step to disassembly is required in order to diagnose the defect and remaining functionalities [9]. Such prior step is a pre-require since returned products are subject to highly variable condition [3,6]. It leads to uncertainty and high variability in the disassembly step while other steps remain less impacted. Disassembly lines

C. Fortin et al. (Eds.): PLM 2019, IFIP AICT 565, pp. 325–335, 2019.
https://doi.org/10.1007/978-3-030-42250-9_31

remain artisanal with versatile workstations at the expense of efficiency. In order to consider disassembly at an industrial level, one has to tackle these variability and uncertainty in returned product quality.

The present paper considers the disassembly process as an industrial process. In such a way, a single type of product is considered as input flow of the disassembly process. Such hypothesis seems realistic when considering mass products such as automobiles, cell phones, laptops, refrigerators, etc. Hence, the disassembly process cannot be considered as an artisanal-work manner as is currently. Thus, disassembly process has to be planned in advance and its financial viability has to be demonstrated. This work proposes a tool in order to define the optimal disassembly depth/level of a product regarding the profit. The originality of the proposed approach is to consider the health state of the product, its parts and sub-parts in the revenue estimation as random variables. The state of a part allows to decide its re-cycling: maintenance, re-use, regeneration or raw material recycling [7]. The re-cycling of a product impacts in a non-linear way its resale price. The recycling decision requires a quantification of the part capacity to re-enter a cycle. For such a purpose, we introduce the Remaining Usage Potential (RUP).

The economical optimization of the disassembly process considers the cost of the disassembly tasks and the revenue of the resale of the disassembled parts. The latter is highly dependent on the re-entering usage cycle whose decision is based on the RUP. The RUPs of a product and its parts are considered as distributions since we consider mass recycling.

This paper is structured as follows. A formal description of the studied problem is presented in Sect. 2. Section 3 presents the developed model along with the solution approach. Numerical experiments and optimization results are presented in Sect. 4. Section 5 concludes the paper with future research directions.

2 Problem Definition and Modeling

In this work, we consider a remanufacturing process where the revenue from retrieved parts (subassemblies and components) depends on the quality of the incoming return products. For an End-of-Life product, the problem consists on the selection of a best disassembly process alternative, among all possible ones, taking into account its RUP and precedence relationships amongst all disassembly tasks and product parts obtained during the disassembly process.

The following assumptions are used. A single type End-of-Life product has to be partially (or completely) disassembled. All received items contain all initial parts with no addition or removing of components. In the case of industrialized disassembly, as it is for remanufacturing systems, this hypothesis seems realistic when a large percentage of products arrive in these conditions. Each component or subassembly has a resale value which represents its revenue. This revenue depends on the quality of the corresponding component or subassembly. The state or quality of each subassembly is modeled using the concept of RUP which follows a probability distribution. In the optics of industrialized disassembly, i.e. a large number of products of the same category are returned, to obtain such a probability distribution, statistical studies on disassembled products can be conducted.

2.1 *And/or* Graph

All possible disassembly process alternatives of an End-of-Life product, along with the precedence relationships among tasks and product subassemblies and components, are modeled explicitly using an *and/or* graph [1] (see Fig. 1).

Each subassembly is represented by a node labeled $A_k, k \in K$. For a simplification reason of the *and/or* graph, the components generated by all disassembly tasks are not explicitly represented in the graph. Each node labeled $B_i, i \in I$, represents a disassembly task. Two types of arcs define the precedence relations between subassemblies and disassembly tasks: *and* and *or*. The first type imposes a mandatory precedence relation and the second type is employed for optional precedence dependencies. A sink node 'S' is introduced and linked with dummy arcs to all the disassembly tasks to model the case of partial disassembly (Fig. 1). For a detailed description of the *and/or* graph modeling process, see [2,5].

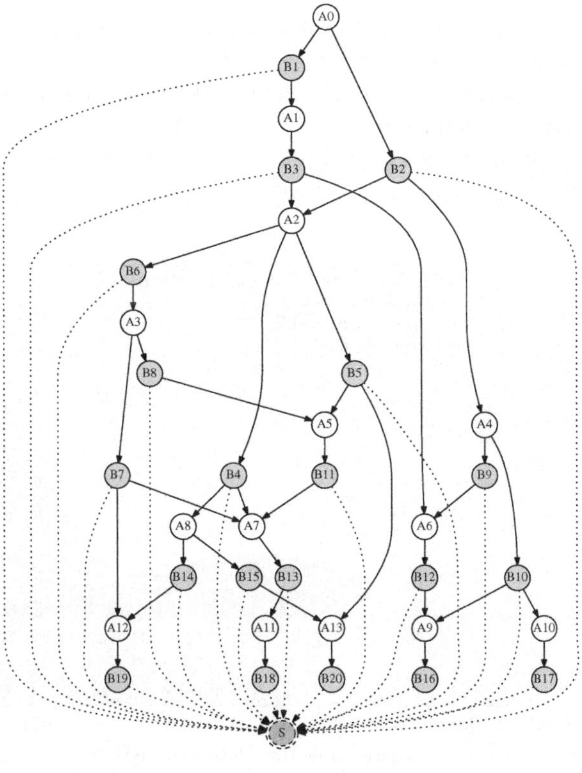

Fig. 1. *And/or* graph of the ball point pen example [1].

2.2 Remaining Usage Potential and Its Probability Density Function

In order to assess the state to be considered for disassembly, we defined the Remaining Usage Potential (RUP). The RUP stands for the "usage" quantity remaining for a product or a part. In our proposition, the RUP is evaluated *prior* to the disassembly. The RUP is evaluated on a $[0, 1]$ scale; 1 corresponds to the product state at the beginning of its exploitation (the product is at its maximal RUP); 0 means that the product/part has reached its end of life and has to be recycled as raw material.

The RUP is modeled as a probability density function since this study considers a mass disassembly process. As such, the number of products to be considered is high and the RUP shall be considered in a statistical way. We consider the RUP as a normal probability density function truncated in 0 and 1. The RUP follows a truncated normal distribution on $[0, 1]$ with μ and σ parameters: RUP $\rightsquigarrow \mathcal{N}_{[0,1]}(\mu, \sigma)$; μ and σ are respectively the mean and standard deviation of the original non truncated normal distribution. Figure 2 shows, over $[0, 1]$ interval, 3 truncated normal distribution functions with parameters: $(\mu = 0, \sigma = 0.2)$, $(\mu = 0.5, \sigma = 0.3)$ and $(\mu = 1, \sigma = 0.2)$. Curves in Fig. 2 shall stand for the RUP of either a product, a part (component) or a sub-part (subassembly):

- The yellow curve, with $\mu = 0$ and $\sigma = 0.2$, shows a heavily worm part whose RUP is statistically low.
- The blue curve, with $\mu = 1$ and $\sigma = 0.2$, shows a slightly used part whose RUP is statistically high.
- The red curve in the middle, with $\mu = 0.5$ and $\sigma = 0.3$, shows a middle term part whose RUP is statistically average.

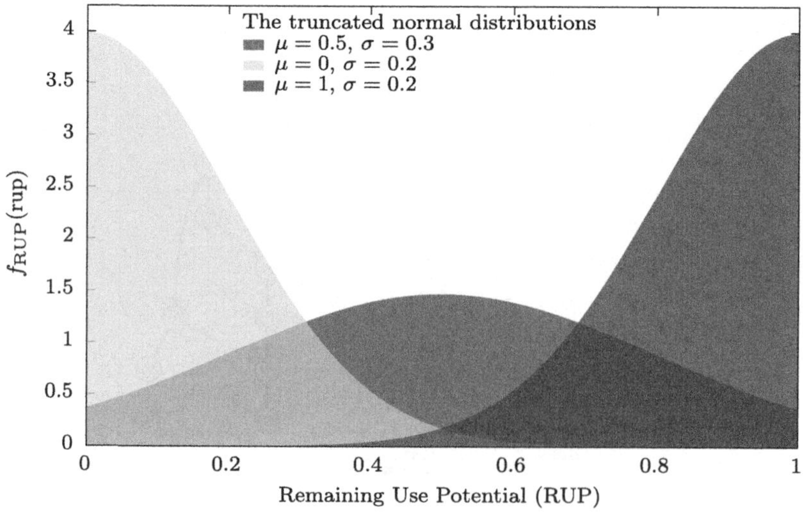

Fig. 2. RUP distribution examples as normal distributions truncated on [0, 1]. (Color figure online)

2.3 Part Revenue with Respect to Its RUP

Since the items have not the same RUP, their resale prices have to be considered as functions of their RUPs. The resale price represents the revenue (R_e) due to recycling recovery of disassembly items. Obviously, the higher the RUP, the higher the revenue. We defined the revenue R_e as a function of the RUP: $R_e(\text{RUP})$. In addition, we assume that the resale price is bounded. The upper bound corresponds to the resale price of an "almost new" used item. Indeed, it is not realistic to consider the sale price as upper bound since as soon as an item is used it depreciates. The lower bound corresponds to the resale price of the raw material of the item. The upper bound, resp. the lower one, corresponds to $R_e(\text{RUP} = 1) = b$, resp. $R_e(\text{RUP} = 0) = a$, with $b > a > 0$. We defined 3 cases for R_e according to the RUP, with the corresponding definition of $R_e(\text{RUP})$:

- The first case considers a linear RUP revenue function, i.e. R_e is proportional to the item's RUP: $R_e = (b - a) \cdot \text{RUP} + a$, affine function.
- The second case considers a rapid growth of the R_e revenue according to the item's RUP with a stabilization when the item's RUP becomes medium. Such a R_e revenue variation is modeled with a root function. Such a case means that the re-sale price of an item remains hight the long "RUP" term despite the drop of the RUP: $R_e = (b - a) \cdot \sqrt[4]{\text{RUP}} + a$, root function.
- The third one considers R_e low for low and medium RUP levels and increases rapidly for high levels of the RUP:
$R_e = e^{\frac{1}{e-1}\left(e\ln(a)-\ln(b)\right)} e^{\frac{1}{e-1}\left(\ln(b)-\ln(a)\right)e^{\text{RUP}}}$, exponential function.

2.4 Part Revenue Probability Density Function

Combining the RUP probability density function with the part revenue function gives the part revenue probability density function. For the 3 R_e functions presented above, the corresponding probability density functions are:

$$f_{R_e}(r_e) = \frac{1}{b-a} \frac{\phi(\mu, \sigma, \frac{r_e - a}{b-a})}{\Phi(\mu,\sigma,1) - \Phi(\mu,\sigma,0)} \mathbb{I}_{[a,b]} \qquad \textbf{(pdf-affine)}$$

$$f_{R_e}(r_e) = \frac{4}{(b-a)^4} (r_e - a)^3 \frac{\phi(\mu, \sigma, (\frac{r_e - a}{b-a})^4)}{\Phi(\mu,\sigma,1) - \Phi(\mu,\sigma,0)} \mathbb{I}_{[a,b]} \qquad \textbf{(pdf-root)}$$

$$f_{R_e}(r_e) = \frac{1}{r_e\,(\ln(r_e) - \alpha)} \frac{\phi(\mu, \sigma, \ln(\frac{\ln(r_e) - \alpha}{\beta}))}{\Phi(\mu,\sigma,1) - \Phi(\mu,\sigma,0)} \mathbb{I}_{[a,b]} \qquad \textbf{(pdf-expo)}$$

where $\alpha = \dfrac{1}{e-1}\,(e\ln(a) - \ln(b))$ and $\beta = \dfrac{1}{e-1}(\ln(b) - \ln(a))$;

$e = 2.71828 \cdots$ is the Euler's constant

$\phi(\mu, \sigma, x) = \frac{1}{\sigma\sqrt{2\pi}} e^{-\frac{1}{2\sigma^2}(x-\mu)^2}$ defines the normal probability density function of mean μ and standard deviation σ and $\Phi(\mu, \sigma, \cdot)$ defines its cumulative distribution function. We consider 3 cases for the RUP distribution, i.e. RUP $\rightsquigarrow \mathcal{N}_{[0,1]}(\mu, \sigma)$, according to the part quality (see Fig. 2): bad ($\mu = 0, \sigma = 0.2$), medium ($\mu = 0.5, \sigma = 0.3$) and good ($\mu = 1, \sigma = 0.2$).

3 Optimization Model and Solution Approach

To model the defined disassembly process planning problem, the following notations are introduced.

3.1 Adopted Notation

A_k : a subassembly: $k \in K$;
B_i : a disassembly task: $i \in I$;
c_i : cost of disassembly task B_i, $i \in I$: $c_i = c \cdot t_i, \forall i \in I$; t_i is the processing time of task B_i and c is a fixed cost per disassembly time unit, $i \in I$;
D_ℓ : set of indices of tasks disassembling subassembly $\ell, \ell \in L$;
G_ℓ : set of indices of tasks generating subassembly or component $\ell, \ell \in L$;
I : set of disassembly task indices: $I = \{1, 2, \ldots, \mathsf{N}\}$, $\mathsf{N} \in \mathbb{N}^*$;
K : set of indices for the generated subassemblies: $K = \{0, 1, \ldots, \mathsf{K}\}$, $\mathsf{K} \in \mathbb{N}$;
L : set of all product part indices (subassemblies and components): $L = \{1, 2, \ldots, \mathsf{L}\}$, $\mathsf{L} \in \mathbb{N}^*$;
L_i : set of indices of retrieved subassemblies and components by the execution of disassembly task $B_i, i \in I$;
P_k : set of indices of A_k predecessors, $k \in K$: $P_k = \{i |\ B_i \text{ precedes } A_k\}$;
$\widetilde{Re_\ell}$: revenue generated by a subassembly or component $\ell, \ell \in L$, where $\widetilde{Re_\ell}$ is a function of $\widetilde{\mathrm{RUP}_\ell}$: $\widetilde{Re_\ell}(\widetilde{\mathrm{RUP}_\ell})$, $\ell \in L$; $\widetilde{\mathrm{RUP}_\ell}$ represents the remaining usage potential of a subassembly or component $\ell, \ell \in L$;
S_k : set of indices of A_k successors, $k \in K$: $S_k = \{i |\ A_k \text{ precedes } B_i\}$.

3.2 Decision Variables

$$x_i = \begin{cases} 1, & \text{if disassembly task } B_i, i \in I \text{ is selected;} \\ 0, & \text{otherwise.} \end{cases}$$

$$y_\ell = \begin{cases} 0, & \text{if } \sum_{i \in G_\ell} x_i = 1, \ell \in L \text{ and } \sum_{i \in D_\ell} x_i = 1 \ (\ell \text{ subassembly});\\ 1, & \text{otherwise.} \end{cases}$$

Variable $y_\ell, \ell \in L$ means: for a subassembly with index $\ell \in L$, if a disassembly task with index $i, i \in G_\ell$ which generates ℓ is chosen and, next, another disassembly task $j, j \in D_\ell$, of the same disassembly process alternative, which disassembles it is also chosen, then its revenue $\widetilde{Re_\ell}$ is not taken into account while calculating the revenue of the whole disassembly process.

3.3 Objective Function and Constraints

The objective is to determine a disassembly process alternative with the maximum profit while considering the quality or states of the subassemblies and components generated during the disassembly process. The objective function and associated constraints are formulated as follows:

$$\max\left\{\sum_{i\in I}\sum_{\ell\in L_i}\widetilde{R_{e\ell}}\cdot y_\ell\cdot x_i-\sum_{i\in I}c_i\cdot x_i\right\} \tag{1}$$

s.t.

$$\sum_{i\in S_0} x_i = 1 \tag{2}$$

$$\sum_{i\in S_k} x_i \leqslant \sum_{i\in P_k} x_i, \forall k \in K\backslash\{0\} \tag{3}$$

$$\text{If } \sum_{i\in D_\ell} x_i = 1 \text{ and } \sum_{i\in G_\ell} x_i = 1 \text{ then } y_\ell = 0, \forall \ell \in L\,(\ell \text{ subassembly}) \tag{4}$$

$$y_\ell = 1, \forall \ell \in L\,(\ell \text{ component}) \tag{5}$$

$$x_i, y_\ell \in \{0,1\}, \forall i \in I, \forall \ell \in L \tag{6}$$

The terms of the objective function represent, respectively, the earned profit of retrieved parts and the cost of the corresponding disassembly tasks. Precedence constraints, partial disassembly and possible values of the decision variables are defined by constraints (2)–(6).

3.4 Solution Approach

In order to solve the developed model, we consider different values of the revenue $\widetilde{R_{e\ell}}, \forall \ell \in L$, where ℓ represents a subassembly or a component. These values depend on: $\widehat{\mu}_\ell$ (mean of $\widetilde{R_{e\ell}}$) and $\widehat{\sigma}_\ell$ (standard deviation of $\widetilde{R_{e\ell}}$), $\forall \ell \in L$.

Concretely, 3 values of $\widetilde{R_{e\ell}}, \forall \ell \in L$ will be considered: $R_{e\ell} = \widehat{\mu}_\ell$ and $R_{e\ell} = \widehat{\mu}_\ell \pm \widehat{\sigma}_\ell$, $\forall \ell \in L$. The values of $\widehat{\mu}_\ell$ and $\widehat{\sigma}_\ell$ of the revenue $\widetilde{R_{e\ell}}$ of each subassembly and component $\ell, \ell \in L$, are calculated using numerical integrations. Subsequently, the obtained problems will be solved using the IBM solver CPLEX 12.6.

4 Numerical Illustration: Application to an Industrial Case

Model (1)–(6) is implemented in Linux using C++ on a PC with 8×CPU 2.80 GHz and 32 Go RAM. It is solved using ILOG CPLEX 12.6. It is applied to a case product in the automotive part remanufacturing: a Knorr-Bremse EBS 1 Channel Module. Such a product is composed of at least 45 components; see here for detailed example of End-of-Life EBS 1 Channel Module disassembly.

Figure 3 represents its *and/or* graph and gathers the obtained optimization results for different values of $R_{e\ell}, \ell \in L$. The obtained results can be summarized as follows: the profit of the disassembly process depends not only on the sequence and level of disassembly but also on the state or quality of the product. In fact, profit is the difference between revenues (R_e) of the components and/or subassemblies and costs c_i of the disassembly tasks. As disassembly costs are known and fixed, then the profit in our case depends mainly on the revenues of the components and/or subassemblies. Revenues are random and they are functions of states of the components and subassemblies. Thus, the profit of the disassembly process depends on the sequence and level of disassembly of the product. The level of disassembly is itself dependent on the states (quality) of the components and subassemblies.

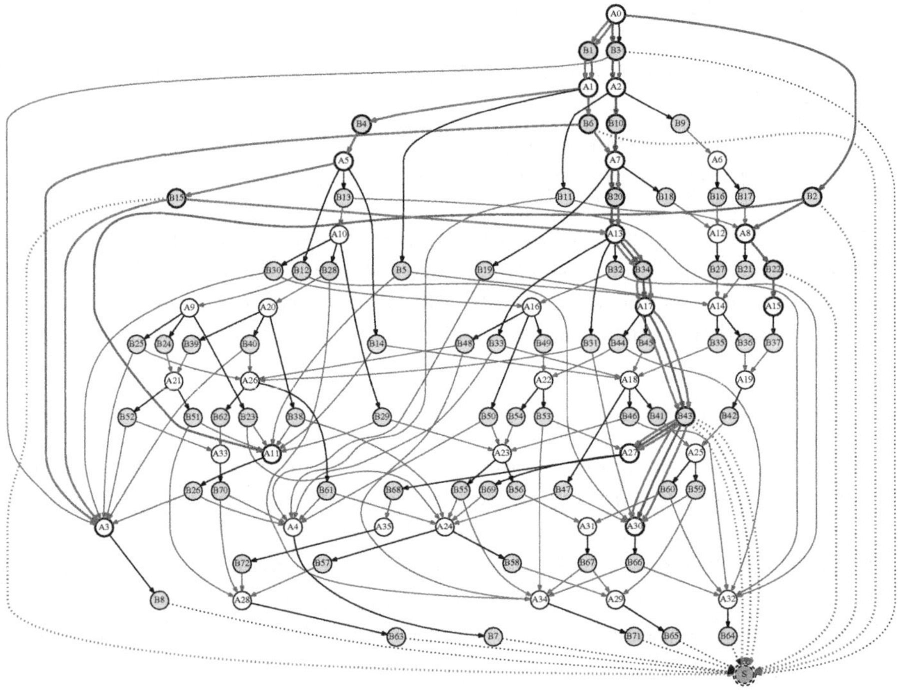

Fig. 3. Alternatives and disassembly levels returned according to the type of revenue functions: EBS 1 Module.

Figure 3 shows in detail the alternative and the level of disassembly returned for each revenue function type of components and subassemblies. In order to identify easily the disassembly alternatives in Fig. 3, a color is assigned to each alternative as shown in Table 1. Table 2 illustrates the obtained disassembly alternative and objective value for each type of revenue function and each value of this revenue ($R_{e\ell}, \forall \ell \in L$). The results, as example, show that for the same

Table 1. Colors representing all obtained disassembly alternatives.

Disassembly alternative	Alternative color	
B_2 B_{22}		EBS 1 Module
B_1 B_4 B_{15} B_{34} B_{43}		
B_3 B_{10} B_{20} B_{34} B_{43}		
B_1 B_6 B_{20} B_{34} B_{43}		

Table 2. Obtained disassembly alternatives and their objective values (cents €).

	$R_{e\ell} = \widehat{\mu}_\ell$	$R_{e\ell} = \widehat{\mu}_\ell - \widehat{\sigma}_\ell$	$R_{e\ell} = \widehat{\mu}_\ell + \widehat{\sigma}_\ell$	
Affine	63550.2	54146.7	72953.7	EBS 1 Module
Root	72710.7	69702.4	76084.2	
Expo	26689.4	6782.7	46828.7	

alternative and the same level of disassembly, values of the corresponding profits depend on the type of the revenue functions considered. These objective values are relatively important for functions of type root, relatively low for functions of type expo and are rather average for functions of type affine.

The results of this section show the applicability of the developed optimization model and solution approach in real disassembly context. Indeed, the computational time is short enough (maximum solution time is less than 5 s) to give to the decision maker the opportunity to generate different disassembly alternatives depending on the profit expected from the retrieved parts. The profit itself depends on the quality of the products. This model helps to make a decision on the disassembly alternative to be retained as disassembly process. Therefore, the choice between complete or partial disassembly can be made on the basis of the economic arguments.

5 Conclusion

To define effective disassembly and derive the economic benefits of the disassembly process, product quality uncertainty must be taken into account. In order to provide an answer to this expectation, we presented in this work a decision tool on the disassembly process planning taking into consideration the quality of the products to be disassembled. The quality of a product is modeled using the Remaining Usage Potential (RUP) concept. RUP models the amount of use remaining before disassembling a product (or subassembly). At the beginning of the operation phase of a product, RUP has a value of 1; a value 0 of RUP means that the product must undergo a recycling of its material. The RUP is taken as a random variable with known normal probability distribution truncated on 0 and 1. To model this problem, a stochastic program is developed. The objective is to maximize the profit of the disassembly process. The latter is the difference between revenues of subassemblies and components and costs of the disassembly tasks. Subassemblies and components revenues are defined as functions of the RUP.

The developed methodology is evaluated and applied to an industrial product, a Knorr-Bremse EBS 1 Channel Module, which represents a real case study, in the automotive part remanufacturing sector, to show the industrial applicability of the developed optimization tool. The optimization results have shown that the profit of the disassembly process depends on the alternative and level of disassembly of the product, and that the disassembly alternative and level are themselves dependent on the states or quality of the components and subassemblies. The results also showed that the level of disassembly for the same sequence or disassembly alternative depends on the type of variation of components and subassembly revenues according to RUP.

The obtained results are promising and have shown the applicability of the developed methodology to real industrial case. The modeling process and optimization tool presented can be easily adapted for more real life cases like End of Life Vehicles (ELV) or Waste Electrical and Electronic Equipment (WEEE). Undertaking such case studies is one of our next research objectives.

References

1. Bentaha, M.L., Battaïa, O., Dolgui, A.: Disassembly line balancing and sequencing under uncertainty. Procedia CIRP **15**, 239–244 (2014)
2. Bentaha, M.L., Battaïa, O., Dolgui, A.: A sample average approximation method for disassembly line balancing problem under uncertainty. Comput. Oper. Res. **51**, 111–122 (2014)
3. Bentaha, M.L., Battaïa, O., Dolgui, A., Hu, S.J.: Dealing with uncertainty in disassembly line design. CIRP Ann. - Manuf. Technol. **63**(1), 21–24 (2014)
4. Bentaha, M.L., Battaïa, O., Dolgui, A., Hu, S.J.: Second order conic approximation for disassembly line design with joint probabilistic constraints. Eur. J. Oper. Res. **247**(3), 957–967 (2015)
5. Bentaha, M.L., Dolgui, A., Battaïa, O., Riggs, R.J., Hu, J.: Profit-oriented partial disassembly line design: dealing with hazardous parts and task processing times uncertainty. Int. J. Prod. Res. **56**, 7220–7242 (2018)
6. Colledani, M., Battaïa, O.: A decision support system to manage the quality of end-of-life products in disassembly systems. CIRP Ann. **65**(1), 41–44 (2016)
7. Diez, L., Marangé, P., Mayer, F., Levrat, E.: Maintenance as a cornerstone for the application of regeneration paradigm in systems lifecycle. In: Auvray, G., Bocquet, J.C., Bonjour, E., Krob, D. (eds.) Complex Systems Design & Management, pp. 185–197. Springer, Cham (2015). https://doi.org/10.1007/978-3-319-26109-6_14
8. Nasr, N., Thurston, M.: Remanufacturing - a key enabler to sustainable product systems. In: Industrial and consumption challenges for life cycle engineering: Proceedings of the 13th CIRP International Conference on Life Cycle Engineering, pp. 15–18. Leuven (2006)
9. Rolf, S.: Automotive service engineering and remanufacturing: new technologies and opportunities. In: 15th CIRP International Conference on Life Cycle Engineering : Applying Life Cycle Knowledge to Engineering Solutions (2008)

10. Schau, E., Traverso, M., Finkbeiner, M.: Life cycle approach to sustainability assessment:a case study of remanufactured alternators. J. Remanuf. **2**(5), 1–14 (2012)
11. Steinhilper, R., Weiland, F.: Exploring new horizons for remanufacturing an up-to-date overview of industries, products and technologies. Procedia CIRP **29**, 769–773 (2015). The 22nd CIRP Conference on Life Cycle Engineering
12. The European Factories of the Future Research Association: Factories of the future: multi-annual roadmap for the contractual PPP under horizon 2020. Technical report (2013)

The Integration of True Lean and Industry 4.0 to Sustain a Culture of Continuous Improvement

M. Abbot Maginnis[1](✉), Buddhika M. Hapuwatte[2](✉), and David Keown[3](✉)

[1] Institute of Research for Technology Development (IR4TD), Lean System Program, Department of Mechanical Engineering, University of Kentucky, Lexington, KY, USA
amaginnis@uky.edu

[2] Institute for Sustainable Manufacturing (ISM), Department of Mechanical Engineering, University of Kentucky, Lexington, KY, USA
hapuwatte@uky.edu

[3] Toyota Motor Engineering & Manufacturing North America (TEMA), Plano, TX, USA
david.keown@Toyota.com

Abstract. Recent advances in information and communication technology and the Internet of Things (IoT) are driving the development of Industry 4.0. Its objective is to enable real-time information exchange between people, machines, products and resources, providing new opportunities for improved safety, quality, productivity and cost factors which can be applied in all stages of Product Lifecycle Management (PLM). The application of lean principles and practices where Industry 4.0 is deployed can leverage real-time processing visibility into even greater productivity improvements if implemented correctly. To do this, companies need to go beyond the implementation of the familiar lean tools and practices such as 5S, visual management and management directed kaizen activities etc. to consider the thinking behind the tools, especially the role of the team members. An over-reliance on technology risks undervaluing the importance of human innovative capacity which can significantly impact the ability to conduct systematic problem solving, adversely effecting daily operational performance and significantly reducing continuous improvement (CI) capacity. This conceptual paper introduces the major elements and thinking of the Toyota Production System (TPS), also referred to as 'True Lean', which are often hidden or underdeveloped within the popular understanding of lean. This paper illustrates how TPS-thinking can be operationalized to support and sustain a CI environment while leveraging the improved visibility possible with Industry 4.0 to integrate all stages of PLM.

Keywords: True Lean · Toyota Production System · Industry 4.0 · Lean · Product Lifecycle Management · PLM

1 Introduction

Much of the promise of Industry 4.0 is due to the level of automation possible and the interconnectability of people, machines, products and resources through the entire value chain. The massive amounts of real-time process data generated greatly increases

C. Fortin et al. (Eds.): PLM 2019, IFIP AICT 565, pp. 336–345, 2019.
https://doi.org/10.1007/978-3-030-42250-9_32

process visibility at all levels and is therefore reasonably expected to boost problem solving and improvement activities. The application of proven lean tools such as 5S, visual management and kanbans etc. to eliminate waste, improve quality and productivity while reducing cost, without requiring a significant culture shift to implement, seems obvious and is currently being explored by several authors [1–3]. While the integration of lean tools will greatly improve stability, they will not in themselves lead to systemic improvements and keep problems from recurring, which is the driving force of Toyota Production System (TPS) and the foundation of Continuous Improvement (CI).

Striving to eliminate problem reoccurrence and setting new targets are at the heart of CI but cannot happen without the full engagement of the team members (T/Ms) doing the work. Industry 4.0 may create situations where organizations become too dependent on automated processes and analytics at the expense of human involvement, which may in-turn reduce human capacity and the creativity driving problem solving and CI [4]. This is important because regardless of the level of technology and the level of automation employed in production, without effective problem solving and CI, the system will ultimately stagnate and degrade.

The University of Kentucky Lean Systems Program (LSP) is a benchmark organization initiated by Fujio Cho in 1994 while he was the president of Toyota Motor Manufacturing of Kentucky (TMMK). Its purpose is to help non-Toyota companies apply the principles and practices of TPS in any industry. The LSP is composed primarily of first generation TMMK employees who were trained and mentored directly by Fujio Cho and a select group of Japanese sensei's to replicate the TPS culture at Toyota's first fully owned manufacturing facility outside Japan. Before coming to Kentucky, Mr. Cho was mentored for many years by Kikuo Suzumura and Taiichi Ohno - often described as the "*father of the Toyota Production System*" [4]. Members of the LSP, which is led by an acting Toyota Executive serving on a rotating basis, represent over 400 years of direct TPS experience. The program coined the term "*True Lean*" as a synonym for TPS as it is practiced inside Toyota in response to the intellectual and experiential 'drift' occurring throughout the world as the popularity of lean has increased over the decades [5].

This paper introduces the two key principles ('Respect for People' and 'Continuous Improvement') and the resulting major elements and thinking of True Lean and TPS which include the importance of team member engagement in standardization and effective systematic problem solving but are often hidden or underdeveloped within the popular understanding of lean. We will use material from our current program and our member's experience to show how TPS Thinking is operationalized to support a problem-solving environment which can help utilize the full potential of Industry 4.0 for CI.

2 Literature Review

2.1 Industry 4.0

Industry 4.0 is seen as the next generation of industry, leveraging the advancements of information and communication technology (ICT) to the manufacturing sphere to integrate the systems involved and facilitate automation. While the term Industry 4.0 was popularized by the German Government in 2011, there is no universally accepted definition for this term. Liao et al. reviews a large number of recent publications and shows the continuing increase of publications in this area [6]. Previous work of Hermann et al. [7] summarizes the three major components of Industry 4.0: (i) Internet of Things (IoT) – this includes the inanimate objects (sensors and other smart components) that connect through internet to communicate between themselves. (ii) Cyber Physical Systems (CPS) – integrated computational and physical processes with feedback loops. (iii) Smart Factories – context-aware factories which assist the people and machines in the execution of their work [7]. This work also identifies four design principles involved in implementing Industry 4.0. These include: (i) Interconnection – of machines, devices and people over technologies such as IoT. (ii) Information transparency – to all objects and people involved in the system, especially by methods such as virtual models of the plants. (iii) Decentralized decisions – made by involved parties utilizing local and global information available for increased productivity. (iv) Technical assistance – as the main role of humans, contrasting the role as 'operators' in conventional manufacturing systems to the 'strategic decision-maker' in smart factories. While other literature [8, 9] suggests slightly different principles, the underlying concepts are variations of these. There are also works available in literature which study what is involved in the transition to the Industry 4.0, and what can be learnt from past technological shifts [10]. Kopp et al. published a critical look at the application of Industry 4.0 from a German perspective and illustrated the importance of ongoing human innovation in advanced technical systems [11].

The common thread running between all these components and principles of Industry 4.0 can be identified as information. Thus, collecting, communicating, analyzing and using information can be expected to be among the most important aspects to ensuring the optimal use of Industry 4.0.

2.2 Conventional Lean and True Lean (TPS)

While lean manufacturing [12, 13] was originally based on TPS [14], previous literature [15] discusses how the term lean has been used in different contexts and with varying definitions (even within academic research). TPS was conceived as a method to fulfill customer expectations for high quality products while eliminating waste and reducing cost within the entire manufacturing system by fully utilizing each T/M's capabilities. As the previous work [15] detailed, most of the available literature focuses on the individual technical tools of lean. The technical tools of lean are just one of the three integral elements required to create and sustain a TPS or lean culture, the other two being the managerial role and the philosophy [16]. TPS Philosophy is the integral element that is the main concern of this paper with respect to the implementation of PLM and IoT. TPS Philosophy includes: *1. Customer First; 2. People are the Most Valuable Resource; 3. Shop Floor Focus (a focus on the workplace); 4. Kaizen (continuous improvement).* Our concern is that the second component of the philosophy, "P*eople are the Most Valuable Resource*", is in danger of being be overlooked in the implementation of Industry 4.0. Focus on *"Respect for People"* and *"People are the Most Valuable Resource"* are the most common yet critical missing considerations in most conventional lean initiatives. [15, 17]. Not utilizing each T/M's full capability is a form of disrespect by not developing their God-given ability (Chie) for innovation [4]. In TPS, a Key Principle of Respect for

People at every level is practiced by developing all T/M's in an environment designed to fully utilize their capability [18]. CI is the other Key Principle embodied in TPS, focusing on reducing cost and improving quality through waste elimination [14, 18] which would not be possible without the Key Principle of Respect for People.

Due to the use in differing contexts, the term 'lean' itself has no standard definition. As a result, organizations attempting to apply lean are subjected to significant variations in what it actually means to be lean and therefore how to create and sustain it. To help overcome this problem, the LSP trademarked the term "True Lean" to describe the basic operational condition of TPS as it is practiced inside Toyota. True Lean is defined as; "*the group by themselves, using systematic problem solving to improve the work they do, towards the achievement of the company's targets and goals, when and only when the company culture is the reason the improvement occurs*" [5]. Similarly, but slightly different, TPS is defined by Toyota as: *"An organization culture of highly engaged people solving problems (or innovating) to drive performance that is created and sustained by a system of philosophy, technical tools and practices and a managerial role."* [19].

2.3 Industry 4.0 and Lean

Previous literature has different views on how Lean and Industry 4.0 are related. Some literature [8] argues Industry 4.0 as an enabler for Lean, by correlating the 'ten dimensions of lean' to the concepts in Industry 4.0. Other work has focused on "the new level of visibility and access to real-time performance data across global operations" provided by Industry 4.0 which will lead to increased productivity, lower costs and shorter lead time [2]. This same source states the opportunities inherent with the increased interconnectedness of devices, systems and even plants create huge increases in complexity, which seems contrary to Lean's traditionally understood focus on process simplification but adds that the proper lean processes and infrastructure could unleash the potential of IoT, resulting in 'Lean on steroids' [2]. This work concludes that for lean to achieve this new level of capability, fully integrated software management systems to generate real-time, actionable information will be required. Other researchers [3] have extended 'Lean Automation' as the combination of Lean and Industry 4.0, providing e-Kanban systems and robot-supported Chaku-Chaku (fully automated) lines as examples of initial Industry 4.0 applications within Lean environments. Unfortunately, all these works seem to rely heavily, if not exclusively, on automation to provide solutions and tend to understate the core aspect of 'people' to implement and sustain effective continuous improvement.

It's important to note that Toyota itself, which lean was based upon, takes a more cautionary stance on combining TPS and Industry 4.0 (and its related technologies). Toyota IT manager, Satoshi Kuroiwa [20] repeated the philosophy of "*first people, then the machines*", explaining Toyota will invest in ICT only after applying Kaizen to improve the process, and only when there are no other options. However, Satoshi also acknowledges the use of digital systems in certain areas such as product development where there are opportunities in doing so. Toyota Motor North America executives on the other hand have acknowledged [21] the possibility of using technologies such as 'Big data' for predictive analytics and using information systems that are based on Industry 4.0 to capture conditions in real-time to support the decision-making process of T/Ms [21]. Examples from Toyota North America includes IoT sensor-enabled equipment capturing data in paint departments, which enabled faster problem identification and resolution by the T/M [21]. Industry 4.0 applications are used to reduce time spent on data gathering and analysis, enabling T/Ms to focus on problem solving [21]. Their response is to remain focused on the decision-making capabilities of their people, using Industry 4.0 and its related technologies as a resource.

3 Discussion

3.1 The Challenges of Industry 4.0 and PLM, and the True Lean Advantage

The integration of True Lean and PLM along with sustainable manufacturing was discussed in a previous paper [14]. In that paper, the concept of the Benevolent Production System was also introduced to illustrate the integration of True Lean (TPS) principles and practices at all stages of PLM and production within the circular economy.

Figure 1 illustrates the conceptual relationship between Industry 4.0 and True Lean.

According to the model, a company implements Industry 4.0 through the use of ICT. Which greatly enhance process visibility, enabling companies to significantly improve performance. This condition is dependent on technology for performance and includes common lean tools as needed. Real-time process visibility can speed up problem identification and reaction but cannot prevent problem reoccurrence. It may be effective to keep the process running and initial costs down, but as unresolved problems accumulate, costs will increase and performance decrease. Changing this condition can be very difficult as T/Ms and management develop a level of comfort and confidence in their ability to address familiar problems quickly.

The addition of True Lean in the model illustrates fundamental TPS thinking, especially the drive to keep problems from coming back, which makes standardization critical. But strict adherence to following standardized work means there must be a system to respond when T/Ms are unable to perform their standardized work and feel safe to let someone know they have a problem. Therefore, they must trust there will be no recriminations as a result.

Toyota's people-friendly philosophy captured in their Key Principle of Respect for People is not there just because it's the right thing to do. It is based on "*economic rationality*" [4] since it helps promote trust and enables Toyota to sustain a standard-based culture maintained by a workforce with the strong belief that problem reoccurrence is not acceptable. This enables problem solving activities that identify and eliminate underlying causes (root cause analysis). Since eliminating the cause of a problem involves changing someone's work, it results in a change in standardized work that keeps the problem from coming back, which as mentioned before, is the foundation of TPS and True Lean. This is the genesis of the central features of the operational side of TPS, which are; 8-Step Problem Solving, also called Toyota Business Practices (TBP) [18], and Standardized Work. These are the engines that drive sustainable productivity and quality [22].

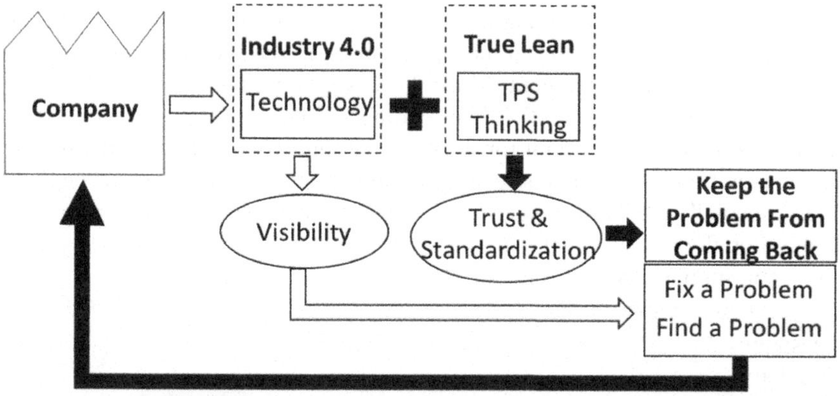

Fig. 1. Conceptual model illustrating the relationship between Industry 4.0 & True Lean

Toyota's key principles of Continuous Improvement and Respect for People are fundamental to T/M engagement. As illustrated in the model above, it is TPS thinking along with Trust and Standardization that provides the ability to eliminate problem recurrence and True Lean defines the operational conditions necessary to accomplish that.

3.2 Operational True Lean (TPS)

Team members in a True Lean system practice problem solving with the objective of eliminating waste, reducing processes and re-aligning T/Ms in production and non-production areas.

A model depicting the True Lean operations environment is presented in Fig. 2. The model illustrates seven conditions which must be met in a True Lean environment. It is most easily explained starting at the customer and working backwards through the annotated conditions as follows. The goal for most organizations is to achieve the Highest Customer Satisfaction using a series of processes to create a product or deliver a service. To do that, there must be a way to eliminate problems which adversely impact the customer. In True Lean, this is 8-Step Problem Solving or TBP. Effective problem-solving practice and thinking is critical for Abnormality Management in which both implementing temporary (fighting fires) and permanent countermeasures are essential activities. These activities require Standard Processes (standardized work) so T/Ms can distinguish normal from abnormal and identify problems. Notice in the model that standard processes, i.e. standardization, is essential for improvement. The primary conditions for the operating system (illustrated in the top half of Fig. 1) is to have stable processes where problems can be quickly identified and a systematic problem-solving methodology capable of permanently eliminating problems. Technologies associated with Industry 4.0 can increase the amount and quality of information and appropriate analytics can assist in finding problems and in some instances even self-correcting them, but without a systematic problem-solving methodology, cannot keep them from recurring. To create and maintain this system requires Engaged Staff. This may be the most essential element of all since they are the ones doing the work and are the most knowledgeable of how the work is performed. They are in the best position to see problems and to contribute meaningful ideas for improvement. Since the T/Ms doing the work are the only ones who are doing value-added work (i.e. providing products or services the customer is willing to pay for), it is important for them to react quickly to all abnormalities so they can continue normal work. This is accomplished in a True Lean system, through the use of Roles, especially the Team Leader role, who is responsible for managing abnormalities at the shop floor level. Finally, for all the above conditions to be sustained, a strong Management Support Culture is required.

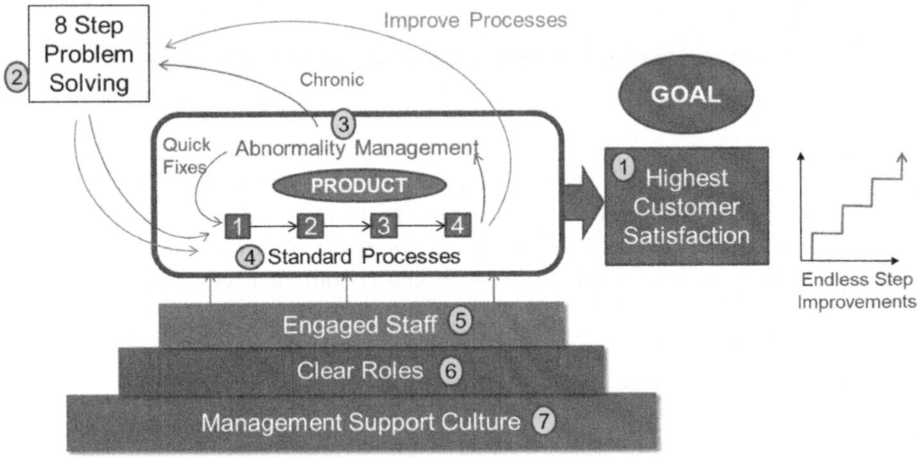

Fig. 2. True Lean Operating Environment model [23]

Meeting the conditions described above often requires an adjustment in how work is performed. The shift (illustrated in Fig. 3) is from the simultaneous performance of normal and abnormal work by T/Ms to one where their primary role is to only perform 'normal' work which is defined as the T/M's repeatable work elements. This contrasts with abnormal work, which disrupts the T/M's ability to perform their repeatable work elements, reducing the amount of value-added work being performed. The role of the Team Leader (T/L) is to eliminate abnormality so the T/Ms can complete their normal work.

When T/Ms are expected to perform both normal and abnormal work, the abnormal eventually becomes normal. This adds variation in processing time, making it impossible to predict the overall lead time for delivering the product or service to the customer and hides problems. In short, problems become normal and will never be eliminated.

As seen in the right-side Fig. 3, introducing the role of T/L helps remove abnormal work which allows the T/M to concentrate on performing normal or value-added work. This provides operational stability and enables processes to be standardized making abnormalities more visible and allows for more effective problem solving and leads to CI. In Industry 4.0 the T/M-T/L roles may be even more critical because with increased visibility will come increased abnormality detection and therefore even more pressure to respond effectively.

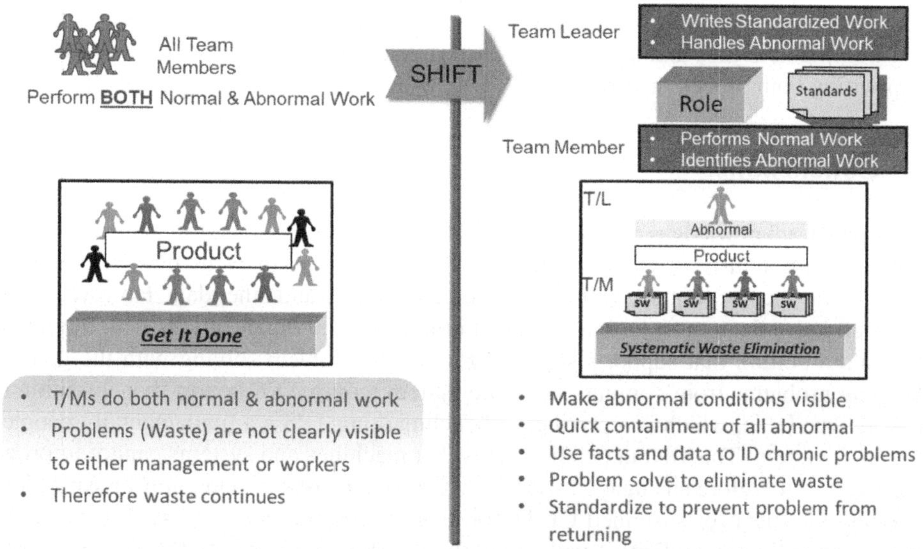

Fig. 3. True Lean Operations Environment shift model [23]

Once the processes are standardized and abnormalities become visible, systematic problem solving can be performed. Adherence to following standardized work is important for two reasons. The first is to provide an environment where problems (abnormalities) can be quickly seen and defined. The second is to provide a foundation on which problem-solving countermeasures can be implemented. Knowing the root cause and implementing the solution to a problem will not ensure CI unless the standardized work is adjusted to accommodate the new work and is adhered to consistently. The importance of this and the T/M-T/L relationship cannot be overstated.

The people side of lean is the most important and most overlooked part of lean transformations. As discussed earlier, engaging T/Ms to participate in systematic problem solving is critical to successfully keep problems from coming back and the key to that is trust. This will be even more difficult to achieve in mostly automated systems such as Industry 4.0 as more problems may be missed as the relationship of workers to the system becomes more impersonal. Therefore, from the outset it is important to promote T/M engagement by not disrespecting them by just relegating them to mindless monitoring status [4, 18].

Toyota believes firmly in the value of people and the importance of providing development opportunities for all their T/Ms, not just because it's the right thing to do morally but because it makes economic sense [4]. Workers must feel safe to call attention to problems, if not, meaningful CI cannot take place. Establishing trust in True Lean requires creating a balanced system that meets the expectations of both the company and the workers through two-way communication. Creating policies to help meet and advocate on behalf of both the T/M's and company's expectations is the role of HR. Often HR policies affecting work and management performance need to be adjusted to support

True Lean operation requirements such as ensuring a safe work environment, supporting training activities and aligning job performance evaluations to reflect their actions supporting both process and results.

4 Conclusions

This paper acknowledges the advantages of utilizing lean tools and concepts in conjunction with Industry 4.0 to leverage the improvements possible with increased process visibility as the result of access to real-time performance and other data. However, to be most effective, lean must be implemented in Industry 4.0 organizations with the intent to build a culture that supports standardization and problem solving with the goal of keeping problems from coming back. The system required to support this condition is called True Lean, which is a product of benchmarking TPS – a fundamentally people-oriented system. The Toyota perspective is that machines and systems cannot improve themselves, therefore an engaged workforce capable of creative and innovative problem solving is critical for sustained CI. Unfortunately, current and accurate Toyota thinking is generally not explicitly available in the lean literature, especially with respect to how fundamental concepts are operationalized. This paper's contribution is to introduce some basic operational models developed by the University of Kentucky Lean Systems Program to help explain TPS critical thinking behind the common tools in an understandable manner, especially in the context of automated manufacturing environments such as I4.0. To promote this outcome, operational models were introduced to illustrate the operating environment and the required environment shift to prevent problem reoccurrence. The Operating Environment model shows the relationship of both temporary countermeasures (quick fix) and permanent countermeasures to standardization. It also illustrates the importance of T/M engagement, clear roles and a strong management support structure to succeed. The Operations Environment Shift model highlights the importance of separating normal (standardized work) from abnormal work to perform effective problem solving and CI.

In highlighting the importance of T/M development this paper exposes the potential risk of developing an over-reliance on data and technology while under-valuing the role of T/Ms to conduct systematic problem solving and sustain CI within Industry 4.0. Undervaluing their importance may alienate people in the system, limiting their engagement and ultimately undermine the system's ability to achieve the full potential of Industry 4.0 and its application within PLM.

References

1. Sanders, A., Elangeswaran, C., Elangeswaran, C., Wulfsberg, J.: Industry 4.0 implies lean manufacturing: research activities in industry 4.0 function as enablers for lean manufacturing. J. Ind. Eng. Manag. **9**(3), 811–833 (2016)
2. How to leverage the IoT in lean manufacturing. Manufacturing engineering (SME). http://www.sme.org/MEMagazine/Article.aspx?id=8589937316. Accessed 15 Mar 2018
3. Kolberg, D., Zühlke, D.: Lean automation enabled by industry 4.0 technologies. IFAC-PapersOnLine **48**(3), 1870–1875 (2015)

4. Saito, A., Saito, A., Kozo, S., Cho, F.: Collection of Goroku Seeds of Collaboration: Seeking the Essence of the Toyota Production System, pp. 60–61. Larkspur Press, Monterey (2012)
5. Kreafle, K.: Models to support type 3 lean implementations. Lean Certification Program Material (2007)
6. Liao, Y., Deschamps, F., Loures, E.D.F.R., Ramos, L.F.P.: Past, present and future of industry 4.0 - a systematic literature review and research agenda proposal. Int. J. Prod. Res. **55**(12), 3609–3629 (2017)
7. Hermann, M., Pentek, T., Otto, B.: Design principles for industrie 4.0 scenarios. In: 2016 49th Hawaii International Conference on System Sciences (HICSS), pp. 3928–3937 (2016)
8. Sanders, A., K. Subramanian, K.R., Redlich, T., Wulfsberg, J.P.: Industry 4.0 and lean management – synergy or contradiction? In: Lödding, H., Riedel, R., Thoben, K.-D., von Cieminski, G., Kiritsis, D. (eds.) APMS 2017. IAICT, vol. 514, pp. 341–349. Springer, Cham (2017). https://doi.org/10.1007/978-3-319-66926-7_39
9. Jazdi, N.: Cyber physical systems in the context of industry 4.0. In: 2014 IEEE International Conference on Automation, Quality and Testing, Robotics, pp. 1–4 (2014)
10. Maghazei, O., Netland, T.: Implementation of industry 4.0 technologies: what can we learn from the past? In: Lödding, H., Riedel, R., Thoben, K.-D., von Cieminski, G., Kiritsis, D. (eds.) APMS 2017. IAICT, vol. 513, pp. 135–142. Springer, Cham (2017). https://doi.org/10.1007/978-3-319-66923-6_16
11. Kopp, R., Howaldt, J., Schultze, J.: Why Industry 4.0 needs Workplace Innovation: a critical look at the German debate on advanced manufacturing. Eur. J. Workplace Innov. **2**(1), 17 (2016)
12. Womack, J.P., Jones, D.T., Roos, D.: The Machine That Changed the World. Simon & Schuster, London (1990)
13. Sugimori, Y., Kusunoki, K., Cho, F., Uchikawa, S.: Toyota production system and kanban system materialization of just-in-time and respect-for-human system. Int. J. Prod. Res. **15**, 553–564 (1977)
14. Maginnis, M.A., Hapuwatte, B.M., Jawahir, I.S.: Implementing total lifecycle product sustainability through true lean thinking. In: Ríos, J., Bernard, A., Bouras, A., Foufou, S. (eds.) PLM 2017. IAICT, vol. 517, pp. 544–553. Springer, Cham (2017). https://doi.org/10.1007/978-3-319-72905-3_48
15. Bhasin, S., Burcher, P.: Lean viewed as a philosophy. J. Manuf. Technol. Manag. **17**(1), 56–72 (2006)
16. Toyota Production System Support Center. https://www.tssc.com/about.php. Accessed 01 May 2019
17. Shah, R.: Lean manufacturing: context, practice bundles, and performance. J. Oper. Manag. **21**(2), 129–149 (2003)
18. Toyota Way: Toyota Motor Corporation (2001)
19. Bonini, J.: Vice President of Toyota Production System Support Center (TSSC). In-person, informal lecture on the definition of TPS, April 2019
20. World Class Manufacturing in Japan - Hoe Toyota Naar Industrie 4.0 Kijkt, Sirris. http://www.sirris.be/nl/blog/world-class-manufacturing-japan-hoe-toyota-naar-industrie-40-kijkt. Accessed 15 Mar 2018
21. IoT at M&T: An inside look at toyota operations technology. IndustryWeek, http://www.industryweek.com/industryweek-manufacturing-technology-conference-expo/iot-mt-inside-look-toyota-operations-technolog. Accessed 15 Mar 2018
22. Maginnis, M.A.: The impact of standardization and systematic problem solving on team member learning and its implications for developing sustainable continuous improvement capabilities. J. Enterp. Transform. **3**(3), 187–210 (2013)
23. University of Kentucky Lean Systems Program, 3-Week Lean Certification Course (2017)

Robot Coalition Formation Based on Fuzzy Cooperative Games over Blockchain-Based Smart Contracts

Alexander Smirnov[1], Leonid Sheremetov[2], and Nikolay Teslya[1(✉)]

[1] SPIIRAS, 14th Line 39, 199178 St. Petersburg, Russia
{smir,teslya}@iias.spb.su
[2] Mexican Petroleum Institute, Eje Central Lázaro Cárdenas Norte, 152, 07730 Mexico City, Mexico
sher@imp.mx

Abstract. In production cyber physical systems robots perform most operations. On the way to Industry 4.0 robots have to be automated and perform operation in coalition to reach common goals. The paper describes an approach to dynamic formation of coalitions of autonomous robots based on the integration of fuzzy cooperative games and smart contracts. Each robot is viewed as an agent, negotiating and bidding with others during the coalition forming for distribution of joint winnings. It is necessary to find combination of robots in way to maximize efficiency of joint work, while the efficiency of the entire coalition is unknown beforehand. A cooperative game with fuzzy core is used to form a coalition of robots allowing coordinating the actions of individual members to achieve a common goal, as well as to evaluate and distribute the overall benefit. To implement the negotiation process and record the composition of the coalition and the responsibilities of individual participants, it is proposed to use the smart contract technology, which now become a part of the blockchain technology. Smart contracts are proposed to be used as entity holding requirements and expected winnings of each participant in the immutable structure of a blockchain network. The final agreement can also be stored by all participants in form of smart contract that contains the distribution coefficients of the winnings given all the conditions of participation in the coalition. The availability of smart contracts to all participants in the coalition makes it possible to ensure joint control over the fulfillment of the task assigned to the coalition.

Keywords: Fuzzy logic · Coalition · Coalition game · Smart contract · Robot

1 Introduction

The development of robots for production cyber-physical systems has reached a level where it is highly important to organize their joint work. The coalition is viewed as the most effective form of joint work organization [1]. Robots in swarms or flocks are limited in actions by strong rules and actions of nearest neighbors. In contrast, robots

Published by Springer Nature Switzerland AG 2019
C. Fortin et al. (Eds.): PLM 2019, IFIP AICT 565, pp. 346–355, 2019.
https://doi.org/10.1007/978-3-030-42250-9_33

in coalitions calculate next steps based on the common goal reaching according to the current coalition state and set of alternatives provided by norms of coalition. Existing models of task solving in coalition define that a robot can receive a reward for the successful problem solving according to its contribution. The independency of robots makes it important to develop an approach to organize coalition formation and interaction between robots for making joint decision during joint problem solving.

Usually production cyber ephysical systems consist of independent robots with different equipment and software that can perform various tasks and expect different levels of reward [2]. In case of production system, the reward is introduced as measure of robot contribution to the success of production and viewed as way to "motivate" robot in doing actions. It is important to consider the heterogeneity and provide common model to consensus reaching during task decomposition and resolving. Each robot is an independent agent with own competencies and goals. The coalition can be considered then as a union of such an agents, which through the negotiation make a decision on a joint solution of the production problem and the distribution of the reward.

The coalition is characterized by dynamic nature and implies a change in its structure, depending on changes in the conditions of the problem being solved. New robots should be quickly familiarized with the current state of the problem solution and provide description of own competences to help to solve the problem. At the same time, existing coalition members should operate without any changes according to the plan. This problem is usually solved by external or internal knowledge bases for storing the history of interaction between coalition members [3, 4].

Most of the existing approaches to coalition formation are characterized by the exponential nature of the computations and communications complexity. To reduce complexity to polynomial the number of agents in one coalition, the number of coalitions, and the rationality of agents are usually limited [5]. The additional complexity is caused by the inability to accurately estimate the size of the gain received after problem solving, which introduces fuzziness into the formulation of the problem.

To solve the problems described above this paper proposes to use the cooperative games with fuzzy core to form a coalition of robots. This model provides the following advantages: robots share own competencies and their expected individual benefit while coalition actions are controlled by one of its member with calculated coalition core. The core coordinates the actions of individual members to achieve a common goal, as well as to evaluate and distribute the overall benefit. The change of environmental conditions leads to a dynamic change in the composition of the coalition, if necessary. A negotiation algorithm and architecture of robot interaction framework has been developed in previous work by the authors [6]. In this paper, it is proposed to use of blockchain technology to store and process fuzzy coalition game's rules for robot negotiation during the coalition formation.

To store the game rules, competencies and requirements of robots, as well as information about the current state of coalitions and tasks, smart contracts over blockchain technology are used. With smart contracts, two types of the rules are defined: (i) for forming a coalition, and (ii) for changing the composition of the coalition, defined with the theory of fuzzy sets. Smart contracts and the current state of the problem solution, are stored in the blockchain.

The rest of the paper is organized as follows. Related work is revised in the following section. A fuzzy cooperative game (FCG) model with core is described in Sect. 3. In Sect. 4, different criteria of dynamic robot coalition formation are analyzed. Finally, the implementation scheme of a FCG over blockchain-based smart contracts is proposed following by conclusions.

2 Related Work

The cooperative nature of modern robotic complexes in production cyber-physical systems causes necessity of considering them within the context of cooperative game theory in order to model and understand their cooperative behavior. The main questions of coalition formation are: what coalitions will be formed, how the common winnings will be distributed among members and if the obtained coalition structure is stable. Once coalitions are formed and they have a feasible set of payoffs available to its members, the question is the identification of final payoffs awarded to each player. That is, given a collection of feasible sets of payoffs, one for each coalition, can one predict or recommend a payoff (or set of payoffs) to be awarded to each player?

The payoff distribution should guarantee the stability of the coalition structure when no one player has an intention to leave a coalition because of the expectation to increase its payoff. The benefit distribution among the coalition members has proved to be fuzzy, uncertain, and ambiguous [7]. Using the theory of fuzzy cooperative games (FCGs), the uncertainty is processed by means of the introduction of a fuzzy benefit concept through the bargaining process to the conclusion about the corresponding fuzzy distribution of individual benefits among the coalition members [8].

The predictions or recommendations of payment distribution are embodied in different solution concepts. According to [9], cooperative games are divided into two classes based on the way a solution is obtained: games with a solution set and games with a single solution. Games with core considered in this paper, belong to the former class and represent a mechanism for analyzing the possible set of stable outcomes of cooperative games with transferable utilities [10]. The concept of a core tends to maximize the sum of coalition utilities in the particular coalition structure (C-stable coalition). The core of a game with respect to a given coalition structure is defined as a set of such imputations that prevent the players from forming small coalitions by paying off all the subsets an amount, which is at least as much they would get if they form a coalition. Thus the core of a game is a set of imputations which are stable.

The drawbacks of the core is that, on the one hand, the computational complexity of finding the optimal structure is high since for the game with n players at least $2^n - 1$ of the total $n^{n/2}$ coalition structures should be tested. On the other hand, for particular classes of the game a core can be empty. Because of these problems, using the C-stable coalition structures was quite unpopular in practical applications [11] and only recently has attracted more attention of the researchers, when the concept of fuzzy cooperative games with core was introduced [12, 13]. For realistic applications like collaborative work of groups of robots, additive environments and the absence of the restrictions on the type of membership functions should be considered [14].

With regard to the organization of robots interaction, the blockchain is mostly used as immutable storage for information exchange and platform for smart contracts. Information stored in the blockchain could contain records about task and consumables distribution [15, 16], smart contracts and reward transactions [17], as well as global knowledge about coalition previous actions [18]. In combination with cooperative games blockchain technology can provide more trust for communication between robots, due to the storing information about transactions in immutable log that can be verified by every coalition participant. In contrary to existing approaches, blockchain does not require central authority that provide trust for all nodes. All nodes negotiate with each other coming to consensus with one of possible mechanisms: Proof of Work, Proof of Stake, or practical byzantine fault tolerance [19].

The combination of the peer-to-peer network and the cryptographic algorithms used in blockchain technology allow for a negotiation process and consensus building without any controlling authorities. Blockchain had already been used in swarm robotics to store global knowledge about swarm actions [18]. The availability of a distributed transaction ledger also allows new robots to join the swarm and gain all the knowledge prior to the moment of inclusion by downloading and analyzing the transaction history.

3 Fuzzy Cooperative Game Model with Core

A generalized model of a fuzzy cooperative game (FCG) with core was proposed in [14, 20, 21]. As shown in [14], the concept of a core tends to maximize the sum of coalition utilities in the particular coalition structure. The core of a game is a set of imputations, which are stable. The proposed model helped solving the problems of the computational complexity of finding the optimal structure and of the empty core, which enabled its use in practical applications of selecting robots in coalitions.

A FCG is defined as a pair $(Robot, w)$, where $Robot$ is nonempty and finite set of players, subsets of $Robot$ joining together to fulfil some task T_i are called coalitions K, and w is called a characteristic function of the game, being $w : 2^n \rightarrow \Re^+$ a mapping connecting every coalition $K \subset Robot$ with a fuzzy quantity $w(K) \in \Re^+$, with a membership function $\mu_K : R \rightarrow [0, 1]$. A modal value of $w(K)$ corresponds to the characteristic function of the crisp game $v(K)$: $\max \mu_K(w(K)) = \mu_K(v(K))$. For an empty coalition $w(\emptyset) = 0$. A fuzzy core for the game $(Robot, w)$ with the imputation $X = (x_{ij})_{i \in I, j \in Robot} \in \Re^+$ is a fuzzy subset C_F of $\Re^+$:

$$C_F = \left\{ x_{ij} \in \Re^+ : \nu f = \left(w(Robot), \sum_{\substack{i \in I, \\ j \in Robot}} x_{ij}\varphi_{ij} \right), \min_{\substack{K_i \in k \\ j \in Robot}} \left(\nu f = \left(\sum\nolimits_{j \in K_i} x_{ij}\varphi_{ij}, w(K_i) \right) \right) \right\}, \quad (1)$$

where x_{ij} is the fuzzy payment of a robot j participating in a coalition i, $i = 1, 2, \ldots, I$, $j = 1, 2, \ldots, N$, $\bar{k} = [K_1, K_2, \ldots, K_l]$ is the ordered structure of effective coalitions; φ is a fuzzy partial order relation with a membership function $\nu f =: R \times R \rightarrow [0, 1]$, and φ_{ij} is a binary variable such that:

$$\varphi_{ij} = \begin{cases} 1, if\ robot\ j\ participates\ in\ a\ coalition\ i; \\ 0, otherwise. \end{cases}$$

The φ_{ij} is considered here as a result of some robot's strategy on joining a coalition.

A fuzzy partial order relation is defined as follows (for more details see [22]). Let a, b be fuzzy numbers with membership functions μ_a and μ_b respectively, then the possibility of partial order $a\phi = b$ is defined as $\nu\phi = (a, b) \in [0, 1]$ as follows:

$$\nu\phi = (a, b) = \sup_{\substack{x,\, y \in R \\ x \geq y}} (\min(\mu_a(x), \mu_b(y))). \tag{2}$$

The core C_F is the set of possible distributions of the total payment achievable by the coalitions, and none of coalitions can offer to its members more than they can obtain accepting some imputation from the core. The first argument of the core C_F indicates that the payments for the grand coalition are less than the characteristic function of the game. The second argument reflects the property of group rationality of the players, that there is no other payoff vector, which yields more to each player. The membership function $\mu_{C_F} : R \rightarrow [0, 1]$, is defined as:

$$\mu_{C_F}(x) = \min\left\{ \nu f = \left(w(Robot), \sum_{\substack{i \in I \\ j \in Robot}} x_{ij}\varphi_{ij} \right), \min_{\substack{K_i \in k \\ j \in Robot}} \left(\nu f = \left(\sum_{j \in K_i} x_{ij}\varphi_{ij}, w(K_i) \right) \right) \right\} \tag{3}$$

The solution of a cooperative game is a coalition configuration (S, x) which consists of (i) a partition S of $Robot$, the so-called coalition structure, and (ii) an efficient payoff distribution x which assigns each robot in $Robot$ its payoff out of the utility of the coalition it is member of in a given coalition structure S. A coalition configuration (S, x) is called stable if no robot has an incentive to leave its coalition in S due to its assigned payoff x_i.

It was proved that the fuzzy set of coalition structures forming the game core represents a subset of the fuzzy set formed by the structure of effective coalitions. In turn, this inference allows us to specify the upper possibility bound for the core, which is a very important condition for the process of solution searching, because in this case, the presence of a solution that meets the efficiency condition may serve as the signal to terminate the search algorithm [21].

The game purpose is to generate an effective structure of robot coalitions for executing some production task. In turn, the generated structure of robot coalitions represents the optimal configuration of the grand coalition. Individual robots use the technique of nonlinear fuzzy regression to estimate the parameters of utility functions for their payments [23]. A "coalition robot" is enabled for constructing membership functions (MF) of coalitions and generating the game core (fuzzy-number generator). The sum operation is based on Zadeh extension principle [22] for fuzzy numbers a and b (which are convex sets normalized in R):

$$\mu_{a(*)b}(Z) = \sup_{z=x*y} \min(\mu_a(x), \mu_b(y)) \tag{4}$$

where * can designate the sum $\oplus$ or the product • of fuzzy numbers. Each fuzzy set is decomposed into two segments, a non-decreasing and non-increasing one. The operation * is performed for every group of n segments (one segment for each fuzzy set) that belong to the same class (non-decreasing or non-increasing one). Thus, a fuzzy set is generated for every group of n segments.

4 Criteria for FCG in Dynamic Robot Coalition Formation

Group problem solving in cyberphysical production systems requires a well-coordinated interaction of the participants' actions during the coalition formation for production task. Regardless of the coalition model used, its formation can be considered as three types of interrelated actions that are performed sequentially:

- Generation of a coalition structure; a framework in which agents within each coalition coordinate their activities;
- Optimization of each coalition; agents have to be united by competencies for effective problem solving;
- Profit sharing between coalition members.

If these actions are performed before problem solving, a static coalition formation is considered. The structure of static coalitions does not change over time. At the time of optimization of the coalition, also a plan for solving the problem is calculated as well as all possible deviations from the plan. In case of failure, the correction of the plan is carried out with coalition members that are still operate, taking into account the changed conditions in order to get back to the original plan with minimal losses.

A more complex case of a coalition formation is the dynamic coalition. In this case a plan of problem solving is formed during the optimization stage same as for the static coalition. However, in case of deviation from the plan, a fix is based on changing the structure of the coalition, for example, by adding a new participant. To do this, the rules for the formation of the coalition should describe actions for unknown situations with fuzzy parameters, and the overall benefit of the coalition and plan are dynamically recalculated considering the context of the task has changed.

To evaluate the coalition efficiency the following parameters can be used:

- *Energy spent* to task solving. The solution of each task or sub-task can be estimated by the energy (charge of the battery) $E_k(T_i)$ of the robot k that was spent to solve it:

$$E_k(T_i) = \sum\nolimits_j f_{T_i}\left(b_j^k\right) \cdot \varphi(T_i, k, j) \quad (5)$$

  Based on aggregated data over similar problems, it is possible to obtain an approximate estimation, which, however, introduces fuzziness into the final coalition formation. The coalition efficiency can be estimated as the total energy expended:

$$v\left(K_{T_i}\right) = Payoff(T_i) - \min_{K_i \in k} \sum\nolimits_{j \in K_i} E_j(T_i) \quad (6)$$

- An analogue to the estimated energy expended is a *robot uptime* based on failure probability. The estimation of failure probability is the ratio of difference between the time of the node work and the average uptime of the same kind of robot units: $P_{C_i} = T_{C_i}^{w} - T_{C_i}^{m} / T_{C_i}^{avg}$, where P_{C_i} – failure probability of unit c_i by robot $\mathrm{r_j r_j}$, $T_{C_i}^{w}$ – total work duration of the unit c_i, $T_{C_i}^{m}$ – last service time point. The probability of entire robot failure is evaluated according to the maximum probability of nodes failure $\mathrm{P_r = max_i\, P_{c_i}}$. The efficiency criterion in this case will be the maximum duration of the coalition's overall work to the next maintenance.

- Maximizing the coalition benefit. For example, in relation to cyberphysical production system, the coalition's benefit is the cumulative product of the system. The value of the solution of the problem decreases with the passage of time: the longer the task is postponed, the less benefit it can provide.

5 Robot Interaction over Smart Contracts with FCG

In this Section, the scheme of interaction of robots during the coalition formation, is proposed. The ability of smart contracts within the scope of blockchain technology to describe complex algorithms by using the Turing-complete programming language is used to define game rules in smart contracts. Examples of blockchain platforms with support of smart contracts include the Ethereum platform and Hyperledger Fabric.

Figure 1 shows the scheme of interaction of robots in the coalition through a blockchain. Two kinds of chains for storing resources and contracts is proposed to use in the blockchain for robot interaction. All system resources including consumables, energy, reward, which are represented by tokens, are stored in the resources chains. In the contracts chain the rules of cooperative game are stored, which are used by the robots coordinators during the coalition forming and the distribution of tasks. The contracts also contains rules for processing tasks and assigning coalition core. The need for the presence of coalition core, which will assess the complexity of the solution of the problem or the effectiveness of its solution and then distribute tasks among the performers is noted in previous works [20, 21]. New tasks can be formed both inside and outside of the system and are recorded in the contract chain, where they become available for all coalition cores. Tasks contain a formalized description of the goal, the initial parameters and the amount of reward for the solution.

The robot coordinator ($Robot_{CORE1}$ or $Robot_{CORE2}$ on Fig. 1) selects robots using smart contracts based on their competencies and reward expectations, as well as the rules of the cooperative game, defined for the subject area to which the task belongs. If the robot can participate in several coalitions, each robot coordinator calculates the cooperative game core and winning for each of the coalitions, as well as the availability of sufficient resources for the robot successful work. If there are enough resources for robot's operations, it can participate in several coalitions. Otherwise, the robot is assigned to a coalition for which it can bring the largest benefit. The reward for the successful solution of the problem is distributed among the robots participating in the coalition based on the reward rules for the cooperative game, described in the code of the relevant contract.

The presented approach provides the following advantages. First, the use of the blockchain guarantees the authorship of the information and its immutability, which is an important aspect in dynamic coalitions of robots. Built-in authentication algorithms and digital signatures allow to get rid of the complex infrastructure of certification centers, which simplifies the deployment and operation of the system. Separation of chains with resources and contracts provides an independent storage and exchange of the state of the coalition between performers and control robots. This provides a trusted knowledge base for robots to share coalition state including task and reward distribution. Since the data in the blockchain is bounded by the blocks' hash, no block can be changed. It makes process logs immutable and history of operations can be traced back, to find a failure points, and enhance the effectiveness of future organized coalitions. The Hyperledger platform that is proposed to be used for the organization of interaction provides a high speed of processing and exchange of transactions (up to 3500 transactions per seconds [24]).

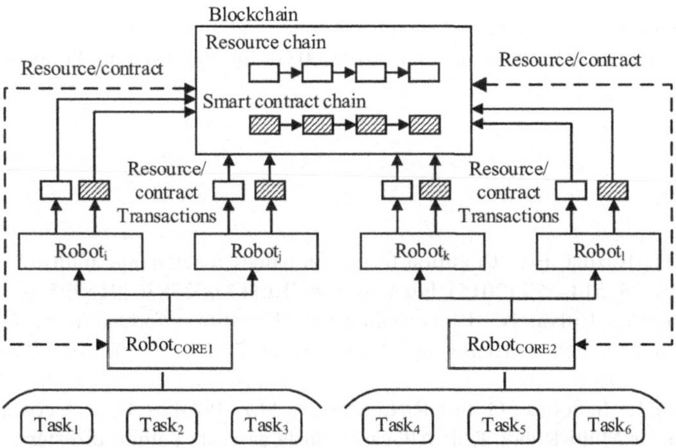

Fig. 1. Robot interaction in coalition through blockchain and smart contracts.

Secondly, the architecture of Hyperledger platform, which includes three levels (clients, peers and orderers), reflects the interaction structure presented on Fig. 1: the clients correspond to the coalition robots, peers is robots with the coalition core and orderer is a cloud service for storing chains. Each chain is corresponds to channel in Hyperledger. Due to this, the computation of the core and the exchange of tasks and the solutions obtained is carried out without the involvement of robots with a small computing power. Turing-complete language can be used to formalize a contract of any complexity.

6 Conclusion

In this paper, the integrated model of application of games with fuzzy coalitions and fuzzy smart contracts, which can be applied to coalition formation between multiple robots has been described. Fuzziness serves as the fundamental component of realistic cooperation models when there exist fuzzy expectations of player and coalition benefits. When an effective solution is found, individual benefits for players (the agreement efficiency) increase, as well as the capability of the coalition to find an effective and stable agreement. Fuzzy payments may have any utility function, which enables the use of the model in real-world applications. The blockchain model allows to avoid the synchronization problem, which is critical for distributed negotiation algorithms with large robot populations.

The integration of this FCG model with smart contracts can make robot coalitions more transparent. The use of Internet of Things (IoT) sensors, which track robots' actions though the chain, provides opportunity to control and analyze all process of joint problem solving. If any robot in coalition fails to meet the terms of the contract, for instance if it did not finish an operation on time, it would be clear for every party to see and new coalitions can be arranged dynamically. The blockchain can be used to safe and trustiness logging of robots' task and reward distribution and for task solving.

Acknowledgments. The present research was supported by the projects funded through grants number 17-29-07073, 17-07-00247 and 17-07-00327 of the Russian Foundation for Basic Research.

References

1. Bayram, H., Bozma, H.I.: Coalition formation games for dynamic multirobot tasks. Int. J. Robot. Res. **35**, 514–527 (2015). https://doi.org/10.1177/0278364915595707
2. Kashevnik, A., Teslya, N.: Blockchain-oriented coalition formation by CPS resources: ontological approach and case study. Electronics **7**, 16 (2018). https://doi.org/10.3390/electronics7050066
3. Mouradian, C., Sahoo, J., Glitho, R.H., Morrow, M.J., Polakos, P.A.: A coalition formation algorithm for Multi-Robot Task Allocation in large-scale natural disasters. In: 2017 13th International Wireless Communications and Mobile Computing Conference (IWCMC), pp 1909–1914. IEEE (2017)
4. Guerrero, J., Oliver, G.: Multi-robot coalition formation in real-time scenarios. Robot. Auton. Syst. **60**, 1295–1307 (2012). https://doi.org/10.1016/j.robot.2012.06.004
5. Jennings, N.R., Faratin, P., Lomuscio, A.R., Parsons, S., Wooldridge, M., Sierra, C.: Automated negotiation: prospects, methods and challenges. Group Decis. Negot. **10**, 199–215 (2001). https://doi.org/10.1023/A:1008746126376
6. Smirnov, A., Teslya, N.: Robot interaction through smart contract for blockchain-based coalition formation. In: Chiabert, P., Bouras, A., Noël, F., Ríos, J. (eds.) PLM 2018. IAICT, vol. 540, pp. 611–620. Springer, Cham (2018). https://doi.org/10.1007/978-3-030-01614-2_56
7. Hosam, H., Khaldoun, Z.: Planning coalition formation under uncertainty: auction approach. In: Proceedings - 2006 International Conference on Information and Communication Technologies: From Theory to Applications, ICTTA 2006, pp. 3013–3017. IEEE (2006)
8. Aubin, J.-P.: Cooperative fuzzy games. Math. Oper. Res. **6**, 1–13 (1981). https://doi.org/10.1287/moor.6.1.1
9. Kahan, J.P., Rapoport, A.: Theories of Coalition Formation. Lawrence Erlbaum Associates Inc, Routledge (1984)
10. Gillies, D.B.: Some theorems on n-person games. Princeton University (1953)
11. Klusch, M., Gerber, A.: Dynamic coalition formation among rational agents. IEEE Intell. Syst. **17**, 42–47 (2002). https://doi.org/10.1109/MIS.2002.1005630
12. Mareš, M.: Fuzzy Cooperative Games. Physica-Verlag HD, Heidelberg (2001)
13. Shen, P., Gao, J.: Coalitional game with fuzzy payoffs and credibilistic core. Soft. Comput. **15**, 781–786 (2010). https://doi.org/10.1007/s00500-010-0632-9
14. Smirnov, A.V., Sheremetov, L.B.: Models of coalition formation among cooperative agents: the current state and prospects of research. Sci. Tech. Inf. Process. **39**, 283–292 (2012). https://doi.org/10.3103/S014768821205005X

15. Verma, D., Desai, N., Preece, A., Taylor, I.: A block chain based architecture for asset management in coalition operations. In: Pham, T., Kolodny, M.A. (eds.) Proceedings of the SPIE 10190, Ground/Air Multisensor Interoperability, Integration, and Networking for Persistent ISR VIII, p. 101900Y (2017)
16. Dorri, A., Kanhere, S.S., Jurdak, R.: Towards an optimized BLOCKCHAIN for IoT. In: Proceedings of the Second International Conference on Internet-of-Things Design and Implementation - IoTDI 2017, pp. 173–178 (2017). https://doi.org/10.1145/3054977.3055003
17. Zhang, Y., Wen, J.: The IoT electric business model: using blockchain technology for the internet of things. Peer-to-Peer Netw. Appl. **10**, 983–994 (2017). https://doi.org/10.1007/s12083-016-0456-1
18. Castelló Ferrer, E.: The blockchain: a new framework for robotic swarm systems. In: Arai, K., Bhatia, R., Kapoor, S. (eds.) FTC 2018. AISC, vol. 881, pp. 1037–1058. Springer, Cham (2019). https://doi.org/10.1007/978-3-030-02683-7_77
19. Cachin, C., Vukolić, M.: Blockchain consensus protocols in the wild 24 (2017). https://doi.org/10.4230/LIPIcs.DISC.2017.1
20. Sheremetov, L.B., Smirnov, A.V.: A fuzzy cooperative game model for configuration management for open supply networks. Contrib. Game Theory Manag. **4**, 433–446 (2011)
21. Sheremetov, L.B.: A model of fuzzy coalition games in problems of configuring open supply networks. J. Comput. Syst. Sci. Int. **48**, 765–778 (2009). https://doi.org/10.1134/S1064230709050116
22. Zadeh, L.A.: Similarity relations and fuzzy orderings. Inf. Sci. **3**, 177–200 (1971). https://doi.org/10.1016/S0020-0255(71)80005-1
23. Haekwan, L., Tanaka, H.: Fuzzy approximations with non-symmetric fuzzy parameters in fuzzy regression analysis. J. Oper. Res. Soc. Japan **42**, 98–112 (1999)
24. Androulaki, E., Manevich, Y., Muralidharan, S., Murthy, C., Nguyen, B., Sethi, M., et.al.: Hyperledger fabric. In: Proceedings of the Thirteenth EuroSys Conference on - EuroSys 2018, pp 1–15. ACM Press, New York (2018)

Integration Between PLM and MES for One-of-a-Kind Production

Emiliano Traini, Giulia Bruno(✉), Ahmed Awouda, Paolo Chiabert, and Franco Lombardi

Politecnico di Torino, Corso Duca degli Abruzzi 24, 10129 Torino, Italy
{emiliano.traini,giulia.bruno,ahmed.awouda,paolo.chiabert, francolombardi}@polito.it

Abstract. Despite the amount of research addressing the formalization of product-related knowledge, the practical use of tools for knowledge management is still very low at the corporate level. Several commercial software applications are already available for product lifecycle management (PLM) and manufacturing execution system (MES). Unfortunately, these two applications are scarcely integrated thus preventing an efficient and pervasive collection of data and the consequent creation of useful information. This is more critical in One-of-a-kind Production (OKP), where each product is unique, the process is not completely defined at the design stage, but it is continuously improved at the shop floor level by skilled operator. In such situations, most of the company's knowledge relies on the lessons learnt by operators in years of work experience, and their ability to reuse this knowledge in order to face new problems. Because OKP must develop unique product and complex processes in a short time, it is mandatory to reuse the acquired information in the most efficient way. It is therefore necessary to collect all the data from the shop floor and transform them in information that will be used in the development of the next product and process. The aim of this paper is to design a framework able to integrate data, from both design and manufacturing phases. To this aim, a framework has been designed to structure and relate information from the PLM and the MES systems. A case study has been developed for a car prototyping company to prove the efficiency of the proposed solution.

Keywords: Industry 4.0 · PLM · Knowledge management · OKP

1 Introduction

Product innovation and customization are the main weapons in the hands of small and medium sized companies to compete in a market characterized by high volatility and quick dynamics. Customization strategies can be particularly observed in companies whose manufacturing processes are dedicated to the manufacture products so customized as to be considered unique specimens, known as "one-of-a-kind production", OKP [1, 2]. This production method is characterized by a very high level of product customization, a strong variability in the production process, a complex and dynamic supply network,

Published by Springer Nature Switzerland AG 2019
C. Fortin et al. (Eds.): PLM 2019, IFIP AICT 565, pp. 356–365, 2019.
https://doi.org/10.1007/978-3-030-42250-9_34

and a versatile and dynamic production plant, often controlled in an empirical way [3]. Several Italian and European SMEs meet this definition and many of them are able to compete with larger companies, offering products (and services) highly personalized, with more content than a large delivery company and with higher quality standards used for similar products (possibly "custom") from global companies.

Effective collaboration and knowledge sharing among experts and technicians at all levels is the "secret strategy" for OKP systems. OKP decision making mainly relies on the life-long human learning process based on product case-histories, which enables operators to react autonomously and adapt and/or recover the manufacturing process, or even suggest product modifications to improve the manufacturability.

In recent years, embedded technology, connected devices, and Internet of Things (IoT) have been introduced in industrial environments to provide sensors, actuators and networks able to interact with the working processes in real time and giving rise to the so-called "fourth industrial revolution" (Industry 4.0). Currently, the usage of IoT data is limited to analyze shop floor behavior by monitoring environment parameters. However, the most significance challenge is to integrate IoT data with data generated in the product design phase, in order to increase the knowledge about products and infer correlations among product geometrical features, product manufacturing process parameters and product failures. This challenge is even more important in OKP, where the knowledge of previous failures of similar products would improve the design of the process of a new product by reducing the time spent for trial-and-error.

Several commercial software applications are already available for product lifecycle management (PLM) and manufacturing execution control (MES). PLM systems bring at the disposal of designers shared product databases. The fact that PLM systems are accessible by different people and departments allows the collaborative development of products, enabling sharing and reuse of information. However, PLM systems are not integrated with the manufacturing execution systems (MES), which control the factory operations, from production order release to testing of the finished product. MES systems are used to control in real time the progress of orders and to associate to each production order the information about the parameters and results of the operations. Through real-time monitoring, it is therefore possible to release and/or modify work orders, to intervene promptly in case of unforeseen problems, and to rebalance workloads of machines and operators.

The full exploitation of PLM and MES systems is limited by two factors: first, the lack of integration between them, thus requiring a third application of interconnection, and second, the need of deriving more explicit knowledge from the data generated in terms of correlations of events and prediction of future failures. The lack of a formalized, structured and effective knowledge management system to capture and represent the tacit knowledge results in such knowledge to remain in the minds of people, or at best, transferred verbally, and then, over time, inevitably lost [4, 5].

To catch such knowledge, there is a need to use more advanced systems to store and correlate all the information coming from the plant. The aim of the paper is to develop a framework to integrate knowledge coming from the design and the execution phases in manufacturing.

The rest of the paper is organized as follows. Section 2 summarizes the relevant literature available on the topic. Section 3 describes the proposed framework and the definition of the data model to structure the product and process knowledge. Section 4 presents the application of the framework for the case of an Italian company producing car prototypes. Finally, Sect. 5 draws conclusions and states future work perspectives.

2 Related Works

In the last ten years, several research papers were published which addressed the issue of structuring and formalizing product-related knowledge, mainly related to modelling product geometrical features and manufacturing process parameters [6–9]. Also, several international research projects addressing the development of industrial knowledge sharing systems were recently funded (e.g., amePLM [10], ICP4Life [11], Know4car [12], Manutelligence [13]). However, the practical use of tools for supporting knowledge management is still very low at the corporate level. A study conducted in 2013 by the GeCo Observatory [14] on a sample of more than 100 Italian manufacturing companies, found that the most used methods to store explicit knowledge remain the traditional verbal communication, the practices based on paper, and the basic IT supports for collaboration such as shared folders, forums, and intranet portals. It is also severely limited by the use of more structured software systems.

Two weaknesses can be identified in both current scientific literature and research projects. The first one is that they did not address specifically the OKP domain, where the presence of many alternative routings and operations makes very difficult to manage all the manufacturing variables together in an efficient and profitable way, without increasing wastes of time and costs. The second one is that there is no overall view of the IoT architecture (in terms of types of data to be measured at the plant level, together with the kind of sensors needed to measure such data) and also on processing intelligence to analyze such data in an efficient way. It is therefore essential, both for industrial efficiency and for customer satisfaction, to develop an integrated knowledge management system, able to take systematic tracks of the experience accumulated over time through the manufacturing activities.

3 Framework

The proposed framework is a knowledge management system able to collect and store data both from product design and process execution. As shown in Fig. 1, this framework is based on a central database (DB) containing the subset of data relevant for both PLM and MES and acting as a bridge between them.

The proposed framework will allow (i) to collect all the information regarding the critical realizations of new components in a structured way, so that the added values of the experience breakthrough, as well as other useful tips, could be provided to the end-user, and (ii) to reuse the knowledge, i.e. help designers to define more reliable processes for new products, reducing the "trial-and-error" cycles in the development of forming processes.

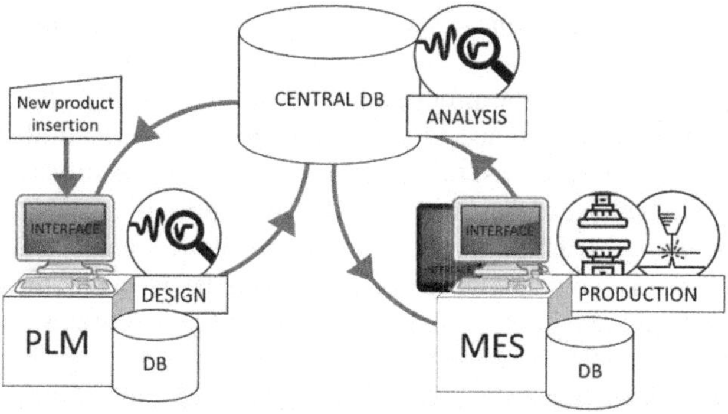

Fig. 1. Conceptual model of the framework.

In fact, when a customer makes an order, it means that the company must define the sequence of activities to obtain the required product. If the historical data regarding previous products are stored in the central DB, it can be used to find the closest product already produced in the past that needs less changes to be adapted to the new shop order. The chosen product is then found in the PLM platform where the needed changes can be done. The information associated to the new product is sent to the central DB and made accessible to the MES. The MES uses the product information to manage the production and, when the production is finished, it reports in the central DB the information related to the execution of each activity and the success or failure of the product. In case of failure, the company can check the intermediate results reported for each activity and decide how to proceed to obtain a better solution.

The content of the central DB and the data flow to and from PLM and MES systems are described in the following subsections.

3.1 Data from PLM

Through the PLM, in the design phase, the following data regarding the product and its activities are generated and sent to the central DB.

- *BOM*. This is a list of the raw materials, sub-assemblies, intermediate assemblies, sub-components, parts, and the quantities of each needed to manufacture an end-product.
- *CAD file*.
- *List of activities*. This is not a typical information stored in PLM. Practically, this is an ordered list of all required activities to obtain the final product.
- *Activities description*. It is related to the company department where the activity must be done, the specification of the activity, the need or not of a machine and, in case of a need, the identification of the machine.
- *Check start*. It regards the necessary condition for the beginning of the activity. If the considered activity is manual, all the tools and raw materials needed by the operator are included. If the activity needs a manufacturing equipment, the set up and all the necessary tools are included. Furthermore, the condition on the semi-finished goods

need to be added (the operator needs to be able to see an error that comes from the previous activities).
- *Check end.* It is related to the production and product quality check. The operator needs to be able to know the necessary parameters to discern similar products from the other. Related to the process, the operator can have information about not only the product lifecycle but also about the CAD files related to it.
- *Machine description.* It is the list of available machines, characterized by the type and other parameters, so that when an activity has to be executed, the operator knows which type of machine he must use and which specific ones are available.

To allow the retrieval of similar products, it is also useful to define a classification of products in groups of similar objects. The selection of good classification parameters is fundamental for the analysis, and the more these parameters are, the more accurate the classification for a future shop order will be. The following three classification parameters were used:

1. *Family.* The first classification parameter generates a macro-division of products, which considers the major differences in production process and material (e.g., structural elements, non-structural elements, panels).
2. *Subfamily.* Once divided into families the products are classified according to their use and their shape (e.g., the panel family is further divided into the subfamily of doors, sides, trunks, fenders and roofs).
3. *Complexity.* The last parameter discriminates products that belong to a very homogeneous group, by considering more complex the products in which an activity is repeated several times to achieve a better degree of refinement.

3.2 Data from MES

The role of the MES is the production monitoring, thus it sends to the Central DB the information related to the process of a specific shop order. The production information to be collected is the following:

- *Check start results.* If it is not possible to start a new activity, the MES needs to be able to receive information about the causes.
- *Check end results.* It is fundamental to collect information regarding the problems occurred during the process at the end of the activity.
- *Machine failure.* In the OKP it is fundamental in addition to the production also the monitoring of the machine failures. In fact, from this information it is possible to improve the machine assignment to different activities in order to minimize downtime.
- *Activity information.* The MES platform need to be able to record information related to the performed activities. Among these parameters, the main ones are the actual cycle time, the machine set up and the waiting time for the operator.

This structure, able to accommodate a prefixed type of information, risks not being enough to capture all the knowledge generated during the production. To overcome this problem, the MES must be thought out and developed in order to allow to receive unforeseen information about the production. A basic example is the possibility for the operator to freely write a description of the incident or to use cameras in the production sector.

In the OKP the MES needs a last degree of freedom: the possibility of changing the activities of the product to production in progress. In fact, this kind of manufacturing companies are still very dependent on the experience of their operators. For this reason, it often happens that the operators take decisions in slight contrast to the ones of the Analyst Office that remain a-priori and non-dynamic decisions. Then the MES must be able to communicate to the central DB that the production cycle has been modified for a single shop order.

3.3 Knowledge DB

The central DB is structured to receive and integrate data coming from both PLM and MES, and to make them available for further analysis.

Figure 2 shows the structure of the central DB through an entity-relationship model. The product entity contains information about the classification, the CAD file, the BOM and other general characteristics of the products. The amount of the semi-finished product is connected to it, which identifies the status of the semi-finished products specifying the next activity to be carried out. This is the reason why there is also the activity entity that characterizes the particular activity, explaining the check start, the check-ends and the machines necessary to carry it out. All the physical machines available in the company are then associated to the corresponding type. This information is provided by the PLM and is subsequently used by the MES.

To the entities associated with the PLM activity are added entities that model the data provided by the MES, i.e. the data coming from the production. The fundamental entity is the one related to the shop order. In the central DB all the shop orders taken in charge and on which the company has worked are stored. This entity is obviously connected to the product, as each shop order concerns a single and specific product, so a single and specific product lifecycle. The shop order is also connected to the activity carried out, connected itself to the verification checks. It models the data structure from which we can extract the history of all the activities divided by shop order and consequently by product and results obtained.

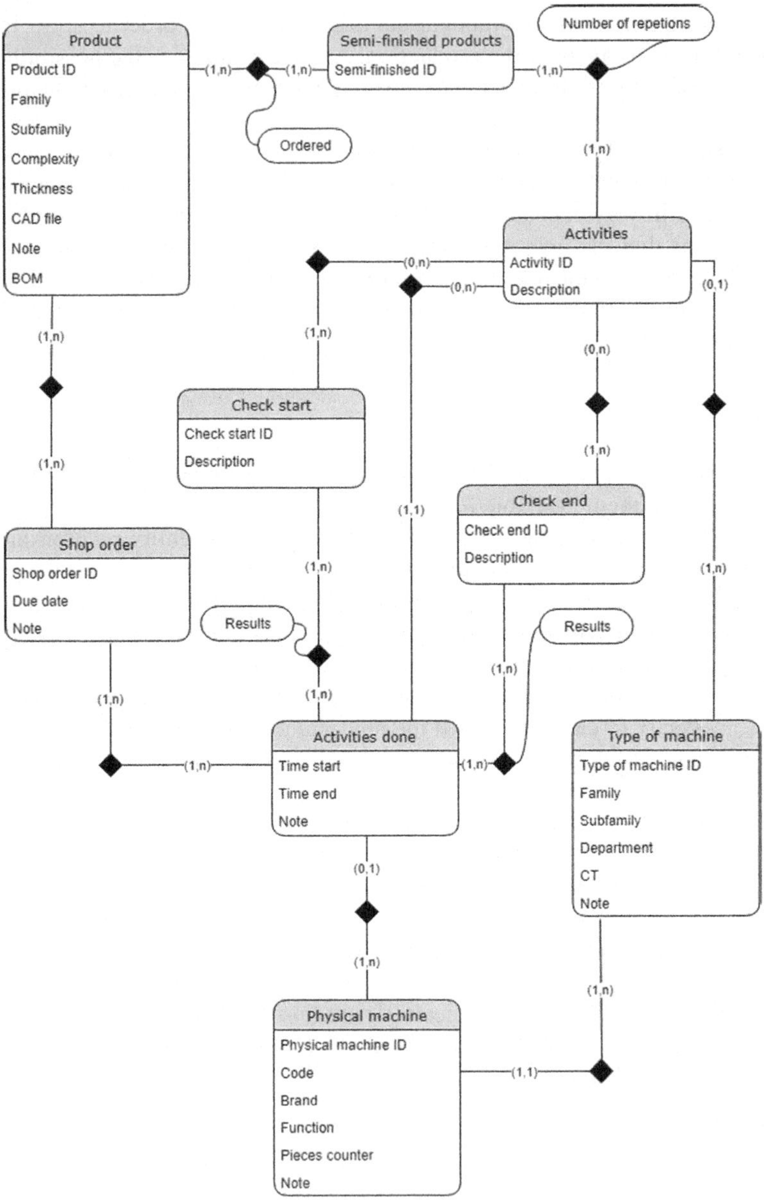

Fig. 2. Entity-relationship model of the knowledge DB.

4 Use Case

The study was conducted in an Italian company that operates in the automotive sector, producing prototype bodywork components for passenger cars and other kinds of vehicles. The company is a tier 2 supplier for worldwide known automotive manufacturers.

The strength of the company relies in its ability of developing complex manufacturing processes in short time providing prototypes and pre-series products. According to this goal the company is a perfect example of the OKP approach to produce customized products based on requirements of individual customers.

4.1 Complexity of the OKP Process

Due to the production nature of the company, it is difficult to forecast the production trend, and there may be problems and mishaps that prevent the plant from having a linear production. Unlike series production, the production of prototypes is characterized by an extremely variable production rate, with high material waste. The problems faced by the company can be attributed to two main aspects. The first is the separation between design phase and production phase (i.e. the separation between product design and process design). When the design of the dies is approved by the responsible person, his role is over, and the designer does not receive any feedback on possible problems caused by the dies during production. Furthermore, the shop floor operators do not receive the results of the simulation that should theoretically indicate which zones of the piece are the most critical.

This lack of bidirectional information flow impedes the process of continuous learning for both parties: the designer who, without receiving feedback on his work, cannot modify his work methodology or make the simulation more reliable. For the operators, the lack of information about the results of the simulation makes their job harder, since they do not know what the outcome of their work should be. The second aspect is the absence of data collection during production. The only relevant data is the quantity of pieces produced at the end of the shift. No data is collected about the exact quantity of defectives or of material waste. No information is stored, about the main problems that the operators had to face during the shift: such information, if available, is found only in the minds of experienced operators, this lack of a structured knowledge management system results in production mishaps and delays when such key employees are absent and creates a dependency on specific personnel which is not efficient for a production plant.

4.2 "As is" Situation

The industrial process for the realization of a prototype bodywork component starts with the delivery, by the costumer company, of the CAD model of the requested piece. The CAD model is received by the technical office that defines the production process, the design of the dies and the material to be used. After that, the model is sent to the CAD office in order to be validated via simulations. If the simulation does not highlight critical issues, the models of the dies are approved and sent to the CAM department, where the toolpaths for the milling machines are studied and defined in order to start the dies construction.

Once the dies have been constructed and ready the metal sheets used to make the body part are sent to the Laser office where the metal sheet is trimmed using a two-dimensional laser to obtain the appropriate shape outline. After the sheets have been cut, they are transported to the presses area where they undergo the first press operation (also known as drawing). The semi-finished items are then returned to the laser section where 3D lasers cut the metal sheet according to specific laser paths obtaining the final measures of the piece and creating slots and holes. Depending on the complexity of the piece a redrawing operation may be required where the piece is pressed again and trimmed by the 3D laser to obtain a component that perfectly satisfies the requested dimensional and geometric tolerances. All the information generated during the process is only written in paper, thus over time, inevitably lost.

4.3 "To be" Situation

In the "to be" situation, essentially the process remains the same but with a different management of the information. There are a dynamic and a historical management of the data.

The first one improves the circulation of information between different departments of the company. In the OKP, in fact, an efficient communication between offices with different manages is necessary to respond to the continuous process changes made during the production itself. The MES is the main proponent of this management. It stores process information and makes it dynamically available to the various operators, according to the task and responsibilities that each of them possesses. As explained above, the MES extracts the product and production indications from the central DB previously filled by the PLM.

The second management of data consists in the digitization of the company know-how. In this way, the technicians responsible for defining the product life-cycle insert the information into the PLM. It automatically makes this information available to the MES in the central DB. In this case Aras PLM platform was chosen to develop the PLM. Aras solution meets all the needs for the management of the OKP, including the possibility of adding a report to a shop order that allows analysts to know that products have encountered problems or changes, and to get an initial description of these. At this point to deepen the analysis of the problems, there is a link to the central DB which will provide more details of what happened: what activities were repeated or added, the results of the check start and check end and all that is related to that shop order. In this way, the company has a detailed history of production and above all of what has not worked, to understand what changes to make for a current shop order and to be more accurate about future ones.

5 Conclusion and Future Works

This paper aims to present a methodology to build a framework to integrate design and production data. Besides the storage of product and process knowledge into a structured archive, the proposed framework is a tool which allows the data retrieval of previous products and its re-usage to define variants and changes to them. Changes in the production operations or parameters can be done more easily starting from the knowledge of a previous product instead of redoing from scratch.

Some limitations of the work are that it is focused on the knowledge related to the production phase of products, without considering other important aspects related to customers or maintenance. Furthermore, the model also lacks additional information, such as the cost, time and quality associated to the operation, which can be inserted to allow more complex reasoning.

References

1. Wortmann, J.C., Muntslag, D.R., Timmermans, P.J.M.: Customer-Driven Manufacturing. Chapman & Hall, London (1997)
2. Tu, Y.: Production planning and control in a virtual one-of-a-kind production company. Comput. Ind. **34**(3), 271–283 (1997)
3. Dean, P.R., Tu, Y.L., Xue, D.: An information system for one-of-a-kind production. Int. J. Prod. Res. **47**(4), 1071–1087 (2009)
4. Bruno, G., Antonelli, D., Korf, R., Lentes, J., Zimmermann, N.: Exploitation of a semantic platform to store and reuse PLM knowledge. In: Grabot, B., Vallespir, B., Gomes, S., Bouras, A., Kiritsis, D. (eds.) APMS 2014. IAICT, vol. 438, pp. 59–66. Springer, Heidelberg (2014). https://doi.org/10.1007/978-3-662-44739-0_8
5. Bruno, G., Taurino, T., Villa, A.: An approach to support SMEs in manufacturing knowledge organization. J. Intell. Manuf. **29**(6), 1379–1392 (2018)
6. Chungoora, N., et al.: A model-driven ontology approach for manufacturing interoperability and knowledge sharing. Comput. Ind. **64**(4), 392–401 (2013)
7. David, M., Rowe, F.: What does PLMS (product lifecycle management systems) manage: data or documents? Complementarity and contingency for SMEs. Comput. Ind. **75**, 140–150 (2015)
8. Efthymiou, K., Sipsas, K., Mourtzis, D., Chryssolouris, G.: On knowledge reuse for manufacturing systems design and planning: a semantic technology approach. CIRP J. Manufact. Sci. Technol. **8**, 1–11 (2015)
9. Igba, J., Alemzadeh, K., Gibbons, P.M., Henningsen, K.: A framework for optimizing product performance through feedback and reuse of in-service experience. Robot. Comput.-Integr. Manuf. **36**, 2–12 (2015)
10. Bruno, G., Korf, R., Lentes, J., Zimmermann, N.: Efficient management of product lifecycle information through a semantic platform. Int. J. Prod. Lifecycle Manag. **9**(1), 45–64 (2016)
11. Elgamma, A., Papazoglou, M., Krämer, B., Constantinescu, C.: Design for customization: a new paradigm for product-service system development. Procedia CIRP **64**, 345–350 (2017)
12. Ebrahimi, A.H., Johansson, P.E.C., Bengtsson, K., Åkesson, K.: Managing product and production variety – a language workbench approach. Procedia CIRP **17**, 338–344 (2014)
13. Petrucciani, M., Marangi, L., Agosta, M., Stevanella, M.: A platform for product-service design and manufacturing intelligence. In: Cattaneo, L., Terzi, S. (eds.) Models, Methods and Tools for Product Service Design. SAST, pp. 45–61. Springer, Cham (2019). https://doi.org/10.1007/978-3-319-95849-1_4
14. http://www.homeappliancesworld.com/2015/06/01/italian-manufacturing-innovation-is-possible. (2013)

Integration of In-service and Operation

Towards Understanding the Role of Product Usage Information in Product Design Improvement

Quan Deng[1(✉)], Stefan Wellsandt[1], Karl A. Hribernik[1], and Klaus-Dieter Thoben[2]

[1] BIBA-Bremer Institut für Produktion und Logistik GmbH, Hochschulring 20, 28359 Bremen, Germany
{dqu,wel,hri}@biba.uni-bremen.de

[2] Faculty of Production Engineering, University of Bremen, Badgasteiner Straße 1, 28359 Bremen, Germany
tho@biba.uni-bremen.de

Abstract. A critical factor that makes a product successful is its acceptance in its market. To achieve this goal, producers oftentimes collect and analyze feedback information from the market. This information allows them to get a deeper understanding about the product behaviors, customers, their usage patterns, future needs and expectations. The academic literature describes a variety of use cases that outline how development-related tasks can benefit from Product Usage Information (PUI). They differ, for instance, in the investigated product, task, communication channel, information source, and the type of the result. This diversity and the lack of a generally agreed vocabulary in this research domain facilitates a fragmentation of PUI-related research. This paper provides a first systematic overview of a selection of PUI application cases in product design improvement. The study sample consists of 17 research papers from the last 20 years. We characterize and classify the papers mainly through three dimensions: product type, product development phase, and information sources and channels. The results indicate that PUI can support different tasks during product improvement, both in the task clarification phase and in the product conceptual, embodiment and detailed design phases. Our findings suggest that organizations need to know more about PUI-related information sources and channels.

Keywords: Product Usage Information · Product design · Product improvement · Closed-loop PLM

1 Introduction

A critical factor that makes a product successful is its acceptance in its market. To achieve this goal, producers oftentimes use a quality management system (QMS) to monitor and improve customer satisfaction (ISO 9001:2015). Approximately 300,000 producers of durable products maintained an ISO 9001 QMS in 2017 [1]. Essential for this QMS is that the producer's employees collect and analyze feedback information

Published by Springer Nature Switzerland AG 2019
C. Fortin et al. (Eds.): PLM 2019, IFIP AICT 565, pp. 369–378, 2019.
https://doi.org/10.1007/978-3-030-42250-9_35

from the market. This information allows them to get a deeper understanding about the customer, their future needs and expectations, and it supports the employees during root cause investigation in the case of low customer satisfaction or customer complaints (ISO 9001:2015). Employees from different departments – especially product development – collaborate in these activities.

In the last decade, new information sources and computer-supported tools emerged that collect and analyze feedback information. Customers can give feedback via customer hotlines, online discussion forums, online review platforms, and weblogs. They review products, issue complaints, or discuss product features with other customers [2]. For products with a distinct usage phase, such as durable consumer goods and industrial goods, producers can create feedback information through product-embedded information devices (PEIDs) [3]. They measure, for instance, user interactions and environmental conditions, and send them to the producer. *Product usage information* (PUI) is a term that subsumes all product-related information that emerges in the usage phase of the product life cycle [2, 4].

We identified more than 70 scientific articles that describe the application of PUI in development-related tasks. These application cases differ in, for instance, the targeted product, task, information source, and communication channel. Their results include approaches, concepts, methodologies, methods and tools. This diversity and the lack of a generally agreed vocabulary in this research domain facilitates a fragmentation of PUI-related research. We experienced this when we started to collect the application case descriptions in 2016. Our sample indicates the existence of several researcher communities with few connections between each other. A problem that results from this fragmentation is that other researchers require significant effort and time to understand the maturity of this research domain. An overview of existing application cases can help other researchers to identify related work and to position their contributions better within the research domain.

This paper provides a first systematic overview of a selection of PUI application cases. It focuses on product design improvement, because the identified case descriptions mainly address this part of product development. Section 2 introduces important concepts and terminology that characterize PUI application cases. Section 3 outlines the methodology used for our literature analysis. Section 4 presents the results and Sect. 5 discusses two aspects of the role of PUI in product design improvement. Section 6 concludes this paper and provides an outlook for follow-up activities.

2 Concepts and Terminology

This section clarifies important concepts that characterize PUI application cases in product development. It focuses on product-related typologies, information feedback, and the product development process. They refer to the main elements of many PUI application cases: product, information, and task.

2.1 Product-Related Typologies

Products with a distinct usage phase are durable. They degrade and are subject to service activities, such as maintenance and repair. A durable product can be a *consumer good*

(CG) or an *industrial good* (IG) [5]. The former is for personal use and the latter for the production of other goods. Producers can use durable products in combination with services, which results in *Product-Service Systems* (PSS). Complex PSS typically contain hardware, software and service components.

2.2 Information Feedback

Information is data with meaning and oftentimes a critical resource in product development. *Product lifecycle management* (PLM) differentiates forward-oriented and backward-oriented information flows as illustrated in Fig. 1.

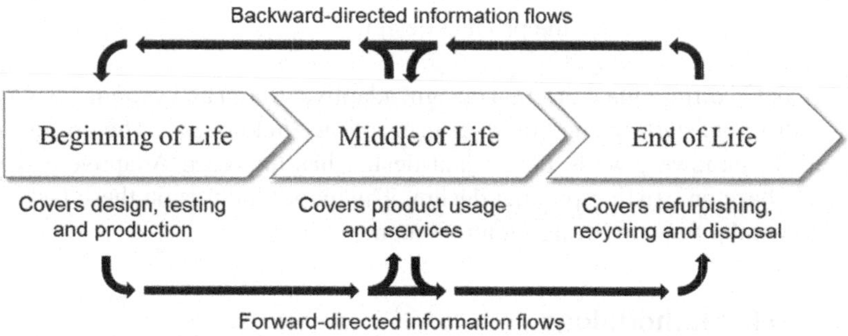

Fig. 1. Information flows in the product life cycle [2]

The product development process can have two information flows. Forward-directed information flows provide information for subsequent activities, such as product testing and production. Backward-directed information flows convey information from other business or stakeholder processes. Wellsandt et al. [6] identified this feedback as "*[…] any response that the producer or its employees receive when they present their work to a stakeholder such as a customer, user, supplier or co-worker*". Employees that receive feedback include engineers, sales persons, service staff, quality managers, and product managers. Responses emerge for different reasons such as complaints, commendation, constructive critique, observation, and inspections. The employees can assess feedback information and use it to support decisions, for instance, about product design changes. This paper focuses on feedback from product usage to product design.

PUI can describe a specific product or groups of them. The former requires that the product has a unique identifier, such as a Serial Global Trade Item Number (SGTIN). Groups of products typically reference a product model (e.g. VW Golf or iPhone) or include shared characteristics, such as geography, user profile, timeframe, and performance. Information about specific items describes products on the so-called "item level". Otherwise, it describes them on the "class level".

2.3 Product Development Process and Tasks

Many product development methodologies and process models are available in the literature. This paper uses the development process proposed by Pahl et al. [7]. We use it to ensure that this paper does not miss critical activities. Their process includes:

- *Product planning*. Analyses the company situation, develops and assesses product ideas. This task results in the requirements list.
- *Task clarification*. Plans the following work activities, and clarifies the requirements list where necessary.
- *Conceptual design*. Abstracts the essential problems, identifies function structures and working principles, and combines them into a working structure. This task results in the principle solution (concept).
- *Embodiment design*. Creates the technical layout in line with the requirements. After several iterations, this task results in the definitive layout.
- *Detail design*. Defines the arrangement, forms, dimensions and surface properties of the individual parts of the solution. This task results in the production documentation that is necessary to produce the product design.

Pahl et al. [7] differentiate original design, adaptive design and variant design. These tasks have different starting conditions in terms of the "unknowns". The original design has the most unknowns, while the variant design has the least. Adaptive and variant design tasks base on existing product design. This paper focuses on these tasks, which we subsume under the term design improvement.

3 Research Methodology

This paper uses a literature review to identify and analyze PUI application cases. Paré et al. [8] outline nine types of literature reviews, such as systematic review, descriptive review, and scoping review. Each type has a specific approach and research goal. This study seeks to provide an initial overview of the application of PUI in product improvement. It bases on 17 case descriptions identified in the literature. This is not an exhaustive review, but sufficient to provide a first overview about the nature of cases.

Our research has three steps: (1) literature search (2) screening (3) data extraction and classification. The literature search started in 2016 and contains more than 70 relevant articles about the usage of PUI in product design. In the screening stage, we include only publications that have concrete examples or use cases. In the stage of data extraction and classification, we characterize and classify the papers mainly through three dimensions: product type, product development phase, and information sources and channels.

In this paper, we group the aforementioned product design tasks into two phases: *task clarification phase*, and *product conceptual, embodiment and detailed design phase*. Product planning, as introduced in Sect. 2.3, is more relevant to new product development. This paper does not focus on this task, though several application cases aim to support product planning.

We use the Big Data source classification schema proposed by the United Nations Economic Commission for Europe (UNECE) to structure the PUI sources and channels [9]. The UNECE uses it in their official statistics and thus we consider it as an acknowledged and credible schema. Furthermore, it aligns well with our previous PUI classifications derived from earlier use case analyses [6]. The schema differentiates three classes of data sources: human sourced information, process mediated data, and machine generated data.

- *Human sourced information* (HSI) is the record of human experiences. It is available through, for instance, Social Networking Services, weblogs, online discussion forums, and email. This information is weakly structured (e.g. XML or JSON format) and often ungoverned. Example PUI in this category include online discussion forum threads, call center transcripts and audio records, product reviews, and emails.
- *Machine-generated data* (MGD) originates from sensors and actuators integrated into products or installed in rooms and areas. This data typically has a structure and specialized databases for documents and time series store it. Example PUI in this category include data from product-embedded sensors and actuators.
- *Process mediated data* (PMD) emerges from business processes and records, for instance, related events. It includes transaction data, reference tables and relationships, and metadata. Information systems for business areas, such as Enterprise Resource Planning and Manufacturing Execution, create, store and convey these data. Process mediated data is highly structured. Example PUI in this category includes service records and warranty claim records.

The next section presents the first results of our analysis. It is not comprehensive, but it gives a rough overview of the nature of our findings and a preliminary insight into the literature about PUI applications in product improvement.

4 Results

The identified literature includes case descriptions from the last 20 years. The earliest article is from 1997 and the most recent ones from 2018. One of the main findings of our analysis is that the identified PUI application cases differ in the focused product type, product development phase, and the information sources and channels. Many articles about application cases take a position somewhere between engineering, business administration and informatics. Oftentimes, they focus on the former or the latter. An engineering focus means that the authors describe the benefits of PUI in a specific development-related task. An informatics focus typically details the applied methodology to collect and process data into information or even more useful knowledge. Table 1 contains characteristic example cases that clarify the nature of the investigated articles.

The identified application cases cover a range of different products. They include comparably simple and low cost fly fishing equipment and toys, cell phones, and more complex and expensive components of machinery. Table 2 summarizes the application of PUI in the two product development phases and the used data source types. Some cases used more than one data source type to support a task. We use the category "mixed data" in the tables for this purpose. An article's focus on one source type does not exclude other sources from being useful for development-related tasks.

Most of the identified cases focus on CG, while only three of them concern IG. The majority uses HSI, especially conveyed through channels on the Internet. Relevant channels include online discussion forums, shopping websites (typically Amazon) and Social Networking Services (typically Facebook). The PUI is typically a part of product review texts and text posts within discussions. The applications oftentimes use it with

Table 1. Excerpt of the identified PUI application cases

Ref.	Topics	Products	Channels
[10]	Support for quality improvement methods	Fly fishing equipment	Usenet
[11]	Decision support for product developers in product improvement	Centrifugal pumps	Sensor data repository
[12]	Product defect discovery with social media information	Cars and car components	Online discussion forum
[13]	Discovering safety concerns mentioned in children's toy reviews	Children's toys	Online customer review platforms
[14]	Analysis of service records to identify improvement potential	Rotary spindle unit	Service records
[15]	Insight on quality of product attributes with correlation to online reviews	Cell phone	Online customer review platforms

Table 2. Overview of PUI application cases in product improvement

Source types	Task clarification phase		Conceptual, embodiment and detailed design phase	
	CG	IG	CG	IG
HSI	[12, 13, 15–17]	–	[10, 18]	–
MGD	[19–21]	–	[22, 23]	[11]
PMD	[24]	[14]	–	–
Mixed	–	[25]	[26]	–

a methodology that uses machine learning, which is a sub-domain of artificial intelligence. These methodologies oftentimes use existing algorithms that the article authors customized to work with the specific sources, channels and tasks of the respective case.

Sensors are the second most used source type. They are oftentimes a component of the targeted product (e.g. a component of a machine). Some application cases refit a small number of products with sensors. The collection and processing of MGD use methodologies that use machine learning as well.

5 Discussion

Our study sample consists of 17 research papers. 65% of them relate to the task clarification phase, and 35% relate to product conceptual, embodiment and detailed design phase. Regarding data sources, most of them are HSI (41%) and MGD (35%). These numbers are sensitive to the selected sample of case descriptions. The following observations are only indicative and may provide useful information to build hypotheses for a larger sample.

5.1 Support in Product Development Tasks

This paper's results indicate that PUI can support different tasks in product improvement. In the *task clarification phase*, the support focuses on changing the requirements list by adding, removing or editing entries. The main role of PUI is to change the employees' understanding about, for instance, product behavior, usage conditions, failure causes, and customer opinions. In the *product conceptual, embodiment and detailed design phase*, the focus is on the evaluation of product designs under market conditions. The application case acquires information from product usage to solve a specific technical problem for the next product generation. We assume that the analysis of more application cases can lead to detailed recommendations when and how to apply PUI for product improvement.

5.2 Role of Information Sources and Channels

The application of PUI in product development can benefit from a detailed understanding of the information sources and channels. This is because each source/channel requires different approaches, methods and tools to extract the PUI from the available information. A second reason is that processes, such as data creation, storage, processing and distribution, differ amongst source types and channels. Different factors related to these processes influence, for instance, the PUI's accuracy, precision, timeliness, accessibility and credibility. The lack of regular sensor calibration, for instance, can turn accurate measurements into information that gives employees a false understanding of environmental conditions or product behavior. A second example why quality matters is the influence of the data format on the information's accessibility. Computer programs can access and process structured data with less effort compared to semi-structured or unstructured data. The tools that process unstructured data typically require that an organization involves experts that are familiar with machine learning. They are an important cost factor that affects the applicability of PUI from these sources and channels.

Table 3. PUI channels usable in product development

Channels	Typical contents	Data formats	Source types
Sensor data repository	Environmental information; performance	S/SS	MGD
Log file of embedded control system	Product behavior	SS	
Service report	Maintenance, repair and failure information; product condition	SS/US	PMD
Online discussion forum	Opinions; ratings; complaints; customer/user profiles; constructive critique		HSI
Online customer review platforms			
Telephone	Opinions; complaints; customer profiles		
Email	Opinions; complaints; customer/user profiles; constructive critique	US	

S = structured; SS = semi-structured; US = unstructured

Table 3 provides an overview of information channels mentioned in the application cases. It is not comprehensive but provides a first overview of relevant characteristics of PUI-related sources and channels.

MGD is mostly structured or semi-structured. It typically originates from sensors and the log files of product-embedded control systems. Producers can control the quality of MGD if their employees take the product development's information needs into account during the design of the product's sensor systems.

PMD integrates HSI and MGD. Service records, for instance, have text input from service personnel and data from measurements. They contain maintenance, repair and failure information, which are helpful for producers to identify a product's weaknesses.

HSI is mainly semi-structured or unstructured data created by consumers. The latter can provide feedback information as opinions, complaints and expectations. This feedback refers to the product instances of the respective consumer but there is often no unique identifier. This is a problem, because the employees cannot combine it with other information about an instance (e.g. sensor data). Therefore, HSI can provide insights about many product aspects but often without much detail. The amount and quality of this kind of information rely on the involved consumers and the available channels.

This research focuses on product-related information that emerges after the product was delivered to the user. One subset of the investigated articles (e.g. [21]) describes applications for product prototypes, i.e. products used by test users. They collect information about product usage and then improve product designs accordingly. In comparison to PUI, the usage information from prototypes entails the same features, but likely contains contents for different purposes. Producers can try sensors in prototypes, which may not appear in the marketed product. They can choose lead users to test prototypes, but the involvement of consumers at a larger scale for testing and feedback is typically too expensive and time consuming.

6 Conclusion

This paper presented an initial overview of PUI application cases in product design improvement. We identified 17 cases and analyzed them along three dimensions: product type, product development phase, and information sources and channels. The results indicate that PUI can support the task clarification phase and the product conceptual, embodiment and detailed design phases. We cannot provide more detailed recommendations without analyzing more cases. The main conclusion of this paper is that organizations need to know more about PUI-related information sources and channels. This is important because each source type and channel requires different approaches, methods and tools to extract the PUI from the available sources. Producers could design solutions that supply their employees with PUI, if they gain a precise understanding in this domain. A *limitation* of this research is the risk of sample bias. The investigated sample is small and the inclusion or removal of papers can have a substantial impact on the conclusion. We will perform a review with a larger sample to address this issue.

Acknowledgments. This research has received funding from the European Union's Horizon 2020 research and innovation programme under grant agreements No. 791875 (REALCOE), No. 636951 (MANUTELLIGENCE) and No. 605389 (FALCON).

References

1. ISO. The ISO Survey of Management System Standard Certifications - ISO 9001 - Quality Management Systems – Requirements - Data from 1993 to 2017. https://isotc.iso.org/livelink/livelink/18808108/01._ISO_9001_-_data_per_country_and_sector_-_1993_to_2017.xlsm?func=doc.Fetch&nodeid=18808108. Accessed 25 Mar 2019
2. Wellsandt, S., Hribernik, K., Thoben, K.-D.: Sources and characteristics of information about product use. Procedia CIRP **36**, 242–247 (2015)
3. Kiritsis, D.: Closed-loop PLM for intelligent products in the era of the Internet of things. Comput. Aided Des. **43**(5), 479–501 (2011)
4. Wellsandt, S., Thoben, K.-D.: Approach to describe knowledge sharing between producer and user. Procedia CIRP **50**, 20–25 (2016)
5. Kotler, P., Keller, K.L.: Marketing Management, 14th edn, pp. 325–328. Prentice Hall, Upper Saddle River (2012)
6. Wellsandt, S., Thoben, K.-D., Klein, P.: Information feedback in product development: analysing practical cases. In: 15th International Design Conference, Glasgow, UK, 21–24 May 2018, pp. 1745–1756 (2018)
7. Pahl, G., Beitz, W., Feldhusen, J., Grote, K.-H.: Engineering Design. Springer, London (2007). https://doi.org/10.1007/978-1-84628-319-2
8. Paré, G., Trudel, M.-C., Jaana, M., Kitsiou, S.: Synthesizing information systems knowledge: a typology of literature reviews. Inf. Manag. **52**(2), 183–199 (2015)
9. United Nations Economic Commission for Europe (UNECE). Classification of Types of Big Data. https://statswiki.unece.org/display/bigdata/Classification+of+Types+of+Big+Data. Accessed 03 Mar 2019
10. Finch, B.J., Luebbe, R.L.: Using Internet conversations to improve product quality: an exploratory study. Int. J. Qual. Reliab. Manag. **14**(8), 849–865 (1997)
11. Abramovici, M., Lindner, A., Dienst, S.: Use case of providing decision support for product developers in product improvement processes. In: Fathi, M. (ed.) Integration of Practice-Oriented Knowledge Technology: Trends and Prospectives, pp. 171–182. Springer, Heidelberg (2013). https://doi.org/10.1007/978-3-642-34471-8_14
12. Abrahams, A.S., Fan, W., Wang, G.A., Zhang, Z.J., Jiao, J.: An integrated text analytic framework for product defect discovery. Prod. Oper. Manag. **24**(6), 975–990 (2015)
13. Winkler, M., Abrahams, A.S., Gruss, R., Ehsani, J.P.: Toy safety surveillance from online reviews. Decis. Support Syst. **90**, 23–32 (2016)
14. Abramovici, M., Gebus, P., Göbel, J.C., Savarino, P.: Utilizing unstructured feedback data from MRO reports for the continuous improvement of standard products. In: ICED 2017, Vancouver, Canada, 21–25 August 2017 (2017)
15. Singh, A., Tucker, C.S.: A machine learning approach to product review disambiguation based on function, form and behavior classification. Decis. Support Syst. **97**, 81–91 (2017)
16. Zhang, X., et al.: Identifying Product Defects from User Complaints: A Probabilistic Defect Model (2016). http://hdl.handle.net/10919/64902
17. Bae, J., Cho, K., Kim, C.: Developing a framework of new mixed method, social networking services group diary and its application in practice. In: Proceedings of the 20th International Conference on Engineering Design (ICED 2015), Milan, Italy (2015)
18. Wang, B., Miao, Y., Zhao, H., Jin, J., Chen, Y.: A biclustering-based method for market segmentation using customer pain points. Eng. Appl. Artif. Intell. **47**, 101–109 (2016)
19. van Horn, D., Olewnik, A., Lewis, K.: Design analytics: capturing, understanding, and meeting customer needs using big data. In: Proceedings of the ASME 2012 IDETC & CIE. ASME, pp. 863–875 (2012)

20. Funk, M., Rozinat, A., Alves de Medeiros, A.K., van der Putten, P., Corporaal, H., van der Aalst, W.: Improving product usage monitoring and analysis with semantic concepts. In: Yang, J., Ginige, A., Mayr, H.C., Kutsche, R.-D. (eds.) UNISCON 2009. LNBIP, vol. 20, pp. 190–201. Springer, Heidelberg (2009). https://doi.org/10.1007/978-3-642-01112-2_20
21. Rohlmann, A., et al.: Monitoring the load on a telemeterised vertebral body replacement for a period of up to 65 months. Eur. Spine J. **22**, 2575–2581 (2013)
22. Simonite, T.: How Tesla uses its customers' cars to develop and test new self-driving software. https://www.technologyreview.com/s/601567/tesla-tests-self-driving-functions-with-secret-updates-to-its-customers-cars/. Accessed 03 Mar 2019
23. van der Vegte, W.F., Kurt, F., Şengöz, O.K.: Simulation of product performance based on real product-usage information: first results of practical application to domestic refrigerators. In: 38th Computers and Information in Engineering Conference, Quebec City, Quebec, Canada (2018). https://doi.org/10.1115/DETC2018-85899
24. Yang, K., Cekecek, E.: Design vulnerability analysis and design improvement by using warranty data. Qual. Reliab. Eng. Int. **20**(2), 121–133 (2004)
25. Hussain, R., Lockett, H., Vijaykumar, G.A.V.: A framework to inform PSS conceptual design by using system-in-use data. Comput. Ind. **63**, 319–327 (2012)
26. Tucker, C.S., Kim, H.M.: Data-driven decision tree classification for product portfolio design optimization. J. Comput. Inf. Sci. Eng. **9**(4), 41004 (2009)

Hybrid Data-Driven and Physics-Based Modelling for Prescriptive Maintenance of Gas-Turbine Power Plant

Sergei Nikolaev(✉), Sergei Belov, Mikhail Gusev, and Ighor Uzhinsky

Laboratory of Cyber-Physical Systems, Skolkovo Institute of Science and Technology, Moscow, Russia
s.nikolaev@skoltech.ru

Abstract. The methodology for prescriptive maintenance of complex technical systems is presented. The proposed methodology is based on a hybrid physics-based and data-driven modelling of complex systems. This approach integrates traditional physics-based simulation techniques such as finite-element modelling, finite-volume modelling, bond-graph modelling and data-driven models, with machine learning algorithms. Combined implementation of the both approaches results in the development of a set of reliable, fast and continuously updating models of technical systems applicable for predictive and prescriptive analytics. The methodology is demonstrated on the jet-engine power plant preventive maintenance case-study.

Keywords: Prescriptive analytics · Machine learning · Hybrid modelling · Jet-engine simulation

1 Introduction

1.1 Digital Twin Concept

Traditionally, PLM systems and tools are focused on the development and production stages of a product lifecycle, including design, testing, validation of the developed models and manufacturing. Since 1980–1990-s (the time of initiation of the PLM concept) huge amount of data have been generated that is used for the development and manufacturing of complex products in aerospace, automotive, machinery and other industries [1]. The use of CAD, CAE and digital manufacturing tools now is considered as a standard for the product development. Nowadays more and more attention is paid to the multi-level simulation of a product functionality to support the development process and to reduce the needed number of physical tests. Demand in numerical models is one of the main drivers of the PLM market growth.

The original version of this chapter was revised: the missing acknowledgment has been added. The correction to this chapter is available at https://doi.org/10.1007/978-3-030-42250-9_39

Published by Springer Nature Switzerland AG 2019
C. Fortin et al. (Eds.): PLM 2019, IFIP AICT 565, pp. 379–388, 2020.
https://doi.org/10.1007/978-3-030-42250-9_36

The high-level models, built using systems modelling languages (SysML), functional models, built in Modelica-oriented environments, finite-element and finite-volume models, built in FEA and CFD codes are managed using special modules in PLM systems called Simulation Data and Process Management modules.

All the mentioned above factors, together with increasing computing power led to introduction of the digital twin concept. Digital twin is an integrated set of virtual physics-driven models of a product, system or process which enables real-time monitoring and avoids problems before they occur with its physical counterpart and prevents downtimes [2]. Also, digital twin aims to reduce the cost of system testing and verification. Unlike ordinary virtual model, which describes the product without any imperfections, digital twin of the product represents a particular its instance at different stages of the lifecycle (testing, production, maintenance, disposal). The digital twin concept along with descriptions of the entire digital twin technology were presented and discussed in a number of research papers [3, 4].

1.2 Preventive Maintenance and Performance Optimization Using Digital Twins

Among other applications, digital twin should be used for prescriptive maintenance of a system or a product in operation. There are different ways to perform preventive maintenance of a functioning product (Fig. 1), including descriptive, diagnostic, predictive and prescriptive analytics.

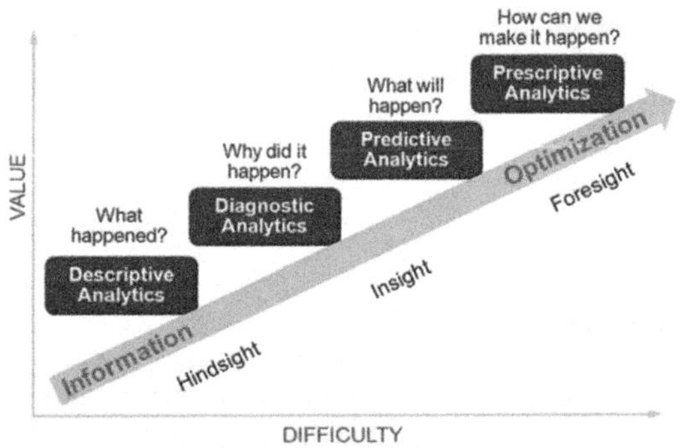

Fig. 1. The way to prescriptive analytics (courtesy of Gartner)

Descriptive and Condition-Based Maintenance

This type of maintenance became a widely-used option with automation and sensors cheapening. Instead of maintaining of the equipment based on a pre-defined schedule, the condition-based maintenance evaluates the asset's actual conditions to determine the need for the maintenance. Most of the modern machines have built-in sensors which provide real-time data transfer to centralized systems and help maintenance teams in maintaining of equipment before problems occur. Following IBM research, advanced maintenance teams have either adopted or are working towards implementing of condition-based maintenance programs to reduce cost and increase uptime.

Predictive Maintenance

The predictive maintenance is the next step further towards implementation of the condition-based maintenance. Once data is coming from the equipment in real-time or near real-time, advanced analytics are used to identify the asset's reliability risks that could impact business operations. By applying machine learning techniques and analytics to operational data, companies can act on these insights as part of a continuous improvement process. Companies with advanced processes and high-value equipment are rapidly adopting predictive maintenance solutions. But right now, these solutions aren't for everyone – they require firms to have condition-based processes in place and are usually data intensive.

Prescriptive Maintenance

The prescriptive maintenance is the next step in implementation of the condition-based maintenance. It uses advanced analytics to make predictions about maintenance, but the main difference is that prescriptive systems not only make recommendations but also act on recommendations, so it should be able to make decisions and be cognitive.

By evolving from time based, to condition based, to predictive and prescriptive maintenance, companies are evolving their maintenance systems from being simply efficient to becoming truly strategic.

One of the cornerstones of prescriptive analytics solutions is that it should be based on use of the maintained product's digital twin, which includes physics-based and data-driven models of a particular instance.

1.3 Hybrid Modeling Approach

The era of IIoT (Industrial Internet of Things) made a huge amount of data affordable, generated by technical systems during exploitation. Machine learning techniques became a very popular tool to build data-driven models and to predict failures or to optimize performance. These models are as efficient as the quantity and quality of data that is used to train them. The popularity of machine learning methods is so high, that sometimes a set of such data-driven models is also called a digital twin. This is not correct since the data-driven models are "blind" in sense of knowing the nature of processes, causes of defects and faults, etc. From another hand, physics-based models are usually quite slow and have to be adjusted to fit real-time data using verification experiments. An approach for overcoming of the described issues is presented below.

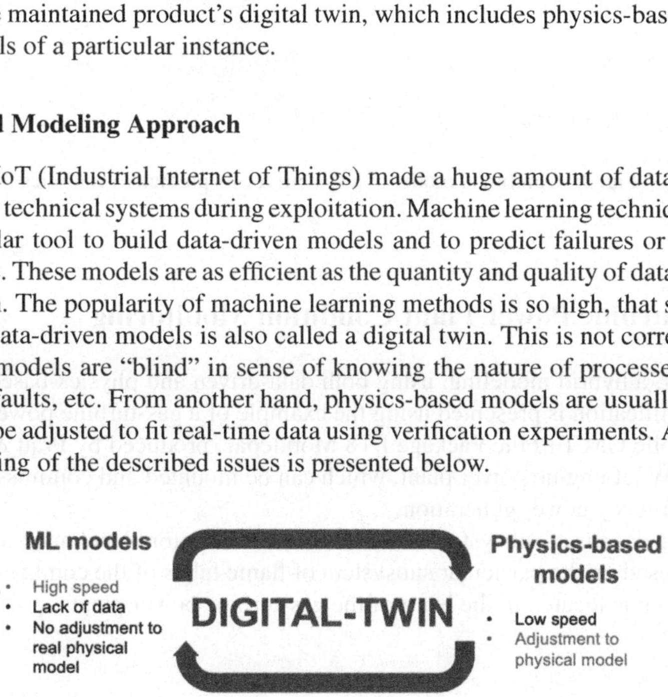

Fig. 2. Digital twin as a combination of data-driven and physics-based models

The general idea is in putting together the data-driven models with physics-based models in order to increase the benefits from digital twin as it's shown in Fig. 2. Despite its obvious advantage, quite few researches discuss the hybrid modelling approach to build digital twin. The hybrid approach to the digital twin development should include two-phase methodology for prognostics, where the first phase develops a physics-based model for both healthy and damaged conditions and the second phase computes the residuals when comparing the measurements with the simulation results [5]. These residuals are indicative of the state of the monitored instance, and the remaining useful life (RUL) can be computed by comparing the residuals with a predefined performance. A comprehensive review of different hybrid modelling approaches for the RUL estimation is presented in [6]. The authors of this paper propose to use the physics-model in order to simulate systems behavior with the presence of different types of defects and then use it for defect detection and identification. The scheme is shown on Fig. 3.

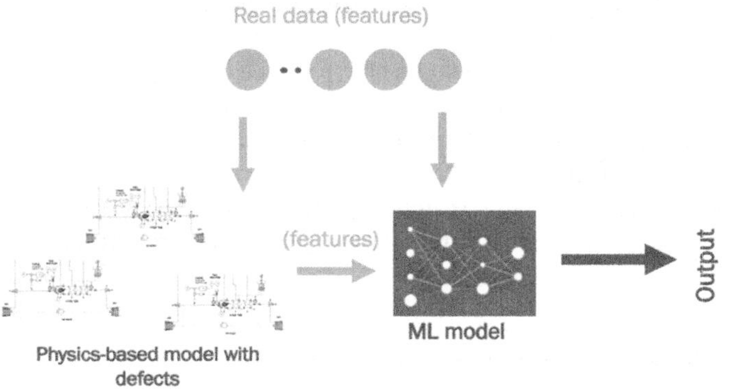

Fig. 3. Combined model of a system for its predictive analytics

2 Gas-Turbine Power Plant Condition Monitoring

In this paper, a hybrid modeling, using both data-driven and physics-based models for defects identification is presented using the example of a gas-turbine power plant monitoring. Mobile Gas Turbine Package FT8 Mobilepac, produced by Pratt & Whitney is about 25 MW jet-engine power plant, which can be mounted and commissioned in one day for emergency power generation.

There are dozens of subsystems which should be monitored and maintained, but this paper is focused on the particular subsystem of flame tubes of the combustion chamber (Fig. 4), which is located in the heart of the gas-turbine power plant – gas-engine.

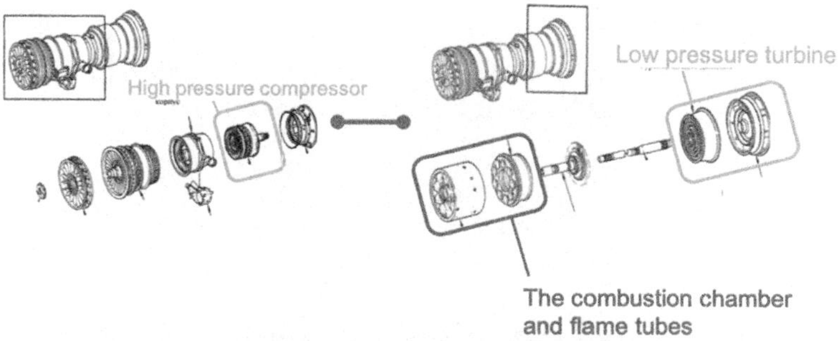

Fig. 4. Main parts of gas-engine

2.1 Data-Driven Model Description

To design data-driven model 25 features were used as presented in the Table 1.

Table 1. Features for machine learning model

Features		
Generated power	Pressure before low pressure compressor (LPC)	Power turbine (PT) rpm
Thermocouples 1–9 temperature	Pressure after high pressure compressor (HPC)	LPC rpm
Mean outlet gas temperature	Pressure after low pressure turbine (LPT)	HPC rpm
Fuel consumption	LPT outlet gas temperature	Environment temperature

One of the most important industrial tasks in the gas turbine prescriptive maintenance is detection of the flame tube breakage. It could be detected by the temperature profile of thermocouples, placed at the different distance from combustion chamber. The point is that the profile deviation could be caused by the different reasons (injector lags, hydraulic system malfunctions and so forth). Monitoring of the combustion process health is a method commonly used in the industry [7].

Initial data analysis has shown, that the correlation between such parameters as generated power, thermocouple temperatures, LPT and HPT rotary speed is more than 0.85. The correlation tab for the whole amount of the data is presented on the Fig. 5.

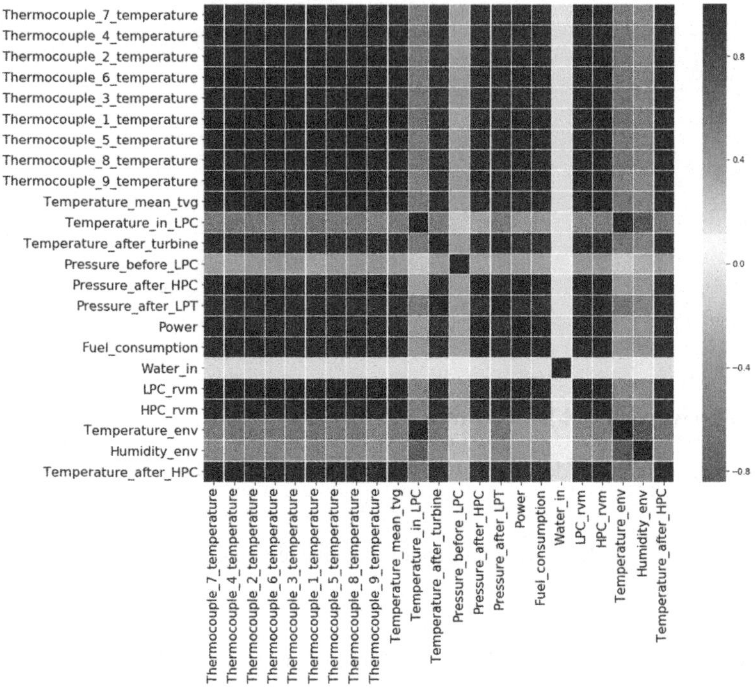

Fig. 5. Correlation tab for the data used in the machine learning model

As the turbine thermodynamics determines the turbine behavior [8] the artificial neural networks, which are well suited for non-linear dependencies, were used to predict the thermocouple temperatures. Training dataset consisted of 25 000 min of exploitation data (excluding the region where flame tubes were broken). The test results are shown on the Fig. 6.

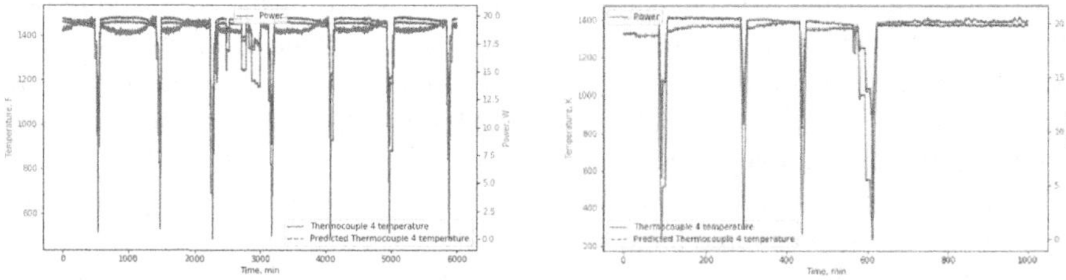

a) b)

Fig. 6. Thermocouple "4" temperature prediction in the regions with broken flame tubes (a) and repaired flame tubes (b)

The best result was shown on the model with configuration of 4 hidden layers and totally 2459 parameters. The machine learning model solves the problem of an abnormal behavior detection, and answering the questions about condition of the tubes. With available amount of data, there is no opportunity to identify the reason of the breakage.

2.2 Physics-Based Modeling

The physics-based model was built to identify the cause of the defect and to enrich the results of the data-driven modelling with physical dependencies. Siemens LMS Amesim software was used to create the functional model of the gas turbine. Amesim is a software platform for multi-physical dynamical systems modelling, which uses bond-graph theory. The problem arises at the stage of detailed design, as the most important parameters for the modelling are usually unknown (compressors and turbine performance maps). To find out the performance map of the HPC the scaling of preloaded performance maps in the Amesim was used. The model of the compressor was used as it shown on the Fig. 7.

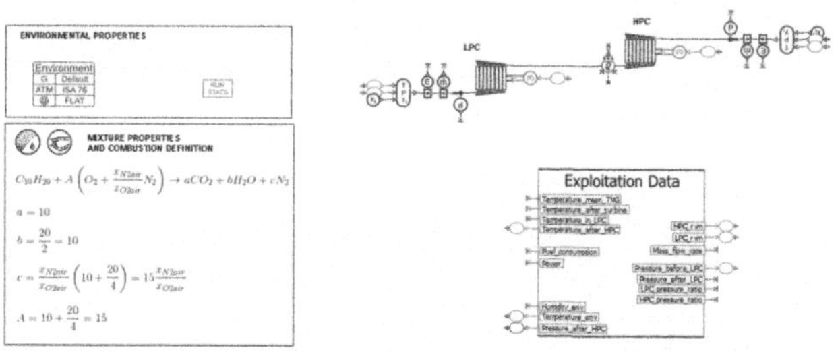

Fig. 7. Amesim model for compressor validation

Real exploitation data was uploaded to the Amesim model, which in conjunction with digitized LPC performance [9] allowed us to select HPC parameters. The results of the model simulation on the real exploitation data are shown on the Fig. 8.

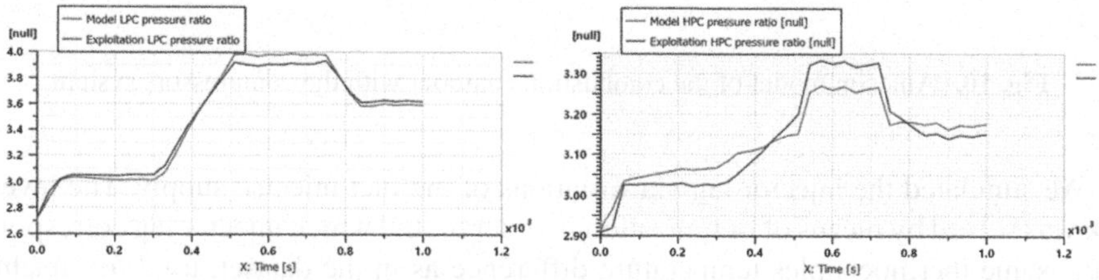

Fig. 8. Simulation data in comparison with exploitation data

The Fig. 9 represents performance maps of the compressors.

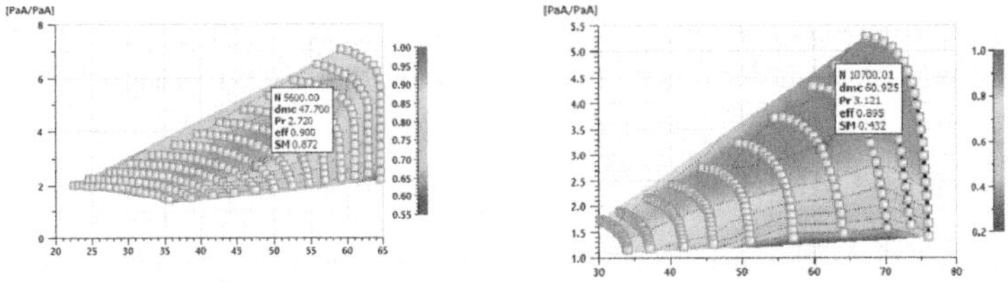

a) b)

Fig. 9. Performance map of the LPC (a) and HPC (b)

2.3 Using Physics-Based Model to Identify the Cause of Defect

For the flame tube breakage simulation, the full gas-engine Amesim model was created. It consisted of a compressors system and a combustion chamber models with real exploitation data uploaded (Fig. 10).

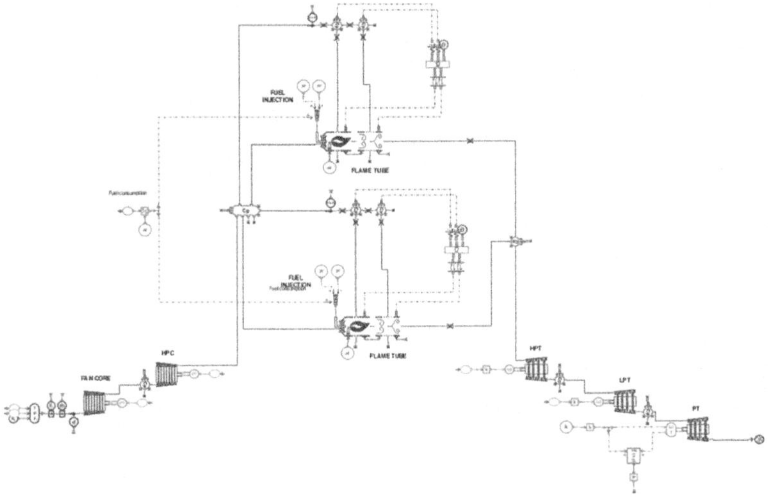

Fig. 10. Amesim model of the combustion chamber with the compressors system

We simulated the injector lag via variations of the fuel injected supply. The inverse task was solved by means of optimization in order to find which injector lag corresponds to the same thermocouples temperature difference as in the dataset, used for machine learning. It was found that the injector lag in flame tube #4 that was equal to 4% led to the difference in temperature of the thermocouples of about 50 °C (Fig. 11) that matched well the machine learning results.

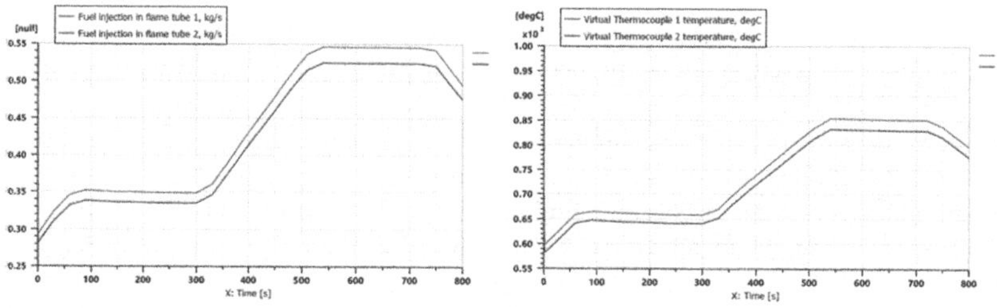

Fig. 11. Simulation of the lag in injector

Combining of applications of physics-based and data-driven models allowed not just to identify the problem in particular flame tube, but also to find out the reason of this defect and to prevent an expensive procedure of the tube replacement, by replacement of just the injector.

3 Conclusion

The approach of hybrid modeling for prescriptive analytics was tested on the gas-turbine flame tubes maintenance. The presented approach consists of two stages: implementation of the data analysis, development of a physics-based model, and its combination in order to identify the causes of anomalies and defects. The presented case study is devoted to the defect identification inside one of the flame tubes in the engine. By using simulation and machine learning modeling of the injector lag, which corresponds to the measured temperatures, the problem was identified and the injector has been replaced.

It's worth noting that, in most cases, there is no need to build a detailed 3D model of the investigated system for its predictive and prescriptive analytics. Usually, the functional model (built in Amesim, Modelica, etc.) can vastly improve the quality of prediction, made just on data analysis. Such models can be developed quite fast and don't need a lot of computational resources.

Our future work will be devoted to automatization of multiple simulations with various types of defects in order to add the datasets for machine learning and to identify the causes of defects and of the product's residual useful life.

Acknowledgments. This work was supported by the Federal program «Research and development in priority areas for the development of the scientific and technological complex of Russia for 2014-2020» via grant RFMEFI60619X0008.

References

1. Terzi, S., Bouras, A., Dutta, D., Garetti, M., Kiritsis, D.: Product lifecycle management – from its history to its new role. Int. J. Prod. Lifecycle Manag. **4**, 360 (2010)
2. Madni, A.M., Madni, C.C., Lucero, S.D.: Leveraging digital twin technology in model-based systems engineering. Systems **7**(1), 7 (2019)

3. Schluse, M., Priggemeyer, M., Atorf, L., Rossmann, J.: Experimentable digital twins—streamlining simulation-based systems engineering for industry 4.0. IEEE Trans. Ind. Inform. **14**, 1722–1731 (2018)
4. Schluse, M., Rossmann, J.: From simulation to experimentable digital twins: simulation-based development and operation of complex technical systems. In: Proceedings of the 2016 IEEE International Symposium on Systems Engineering (ISSE), Edinburgh, UK (2016)
5. Leturiondo, U., Salgado, O., Galar, D.: Methodology for the physics-based modelling of multiple rolling element bearing configurations. Proc. Inst. Mech. Eng. Part K: J. Multi-body Dyn. **231**(1), 194–212 (2016)
6. Liao, L., K'ottig, F.: A hybrid framework combining data-driven and model-based methods for system remaining useful life prediction. Appl. Soft Comput. **44**, 191–199 (2016)
7. Weizhong, Y., Lijie, Y.: On accurate and reliable anomaly detection for gas turbine combustors: a deep learning approach. In: Annual Conference of the Prognostics and Health Management Society (2015)
8. Turan, O.: First law approach of a low bypass turbofan engine. J. Autom. Control Eng. **2**(1) (2014)
9. Monhardt, R.J., Richardson, J.H.: Design and test of the FT8 gas turbine low pressure compressor. In: The American Society of Mechanical Engineers, 89-GT-295 (1989)

Product-Service Systems Lifecycle Management in Industry: Interests and Exploited Data

Juliana Cavalcante(✉) and Lilia Gzara

G-SCOP Laboratory, 46 Avenue Félix Viallet, 38000 Grenoble, France
juliana.cavalcante-da-silva@grenoble-inp.fr

Abstract. Product-Service Systems (PSS) emerged as a response to the market demand for specific solutions to meet their needs in a competitive and sustainable way. In order to manage and improve the value offered to the customer, lifecycle information needs to be gathered and exploited. In this paper, we present a survey realized among PSS providers, aiming to identify the exploitations and anticipations serving best industry's current interests. These exploitations were divided in five categories, which the respondents were invited to rank according to the pertinence to their business. The survey also covers the investigation of which data the providers dispose to achieve these exploitations. The answers were compared to general information about the PSS offered by the respondents, such as the type of PSS, product smartness level and type of services offered. The results indicate an initial stage of PSS development, with an important potential to improve. This analysis will further guide the proposition of an information system architecture for PSS lifecycle management in closed-loop, which may integrate the exploitations highlighted by the survey.

Keywords: Product-Service Systems · Lifecycle management · Data exploitation · Feedback data · Industrial survey

1 Introduction

This paper fits into the context of PSS lifecycle management in closed-loop. Lifecycle management aims to efficiently handle information during the whole lifecycle, but these information flows are interrupted shortly after the PSS is delivered. The advantage of a closed-loop approach is the possibility to close these information loops, allowing the feedback and reuse of all lifecycle data. In this sense, the focus of the current work is the investigation on how lifecycle data can be used to propose improvements to the PSS offer.

The survey described in this paper confronts possible exploitations, based on literature review and theoretical methods, with the current interests of industrial PSS providers. The second section briefly describes the path to the survey motivation, from the PSS lifecycle model to a method to propose anticipations and exploitations from indicators. The survey building and the target diffusion are detailed in the third section. The survey results are presented in the fourth section and discussed in the section five.

C. Fortin et al. (Eds.): PLM 2019, IFIP AICT 565, pp. 389–398, 2019.
https://doi.org/10.1007/978-3-030-42250-9_37

2 Problem Space

An adapted PSS lifecycle model was proposed in order to identify the activities and data involved in each stage [1]. It is composed by four main phases: Idea & Design, Realization, Use and End of Life. Idea & Design consists on the identification of product and services opportunities, selection of the best alternative and conversion into requirements. The second phase corresponds to product and service prototyping, product manufacturing and service implementation, testing and delivery. PSS assistance and monitoring are included in the Use phase. Finally, the End of Life considers product reuse, remanufacturing or recycling, and service decommissioning or redesign.

Based on this lifecycle model, a literature review was driven to identify the data exploitations, from downstream phases to upstream phases, already treated in previous works. These exploitations were divided according to the origin of the data and the phase where it is applied. Most works considered the application of realization [2, 3], use [4, 5] and end of life [6, 7] data to improve design.

In this step, a great amount of underused use phase data was highlighted as well as the low number of exploitations performed in realization phase. It guided the choice of focusing the following steps on the exploitation of PSS use data in realization phase.

In sequence, a method to propose exploitations from use data was developed. Key use data from a semantic model representing PSS lifecycle data [8] were combined in pairs to create indicators. From these indicators, a list of exploitations to realization phase was prospected and further divided in categories.

The main goal of the survey was to identify the exploitations that best meet the industry's needs and interests. For that, the survey invites the respondents to rank the exploitations categories according to their pertinence to their business, and also to identify the data available to perform these exploitations.

3 Survey Building

The proposed survey was divided into three main blocks: contextualization, categories ranking and data availability.

3.1 Contextualization

Aiming to identify possible patterns in different PSS providers, this block proposes a series of questions related to the company, the PSS offer and management, and relationship with the clients and their data. For all questions, a free space was left for further details or controversies.

Company Size. Considering the number of employees (E) and the turnover (T), a company can be classified as: micro ($E \leq 10$, $T \leq 2$ million euros), small ($E \leq 50$, $T \leq 10$ million euros), medium ($E \leq 250$, $T \leq 50$ million euros), or big ($E > 250$, $T > 50$ million euros).

Type of PSS Offer. There are some divergences on the types of PSS. Although [9] defends that there are at least eight types of PSS, most authors consider only three main groups [10–12]: product-oriented, use-oriented and result-oriented PSS. In a product-oriented PSS, the business model is mainly geared towards the sale of products, having extra services being added to them. A use-oriented PSS offer does not include a product being sold and the ownership remains with the provider. In this case, the product is made available in a different form, and sometimes it is shared by a number of users. The result-oriented PSS is offered through an agreement between client and provider on the result, and there is no pre-determined product involved.

Product Nature. The product component of a PSS can be a manufacture or a software example, which might influence on the preferred exploitations and on the data access.

Product Smartness Level. Considering the rise of smart products, it is necessary to identify the level of connectivity and information management of products that are part of PSS. According to [13], the simplest type of integration would be physical products with embedded simple sensors, such as a refrigerator with a thermostat. In a higher level, these products embedded with sensors would have memory and data process capabilities, as in a car with an ETS system. Finally, the most connected would include not only sensors but also information devices (e.g. RFID tags, sensors networks and on-board computers), such as airplanes with tagged components and networks that allow Predictive Maintenance.

Services Offered. A PSS might offer a cascade of services, each layer including the previous services and new ones. From the lowest to the highest level, it could be based on monitoring, controlling, optimization or autonomy-related services.

Type of Use. Individual use stands for products that are used by only one customer for the whole duration of PSS lifecycle. Shared use includes the cases of renting and leasing, such as most city bikes offers.

Type of Installation. A huge part of known PSS examples is based on mobile products, such as transport solutions. This kind of offer must consider not only the product identification but also the different uses of it – client type of use and location. Otherwise, many PSS are based on physically installed products, such as industrial machines or Xerox's copiers leasing business [14].

Access to Product. Considering the access to the product, the PSS provider usually have three different alternatives: accessing the product on the customer site, taking the product to their own site or having remote access to the product.

Software Tool Used for PSS Management. Commercial information tools dedicated to PSS lifecycle management are not available yet. For this reason, PSS providers might use PLM (Product Lifecycle Management) or SLM (Service Lifecycle Management) tools, combined or separately, to perform PSS management. Providers might also dispose of a customized software dedicated to PSS management.

Access to Data on the PSS During Use Phase. PSS providers might have different levels of access to PSS data. The access can be autonomous to all data or part of it, or it can be given under request to the customer. The under request access can concern the integrality of data or only a pre-defined part. In the most restrictive scenario, the provider may not have access to PSS data at all.

3.2 Categories Ranking

As previously discussed, this work focuses on the possible exploitations of PSS use data to improve PSS realization. According to the PSS lifecycle model in [1], the use phase includes all data related to the monitoring of the product status, product replacement, part changes, product transport, service request, service offerings, service adaptation, consumable management etc. The activities of the realization phase, on which the improvements will be focused, are: manufacturing and assembly of products, implementation of services, product use training, service realization training, tests of products and services, scheduling for product and service demand, delivery of PSS etc.

In Sect. 2, a method to combine data into indicators, and to use indicators to prospect exploitations was discussed. From this method, an important list of possible exploitations was proposed. This list was divided in five main categories of exploitation:

- Adapt PSS offer according to the customer: replace product, replace service, replace both;
- Improve product realization: improve product prototyping, improve product manufacturing, improve training for product use, improve product testing;
- Improve service implementation: improve service simulation, improve resources allocation, improve training for service realization, improve service testing;
- Manage PSS demand: predict product demand, predict service demand, predict PSS demand, improve product demand scheduling, improve service demand scheduling;
- Manage PSS contract: change the number of products and/or services per contract, change the diversity of products and/or services per contract, change the availability of products and/or services per contract.

In this block, the respondents were asked to rank the categories from the most to the least pertinent to their business.

3.3 Data Availability

In order to arrive at the exploitations identified as important, it is essential to determine the data available for this purpose. In this part of the survey, the respondents were asked to identify, from the proposed lists of internal data and data from the customer, whether the data is available or not. For the unavailable data, the providers might specify how difficult it would be to have them (easy, medium, difficult, and unknown).

Data from the Customer. Includes: product identification, product location, product operating state (e.g. normal, disturbed, off.), data recorded by product sensors (e.g. pressure, temperature, vibration), type of event trigger (e.g. max temperature exceeded, max vibration exceeded, expected duration exceeded), date/hour of event trigger, customer feedback after service intervention, and material resource stock at the customer (e.g. spare parts, tools, consumables).

Internal Data. Includes: date/hour of intervention, activities performed at each service intervention, duration of interventions, material resources used during intervention, software resources used during intervention, human resources used during intervention, contract conditions, material resource availability for service execution, software resource availability for service execution, human resource availability for service execution, human resource availability for product realization (e.g. manufacture, delivery), product availability at the provider, spare parts availability at the provider, production planning, delivery planning, data recorded by sensors installed in the material components of service (e.g. location of the intervention vehicle), service performance indicators, reference values (expected behavior) for product sensors, PSS offer configuration (e.g. possible combinations of product-service, relationships between services).

3.4 Target and Diffusion

This survey was intended for industrial PSS providers, who were reached through LinkedIn community. In the absence of a group dedicated to PSS, other pertinent groups were selected for investigation: Product Information Management Professional Association, Service Lifecycle Management and Service in Industry – Management | Servitization | Innovation | Digitalization.

Product Information Management Professional Association unites near 5,5k members, among professionals and people interested not only in Product Information Management (PIM), but also Product Data Management, Product Resource Management, Product Lifecycle Management and Product Catalogue Management. Service Lifecycle Management is a group whose access is made by invitation only, has more than 7k members. It is a collaboration group that puts together professionals from different fields to discuss and collaborate on solutions to industry challenges and opportunities. Service in Industry and its 2k members incite discussions and share insights and news on services and its advantages for industrial companies, focused on Business to Business activities.

The diffusion was made, at first, by sharing the survey in public discussions in these groups. After that, a research among the members of the group took place, targeting professionals working with product and/or service lifecycle management subjects or in companies that provides PSS. One-hundred-twelve potential respondents were contacted by private message on the LinkedIn platform.

4 Results

The complete responses received (21) will be detailed in the following sub-sections.

4.1 Respondents' Profile

Type of PSS Offered. The majority of the respondents offers product-oriented PSS (11), which is the most established type of PSS. It is followed by result-oriented (2) and use-oriented PSS (1). Some of the respondents offer more than one type of PSS: product and result-oriented (2); use and result-oriented (1); product, use and result-oriented (1). Three of the respondents selected "other" as an answer. Two of them are consulting companies offering support for clients having the three types of PSS and they compromise to answer from the point of view of their clients. The third offers PLM solutions.

Nature of the Products. Eleven respondents offer only manufactured products, against two offering only software ones. Two offer both types of products and three offer consulting services besides manufactured and software products.

Level of Smartness of the Products. Most of the respondents have only physical products with embedded simple sensors (5), followed by the ones that have also memory and data processing capabilities (3), and the ones equipped with information devices (2). Some respondents have more than one level of smartness in their products: four of them deal with all three levels of smartness and two with both, products with simple sensors and products with memory and data processing capability. Five respondents answered "other" for different reasons: offering simple products with no sensors or offering consulting services for companies having the three levels of smartness.

Type of Services Provided. One respondent offers only monitoring services, the others have more complete solutions such as control (5), optimization (7) and autonomy (6).

Type of Use. Eleven respondents manage products for individual use, versus four having shared use. Three of them have both types of products, and the other three considered the question not applicable.

Type of Installation. Thirteen respondents identified the installation of their products as fixed, while only five have mobile units. The other two have the two types of installation.

Access to Product. Many respondents have access to the product exclusively on the customer site (7), and just one mentions to offer the only option to take the product to their site in case of intervention; two of them have both of the previous options. The rest of respondents have remote connection to the product, which can be the only access (2), combined with access on the customer site (6) or the three combined (3).

Software Tools to Manage PSS Data. Most respondents have a customized software dedicated to PSS management (4), or a combination of PLM and SLM (4). They also use the combination of customized PSS management software with a commercial PLM solution (3), and one of them uses the three types of software to manage PSS. Two respondents declared to use only a commercial PLM solution and another one, only commercial SLM solution. Five respondents answer "other" for not having a software at all or because they use a different software than the ones specified.

Access to PSS Use Data. Considering autonomous access, eight respondents have access to all data, while three, only to part of it. For under request access, three have access to all data, while six, only to part of it.

4.2 Categories Analysis

Categories Ranking. Evaluating the ranking position chosen for each of the exploitation categories, we noticed that "Adapt of the PSS offers according to the customers" was strongly preferred in the first place (11). The categories that appeared the most in the second place of the ranking were "Improve service implementation" (9) and "Improve of product realization" (8), that were also the second most voted for the first place. The categories presenting other anticipations, such as "Manage PSS demand" or "Manage PSS contracts" were mostly poorly ranked from third to fifth places.

Categories per Respondent Profile. In order to identify possible patterns in the choice of categories, they were compared with the PSS offers information.

Type of PSS. The identification of patterns concerning the preferred exploitations according to the PSS offer was made by identifying the best-ranked categories (first and second places) per each type of PSS (product, use or result-oriented). Besides the fact that most of the respondents offer product-oriented solutions, the distribution of categories chosen is balanced between the different types of PSS.

Smartness Level. The profile of the respondents in terms of smartness level was also analyzed considering the categories ranked in first and second places. When comparing the choice of categories with the level of smartness offered by the PSS providers, it is possible to notice that for "Adapt PSS offer according to the customer", "Manage PSS contracts" and "Manage PSS demand", the ranking is well distributed between the different levels of smartness. On the other hand, the categories related to the improvement of service implementation and product realization are less demanded by the providers offering products with higher levels of smartness.

Service Level. The levels of service proposed in this survey are considered as having increasing complexity. It means that monitoring represents the simplest type of service offer and autonomy the most complete, frequently grouping the functionalities of the previous levels (monitoring, control and optimization). In this analysis, the highest level of service offered by PSS providers was compared to their preferred categories (the ones ranked in first and second places). The unique respondent offering only monitoring services considers "Improve product realization" and "Improve service implementation" the most important categories. This preference is shared with providers offering control-level services, having voted three times for each of these two categories. On the other hand, PSS providers offering more complete services, such as optimization and autonomy highlight the importance of "Adapt PSS offer to the customer" and "Improve service implementation" categories (5 votes from optimization level and 3 from autonomy, for both categories).

4.3 Data Availability

In order to evaluate the general access to data, the comparison was made between data assigned as already available or easily accessible versus data having medium, difficult or unknown access. Product operating state, sensors data, material resource stock at the customer, software resource availability, product availability at the provider, sensor reference values and PSS offer configuration were voted as hardest to access.

5 Discussion

5.1 Respondents' Profile

The responses about the provider's profiles and the type of PSS they offer, indicate an initial stage of PSS development. Most respondents classify their PSS as product-oriented and offer manufactured individual (non-shared) products with low smartness level, i.e. products having embedded simple sensors. These providers might go through a process similar to the productization, developing their products to respond to the needs of services in terms of data and connection [15].

The services provided, on the other hand, correspond to more complex solutions, such as optimization and autonomy, instead of simple monitoring. This might represent that former product providers have been moving towards servitization: the evolution of product identity to a position where it is inseparable from the service system, becoming a PSS [10].

Considering the access to the product and to PSS data, there are some barriers to the provider's autonomy in lifecycle management. An important part of the respondents declared depending on visiting the customer site to have access to the product. The management of PSS data is also a delicate subject since it is mostly handled by a combination of two or more software tools. PLM, SLM and customized PSS lifecycle management tool have to be combined to cover PSS lifecycle data.

However, part of the respondents claims to have remote access to the product, and the types of access are divided in two main groups: the ones that have autonomous access to all data and the ones having partial access to the data under request.

As discussed, the products are still the core of the PSS offer and the simple sensors they dispose do not allow complete access to their data. It limits the type of data analytics they can perform.

5.2 Categories Analysis

The highest ranked category is the one offering exploitations that allow the adaptation of the PSS offer according to the customer. Besides this fact, some other information can be gathered from the respondent's profile and the categories they chose.

Considering the categories preferred by the different types of PSS, the results were quite balanced. Which means that PSS providers believe that the five exploitations categories could be equally beneficial for all three types of PSS.

On the levels of product smartness and services offered, however, there are some clear differences. Providers offering lower levels of smartness are frequently more interested in improving the process of product realization and service implementation. It might be explained by the fact that they remain focused on an offer in one of the two components, product or service, instead of improving the offer as a system. On the other hand, those proposing smarter products and more complex services, might think on how to improve the offer as a whole.

5.3 Data Availability

As expected, the majority of data previously classified as internal data was identified as available or easy to access by the respondents. This group of data is mostly related to the services offered by the providers.

On the other hand, part of the product-related data coming from the customer, was identified from medium-difficulty to unknown access. This might relate to the fact that an important part of the respondents has access to the product only on the customer site and only partial access to product data under request.

Another remarkable information is that few of them have access to the PSS offer configuration or to the expected values for product sensors. These facts might be linked to the great majority of product-oriented PSS providers who responded to the survey, which signalizes an eventual initial stage of PSS development.

6 Conclusions

The survey results will be used to align the next steps of this project on closed-loop PSS lifecycle management. The following step consists in proposing an information system architecture for PSS lifecycle management. This architecture should integrate the exploitations identified as important for the PSS providers, considering the data they have available.

Following the current results, the architecture will be focused on the exploitations of the category "Adapt PSS offer according to the customer", proving decisions on when and how to replace products and/or services for different clients.

It was also noticed that the data coming from the customers is limited, probably due to the early stage of PSS offers development. The decision is to consider these data in the IS architecture, previewing their future availability. However, data such as PSS offer configuration can be put aside with no major prejudice.

Most respondents use a mix of PLM and other software to manage PSS data. For this reason, the architecture must consider data from different sources and ensure interoperability between them.

References

1. Cavalcante, J., Gzara, L.: Product-service systems lifecycle models: literature review and new proposition. Procedia CIRP **73**, 32–38 (2018)
2. Kurilova-Palisaitiene, J., Lindkvist, L., Sundin, E.: Towards facilitating circular product life-cycle information flow via remanufacturing. Procedia CIRP **29**, 780–785 (2015)
3. Mourtzis, D., Fotia, S., Gamito, M., Neves-silva, R.: Product-service systems across life cycle PSS design considering feedback from the entire product-service lifecycle and social media. Procedia CIRP **47**, 156–161 (2016)
4. Chierici, E., Copani, G.: Remanufacturing with upgrade PSS for new sustainable business models. Procedia CIRP **47**, 531–536 (2016)
5. Petkova, V.T., Sander, P.C., Brombacher, A.C.: Role of the service centre in improvement processes. Qual. Reliab. Eng. Int. **15**, 431–437 (1999)
6. Mamrot, M., Nicklas, J., Schlüter, N., Winzer, P.: Concept for a sustainable industrial product service systems based on field data. Procedia CIRP **40**, 687–692 (2016)
7. Mien, L.H., Feng, L.W., Gay, R., Leng, K.: An integrated manufacturing and product services system (IMPSS) concept for sustainable product development. In: International Symposium on Environmentally Conscious Design and Inverse Manufacturing, pp. 656–662 (2005)
8. Hajimohammadi, A., Cavalcante, J., Gzara, L.: Ontology for the PSS lifecycle management. Procedia CIRP **64**, 151–156 (2017)
9. Tukker, A.: Eight types of product-service system: eight ways to sustainability? Bus. Strat. Environ. **13**, 246–260 (2004)
10. Baines, T.S., et al.: State-of-the-art in product-service systems. Proc. Inst. Mech. Eng. Part B: J. Eng. Manuf. **221**(10), 1543–1552 (2007)
11. Zhu, H., Gao, J., Li, D., Tang, D.: A web-based product service system for aerospace maintenance, repair and overhaul services. Comput. Ind. **63**, 338–348 (2012)
12. Matsumoto, M., Yang, S., Martinsen, K., Kainuma, Y.: Trends and research challenges in remanufacturing. Int. J. Precis. Eng. Manuf. Technol. **3**, 129–142 (2016)
13. Kiritsis, D.: Closed-loop PLM for intelligent products in the era of the internet of things. CAD Comput. Aided Des. **43**, 479–501 (2011)
14. Wang, P.P., Ming, X.G., Li, D., Kong, F.B., Wang, L., Wu, Z.Y.: Status review and research strategies on product-service systems. Int. J. Prod. Res. **49**, 6863–6883 (2011)
15. Pirayesh, A.E., Seregni, M., Doumeingts, G., Zanetti, C.: A Conceptual Model for Product Service System (PSS), pp. 1–21 (2018)

Implementation of Pay-Per-Output Business Models and Advanced Automation Systems in Capital Goods Manufacturing SMEs

Mikko Uuskoski(✉), Hannu Kärkkäinen, and Karan Menon

Tampere University, Tampere, Finland
{mikko.uuskoski,hannu.karkkainen,karan.menon}@tuni.fi

Abstract. Manufacturing small and medium enterprises (SMEs) are recognized as a major driving force in European Union (EU) and elsewhere both economically as well as technologically in this ever-changing manufacturing paradigm. SMEs have major difficulties in implementing digital technologies such as the industrial internet enabled technologies that can lead towards a change in the business models, especially towards pay-per-output type business models. In this paper, we have studied pioneering manufacturing SMEs that have implemented pay-per-output business models as well as the related advanced automation systems. Both case companies were able to demonstrate the benefits and difficulties that they faced because of the size (SME) during the implementation process of both the pay-per-output business model and the related advanced automation system.

Keywords: Industry 4.0 · Business models · Nonownership business model · Pay-per-output · Capital goods · IIoT · Automation system · SME

1 Introduction

Manufacturing industry - like many other industries - are facing a new era which is caused by digitalization of processes. This change is affecting both products and services, as well as production lines, and increases the need for their interaction. For example, the German initiative Industry 4.0 is defining the changes very well in different operation levels. Manufacturing Small and Medium-sized Enterprises (SMEs) are recognized as a major driving force in EU and elsewhere both economically as well as technologically in this manufacturing paradigm change. However, SMEs have major difficulties in digitalization, Industrial Internet of Things (IIoT)/Industry 4.0 and the implementation of novel business models, such as pay-per-output type business models enabled significantly by the afore-mentioned technologies. This is partly due to the fact that SMEs have different types of challenges, barriers and also benefits related to business decision making compared to large companies. While it is known that existing academic research concentrates almost solely on large companies in the topics of digitalization, IIoT and Industry 4.0 [1], this research cannot be used as such, or can be used only marginally by SMEs due to the special characteristics of SMEs.

Published by Springer Nature Switzerland AG 2019
C. Fortin et al. (Eds.): PLM 2019, IFIP AICT 565, pp. 399–410, 2019.
https://doi.org/10.1007/978-3-030-42250-9_38

There are few studies that focus on the SME perspective and supporting the SME's in their implementation of Industry 4.0/IIoT and Smart Manufacturing [2]. Furthermore, the actual implementation of IIoT and advanced Automation Systems (AS), as well as related pay-per-output type business models especially in SME-companies are very little studied and reported in academic literature. There are existing recent studies for instance on novel advanced automation and IIoT supported or enabled services and advanced non-ownership business models, including pay-per-use (PPU) and pay-per-performance (pay-per-output/outcome (PPO)) business models (BMs). However, these studies do not consider how the relatively small SME company size matters in the implementation process. Furthermore, the advanced PPU/PPO type-of models are still extremely little adopted and made use of in SMEs: for instance, in the survey [3] of European capital goods manufacturing companies (54% of respondents were SMEs or smaller companies), only as few as 0,2% of studied machinery and 0,1% of automation companies' turnover was derived from PPU or PPO contracts. Thus, there seems to be a strong need for SME-oriented research particularly in IIoT/Industry 4.0 and advanced pay-per-use, pay-per-output and pay-per-outcome BM context. Accordingly, our research questions were defined as follows:

RQ1 "How were the pay-per-output business models and automation system implemented in the studied pioneering capital goods manufacturing SMEs?"
RQ2 "How did the business model and the automation system interact in the implementation process?"
RQ3 "How did the SME size matter in the implementation process?"

The studied two capital goods manufacturing companies can be considered as pioneering companies in their own capital goods businesses in making use of pay-per-output business models in the SME company category. The structure of this study is as follows: we first review existing research and the research gap in more detail. Second, we introduce the methodology of this paper, describe the cases and explain the questionnaire themes. Third, we present the results, and discuss them, leading finally into the conclusions and managerial implications.

2 Theoretical Background

2.1 IIoT Based Technologies and Advanced Automation Systems

High level topics concerning today's production of goods and services include sustainability, flexibility, efficiency and competitiveness [4]. Many companies are currently fighting high costs to make small changes to their ISA-95-based production automation systems and thus are calling for new models and architectures for dynamic and digitized production [5]. Several current technological trends that are receiving substantial attention include the following: internet of things (IoT), system of systems (SoS), cyber physical systems (CPS), clouds, big data and service oriented architecture (SOA) [4]. Delsing [4] and Porter et al. [6] show the need to extend the ISA-95 framework, and we decided to select the technology stack from [6] as one base for our interview framework, when discussing the changes in Automation Systems. The former ISA-95 standard doesn't include IIoT (Industrial internet of things) - enabled extended connectivity to the cloud and other systems [5].

An IIoT system connects and integrates industrial control systems with enterprise systems, business processes and analytics [7]. Related automation control systems contain sensors and actuators, and systems are typically large and complicated (Fig. 1).

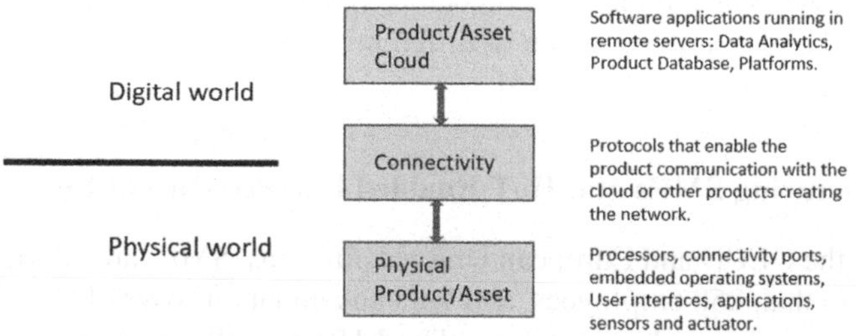

Fig. 1. Industrial Internet technology stack [6]

Into this stack, we can place all hardware and software components needed to realize modern and connected automation system required by Pay-per-output. In the physical product/platform software level, we included controller parameters, fieldbus technologies and programming, and runtime software as well as that at the sensor level. At the connectivity level, we were interested in used hardware connection types and used protocols. The cloud level gave us information about used cloud/server types and tools used in the cloud.

2.2 Pay-Per-Output Business Model in Manufacturing Companies

In the manufacturing sector, Nonownership model can be defined as *"service in which customers acquire some property rights to an asset and are offered a certain degree of freedom in using this asset for a specified period of time while the burdens of ownership remain with the owner"* [8].

The above definition describes the concept of nonownership in a clear manner from the customers point of view as it talks about how a customer can use the asset but not own it, by keeping the ownership with the manufacturer. In order to take the manufacturer's point of view into consideration, the earning logic of nonownership business models has to be described. This can be done by dividing the nonownership model into pay-per-use, pay-per-output and pay-per-outcome models.

Literature has covered the nonownership models from various different sectors; such as, software industry [9], B2C product manufacturers such as washing machine manufacturers [10], manufactured products such as the copier and printer [11]. The above-mentioned product ranges are easy to scale because the economies of scale work very well for software products, B2C products and use intensive copiers and printers. B2B manufacturers that make equipment's or machines that are critical in the customers process, such as the air-compressors or jet engines (critical components for an airplane manufacturer) have a very different risk profile when it comes to these nonownership models when compared to the above-mentioned products. There are some authors that discuss the risk profile for these kind of manufacturing companies [12, 13].

In order to understand the implementation of the pay-per-output model, we follow the implementation process described by [14] where the business model implementation is divided into four phases or 4I's, Initiation, Ideation, Integration and Implementation. Initiation, ideation and integration belong to the design part of the business model innovation process whereas implementation belongs to the realisation part. All these phases are intertwined and require iteration at different times in order to create a near perfect business model for the customers [14].

2.3 Manufacturing SMEs and IIoT Enabled Pay-Per-Output Business Model

According to the OECD and European Union definitions, SMEs are defined as the enterprises with less than 250 employees, and with an annual turnover of 50 million euros or less or an annual balance sheet not exceeding EUR 43 million[1]. In this section, we discuss in more detail the overall SME specific characteristics that differentiate SME-related operations and business from larger companies' operation and business. Furthermore, we discuss the significance of SME-related research in IIoT and automation, and related novel business models, as well as the research gap of this study.

Manufacturing SMEs are recognized as a major driving force of many economies. For instance, in Germany, as well as in the EU, ca. 99% of all companies are SMEs, and only 1% are large companies [1]. In addition, it is found that SME's can have a significant impact on the Fourth Industrial Revolution, which is related to the rise in the role of IIoT in the manufacturing sector [2]. However, SMEs have different types of challenges, barriers and also benefits related to business decision making, compared to large companies [2, 15]. For this reason, the Smart manufacturing and IIoT research carried out from the perspective of large companies, which forms a very extensive part of all related research, cannot be directly applied and is not considered credible in most cases in SMEs. According to [2], only a few studies focus on supporting SME's in their implementation of Industry 4.0/IIoT and Smart Manufacturing.

Many studies have listed major differences between SMEs and large companies or (Large) Multi-National Enterprises (MNEs). Mittal et al. [2] provides a good condensed description of main SME characteristics compared to large MNEs: they sum up these to include 8 overall clusters of characteristics, including the following: finance, technical resource availability, product specialization, standards, organizational culture, employee participation, alliances and collaboration. Various studies, e.g. [1] demonstrate that academic research on Industry 4.0/IIoT focuses strongly on large enterprises [16], and only marginally on SMEs [17]. Also, a recent review study by Mittal et al. [2] recognized a few studies to have at least some focus on SME-specific needs in the field of Smart manufacturing and Industry 4.0. Thus, there seems to be a strong need for SME-oriented research, in general, in manufacturing, as well as in the IIoT/Industry 4.0 context in particular.

We found one very recent paper [1] which discusses specifically IIoT/Industry 4.0 - facilitated business models and business model innovations from the specific angle

[1] https://stats.oecd.org/glossary/detail.asp?ID=3123.

of SMEs. It discusses Industry 4.0 implementation and related business model implementation from the perspective of interviewed SMEs. They also discuss the impact of Industry 4.0 on the business model elements of manufacturing SMEs. However, it does not address the advanced NOBMs and their implementation process from SME perspective. Our study will go further than the above study in analysing the PPO BMs and their implementation and impacts to AS from an SME perspective in more detail. We used also recent literature reviews in confirming the research gap (e.g. reviews on links of IoT and BM: [18, 19], and academic studies discussing advanced automation and IIoT technologies' various roles in novel business models: [11, 20–22]), revealing no other studies considering the SME company size in the context of BM (and AS) implementation. To the best of our knowledge, our study is the first to consider SME company size, as a central focus of the study, in understanding its impact in the BM and AS implementation, as well as the BM and AS interaction in the case of PPO NOBMs.

3 Research Methodology

The aim of this research is to understand the implementation process of pay-per-output business model and IIoT enabled automation systems for capital goods manufacturing SMEs. To study this, we have used the case study methodology, by selecting pioneering SME capital goods manufacturing companies that have implemented the pay-per-output business model and have implemented the related IIoT enabled automation systems. In order to answer the research questions appropriately, we designed a selection criterion, under which we selected companies that were capital goods manufacturing SMEs, pioneering in their business, B2B businesses, companies that had already implemented the pay-per-output business model, companies that had implemented the IIoT enabled automation system.

Based on the above selection criteria, we selected two companies, Company A and Company B from Finland. We have signed a confidentiality agreement with the companies, that does not allow us to mention their names and details of their businesses. On a broader level, they are B2B capital goods manufacturing SMEs, pioneering in their business and have implemented the pay-per-output business model as well as IIoT enabled automation system with many of their customers.

We conducted a qualitative interview session with both the companies that lasted for about 2 h each. In both companies, we interviewed R&D managers who were responsible for strategizing the implementation of both the business model (pay-per-output) as well as the IIoT enabled automation system. Due to the lack of space, we are not able to attach the entire interview questionnaire, but we will describe the major interview themes in the following paragraph. We designed a semi-structured questionnaire with a few open questions and some specific structured questions. All the questions are categorized under the following five categories:

1. Background questions
2. Planning of the business model implementation and main drivers
3. Business model implementation process
4. Automation system implementation process

We recorded the interview and then transcribed it manually in order to extract the data for the result section.

4 Results

4.1 Drivers and Motivation for Implementation of PPO Business Model and Automation System (See Tables 1 and 2)

Both studied SME-companies explained that internal motivation to develop new business models came from strategic needs to develop new sources of income. According to the interviews, one of the main external drivers to the implementation of the PPO BM in both companies was the needed transparency to the real created value from their products to the customers. In the starting phase, company A had large technological limitations to implement the PPO BM, while e.g. industrial internet and automation data collection and analysis technologies were not too developed from PPO perspective. For company B, technological readiness was good.

Pay-per-output (PPO) business model was experienced in the interviews as significantly important for the business of both the interviewed companies A and B in many ways, which were not only about the proportion of turnover from PPO to the whole turnover. As far as company A was concerned, the traditional business, where they sell the machine and later on in the lifecycle of the machine sell spare parts and components of the machine, was not enough to generate profits. Hence, company A implemented the PPO based optimization service. Company B has a product which is unique when compared to the competitor's product but very expensive. Hence, company B designed a PPO model where the customer can use the entire product and related system and pay under the PPO model (i.e. pay as per output of the machine and the related system). In the last couple of years, this has led to a situation where 20% of their overall business is now under PPO business model. Company B expects that it will be almost 100% of their business under the PPO model in near future. Table 1 describes the advantages and the disadvantages of being an SME that company A experienced while implementing the PPO business model and the advanced automation system, and Table 2 company B's experiences.

Table 1. SME related advantages and hindrances for company A from BM and AS point of view.

Company A	Advantages from the size (SME), PPO	Hindrances from the size (SME), PPO	Advantages from the size (SME), AS	Hindrances from the size (SME), AS
Initiation – analyzing the ecosystem	Motivation to find niche BM to grow Decision making process was dynamic	Harder to convince customer for novel BMs Limited resources for experimenting with customers	Limited resources forced team to concentrate on relevant, focused tasks	Not possible to collect data about customer needs extensively

(continued)

Table 1. (*continued*)

Company A	Advantages from the size (SME), PPO	Hindrances from the size (SME), PPO	Advantages from the size (SME), AS	Hindrances from the size (SME), AS
Ideation – generating new ideas		Limited resources forced decision making more by gut-feeling. Not clear road map	Good customer knowhow about needs to fulfill requirements to engineer AS	Resources were limited, not possible to explore and test many ideas
Integration – building a new business model	Fast decision making Goal was clear Not too much internal resistance	Had to accept customers which were willing for testing. Risk taking capacity was rather small	Clear goal Team motivated and independent for fast decision making Objective supplier selection	
Implementation	Management supporting decision making towards new BM. Full commitment from the whole team	Development steps were limited because of the resources, not possible to jump fast towards PPO	Information flow between customer and supplier was better in small organization, better customer insight	Limited resources, which had potential to slow down technology development towards to the technology required by PPO
	Found own niche business area, which was enough to fulfill SMEs needs	Limitation to execute larger development projects fast, for example general IT data secure system	New opportunity to sell also hardware to larger customers. Was not be possible without PPO BM	Sales forces and production capacity was limited

For both companies that are SMEs, the PPO-model was experienced to provide a way to grow their business and compete in a business and market where there are many large companies. For company A, the growth in the business was triggered because of the ability to manage machines that were manufactured by other manufacturers using their optimization system. For company B growth in the business was triggered because even if the machine they manufacture is expensive, under the PPO model the customer just pays for the output. This allowed them to tap into new customers and grow their business. Through experimenting, both companies believed that the output-based BM was leading to improved earnings in the long term.

4.2 Implementation Process of PPO Business Model and Automation System (See Tables 1 and 2)

The results from interviews related specifically to the advantages and hindrances from the relatively small (SME) company size perspective towards the different phases of the implementation process of PPO BM and automation system (AS) are shown in Tables 1 and 2.

Table 2. SME related advantages and hindrances for company B from BM and AS point of view

Company B	Advantages from the size (SME), PPO	Hindrances from the company size (SME), PPO	Advantages from the size (SME), AS	Hindrances from the size (SME), AS
Initiation – analyzing the ecosystem	Agile. Company sold PPO BM to show performance level	Unknown company and small size (SME)	Team motivation was excellent to develop a good system	
Ideation – generating new ideas			Good customer knows- how to fulfill requirements of the AS	Resources were limited, takes time to get system ready
Integration – building a new business model	Big competitors didn't go to similar PPO model, because it spoiled existing business Fast decision making	To convince customer in different places to believe PPO and measuring of the production, easier in Europe, harder in China and less developed countries	Goal was clear for everyone	Measurement of output was not easy. Took resources to realize measurement system
Implementation	Readiness and capabilities to fulfill customer requirements Possibility to use many selling channels and methods	Biggest problem was financing the customer hardware when sold as a PPO BM	Better information flow between customer and supplier resulted in small organization better customer insight	If the company wants to larger scope of supply with additional system components development resources were limited

Company A mentioned that instead of an intensive pre-study, they started the implementation with experimenting with beta-customers. Company B started implementation at a fast pace from the idea to get new customers faster with PPO BM. In company B, the AS system development towards the PPO BM was not a big step, because the system was already equipped with extensive measurement and data collection system. Only limited modifications were needed to get a reliable AS for PPO based invoicing.

In Company A, the experimentation phase provided a good basis for the BM and AS development. Because of size and its flat organization structure, the companies had freedom to select most suitable AS according to the overall system requirement. Especially company A noticed that it was an important advantage when they compare their success to a larger competitor who selected a system according to internal rules instead of real AS system and PPO BM needs. In company B, the system was selected based on demanding machine control requirements and at the same time, it was serving PPO BM requirements very well.

Company A also told that because of the low hierarchy of the company they were able to take decisions and act quickly. For that reason, the experimentation phase gave fruitful results to the PPO BM and AS development. The same was true for company B, when they decided to implement the PPO BM. Both companies agreed that the AS technology development with connectivity (IIoT) development is important in enabling implementation of the PPO BM. In both companies, at the time when data security issues cause concerns to move towards more open communication systems, for example that based on cloud systems.

Concerning the AS, in Company A I/O-quantity had increased 2–3 times from the beginning. Data was processed and collected at the Physical product/Asset level [6] as well as the Product/Asset cloud level [6]. Because of larger data collection and more advanced analysis also, the calculation capacity of the system was huge compared to the original system. They have basic technical readiness to use real cloud-based system, but because of the customer prejudices about IT-secures issue, it is still marginal. Company B started the automation system development with machine development and additional features was added when they decided to have PPO BM. They have developed a full automation system to collect data from the Machine. I/O-quantity per system is 50-100 points. The current situation is that most of the systems are connected with 3G modem to the company own server. The user interface is playing a major role in opening the critical information for the system operator to optimize the process and create saving or higher performance. The current system is very precise with measurements and enabling PPO invoicing. Company B could also offer connectivity to customer systems with OPC-UA.

4.3 Interaction of PPO Business Model and aS

Both companies A and B noticed that the business model development and automation system development seemed to be strongly interdependent. The AS impacted the PPO BM by enabling the more credible (A and B), more accurate (A and B) and real-time measurement (A and B) of the output. It also enabled invoicing (A and B).

The PPO BMs output results in both companies were related with savings and process optimization to get more output. All value to generate savings or better performance was conveyed by automation system capabilities. That is why automation system played a major role in execution of the PPO BM successfully.

There was no internal resistance, for that reason both BM and AS development were really customer and system based. Motivation to the PPO BM in both companies is transparency to real created value (saving or performance improvements). To enabled PPO BM AS has to fulfil technical requirements for data collection, analysing and measurement and all that should be synchronized with BM. Connectivity to different directions is extremely important for running PPO BM. Both companies have realized online connectivity to the machine. Security concerns and customer prejudice are still limiting larger cloud-based system implementation.

5 Discussion and Conclusions

This study contributed to the academic understanding of the implementation of advanced BMs, especially the very little studied PPO models, in the context of SMEs in particular.

Both studied companies agreed that small size is both advantageous and brings limitations in the implementation process of BM. As for the advantages, both companies due their small size were able to recognize a new niche market, making use of the PPO BM, which were interesting and significant for their SME company, but probably would not have been interesting for larger companies. Secondly, internal small and flat organization of the SME was enabling fast adapting to the BM requirements. Due to the limited size both companies didn't have all needed expertise to implement the PPO BM in a structured and preplanned way, and for that reason they had to take relatively large risks in BM implementation.

Furthermore, their company size seemed to matter in all phases of PPO implementation process: initiation, ideation, integration and implementation (See Tables 1 and 2). The SME company size seemed also to impact in a manner that there was no clear roadmap and no before-planned separate implementation process phases in the PPO implementation, e.g. initiation and implementation were very iterative and intertwined.

Both companies faced that small size is both advantageous and brings limitations in the implementation process of AS. Because of relatively small organization size and freedom from internal strict supplier policies, both companies were able to select most suitable advanced AS parameters according to the system requirement.

Major strategic benefits from PPO BM were access to new markets, better profitability and overall growth opportunities. For both of these two SME companies PPO BM and advanced AS have given opportunities to succeed and differentiate their business from large competitors. In company A, open-minded BM and AS experimentation led them to a new business, relatively free from competition, and at least partly without precise planning, opened to them new markets to sell hardware, both as an investment product as well as a PPO service. In company B, PPO BM enabled the sales of a totally new type of expensive technology to customers which were not able to trust the promised performance of produced machine, sold in the form of an investment product. In both companies there was clear interaction of BM and AS development.

This study brings forth some important managerial implications for manufacturing SMEs, especially those dealing with B2B capital goods. First, we demonstrate that PPO BMs are possible to be achieved also by SMEs, and that there can even be important small size-related benefits enabling SMEs to make use of such advanced PPO BMs that large companies cannot make use of. Among these are that the studied novel type of business models offer these SMEs new possibilities to compete with even larger companies that have e.g. the advantage of economies of scale compared to SMEs, by enabling SMEs for instance to enter interesting niche markets created by pay-per-output services and related BMs.

This study is limited by its approach to studying two case companies, and as such, it does not allow the direct generalization of the results to other companies. The results and conclusions are important, however, already in this case study format, because there are very few studies that focus on SMEs in the field of advanced BMs (such as PPU and PPO models) and advanced automation. It seems viable, however, to make the claim that also other SMEs will very probably find both similar types of benefits and also limitations in their attempts to make use of advanced business models like PPO models. Future research should attempt to include further SMEs, including different types of industries, to enable a more extensive generalization of the conclusions.

References

1. Müller, J.M., Buliga, O., Voigt, K.-I.: Fortune favors the prepared: how SMEs approach business model innovations in Industry 4.0. Technol. Forecast. Soc. Change **132**, 2–17 (2018). https://doi.org/10.1016/j.techfore.2017.12.019
2. Mittal, S., Khan, M.A., Romero, D., Wuest, T.: A critical review of smart manufacturing & Industry 4.0 maturity models: implications for small and medium-sized enterprises (SMEs). J. Manuf. Syst. **49**, 194–214 (2018). https://doi.org/10.1016/j.jmsy.2018.10.005
3. Adrodegari, F., Alghisi, A., Ardolino, M., Saccani, N.: From ownership to service-oriented business models: a survey in capital goods companies and a PSS typology. Procedia CIRP **30**, 245–250 (2015). https://doi.org/10.1016/j.procir.2015.02.105
4. Delsing, J.: Local cloud internet of things automation: technology and business model features of distributed internet of things automation solutions. IEEE Ind. Electron. Mag. **11**, 8–21 (2017). https://doi.org/10.1109/MIE.2017.2759342
5. ANSI/ISA-95.00.01: Enterprise-control System Integration–Part 1: Models and Terminology. American National Standards Institute, Washington, DC (2010)
6. Porter, M.E., Heppelmann, J.E.: How smart, connected products are transforming competition. Harvard Bus. Rev. **92**, 64–88 (2014)
7. Karmarkar, A., Buchheit, M.: The Industrial Internet of Things, Volume G8: Vocabulary, Industrial Internet Consortium (2017)
8. Wittkowski, K., Moeller, S., Wirtz, J.: Firms' intentions to use nonownership services. J. Serv. Res. **16**, 171–185 (2013). https://doi.org/10.1177/1094670512471997
9. Weinhardt, C., Stößer, J., Anandasivam, A., Blau, B.: Business Models in the Service World (2009)
10. Manninen, K., Koskela, S., Antikainen, R., Bocken, N., Dahlbo, H., Aminoff, A.: Do circular economy business models capture intended environmental value propositions? J. Clean. Prod. **171**, 413–422 (2018). https://doi.org/10.1016/j.jclepro.2017.10.003
11. Ardolino, M., Rapaccini, M., Saccani, N., Gaiardelli, P., Crespi, G., Ruggeri, C.: The role of digital technologies for the service transformation of industrial companies. Int. J. Prod. Res. **56**, 2116–2132 (2018). https://doi.org/10.1080/00207543.2017.1324224
12. Uuskoski, M., Menon, K., Kärkkäinen, H., Koskinen, K.: Perceived risks and benefits of advanced pay-per-use type of business models based on Industry 4.0 enabled technologies in manufacturing companies. In: Chiabert, P., Bouras, A., Noël, F., Ríos, J. (eds.) PLM 2018. IAICT, vol. 540, pp. 498–507. Springer, Cham (2018). https://doi.org/10.1007/978-3-030-01614-2_46
13. Gebauer, H., Saul, C.J., Haldimann, M., Gustafsson, A.: Organizational capabilities for pay-per-use services in product-oriented companies. Int. J. Prod. Econ. (2015). https://doi.org/10.1016/j.ijpe.2016.12.007
14. Frankenberger, K., Weiblen, T., Csik, M., Gassmann, O.: The 4I-framework of business model innovation: a structured view on process phases and challenges. Int. J. Prod. Dev. **18**, 249–273 (2013)
15. Sommer, L.: Industrial revolution - Industry 4.0: are German manufacturing SMEs the first victims of this revolution? J. Ind. Eng. Manag. **8**, 1512–1532 (2015). https://doi.org/10.3926/jiem.1470
16. Arnold, C., Kiel, D., Voigt, K.-I.: How the industrial internet of things changes business models in different manufacturing industries. Int. J. Innov. Manag. **20**, 1640015 (2016). https://doi.org/10.1142/S1363919616400156

17. Schmidt, R., Möhring, M., Härting, R.-C., Reichstein, C., Neumaier, P., Jozinović, P.: Industry 4.0 - potentials for creating smart products: empirical research results. In: Abramowicz, W. (ed.) BIS 2015. LNBIP, vol. 208, pp. 16–27. Springer, Cham (2015). https://doi.org/10.1007/978-3-319-19027-3_2
18. Kiel, D., Gasse, L., Arnold, C., Collisi, M., Voigt, K.-I.: The impact of the industrial internet of things on established business models. In: Conference Proceedings, p. 24 (2016)
19. Wnuk, K., Murari, B.T.: The impact of internet of things on software business models. In: Maglyas, A., Lamprecht, A.-L. (eds.) Software Business. LNBIP, vol. 240, pp. 94–108. Springer, Cham (2016). https://doi.org/10.1007/978-3-319-40515-5_7
20. Bock, M., Wiener, M.: Nonownership business models in the manufacturing industry: the role of uncertainty and the industrial internet of things. In: ICIS 2018 Proceedings (2018)
21. Metallo, C., Agrifoglio, R., Schiavone, F., Mueller, J.: Understanding business model in the internet of things industry. Technol. Forecast. Soc. Chang. **136**, 298–306 (2018). https://doi.org/10.1016/j.techfore.2018.01.020
22. Ehret, M., Wirtz, J.: Unlocking value from machines: business models and the industrial internet of things. J. Mark. Manag. **33**, 111–130 (2017). https://doi.org/10.1080/0267257X.2016.1248041

Correction to: Hybrid Data-Driven and Physics-Based Modelling for Prescriptive Maintenance of Gas-Turbine Power Plant

Sergei Nikolaev, Sergei Belov, Mikhail Gusev, and Ighor Uzhinsky

Correction to:
Chapter "Hybrid Data-Driven and Physics-Based Modelling for Prescriptive Maintenance of Gas-Turbine Power Plant" in: C. Fortin et al. (Eds.): *Product Lifecycle Management in the Digital Twin Era*, IFIP AICT 565, https://doi.org/10.1007/978-3-030-42250-9_36

The original version of this chapter was revised. The acknowledgement was inadvertently not included. The missing acknowledgment has been added.

The updated version of this chapter can be found at
https://doi.org/10.1007/978-3-030-42250-9_36

Published by Springer Nature Switzerland AG 2021
C. Fortin et al. (Eds.): PLM 2019, IFIP AICT 565, p. C1, 2021.
https://doi.org/10.1007/978-3-030-42250-9_39

Author Index

The manufacturer's authorised representative in the EU is Springer Nature Customer Service Centre GmbH, Europaplatz 3, 69115 Heidelberg, Germany. If you have any concerns regarding our products, please contact ProductSafety@springernature.com

Printed and bound by CPI Group (UK) Ltd, Croydon, CR0 4YY
30/09/2026
02225442-0020